CB126787

American Language Hub

LEVEL 5
Teacher's Book

BOBBY DUNNETT

macmillan education

Macmillan Education Limited
4 Crinan Street
London N1 9XW

Companies and representatives throughout the world

American Language Hub Level 5 Teacher's Book ISBN 978-0-230-49754-2
American Language Hub Level 5 Teacher's Book with Teacher's App
ISBN 978-0-230-49755-9

Text, design and illustration © Macmillan Education Limited 2020
Written by Bobby Dunnett

The author has asserted their right to be identified as the author of this work in accordance with the Copyright, Designs and Patents Act 1988.

First published 2020

All rights reserved. No part of this publication may be reproduced, stored in a retrieval system, or transmitted in any form or by any means, electronic, mechanical, photocopying, recording, or otherwise, without the prior written permission of the publishers.

Note to Teachers
Photocopies may be made, for classroom use, of pages W1–W51 without the prior written permission of Macmillan Education Limited. However, please note that the copyright law, which does not normally permit multiple copying of published material, applies to the rest of this book.

Teacher's Edition credits:
Original design by emc design ltd
Page make-up by SPi Global
Cover design by Macmillan Education, based on an original design by Restless
Cover photographs by Getty Images/Luís Henrique Boucault; Plainpicture/Cavan Images
Picture research by Emily Taylor

Author's acknowledgements
The author would like to thank Tabbie, Dulcie and Felix.

The authors and publishers would like to thank the following for permission to reproduce their photographs:

Alamy Stock Photo/Matthew Taylor pW6, Alamy Stock Photo/pureshot pW4(cr); Getty Images/Aleksandr Kuzmin/Blend Images pW2, **Getty Images**/Andrew Mayovskyy/iStock pW28, Getty Images/Blend Images/Larry Hirshowitz/Ronnie Kaufman pW17, Getty Images/Caiaimage/Tom Merton pW42, Getty Images/Caiaimage/Tom Merton pW39, Getty Images/Chris Ryan/Hoxton pW30(br), Getty Images/Cultura/Henglein and Steets pW37, Getty Images/DaniloAndjus/iStockphoto pW25, Getty Images/Digital Vision/Hero Images pW22, Getty Images/DigitalVision/Hinterhaus Productions pW27, Getty Images/EyeEm/Yamgata Sohjiroh pW9, Getty Images/Eloy Rodriguez/Moment pW45, Getty Images/EUGEN GEBHARDT/Westend61 pW33, Getty Images/E+/skynesher pW41, Getty Images/E+/skynesher pW43, Getty/Fancy Images/Punchstock pW18, Getty Images/Fuse pW11, Getty Images/Hero Images pW12, Getty Images/Hero Images pW20, Getty Images/Hero Images pW8, Getty Images/Hero Images pW48, Getty Images/Image Source/Stanton j Stephens pW7, Getty Images/iStock/nautiluz56 pW4(tr), Getty Images/iStockphoto/joggiebotma pW14, Getty Images/iStockphoto/monkeybusinessimages pW31, Getty Images/iStockphoto/monkeybusinessimages pW35, Getty Images/Jordan Siemens/Taxi pW10, Getty Images/kan wang pW46, Getty Images/Kieran Stone/Moment pW29, Getty Images/Maskot pW38, Getty Images/Moment/Stefan Cristian Cioata pW44, Getty Images/Photodisc/Rafael Ben-Ari pW36, Getty Images/seng chye teo pW40, Getty Images/Tetra images RF pW32, Getty Images/VICTOR COSCARON/iStockphoto pW30(tr); **Macmillan Education Limited**/COMSTOCK IMAGES pW4(br), Macmillan Education Limited/Corbis/Royalty-Free pW47; **Shutterstock**/MagSpace pW1.

Commissioned photo by **Sharp Focus** TBXIII(br)

The author and publishers are grateful for permission to reprint the following copyright material:

Extracts from: 'Sound Foundations: Learning and teaching pronunciation (2nd Edition): English pronunciation' © Adrian Underhill, 2005. Published by Macmillan Education Limited. Used by Permission. All Rights Reserved.

Extracts from: 'Beyond the Sentence: Introducing Discourse Analysis' © Scott Thornbury, 2005. Published by Macmillan Education Limited. Used by Permission. All Rights Reserved.

Extracts from: 'Teaching Reading Skills in a Foreign Language' © Christine Nuttall, 2009. Published by Macmillan Education Limited. Used by Permission. All Rights Reserved.

Extracts from: 'Learning Teaching: The Essential Guide to English Language Teaching (3rd edition)' © 2011. Published by Macmillan Education Limited. Used by Permission. All Rights Reserved.

Extracts from: 'The New A-Z of ELT: A Dictionary of Terms and Concepts' © Scott Thornbury, 2017. Published by Macmillan Education Limited. Used by Permission. All Rights Reserved.

Extracts from: '700 Classroom Activities New Edition' © David Seymour and Maria Popova, 2005. Published by Macmillan Education Limited. Used by Permission. All Rights Reserved.

Student's Book credits:
Text, design and illustration © Macmillan Education Limited 2020
Written by Jeremy Day and Graham Skerritt

The authors have asserted their right to be identified as the authors of this work in accordance with the Copyright, Designs and Patents Act 1988.

Designed by emc design ltd
Picture research by Emily Taylor

Full acknowledgements for illustrations and photographs in the facsimile pages can be found in the Student's Book ISBN 978-0-230-49748-1.

The author and publishers are grateful for permission to reprint the following copyright material:

Graph from 'Vinyl LP Sales and Market Share' by British Phonographic Industry, 2017. © BPI (British Recorded Music Industry) Limited 2019. All rights reserved. Reprinted with permission of British Phonographic Industry, p6; Extract from 'Tim Smit: how we made the Eden Project' by Anna Tims. Originally published in The Guardian, 29 September 2014. © 2019 Guardian News & Media Limited or its affiliated companies. All rights reserved. Reprinted with permission of Guardian News & Media Limited, p16; Extract from 'Life In An Underwater Skyscraper' by Rex Features. © Rex Features Ltd. 2018. Reprinted with permission of Rex Features Ltd. UK, p27; Extract from 'Architect Unveils Plans For Spectacular Eco-Friendly Resort' by Rex Features. © Rex Features Ltd. 2018. Reprinted with permission of Rex Features Ltd. UK, p27; Extract from 'The 'Lily Pad City' - 03 Jul 2008' by Rex Features. © Rex Features Ltd. 2018. Reprinted with permission of Rex Features Ltd. UK, p27; Extract from 'From Forest Bathing to 'Halotherapy': 5 Ridiculous Wellness Trends' by Loulla-Mae Eleftherious-Smith. Originally published in The Independent, 7 October2016. © Independent Digital News and Media Limited 2019. Reprinted with permission of Independent Digital News and Media Limited, p92; Extract from 'Political activism is as strong as ever, but now it's digital – and passionate' by Ethan Zuckerman. Originally published in The Guardian, 15 October 2013. © 2019 Guardian News & Media Limited or its affiliated companies. All rights reserved. Reprinted with permission of Guardian News & Media Limited, p120

These materials may contain links for third party websites. We have no control over, and are not responsible for, the contents of such third party websites. Please use care when accessing them.

The inclusion of any specific companies, commercial products, trade names or otherwise does not constitute or imply its endorsement or recommendation by Macmillan Education Limited.

Printed and bound in Brazil

2025
23

Contents

Student's Book Introduction

American Language Hub is a new six-level general English course for adult learners, which takes the complexity out of teaching English. It is designed to promote effective communication and helps to build learners' confidence with regular opportunities for meaningful practice. With its firm pedagogic foundation and syllabus aligned to the revised CEFR, American Language Hub has clear learning outcomes which make it easy to use in a variety of teaching situations.

The engaging photograph and famous quotation help teachers to focus students and familiarize themselves with the ideas in the unit. Teachers can also encourage students to label the picture.

Student's Book unit opener
The first page of every American Language Hub unit is the unit opener. It is an exciting visual opportunity for students to engage with the theme of the unit and see at a glance the CEFR learning objectives for each lesson.

There is a quick warm-up speaking activity. Teachers can use this time to prepare the class for their lesson and delay the main start for five minutes until all the students arrive.

Student's Book Lessons 1 and 2 first spread

Vocabulary
American Language Hub teaches vocabulary in topic-related sets to help students categorize the new words they learn. Key vocabulary sets are built on and reviewed in the back of the book.

Skill labels
By focusing students' attention on the skills labels next to each exercise number, teachers can highlight which skills are being practiced and recycled.

Grammar
The American Language Hub approach to grammar is inductive. Students are exposed to new language in context. Each grammar section prompts the student to notice the feature in context and to discover its form and use. Students then have further opportunities for controlled practice before using their new language in more authentic spoken or written output.

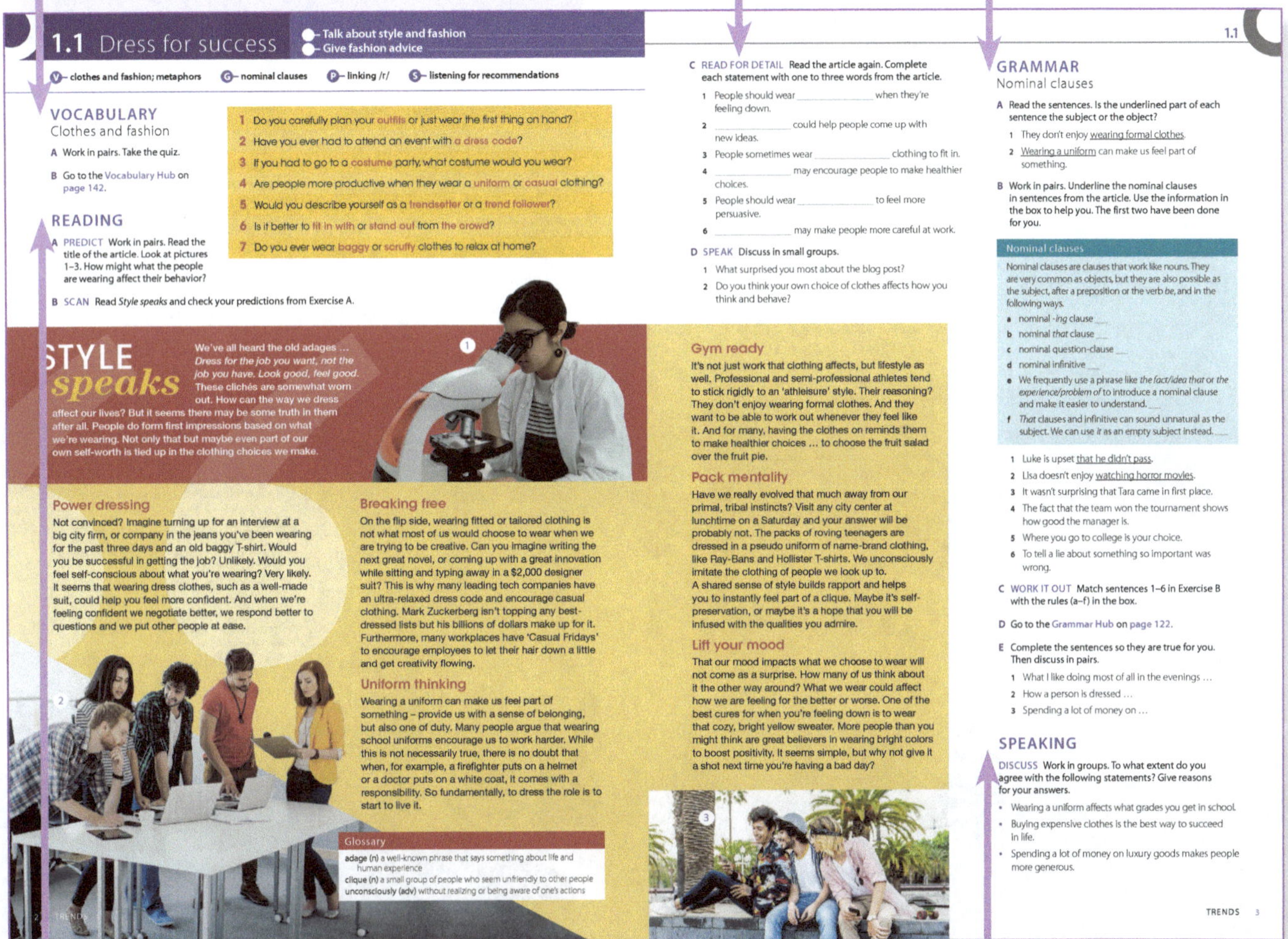

1.1 Dress for success

- Talk about style and fashion
- Give fashion advice

V – clothes and fashion; metaphors G – nominal clauses P – linking /r/ S – listening for recommendations

VOCABULARY
Clothes and fashion

A Work in pairs. Take the quiz.

B Go to the Vocabulary Hub on page 142.

1 Do you carefully plan your outfits or just wear the first thing on hand?
2 Have you ever had to attend an event with a dress code?
3 If you had to go to a costume party, what costume would you wear?
4 Are people more productive when they wear a uniform or casual clothing?
5 Would you describe yourself as a trendsetter or a trend follower?
6 Is it better to fit in with or stand out from the crowd?
7 Do you ever wear baggy or scruffy clothes to relax at home?

READING

A PREDICT Work in pairs. Read the title of the article. Look at pictures 1–3. How might what the people are wearing affect their behavior?

B SCAN Read *Style speaks* and check your predictions from Exercise A.

STYLE speaks

We've all heard the old adages … *Dress for the job you want, not the job you have. Look good, feel good.* These clichés are somewhat worn out. How can the way we dress affect our lives? But it seems there may be some truth in them after all. People do form first impressions based on what we're wearing. Not only that but maybe even part of our own self-worth is tied up in the clothing choices we make.

Power dressing

Not convinced? Imagine turning up for an interview at a big city firm, or company in the jeans you've been wearing for the past three days and an old baggy T-shirt. Would you be successful in getting the job? Unlikely. Would you feel self-conscious about what you're wearing? Very likely. It seems that wearing dress clothes, such as a well-made suit, could help you feel more confident. And when we're feeling confident we negotiate better, we respond better to questions and we put other people at ease.

Breaking free

On the flip side, wearing fitted or tailored clothing is not what most of us would choose to wear when we are trying to be creative. Can you imagine writing the next great novel, or coming up with a great innovation while sitting and typing away in a $2,000 designer suit? This is why many leading tech companies have an ultra-relaxed dress code and encourage casual clothing. Mark Zuckerberg isn't topping any best-dressed lists but his billions of dollars make up for it. Furthermore, many workplaces have 'Casual Fridays' to encourage employees to let their hair down a little and get creativity flowing.

Uniform thinking

Wearing a uniform can make us feel part of something – provide us with a sense of belonging, but also one of duty. Many people argue that wearing school uniforms encourage us to work harder. While this is not necessarily true, there is no doubt that when, for example, a firefighter puts on a helmet or a doctor puts on a white coat, it comes with a responsibility. So fundamentally, to dress the role is to start to live it.

Glossary
adage (n) a well-known phrase that says something about life and human experience
clique (n) a small group of people who seem unfriendly to other people
unconsciously (adv) without realizing or being aware of one's actions

Gym ready

It's not just work that clothing affects, but lifestyle as well. Professional and semi-professional athletes tend to stick rigidly to an 'athleisure' style. Their reasoning? They don't enjoy wearing formal clothes. And they want to be able to work out whenever they feel like it. And for many, having the clothes on reminds them to make healthier choices … to choose the fruit salad over the fruit pie.

Pack mentality

Have we really evolved that much away from our primal, tribal instincts? Visit any city center at lunchtime on a Saturday and your answer will be probably not. The packs of roving teenagers are dressed in a pseudo uniform of name-brand clothing, like Ray-Bans and Hollister T-shirts. We unconsciously imitate the clothing of people we look up to.
A shared sense of style builds rapport and helps you to instantly feel part of a clique. Maybe it's self-preservation, or maybe it's a hope that you will be infused with the qualities you admire.

Lift your mood

That our mood impacts what we choose to wear will not come as a surprise. How many of us think about it the other way around? What we wear could affect how we are feeling for the better or worse. One of the best cures for when you're feeling down is to wear that cozy, bright yellow sweater. More people than you might think are great believers in wearing bright colors to boost positivity. It seems simple, but why not give it a shot next time you're having a bad day?

1.1

C READ FOR DETAIL Read the article again. Complete each statement with one to three words from the article.

1 People should wear ________ when they're feeling down.
2 ________ could help people come up with new ideas.
3 People sometimes wear ________ clothing to fit in.
4 ________ may encourage people to make healthier choices.
5 People should wear ________ to feel more persuasive.
6 ________ may make people more careful at work.

D SPEAK Discuss in small groups.

1 What surprised you most about the blog post?
2 Do you think your own choice of clothes affects how you think and behave?

GRAMMAR
Nominal clauses

A Read the sentences. Is the underlined part of each sentence the subject or the object?

1 They don't enjoy wearing formal clothes.
2 Wearing a uniform can make us feel part of something.

B Work in pairs. Underline the nominal clauses in sentences from the article. Use the information in the box to help you. The first two have been done for you.

Nominal clauses

Nominal clauses are clauses that work like nouns. They are very common as objects, but they are also possible as the subject, after a preposition or the verb *be*, and in the following ways.

a nominal *-ing* clause ___
b nominal *that* clause ___
c nominal question-clause ___
d nominal infinitive ___
e We frequently use a phrase like *the fact/idea that* or *the experience/problem of* to introduce a nominal clause and make it easier to understand. ___
f *That* clauses and infinitive can sound unnatural as the subject. We can use *it* as an empty subject instead. ___

1 Luke is upset that he didn't pass.
2 Lisa doesn't enjoy watching horror movies.
3 It wasn't surprising that Tara came in first place.
4 The fact that the team won the tournament shows how good the manager is.
5 Where you go to college is your choice.
6 To tell a lie about something so important was wrong.

C WORK IT OUT Match sentences 1–6 in Exercise B with the rules (a–f) in the box.

D Go to the Grammar Hub on page 122.

E Complete the sentences so they are true for you. Then discuss in pairs.

1 What I like doing most of all in the evenings …
2 How a person is dressed …
3 Spending a lot of money on …

SPEAKING

DISCUSS Work in groups. To what extent do you agree with the following statements? Give reasons for your answers.

- Wearing a uniform affects what grades you get in school.
- Buying expensive clothes is the best way to succeed in life.
- Spending a lot of money on luxury goods makes people more generous.

TRENDS 3

Reading and Listening
Reading and listening sections allow students to practice their receptive skills. All sections have tasks that move from global to detailed understanding so students can achieve a good overall comprehension. The key skills focus is clearly marked in the activity titles. The texts and scripts also present target vocabulary, grammar or pronunciation.

Speaking
Each lesson starts with a CEFR unit objective which the lesson is designed to address. Students will often use the grammar, vocabulary and pronunciation from the lesson to complete a speaking activity linked to the unit objective. American Language Hub allows students to safely practice speaking in pairs after most sections. This ensures that they feel confident to take an active role in the final speaking task.

Student's Book Lessons 1 and 2 second spread

Reading and Listening Skill

Every unit includes a task designed to practice a key reading or listening skill. This ensures students are given the tools they need to effectively process a wide variety of texts and scripts. By the end of each book, students will have been exposed to 12 different key skills for reading or listening.

Pronunciation

In American Language Hub, lessons focus on both word-level and sentence-level pronunciation. This not only allows students to improve their accuracy, but also their fluency through sentence-level intonation, which helps students understand how to add meaning through pronunciation.

1.1

LISTENING

A SPEAK Work in pairs. Look at the infographic from a fashion magazine. What do you think the results would be in your country?

1.1 B LISTEN FOR RECOMMENDATIONS Listen to a conversation between two friends. What nine tips does Carly give Dan? Use the information in the box to help you.

Listening for recommendations

When listening for recommendations, pay attention to phrases like *it's a good idea to, it's always worth*, or *don't forget to.*

Also listen for phrases that signal a shift from main points to examples (e.g. *for instance, let's say*) and those that move from examples to new main points (e.g. *more generally, that's an example of*).

1.1 C LISTEN FOR DETAIL Listen again. Choose the correct answers (a, b or c).

1 Why is Dan worried?
  a He doesn't know what to wear for his new job.
  b He thinks people won't respect him.
  c He won't earn enough to buy nice clothes.
2 What's good about the suit Dan wants to buy?
  a the price
  b the fit
  c the quality
3 Why did Dan wear baggy sweatpants for his job interview?
  a He knew the interviewers couldn't see them.
  b He wanted to create a good impression.
  c He didn't have any other pants.
4 What should Dan do with his suit pants?
  a mend them
  b sell them
  c put them in the trash
5 According to Carly, what's good about ugly sales pages?
  a You can charge more money.
  b You appear inexperienced.
  c You can buy things cheaply.
6 Where does Carly say you can find good second-hand bargains?
  a expensive parts of town
  b trendy neighborhoods
  c areas near colleges

D SPEAK Work in small groups.

1 Which of Carly's tips do you already follow?
2 Would you try any of them in the future? Why/Why not?

4 TRENDS

FASHION TRENDS
in the US according to our readers

75% of you only buy NAME-BRAND sportswear

45% believe QUALITY is more important than VALUE for money

IMAGE is the first thing that 85% of you notice about someone the first time you meet them

65% THROW ripped clothing away rather than MENDING it

40% of our readers think FASHION is more important than COMFORT

VOCABULARY
Metaphors

A SPEAK Work in pairs. Look at the sentences. What do the underlined words and phrases mean?

1 a I'd love to come out tonight, but I'm on a tight budget. ___
  b They had some nice suits, but they were all too tight. ___
2 a The dress was so finely stitched that it looked seamless. ___
  b It needs to be a seamless process for your customers. ___
3 a Instead of buying a cheap off-the-rack suit, save up for a tailor-made suit. ___, ___
  b Don't use an off-the-shelf template for your company's website. We can design a tailor-made site to help you stand out from the competition. ___, ___

B Work in pairs. Decide whether the underlined words in Exercise A are literal (l) or metaphorical (m). Use the information in the box to help you.

Metaphors

A metaphor is a word or phrase that's used in a different context from its literal meaning. It's easier to understand a metaphor when you know the literal meaning. For example:
Literal: *There is a **breeze** outside. (= a light wind)*
Metaphorical: *It was a **breeze**! I got the job. (= easy and pleasant)*

C Complete the sentences with the correct form of the words in the box.

catch drain peanut run snap wind

1 I'm getting very ______ up about it.
2 You're throwing money down the ______.
3 It's much better in the long ______.
4 Then you'll have two suits in your closet for ______.
5 Choose a template that ______ your eye.
6 All the best stuff will be ______ up immediately.

D Work in pairs. What is the metaphorical meaning of each sentence in Exercise C?

E Complete the questions with the correct form of a word from Exercises A or C.

1 When one person leaves a job and another person takes over, how can they make the transition as ______ as possible?
2 Are you the kind of person who plans for the long ______? Or do you tend to make snap decisions?
3 Have you ever bought anything that was ______ especially for you? Or do you always buy ______ products?
4 Which current trends really ______ you up?

F SPEAK Work in pairs. Discuss the questions in Exercise E.

1.1

PRONUNCIATION
Linking /r/

A Work in pairs. Read the sentences below aloud. Draw a ‿ between any words that you think are connected by a /r/ sound.

1 I saw a nice suit yesterday for 40% off.
2 You're only saving money if you buy something you need.
3 I just wore a jacket from an old suit.
4 They had no idea I was wearing sweatpants.
5 Are auction sites the best place to pick up cheap clothes?
6 Avoid stores in a trendy area or one with a lot of students.
7 Many sales clerks are authorized to offer discounts.

1.2 B Listen to check. Then practice saying the sentences.

SPEAKING HUB

A PREPARE Choose one of the following roles. Spend a few minutes thinking about your character (e.g. your age, background, ambitions, the problems you face, etc).

- **Role 1: The fashion victim.** You always want the latest designer fashions, but you're worried you would spend far too much.
- **Role 2: The reluctant shopper.** You hate shopping and don't care what you wear, but all your clothes are old and scruffy.
- **Role 3: The trendsetter.** You like to take risks and experiment with your clothes. Just one problem: you've run out of ideas!

B DISCUSS Work in groups of two or three. Role-play a conversation between your characters. Ask your partners for more information about their situation. Offer each other (good or bad) fashion advice.

I know it feels good to snap up a bargain, but in the long run, it's just money down the drain, don't you think?

C REFLECT Report back to the class on the best and worst advice for each character.

Talk about style and fashion
Give fashion advice

TRENDS 5

Topics

American Language Hub topics contextualize the language input for the lesson. They have been selected to allow opportunities for personalization.

Speaking Hub

At the end of each lesson, students perform a longer speaking turn which is staged to allow planning and ideas creation. Students should apply their learning from the whole unit in the performance of their long speaking turn.

Student's Book Lesson 3

Topic Video

The first video in the lesson is a real-life news report or documentary clip. This video provides the context and input for the topic of the lesson. All the videos focus on current, real-world issues.

Café Hub

The second video is an episode from Café Hub, an amusing 'situation comedy' series. Meet Sam, Malcolm, Amanda, Harry and Emily as they discuss and face issues related to the topic in the first video.

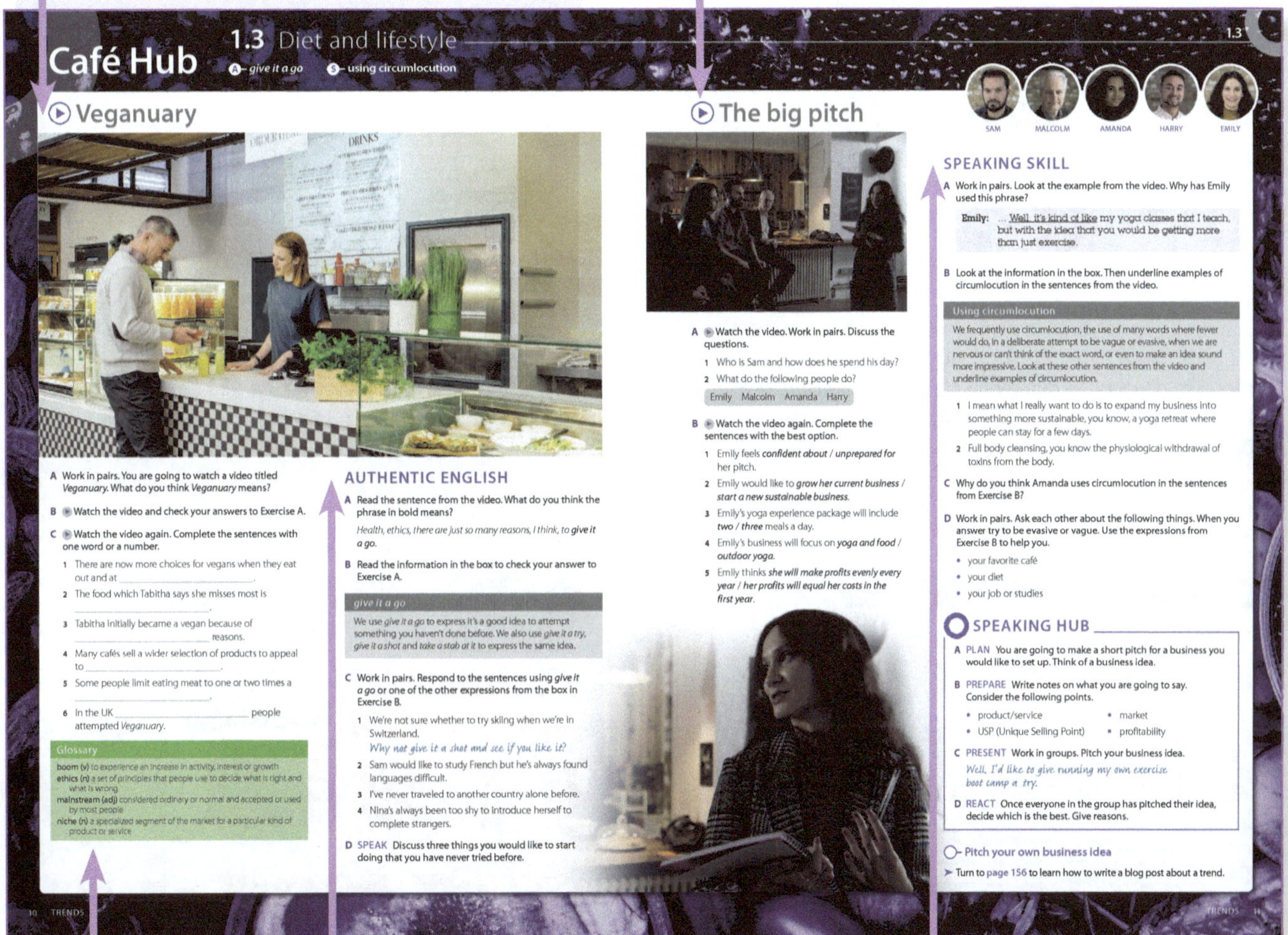

Café Hub

1.3 Diet and lifestyle

A – *give it a go* S – using circumlocution

Veganuary

A Work in pairs. You are going to watch a video titled *Veganuary*. What do you think *Veganuary* means?

B Watch the video and check your answers to Exercise A.

C Watch the video again. Complete the sentences with one word or a number.

1 There are now more choices for vegans when they eat out and at ________.
2 The food which Tabitha says she misses most is ________.
3 Tabitha initially became a vegan because of ________ reasons.
4 Many cafés sell a wider selection of products to appeal to ________.
5 Some people limit eating meat to one or two times a ________.
6 In the UK ________ people attempted *Veganuary*.

Glossary

boom (v) to experience an increase in activity, interest or growth
ethics (n) a set of principles that people use to decide what is right and what is wrong
mainstream (adj) considered ordinary or normal and accepted or used by most people
niche (n) a specialized segment of the market for a particular kind of product or service

AUTHENTIC ENGLISH

A Read the sentence from the video. What do you think the phrase in bold means?

Health, ethics, there are just so many reasons, I think, to ***give it a go****.*

B Read the information in the box to check your answer to Exercise A.

give it a go

We use *give it a go* to express it's a good idea to attempt something you haven't done before. We also use *give it a try*, *give it a shot* and *take a stab at it* to express the same idea.

C Work in pairs. Respond to the sentences using *give it a go* or one of the other expressions from the box in Exercise B.

1 We're not sure whether to try skiing when we're in Switzerland.
Why not give it a shot and see if you like it?
2 Sam would like to study French but he's always found languages difficult.
3 I've never traveled to another country alone before.
4 Nina's always been too shy to introduce herself to complete strangers.

D SPEAK Discuss three things you would like to start doing that you have never tried before.

10 TRENDS

The big pitch

SAM MALCOLM AMANDA HARRY EMILY

A Watch the video. Work in pairs. Discuss the questions.

1 Who is Sam and how does he spend his day?
2 What do the following people do?

Emily Malcolm Amanda Harry

B Watch the video again. Complete the sentences with the best option.

1 Emily feels *confident about / unprepared for* her pitch.
2 Emily would like to *grow her current business / start a new sustainable business*.
3 Emily's yoga experience package will include *two / three* meals a day.
4 Emily's business will focus on *yoga and food / outdoor yoga*.
5 Emily thinks *she will make profits evenly every year / her profits will equal her costs in the first year*.

SPEAKING SKILL

A Work in pairs. Look at the example from the video. Why has Emily used this phrase?

Emily: ... Well, it's kind of like my yoga classes that I teach, but with the idea that you would be getting more than just exercise.

B Look at the information in the box. Then underline examples of circumlocution in the sentences from the video.

Using circumlocution

We frequently use circumlocution, the use of many words where fewer would do, in a deliberate attempt to be vague or evasive, when we are nervous or can't think of the exact word, or even to make an idea sound more impressive. Look at these other sentences from the video and underline examples of circumlocution.

1 I mean what I really want to do is to expand my business into something more sustainable, you know, a yoga retreat where people can stay for a few days.
2 Full body cleansing, you know the physiological withdrawal of toxins from the body.

C Why do you think Amanda uses circumlocution in the sentences from Exercise B?

D Work in pairs. Ask each other about the following things. When you answer try to be evasive or vague. Use the expressions from Exercise B to help you.

- your favorite café
- your diet
- your job or studies

SPEAKING HUB

A PLAN You are going to make a short pitch for a business you would like to set up. Think of a business idea.

B PREPARE Write notes on what you are going to say. Consider the following points.

- product/service
- USP (Unique Selling Point)
- market
- profitability

C PRESENT Work in groups. Pitch your business idea.

Well, I'd like to give running my own exercise boot camp a try.

D REACT Once everyone in the group has pitched their idea, decide which is the best. Give reasons.

Pitch your own business idea

Turn to page 156 to learn how to write a blog post about a trend.

TRENDS 11

Variety of English

The Glossary boxes on these pages point out differences between American English and British English.

Authentic English

The first video also provides an opportunity to learn a variety of phrases that students can use to bring authenticity to their language output.

Speaking Skill

The second video provides a model for a speaking skill. Each skill helps students develop fluency and manage discussions successfully.

Student's Book Hubs

Writing Hub

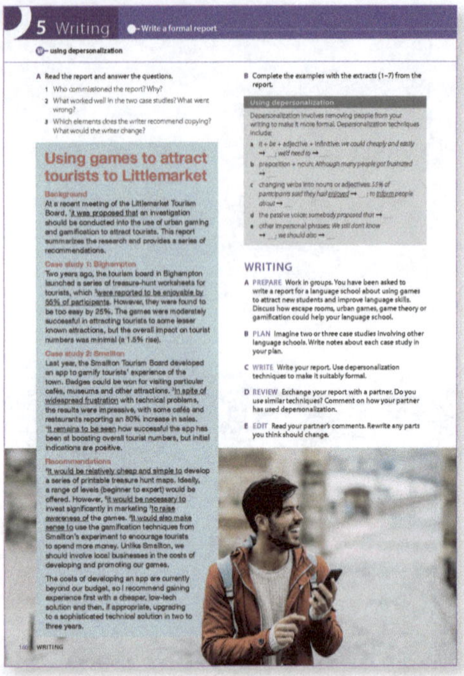

The Student's Book has an individual writing page at the back of the book for each unit. Each writing lesson is aligned to the unit topic and teaches a different writing genre and writing skill. Students can see completed writing models to analyze before they begin to write their own work.

Grammar Hub

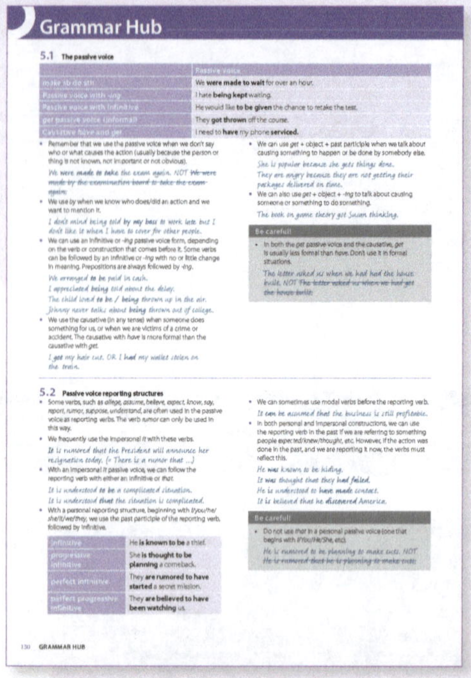

Clear explanations and further practice activities for each grammar point in the syllabus are provided at the back of the book. These can be used in class or set for homework to free up classroom time for communication.

Vocabulary Hub

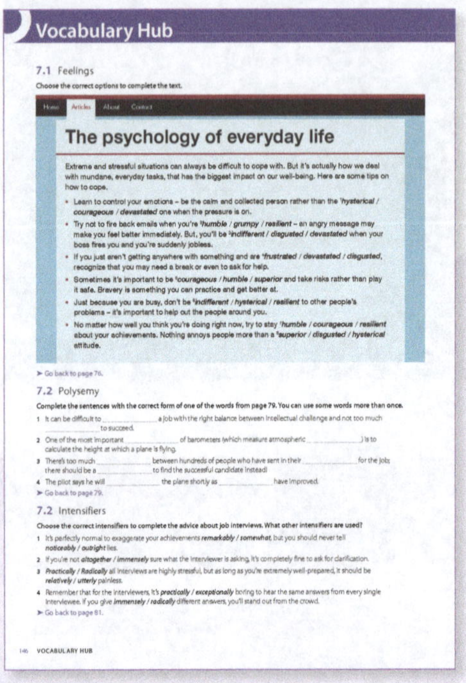

The Vocabulary Hub provides extra practice of key vocabulary presented in each unit. As with the Grammar Hub sections, these can either consolidate work done in class or be used for further self-study.

Communication Hub

The Communication Hub is used to set up longer communicative activities, such as information exchanges, quizzes and role plays.

Workbook

A Workbook is sold separately for American Language Hub. This includes 360 print activities practicing the language from the Student's Book. For each lesson there are corresponding practice exercises of grammar, vocabulary and pronunciation. There is further practice of the reading and listening skills from Lessons 1 and 2. There is also a page dedicated to the unit's writing genre and skill. All of these pages develop learning from the main lessons of the Student's Book.

Vocabulary and Grammar

The Workbook practices vocabulary and grammar that students have attended to in the Student's Book. By reminding themselves of the words and skills they have recently seen, students are better able to imbed learning and have it ready for recall during speaking practice.

Listening and Reading

The Workbook provides additional listening and reading texts that explore the topics in the Student's Book. These give students the opportunity to develop the key receptive skills from the unit.

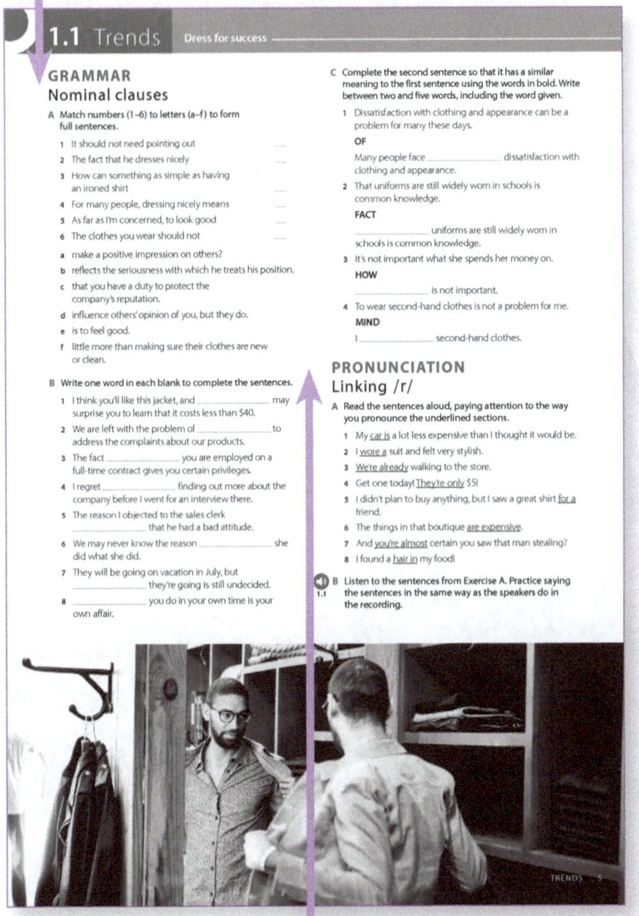

1.1 Trends   Dress for success

GRAMMAR
Nominal clauses

A Match numbers (1–6) to letters (a–f) to form full sentences.

1 It should not need pointing out ___
2 The fact that he dresses nicely ___
3 How can something as simple as having an ironed shirt ___
4 For many people, dressing nicely means ___
5 As far as I'm concerned, to look good ___
6 The clothes you wear should not ___

a make a positive impression on others?
b reflects the seriousness with which he treats his position.
c that you have a duty to protect the company's reputation.
d influence others' opinion of you, but they do.
e is to feel good.
f little more than making sure their clothes are new or clean.

B Write one word in each blank to complete the sentences.

1 I think you'll like this jacket, and ________ may surprise you to learn that it costs less than $40.
2 We are left with the problem of ________ to address the complaints about our products.
3 The fact ________ you are employed on a full-time contract gives you certain privileges.
4 I regret ________ finding out more about the company before I went for an interview there.
5 The reason I objected to the sales clerk ________ that he had a bad attitude.
6 We may never know the reason ________ she did what she did.
7 They will be going on vacation in July, but ________ they're going is still undecided.
8 ________ you do in your own time is your own affair.

C Complete the second sentence so that it has a similar meaning to the first sentence using the words in bold. Write between two and five words, including the word given.

1 Dissatisfaction with clothing and appearance can be a problem for many these days.
OF
Many people face ________ dissatisfaction with clothing and appearance.
2 That uniforms are still widely worn in schools is common knowledge.
FACT
________ uniforms are still widely worn in schools is common knowledge.
3 It's not important what she spends her money on.
HOW
________ is not important.
4 To wear second-hand clothes is not a problem for me.
MIND
I ________ second-hand clothes.

PRONUNCIATION
Linking /r/

A Read the sentences aloud, paying attention to the way you pronounce the underlined sections.

1 My car is a lot less expensive than I thought it would be.
2 I wore a suit and felt very stylish.
3 We're already walking to the store.
4 Get one today! They're only $5!
5 I didn't plan to buy anything, but I saw a great shirt for a friend.
6 The things in that boutique are expensive.
7 And you're almost certain you saw that man stealing?
8 I found a hair in my food!

1.1 B Listen to the sentences from Exercise A. Practice saying the sentences in the same way as the speakers do in the recording.

TRENDS 5

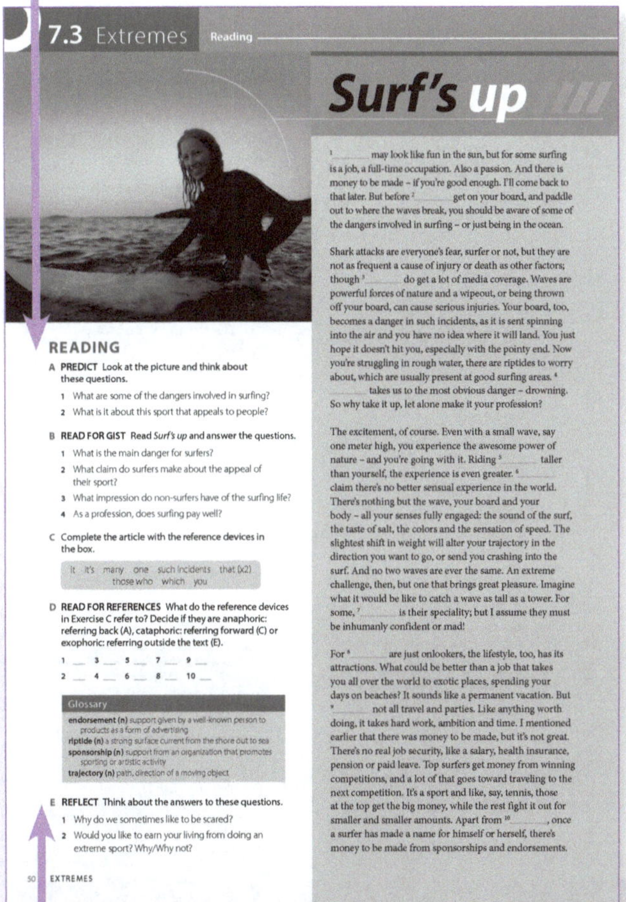

7.3 Extremes   Reading

READING

A PREDICT Look at the picture and think about these questions.

1 What are some of the dangers involved in surfing?
2 What is it about this sport that appeals to people?

B READ FOR GIST Read *Surf's up* and answer the questions.

1 What is the main danger for surfers?
2 What claim do surfers make about the appeal of their sport?
3 What impression do non-surfers have of the surfing life?
4 As a profession, does surfing pay well?

C Complete the article with the reference devices in the box.

it   it's   many   one   such incidents   that (x2)   those who   which   you

D READ FOR REFERENCES What do the reference devices in Exercise C refer to? Decide if they are anaphoric: referring back (A), cataphoric: referring forward (C) or exophoric: referring outside the text (E).

1 ___ 3 ___ 5 ___ 7 ___ 9 ___
2 ___ 4 ___ 6 ___ 8 ___ 10 ___

Glossary
endorsement (n) support given by a well-known person to products as a form of advertising
riptide (n) a strong surface current from the shore out to sea
sponsorship (n) support from an organization that promotes sporting or artistic activity
trajectory (n) path, direction of a moving object

E REFLECT Think about the answers to these questions.

1 Why do we sometimes like to be scared?
2 Would you like to earn your living from doing an extreme sport? Why/Why not?

50 EXTREMES

Surf's up

[1] ________ may look like fun in the sun, but for some surfing is a job, a full-time occupation. Also a passion. And there is money to be made – if you're good enough. I'll come back to that later. But before [2] ________ get on your board, and paddle out to where the waves break, you should be aware of some of the dangers involved in surfing – or just being in the ocean.

Shark attacks are everyone's fear, surfer or not, but they are not as frequent a cause of injury or death as other factors; though [3] ________ do get a lot of media coverage. Waves are powerful forces of nature and a wipeout, or being thrown off your board, can cause serious injuries. Your board, too, becomes a danger in such incidents, as it is sent spinning into the air and you have no idea where it will land. You just hope it doesn't hit you, especially with the pointy end. Now you're struggling in rough water, there are riptides to worry about, which are usually present at good surfing areas. [4] ________ takes us to the most obvious danger – drowning. So why take it up, let alone make it your profession?

The excitement, of course. Even with a small wave, say one meter high, you experience the awesome power of nature – and you're going with it. Riding [5] ________ taller than yourself, the experience is even greater. [6] ________ claim there's no better sensual experience in the world. There's nothing but the wave, your board and your body – all your senses fully engaged: the sound of the surf, the taste of salt, the colors and the sensation of speed. The slightest shift in weight will alter your trajectory in the direction you want to go, or send you crashing into the surf. And no two waves are ever the same. An extreme challenge, then, but one that brings great pleasure. Imagine what it would be like to catch a wave as tall as a tower. For some, [7] ________ is their speciality; but I assume they must be inhumanly confident or mad!

For [8] ________ are just onlookers, the lifestyle, too, has its attractions. What could be better than a job that takes you all over the world to exotic places, spending your days on beaches? It sounds like a permanent vacation. But [9] ________ not all travel and parties. Like anything worth doing, it takes hard work, ambition and time. I mentioned earlier that there was money to be made, but it's not great. There's no real job security, like a salary, health insurance, pension or paid leave. Top surfers get money from winning competitions, and a lot of that goes toward traveling to the next competition. It's a sport and like, say, tennis, those at the top get the big money, while the rest fight it out for smaller and smaller amounts. Apart from [10] ________, once a surfer has made a name for himself or herself, there's money to be made from sponsorships and endorsements.

Pronunciation

The Workbook also consolidates the pronunciation topics from the Student's Book through further controlled practice.

Reflect

Each reading and listening page has a Reflect section so that students can use their Workbooks in class if they wish to reflect on their learning with their peers.

American Language Hub for Teachers

Teacher's Book

Worksheets
The bank of communicative worksheets at the back of the Teacher's Book provides additional controlled and freer practice of every vocabulary and grammar section.

Procedural notes
The lessons include procedural notes for teachers. These offer support to teachers on how to deliver the lesson rather than telling them how to teach. The notes are designed to be brief and easy to read.

Interleaved pages
Every level of American Language Hub has a Teacher's Book interleaved with pages of the Student's Book. The answers to all of the Student's Book activities are annotated on the page so there is no need for teachers to flip back and forth to find information.

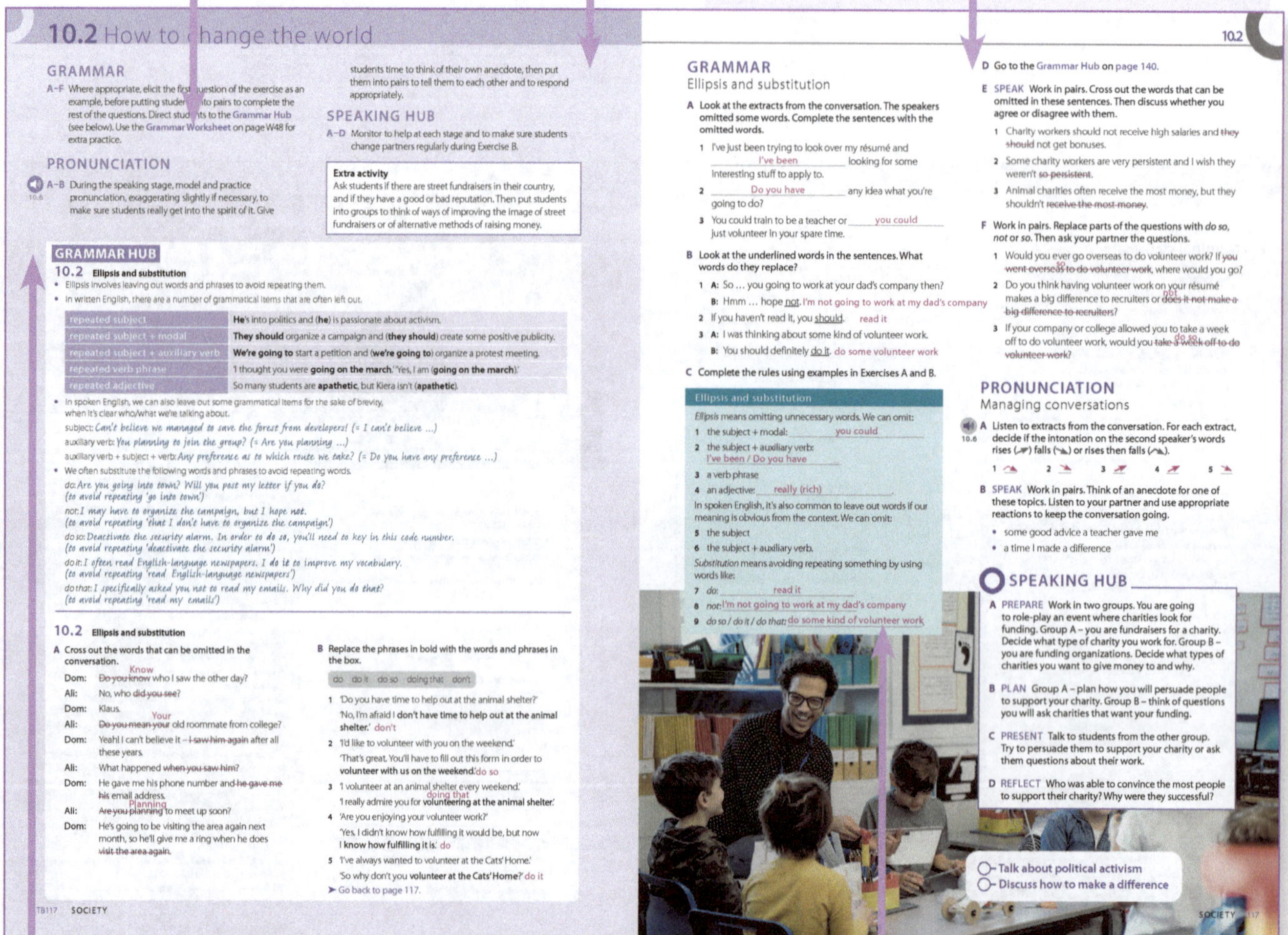

Grammar explanations
Where the Student's Book asks the students to look at the Grammar Hub, the teacher can find this already annotated on the Teacher's Book page. For ease of use, the Grammar Hub reference activities at the end of the Student's Book have been added to the Teacher's Book pages at the location they will be used in the course. This makes it easier for teachers to mark homework in class or refer to succinct grammar explanations.

Annotated answers
The answers are annotated on the interleaved pages of the Student's Book. These provide a quick reference tool for teachers.

Teacher's Book: Macmillan Books for Teachers

Lead-in

Suggested lead-ins can be used to activate prior knowledge, generate interest in the lesson topic or focus on useful lexis.

Extra activities

Extra activity boxes help teachers extend the content of the lesson, both in and out of the classroom.

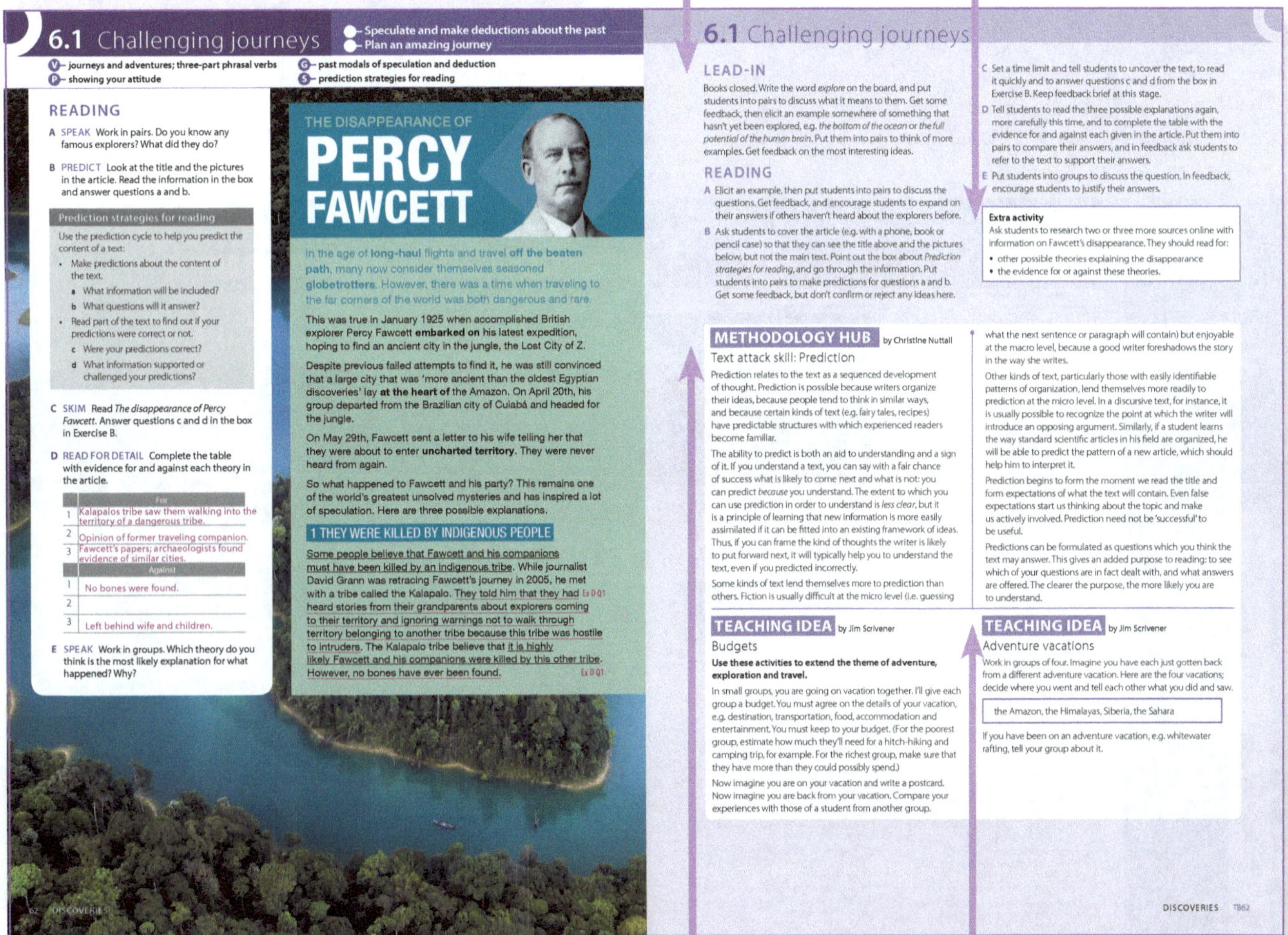

6.1 Challenging journeys

- Speculate and make deductions about the past
- Plan an amazing journey

V – journeys and adventures; three-part phrasal verbs
P – showing your attitude
G – past modals of speculation and deduction
S – prediction strategies for reading

READING

A SPEAK Work in pairs. Do you know any famous explorers? What did they do?

B PREDICT Look at the title and the pictures in the article. Read the information in the box and answer questions a and b.

Prediction strategies for reading

Use the prediction cycle to help you predict the content of a text:

- Make predictions about the content of the text.
  - a What information will be included?
  - b What questions will it answer?
- Read part of the text to find out if your predictions were correct or not.
  - c Were your predictions correct?
  - d What information supported or challenged your predictions?

C SKIM Read *The disappearance of Percy Fawcett*. Answer questions c and d in the box in Exercise B.

D READ FOR DETAIL Complete the table with evidence for and against each theory in the article.

	For
1	Kalapalos tribe saw them walking into the territory of a dangerous tribe.
2	Opinion of former traveling companion.
3	Fawcett's papers; archaeologists found evidence of similar cities.
	Against
1	No bones were found.
2	
3	Left behind wife and children.

E SPEAK Work in groups. Which theory do you think is the most likely explanation for what happened? Why?

THE DISAPPEARANCE OF PERCY FAWCETT

In the age of **long-haul** flights and travel **off the beaten path**, many now consider themselves seasoned **globetrotters**. However, there was a time when traveling to the far corners of the world was both dangerous and rare.

This was true in January 1925 when accomplished British explorer Percy Fawcett **embarked on** his latest expedition, hoping to find an ancient city in the jungle, the Lost City of Z.

Despite previous failed attempts to find it, he was still convinced that a large city that was 'more ancient than the oldest Egyptian discoveries' lay **at the heart of** the Amazon. On April 20th, his group departed from the Brazilian city of Cuiabá and headed for the jungle.

On May 29th, Fawcett sent a letter to his wife telling her that they were about to enter **uncharted territory**. They were never heard from again.

So what happened to Fawcett and his party? This remains one of the world's greatest unsolved mysteries and has inspired a lot of speculation. Here are three possible explanations.

1 THEY WERE KILLED BY INDIGENOUS PEOPLE

Some people believe that Fawcett and his companions must have been killed by an indigenous tribe. While journalist David Grann was retracing Fawcett's journey in 2005, he met with a tribe called the Kalapalo. They told him that they had heard stories from their grandparents about explorers coming to their territory and ignoring warnings not to walk through territory belonging to another tribe because this tribe was hostile to intruders. The Kalapalo tribe believe that it is highly likely Fawcett and his companions were killed by this other tribe. However, no bones have ever been found. Ex D Q1

62 DISCOVERIES

6.1 Challenging journeys

LEAD-IN

Books closed. Write the word *explore* on the board, and put students into pairs to discuss what it means to them. Get some feedback, then elicit an example somewhere of something that hasn't yet been explored, e.g. *the bottom of the ocean* or *the full potential of the human brain*. Put them into pairs to think of more examples. Get feedback on the most interesting ideas.

READING

A Elicit an example, then put students into pairs to discuss the questions. Get feedback, and encourage students to expand on their answers if others haven't heard about the explorers before.

B Ask students to cover the article (e.g. with a phone, book or pencil case) so that they can see the title above and the pictures below, but not the main text. Point out the box about *Prediction strategies for reading*, and go through the information. Put students into pairs to make predictions for questions a and b. Get some feedback, but don't confirm or reject any ideas here.

C Set a time limit and tell students to uncover the text, to read it quickly and to answer questions c and d from the box in Exercise B. Keep feedback brief at this stage.

D Tell students to read the three possible explanations again, more carefully this time, and to complete the table with the evidence for and against each given in the article. Put them into pairs to compare their answers, and in feedback ask students to refer to the text to support their answers.

E Put students into groups to discuss the question. In feedback, encourage students to justify their answers.

Extra activity

Ask students to research two or three more sources online with information on Fawcett's disappearance. They should read for:

- other possible theories explaining the disappearance
- the evidence for or against these theories.

METHODOLOGY HUB by Christine Nuttall

Text attack skill: Prediction

Prediction relates to the text as a sequenced development of thought. Prediction is possible because writers organize their ideas, because people tend to think in similar ways, and because certain kinds of text (e.g. fairy tales, recipes) have predictable structures with which experienced readers become familiar.

The ability to predict is both an aid to understanding and a sign of it. If you understand a text, you can say with a fair chance of success what is likely to come next and what is not: you can predict *because* you understand. The extent to which you can use prediction in order to understand is *less clear*, but it is a principle of learning that new information is more easily assimilated if it can be fitted into an existing framework of ideas. Thus, if you can frame the kind of thoughts the writer is likely to put forward next, it will typically help you to understand the text, even if you predicted incorrectly.

Some kinds of text lend themselves more to prediction than others. Fiction is usually difficult at the micro level (i.e. guessing what the next sentence or paragraph will contain) but enjoyable at the macro level, because a good writer foreshadows the story in the way she writes.

Other kinds of text, particularly those with easily identifiable patterns of organization, lend themselves more readily to prediction at the micro level. In a discursive text, for instance, it is usually possible to recognize the point at which the writer will introduce an opposing argument. Similarly, if a student learns the way standard scientific articles in his field are organized, he will be able to predict the pattern of a new article, which should help him to interpret it.

Prediction begins to form the moment we read the title and form expectations of what the text will contain. Even false expectations start us thinking about the topic and make us actively involved. Prediction need not be 'successful' to be useful.

Predictions can be formulated as questions which you think the text may answer. This gives an added purpose to reading: to see which of your questions are in fact dealt with, and what answers are offered. The clearer the purpose, the more likely you are to understand.

TEACHING IDEA by Jim Scrivener

Budgets

Use these activities to extend the theme of adventure, exploration and travel.

In small groups, you are going on vacation together. I'll give each group a budget. You must agree on the details of your vacation, e.g. destination, transportation, food, accommodation and entertainment. You must keep to your budget. (For the poorest group, estimate how much they'll need for a hitch-hiking and camping trip, for example. For the richest group, make sure that they have more than they could possibly spend.)

Now imagine you are on your vacation and write a postcard. Now imagine you are back from your vacation. Compare your experiences with those of a student from another group.

TEACHING IDEA by Jim Scrivener

Adventure vacations

Work in groups of four. Imagine you have each just gotten back from a different adventure vacation. Here are the four vacations; decide where you went and tell each other what you did and saw.

the Amazon, the Himalayas, Siberia, the Sahara

If you have been on an adventure vacation, e.g. whitewater rafting, tell your group about it.

DISCOVERIES TB62

Methodology Hub

Ideas for professional development from Jim Scrivener's *Learning Teaching Third Edition*, Adrian Underhill's *Sound Foundations*, Christine Nuttall's *Teaching Reading Skills in a Foreign Language*, Scott Thornbury's *Beyond the Sentence* and *The New A–Z of ELT* are presented in every unit to help new teachers pick up helpful tips to add to their repertoire or just reflect on a new way to use American Language Hub with their class.

Teaching Idea

Tips and ideas from the *Macmillan Books for Teachers* series are included in the teacher's notes to give some new ideas for instant communicative activities in the lesson. These can usually be used without paper preparation as warm-ups to get the class moving or as a flexible stage where there is time to fill.

American Language Hub for Teachers

Teacher's App

The American Language Hub Teacher's Book comes with a Teacher's App, which gives access to the Resource Center, Test Generator and Classroom Presentation Kit.

The Classroom Presentation Kit is designed to be displayed on an interactive whiteboard (IWB) or using a projector, and it enables teachers to play video and audio or show interactive activities in class. It is not only user-friendly for the teacher but also for the student, with activities being clearly visible for the whole class. Answer-by-answer reveal enables teachers to elicit student responses and check answers one by one.

Tools

Embedded tools make it possible to highlight and annotate texts to prompt noticing or self-correction. Teachers have the option to turn on an audio script, which is timed to sync with the dialogue, when listening to audio.

Teachers can zoom into each activity with one click. Then they can either move smoothly through the activities or zoom out to see the whole page. They can also create a whiteboard area for additional notes.

Video

Teachers can also access the video and audio for the course, including the authentic video from *The Guardian*.

Homework

The app allows teachers to assign homework directly to their students' devices and alert them when they have activities to complete.

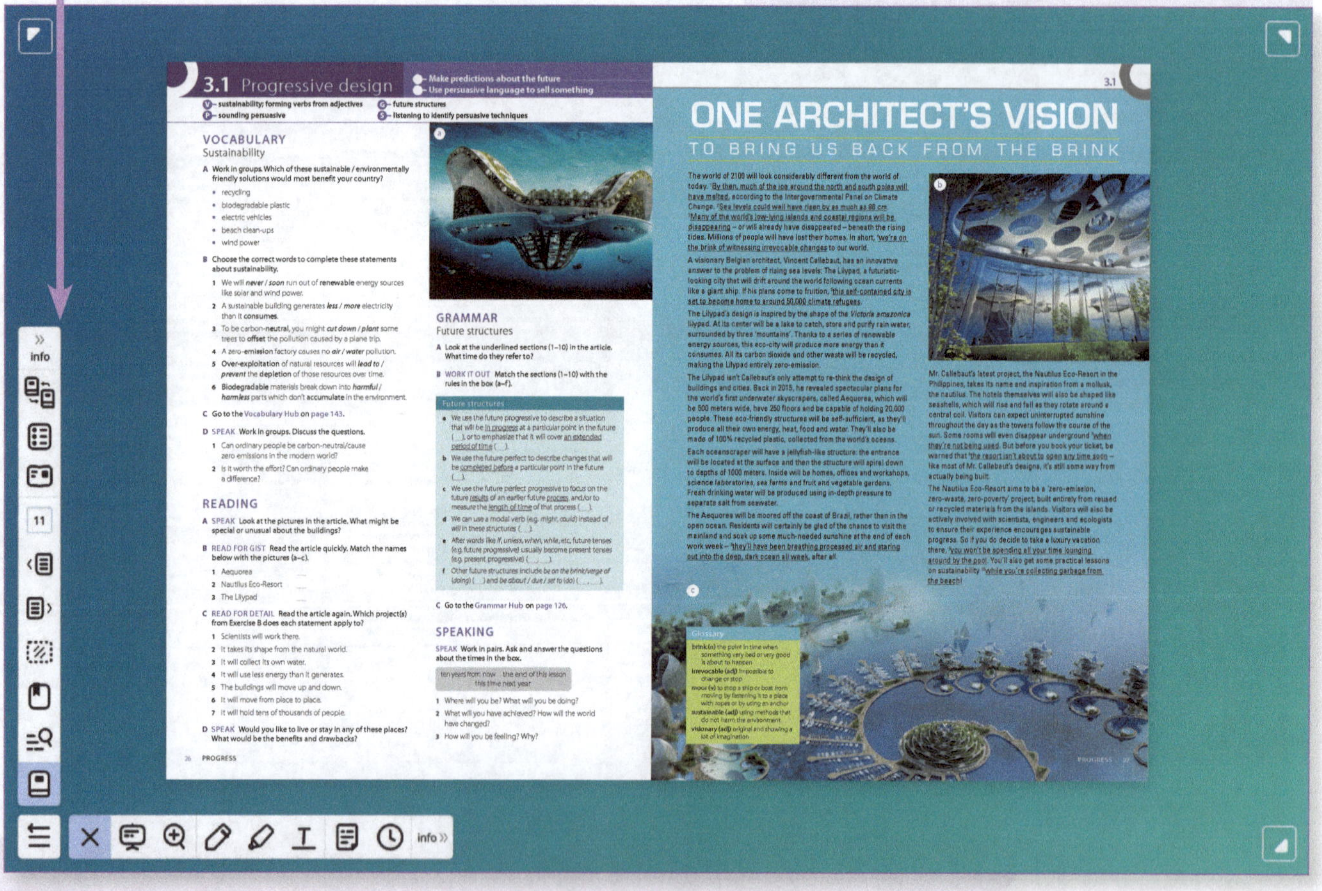

Preparation and Practice

Teachers can also configure student preparation and practice using the Teacher's App. Using the practice activities available, teachers can select and publish content to their students which they will receive through a push notification when they access their app. This enables teachers to personalize the amount and type of practice students do every week and to track their progress. Students can practice the grammar or vocabulary for the week before they go to class, allowing more time in the class for communication.

Test Generator

The Teacher's App also gives access to the Test Generator. In the Test Generator, teachers can create tests or use the pre-built tests for each level of the course and print these to assign to students. There are unit tests, and mid- and end-of-course tests for each level, testing vocabulary, grammar and the four skills.

Student's App

Each Student's Book includes a code for the Student's App, to engage and encourage your students to practice their English on the move. Students can access grammar, vocabulary and pronunciation activities to prepare them for the lesson. Students are able to complete activities with varying levels of challenge and earn points.

Preparation
Allows more time for communicative activities in the class by providing pre-lesson exposure to the language covered in the Student's Book.

Practice
Provides additional practice to consolidate, review and extend areas covered in the Student's Book.

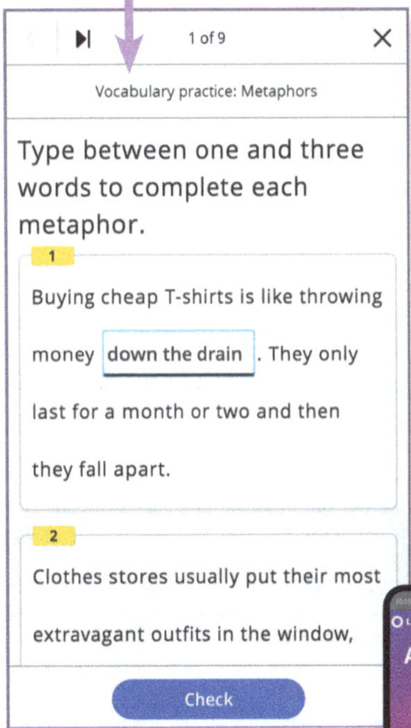

Rewards
A reward system helps to maintain student motivation.

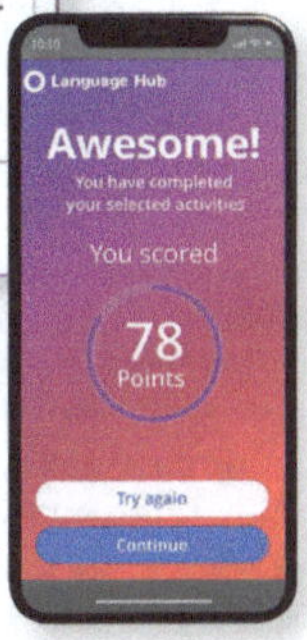

Video

Three types of video are available with the course. The Café Hub contains a real-life news or documentary clip and a situation comedy which models speaking skills. The Video Hub uses content from *The Guardian* as a resource for authentic English. All the videos from the course relate to the unit topics and offer listening practice and scaffolding for speaking output.

Video Hub

Café Hub

Student's Book Contents

Welcome

GRAMMAR

Verb tenses and structures

A Choose the correct option to complete the conversation.

A: Hello. Could you tell me [1]*where is the conversation class* / *where the conversation class is*?

B: Yes, just follow me! [2]*I'm going* / *I'll go* there now. I actually study here myself.

A: Cool. [3]*Did you* / *Have you* been studying English for long?

B: Let me think. Actually [4]*I'll have been* / *I'll be* at this school for two years at the end of this month. Don't worry. You [5]*don't have to* / *must not* bring anything. Just yourself. And there is only one rule: you [6]*don't need to* / *must not* speak in your own language in class.

A: Great, that's really important. In my last school we [7]*used to* / *get used to* do a lot of grammar. But I wasn't [8]*taught* / *didn't teach* any speaking or pronunciation. So I really need to [9]*used to* / *get used to* speaking more.

B: Yes, me too. I [10]*was learning* / *am learning* on my own for a little while, but stopped because I didn't feel like I'd made much progress.

Articles, determiners and quantifiers

B Find and correct the mistakes in the sentences.

1. It's ~~the~~ good to watch videos in English to practice your listening.
2. A lot of problems when learning a language come from lack of confidence not lack of ability.
3. It's best to get personal recommendations when finding ~~the~~ English courses.
4. When you first learn a language you should spend a great deal of time on grammar.
5. ~~A childhood~~ Childhood is a good time to start learning a language.
6. There's never ~~time enough~~ enough time when you're working and learning at the same time.
7. Most ~~the~~ people feel demotivated at some point when learning a new language.
8. Every ~~languages~~ language has it own unique pronunciation and grammar and you can't easily compare them.
9. Languages are neither fixed ~~and~~ nor completely stable but are constantly changing.

C SPEAK Work in pairs and discuss the questions.

1. Do you agree with the speakers in Exercise A? Why/Why not?
2. Do you agree with the statements in Exercise B? Why/Why not?

VOCABULARY

Collocations

A Choose the correct words to complete the collocations.

1. It's *highly* / *deeply* / *absolutely* likely that even jobs in education will be automated in the future.
2. Concerning future problems, I'm *bitterly* / *deeply* / *ridiculously* concerned about extreme weather conditions.
3. There is the possibility *for* / *of* / *about* colonizing another planet to relieve human overpopulation.
4. Young people should have *knowledge* / *ideas* / *opinions* of news sources and searching online to deal with the problem of fake news.
5. Understanding your *focus* / *target* / *regular* audience is important for being an entrepreneur.
6. Not all regeneration projects get a *positive* / *high* / *key* reaction from local communities.

Compound adjectives and nouns

B Complete the sentences with the compound adjectives and nouns in the box.

community spirit	last-minute	old-fashioned
six-bedroom	street parties	up-to-date

1. Visit our website for the most up-to-date travel times and last-minute deals.
2. Mark and Susan have just bought a huge six-bedroom house in the country. It's a little old-fashioned, but they're planning on renovating it.
3. There is great community spirit in my town. The local council usually organize street parties for national holidays.

C SPEAK Work in pairs. Do you agree with the statements in Exercise A?

PRONUNCIATION

0.1 **A Circle the arrows to predict which intonation will be used. Then listen and check.**

1. Is this meeting finishing soon? **(↗)** / [↘]
2. How often do you come to these classes? **(↗)** / [↘]
3. Unless there is a good reason **(↗)** / [↘], you shouldn't work late. [↗] / **(↘)**
4. Take some chocolate bars **(↗)** / [↘], in case you need a quick snack. [↗] / **(↘)**

0.2 **B Listen to the sentences. Draw (‿) between any words that link together.**

1. He's improved‿a lot despite having‿a few problems.
2. We went‿out‿at night‿a lot to see the city.
3. Plenty‿of people find it difficult at first.
4. Hundreds‿of people came out to see her talk.

C Practice saying the sentences in Exercise B.

A flamingo among geese, egrets, swans and herons.

Trend (n) a gradual change or development that produces a particular result.
Synonyms: fashion (n), change (n)

Samuel Johnson means that most people don't think for themselves and simply follow the crowd.

Samuel Johnson (1709–1784) was an English writer. He was a poet and playwright, among other things, but he is most famous for writing *A Dictionary of the English Language*, published in 1755.

OBJECTIVES

- talk about style and fashion
- give fashion advice
- compare different trends
- make a podcast or vlog
- pitch your own business idea
- write a blog post

Work with a partner. Discuss the questions.

1 Look at the picture. How does it relate to trends?
2 Read the quote. What do you think it means? Do you agree?
3 How important are trends in the following areas to you?
- fashion
- music
- design
- lifestyle

TRENDS 1

OBJECTIVES

Read the unit objectives to the class.

UNIT OPENER QUESTIONS

1 Put students in pairs to discuss the picture's message and how it is related to the topic of trends. Get some whole-class feedback.

2 Tell students to discuss the meaning of the quote and if they agree with it. Encourage them to think of examples to support their opinion (e.g. a trend that a lot of people are currently following).

3 Give your own example of how important some of those trends are to you before students discuss the question in pairs. Again, encourage students to give examples and to expand on these in class feedback.

WORKSHEETS

Lesson 1.1 Dress for success

Vocabulary: Clothes and fashion (W1)

Grammar: Nominal clauses (W2)

Vocabulary: Metaphors (W3)

Lesson 1.2 Trendsetting

Grammar: Comparatives and superlatives (W4)

Vocabulary: Experimenting with prefixes and suffixes (W5)

1.1 Dress for success

- Talk about style and fashion
- Give fashion advice

V – clothes and fashion; metaphors   G – nominal clauses   P – linking /r/   S – listening for recommendations

VOCABULARY
Clothes and fashion

A Work in pairs. Take the quiz.

B Go to the Vocabulary Hub on page 142.

1. Do you carefully plan your **outfits** or just wear the first thing on hand?
2. Have you ever had to attend an event with **a dress code**?
3. If you had to go to a **costume** party, what costume would you wear?
4. Are people more productive when they wear a **uniform** or **casual** clothing?
5. Would you describe yourself as a **trendsetter** or a **trend follower**?
6. Is it better to **fit in with** or **stand out** from **the crowd**?
7. Do you ever wear **baggy** or **scruffy** clothes to relax at home?

READING

A PREDICT Work in pairs. Read the title of the article. Look at pictures 1–3. How might what the people are wearing affect their behavior?

Relaxed clothes could make you feel more creative.
A uniform could give a sense of belonging and duty. Bright clothes boost positivity.

B SCAN Read *Style speaks* and check your predictions from Exercise A.

1

STYLE *speaks*

We've all heard the old adages ... *Dress for the job you want, not the job you have. Look good, feel good.* These clichés are somewhat worn out. How can the way we dress affect our lives? But it seems there may be some truth in them after all. People do form first impressions based on what we're wearing. Not only that but maybe even part of our own self-worth is tied up in the clothing choices we make.

Power dressing

Not convinced? Imagine turning up for an interview at a big city firm, or company in the jeans you've been wearing for the past three days and an old baggy T-shirt. Would you be successful in getting the job? Unlikely. Would you
Ex C feel self-conscious about what you're wearing? Very likely.
Q5 It seems that wearing dress clothes, such as a well-made suit, could help you feel more confident. And when we're feeling confident we negotiate better, we respond better to questions and we put other people at ease.

2

Breaking free

Ex B On the flip side, wearing fitted or tailored clothing is not what most of us would choose to wear when we are trying to be creative. Can you imagine writing the next great novel, or coming up with a great innovation while sitting and typing away in a $2,000 designer
Ex B suit? This is why many leading tech companies have an ultra-relaxed dress code and encourage casual clothing. Mark Zuckerberg isn't topping any best-dressed lists but his billions of dollars make up for it.
Ex C Q2 Furthermore, many workplaces have 'Casual Fridays' to encourage employees to let their hair down a little and get creativity flowing.

Uniform thinking

Ex B Wearing a uniform can make us feel part of
Ex C Q6 something – provide us with a sense of belonging, but also one of duty. Many people argue that wearing school uniforms encourages us to work harder. While this is not necessarily true, there is no doubt that when, for example, a firefighter puts on a helmet or a doctor puts on a white coat, it comes with a responsibility. So fundamentally, to dress the role is to start to live it.

Glossary

adage (n) a well-known phrase that says something about life and human experience
clique (n) a small group of people who seem unfriendly to other people
unconsciously (adv) without realizing or being aware of one's actions

1.1 Dress for success

LEAD-IN

Books closed. Put students into pairs and give them one minute to write down as many items of clothing as they can. Then tell them to arrange the items into categories (e.g. men's/women's clothes, summer/winter clothes, items made of cotton/leather, etc). Get class feedback, write on the board any interesting or unusual items. Check understanding and help with pronunciation where necessary.

VOCABULARY

A Point out the words in red and ask students to use the context of the quiz to work out their meanings. Do number 1 as a class example, and tell students to continue in pairs. Monitor to help or prompt where necessary. Lead class feedback, and clarify the meaning of anything students struggled with.

B Direct students to the **Vocabulary Hub** (see TB121). For Exercise B in the **Vocabulary Hub**, check that students understand the differences between the words in whole-class feedback. Use the **Vocabulary Worksheet** on page W1 for extra practice.

Suggested answers

1 *A dress code tells people more or less what to wear (e.g. suits and ties), while a uniform forces everyone to wear exactly the same clothes.*
2 *A trend can be set in fashion, music, etc; after it's started, other people follow it.*
3 *They both describe a complete set of clothes that someone wears together, but a costume is an outfit for somebody who is pretending to be someone else (e.g. an actor) or a traditional set of clothes for a particular place/time.*
4 *They both contrast with dress clothes. Scruffy clothes may be dirty or damaged; casual clothes are comfortable but still typically clean and in good condition.*
5 *If you stand out from the crowd, you look different from everyone else; if you fit in, you look similar to everyone else.*
6 *Both describe clothes that are very loose. Oversized clothes are too big for you; baggy clothes may be the right size for you, but are deliberately designed to be loose-fitting.*

READING

A Draw students' attention to the title of the article and pictures 1–3. Allow them a minute or so to reflect on the question before moving on to Exercise B.

B Set a suitable time limit, and explain that students don't need to read and understand every word to be able to complete the task. Get class feedback, but don't go into too much depth at this stage.

C Tell students to read the article more closely and to complete the sentences. Ask fast finishers to check their answers in pairs, or alternatively, you could put a fast finisher with a weaker student to show them how and where they found the answers. In class feedback, encourage students to refer to the text to justify their answers.

D Put students into small groups to discuss the questions. Elicit some of the most interesting ideas or answers.

TEACHING IDEA by David Seymour and Maria Popova

Uniforms

Use this activity to extend the theme of clothes and fashion.

Why do people wear uniforms? Have you ever worn one? Tell us when it was, and why you wore it. How is a uniform different from a dress code? What is 'dressing down'?

Here is a list of people who dress in a particular way. Describe how they dress. Can you think of any more?

B boys (hip hop), grunge kids, ravers, new age people, goths, surfers, punks

In small groups, discuss why these groups dress as they do. What messages are they trying to send?

TEACHING IDEA by David Seymour and Maria Popova

Kinds of clothes

Use this activity to extend the theme of clothes and fashion.

What does the rhyme 'Something old, something new, something borrowed, something blue' refer to? (*Answer: Traditional advice on what to wear at a wedding.*)

In small groups, think of the best clothes for these situations:

a walk in the snow, a party, a job interview, a naming ceremony, a camel ride in the desert, a nightclub, an expedition into the jungle

Tell each other about a time you had to dress up for a formal occasion or a special event.

TEACHING IDEA by David Seymour and Maria Popova

Fashion statements

Use this activity to extend the theme of clothes and fashion.

In small groups, briefly discuss these questions and choose someone to report the group's opinions and answers to the class.

Where do you buy your clothes?
What is the most expensive garment you've ever bought?
What is good and bad taste in clothes?
Who is the best-dressed person in the class?
Which countries are the most influential in fashion?
What do you think of the fur trade?
Which famous designers do you know about?
What is a 'fashion statement'? Do you ever make your own clothes?
What piece of clothing would you most like to buy?
What piece of clothing would you most hate to wear?
Is fashion important? Why (not)?
What do clothes tell you about the person wearing them?

TEACHING IDEA by David Seymour and Maria Popova

Projects

Use this activity to extend the theme of clothes and fashion.

Write a description of someone you saw today, or an imaginary description of a famous person you'd like to meet. Then work in pairs. Student A, read the beginning of your description. Student B, ask yes/no questions about what the person was wearing. Then swap roles.

Use the internet to find a biography of a famous fashion designer. Write notes for a short presentation. Bring some pictures of his/her designs you feel strongly about. Work in small groups and show the others what you have brought and why you chose the designer.

GRAMMAR

A–C Put students into pairs to complete the exercises.

D Direct students to the **Grammar Hub** (see below).

E Give your own examples, before students discuss in pairs. Use the **Grammar Worksheet** on page W2 for extra practice.

SPEAKING

Put students into groups to discuss the statements. Encourage them to fully explain their reasons for agreeing or disagreeing with each one. Get some feedback and encourage students to expand further on their answers.

GRAMMAR HUB

1.1 Nominal clauses

- Nominal clauses function like nouns. They can be used as the subject or object of a sentence, after a preposition, an adjective or the verb *to be*.
- Nominal *-ing* clause (also known as a 'participle clause'):

Wearing a uniform can help people feel part of the team. (as subject)

I don't enjoy wearing formal clothes. (as object)

I'm excited about buying some new outfits. (after a preposition)

- Nominal *that* clause:

That she won again this year is not surprising. (as subject: this use is rare)

I explained that she would have to buy a new outfit. (as object)

I'm worried that I won't fit in. (after an adjective)

- Nominal question clause:

What you wear is entirely up to you. (as subject)

My appearance certainly affects how I feel. (as object)

Fiona felt embarrassed because of how she looked. (after a preposition)

- Nominal infinitive:

To spend so much money on clothes is totally unnecessary. (as subject: this use is rare)

It's a good idea to wear dress clothes for an interview. (as object)

I was surprised to learn about the dress code. (after an adjective)

- We frequently use phrases like *The fact/idea that …* or *The experience/problem of …* to introduce a nominal clause.

The fact that you got a high grade shows how hard you worked.

The experience of traveling on the Orient Express was one she would never forget.

Be careful!

- Because *that* clauses and infinitive clauses can sometimes sound unnatural as subjects, we usually use *it* as an empty subject.

It doesn't surprise me that you hate shopping.

NOT ~~That you hate shopping doesn't surprise me.~~

1.1 Nominal clauses

A Correct the mistakes in each sentence.

1 It's an unwritten rule ~~what~~ that employees must stick to the dress code.
2 The fact ~~of~~ that you wear a uniform sends a certain message about your status.
3 You'll regret ~~not to wear~~ not wearing / that you didn't wear nicer clothes to yesterday's interview.
4 David insisted on ~~that he pay~~ paying for all the designer clothes I'd chosen!
5 The reason for Sarah's absence ~~that~~ was / is that she never received her invitation.
6 ~~That~~ What I had forgotten was that the restaurant only lets in nicely dressed customers.
7 The clothing company more than ~~double~~ doubled its annual profits.
8 Sandra always wants to buy clothes at the ~~possible lowest~~ lowest possible price.

B Choose the correct options to complete the conversation.

Joey: I'm really eager [1]__*to start*__ / *about starting* my new job next week.

Phoebe: I'm sure [2]*you to* / __*that you will*__ fit in really well.

Joey: They explained [3]__*that they have*__ / *having* a dress code there. So … [4]*that I buy* / __*buying*__ a business suit is my first priority! Will you come and help me choose one?

Phoebe: Of course. I think you should be prepared [5]__*to spend*__ / *that you spend* a lot of money.

Joey: What do you mean?

Phoebe: You must know [6]__*that*__ / *the fact* an expensive suit will last longer than a cheap one?

Joey: Oh, I see [7]__*what*__ / *that* you mean. OK. But [8]*I'm needing to know* / __*what I really need to know*__ is what color to choose!

C Complete the second sentence so that it has a similar meaning to the first sentence, using the word given. Write between two and five words.

1 That designer clothes are hugely expensive is well-known.
FACT
The fact that designer clothes are hugely expensive is well-known.

2 It's none of my business what he does in his free time.
SPENDS
How he spends his free time is none of my business.

3 The purchase of expensive school uniforms is a problem which many parents face.
OF
Many parents face the problem of purchasing expensive school uniforms.

➤ Go back to page 3.

C READ FOR DETAIL Read the article again. Complete each statement with one to three words from the article.

1 People should wear bright colors when they're feeling down.
2 Casual Fridays could help people come up with new ideas.
3 People sometimes wear name-brand clothing to fit in.
4 'Athleisure' clothing may encourage people to make healthier choices.
5 People should wear dress clothes / a well-made suit to feel more persuasive.
6 Uniforms may make people more careful at work.

D SPEAK Discuss in small groups.

1 What surprised you most about the blog post?
2 Do you think your own choice of clothes affects how you think and behave?

Gym ready

It's not just work that clothing affects, but lifestyle as well. Professional and semi-professional athletes tend to stick rigidly to an 'athleisure' style. (Ex C Q4) Their reasoning? They don't enjoy wearing formal clothes. And they want to be able to work out whenever they feel like it. And for many, having the clothes on reminds them to make healthier choices (Ex C Q4) … to choose the fruit salad over the fruit pie.

Pack mentality

Have we really evolved that much away from our primal, tribal instincts? Visit any city center at lunchtime on a Saturday and your answer will be probably not. The packs of roving teenagers are dressed in a pseudo uniform of name-brand clothing, (Ex C Q3) like Ray-Bans and Hollister T-shirts. We unconsciously imitate the clothing of people we look up to. A shared sense of style builds rapport and helps you to instantly feel part of a clique. Maybe it's self-preservation, or maybe it's a hope that you will be infused with the qualities you admire.

Lift your mood

That our mood impacts what we choose to wear will not come as a surprise. How many of us think about it the other way around? What we wear could affect how we are feeling for the better or worse. One of the best cures for when you're feeling down is to wear that cozy, bright yellow sweater. (Ex B) More people than you might think are great believers in wearing bright colors to boost positivity. (Ex C Q1) It seems simple, but why not give it a shot next time you're having a bad day?

3

GRAMMAR

Nominal clauses

A Read the sentences. Is the underlined part of each sentence the subject or the object?

1 They don't enjoy wearing formal clothes. object
2 Wearing a uniform can make us feel part of something. subject

B Work in pairs. Underline the nominal clauses in sentences from the article. Use the information in the box to help you. The first two have been done for you.

Nominal clauses

Nominal clauses are clauses that work like nouns. They are very common as objects, but they are also possible as the subject, after a preposition or the verb *be*, and in the following ways.

a nominal *-ing* clause 2
b nominal *that* clause 1
c nominal question-clause 5
d nominal infinitive 6
e We frequently use a phrase like *the fact/idea that* or *the experience/problem of* to introduce a nominal clause and make it easier to understand. 4
f *That* clauses and infinitive can sound unnatural as the subject. We can use *it* as an empty subject instead. 3

1 Luke is upset that he didn't pass.
2 Lisa doesn't enjoy watching horror movies.
3 It wasn't surprising that Tara came in first place.
4 The fact that the team won the tournament shows how good the manager is.
5 Where you go to college is your choice.
6 To tell a lie about something so important was wrong.

C WORK IT OUT Match sentences 1–6 in Exercise B with the rules (a–f) in the box.

D Go to the **Grammar Hub** on **page 122**.

E Complete the sentences so they are true for you. Then discuss in pairs.

1 What I like doing most of all in the evenings …
2 How a person is dressed …
3 Spending a lot of money on …

SPEAKING

DISCUSS Work in groups. To what extent do you agree with the following statements? Give reasons for your answers.

- Wearing a uniform affects what grades you get in school.
- Buying expensive clothes is the best way to succeed in life.
- Spending a lot of money on luxury goods makes people more generous.

LISTENING

A SPEAK Work in pairs. Look at the infographic from a fashion magazine. What do you think the results would be in your country?

1.1 **B LISTEN FOR RECOMMENDATIONS** Listen to a conversation between two friends. What nine tips does Carly give Dan? Use the information in the box to help you.

Listening for recommendations

When listening for recommendations, pay attention to phrases like *it's a good idea to*, *it's always worth*, or *don't forget to*.

Also listen for phrases that signal a shift from main points to examples (e.g. *for instance*, *let's say*) and those that move from examples to new main points (e.g. *more generally*, *that's an example of*).

1.1 **C LISTEN FOR DETAIL** Listen again. Choose the correct answers (a, b or c).

1 Why is Dan worried?
  a He doesn't know what to wear for his new job.
  b He thinks people won't respect him.
  c He won't earn enough to buy nice clothes.

2 What's good about the suit Dan wants to buy?
  a the price
  b the fit
  c the quality

3 Why did Dan wear baggy sweatpants for his job interview?
  a He knew the interviewers couldn't see them.
  b He wanted to create a good impression.
  c He didn't have any other pants.

4 What should Dan do with his suit pants?
  a mend them
  b sell them
  c put them in the trash

5 According to Carly, what's good about ugly sales pages?
  a You can charge more money.
  b You appear inexperienced.
  c You can buy things cheaply.

6 Where does Carly say you can find good second-hand bargains?
  a expensive parts of town
  b trendy neighborhoods
  c areas near colleges

D SPEAK Work in small groups.

1 Which of Carly's tips do you already follow?
2 Would you try any of them in the future? Why/Why not?

FASHION TRENDS
in the US according to our readers

75% of you only buy **NAME-BRAND** sportswear

45% believe **QUALITY** is more important than **VALUE** for money

IMAGE is the first thing that **85%** of you notice about someone the first time you meet them

65% **THROW** ripped clothing away rather than **MENDING** it

40% of our readers think **FASHION** is more important than **COMFORT**

VOCABULARY
Metaphors

A SPEAK Work in pairs. Look at the sentences. What do the underlined words and phrases mean?

1 a I'd love to come out tonight, but I'm on a <u>tight</u> budget. ___
  b They had some nice suits, but they were all too <u>tight</u>. ___
2 a The dress was so finely stitched that it looked <u>seamless</u>. ___
  b It needs to be a <u>seamless</u> process for your customers. ___
3 a Instead of buying a cheap <u>off-the-rack</u> suit, save up for a <u>tailor-made</u> suit. ___, ___
  b Don't use an <u>off-the-shelf</u> template for your company's website. We can design a <u>tailor-made</u> site to help you stand out from the competition. ___, ___

1.1 Dress for success

LISTENING

A Put students into pairs to discuss the question.

B 1.1
1 *Invest in timeless classics*
2 *Buy oversized clothes (and take them in)*
3 *Learn to sew*
4 *Mix and match (parts of different outfits)*
5 *Go shopping in your closet*
6 *(When selling clothes online) make your sales page look good*
7 *(When buying clothes online) look out for newbie sellers*
8 *Buy (cheap second-hand clothes) from thrift stores*
9 *Haggle (to get the price down)*

C–D 1.1 Put students into pairs then groups to complete the exercises.

AUDIO SCRIPT

1.1

Listening, Exercise B
C = Carly D = Dan

C: So? How did the job interview go, Dan?
D: It was a breeze! I got the job. But the thing is, I start in two weeks and I don't have anything to wear. The job involves meeting important clients. But they won't take me seriously in my scruffy jeans and hoodie! (Ex C Q1)
C: Sounds like you need some new clothes.
D: I know. But I'm on a tight budget until I receive my first few months' salary.
C: Well, it's easy to look good without spending a fortune. Do you have a suit?
D: No, but I saw a suit yesterday for 40% off in a sale, so I'll save almost $100 if I buy that.
C: Well, you're only saving money if you buy something you really need. If you're just buying it because it's cheap, you're throwing money down the drain. It's much better in the long run to invest in timeless classics. (Ex B) For example, instead of buying a cheap off-the-rack suit that you'll need to replace in a few months, save up for a tailor-made suit that will make you look great for many years.
D: OK, I admit that suit was a little cheap-looking. But it was the only one in my size. They had some nice suits in the sale, but they were all too tight or too loose for me. (Ex C Q2)
C: Well, you can always buy oversized clothes (Ex B) – as long as they're good quality, and then take them in.
D: What do you mean, take them in?
C: It's when you unpick the seams, move the pieces of fabric closer together and sew them back together. In fact, more generally, I'd say the best way to look good without spending a lot of money is to learn to sew. (Ex B) But hang on a second. Didn't you have to wear a suit for the job interview?
D: Well, it was an online interview, (Ex C Q3) so I just wore a jacket from an old suit and a nice shirt and tie to create a good impression. They had no idea I was wearing baggy sweatpants under my desk!
C: Haha, no, you're kidding me! It's usually a good idea to mix and match parts of different outfits, (Ex B) which can save you a lot of money, but I'd say mixing a suit with a sweatsuit is taking things a little far! Do you still have the pants to go with that jacket?
D: Yeah, I actually have two old suits with perfectly good jackets but pants that I can't wear! One pair is coming apart at the seams. The other is completely worn out at the knee.
C: Hmm, it sounds like you can start your sewing lessons on those pants! (Ex C Q4) Then you'll have two suits in your closet for peanuts! That's actually a good example of how to go shopping in your closet. (Ex B)
D: Sorry. Where?
C: In your closet. Most people have a lot of clothes that they never wear. The trick is to sort them into four categories: love, mend, sell and trash.
D: Go on.
C: 'Love' is for the clothes that make you look and feel great. 'Mend' is for the clothes that you need to adjust or repair. 'Sell' is for the clothes that you can auction online. And then 'trash' is for everything else. Basically you need to get rid of them!
D: OK, I have a lot of clothes that I could sell, but I've never used an auction website before. Do you think anyone will buy my old clothes?
C: You'd be surprised. I mean, most customers on those sites stick to the professional sellers with beautiful tailor-made sales pages created by web designers. But I actually buy most of my clothes from ugly sales pages, created by inexperienced sellers.
D: What? Are you saying I should create an ugly sales page for my second-hand clothes?
C: No, not at all. The more professional your sales page, the more you can charge for your clothes. And it needs to be a seamless process for your customers from beginning to end. So as a general rule, when you're selling clothes, it's well worth taking the time to make your sales page look good. (Ex B) For example, you can just use one of the off-the-rack templates from the auction site. Choose a template that catches your eye – it's much better than creating your own site from scratch.
D: OK, sounds like good advice. And when I'm buying clothes online, to replace the ones I'm selling?
C: Then you should look out for newbie sellers with bad photos (Ex B) – they're usually good for picking up a bargain. (Ex C Q5)
D: Ah, yes, that makes sense. So are auction sites the best place to pick up cheap second-hand clothes?
C: Sometimes, but the best place to buy them is usually thrift stores, (Ex B) even though they're pretty exhausting! You need to know where to go if you want to avoid wearing yourself out for nothing! For instance, the best thrift stores are in expensive, exclusive neighborhoods. (Ex C Q6) You'd be amazed what you can pick up there. The trick is to avoid stores in a trendy area or one with a lot of students – all the best stuff will be snapped up immediately.
D: OK, good. What about regular stores?
C: They're fine as long as you're not too choosy – the big-name stores are usually no better than others, but they charge a lot more for the same stuff! But wherever you go, don't forget to haggle to get the price down. (Ex B)
D: What do you mean?
C: Ask the sales clerk for a discount. I always ask, 'Is this the best you can do?' Many sales clerks are authorized to offer discounts, so it's always worth haggling. You have nothing to lose but your pride!
D: OK. I'll give it a try. Thanks.

1.1 Dress for success

VOCABULARY

A Do the first pair as a class example, then put students into pairs to continue. In feedback, make sure students fully understand the meaning of each word or phrase.

Suggested answers

1 a *very little money to spend*
b *not big enough*
2 a *smooth without seams or obvious joins*
b *changing or continuing very smoothly*
3 a *available to buy on a store shelf; made to fit a particular customer*
b *sold for general use ; designed for a particular customer*

B Point out the information in the box about metaphors, and use the examples given to make sure students understand the difference between literal and metaphorical meaning.

C Explain that the sentences are all from the conversation between Carly and Dan and that they all contain metaphors. Students fill in the blanks with the words in the box.

D Suggested answers

1 *stressed or irritated* 4 *a small amount of money*
2 *wasting money* 5 *gets your attention*
3 *over a longer period* 6 *bought and sold very quickly*

E Get feedback from one or two pairs.

F Monitor, helping where necessary and put any new vocabulary on the board. Ask one or two pairs to give their opinions on the questions in whole-class feedback. Use the **Vocabulary Worksheet** on page W3 for extra practice.

Note: American English typically uses "off-the-rack" to refer to clothing but "off-the-shelf" for other terms.

PRONUNCIATION

A Do the first one as an example, modeling the pronunciation of the sentence and exaggerating slightly on the underlined words if necessary. Then, put students into pairs to continue with the rest. Encourage them to say the sentences out loud as they do this, so they become more aware of this feature of connected speech.

1.2 **B** Tell students to listen and check and then to repeat the sentences for further practice.

SPEAKING HUB

A Put students into groups of three, and assign each student one of the roles. Tell them to work individually to think about their character. Give your own example, including information about age, background, ambitions and problems. Use some examples of the metaphors from earlier on as you do this.

B Tell the students to remain in character and to work with the other members of their group. With a stronger student, model a short conversation where you explain your situations and give each other some advice. Tell students in their groups to have similar conversations. Monitor to help and prompt if necessary.

C Students report back to the class on the best and worst advice they were given. Finish with feedback on students' language.

Extra activity

Tell each group to compile a list of the three best tips they thought of. Regroup students so each new group contains one representative of each previous group. Tell them to discuss their lists of tips and to agree on the best three overall. Get class feedback and try to reach a consensus on the best three tips.

METHODOLOGY HUB by Adrian Underhill

Linking /r/

In RP the letter *r* in the spelling of a word is not pronounced unless it is followed by a vowel sound. But in connected speech, the final spelling *r* of a word may be pronounced or not, depending on whether the first sound of the next word is a consonant or vowel.

Discovery activity

Say the following phrases and decide if the *r* at the end of the first word is sounded or not:

- her English
- her Spanish
- car seat
- car engine
- brother and sister

Commentary

In the second and third phrases, the *r* is not sounded as the following sound is a consonant. In the first, fourth and fifth phrases, the *r* is a linking **/r/** joining the first word to the second which begins with a vowel.

Note that the term linking **/r/** can be applied only when the letter *r* occurs in the written form.

The notion of linking **/r/** is redundant in rhotic varieties of English that typically pronounce all *r*'s occurring in spelling form. Learner dictionaries show linking **/r/** in parentheses as part of the pronunciation.

TEACHING IDEA by David Seymour and Maria Popova

Clothes lines

Point out that sayings are often metaphorical.

In groups, discuss the meaning of these sayings.

Keep it under your hat. I wear the pants. We'll have to tighten our belts. She has a bee in her bonnet. Keep your shirt on. Put yourself in my shoes. He's too big for his boots.

Tell the rest of the class some clothes sayings from your country.

METHODOLOGY HUB by Adrian Underhill

Intrusive /r/

This refers to the **/r/** sound an English speaker may insert between two words where the first ends in **/ə/** or **/ɔː/** and the following word begins with a vowel sound.

Discovery activity

See if you can make use of intrusive **/r/**. Say these two phrases and notice how you join the first to the second word.

- America and Canada
- law and order

Commentary

Some speakers would say **/əmerɪkə ən kænədə/**, or **/lɔː r ən ɔːdə/**. Use of this intrusive **/r/** is frequent though by no means obligatory. The only difference between linking and intrusive **/r/** is that linking **/r/** is reflected in the written form, while intrusive **/r/** is not. Intrusive **/r/** does not exist in rhotic accents (where *r* in the spelling is always pronounced).

B Work in pairs. Decide whether the underlined words in Exercise A are literal (l) or metaphorical (m). Use the information in the box to help you.

> **Metaphors**
>
> A metaphor is a word or phrase that's used in a different context from its literal meaning. It's easier to understand a metaphor when you know the literal meaning. For example:
>
> **Literal:** *There is a* ***breeze*** *outside. (= a light wind)*
>
> **Metaphorical:** *It was a* ***breeze****! I got the job. (= easy and pleasant)*

C Complete the sentences with the correct form of the words in the box.

catch drain peanut run snap wind

1. I'm getting very ___wound___ up about it.
2. You're throwing money down the ___drain___.
3. It's much better in the long ___run___.
4. Then you'll have two suits in your closet for ___peanuts___.
5. Choose a template that ___catches___ your eye.
6. All the best stuff will be ___snapped___ up immediately.

D Work in pairs. What is the metaphorical meaning of each sentence in Exercise C?

E Complete the questions with the correct form of a word from Exercises A or C.

1. When one person leaves a job and another person takes over, how can they make the transition as ___seamless___ as possible?
2. Are you the kind of person who plans for the long ___run___? Or do you tend to make snap decisions?
3. Have you ever bought anything that was ___tailor-made___ especially for you? Or do you always buy ___off-the-rack___ products?
4. Which current trends really ___wind___ you up?

F **SPEAK** Work in pairs. Discuss the questions in Exercise E.

PRONUNCIATION

Linking /r/

A Work in pairs. Read the sentences below aloud. Draw a (‿) between any words that you think are connected by a /r/ sound.

1. I saw a nice suit yesterday for 40% off.
2. You're only saving money if you buy something you need.
3. I just wore a jacket from an old suit.
4. They had no idea I was wearing sweatpants.
5. Are auction sites the best place to pick up cheap clothes?
6. Avoid stores in a trendy area or one with a lot of students.
7. Many sales clerks are authorized to offer discounts.

1.2 **B** Listen to check. Then practice saying the sentences.

SPEAKING HUB

A **PREPARE** Choose one of the following roles. Spend a few minutes thinking about your character (e.g. your age, background, ambitions, the problems you face, etc).

- **Role 1: The fashion victim.** You always want the latest designer fashions, but you're worried you would spend far too much.
- **Role 2: The reluctant shopper.** You hate shopping and don't care what you wear, but all your clothes are old and scruffy.
- **Role 3: The trendsetter.** You like to take risks and experiment with your clothes. Just one problem: you've run out of ideas!

B **DISCUSS** Work in groups of two or three. Role-play a conversation between your characters. Ask your partners for more information about their situation. Offer each other (good or bad) fashion advice.

I know it feels good to snap up a bargain, but in the long run, it's just money down the drain, don't you think?

C **REFLECT** Report back to the class on the best and worst advice for each character.

- Talk about style and fashion
- Give fashion advice

1.2 Trendsetting

- Compare different trends
- Make a podcast or vlog

G – comparatives and superlatives
P – emphatic stress
V – experimenting with prefixes and suffixes
S – using contrasts to work out meaning

READING

A SPEAK Work in pairs. Think of as many trends from the past five years as you can in one minute. Use the topics below to help you.

- technology
- music
- fashion
- culture

B READ FOR MAIN IDEA Read *The life cycle of a trend* quickly. Match the paragraphs (1–7) with the topics (a–d). Some paragraphs cover more than one topic.

a musical styles 3
b music formats 1, 2, 7
c games 4
d human needs 5, 6, 7

THE LIFE CYCLE OF A TREND

1 Technology trends are very simple at first sight: older technologies become <u>outdated</u> and <u>anachronistic</u>, to be replaced by **newer**, **<u>funkier</u>** technologies, until they are rendered <u>obsolete</u> with the next cycle. In this way, the vinyl records of the 1970s gave way to cassettes in the 1980s. By the 1990s, cassettes were <u>old hat</u> and CDs were <u>state-of-the-art</u>. By the 2000s, we all loved <u>novel</u> gadgets like MP3 players. But by the 2010s, we had cloud-based music streaming services like Spotify. Why limit yourself to the music you own, when you can stream every song ever recorded?

2 But in 2016, the unexpected happened: sales of vinyl records in the UK outstripped digital music sales for the first time. The renewed interest in vinyl is a powerful reminder that trends don't always flow in a straight line from <u>fringe</u> products to mass-market <u>blockbusters</u>. It also reminds us to pay attention to the durability of trends over decades, not just the short-term ups and downs of **the latest** fads.

3 These trends are **clearest** in the world of popular music, which seems to be on a 20-year cycle. In the 1980s, music from the 50s and 60s was cool, while 70s music was <u>tacky</u>. By the 1990s, 70s music was enjoying a revival, but 80s music had become the height of uncool. After 2000, it was OK to like 80s music again but now 90s music was for losers. The 20-year cycle makes **somewhat more sense** when you remember that the average trendsetter is about 22 years old. They <u>feel sheepish about</u> the music they enjoyed when they were 12, but they can look back **a great deal more fondly** at the music from their early childhood.

4 There's a key difference between a trend, a flash-in-the-pan and a fad. A flash-in-the-pan pops up suddenly, grabs everyone's attention, and then disappears again **almost as suddenly**. A few years ago, the whole world went crazy for a new smartphone app called 'Pokémon Go'. At one point, people were playing it everywhere you looked. But within a few months, almost everybody had <u>abandoned</u> it, leaving only a handful of <u>die-hard fans</u> to <u>persevere</u> with it.

Vinyl LP Sales and Market Share

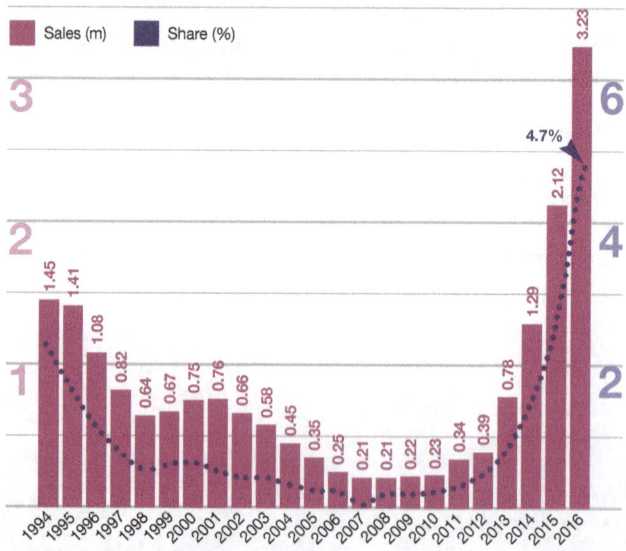

Source: British Phonographic Industry

5 A fad, on the other hand, may be **a little more <u>enduring</u>**, but it too is doomed to disappear sooner or later because it serves no useful purpose. It may be <u>quirky</u> or amusing, but unless it fulfills a basic human need, like 'convenience', 'social status', 'self-expression' or 'security', it will never be **more than a <u>gimmick</u>**.

6 In contrast, an <u>authentic</u> trend always fulfills one of **our very deepest** needs – something that's shared by every human that's ever lived. Of course, nobody really needs **a slightly thinner than usual phone** or every song ever recorded, but we do need things like relaxation, creative stimulation, self-confidence and a sense of belonging to a social group, which those products and services satisfy.

7 This idea of basic human needs also goes some way toward explaining **by far the most curious** feature of the vinyl revival: almost half of buyers of vinyl records never actually listen to them according to a poll by ICM Unlimited! As long as we see vinyl as 'a music format' to fulfill our need for 'relaxation' and 'creative stimulation', this makes no sense. But don't forget, we also have a need to own beautiful <u>physical</u> objects to express our personality, and this is **every bit as important as** those other needs. And of course, the <u>large-sleeved</u> LPs **more than meet** that particular need, to **a much greater extent than** either <u>diminutive</u> CDs or <u>intangible</u> digital downloads.

Glossary

doom (v) to make someone or something certain to fail, be destroyed, be extremely unhappy, etc
durability (n) the ability to continue to exist or work for a long time.
outstrip (v) to become larger than something else
revival (n) the process of becoming active, successful, or popular again

1.2 Trendsetting

LEAD-IN

Books closed. Write *70s*, *80s*, *90s* and *2000s* as column headings on the board. Elicit an example of one thing (e.g. a famous event, a person, a trend or an object) that students associate with each decade, and write this under each heading. Set a time limit, and put students into pairs to think of as many more things as they can for each decade. Get feedback and students' ideas on the board, asking them to explain why they chose what they did, especially in a multilingual class where cultural references may be different.

READING

A Elicit an example of a trend in technology, fashion, music and culture. Put students into pairs to complete the task, reminding them they have one minute to do so. Get feedback and ask students to expand on their ideas and give examples.

B Tell students to look at the picture and elicit how it is connected to trends. Explain the task and point out that some paragraphs cover more than one topic. Set a time limit and tell students not to worry about any unfamiliar vocabulary at this stage, but point out the glossary with definitions of a few words.

C Focus students on the information in the box about using contrasts to work out meaning, and point out one or two examples in the article (e.g. *but* in paragraphs 1 and 2, *while* in paragraph 3). Tell students to think about this as they read the article a second time more closely and answer the questions.

1 *Old: outdated, anachronistic, obsolete, old hat*
New: funkier, state of the art, novel
2 *Fringe products vs mass-market blockbusters; the durability of trends over decades vs short-term ups and downs of the latest fads*
3 *Tacky: bad, the opposite of cool*
Feel sheepish about: embarrassed by, the opposite of look back fondly at
4 *Die-hard fans: somebody who refuses to accept change; contrasts with almost everybody*
5 *Abandoned it vs persevere with it*
6 *Positive: enduring, quirky, authentic*
Negative: gimmick
7 *Diminutive: very short or small, contrasts with large-sleeved*
Intangible: not able to be touched or measured, contrasts with physical

D In pairs, students compare their answers to Exercise C. Check answers as a class.

E Put students into pairs to discuss the question and think of counterexamples. Monitor to prompt if necessary. In feedback, ask students to explain their ideas and encourage others to agree, disagree or ask further questions.

GRAMMAR HUB

1.2 Comparatives and superlatives

- We only use *than* after comparative adjectives and adverbs when it is followed by the thing we are comparing it with.

  CDs are ***more expensive than*** *they used to be.*

Be careful!

CDs are only fractionally more expensive today. NOT *~~CDs are only fractionally more expensive than today.~~*

- We don't put *the* before a superlative when we use a determiner.

  Here's our ***cheapest*** *smartphone.*
  NOT *~~Here's our the cheapest smartphone.~~*
- To compare things that are the same, we can use *as* + adjective/adverb + *as* …

  Dance music is ***as popular as*** *it ever was.*
- We leave out the second + *as* when the adjective/adverb isn't followed by the thing we're comparing it with.

  None of our audiences have been as large!
  NOT *~~None of our audiences have been as large as!~~*
- We can use *the* … *the* with comparatives to show that two changes are closely connected. As one thing changes, it makes the other thing change.

  The cheaper ***the*** *technology, the worse quality it is.*
  The bigger, ***the*** *better!*
- We can use the structure *more than* with a small number of verbs (*compensate for, double, fulfill, make up for, meet*)

  His enthusiasm and intelligence more than compensated for his lack of experience.
- To show that there is a big difference between two things we can use one of these modifiers before the comparative adjective: *a good/great deal, a lot, considerably, dramatically, far, significantly, much*.

  The new building is ***considerably*** *bigger than the old one.*
- To show that there is a small difference, we use these words and phrases before the comparative adjective: *a little, a fraction, fractionally, marginally, rather, slightly, somewhat*.

  The first movie was ***fractionally*** *longer than the sequel.*
- We can modify superlative adjectives using: *by far, far and away, easily, the very*.

  Tom is ***by far*** *the smartest boy in the class.*
  Tom is the smartest boy ***by far***.
- We can also make a superlative stronger by inserting *possible* after the superlative and before the noun.

  The shopping mall was built in the best ***possible*** *location.*
- We can also use modifiers before the structure *as … as*: *almost, at least, easily, every bit, half, just, twice*.

  My old phone was every bit ***as good as*** *this new one.*

1.2 Trendsetting

GRAMMAR

A Elicit that a lot of comparatives and superlatives were used in the article to discuss different trends. Tell students that they will find examples in the article to help them decide if the statements are true or false. In feedback, ask students to give you an example from the article to support their answers.

B In pairs, students find examples from the text. Monitor to help if necessary, then elicit answers from the class. In feedback, check that students understand that in Question 3 we don't use *the* when there's already a determiner such as *this* or *my* and that *the* is optional when there's no noun.

C Students look in the article again for examples of the rules.

D Direct students to the **Grammar Hub** (see TB6 and below).

E Ask students to choose one of the three points and allow them a little time to write some notes if needed. Monitor to check students are using the forms correctly, then get some feedback from a few pairs. Use the **Grammar Worksheet** on page W4 for extra practice.

SPEAKING

Put students into pairs to carry out the task. Elicit or give an example of how this can be done, using some of the structures from this lesson. Monitor to help or prompt if necessary. Get feedback on students' opinions and encourage further discussion at this stage. Finish with feedback on students' use of language during the activity.

Extra activity

Tell students that aliens have come to Earth and are planning to destroy some things forever. As an example, tell them to choose which one out of smartphones, planes, books, jeans or laptops you would save, and why. Elicit ideas for other groups, or give more yourself (e.g. different sports, different school subjects, different types of food, different types of transportation, music, clothes, etc). Put students into groups to discuss, then get class feedback and see if there is a consensus.

GRAMMAR HUB

1.2 Comparatives and superlatives

A Choose the correct options to complete the sentences.

1 Thank goodness I have tech-savvy friends like you – you're ________________.
  (a) the best b the best friend

2 I think we need to replace our company logo with something ________________.
  a funkier than (b) funkier

3 Winning the Young Tech Designer of the Year was ________________ moment!
  a the my proudest (b) my proudest

4 Your handwriting is ________________ Carol. Well done!
  a the neatest handwriting (b) the neatest

5 We've redesigned our website so that it's ________________.
  (a) more user-friendly b user-friendlier

6 CDs weren't around for very long, and CD burners disappeared almost ________________.
  (a) as quickly b as quickly as

B Write one word in each blank to complete the sentences.

1 My sister is a great __deal__ more concerned about appearances than I am.

2 A tailored jacket is __far__ and away the most important item of clothing in your closet.

3 I dress __a__ fraction more informally on Fridays, but I don't feel comfortable in casual clothes.

4 In my opinion, having the right image is every __bit__ as important as saying the right thing.

5 Chelsea only ever buys the __very__ best in terms of clothing and accessories.

C Complete the sentences using a word from the box and your own ideas.

considerably	half	marginally	twice

1 The green dress costs $25. The blue dress costs $27.
  The blue dress costs __marginally more than the green dress/one__.

2 My sister is a fashion vlogger and earns ten times more than I do!
  My sister earns __considerably more than me/I do__.

3 We were expecting 100 people at the fashion show, but only 50 came.
  Only __half as many people as__ we expected came to the fashion show.

4 I believe that you have to do double the work of others to be sure of success.
  I believe that you have to work __twice as hard as others to succeed__.

➤ Go back to page 7.

TEACHING IDEA by David Seymour and Maria Popova

Advertising agency

Use this activity to review comparatives and superlatives.

Tell me things which are typically advertised on TV. (Write the elicited list on the board.) In small groups, choose one of these things and think of a new brand. Write a radio ad explaining why it's better than its competitors, e.g. *For the whitest teeth buy Afterglo. It whitens your teeth and leaves your breath fresher than mountain air. It's more effective than all its leading competitors. Choose Afterglo, for the brightest, most confident smile.*

Read aloud your ad to the class. When you're listening to the other groups' ads, write some notes for a complaint to the Advertising Standards Agency, e.g. *The ad says it's more effective than other toothpastes, but it contains much more sugar than other brands to make it taste better.*

C WORK OUT MEANING Read the article carefully and answer the questions. Use the information in the box to help you.

Using contrasts to work out meaning

It's usually possible to work out the meaning of new words and phrases by looking for contrasts with known words and phrases. Look out for linking words (e.g. *while, but*) that signal a contrast.

1. Which underlined adjectives in paragraph 1 mean *old-fashioned*? Which mean *new*?
2. What do the two underlined words in paragraph 2 contrast?
3. What do the underlined words and phrases mean in paragraph 3?
4. What does the underlined phrase in paragraph 4 mean? What is it being contrasted with in the same sentence?
5. Which two verbs are being contrasted in the last sentence in paragraph 4?
6. Which of the underlined words in paragraphs 5 and 6 have a positive meaning? Which have a negative meaning?
7. What do the underlined adjectives in paragraph 7 mean? Which words in the same paragraph have the opposite meanings?

D Work in pairs. Compare your answers to Exercise C.

E SPEAK Work in pairs. Discuss the questions.

1. Do you agree that all successful trends are popular because they fulfill a basic human need?
2. Can you think of any examples or counterexamples to support your opinion?

GRAMMAR

Comparatives and superlatives

A Are these statements true (T) or false (F)?

1. After a comparative adjective (e.g. *bigger*), we always need *than*. T / F
2. We form the comparative and superlative of *-ly* adverbs (e.g. *quickly*) by changing *-y* to *-ier/-iest*. T / F
3. We always need *the* before a superlative (e.g. *fastest*). T / F

B Work in pairs. Justify your choices in Exercise A with examples in bold from the *The life cycle of a trend*.

1. newer, funkier, a little more enduring
2. more fondly (we always use more/most with *-ly* adverbs)
3. These trends are clearest, our very deepest needs

C WORK IT OUT Complete the rules with an example in bold from the article.

Advanced comparatives and superlatives

1. Some modifiers start with *a/an* (e.g. *a little*). When we use these together with *a/an* + noun, the second *a/an* goes after the comparative: a much greater extent than
2. Only a few words (*anticipated / expected / hoped for / necessary / usual*) can come between *than* and a noun: a slightly thinner than usual phone
3. We can use the structure *more than* with a small number of verbs (*double, make up for, meet*): more than meet

D Go to the Grammar Hub on page 122.

E SPEAK Tell your partner about one of the following. Use comparative and superlative structures.

- a movie that you enjoyed more than you thought you would
- a concert that you went to or an album you really love
- the most enjoyable vacation you've ever had

SPEAKING

DISCUSS Work in pairs. Compare the following things. Use structures from this lesson.

1. fashion from 1 / 5 / 10 / 20 / 50 years ago
2. popular music from 5 / 10 / 20 / 30 years ago
3. technology now / 10 / 20 / 50 years ago
4. society now / 10 / 20 / 100 years ago

LISTENING

A SPEAK Work in pairs. Discuss the questions.

1 What's the difference between the types of people in the box? Do you know any of these types of people?

blogger influencer podcaster trendsetter vlogger

2 Do you listen to any podcasts or watch any vlogs? If so, which ones?

1.3 **B LISTEN FOR GIST** Listen to a podcast about trendsetting. Which topics do the speakers give advice about?

- [ ] 1 making money
- [x] 2 choosing a focus
- [x] 3 using social media to build a community
- [x] 4 the problem with perfection
- [ ] 5 designing your own website
- [ ] 6 learning from statistics
- [x] 7 long-term planning
- [x] 8 learning from mistakes

1.3 **C LISTEN FOR DETAIL** Listen again. Are the statements true (T) or false (F)? Correct the false statements.

1 Dora and Adam are in the same room. T / (F)
They are in different places.
2 Dora regrets that she made so many mistakes. T / (F)
She learned everything by taking risks and making mistakes.
3 Hardly anyone watched Dora's videos at first. (T) / F
4 Dora releases a video at the same time every week. (T) / F
5 Dora replies to every comment on her videos. T / (F)
She only focuses on the people who want to join her community.
6 Dora sees herself as an overnight success. T / (F)
There are years of hard work behind her success.
7 Adam is unsure about filming himself. (T) / F

D SPEAK Discuss in pairs.

1 Do you think the idea of an 'overnight success' is a myth?

2 Have you ever had a blog or vlog? If not, would you ever consider starting one? Why/Why not?

VOCABULARY

Experimenting with prefixes and suffixes

A Complete Dora's advice using the words in the box.

amateurish disaster-prone hyper-influential largish re-editing super-lucky tech-savvy unmute user-friendly

VLOG AWAY!

A lot of the vlogs on the web are very [1] amateurish. Stand out by editing and [2] re-editing until your vlog is as slick and professional as possible.

If you're not particularly [3] tech-savvy, do some research into [4] user-friendly software – one with clear instructions.

Look at some of the videos made by the most [5] hyper-influential vloggers and some with a [6] largish number of subscribers. Success isn't down to being [7] super-lucky, it's about hard work and perfecting the craft.

You don't have to be a [8] disaster-prone person to sometimes forget to [9] unmute the mic. Remember not to be too hard on yourself. We all make mistakes, the important thing is to learn from them. You'll get more confident with experience.

LISTENING

A Write the names of one well-known influencer/podcaster/trendsetter on the board. Elicit who they are and what they are known for. Put students into pairs to discuss the questions. Get class feedback and make sure the difference between the types of people is made clear, eliciting well-known examples.

1.3 **B** Explain that students are going to listen to a podcast about trendsetting. Tell them to read the topics and predict which ones the speakers will give advice about, and what that advice might be. Students then listen to check.

1.3 **C** Put students into pairs to read the statements and to try to remember if they're true or false. Students then listen again to check. In feedback, ask students to justify their answers with reference to what they heard in the podcast.

D Put students into pairs to discuss the questions. Get feedback from one or two pairs.

VOCABULARY

A Explain the task and tell students to fill in the blanks with the words. In feedback, check understanding of the words and practice pronunciation where necessary.

AUDIO SCRIPT

1.3

Listening, Exercise B
D = Dora A = Adam

A: Hello and welcome to the latest 'Website design podcast'. Today, I've invited Dora Cho to talk about becoming a trendsetter. As I'm sure you know, Dora's video channel is the most hyper-influential source of advice on lifestyle trends on the web. Dora, are you there?

A: Sorry. I forgot to unmute Dora's microphone. Dora?

D: Hello? Can you hear me now?

A: Yes. Sorry, Dora. Should we restart?

Ex B 4 **D:** You know what? Keep going. One of the most common mistakes that new vloggers and podcasters make is to expect everything to be perfect. So they edit and re-edit everything again and again. But when things go wrong, we hear the real, authentic 'you', and that's what makes your podcast engaging. You actually need to unlearn all those rules about perfection!

A: OK. But your videos are always amazing. You seem so self-confident and relaxed. How do you do that?

D: It all comes down to experience. My first videos were pretty cheesy and amateurish. I used to be fairly disaster-prone with technology: everything that could go wrong did go wrong. But after a while,
Ex B 8 it got a lot easier! I learned everything by taking risks and making mistakes. It was frustrating at the time but you need to go through that experience. I'm a lot more tech-savvy now, but I'm still learning.

A: Great. So how did you start your vlog?

D: First of all, I set myself a target of one video every week for a year. I figured that if nobody cared after a year, I'd give up. And it did take a while to get noticed, which was frustrating. But after several months, I started to see fairly big audience numbers. By the end of the year, I had 7,000 subscribers.

A: Wow! And now?

D: Six million.

A: Amazing! So what am I doing wrong with my podcasts?

Ex B 2 **D:** Well, there's no need to be negative. The most important thing is that you've found your niche and you've created some excellent content.

A: Really? Oh, thank you.

D: Yeah, it's true. But if you want to move to the next level, you need to be really systematic. I mean, when do your podcasts come out?

A: It depends. Whenever I have a somewhat good idea for a podcast, then I try to make it within a few days.

D: OK, but you can't expect your listeners to check your website every day on the off-chance that you've released another episode – that's not user-friendly at all. But my followers can be absolutely sure that every Wednesday at 10 o'clock, there will be a new video on my channel.

A: OK. But what if you run out of ideas?

Ex B 7 **D:** I won't. I plan everything at least six months in advance, and I set alerts on my phone to tell me what to do and when. I've tried to make my system idiot-proof so that I can't mess up!

A: OK …

Ex B 3 **D:** You also need to be far more social media-savvy: once you've released each episode, tell the world about it. And don't just post a link – you need to engage with your audience, too, by replying to the comments on your site. People love to feel listened to.

A: Every single comment?

D: Well, there are plenty of people who post offensive or spammy comments. The trick is to ignore them
Ex B 3 and focus on the people who want to join your community. You can also ask them what they'd like you to talk about in future podcasts. Once you have an active community behind you, you'll never run out of ideas.

A: Right. OK, so I'll do all that. But it sounds like hard work!

D: It is hard work! Not long ago, a journalist mentioned my blog in an article about overnight successes. I suppose in many people's eyes, I am an overnight success. They probably think I'm super-lucky to have hit the big time. But they don't see the years of hard work behind that success.

A: Right. So I just need to keep working hard on my podcasts, right?

D: Well, your podcasts are great, as I say, but actually I think your content would work much better as smartphone-friendly videos. I mean, you talk about website design, so we really need to be able to see what you're talking about.

A: Maybe, but I'm not as charismatic as you. I hate being in front of the camera.

D: Well, I felt awkward at first, too, but you do get used to it. I really think you should rethink and become a vlogger instead.

A: OK. I'll give it a try. Dora Cho, thanks so much for joining me today. You've given me a long list of jobs to do! I feel super-exhausted just thinking about it.

B Ask students what the words from Exercise A all have in common, and elicit that they all contain prefixes or suffixes. Tell students to complete the examples in the *Experimenting with prefixes and suffixes* box with the words from Exercise A. Do the first one as a class example.

1.4 **C** Tell students to replace the underlined words or phrases with a word containing a prefix or suffix with the same meaning. Do the first one as an example, and make it clear that students will sometimes have to change the order of other words in the sentence to do this.

D Direct students to the **Vocabulary Hub** (see TB121) for further practice.

E Give one example of your own, then put students into pairs to think of more. Get class feedback and ask students to justify their choices. Encourage others to agree, disagree or ask further questions. Use the **Vocabulary Worksheet** on page W5 for extra practice.

PRONUNCIATION

1.5 **A** Play the first sentence only, or model the pronunciation yourself as the sentence was said in the recording, and tell students to listen for which word is stressed most strongly. Then, put students into pairs to try to predict which word will be stressed most strongly in the other sentences. Encourage them to say the sentences aloud as they do this. Play the recording for students to listen and check. In feedback, ask students if they are surprised by which words were stressed, and try to elicit *why* these words were stressed.

B Tell students to practice saying the sentences from Exercise A and to think again about why they're stressed as they are.

Suggested answers

1. *To draw attention to the superlative adjective.*
2. *To emphasize how much easier it got.*
3. *To focus on the positive verb form, which confirmed Dora's expectations.*
4. *To emphasize that Adam has achieved two important things, not just one.*
5. *To turn a prediction (… there'll (probably) be …) into a promise (… there will be …).*
6. *To focus on the positive verb form, which agrees with people's assumption.*
7. *To draw attention to the positive verb – to reassure Adam that he'll be OK.*
8. *To emphasize how grateful he is.*

1.6 **C** Tell students to look back at their answers to Exercise B to help them decide where the stress should go in the sentences. Again, encourage them to say the sentences aloud as they do this. Then, play the recording for students to check. Play the recording a second time for students to repeat.

SPEAKING HUB

A Tell students they're going to make their own podcast or vlog about trends, similar to the one they listened to earlier. Put them into small groups to think about the questions. Monitor to help and prompt if necessary.

B Ask students to share their ideas with the class and to ask for suggestions on what to focus on. Encourage the other students to give feedback. Participate if necessary to generate some enthusiasm for the podcasts.

C Students plan their episode. Make it clear that they shouldn't write a script, however, as they need to sound spontaneous. Monitor to help with language if needed. Encourage students to rehearse before they present their podcast or vlog to the class.

D Instruct students to make their podcast or vlog. They could perform it to the class or record it, then play it to the class if you have the facilities for this. Encourage students to respond to each other's episodes and ask questions or give opinions about it. Give some feedback on students' use of language after this as well.

Extra activity

If students didn't record their podcast or vlog in class, they could do this outside the class after taking in feedback they received from the other students and from you. They could then present their recordings in the next class, either in small groups or to the whole class.

After students have presented, encourage those listening to give feedback, although obviously handle this sensitively.

Allow students time to reflect on what went well and what could have been improved or done differently in their own podcasts.

METHODOLOGY HUB by Jim Scrivener

Word stress

Stress and its opposite – unstress – are very important aspects of English pronunciation. Getting the stress wrong can seriously damage your chances of being understood.

Words have their own stress pattern; for example, *water*, *cricket* and *justice* are stressed on the first syllable, whereas *abroad*, *enough* and *today* are stressed on the second. A stressed syllable in a word is usually noticeable by being slightly louder, longer and higher in pitch than the syllables next to it.

Stress and unstress

Unstressed syllables tend to be pronounced less loudly and with a more 'relaxed' manner; vowel sounds are typically 'weak'. Check this out: try saying the words *water* and *justice* with the stress on the wrong syllable. What happens to the previously stressed syllables?

Commentary

The unstressed syllables become weaker, i.e. shorter, spoken more quickly and with less well-defined (or even altered) sounds, e.g. **/wɒ'tɜːr/, /dʒəs'tɪːs/**.

Word stress is important because when it is wrong, words sound very strange or even incomprehensible. Would anyone understand you saying *secretary*? Sometimes wrong stress changes one word into another: *desert – dessert*. Or it can change the class of a word: *import (v) – import (n)*.

Marking stress

There are a variety of ways of marking stress in a written text and it's important to do this for students. Which of the following do you personally find clearest?

formation	'window	unhappy	impostor
magaZINE	cassette	**wat**erfall	delightful

B Complete the information in the box with examples from Exercise A. Use the information in the box to help you.

Experimenting with prefixes and suffixes

1 Some prefixes (e.g. *un-*, *re-*) allow you to invent completely new verbs: unmute, re-edit
2 *Super-*, *hyper-* and *ultra-* all mean 'much more than usual': hyper-influential, super-lucky
3 You can add *-y* or *-ish* to nouns to invent new informal adjectives: *trashy, babyish,* amateurish
4 You can add *-ish* to an adjective or number to mean 'more or less': *twentyish, smallish,* largish
5 *Friendly, prone, proof, resistant* and *savvy* can be used as suffixes to make adjectives: *environmentally friendly, waterproof, heat-resistant,* disaster-prone, tech-savvy, user-friendly

C Replace the underlined phrases in these extracts with a word with a prefix or suffix. You may need to change the word order in some sentences. Then listen to check.
1.4

1 You actually need to forget all you learned about all those rules about perfection! unlearn
2 Whenever I have a fairly good idea for a podcast, then I try to make it within a few days. goodish
3 You also need to be far more aware of how to use social media. social media-savvy
4 Well, there are plenty of people who post offensive comments that are like spam. spammy (comments)
5 Your content would work much better as videos that work well on smartphones. smartphone-friendly (videos)
6 I really think you should think again and become a vlogger instead. reconsider
7 I feel incredibly exhausted just thinking about it. super-exhausted

D Go to the **Vocabulary Hub** on **page 142**.

E **SPEAK** Work in pairs. Think of examples of the following.

- websites that aren't very user-friendly / smartphone-friendly
- a person who's tech-savvy / fashion-savvy
- any objects you own that are waterproof or water-resistant
- any objects you own that are damage-prone

PRONUNCIATION

Emphatic stress

A Listen to the extracts from the recording. Underline the words that are stressed.
1.5

1 One of the most common mistakes that new vloggers and podcasters make is to expect everything to be perfect.
2 But after a while, it got a lot easier!
3 … if nobody cared after a year, I'd give up. And it did take a while to get noticed.
4 … you've found your niche and you've created some excellent content.
5 Every Wednesday at ten o'clock, there will be a new video on my channel.
6 I suppose in many people's eyes, I am an overnight success.
7 I felt awkward at first, too, but you do get used to it.
8 Dora Cho, thanks so much for joining me today.

B Work in pairs. Why did the speaker use emphatic stress in the extracts in Exercise A? Practice saying the sentences.

C Decide where to add emphatic stress in these sentences. Then listen to check.
1.6

1 That's one of the most popular vlogs on the web.
2 When you reach one million subscribers, it will be worth it!
3 Is it possible to be a trendsetter and an influencer?

SPEAKING HUB

A **PLAN** Work in small groups. You are going to make a podcast or vlog episode about trends. Discuss the following questions.

- What will it be about?
- Why will anyone want to listen/watch?
- What topics could you cover?
- How will you add your own personalities?

B **DISCUSS** Share your initial ideas with the class. Ask your 'audience' what the next episodes should focus on. Try to engage with them to generate enthusiasm.

C **PREPARE** Plan an episode of your podcast/ vlog. Don't simply write a script – you'll need to stay spontaneous.

D **PRESENT** Make your podcast/vlog. If you have recording equipment, e.g. a phone, you can use that. Otherwise, present your episode to the class.

Compare different trends
Make a podcast or vlog

Veganuary

A Work in pairs. You are going to watch a video titled *Veganuary*. What do you think *Veganuary* means?

B Watch the video and check your answers to Exercise A.
It is a UK campaign to encourage eating vegan food in January.

C Watch the video again. Complete the sentences with one word or a number.

1. There are now more choices for vegans when they eat out and at ___grocery stores___.
2. The food which Tabitha says she misses most is ___cheese___.
3. Tabitha initially became a vegan because of ___environmental___ reasons.
4. Many cafés sell a wider selection of products to appeal to ___everybody___.
5. Some people limit eating meat to one or two times a ___week___.
6. In the UK ___78,000___ people attempted *Veganuary*.

Glossary

boom (v) to experience an increase in activity, interest or growth
ethics (n) a set of principles that people use to decide what is right and what is wrong
mainstream (adj) considered ordinary or normal and accepted or used by most people
niche (n) a specialized segment of the market for a particular kind of product or service

AUTHENTIC ENGLISH

A Read the sentence from the video. What do you think the phrase in bold means?

Health, ethics, there are just so many reasons, I think, to ***give it a go****.*

B Read the information in the box to check your answer to Exercise A.

give it a go

We use *give it a go* to express it's a good idea to attempt something you haven't done before. We also use *give it a try*, *give it a shot* and *take a stab at it* to express the same idea.

C Work in pairs. Respond to the sentences using *give it a go* or one of the other expressions from the box in Exercise B.

1. We're not sure whether to try skiing when we're in Switzerland.
   Why not give it a shot and see if you like it?
2. Sam would like to study French but he's always found languages difficult. Why doesn't he give it a shot? It might be easier than he thinks.
3. I've never traveled to another country alone before. Give it a try, see how you feel.
4. Nina's always been too shy to introduce herself to complete strangers. She should take a stab at it – what's the worst that could happen?

D **SPEAK** Discuss three things you would like to start doing that you have never tried before.

The big pitch

SAM MALCOLM AMANDA HARRY EMILY

A Watch the video. Work in pairs. Discuss the questions. *the café owner; making coffee; doing calculations; talking to customers*

1 Who is Sam and how does he spend his day?

2 What do the following people do? *Emily: yoga teacher; Malcolm: retired professor; Amanda: journalist; Harry: Sam's assistant*

Emily Malcolm Amanda Harry

B Watch the video again. Complete the sentences with the best option.

1 Emily feels *confident about* / *unprepared for* her pitch.

2 Emily would like to *grow her current business* / *start a new sustainable business*.

3 Emily's yoga experience package will include *two* / *three* meals a day.

4 Emily's business will focus on *yoga and food* / *outdoor yoga*.

5 Emily thinks *she will make profits evenly every year* / *her profits will equal her costs in the first year*.

SPEAKING SKILL

A Work in pairs. Look at the example from the video. Why has Emily used this phrase? *Emily is nervous, can't think of the exact words, may want to buy time.*

> **Emily:** ... Well, it's kind of like my yoga classes that I teach, but with the idea that you would be getting more than just exercise.

B Look at the information in the box. Then underline examples of circumlocution in the sentences from the video.

Using circumlocution

We frequently use circumlocution, the use of many words where fewer would do, in a deliberate attempt to be vague or evasive, when we are nervous or can't think of the exact word, or even to make an idea sound more impressive. Look at these other sentences from the video and underline examples of circumlocution.

1 I mean what I really want to do is to expand my business into something more sustainable, you know, a yoga retreat where people can stay for a few days.

2 Full body cleansing, you know the physiological withdrawal of toxins from the body.

C Why do you think Amanda uses circumlocution in the sentences from Exercise B? *may be looking for the right words; may want to make this sound impressive*

D Work in pairs. Ask each other about the following things. When you answer try to be evasive or vague. Use the expressions from Exercise B to help you.

- your favorite café
- your diet
- your job or studies

SPEAKING HUB

A PLAN You are going to make a short pitch for a business you would like to set up. Think of a business idea.

B PREPARE Write notes on what you are going to say. Consider the following points.

- product/service
- USP (Unique Selling Point)
- market
- profitability

C PRESENT Work in groups. Pitch your business idea.

Well, I'd like to give running my own exercise boot camp a try.

D REACT Once everyone in the group has pitched their idea, decide which is the best. Give reasons.

Pitch your own business idea

➤ Turn to page 156 to learn how to write a blog post about a trend.

1.3 Diet and lifestyle

Veganuary

A Write *Veganuary* on the board and ask students what they think it means. Tell them that it is a recently invented word, formed by combining two more common words (a portmanteau word).

B ▶ Before they watch, point out the glossary containing definitions of some of the words they will hear.

C ▶ Tell students they're going to watch the video again. Before they do, tell them to look at the sentences and to try to fill in the blanks from memory.

AUTHENTIC ENGLISH

A Put students into pairs to read the sentence and to discuss what they think the phrase means.

B Check understanding with another example of how you could use *give it a go* or one of the other similar expressions.

C Point out the example, then tell students to work in pairs to think of how they could reply to the other sentences.

D Give an example of your own, then put students into pairs to discuss the question.

The big pitch

A ▶ Point out the picture and ask students what they think is happening. Tell them to watch the video and to answer the questions.

B ▶ Tell students to read the sentences and to try to choose the correct alternative from memory, before playing the video again. You can find the **video script** for *The big pitch* on the Teacher's Resource Center.

SPEAKING SKILL

A Put students into pairs to discuss the question. In feedback, ask students if they use similar phrases in their language.

B Go through the information in the *Using circumlocution* box with the class. Do the first sentence with the whole class, before students complete the rest.

C Give an example of your own, using a few of the phrases from Exercise B. Then, put students into pairs to practice. Monitor to help where necessary.

SPEAKING HUB

A Ask students to think of an idea for what their business might be.

B Ask students to write notes about the different points. Make sure students are just writing notes and not writing their pitch out in full.

C Put students into small groups to pitch their ideas to each other. Encourage them to ask each other questions at the end of each pitch.

D Students decide which pitch was the best in their group. In feedback, ask each group to explain which was the best idea and why.

Extra activity
Elicit or give an example, then put students into pairs to talk about any new businesses they have heard about recently and to discuss why they think they are good or bad ideas. Get whole-class feedback and find out if the class agrees.

▶ VIDEO SCRIPT

Veganuary
D = Danny Savage (journalist) V = Vegan customer
T = Tabitha El = Ellie (baker) Ex = Expert

D: A vegan café in Leeds – there's no meat or dairy products in any of the food here, and for the last month, non-vegans have been encouraged to give it a go. And those behind Veganuary say it's a lot easier today than it was a few years ago.

V: When I went vegan seven years ago, there was none of the chain restaurants doing vegan options, now, nearly all of them have either got vegan options on the menu or they've got a vegan menu itself. [Ex C Q1] Um, a lot of the supermarkets now, the range of products that are available to … to people going vegan is a lot better than it was six or seven years ago. So it's moving in the right direction.

D: What's the one thing you miss?

Ex C Q2 **T:** Cheese.

D: Haha! That's your …

T: Yeah, cheese.

D: Tabitha went vegan for January. Despite some cravings, she's stuck to it and will continue.

Ex C Q3 **T:** The thing that got me in the first place was actually the environmental impacts of veganism and vegetarianism. Um, but, yeah, health, ethics, there's just so many reasons, I think, to give it a go.

D: And it's been OK?

T: Yeah.

D: You haven't struggled?

T: Yeah. No, I haven't actually struggled.

D: You've completed it.

T: Yeah, I've done it.

D: You haven't fallen off the wagon, as such.

T: No, I haven't.

D: At a nearby bakery, Ellie has built up a business making vegan cakes. Production has grown rapidly because veganism is no longer a niche – it's becoming mainstream.

Ex C Q4 **El:** It's been crazy busy. Um, I mean, lots of cafés have just started doing, a lot, they've, you know, they want to accommodate everybody so they're wanting to offer a really good range and, just the general public as well, you've noticed, you know, you'll go to a market or even just going to, like, the big vegan fairs, there's, er, much, much bigger crowds.

D: And the growth in trade is reflected by a growing change in people's attitudes.

Ex: Veganism as a lifestyle choice has definitely boomed in the last few years. But for a lot of other people, they're choosing a more flexible approach, even part-time, um, [Ex C Q5] perhaps reducing their meat intake to once or twice a week, taking a more vegetable-centric approach the other days, and for these people Veganuary is a brilliant introduction and a way to test the waters.

Ex C Q6 **D:** The organizers say about 78,000 people in the UK tried going vegan in January. They think even more will have a go next year. Danny Savage, BBC News, Leeds.

1 Writing — Write a blog post

W– making your blog post successful

A Look at the buttons. What do you think *skeuomorphism* means?

B Read *4 things you need to know about skeuomorphism*. Complete the article with the headings (a–d).

- a Is skeuomorphism cool?
- b Is skeuomorphism useful?
- c What are some examples of skeuomorphism in real life?
- d What is skeuomorphism?

4 things you need to know about SKEUOMORPHISM

Have you ever wondered why the best websites look fresher and smarter than yours? Do you want to learn the powerful secret of great web design? Then you need to know about skeuomorphism.

1 d

Here's a simple definition: skeuomorphism involves making digital objects look like things in the real world. The earliest websites just had a lot of text. Instead of a 'click here' button, you simply had the words 'click here'. But web designers soon realized that users prefer life-like buttons and switches.

2 c

Examples of skeuomorphism are everywhere. Is there a trash can on your phone for 'delete'? A cogwheel for 'settings'? An envelope for 'messages'? The list of examples is endless. Skeuomorphism even brings outdated technologies – like floppy disks and sand-filled hourglasses – back to life.

3 a

It depends. Early web designers got carried away with skeuomorphism. Every button had a 3D appearance, with shadows and reflections. This led to a backlash in the early 2010s called 'flat design', which gave a cleaner, less fussy appearance. Flat design managed to appear both retro and modern … but also a little boring.

4 b

Yes and no. Skeuomorphism does make things more user-friendly and intuitive. We all know that a green phone means 'start a call' and a red one means 'end a call', but what if you've never seen an old-fashioned phone? What if you're color-blind? By all means use skeuomorphism in your web design, but don't assume your users can work out what everything means!

Want to learn more about web design trends? Click here to sign up for our online course.

C SPEAK Work in pairs. Discuss the questions in the headings.

D Match the objectives (1–3) with the strategies (a–g).

Making your blog post successful

A successful blog post achieves three objectives:

1. People will find it using search engines. a, d, e, g
2. They will read it from start to finish. c, f
3. They will take some action that helps the writer. b

- a Include a number in your title (i.e. 7, not seven). Search engines prefer them!
- b End with a clear call to action (CTA), e.g. 'sign up for our newsletter'.
- c Ask questions in your first paragraph, but only answer them later in your blog post.
- d Choose one key word or phrase and use it as many times as possible in your blog post.
- e Use questions as section headings. Many people use questions to search. *All four headings are questions that might be asked in a search.*
- f Speak to readers as 'you' and offer to solve their problems.
- g Include a lot of common search terms like 'definition' and 'examples'.

E Find examples of the strategies (a–g) in the blog post.

WRITING

A PREPARE Work in groups. You are going to write a blog post about a trend or trends in general. Think of ideas for topics.

B PLAN Choose your key word or phrase (to be repeated many times in your blog post), your title and a series of questions to use as section headings.

C WRITE Write your blog post. Make sure the first paragraph encourages the reader to keep going to the CTA!

D REVIEW Read some other people's blog posts. Use the box above to evaluate the posts.

156 WRITING

Refer students to this article as a model for their blog post.

Remind students to refer back to the box on making a successful blog post as they write.

Ask students to compare blog posts in small groups.

WRITING

A Write *skeuomorphism* on the board and ask students what they think it means. Put them into pairs and tell them to look at the pictures and ask them to think about it again. Get some feedback but don't confirm or reject any suggestions at this stage.

B Tell students they're going to find out all about skeuomorphism. Students read the blog post and match the headings to the paragraphs.

C Put students into pairs to discuss the questions from Exercise B. Get some feedback to find out how similar or different students' opinions are.

D Point out the information in the box about *Making your blog post successful*. Elicit which of the objectives strategy *a* is an example of, then tell students to match the other strategies to an objective.

E Tell students to look at the blog post again and to find more examples of the strategies from Exercise D.

WRITING TASK

A Tell students that they're going to write a blog post about a particular trend or trends in general. Put them into groups, and tell each group to choose a topic to write about and to brainstorm ideas.

B Students work individually to plan the specifics of their post. Monitor to help or prompt if necessary.

C Remind students about all the strategies for writing a successful blog post, then tell them to write their post. This could be done for homework if there isn't time to do it in class.

D Either display the blog posts on the walls for students to walk around and read, or pass the posts around so everyone has a chance to read several. Ask students to evaluate the posts with reference to the strategies they saw earlier. In feedback, ask students which blog posts they think are the most successful and why. Finish with feedback on the organization, style and language used in the posts.

Unit 1 Review

GRAMMAR

A Put the words into the correct order to make nominal clauses.

A: Why are you getting rid of those pants? There's nothing wrong with them!

B: Well, the fact [1]**aren't / in the knees / holes / that / there** doesn't mean I can wear them forever. These pants are so last year! *that there aren't holes in the knees*

A: Come on! [2]**your clothes / people / think about / what** isn't important! What counts is [3]**on / what's / inside / the**! *What people think about your clothes* *what's on the inside*

B: Exactly! But you know what they say: [4]**on / good / to look / outside / the** is to feel good on the inside. And anyway, [5]**fashion / gives / following** me a lot of pleasure. *to look good on the outside* *following fashion gives*

A: Yeah, apart from the fact [6]**you can afford / that you spend / more than**. *that you spend more than you can afford*

B: [7]**much / I spend / How** is up to me! *How much I spend*

B Choose the correct options (a, b, c or d) to complete each sentence.

1 This is the ___ worst movie I've ever seen.
- a just
- b marginally
- c somewhat
- (d) absolute

2 There was a slightly larger than ___ crowd at the game.
- (a) anticipated
- b believed
- c hope for
- d previous

3 Some online stores are ___ as cheap as high-end stores.
- a by far
- b double
- c far and away
- (d) twice

4 My achievements are ___ as impressive as yours.
- a considerably
- (b) every bit
- c rather
- d significantly

5 The hotel offers ___ best views across the bay.
- a at least
- b fractionally
- (c) the very
- d dramatically

VOCABULARY

A Match numbers (1–6) to letters (a–f) to form full sentences.

1 If Jon decides to come to the wedding, *d*
2 If you get a new job in an office, *e*
3 If celebrities dress in a stylish way, *f*
4 If you wear creative and original clothes, *b*
5 If you want to stay cool in the summer, *a*
6 If you're going away for the weekend, *c*

a wear light, baggy clothes.
b you'll fit in well here – everyone has a very unique style.
c pack at least four outfits.
d make sure he doesn't wear his usual scruffy clothes.
e check the company's dress code before you start.
f they usually set a trend.

B Complete the words in the sentences. Some of the letters have been given to help you.

1 I can't afford to eat out again this week – I'm on a very _t_ _i_ g _h_ _t_ budget.
2 We offer a range of _o_ _f_ _f_-the-_r_ _a_ _c_ _k_ and _t_ a _i_ _l_ _o_ _r_-m _a_ _d_ _e_ suits for our customers.
3 I got really _w_ _o_ u _n_ _d_ up this morning when I couldn't find a parking space.
4 I know it seems expensive now, but it's worth it in the long _r_ _u_ _n_.
5 If we are late getting to the store, all the bargains will have been _s_ _n_ _a_ p _p_ _e_ _d_ up!
6 If you have the time to look, you can buy great clothes for p _e_ _a_ n _u_ _t_ _s_ in thrift stores.
7 The exam was an absolute _b_ _r_ _e_ _e_ z _e_ – I'm sure I got a great grade!

C Complete the ad using a prefix or suffix from the box with the words in parentheses. Each prefix or suffix may be used more than once. Other changes may be necessary.

-ish ultra- -savvy -prone -y -friendly -proof

TRENDY KID

Are you looking for an [1] ultra-cool (*cool*) fashion gadget for an [2] accident-prone (*accident*) child?
Our new unbreakable 'Trendy Kid' smartwatch is completely [3] childproof / child-friendly (*child*).
No need to be [4] tech-savvy (*tech*)!
This watch uses the latest skeuomorphic design principles to make it as [5] user-friendly (*user*) as possible.
Available in [6] flowery (*flower*) pink or [7] muddy (*mud*) brown.
Do you love the design but worry that you'll look too [8] childish (*child*) wearing a 'Trendy Kid' watch? Head over to our store for a huge range of on-trend adult smartwatches!

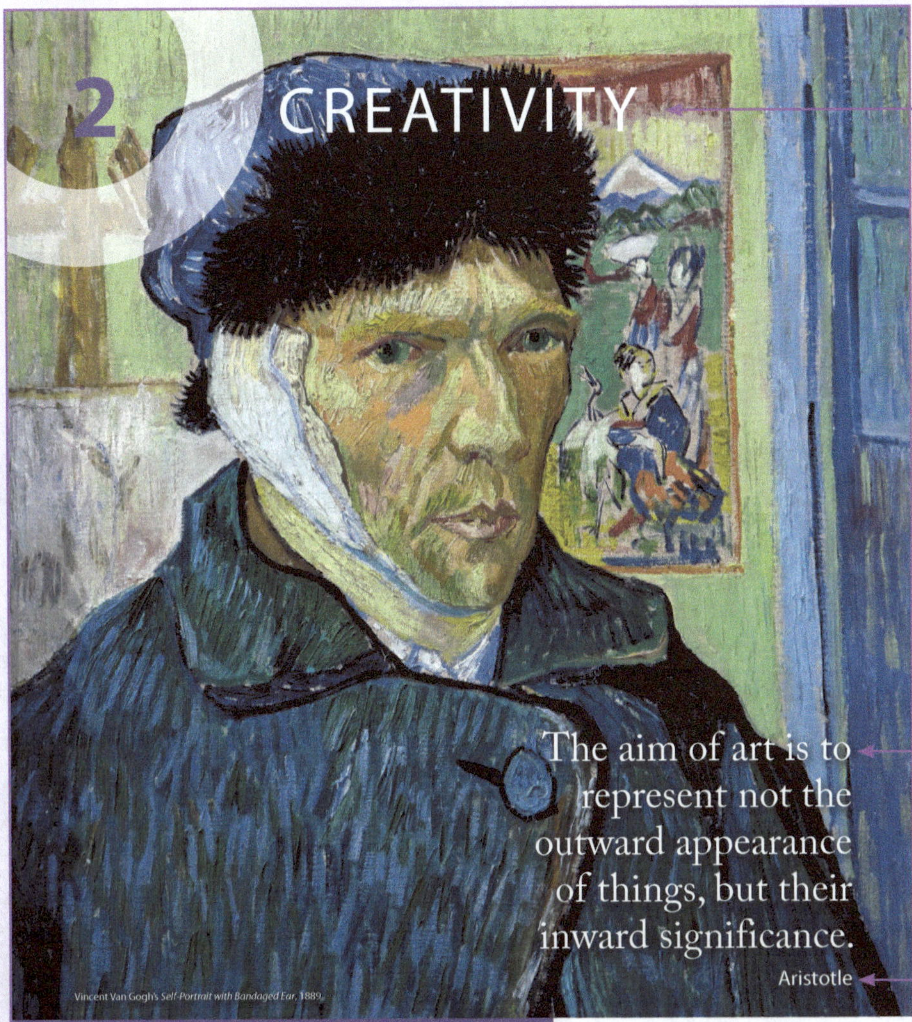

Vincent Van Gogh's *Self-Portrait with Bandaged Ear*, 1889.

Creativity (n) the ability to create new ideas or things using your imagination.
Synonyms: imagination (n), originality (n)

Aristotle means that art should look beyond the surface and reveal something that is true, but not immediately obvious.

Aristotle (384 BCE–322 BCE) was an ancient Greek philosopher and scientist. He is considered to be one of the fathers of Western philosophy, and his ideas remain influential today.

OBJECTIVES

- give a presentation about art
- talk about creative projects
- talk about finding inspiration
- describe a life-changing moment
- discuss a work of art
- write a review

Work with a partner. Discuss the questions.

1 Look at the picture. What is your opinion of works of art like this?
2 What does Aristotle mean in the quote? Do you agree with him?
3 Is the main aim, or goal of art:
- to tell a story
- to celebrate an event
- to express emotion
- to create beauty
- to persuade
- to entertain?

CREATIVITY 13

OBJECTIVES

Read the unit objectives to the class.

UNIT OPENER QUESTIONS

1 Focus students on the photo and elicit what it shows and where students think it was taken. Put them into pairs to discuss the question, and encourage students to express different opinions in feedback.

2 Students discuss the quote in pairs. Elicit some ideas from around the class.

3 Put students back into pairs to discuss the questions. In feedback, encourage students to give examples to support their answers. Write on the board any useful language that comes up.

WORKSHEETS

Lesson 2.1 The story behind it

Vocabulary: Describing art (W6)

Grammar: Narrative tenses (W7)

Lesson 2.2 Creative people

Vocabulary: Ideas and inspiration (W8)

Vocabulary: Compound adjectives (W9)

Grammar: Future in the past (W10)

2.1 The story behind it

- Give a presentation about art
- Talk about creative projects

V – describing art **P** – contrastive stress **G** – narrative tenses **S** – anticipating content before listening

VOCABULARY
Describing art

A **SPEAK** Work in pairs. Look at the pictures (a–e) and discuss the questions.

1 Do you know any of these works of art?

2 Which do you prefer? Why?

B Choose the correct adjectives to complete the comments (1–5).

C Go to the **Vocabulary Hub** on **page 142**.

D What art forms are being described in Exercise B?

1 a painting 2 a (comedy) movie 3 a sculpture / an installation 4 a photograph 5 a musical / a dance performance

E **SPEAK** Think of an example of an art form from Exercise D. Describe it to your partner.

I find this installation groundbreaking. It makes you think about space in a different way.

It's actually fairly … It's not that … It's somewhat …

1 I think some famous works of art are ***overrated*** / ***repetitive***. But that isn't the case here. The artist's use of light and shade in this composition was different from anything that had come before – it was truly ***pretentious*** / ***groundbreaking***.

2 It was ***hilarious*** / ***tedious***! I couldn't stop laughing. OK, the same jokes again and again become a little ***underrated*** / ***repetitive***, but the comic performances were ***awesome*** / ***appalling***.

3 It's a very ***unconventional*** / ***repetitive*** piece. I can see why some people wouldn't want something so big and strange put up in a public space. They probably think it's a little ***acclaimed*** / ***pretentious***, as if the artist is trying too hard to be different.

4 Most people recognize this image. It's so ***iconic*** / ***hilarious***, capturing the mood of the time it was taken. It's ***thought-provoking*** / ***unconventional***, too – it really makes you consider the human story behind this historical event.

5 The risk with performances like this is if the songs are ***appalling*** / ***iconic*** then it's really not enjoyable. It just makes them really ***tedious*** / ***awesome*** – so long and slow. Fortunately the music, lighting and costumes in this show were really special. It was a truly ***sensational*** / ***iconic*** experience. I can see why it's been ***overrated*** / ***acclaimed*** by critics and audiences.

2.1 The story behind it

LEAD-IN

Books closed. Tell all students to stand up. Give one example of an art form, e.g. *movies*, then nominate another student (either by name or by throwing a soft object to catch) to say another. They then nominate another student and so on. When a student can't think of anything, or repeats one previously said, they have to sit down. The last student left standing is the winner. Record any new language that comes up on the board, and encourage students to challenge and justify any answers that aren't typical art forms.

VOCABULARY

A Tell students to look at the pictures and elicit that they all show art forms. Put them into pairs to discuss the questions. In feedback, check all students are familiar with each art form, and record any useful language that came up during their conversations.

B Do the first one as a class example, and demonstrate how the sentences help students understand the meaning of the words. Put students into pairs to do the rest. In feedback, check students fully understand the meaning of the words, and practice pronunciation where necessary.

C Direct students to the **Vocabulary Hub** (see TB121).

D Tell students to look at the comments in Exercise B again, and explain that they all refer to different art forms. Elicit the first one as an example before students do the rest.

E Give an example of your own, using some of the phrases to describe a movie, painting, art installation, photograph or show that you know. If there is time, this could be done as a quick activity, with students reconstructing your short text or completing a fill-in-the-blank version to draw their attention to how they can use the language. Put students into pairs to describe three examples of their own. Monitor to help with language and to collect examples of good language use. In feedback, encourage students to expand on their answers and to ask each other questions. Use the **Vocabulary Worksheet** on page W6 for extra practice.

Extra activity

Ask students to find two or three short texts describing different works of art, e.g. online reviews of movies, plays, exhibits, etc. Ideally they should find both positive and negative reviews. Get students to underline any adjectives used to describe works of art. Students should bring these to class. Put students into small groups and ask them to read aloud only the adjectives from their texts, while the rest of the group guesses if the review is positive or negative. Groups can then read their reviews and write down examples of common or useful vocabulary. In whole-class feedback, ask each group to write on the board examples of new vocabulary, which the class can then sort (e.g. into positive and negative categories).

METHODOLOGY HUB by Christine Nuttall

Top-down processing

These are complementary ways of processing a text. They are both used whenever we read; sometimes one predominates, sometimes the other, but both are needed. And, though normally unconscious processes, both can be adopted as conscious strategies by a reader approaching a difficult text.

The top-down approach

In top-down processing, we draw on our intelligence and experience – the predictions we can make, based on the schemata we have acquired – to understand the text. This kind of processing is used when we interpret assumptions and draw inferences. We make conscious use of it when we try to see the overall purpose of the text, or get a rough idea of the pattern of the writer's argument, in order to make a reasoned guess at the next step (on the grounds that having an idea of what something *might* mean can be a great help in interpreting it).

We might compare the approach to an eagle's view of the landscape. From a great height, the eagle can see a wide area spread out below; it understands the nature of the whole terrain, its general pattern and the relationships between various parts of it, far better than an observer on the ground.

A reader adopts an eagle's view of the text when he considers it as a whole and relates it to his own knowledge and experience. This enables him to predict the writer's purpose, the likely trend of the argument and so on, and then use the framework to interpret difficult parts of the text. The top-down approach gives a sense of perspective and makes use of all that the reader brings to the text: prior knowledge, common sense, etc, which have sometimes been undervalued in the reading class.

TEACHING IDEA by David Seymour and Maria Popova

High culture

Use this activity to extend the theme of describing art.

What cultural activities do you take part in? In pairs, tell each other about what you do and the places you go, e.g. movie theaters, theaters, galleries, museums, etc. (Ask students to specify movies, plays and exhibits.)

Mingle with the rest of the class and find out everyone's favorite painting, building and piece of music. Write down the name of anyone who shares your opinion. Did anyone find someone with the same three favorites?

LISTENING

A–B Put students into pairs to discuss the review and make predictions.

Suggested answers

1 *Background of the painting and artist – the review tells us the guest speakers have specialized knowledge; the story behind the painting – there are many subjects in the composition and the show title suggests a puzzle; the reason why the painting is special – the review mentions that guest speakers have a personal connection.*

2 *When and where was the piece of art painted? Why does the guest speaker like it? Why is the painting of special interest? Who are the subjects in the painting? How did the painting affect the guest speaker's life?*

2.1; 2.2 **C–E** Check answers as a class or give feedback after students complete each stage.

PRONUNCIATION

2.3; 2.4 **A–C** Make sure students have realized that the type of intonation introduced is used to contrast two ideas before they complete the rest of the exercises.

SPEAKING

A–D Ensure students have chosen a work of art and write notes before they give their presentations. Encourage them to ask questions about their partner's presentations before whole-class feedback.

Extra activity

Ask students to design a cultural tour of their city or country. If you have students from the same countries, put them in groups to work together before presenting to the class. If your students are from very different countries, they can prepare individually and then present in small groups.

AUDIO SCRIPT

2.1

Listening, Exercise C

P = Presenter C = Caroline

P: This week's guest on *More than meets the eye* is art historian Caroline Bishop. Caroline, thanks for joining us.

C: It's my pleasure. Thank you for having me.

P: So the painting you've picked also happens to be one of the great masterpieces. Could you start by telling us its name and a little about the painter?

C: Sure. It's a painting by Velázquez, called *Las Meninas*. Velázquez is one of Spain's most important artists. He painted in a Baroque style, which means his paintings are very ornate, detailed and realistic. He mainly painted historical scenes and portraits. He painted *Las Meninas* after he'd been given a prominent position in the royal court.

P: And can you describe the painting to us?

C: Well, it depicts a scene in the artist's studio. In the center foreground, we have the young Infanta Margaret Theresa, the daughter of the King and Queen – the word 'Infanta' is similar in meaning to 'princess'. The *Infanta* is framed on either side by her two ladies-in-waiting. Then, to the right, we have two other women from the royal court and a dog. Behind them are the Infanta's attendants – a chaperone and bodyguard – and further in the background, there's a royal official in a doorway.

P: OK. So, we are probably looking at the Infanta's entourage?

C: Hmm … yes we can see her entourage on the right, but to the left, we can see the artist himself, standing next to a gigantic canvas. The inclusion of the artist in the painting is one of the things that makes this such an interesting piece. It seems more like a snapshot, taken behind the scenes of the royal court, rather than the typical posed portraits of the time. It was a very original composition – groundbreaking at the time.

P: So, do you know why he chose such an unconventional composition?

C: Actually, there are several theories about this – which is one of the things I like best about the painting. There's been a lot of debate about who the subject of the painting really is. (Ex D Q1) On first inspection, it seems that the Infanta is the subject – after all, she's in the center of the painting. But then, if you look in the background, (Ex D Q2) there appears to be a mirror that shows the King and Queen. This suggests that the artist is actually painting *their* portrait. So we, the viewer, are actually seeing the world through the eyes of the King and Queen. The Infanta and her companions are merely watching.

P: So, it's a portrait of the King and Queen, not the Infanta. Is that right?

C: Well … some people think so, yes. Even though the image of them is really small.

P: That's a very imaginative idea – and really unusual for a royal portrait I'm guessing.

C: Yes, absolutely. However … there's one other interpretation that I like. Some people believe that the scene we see is actually just the reflection in a large mirror. (Ex D Q3) What we're seeing is the artist at work in his studio.

P: So this may even be a self-portrait?

C: Exactly. The point of the picture may be to show us the artist's life – this is his studio, this is what it was like when he was painting a portrait. It's actually a very complex composition. It's like a puzzle for the viewer to decide what is really happening.

P: It's fascinating – and I'm not sure which interpretation I like best. Anyway, why did you choose it as your favorite painting? Do you have a personal connection to the work?

C: Well, I first saw this painting in the Prado Gallery in Madrid over 20 years ago when I was a student. And the first time I saw it, I was astounded. It's sensational. I'd never seen anything like it. In fact, I switched to art history a couple of months later.

P: So this painting helped you to choose your career?

C: Yes, yes it did.

LISTENING

A Work in pairs. Read a review of the radio show *More than meets the eye*. Are there similar radio shows in your country?

> ### More than meets the eye
>
> gives an analysis of one different piece of groundbreaking fine art each week. The guest speakers make these discussions unique and sometimes fairly unconventional. They don't just have specialist knowledge of the artist, but also some personal connection to the pieces.

B **ANTICIPATE CONTENT** You're going to listen to an episode of *More than meets the eye* about picture b. Work in pairs and answer the questions below. Use the information in the box to help you.

> **Anticipating content before listening**
>
> You can use different types of information to predict what you will hear.
>
> - Read notes, reviews, handouts, etc.
> - Look at titles or images for clues about what the speaker will cover.
> - Use your own knowledge to predict topics or themes.
> - Use information to think of questions you expect to be answered.

1 What topics will be discussed in the show?

____

2 What questions will be answered?

____

2.1 **C** **LISTEN FOR GIST** Listen to the show and check your predictions in Exercise B.

2.2 **D** **LISTEN FOR DETAIL** Listen and write down the different ideas about who the main subject of the painting is.

1 The Infanta

2 The King and Queen

3 The artist (Velázquez)

E **SPEAK** Work in pairs and discuss the questions.

1 Who do you think the subject of the painting is?

2 Why do you think the artist chose this composition?

PRONUNCIATION

Contrastive stress

2.3 **A** Listen to these extracts from the radio show. Draw arrows to show whether the intonation rises (↗) or falls (↘).

1 Yes, we can see her entourage on the right (↗), but to the left (↘), we can see the artist himself, standing next to a gigantic canvas.

2 So, it's a portrait of the King and Queen (↘), not the Infanta (↗).

2.4 **B** Underline the words you think will be stressed and draw arrows to show where you think the intonation will rise (↗) or fall (↘). Then listen to check.

1 Actually, Mondrian wasn't American, he was Dutch.

2 Although I like his landscapes, his portraits are much better.

3 Why don't we watch a movie instead of going to the gallery?

4 I don't think it's tedious. I just think it's overrated.

5 It was painted in 1656 – you said 1666.

6 **A:** You study art history, don't you?

B: No, I study fine art, not art history.

C **SPEAK** Guess whether your partner likes these things or not. Respond to your partner's guesses. Use contrastive stress when appropriate.

> classical music   comic books   crime novels   heavy metal   Hollywood movies   modern art   musicals   science fiction movies   soap operas

A: You like Spider-Man comicbooks.

B: No, I like Batman not Spider-Man.

SPEAKING

A Choose a work of art that you really like. It could be a painting, a sculpture, a photograph, a movie, a book, a play, a poem or a song.

B **PLAN** Write notes so that you can talk about:

- information about the artist / writer / singer
- a description of the work of art
- your interpretation of the work of art
- the reasons why you like this work of art.

C **PRESENT** Give a short presentation to your partner about the work of art you have chosen.

D **DISCUSS** Ask your partner about the work of art he or she chose.

READING

A PREDICT Look at the pictures in the article. What kind of place is this? Do you know anything about it?

B SKIM Read the box below about the Eden Project. Check your answers to Exercise A.

The Eden Project is a spectacular tropical garden housed inside huge plastic bubbles within a crater the size of thirty soccer fields.

C READ FOR DETAIL Read *How we made the Eden Project*. Put the events (a–h) in the correct order. Two events are not needed.

4 **a** They hired a lot of people to work on the project.
6 **b** They did a lot of tests to make sure the building would be safe.
5 **c** They tried out some innovative techniques.
___ **d** They had to stop working until they found more money.
2 **e** They started working on designs without a specific location in mind.
1 **f** Tim Smit had the inspiration for the project.
3 **g** They found the ideal location.
___ **h** They conducted a feasibility study.

How we made the Eden Project

Tim Smit, *founder*

We started the construction with just $3000 in the bank. To persuade government officials to part with public funds, you have to do a feasibility study and that's expensive. So we simply progressed on faith, and hope, promising ourselves that we'd never use the word *if* only *when*.

The idea for a huge horticultural expo had come to me as I worked on the Lost Gardens of Heligan. [1]I'd always loved the thought of a lost civilization in a volcanic crater, and when I saw the lunar landscape of the old Cornish clay pits, [2]I realized they'd be the perfect site.

A friend put me in touch with an architecture firm. Ex D I hadn't received a penny in funding at that point, or even a site, just a belief that the idea of a lost world in a crater would appeal to anyone who's ever been 12. They thought the idea was crazy, but it struck them as an adventure and they agreed to start work for nothing. Meanwhile, a construction firm put some money into the project in return for a share of the profits. Everyone was now suddenly highly motivated.

Our two horticultural directors recruited anyone they'd ever worked with and debated what to put in the buildings. I'd envisaged rainforest and Mediterranean areas, eager for it to be the greatest ever collection of plants useful to humans. But it was also a question of finding a balance between the wow factor and more meditative moments. So we have a giant waterfall along with a prairie that, in the winter, is about the most boring thing you can see – then, for six weeks a year, it bursts into spectacular life.

Glossary

arch (n) a structure with a curved top and straight sides that you can walk through
camaraderie (n) friendship and trust between people in a group
crater (n) a large round hole in the ground
pioneer (n) one of the first people to do something important
pit (n) a very large hole dug in the ground in order to obtain a particular substance or type of stone
quarry (n) a place where stone is dug out of the ground.

2.1 The story behind it

READING

A Tell students to look at the pictures and to discuss the questions. Get some feedback on their predictions, but don't confirm or reject any ideas yet.

B Students read the first paragraph and work in pairs to compare their predictions.

C Ask students to read the article quickly and to put the events in the correct order. Make sure students realize that two of the events are not needed. Set a time limit and tell students not to worry about unknown vocabulary at this stage.

D Students read the article again to answer the questions. Encourage them to underline in the text where the obstacles are mentioned. Tell students to compare their answers in pairs before taking feedback from the class. If necessary, change pairs so that fast finishers can help others. In feedback, ask students to justify their answers with reference to the parts of the text they underlined.

E Put students into pairs to discuss the questions. Get feedback and ask students to expand on their answers or ask each other further questions.

Extra activity

Divide the class into groups of equal numbers. Give each group one of the following projects:

- a public art mural or sculpture
- a community garden
- a public space with free musical instruments
- free art education classes for younger people

Ask students to discuss why their project deserves funding. Regroup students into groups of at least four, with one representative of each project. Students take turns presenting their arguments, before a class vote on the worthiest project.

METHODOLOGY HUB by Christine Nuttall

Making sense of a text

The writer has an advantage over the speaker; she has the time to help the reader by making the text as straightforward as possible. The reader also has time at his disposal: he can stop and think, go back to check an earlier passage, reread the difficult parts. Unless the text takes for granted a body of knowledge that he simply does not have, a careful reader should be able to reconstruct most of the assumptions on which it is based. To do this he must assess the evidence – choice of words, selection of facts and so on – and draw appropriate inferences, so he gets the message intended rather than the message he expected.

The text functions like a do-it-yourself construction kit. The message in the writer's mind is the perfect piece of furniture. The process of separating this into its component parts and packing them into a box with instructions for reassembly is a little like the process of putting thoughts into words and organizing them into a coherent text. A reader tackling a text resembles the amateur furniture maker unpacking his do-it-yourself kit and trying to work out how the pieces fit together.

It would not be wise to press this analogy far, but it does demonstrate the force of the metaphor *making sense*. The writer has to make sense (like a designer envisioning a perfect table and then shaping each part to be right for its purpose and to fit with all the others). The text itself has to make sense (like a kit containing all the pieces and clear instructions).

Finally, the reader has to make sense, like the amateur making the table; whether it turns out as planned depends not only on the kit, but on whether he understands the basic principles, follows the instructions properly and does not lose many of the pieces. Sometimes, moreover, he may supply pieces of his own and make a table better suited to his purpose – or even a different piece of furniture altogether; but he needs to be a skilled carpenter to risk doing this.

METHODOLOGY HUB by Christine Nuttall

Scanning and skimming

The idea that some parts of a text may be ignored or skipped is strange to some students, but efficient reading, and specifically the techniques of scanning and skimming, require it.

By scanning we mean glancing rapidly through a text either to search for a specific piece of information (e.g. a name, a date) or to get an initial impression of whether the text is suitable for a given purpose (e.g. whether a book on gardening deals with a particular plant disease).

By skimming we mean glancing rapidly through a text to determine its gist, for example, in order to decide whether a research paper is relevant to our own work (not just to determine its field which we can find out by scanning) or to keep ourselves superficially informed about matters that are not of great importance to us; much of newspaper reading is skimming.

The distinction between the two is not particularly important. In both, the reader forces their eye over print at a rate which permits them to take in only, maybe, the beginnings and ends of paragraphs (where information is usually summarized), chapter headings and so on.

Scanning and skimming are important techniques; they do not remove the need for careful reading, but they enable the reader to select texts, or parts of texts, that are worth spending time on. And skimming to get a top-down view is valuable as a way of approaching difficult texts.

Students need plenty of practice in these techniques; it is a good idea to devise races to practice them, to ensure the necessary pace. Many tasks can be done in groups, which makes the supply of materials more feasible.

2.1 The story behind it

GRAMMAR

A–B Put students into pairs to check their answers after each exercise.

C Direct students to the **Grammar Hub** (see below).

D Use the **Grammar Worksheet** on page W7 for extra practice.

SPEAKING HUB

A–D Make sure students do not write down their anecdotes word for word first and give whole-class feedback at the end.

GRAMMAR HUB

2.1 Narrative tenses

	Active Voice	Passive Voice
Simple past	**I realized** it was a great idea.	**We were given** a month to finish the job.
Past progressive	**We were hoping** for a better result.	**The plans were being drawn up** at the time.
Past perfect	**They had already bought** the site.	**The architects had been chosen.**
Past perfect progressive	**We had been walking** for hours.	

- We use the simple past in a story or narrative to explain the main events.

  *We **met** on Saturday, outside Victoria train station.*
- We use the past progressive to describe the background to a story, actions in progress at a particular point or together with the simple past, to describe actions or situations that were interrupted by shorter events.

  *The sun **was shining** when Amy **left** the house.*
- We use the past perfect to show that one event happened before the other.

  *He **had waited** for over an hour by the time she finally arrived.*
- We usually use the past perfect progressive together with the simple past, for actions that were in progress before another action in the past.

  *I **had been working** all day so I **decided** not to go out that night.*
- We can use the simple past with *did* + base form for emphasis.

  *He **did** look very anxious when he left.*

Be careful!

- We don't usually use the passive voice form of past perfect progressive.

  Someone had been watching us. NOT ~~*We had been being watched.*~~

2.1 Narrative tenses

A Choose the option in each sentence that is NOT correct.

1 I ___ what he meant.
- (a) had finally been understanding
- b finally understood
- c had finally understood

2 ___ to wait in the reception area.
- a They told me
- (b) I was telling
- c I was told

3 Jim had been swimming earlier and his hair ___ wet.
- a was
- b had got
- (c) was getting

4 Angie was shocked by what she ___ at the film festival.
- a had seen
- b saw
- (c) has seen

5 He had gotten the job but he ___ the starting date.
- (a) hadn't been being told
- b wasn't told
- c hadn't been told

6 It was a terrible day and it ___ heavily.
- a was raining
- b had been raining
- (c) had been rained

B Correct the underlined mistakes. Sometimes more than one answer is possible.

1 I realized I <u>left</u> my money at home. had left

2 When I looked out of the window, I saw that it <u>rained</u>. was raining / had been raining

3 I <u>did to realize</u> that I had forgotten my keys before I left. did not realize

4 Janine changed her mind about the theater but it was too late as I <u>already bought</u> the tickets. had already bought

5 We arrived a little early and we <u>told</u> to wait until the manager was free. were told

6 Greg went to see the doctor because he <u>wasn't being feeling</u> well. wasn't feeling / hadn't been feeling / didn't feel

7 As soon as we had finished the discussion, we <u>had left</u>. left

C Complete each sentence with the correct form of the verb in parentheses, active voice or passive voice. Sometimes more than one answer is possible.

1 I was angry because I had been kept / was kept (*I / keep*) waiting for an hour.

2 The sun was shining and the birds were singing (*sing*) in the trees.

3 The reason I was tired was that I had to walk / had had to walk / 'd had to walk (*have to / walk*) all the way home.

4 We had only been working / had only worked (*only / work*) on the project for a week when it was canceled.

5 Pete had not been told / was not told (*not / tell*) about the change of plans so he knew nothing.

6 We couldn't use the living room because it was being decorated (*decorate*).

➤ Go back to page 17.

D SCAN Read the article again. What were the obstacles they had to overcome to build the Eden Project?

E SPEAK Work in pairs. Discuss the questions.

1. Why do you think people agreed to work on the project while funding was uncertain?
2. Why do you think this project succeeded?
3. Would you like to have worked on this project?
4. What other kinds of projects would you like to work on?

Jolyon Brewis, *architect of Grimshaw Architects*

Most architects dream of creating a new world on a scale that eclipses all that's gone before. So, in the early days, when there was always the threat of construction being stopped because of lack of money, all the companies involved carried on regardless: we were so enthralled by the vision.

Our first designs were for different locations, including a tent-like structure for a hillside, then Smit discovered the china clay quarry at Bodelva. It had a romantic, lost world feel since it would be hidden from view until you were almost upon it. For a long while it all seemed like a terrific gamble. Usually, the one thing an architect can rely on is solid ground, but since it was still a working quarry there was a lot of movement. What's more, to figure out costs, we had to design our buildings right down to the last detail, even though no one knew if there'd even be enough money to buy the site.

[3]We'd been working on a series of snaking arches linked with glass, but while one of our design teams [4]were cleaning up, they realized that bubbles would have far more stability on the shifting soil. Building on such a huge scale involved untried technology: this was a leap into the unknown. Glass would have been too heavy so we pioneered 11-meter hexagonal pillows of inflated plastic. It had never been used so big before and we had no idea how it would behave. So we had to work through various disaster scenarios, such as what would happen if one deflated, then filled up with water and brought down the entire structure.

The worst moments were at the beginning when we [5]hadn't been given the funding yet and some of the foundations [6]got washed away during one of the wettest winters in memory. But there was a great feeling of camaraderie. We felt there was nothing we couldn't cope with.

GRAMMAR

Narrative tenses

A Match the underlined words (1–6) in the article with the tenses.

simple past	2	past perfect progressive	3
past progressive	4	simple past passive voice	6
past perfect	1	past perfect passive voice	5

B WORK IT OUT Complete the rules with the tenses in Exercise A.

Narrative tenses

1. When we tell a story, we use the ___simple past___ and ___simple past passive voice___ to explain the main events.
2. We use the ___past perfect___ and ___past perfect passive voice___ to give background information for actions that were completed before the main events of the story.
3. We use the ___past progressive___ and ___past perfect progressive___ to give background information for actions that were in progress before the main events of the story.

C Go to the **Grammar Hub** on **page 124**.

D Choose a sentence and continue the story. (It doesn't have to be a true story!)

1. I had been working for several hours when …
2. I had been planning to go to … for months, but …
3. I had just gone to bed when …
4. It had been raining all day, so …
5. I had been feeling sick all day because …
6. I had already eaten a big breakfast, but …

SPEAKING HUB

A PREPARE Think of an anecdote about an interesting project you worked on or a piece of work you have done. Use the ideas below to help you prepare what you are going to say.

- what was the project or piece of work
- what went well
- what went badly
- what would you do differently if you could do it again

B PRESENT Work in groups. Tell your anecdote about the project or piece of work.

C DISCUSS Listen to your classmates' anecdotes, react to what they say and ask questions.

D REFLECT Choose the best anecdotes.

- Give a presentation about art
- Talk about creative projects

2.2 Creative people

- Talk about finding inspiration
- Describe a life-changing moment

V – ideas and inspiration; compound adjectives
P – questions for comment or criticism
G – future in the past
S – inferring meaning

VOCABULARY
Ideas and inspiration

A Read the blog post *Sparking ideas*. Choose the correct definition (a or b) for the underlined phrases (1–10).

1 a find the right location
(b) find the right mood

2 a abandon an idea
(b) develop an idea

3 (a) working from nothing
b working with no equipment

4 a steal someone's ideas
(b) discuss something with someone

5 (a) get ideas from
b paint a picture of

6 a escape a problem
(b) help you to think of some ideas

7 (a) become very involved with something
b are about to finish

8 a feel more energetic about
(b) get a different view of

9 a find a good idea
(b) am unable to progress

10 a think carefully
(b) rely on your feelings

SPARKING IDEAS

Jasmine, artist

'Some people are very practical about finding ideas. But not me. I need to [1]<u>get into the right state of mind</u>, whatever it takes. It means traveling miles to get away from everyone, working through the night or going for a walk – until I find inspiration or it finds me. Then I just [2]<u>run with an idea</u> and see where it takes me.'

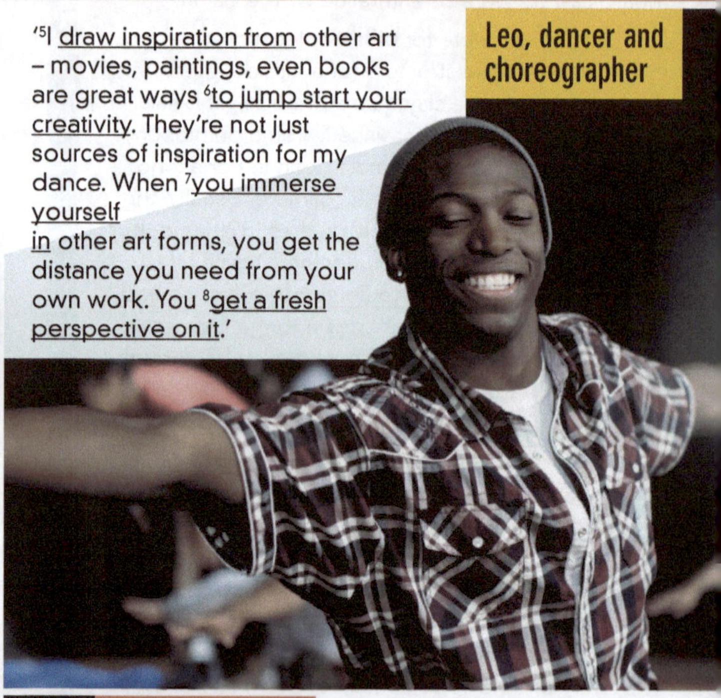

Leo, dancer and choreographer

'[5]I <u>draw inspiration from</u> other art – movies, paintings, even books are great ways [6]<u>to jump start your creativity</u>. They're not just sources of inspiration for my dance. When [7]<u>you immerse yourself in</u> other art forms, you get the distance you need from your own work. You [8]<u>get a fresh perspective on it</u>.'

Michelle, director

'[3]<u>Working from a blank canvas</u>, with no idea where you are going to start, can be really scary. So, … I call my mom! It's great [4]<u>to bounce ideas off someone</u>. Even if you disagree, it can help you move forward.'

Sam, playwright

'Although writing is my job, when [9]<u>I hit a wall</u> and just can't find the ideas, I start doodling cartoons, shapes. It really helps me to think. Then when the ideas start to come, [10]<u>you trust your instincts</u>. You just know which ideas to use, which to combine and which to just forget.'

2.2 Creative people

LEAD-IN

Books closed. Write the word *inspiration* on the board. Tell students to write down as many words as they can, using only the letters in the word. Give one or two examples, e.g. *into* or *arts*. Tell them to try to make the longest word they can as well. There are 434 possible words. The longest that students are likely to have heard before are seven letters. Below are some suggested answers:

aspirin, patrons, nations, rations, pianist, anoints

VOCABULARY

A Direct students to the pictures and elicit ideas as to what the people are doing and what the photos have in common. Elicit that they all show people doing some kind of creative work. Tell students to read the four quotes and to think about whether they know the meaning of the underlined phrases. Students choose the correct definitions for the underlined phrases. Encourage them to read the full quotes again to help them use the context to work out the meaning. Do the first one as a class example to demonstrate how to do this. In feedback, be prepared with further examples to ensure all students fully understand the meanings.

B Explain the task and do the first one as an example, referring back to the definitions from Exercise A to check students understand how to do the task and to consolidate understanding of the meaning. In feedback, ask further questions again to make sure students have understood the meaning of the phrases.

C Put students into pairs to discuss the questions. In feedback, encourage students to expand on and justify their answers and to ask each other questions. Monitor, helping where necessary, then get feedback from a few pairs. Use the **Vocabulary Worksheet** on page W8 for extra practice.

Extra activity

Ask students to think of the best idea they've ever had at work or when studying. Give your own example. Tell students to think about:

- what the idea was
- how, when and where they came up with it
- why it was such a good or important idea.

Put students into small groups to share their experiences. Get feedback on some of the most interesting ideas and highlight any good uses of the new lexis you heard as you monitored discussions.

METHODOLOGY HUB by Jim Scrivener

Lexis and skills work

A great deal of lexis work in class occurs in relation to reading and listening tasks. There are definite advantages in this, most importantly because learners meet the language in realistic contexts and see how the items fit into the meaning and style of a whole text.

The text that immediately surrounds a lexical item is referred to as **co-text**. Co-text provides important exposure for learners to samples of language being used. This suggests why texts are usually more useful for teaching lexis than lessons that focus on lexis as separated, stand-alone items without such surrounding language. When using reading or listening texts, a focus on lexis may occur before, while or after the students read or listen.

Pre-teaching lexis

The teacher may select some activities specifically designed to review, teach and practice lexis before moving on to work on the text or recording. The lexis selected for teaching is likely to be that most needed for completion of whatever listening or reading tasks are to be set. Although this is usually called pre-teaching, remember that this work may be helping students to recall items they already know as much as introducing new items. The main aim is to help ensure that the following activity will work (because there will be fewer stumbling blocks of unknown lexical items). This work may, of course, also teach or review some lexis that may be useful in its own right.

After the first phase of listening or reading work

Once the learners have become comfortable with the text, you can focus attention on lexical items in the text and how they are used. Here are some things that you could ask:

- Can you guess the meaning of this word from the meaning of the text around it?
- Find some words in the text that mean …
- Find some words in the text connected with the subject of …
- In line X, what does … mean?
- Find words and sort them into three separate groups under these headings: …
- Why does the writer use the word … here?
- Find words in the text that match this list of synonyms.
- What words come before/after the word … What other words collocate with this word?
- Can you remember any other phrases you know with this word in them?
- Can you find any multi-word items (i.e. groups of words that go together / chunks)?
- What's the opposite of this word?
- How many different words does the writer use to describe the …?

Dealing with lexis during reading or listening work

While students are mainly working on reading or listening skills, you are less likely to spend time on lexis, since this might clash with the reading, listening or other goals. During such stages, you are likely only to:

- deal with an item when a student specifically asks about it;
- give brief, to-the-point explanations or translations, rather than detailed presentations;
- offer help quietly to the one or two students who ask, rather than to the whole class;
- sometimes refuse help and tell students to do their best without knowing some items.

Lexis work after the main stages of reading or listening work

Textbooks frequently offer follow-up tasks and exercises that focus on the use of lexis in the text and encourage learners to try using the items themselves.

2.2 Creative people

LISTENING

2.5 **A** Let students compare their answers in pairs, then in feedback record the answers on the board.

2.5 **B** Tell students to listen again and to decide which tip Mark likes best. In feedback, ask students to justify their answers.

C Put students into pairs to discuss the question. In feedback, ask students to give more information on what they have tried.

PRONUNCIATION

2.6 **A** Ask them to decide if the speaker's intonation rises or falls in each question. If students seem unsure about what this means, you could demonstrate rising and falling intonation yourself.

2.7 **B** Encourage students to use the questions in Exercise A to help them decide on the intonation patterns. Students work in pairs, and encourage them to say the questions aloud as they do the task.

C As an example, ask a student to ask you one of speaker A's questions in Exercise B. Reply with a question for comment or criticism, using the appropriate intonation. Put students into pairs for further practice.

SPEAKING

A Tell students to work individually to look at the suggestions for stimulating creativity and to think about the advantages and disadvantages of each.

B Put students into pairs to compare their ideas. Get some feedback to see how similar their ideas were.

C Ask students to work with their partner to agree on the best suggestion.

D Put students into new pairs to discuss the questions. In feedback, encourage them to expand on their answers. Finish with feedback on students' use of language during the activity.

AUDIO SCRIPT

2.5

Listening, Exercise A
M = Mark L = Lauren

L: Hi Mark, how's the dissertation going?
M: Terrible, Lauren. I'm stuck. I have no ideas today. Zero.
L: Oh, no. How awful! But did you see that article Simon shared about how people find inspiration? It's really interesting.
M: Yeah? He's always sharing self-help stuff, but …
L: No, but this one's different. It's real artists, writers, directors, musicians and dancers talking about how they come up with their ideas.
M: Hmm … So, what did they say then?
L: Oh … let me find it. Here we go. OK. This person's a fashion designer and he says, 'Inspiration can strike at any time. I sometimes get ideas when I'm out shopping or walking in the park. (Ex A) I always carry a pen and paper with me, so I can sketch it or write it down. Sometimes the smallest thing can trigger an idea. A flower, a smile, a color.'
M: OK. Isn't that somewhat pretentious? Can't he just use his phone to write notes? And anyway a blank notebook is still a blank notebook.
L: OK, here's an artist – he says the best time for him to get ideas is very early in the morning – when you're not exactly awake and not exactly asleep. (Ex A) He often sets his alarm for 4 am, so he can get into the right state of mind to have ideas.
M: What! Is he crazy? He must never get enough sleep.
L: Yeah, but come on, I know what he means. A few times, I've had a good idea just before waking up – usually when I have a problem that I'm trying to solve.
M: Well, I don't think it's going to work for my dissertation.
L: (Ex A) OK. But here's an actual writer. Apparently, she thinks you have to be really disciplined and get into a regular routine. You just sit down and write, because if you wait for ideas to come, you'll never do anything. She says choose a time and stick to it – even if you don't feel like it or even if your writing is terrible, you just need to shut the door, remove all distractions and write.
M: Why does she keep writing if it's terrible? I don't want my dissertation to be terrible!
L: (Ex A) How about this then? You should immerse yourself in other things. Do something completely different – like watch a movie. Then when you get back to your desk, you'll be refreshed and ready to be creative again.
M: (Ex B) That's the first thing that I agree with! I need to take a break. I think I need a change of scenery … right now.
L: (Ex A) Yeah, it doesn't hurt, does it? I also think it helps to talk to people – you know, bounce ideas around with someone and see if they can improve your idea. It can really help to get a fresh perspective on something.
M: Isn't that a little … scary? I don't think I want to share this dissertation until it's finished.
L: Well, it has to be someone you trust. Celia and I usually read each other's work, so we're used to helping each other. She also thinks that if you're working from a completely blank canvas, the possibilities can seem limitless, so (Ex A) she likes to impose some restrictions – such as using a particular genre or restricting herself to a particular format. I think she likes to set herself a challenge. That's pretty fun, don't you think?
M: (Ex B) OK, it's very interesting – and I guess it makes sense. It must be easier to decide what to do if you have fewer choices.
L: Yeah, and I really like the idea of giving yourself a challenge like that. There's one other thing you could do. An artist here says (Ex A) it's important to take risks. You might not fully understand what you're doing, but you just have to trust your instincts and run with it.
M: Is she serious? How can you make something when you don't know what you're doing?
L: Haven't you ever started doodling a picture without knowing what it was going to be?.
M: Hmm … I guess so …
L: Well, I think that's what she means. So … anyway, good luck with the dissertation, Mark.
M: Thanks, Lauren!

B Choose the correct phrases to complete the sentences.

1 I've just *gotten into the right state of mind* / *hit a wall* with this project. I have no inspiration and can't get any further with it.

2 With art projects, you can't always know for certain you have the best idea. Sometimes you just have to *trust your instincts* / *work from a blank canvas*.

3 When you're feeling uninspired, talk to other people. *Bouncing ideas off someone* / *Running with an idea* can only help.

4 When there are no distractions and you are completely focused, you can truly *get a fresh perspective on* / *immerse yourself in* something.

5 We had no idea where we could begin with the design. We were *jump starting our creativity* / *working from a blank canvas*.

C SPEAK Work in pairs. Do you ever have to be creative in your daily life? How do you come up with ideas?

LISTENING

2.5 **A LISTEN FOR MAIN IDEA** Listen to Mark and Lauren discussing an article about inspiration. What seven tips for getting inspiration do they discuss?

SEVEN TIPS FOR GETTING INSPIRATION

1 Always carry a pen and paper and write down ideas
2 Set your alarm early and try to have ideas as you wake up
3 Get into a regular routine
4 Immerse yourself in other things
5 Bounce ideas around with someone else
6 Impose some restrictions
7 Trust your instincts

2.5 **B LISTEN FOR DETAIL** Listen again. Which of the tips does Mark like? 4, 6

C SPEAK Work in pairs. Have you ever tried any of the ideas mentioned in Exercise A? Why/Why not?

PRONUNCIATION

Questions for comment or criticism

2.6 **A** Listen to the questions from the discussion. Draw arrows in the parentheses to show whether the intonation rises (↗) or falls (↘) at the end of each sentence.

1 Isn't that somewhat pretentious? (↘)
2 Is he crazy? (↗)
3 Why does she keep writing if it's terrible? (↘)
4 Don't you think? (↘)
5 Is she serious? (↗)
6 How can you make something when you don't know what you're doing? (↘)

2.7 **B** Choose the correct intonation for the questions. Then listen to check your answers.

1 **A:** Do you think it's sensible to schedule time for creativity?
B: What's the point of that? (*rise* / *fall*) You can't be creative if you're not in the right state of mind.

2 **A:** Do you ever have creative ideas while you're dreaming?
B: Yes, but I can never remember them. Isn't that frustrating? (*rise* / *fall*)

3 **A:** Do you find it easier to be creative when you're listening to music?
B: Are you serious? (*rise* / *fall*) I can't think properly unless it's quiet.

4 **A:** Do you feel more creative early in the morning or late at night?
B: Late at night. Definitely. Who feels creative first thing in the morning? (*rise* / *fall*)

C SPEAK Ask your partner the questions in Exercise B. Try to use a question for comment or criticism in your answer.

SPEAKING

A Look at the infographic. Think of an advantage and disadvantage for each suggestion.

B Work in pairs. Compare your ideas with your partner.

C Now decide which is the best suggestion for finding ideas. Talk for about one minute.

D DISCUSS Work in pairs and discuss the questions.

1 Are you a creative person?
2 How important is the ability to be creative?
3 Do you think everyone should try to do something creative from time to time?

VOCABULARY
Compound adjectives

A Complete the fame quiz.

ARE YOU CUT OUT FOR FAME?

RATE YOURSELF ON A SCALE OF 1 to 5.
1 = Strongly agree 5 = Strongly disagree

Ex C **1** You would trade having privacy for being world famous. 1 2 3 4 5

Ex C **2** You are very focused on one kind of career. You are not open-minded to other career choices. 1 2 3 4 5

Ex C **3** You would describe yourself as a highly-motivated person. 1 2 3 4 5

Ex C **4** You are thick skinned. You don't mind being criticized. 1 2 3 4 5

Ex C **5** You would rather be self-employed than do part-time work for someone else for the same money. 1 2 3 4 5

Ex C **6** You'd prefer to be paid less in a fun creative job than well paid and bored at work. 1 2 3 4 5

Ex C **7** You can handle working long days and doing late-night shifts. 1 2 3 4 5

B Work in pairs. Turn to **page 149** of the **Communication Hub** to see what your answers say about you.

C Find eight compound adjectives in the quiz. Use the information in the box to help you.

Compound adjectives

Compound adjectives can be formed in several ways, including:

- adjective + noun: *last-minute*
- adjective + participle: *left-handed*
- adverb + participle: *never-ending*
- noun + adjective: *sun-dried*
- noun + participle: *career-ending*

We always hyphenate compound adjectives before a noun, but not after a noun. However, some compound adjectives are written as one word (e.g. *heartwarming*) or always hyphenated (e.g. *self-important*).

D Go to the **Vocabulary Hub** on **page 142**.

E **SPEAK** Work in pairs and discuss the questions. Use some of the adjectives in Exercise C.

1 Would you like to be famous?
2 What do you think are the good and bad points of being famous?

CHANGE OF PLANS

Some people choose a career at a young age and stick with it. However, here are four famous people who ended up with very different careers from what they expected.

CHARLIZE THERON

Charlize Theron, originally from South Africa, was to have been a ballerina. However, she suffered a career-ending injury to her knee that meant she had to abandon her childhood dream. Instead, she decided she would turn to acting. After finding it difficult to land speaking roles, she watched hours of television to try to pick up an American accent. (Ex C Q1) But, the roles still didn't come and although she was getting modeling work, money was tight. One day she was trying to cash a check at the bank but the teller said he was not going to accept it. Theron started to argue with the teller, making a scene in the bank as she tried to explain that she was about to be thrown out of her apartment if she couldn't cash the check. Eventually a man in the line behind her came over to help resolve the situation and, after she had her money, he gave her his business card – he was an agent. A couple of months later, Theron had landed her first movie role.

ANDREA BOCELLI

(Ex C Q2) World-famous opera singer Andrea Bocelli was supposed to have a very different career. Although he displayed a clear talent for music from an early age, his parents encouraged him to study law so that he would always have a steady income. (Ex C Q2) Following his parents' advice, he attended law school and became a lawyer. However, he also continued with his music – playing in piano bars in the evenings to earn money for singing lessons. It was at one of these bars where he got the lucky break that was to launch his career. Zucchero, a famous Italian singer, heard him sing, and thought that (Ex C Q2) he would be perfect for a demo he wanted to make. As a result of that meeting, Bocelli ending up going on tour with Zucchero. Bocelli even sang at Zucchero's birthday party – and was immediately signed up by an agent at the party. The agent knew he was going to be a big star – and she was right.

Glossary

renovate (v) to make something old look new again by repairing and improving it, especially a building

embroidery (n) the activity of decorating cloth with colored stitches

2.2 Creative people

VOCABULARY

A Put students into pairs to discuss the questions. In feedback, ask the students which of their classmates they think are cut out for fame and why.

B Direct students to the **Communication Hub** (see TB121).

C Draw students' attention to the information in the *Compound adjectives* box to help them find the compound adjectives. Remind them that all the compound adjectives are from Exercise A, but you could also ask if they remember any compound adjectives, without looking back at the quiz yet. When students have finished, tell them to look at the quiz to check. Finish with class feedback, and check understanding of the compound adjectives where necessary.

D Direct students to the **Vocabulary Hub** (see TB121).

E Put students into pairs to discuss the questions. Give your own example, and use some of the compound adjectives from Exercises A and C if possible. Get feedback on some of the students' opinions. Use the **Vocabulary Worksheet** on page W9 for extra practice.

Extra activity

If students had very strong and differing opinions on the questions, you could turn it into a debate. Split the class into two groups, one that is positive about fame and one that is negative about it. Give them time to prepare their arguments before holding the debate. For a small class, this could be done as a whole-class activity. For a larger class, make groups of four with two for and two against the statement. Finish with feedback on whose arguments were more convincing and also on students' use of language during the debate.

TEACHING IDEA by David Seymour and Maria Popova

My hero

Use this activity to extend the theme of celebrities and role models.

- What makes someone a hero?
- Did you have a hero at school? Tell us about him/her.

Think of a famous hero and imagine you are that person. Stand at the front of the class and answer the students' questions. You can only answer *yes* or *no*. They will try to guess who you are. (If they can't think of a hero, give them one of these.)

Mahatma Gandhi, James Bond, Nelson Mandela, Superman, Robin Hood, Bob Marley, Princess Diana, Che Guevara, Neil Armstrong, Mother Theresa, Abraham Lincoln, Leonardo da Vinci, Joan of Arc, Martin Luther King, J. K. Rowling, Muhammad Ali, Elvis Presley, Rosa Parks, Desmond Tutu, Stephen King, Anne Frank, Stephen Hawking, Audrey Hepburn, Billie Holiday, Serena Williams, Eva Perón

GRAMMAR HUB

2.2 Future in the past

	Future in the past
Past progressive	We **were traveling** to Australia the next day.
was/were going to	Sam **was going to start** looking for another job.
would + base form	I thought it **would be** nice to take a gift.
was/were + infinitive	Jody **was to contact** me as soon as her plane landed.
was/were + perfect infinitive	Jody **was to have contacted** me as soon as her plane landed.
was/were about to + base form	We **were about to leave** the house when the phone rang.

- When we are talking about the past, we sometimes need to talk about things that had not yet happened. We can use the past progressive or *was/were going to* for this.

  *When I saw her, she **was leaving** the next day.*

  *Jim **was going to** meet Mary that evening.*
- We can use the past form of *will* (*would*).

  *That discovery **would turn** out to be important later on.*
- We can also use past forms of the verb *be* with the infinitive or the perfect infinitive. The infinitive can be used for events that came true or didn't come true.

  *He **was to deliver** the report on Tuesday. (And he did.)*

  *He **was to deliver** the report on Tuesday. (But he failed.)*

  The perfect infinitive is usually only used for events that didn't come true.

  *He **was to have delivered** the report on Tuesday. (But he failed.)*
- We can also use past forms of *be* + *supposed to* + base form or perfect infinitive. These are often, but not always, used for events that didn't come true.

  *He **was supposed to have delivered** the report on Tuesday. (But he failed.)*

  *He **wasn't supposed to look** at the files. (But he did anyway.)*
- To describe something that was going to happen soon, we use the past form of the verb *be* with the word *about*. Sometimes we add the word *just*.

  *She had her coat on because she **was (just) about to take** the dog for a walk.*

Be careful!

- You may need to make other changes to pronouns, times, places, etc, in the same way as you do in reported speech.

  Anna was leaving for Canada the following day.

  NOT ~~Anna was leaving for Canada tomorrow.~~

2.2 Creative people

READING

A Draw students' attention to the pictures, and elicit what they know about the people shown.

B Set a time limit and tell students to read the article quickly to find out what the four people's stories have in common. Let students compare their ideas in pairs before taking class feedback.

C Tell students to read the information in the *Inferring meaning* box, and ask students if they think this is true about the way articles are written in their language(s). Tell them to think about this as they read again and answer the questions.

D Put students into pairs to discuss the questions and monitor to help with ideas or language where needed.

GRAMMAR

A Refer students to the underlined phrases in the article and elicit what they have in common. Tell them to use these examples to help them complete the rules in the *Future in the past* box.

B Direct students to the **Grammar Hub** (see TB20 and below).

C Elicit one or two examples for the first one, then put students into pairs to continue. In feedback, record the students' ideas on the board, and see how many different sentences the class can think of for each situation. Use the **Grammar Worksheet** on page W10 for extra practice.

SPEAKING HUB

A Give your own example, explaining what the change of plans was and what effect it had on your life. Encourage students to react to your story and ask you further questions. Tell students to choose one of the situations to talk about for themselves or to think of their own idea.

B Students write notes to prepare to tell their anecdote. Monitor to help with language if needed, and make sure students are just writing brief notes and not writing out their whole story word for word.

C Put students into pairs to share their experiences. Circulate, prompting and helping out where necessary. You can also collect examples of good language use and errors as you monitor.

D Encourage students to listen carefully and to ask each other follow-up questions. When both students have told their story, re-pair students to repeat the task with a new partner. In feedback, ask students to tell the class something interesting they learned about one of their partners. Encourage the rest of the class to ask questions as well.

Extra activity

Use this activity for further practice of future in the past structures.

Brainstorm an example of an event that has changed someone's life, e.g. *winning a large sum of money.* Brainstorm some sentences for what the person was going to do, was about to do, was supposed to do, etc before winning the money. Then tell students to think of a different life event and to write some sentences using the future in the past structures from this lesson to explain what the person's life was like just before it happened. Tell students that their partner will have to guess what the event is, so they shouldn't make their sentences too obvious or repetitive. Put students into small groups to read their sentences and to guess what each other's events were. Finish with feedback on students' use of language in the activity.

GRAMMAR HUB

2.2 Future in the past

A Choose the correct options to complete the sentences.

1 I couldn't go to the party because I *would take* / *<u>was taking</u>* a test the next day.

2 When we were at school together, he was *becoming* / *<u>going to become</u>* a doctor.

3 They thought it *will* / *<u>would</u>* be fun to play a trick on us.

4 Our new TV was to have been *<u>delivered</u>* / *delivering* yesterday but it didn't come.

5 I was *about* / *<u>about to</u>* ask him where he got the money when he made an excuse and left.

6 When the movie was released, few people thought it *<u>would be</u>* / *was being* a success.

7 The fingerprints found at the scene of the crime *were being* / *<u>were to be</u>* vital in solving it.

8 Thinking there was no way he *<u>was going</u>* / *would* to get into college, he didn't even apply.

B Write one word in each blank to complete the sentences.

1 Sonja ___was___ about to get on the train when she realized she'd left her ticket at home.

2 Philippe couldn't believe he was actually ___going___ to graduate in three weeks' time.

3 We all knew it ___would___ be fun to enter the competition.

4 Both girls truly believed they ___were___ going to be famous one day.

5 At that point it dawned on me that London ___was___ to be my new home.

6 Marie was ___just___ about to give in her report when she spotted the mistake.

➤ Go back to page 21.

READING

A SPEAK Look at the pictures of the people in the article *Change of plans*. What do you know about them?

B READ FOR DETAIL Read *Change of plans*. What do the four people's stories have in common? All four started their careers after meeting someone by chance.

C INFER MEANING Read the article again and answer the questions. Use the information in the box to help you.

Inferring meaning

Writers do not always explain everything in detail. They sometimes provide readers with the facts and allow them to infer the meaning by drawing a conclusion from the available information.

1 Why was Charlize Theron unable to get speaking roles?
She didn't have an American accent and most roles probably needed one.

2 Does Andrea Bocelli still work as a lawyer?
No. He became a lawyer, but he probably had to give it up to go on tour.

3 What do we know about Harrison Ford's personality when he was younger? Probably fairly independent and ambitious – he left college to move to Hollywood, got frustrated about not getting roles.

4 How did Grandma Moses learn to paint? Probably self-taught. No formal training and started painting as a hobby.

D SPEAK Work in pairs and discuss the questions

1 Which was the most interesting story? Why?
2 Which person do you think was the luckiest?

HARRISON FORD

Harrison Ford first became interested in acting at the age of 18 because he thought it would be an easy way to get a good grade on his English course. He dropped out of college and moved to Hollywood in his early 20s. Ex C Q3 He managed to get some small acting jobs, but after a few years he became frustrated with the kind of roles he was being offered. Ex C Q3 While renovating his house, he decided to use the tools he had bought and the skills he had learned to become a self-employed carpenter. Ex C Q3 One day, movie director George Lucas hired Ford to make some cabinets for his home and after meeting him, decided to cast him in a movie he was making called *American Graffiti*. When Lucas was auditioning actors for his next movie, he was one actor short so he asked Ford to help out. In the end, he cast Ford and the movie, *Star Wars*, would go on to become a huge hit and make Ford a star.

GRANDMA MOSES

Grandma Moses (Anna Mary Robertson Moses) became a famous painter at the age of 80 – despite not having had any formal training. Ex C Q4 She was born in 1860 and raised on her parents' farm. She didn't attend school regularly, because she knew she would be leaving home to start working on another farm when she was 12. She married at 17, was widowed at 47, and retired at 76. In fact, she didn't start painting until she took it up as a hobby at the age of 78. Ex C Q4 She only started because she was giving up embroidery due to pain from arthritis. She painted rural scenes from her childhood, which she gave away or sold cheaply. However, one day an art collector saw her paintings in a local store. He drove straight to her farm and asked to buy all the paintings she had, and, later that year, he exhibited some of her paintings at a show for new painters. This led to solo exhibitions, and soon her shows would break attendance records around the world. She died in 1961.

GRAMMAR

Future in the past

A WORK IT OUT Look at the underlined phrases in the article. Then choose the correct words to complete the rules.

Future in the past

1 When we talk about plans, intentions and predictions that we had in the past, we use ***past* / *present*** forms of the verbs we usually use to talk about the future.

2 We use *be* + *to* + base form for events that ***came true* / *didn't come true*** and *be* + *to* + *have* + past participle (or *be* + *supposed to* + verb) for events that ***came true* / *didn't come true***.

B Go to the **Grammar Hub** on **page 124**.

C Write sentences using the future in the past to explain the situations (1–5). Then share your ideas with a partner.

1 You didn't get up early today.
2 You missed your train or bus this morning.
3 You didn't eat lunch yesterday.
4 You got lost in the city.
5 You went to see a movie with a friend.

I was going to get up early, but I forgot to set my alarm clock.

SPEAKING HUB

A PLAN Think of a time when a change of plans had a big effect on your life. Choose one of these situations or think of your own idea.

- You changed your mind about something.
- You suddenly had an unexpected opportunity.
- Something did not go as you had planned.
- Something good came out of a bad situation.

B PREPARE Write notes to prepare to talk about this event.

C PRESENT Tell your partner about what happened.

D DISCUSS Listen and ask your partner questions.

Talk about finding inspiration
Describe a life-changing moment

Café Hub

2.3 Art and design

A – *nowhere* phrases S – managing a discussion

City design festival

a

b

A Work in pairs. Look at the pictures (a and b) and discuss the questions.

1 Where are they? Behind Liverpool Street station, London; Granary Square, London

2 What do you think they are? Both form part of the London Design Festival.

B Watch the video and check your answers to Exercise A.

Glossary

accessible (adj) art, music, literature, etc, which is easy to understand and enjoy

ceramic (adj) made from clay baked at a high temperature so that it has become hard

eccentricity (n) the state of behaving in a strange and unusual way, sometimes in a humorous way

installation (n) a piece of art that consists of several objects or pictures arranged to produce a particular effect

C Watch the video again. Check (✓) the things you see.

1 People walking inside an installation. ✓

2 A designer creating an installation. ☐

3 An indoor design exhibition. ✓

4 A man sitting at a table with a cup of coffee. ✓

5 Children playing on the installation. ☐

6 A person taking a photo of an installation. ✓

7 People walking through arches. ✓

8 A designer showing a group of people around an installation. ☐

D Watch the video again. Complete the sentences with the best option.

1 What Camille Walala loves most about an outdoor art installation is that it *makes art easier for people to understand and enjoy* / *allows her to be more creative*.

2 Camille has lived in London for *fifteen* / *twenty* years.

3 A woman says Camille Walala's installation looks like a *theme park* / *bouncy castle*.

4 Adam Nathaniel Furman says people think ceramics are something *found in your bathroom and kitchen* / *used to cover buildings*.

5 Ben Evans says *a minority* / *the majority* of London's design community have British passports.

AUTHENTIC ENGLISH

A Work in pairs. Read the sentences from the video. Then choose the correct words to complete the information in the box.

There's ***nowhere quite like*** *it, especially when it comes to design.*

I absolutely love London, it's like an eccentricity that you've got ***nowhere else****.*

There's nowhere else *really in the UK where you can just walk down the street and see exciting things like this every day.*

nowhere phrases

We use *there's nowhere quite like*, *that you've got nowhere else* and *there's nowhere else where* to express that a place is ***ordinary*** / ***unique***.

We have many other phrases with *nowhere like*: *nowhere on Earth*, *… but nowhere more so than …*, *out of nowhere*, *go nowhere*, *be going nowhere fast*, *in the middle of nowhere*, *nowhere near* and *nowhere to be found*.

B Write sentences using phrases with *nowhere* about these places.

1 Paris *There's nowhere on earth like Paris for culture.*

2 London There's nowhere quite like London.

3 Dubai There's nowhere else where you have the range of stores.

4 New York There's nowhere on Earth like New York for bookstores.

5 Italy There's nowhere quite like Italy when it comes to food.

6 Brazil There's nowhere else on Earth like Brazil during Carnival.

C Work in pairs. Tell each other about some of your favorite places (countries, cities, restaurants, stores, museums, etc) and why they are unique.

Art critics

SAM MALCOLM AMANDA HARRY EMILY

A Work in pairs. Discuss the questions.

1 Do you like modern art? Why/Why not?

2 What do you think about art criticism?

B Watch the video and answer the questions.

1 What does Malcolm like about the painted paper? use of color

2 What does each of the following people think the message of the painted paper is?

- Amanda about feelings of isolation in the digital age
- Malcolm exposing how superficial connections are
- male customer comment on the current political situation

3 Whose opinion is most popular among the three of them? the male customer's

4 What misunderstanding has occurred? The 'art' is just samples used by Sam and Harry to decide what color to paint the wall.

SPEAKING SKILL

A Work in pairs. Look at the underlined expression from the video and answer the questions.

Amanda:	The artist is clearly making a comment on ...
Sam:	I think you're a little confused ...
Amanda:	Sam ... <u>Can you let me finish?</u> Thanks. The artist is clearly making a statement on feelings of isolation ...

1 What has happened in the exchange between Sam and Amanda? Sam interrupted Amanda; Amanda wants to finish her point.

2 Why do we use expressions like this when we're speaking? when we want to finish our point

Read the information in the box. Which of the ways of managing a discussion (1–5) are used in the exchange in Exercise A? 1, 4

B Match the ways of managing a discussion (1–5) with the examples from the video (a–e) below.

Managing a discussion

1 Interrupting: Say something to stop someone speaking so that you can speak instead. d

2 Taking the floor: Signal that you are now going to join a debate or discussion. c

3 Returning to a point: Indicate that you want to further discuss a point that you previously made. a

4 Stopping an interruption: Tell the person who is trying to interrupt that you want to finish your point first. b

5 Pre-empting an interruption: Anticipate that someone will interrupt you and briefly state all the points you want to cover before they cut in. e

a Well that leads back to my point ... without meaning there is no relationship.

b If I could just finish ... my main point though is that it doesn't really matter what it is.

c I couldn't agree more ... it does evoke some really intense emotions.

d I don't mean to cut you off, Amanda, but I think it's the exact opposite.

e And that's my point exactly. When you are using bold colors like this artist has, you are clearly trying to expose just how superficial those connections are.

C Work in small groups. Discuss one of the following topics. Use the strategies from Exercise B.

- Art in the past and now
- The greatest artist ever
- Different forms of art

SPEAKING HUB

A PREPARE You are going to talk about a work of art in a small group. Look at the picture on page 13. Think about what you want to say about the picture and art in general.

B PRESENT Work in small groups. Discuss the picture and present your views.

A: I usually tend to prefer landscapes rather than portraits ...
B: Can I just stop you there? ... The style of painting is what makes it special.
A: Exactly. What I was actually saying was that while I usually prefer landscapes, in this case ...

Discuss a work of art

➤ Turn to page 157 to learn how to write a review about a classic book or movie.

2.3 Art and design

City design festival

A Put students into pairs to look at the pictures and to discuss the questions. Get some feedback on their ideas, but don't confirm or reject any answers at this stage.

B ▶ Tell students to watch the video to check their answers. Before playing the video, point out the glossary with definitions of some vocabulary that appears in it, and check for understanding.

C–D ▶ Put students into pairs to check answers before whole-class feedback.

AUTHENTIC ENGLISH

A Point out the sentences from the video and the information in the box about *nowhere phrases*. Give some examples of your own of how you could use some of the phrases in the box.

B Tell students to look at the example then to write some similar sentences about the other places. In feedback, write some of the students' sentences on the board. Make it clear that there are a lot of possible answers, but correct or reformulate any that sound awkward or unnatural.

C Give your own example, then put students into pairs to tell each other about some of their favorite places. Get feedback from a few students, and see if others know the places and if they agree.

Art critics

A Put students into pairs to discuss the questions. Get feedback to find out how similar or different their opinions are.

B ▶ Tell students to watch the video and to answer the questions. In feedback, ask students to justify their answers with reference to what exactly the speakers said. You can find the **video script** for *Art critics* on the Teacher's Resource Center.

SPEAKING SKILL

A Put students into pairs to read the extract from the video and to answer the questions. In feedback, ask students if they use similar expressions in these situations in their language(s).

B Point out the information in the box about *Managing a discussion*. Draw students' attention to sentences a–e, and point out that these are examples of each of these five ways. Elicit the first one as an example, then tell students to underline the phrases used to manage a discussion in sentences a–e.

C Elicit the first one as an example, then tell students to match the other sentences to the other ways. Ask students to check their answers in pairs before checking as a class.

D Demonstrate with a couple of stronger students, then put students into small groups to discuss the other topics. Monitor attentively, then give feedback on how well students managed the discussion.

SPEAKING HUB

A Explain that students are going to be speaking in a small group, but first to prepare their ideas individually. Draw their attention to the picture on page 13 and allow them time to think of ideas.

B Instruct students to discuss the work of art. Encourage them to interrupt, ask questions and use the strategies for managing a conversation seen earlier.

Extra activity
Tell students to think of more examples of works of art they like or admire. Encourage them to find pictures on their phones and to research background information about the works of art. Put students into small groups to tell each other about the works of art and why they like them.

▶ VIDEO SCRIPT

City design festival
N = Narrator C = Camille Walala F1 = Female 1
F2 = Female 2 A = Adam Nathaniel Furman
B = Ben Evans

N: A dramatic splash of color lurks behind Liverpool Street Station, creating a surprise and playful environment. Something its designer, Camille Walala, was keen to create.

C: When I saw the place, I just thought I wanted to do something a bit like fun and, and bring an element of surprise for people who work around here. What I love about doing installation, like outdoor installation, it can be, it makes design much more accessible and people might just come here by surprise and yet finally stay one hour or two.

N: The textile designer was born in France but has lived in London for the past 20 years and says there's nowhere quite like it, especially when it comes to design.

C: I absolutely love London, it's like … it's like an eccentricity that you've got nowhere else, and I think, um, yeah, to be able to do something like this in London is pretty amazing.

F1: I think it's fantastic. There's nowhere else really in the UK where you can just walk down the street and see exciting things like this every day.

F2: I really, really like it. I think it's fun, it's playful. It looks like a bouncy castle, although, we're, I guess, we're not really allowed to bounce off of it, er, but it's what London needs, I think, at the moment.

N: Not far away, four giant colorful tiled gates are dominating Granary Square, drawing inspiration from some of London's tiled Underground stations.

A: I think people very often tend to think that ceramics are something you have on your bathroom floor or in the splashback in your kitchen, but, actually, across countries from Turkey to Iran to Italy to the United Kingdom, there is an incredible tradition for hundreds and hundreds of years of covering buildings in monumental ways, monumental architectures with ceramic products.

B: London's design community is very international. Most of our designers don't have British passports, but they've chosen to live and work in our great city, and it's easy for them to go and work anywhere they like in the world.

N: But for now London is celebrating its dominance in a very bold way.

2 Writing — Write a review

W– writing concisely

A Read this announcement and answer the questions.

Reviews wanted

Have you recently read a classic book or watched a classic movie? We're starting a series of reviews of classic books and movies and we want your opinions.
Is the book or movie as good as everyone says it is? Is it still relevant today? Please send us a review for the college paper. Write 220–260 words.

1 What should be reviewed?
2 What questions should be addressed by the review?
3 Who is the target audience?
4 How long should the review be?

B Read the review. Does the writer agree that the book deserves its reputation as a classic? Which parts of the review tell you this?

Alice's Adventures in Wonderland

Ex E Ex E Ex B 1 Fantasy children's novel *Alice's Adventures in Wonderland* was published in 1865. The book, adapted for movies and television and translated into over 100 languages, fully deserves its reputation as a classic and is just as fun today as it always was.

Ex E 2 At the beginning of the story, Alice sees a white rabbit wearing clothes and talking to himself. Following the rabbit, she falls down a hole into a bizarre world of strange and wonderful creatures, including a snooty caterpillar and the mysterious, grinning Cheshire Cat.

3 One of the reasons that *Alice's Adventures in Wonderland* is so popular is that it is a nonsense story. It's not a typical linear story or a story with logic and a moral. It's about the strange situations and unusual characters created by the author, and they surprise and delight readers.

4 Another reason for the book's enduring popularity is Lewis Carroll's playful use of language. The story is full of riddles, puzzles, puns and made-up words. One of the most famous examples is the 'unbirthday party' at the Mad Hatter's tea party.

Ex B 5 *Alice's Adventures in Wonderland* is without a doubt a classic book that has captured the imaginations of generations of children and adults. Its creative story, characters and playful use of language make it a unique story – and one that everybody should read at least once.

C Look at the review and identify which paragraph contains the following information.

a an overall opinion of the work and a recommendation 5
b key information about the work and a general opinion of it 1
c analysis of a second positive or negative aspect of the work 4
d a plot summary or description of the work 2
e analysis of one positive or negative aspect of the work 3

D Read the review again and answer the questions.

1 Which characters from the book are mentioned? Alice, the white rabbit, a snooty caterpillar, the Cheshire Cat, the Mad Hatter
2 How is the story of this book different to most other books? it is not linear; it has no logic/moral
3 What example of playful use of language does the writer give? 'unbirthday party'

E Find features of concise description in the text. Use the information in the box to help you.

Writing concisely

If you need to write concisely, you can use some of the following features:

- noun phrases: *English writer and mathematician Charles Dodgson*
- reduced adjective clauses: *Charles Dodgson, writer and mathematician, published his first book.*
- participle clauses: *Educated at home, Dodgson wrote poems and short stories.*

WRITING

A PREPARE Look again at the announcement in Exercise A.

B PLAN Plan your review. Use your answers to question 2 in Exercise A to help you.

C WRITE Write your review. Use your plan to help you.

D REVIEW Exchange your review with a partner. Do you have similar information? Underline any information that you don't think is correct.

E EDIT Read your partner's comments. Rewrite any parts you think should change.

WRITING 157

Answers

1 a classic book or movie
2 Is it as good as everyone says it is? Is it still relevant today?
3 college students
4 220–260 words

Answers

Yes. The end of the first paragraph and the final paragraph.

Refer students to this review as a model for the writing task.

Remind students to refer back to the box on writing concisely as they write.

Again ask students to refer to the box when evaluating and editing their partner's review.

WRITING

A Elicit *review* and ask students what kind of things can be reviewed, e.g. *movies*, *books*, *restaurants*, *hotels*, etc. Tell students to read the announcement and to answer the questions.

B Students read the review and answer the questions. Encourage them to underline the parts of the review where they find the answers, and in feedback ask them to refer to these.

C Tell students to look at the review again and explain the task. They check their answers in pairs before whole-class feedback.

D Students read the review one more time and answer the questions.

E Point out the information in the box about *Writing concisely*. Elicit one example from the review, then tell students to find more.

WRITING TASK

A Explain that students are going to write a review as described in the announcement in Exercise A. Tell them to read the announcement again and to decide what book or movie they want to review.

B Students plan their review, thinking about the questions posed in the announcement. Remind them about how the information is organized into different paragraphs in the review from Exercise B.

C Tell students to use their plan to help them write their review. If there isn't time in class, this can be set as homework. Remind them about the tips for writing concisely.

D Ask students to swap reviews with a partner and to read each other's. Tell them to add comments and to underline anything they don't think is correct. Monitor to help and prompt where necessary.

E Tell students.to swap reviews back, read their partner's comments and to make any changes they think necessary. Finish with some whole-class feedback on how similar students' reviews were. How similar are the students' tastes?

Unit 2 Review

VOCABULARY

A Complete the conversations with the words in the box.

groundbreaking hilarious repetitive sensational tedious unconventional

1 **A:** That was a really funny movie. I was crying with laughter.
B: Yes, it was hilarious.

2 **A:** I thought her performance was amazing.
B: She was sensational. She deserves an Oscar.

3 **A:** Have you read this book? I'm finding it pretty dull.
B: Yeah, it's a little tedious, isn't it?

4 **A:** It was such an innovative musical. I loved it.
B: Me, too. As you say, it was groundbreaking.

5 **A:** Can we turn this off? It's just car chase after car chase.
B: Yeah, it's kind of repetitive, isn't it?

6 **A:** Do you like her work? Her pieces are very unusual.
B: She's unconventional, but I find her work exciting.

B Complete the sentences with the words in the box. Then choose which ideas help you feel most creative.

bounce draw fresh trust immerse run stimulate hit

1 Take a break. Immerse yourself in a TV show for 30 minutes.
2 Bounce ideas around with your best friend. Ask them for a fresh perspective.
3 Draw inspiration from a piece of music.
4 Whenever you hit a wall, take a walk.
5 Drink coffee to stimulate your creativity.
6 Don't think carefully – just run with an idea. Trust your instincts.

C Match numbers (1–8) to letters (a–h) to form full sentences. Then think of some jobs which match each sentence.

1 You need to be thick- g
2 It's a well- d
3 You need to be highly f
4 Most people won't become world- h
5 It's like being self- c
6 There are a lot of late- a
7 You have to be open- e
8 It's a high- b

a night shifts, so you'll have an irregular sleeping pattern.
b risk job, so it pays well.
c employed, because you can work from home.
d paid job.
e minded, because things change all the time.
f motivated, because it's competitive.
g skinned to handle the criticism.
h famous, but they still make a living.

GRAMMAR

A Complete the text with the correct form of the verbs in parentheses.

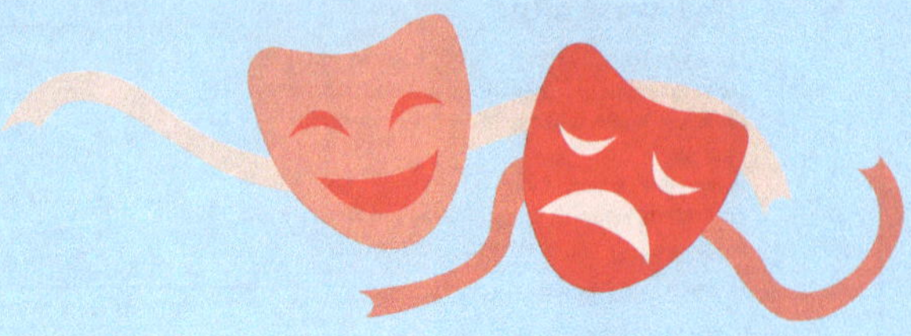

My first role

When I was about ten, I [1] joined (*join*) a drama group in a nearby town and they [2] performed (*perform*) a show every year. That year, we [3] were doing / did (*do*) *Peter Pan*. We [4] had been rehearsing / rehearsed (*rehearse*) for weeks. I [5] had been given / was given (*give*) a pretty big role – I [6] was playing / played (*play*) Michael, the smallest of the children Peter Pan [7] brings / brought (*bring*) to Neverland. I [8] remember (*remember*) how nervous I [9] was (*be*) when we [10] peeked (*peek*) out from behind the curtain to see the people in the audience.

However, it was worth all the nerves when the audience [11] applauded (*applaud*) at the end. I [12] felt (*feel*) so proud – and I couldn't wait to start practicing for the next show.

B Choose the correct option to complete the sentences.

1 The band did not know they *would have* / *were going to be* the biggest selling rock group this decade.
2 Little did he know, it was this discovery that *would change* / *is to have changed* the experiment completely.
3 This *was supposed to be* / *would be* a dream vacation, but it turned into a nightmare.
4 They *were supposed to finish* / *be finished* in May, but the deadline was pushed back until June.
5 The highway was *due* / *meant* to be completed by now.
6 Carlos had been *about* / *set* to go through airport security when he realized he didn't have his passport.

Blazing a trail at thirty thousand feet.

Progress (n) the process of developing or improving. Synonyms: development (n), advance (n)

Frederick Douglass means that important things cannot be achieved without hard work.

Frederick Douglass (1818–1895) escaped from slavery in the US and became a social reformer and statesman, whose speeches and writings played a significant role in the abolition of slavery.

OBJECTIVES

- make predictions about the future
- use persuasive language to sell something
- discuss progress and society
- evaluate costs and benefits
- discuss renewable energy
- write a persuasive email

Work with a partner. Discuss the questions.

1 Look at the picture. What does it say about progress? What other examples can you think of to illustrate the same idea?

2 Read the quote. What does Douglass mean?

3 How could you measure 'progress':

- in your own life
- in your city/country
- in the world?

PROGRESS 25

OBJECTIVES

Read the unit objectives to the class.

UNIT OPENER QUESTIONS

1 Put students into pairs to discuss the picture and the questions. Get some class feedback and encourage students to expand on and justify their opinions.

2 Draw students' attention to the quote and elicit how it is related to the topic of progress. Get feedback on some of the most interesting ideas students come up with.

3 Give or elicit an example of how progress could be measured, then put students into pairs to think of more ways. Again, get feedback on the most interesting ideas. Give feedback on students' use of language during these tasks, and record any useful language that comes up on the board.

WORKSHEETS

Lesson 3.1 Progressive design

Vocabulary: Sustainability (W11)

Grammar: Future structures (W12)

Vocabulary: Forming verbs from adjectives (W13)

Lesson 3.2 Better … or worse?

Grammar: Negative inversion (W14)

Vocabulary: Verb–noun collocations (W15)

3.1 Progressive design

- Make predictions about the future
- Use persuasive language to sell something

V – sustainability; forming verbs from adjectives
P – sounding persuasive
G – future structures
S – listening to identify persuasive techniques

VOCABULARY
Sustainability

A Work in groups. Which of these sustainable / environmentally friendly solutions would most benefit your country?

- recycling
- biodegradable plastic
- electric vehicles
- beach clean-ups
- wind power

B Choose the correct words to complete these statements about sustainability.

1 We will *never* / *soon* run out of **renewable** energy sources like solar and wind power.
2 A sustainable building generates *less* / *more* electricity than it **consumes**.
3 To be carbon-**neutral**, you might *cut down* / *plant* some trees to **offset** the pollution caused by a plane trip.
4 A zero-**emission** factory causes no *air* / *water* pollution.
5 **Over-exploitation** of natural resources will *lead to* / *prevent* the **depletion** of those resources over time.
6 **Biodegradable** materials break down into *harmful* / *harmless* parts which don't **accumulate** in the environment.

C Go to the Vocabulary Hub on page 143.

D SPEAK Work in groups. Discuss the questions.

1 Can ordinary people be carbon-neutral/cause zero emissions in the modern world?
2 Is it worth the effort? Can ordinary people make a difference?

READING

A SPEAK Look at the pictures in the article. What might be special or unusual about the buildings?

B READ FOR GIST Read the article quickly. Match the names below with the pictures (a–c).

1 Aequorea b
2 Nautilus Eco-Resort c
3 The Lilypad a

C READ FOR DETAIL Read the article again. Which project(s) from Exercise B does each statement apply to?

1 Scientists will work there. Aequorea, Nautilus
2 It takes its shape from the natural world. Lilypad, Aequorea, Nautilus
3 It will collect its own water. Lilypad, Aequorea
4 It will use less energy than it generates. Lilypad
5 The buildings will move up and down. Nautilus
6 It will move from place to place. Lilypad
7 It will hold tens of thousands of people. Lilypad, Aequorea

D SPEAK Would you like to live or stay in any of these places? What would be the benefits and drawbacks?

GRAMMAR
Future structures

A Look at the underlined sections (1–10) in the article. What time do they refer to?

B WORK IT OUT Match the sections (1–10) with the rules in the box (a–f).

Future structures

a We use the future progressive to describe a situation that will be in progress at a particular point in the future (3), or to emphasize that it will cover an extended period of time (9).
b We use the future perfect to describe changes that will be completed before a particular point in the future (1).
c We use the future perfect progressive to focus on the future results of an earlier future process, and/or to measure the length of time of that process (6).
d We can use a modal verb (e.g. *might*, *could*) instead of *will* in these structures (2).
e After words like *if*, *unless*, *when*, *while*, etc, future tenses (e.g. future progressive) usually become present tenses (e.g. present progressive) (7, 10).
f Other future structures include *be on the brink/verge of (doing)* (4) and *be about / due / set to (do)* (5, 8).

C Go to the Grammar Hub on page 126.

SPEAKING

SPEAK Work in pairs. Ask and answer the questions about the times in the box.

ten years from now   the end of this lesson   this time next year

1 Where will you be? What will you be doing?
2 What will you have achieved? How will the world have changed?
3 How will you be feeling? Why?

3.1 Progressive design

LEAD-IN

Books closed. Ask students to imagine the world in the year 2100. Tell them to write down five predictions about how the world will be different then. Put students into pairs to compare their ideas. Get class feedback, and encourage students to expand on or explain their predictions where appropriate. Record any useful language that comes up on the board.

VOCABULARY

A Elicit or give an example for the first one, then put students into groups to discuss how sustainable the activities are and how they could be made more so. Get feedback on students' ideas, and write on the board any useful language that comes up, especially if it is relevant to the topic.

B Tell students to choose the correct word to complete the statements. Do the first one as an example to demonstrate how the sentences define the words in bold. In feedback, fully check understanding of the vocabulary with further examples where necessary. Model and practice pronunciation of some words and phrases (e.g. *renewable energy, depletion, biodegradable materials, accumulate*) where appropriate.

C Direct students to the **Vocabulary Hub** (see TB121).

D Give an idea or example of your own, then put students into groups to discuss the questions. Get feedback and encourage students to ask each other questions and to agree or disagree with each other. Use the **Vocabulary Worksheet** on page W11 for extra practice.

TEACHING IDEA by David Seymour and Maria Popova

Eco-warrior

Use this activity to extend the theme of environmental problems and sustainability.

What is an 'eco-warrior'? What kind of issues do they fight for and how do they fight for them?

In pairs, imagine a highway is being built through an area of outstanding natural beauty.

- How would you oppose it if you were an eco-warrior?
- What arguments would you make, and what arguments would you expect from the developer?

Role-play an interview between a journalist and an eco-warrior chained to a tree. Discuss the planned development, how long he/she has been there and what he/she plans to do when the bulldozers arrive.

TEACHING IDEA by David Seymour and Maria Popova

Public consultation meeting

Use this activity to extend the theme of environmental problems and sustainability.

A paper factory is planned for your town, which is very beautiful but high in unemployment. There are concerns about pollution and the destruction of a forest nearby. In groups of eight, you are going to role-play a public consultation meeting to listen to local views. (Allocate these roles. If the class does not divide into groups of eight, drop one or two of the roles.)

In favor of the factory: the mayor, a representative of the paper company, the building contractor, an unemployed person.

Against the factory: a member of the Green Party, an environmental scientist, a local craftsman, a local hotel owner.

Role-play the meeting.

GRAMMAR HUB

3.1 Future structures

- We can use a variety of grammatical forms to express the future, such as future forms with *will*, the simple present, the present progressive and *be going to*.

  They'll plant some more trees over the next few weeks.
  When does the presentation begin?
  I'm going to install solar panels on my roof.

- We use the future progressive (*will be* + *-ing*) to describe a situation that will be in progress at a particular point in the future.

  Scientists will be making an important announcement at 3 pm.

- We use the future perfect (*will have* + past participle) to describe changes that will be completed before a particular point in the future.

  He will have fixed the air-conditioning by the end of the day.

- We can use the future perfect with adverbs in the middle position after *will*.

  *Pollution in our city will **surely** have impacted quality of life by the end of the next decade.*

- We use the future perfect progressive (*will have been* + *-ing*) to focus on the future results of an earlier future process, and/or to measure the length of time of that process.

  The crew will have been tearing down the old factory for twelve weeks by the end of June.

Be careful!

- We usually don't use *will* after words which signal conditional sentences such as *if, unless, when, while*. So we use present progressive instead of future progressive, and present perfect instead of future perfect.

  She'll be hanging up flyers while I'm meeting with the council. NOT ~~*She'll be hanging up flyers while I'll be meeting with the council.*~~

- We can use a modal verb such as *may, might* or *could* instead of *will* in these future structures to express possibility.

  They'll be switching to renewable energy soon. (= definitely)
  They could be switching to renewable energy soon. (= it's possible)

- We also use phrases such as *be on the verge of* + *-ing*, *be on the brink of* + *-ing*, *be due to* + base form, *be set to* + base form, and *be about to* + base form to refer to the future.

  *Danielle **was on the verge of achieving** her goal.*

3.1 Progressive design

READING

A Get some class feedback, but don't confirm or reject any of their ideas yet.

B Set a time limit and ask students to read the article quickly to match the names to the pictures. Stress that they don't need to worry about unknown vocabulary to do this.

C Students read the article again, more carefully this time, to match the statements to one of the projects. Encourage them to underline the parts of the text that help them find the answer. Let students compare answers in pairs before feedback.

D Give an example of your own, then put students into pairs to discuss the questions. Get feedback on some of the most interesting conversations.

GRAMMAR

A Suggested answers

1, 2 Between now and 2100; 3 In 2100; 4 Now ('we're on the brink') / the very near future ('witnessing'); 5 Some time in the future (after the Lilypad is finished); 6 A point in the future ('at the end of a work week') looking back at an earlier period of time ('all week'); 7 Around a series of points in the future, i.e. whenever the rooms disappear underground; 8 The very near future; 9 Over a period of time in the future, i.e. during your vacation; 10 At the same time ('while') as another process in the future ('you'll also get some practical lessons')

B Point out the rules in the *Future structures* box, and explain that the underlined structures are all examples of those rules. Elicit the first one as a class example, then tell students to match the other sentences to the rules.

C Direct students to the **Grammar Hub** (see TB26 and below). Use the **Grammar Worksheet** on page W12 for extra practice.

SPEAKING

Give some examples of your own, then put students into pairs to discuss the questions. Get feedback on students' answers, and encourage them to expand on what they say and to ask each other further questions. Give feedback on students' use of language during the activity, especially in terms of how well they used future structures.

> **Extra activity**
> Remind students about the predictions they made in the lead-in. Put them into small groups to write down five more predictions about the year 2100, using one of the future structures from this lesson in each. Groups can then swap sheets of paper, and discuss how likely they think the other group's predictions are to come true. Swap again and repeat so that every group gets to discuss each other group's predictions. Finish with whole-class feedback. Establish which predictions the class thinks are the most plausible. Are the students generally optimistic or pessimistic about the future? Why?

GRAMMAR HUB

3.1 Future structures

A Match the statements (1–7) with their purposes (a–g).

1 We're going to build a zero-emissions home. b
2 I'll call the manager, if you like. e
3 I think you'll be famous someday! d
4 When are they going to close down that factory? f
5 The talk begins at 10 am. c
6 I think I'll just take the bus instead. g
7 With all these clouds, it's going to rain very soon! a

a making a prediction from strong evidence
b explaining plans
c talking about a fixed scheduled event
d making a prediction based on opinion more than evidence
e making an offer
f asking about plans
g making a decision while speaking

B Choose the correct options to complete the sentences.

1 We'll *be testing* / *have tested* the new equipment for a few hours tomorrow.
2 They'll have *been laying* / *laid* the foundation by the end of next week.
3 I'll *be meeting* / *have met* Jim later today, if you'd like to join us.
4 Will you have *be working* / *been working* with the company for very long when you retire?
5 The company will have *built* / *been building* two new hotels by the end of the year.
6 They won't *have taken* / *be taking* questions from the audience after the talk.
7 By the time she finishes the marathon, Kayla will have *jogged* / *been jogging* for six hours.
8 He'll probably still be working unless he *decides* / *will decide* to leave it for next week.

C Complete the second sentence so that it has a similar meaning to the first sentence. Use between two and five words, including the word in bold.

1 Thirty minutes from now, the meeting will conclude. **DUE**
The meeting is due to conclude in half an hour.
2 The scientists will make the discovery any day now. **VERGE**
The scientists are on the verge of making the discovery.
3 In less than a minute, the rocket will launch. **ABOUT**
The rocket is (just) about to be launched.
4 The two companies are close to sealing the deal. **BRINK**
The two companies are on the brink of sealing the deal.
5 By the end of the year, the agreement will have expired. **SET**
The agreement is set to expire by year's end.
6 I'll be collecting samples and she'll be recording them. **WHILE**
She'll be recording samples while I'm collecting / while I collect them.

➤ Go back to page 26.

ONE ARCHITECT'S VISION

TO BRING US BACK FROM THE BRINK

The world of 2100 will look considerably different from the world of today. [1]By then, much of the ice around the north and south poles will have melted, according to the Intergovernmental Panel on Climate Change. [2]Sea levels could well have risen by as much as 88 cm. [3]Many of the world's low-lying islands and coastal regions will be disappearing – or will already have disappeared – beneath the rising tides. Millions of people will have lost their homes. In short, [4]we're on the brink of witnessing irrevocable changes to our world.

A visionary Belgian architect, Vincent Callebaut, has an innovative answer to the problem of rising sea levels: The Lilypad, a futuristic- Ex C Q6 looking city that will drift around the world following ocean currents like a giant ship. If his plans come to fruition, [5]this self-contained city is set to become home to around 50,000 climate refugees. Ex C Q7

The Lilypad's design is inspired by the shape of the *Victoria amazonica* Ex C lilypad. At its center will be a lake to catch, store and purify rain water, Q2 surrounded by three 'mountains'. Thanks to a series of renewable Ex C Q3 energy sources, this eco-city will produce more energy than it Ex C Q4 consumes. All its carbon dioxide and other waste will be recycled, making the Lilypad entirely zero-emission.

The Lilypad isn't Callebaut's only attempt to re-think the design of buildings and cities. Back in 2015, he revealed spectacular plans for the world's first underwater skyscrapers, called Aequorea, which will be 500 meters wide, have 250 floors and be capable of holding 20,000 Ex C Q7 people. These eco-friendly structures will be self-sufficient, as they'll Ex C Q3 produce all their own energy, heat, food and water. They'll also be made of 100% recycled plastic, collected from the world's oceans.

Each oceanscraper will have a jellyfish-like structure: the entrance Ex C Q2 will be located at the surface and then the structure will spiral down to depths of 1000 meters. Inside will be homes, offices and workshops, Ex C Q1 science laboratories, sea farms and fruit and vegetable gardens. Fresh drinking water will be produced using in-depth pressure to separate salt from seawater.

The Aequorea will be moored off the coast of Brazil, rather than in the open ocean. Residents will certainly be glad of the chance to visit the mainland and soak up some much-needed sunshine at the end of each work week – [6]they'll have been breathing processed air and staring out into the deep, dark ocean all week, after all.

b

Mr. Callebaut's latest project, the Nautilus Eco-Resort in the Ex C Q2 Philippines, takes its name and inspiration from a mollusk, the nautilus. The hotels themselves will also be shaped like seashells, which will rise and fall as they rotate around a Ex C Q5 central coil. Visitors can expect uninterrupted sunshine throughout the day as the towers follow the course of the sun. Some rooms will even disappear underground [7]when they're not being used. But before you book your ticket, be warned that [8]the resort isn't about to open any time soon – like most of Mr. Callebaut's designs, it's still some way from actually being built.

The Nautilus Eco-Resort aims to be a 'zero-emission, zero-waste, zero-poverty' project, built entirely from reused or recycled materials from the islands. Visitors will also be Ex C Q1 actively involved with scientists, engineers and ecologists to ensure their experience encourages sustainable progress. So if you do decide to take a luxury vacation there, [9]you won't be spending all your time lounging around by the pool. You'll also get some practical lessons on sustainability [10]while you're collecting garbage from the beach!

c

Glossary

- **brink (n)** the point in time when something very bad or very good is about to happen
- **irrevocable (adj)** impossible to change or stop
- **moor (v)** to stop a ship or boat from moving by fastening it to a place with ropes or by using an anchor
- **sustainable (adj)** using methods that do not harm the environment
- **visionary (adj)** original and showing a lot of imagination

LISTENING

A SPEAK Work in pairs. Read *(Very) Smart Materials.* Discuss why each material mentioned might be useful.

> **Glossary**
>
> **smart materials (n)** technologically advanced materials with properties (e.g. color, shape, magnetism, etc) that can change in response to stimuli such as light, temperature, pressure or moisture

(VERY) SMART MATERIALS

COLOR-CHANGING PAINT:
The roof and walls of a building automatically change color during the day, depending on the temperature.

PIEZOELECTRIC SHOES:
Walking in the shoes causes crystals in the soles to change shape, generating an electric current.

SHAPE-CHANGING AIRPLANE WINGS:
The wings detect the plane's height (using atmospheric pressure) and change shape automatically.

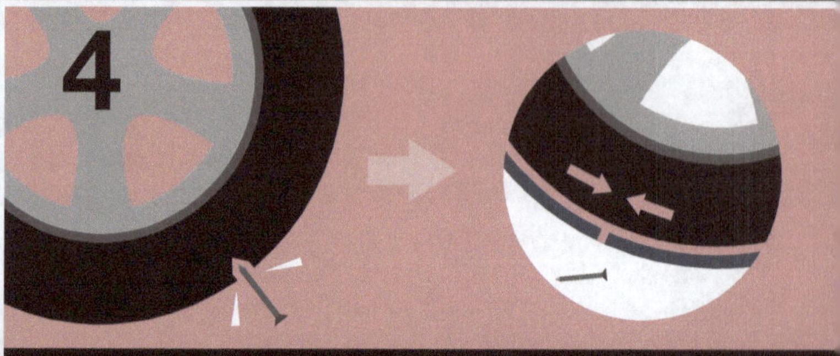

SELF-REPAIRING RUBBER TIRES:
The rubber contains tiny balls of glue. If the tire is damaged, the balls open, glue is released and solidifies, and the holes are repaired.

B LISTEN FOR DETAIL 3.1 Listen to a conversation about smart materials. Choose the correct options (a, b or c) to answer the questions.

1 What is the woman trying to do?
   a make friendly conversation
   b teach the man something
   (c) sell something
2 How does the hat work?
   (a) Its fibers change shape to control air flow.
   b It uses electricity to warm your head.
   c You can adjust its shape based on the weather.
3 What must the man do to keep the hat?
   a write a detailed report about his experiences of wearing it
   b pay $50
   (c) test it in the rain
4 Why does the woman call her boss?
   a to ask for advice about the jacket
   b to persuade her boss to lower the price
   (c) to put the man under pressure to buy the jacket

C LISTEN FOR TECHNIQUES 3.1 Listen again. Which persuasive techniques does the woman use for 1–6? Use the information in the box to help you.

> **Listening to identify persuasive techniques**
>
> People sometimes use tricks to persuade us to do things. When someone is trying to persuade you, listen for these tricks.
>
> **Exaggeration:** listen for words like *absolutely* and *extremely.* E = Exaggeration
>
> **Leading questions:** listen for questions that 'push' you toward a particular answer, including question tags (e.g. *isn't it?*). L = Leading questions
>
> **Personalization:** listen for phrases like *if you imagine* and overuse of *you/your.* P = Personalization

1 biking more frequently P (I bet you can't wait … your bike); L (can you?)
2 how the hat works P (Just imagine you're …; … your hat); L (Amazing, isn't it?)
3 testing the hat E (absolutely love; incredibly useful); P (You wear your hat …); L (Would that be OK?)
4 the problem and the solution L (Did you say …?; E (… this is really embarrassing; That would be amazing …)
5 the smart jacket L (Do you mind waiting …?); P (… an exception, just for you)
6 paying for the jacket L (Would that be better? Will you be paying by …?); E (Thanks so much for …; I really appreciate it)

D SPEAK Work in pairs. Discuss the questions.

1 Is it acceptable to use techniques like these to persuade or manipulate other people? In what situations is it OK? When is it unfair?
2 What techniques do you use when you're trying to persuade someone?

LISTENING

A Put students into pairs to discuss the questions. In feedback, get as many suggestions from the class as you can and write them on the board.

Suggested answers

1 *It may make buildings look more attractive. A more practical use might be to use color-changing paint on the outside of buildings to reduce electricity consumption.*

2 *Most useful in extreme situations where a damaged tire can't be easily changed/repaired.*

3 *They may generate heat to keep your feet warm, or light to help you see and be seen in the dark.*

4 *This will dramatically improve the fuel efficiency of planes, with benefits in terms of cost and sustainability.*

3.1 **B–D** Students check answers or discuss questions in pairs before whole-class feedback.

AUDIO SCRIPT

3.1

Listening, Exercise B
S = Saleswoman M = Man W = Woman

S: Excuse me, sir. Do you ride a bike, by any chance?
M: Well, I have a bike yes. Why do you ask?
S: You just look like a very healthy and athletic person.
M: Really? Thank you. Well, I haven't ridden my bike for months. It's too wet right now.
Ex C Q1 **S:** Yeah, tell me about it! I bet you can't wait for the weather to warm up so you can get out on your bike, can you?
M: Uh, no. I guess not. It's not much fun bike riding in the rain!
S: Hmm, I know exactly what you mean. It sounds like you need some smart biking clothes.
M: Uh, sorry? I don't …
S: Smart biking clothes are made from smart materials, which change their form depending on their environment. Let me show you an example. This biking hat is made from an advanced material that responds to your body temperature. It's somewhat complicated technology, but I'll try to simplify it
Ex C Q2 for you. Just imagine you're out on your bike early
Ex B Q2 one morning. When you leave home, the fibers in your hat respond to the cold temperature by tightening up. That ensures there's no heat loss from
Ex B Q2 your head and keeps you nice and warm. But as you warm up, the gaps between the fibers in your hat automatically enlarge to allow air to flow freely around your head, to cool you down. But then let's imagine it starts to rain. As the hat gets wet, the water strengthens the fibers and the gaps close to
Ex C Q2 keep your head dry. Amazing, isn't it?
M: Yes. It sounds very inventive.
S: It is inventive! This technology is straight out of the laboratory. You won't find these in any stores for years!
M: Really?
S: No. We're still at the testing stage. Hey, would you be
Ex C Q3 willing to test it for us? We'd absolutely love to hear how you do with it. It would be incredibly useful for us.
M: Uh, possibly. What would it involve?
Ex C Q3 **S:** You wear your hat for a few weeks while you're biking, and then you fill in a five-minute questionnaire about your experiences. And of course
Ex C Q3 you get to keep your hat at the end! Would that be OK?
M: Really? Yeah, why not?
S: Great! Thanks. Here's your hat. Congratulations! I just need you to sign this form to formalize our agreement.
M: OK, no problem.
S: Thanks. We're planning to sell the hats for $50 in the future, so I think you got yourself an excellent deal there, sir. I can see you're a very smart negotiator!
M: Am I? Yes, I suppose so. Thanks a lot.
Ex C Q4 **S:** No problem. Actually, maybe there is a problem. Did you say you never go biking in the rain?
M: Yes. Why?
Ex B Q3 **S:** Ah … well we really need people to describe their experiences of wearing the hat in different weather conditions over the next couple of weeks, including
Ex C Q4 rain. I'm so sorry – this is really embarrassing. Should I take the hat back?
M: Uh, no. I don't mind biking in the rain once or twice. I'll just have to get a little wet, I suppose!
Ex C Q4 **S:** Really? Oh that would be amazing if you could. And
Ex B Q1 you know what? Maybe I can help you out there. You see, we also have some smart biking jackets. They're made of tiny fibers that flatten when they're wet, making the coat completely waterproof, and they open up again when dry, enabling your skin to
Ex B Q4 breathe. Again, they're not available for sale for a
Ex C Q5 while, but maybe I can make exception for you. Do you mind waiting a second while I call my boss?
M: No, not at all. Go ahead.
S: Great! Oh hi, Debbie. Listen, I have a gentleman here who's interested in buying the biking coat. I know we're not allowed to sell them yet, but … No way, huh? Are you sure? He's going to help us test our hat. Really? Oh, that's great. Thanks, Debbie! I owe you one. Good news! She says she's willing to make an exception, just for you.
M: Oh, great. Thanks. Uh, how much is it?
Ex B Q1 **S:** Well, we're planning to sell them for $500. But … hmm … maybe … I can offer you … a special price …
Ex C Q6 to thank you for your help. I'll give you 10% off … would that be better?
M: Yes, I guess so.
Ex C Q6 **S:** Excellent. So that's $450, please. Will you be paying by cash or credit card?
M: Uh, credit card, I suppose.
S: Yes. Of course. Just put in your PIN here.
Ex C Q6 **S:** OK, perfect. Thanks. And here's your coat. Thanks so much for helping us out with the testing. I really appreciate it.
M: You're welcome. And thank you. You've been very kind. Goodbye.
S: Goodbye.

3.1 Progressive design

PRONUNCIATION

3.2 **A** Draw students' attention to the information in the *Sounding persuasive* box. Make sure they understand the different techniques, then play the recording. If students seem unsure, stop the recording after the first extract and do the first one as a class.

B Put students into pairs to practice saying the sentences as persuasively as possible. Demonstrate the first one yourself as an example, and practice pronunciation with the class. Exaggerate so that students make an effort to sound persuasive.

Extra activity

Ask students to find two examples of conversations that use persuasive techniques. These could come from ads available online, but also podcasts, movies or even comedy sketches. Ask students to answer the following questions while they watch or listen to the clips.

- Is the persuasion effective? Why/Why not?
- What persuasive techniques are used?

If you have internet access in class, students can compare and discuss their examples in the next class. As the class watches or listens to each conversation, they can also use the two questions above.

VOCABULARY

A Point out that all the sentences come from the conversation students heard earlier. Tell them to complete the spaces with the correct form of the verb in the box. Elicit the first one as a class example. In feedback, point out an adjective that one of the verbs is formed from and make sure the students understand the connection in meaning between the two words.

B Students do the task individually, then check answers in pairs.

C Do the first group as a class example to ensure students realize that the same prefix or suffix is needed for the three adjectives in each group. Point out that spelling changes to the root word are also needed in some cases. Put students into pairs to convert the other groups of adjectives into verbs.

D Tell students to read the advice and to fill in the blanks with the correct form of a verb from Exercise C. Fast finishers could work in pairs or small groups to decide on the three most useful tips. In feedback, check understanding where necessary if students have struggled to choose the correct verb, and ask students which tips they thought were the most useful. Use the **Vocabulary Worksheet** on page W13 for extra practice.

SPEAKING HUB

A Put students into pairs and tell them they are going to try to persuade somebody to buy something made from smart materials. Remind them of the ideas they saw in Listening Exercise A and explain that they could choose one of those or think of their own idea.

B Put students into pairs to tell each other about their idea. Give your own example first, explaining how the product works and why it's useful.

C Explain that students are going to try to sell their product. Remind them of the persuasive techniques they saw earlier, and give them time to prepare their sales strategy. Monitor to help with ideas or language where needed.

D Put students into new pairs to try to persuade their new partner to buy their product. If time allows, they can change partners again to repeat the task.

E Ask students whether or not they would buy their partners' products and why. Finish with feedback on students' use of language in this activity.

Extra activity

Elicit an example of a change that students would like to make to their class or school (e.g. having all classes earlier in the morning or later in the evenings). Put students into small groups to think of their own proposed change and to prepare how they will persuade the others of its benefits. Ask each group to present their proposal, and encourage the other students to listen carefully and to ask questions at the end. When all groups have made their presentations, take a class vote to decide which proposal should be implemented.

TEACHING IDEA by David Seymour and Maria Popova

Mission

Use this activity before or after the listening to extend the themes of smart materials and technology.

Imagine you are James Bond and you are on a mission to save the planet from a master criminal who plans to dominate the whole world. You have a briefcase containing a recording of your instructions about the mission, including the location, name and description of the criminal. It also contains instructions on how to use the high-tech and extremely dangerous gadgets in the briefcase.

In groups, write the recorded message for James Bond. Choose five of your possessions to include as 'gadgets', e.g. a pen that fires poisonous darts when you twist the nib counter-clockwise. Swap instructions and gadgets with another group. You have one minute to memorize the instructions and learn how to use the gadgets.

Explain your mission and your gadgets to the class. The group who wrote the instructions will listen for any mistakes.

In your groups, tell each other about a movie you have seen in which there were some interesting gadgets.

TEACHING IDEA by David Seymour and Maria Popova

Hard sell

Use this activity before or after the listening to extend the theme of persuasive techniques.

In pairs, think of arguments to persuade people to buy these objects, e.g. empty soda can – you could use this as a vase.

a snowball, a dirty comb, one sock, a used teabag, a broken plate, cold burger and fries, a clock with no hands, a house with no roof, a bucket with a hole, a piece of string

(Invite volunteers to try to persuade the class of the value of each object.)

TEACHING IDEA by David Seymour and Maria Popova

Time-saving devices

Use this activity before or after the listening to extend the themes of smart materials and technology.

In small groups, brainstorm ten time-saving devices we use for doing ordinary jobs. Put them in order from the most to the least useful. Compare lists with another group.

PRONUNCIATION
Sounding persuasive

3.2 **A** Listen to the extracts which include the sentences below. How is the woman trying to sound persuasive? Use the information in the box to help you.

1 You just look like a very healthy and athletic person. a (flattery)
2 Yeah, tell me about it! c (empathy)
3 Hmm, I know exactly what you mean. c (empathy)
4 I think you got yourself an excellent deal there, sir. I can see you're a very smart negotiator! a (flattery)
5 You know what? Maybe I can help you out there. a (exceptionalism)
6 But … hmm … maybe … I can offer you … a special price … to thank you for your help. a (exceptionalism)

Sounding persuasive

a Speak fairly quietly (as if you're sharing a secret) and slowly, with a lot of pauses (as if you're thinking of new ideas while speaking).
b Start fast and then slow right down, placing extra stress on all positive words.
c Use slightly exaggerated rising and falling intonation on key words to express emotions.

B SPEAK Work in pairs. Practice saying the sentences in Exercise A as persuasively as possible.

VOCABULARY
Forming verbs from adjectives

A Complete the extracts with the correct form of the verbs in the box.

ensure formalize simplify strengthen tighten warm

1 I bet you can't wait for the weather __to warm__ up!
2 It's fairly complicated technology, but I'll try __to simplify__ it for you.
3 The fibers in your hat respond to the cold temperature by __tightening__ up.
4 That __ensures__ there's no heat loss from your head.
5 As the hat gets wet, the water __strengthens__ the fibers.
6 I just need you to sign this form __to formalize__ our agreement.

B What adjective is each verb from Exercise A formed from?
warm, simple, tight, sure, strong, formal

C Use the affixes in the box to create verbs. The same affix is used for all words in each group. Other spelling changes may also be needed. One group doesn't require any change.

-en -ify en- -ize

1 strong long short
strengthen lengthen shorten
2 final visual equal
finalize visualize equalize
3 empty smooth narrow
empty smooth narrow
4 pure solid simple
purify solidify simplify
5 danger able large
endanger enable enlarge

D Complete the advice with the verbs you formed in Exercise C. Sometimes more than one answer is possible.

How to be persuasive

1 Don't just offer weak opinions. __Strengthen__ your arguments with evidence and examples.
2 Help your potential customers to __visualize__ themselves using your product.
3 Don't try to persuade everybody at the same time: __narrow__ your focus to a small group of key people.
4 __Simplify__ complicated explanations to make them easier to understand.
5 __Smooth / Simplify__ the decision-making process for your customers by removing any barriers that make their decisions harder.
6 Don't speak too quickly. Try to __lengthen__ the pauses between key words.

SPEAKING HUB

A PREPARE Work in pairs. You are going to try to persuade somebody to buy a product made from smart materials. Choose one of the ideas from Listening Exercise A or use your own idea.

B DISCUSS Discuss how your product works and why it's useful.

C PLAN Plan a sales strategy using the persuasion techniques from Listening Exercise C.

D PRESENT Swap partners. Take turns to try to persuade your new partner to buy your product.

E REFLECT Share your experiences with the class. Would you buy your partner's product? Why/Why not?

- Make predictions about the future
- Use persuasive language to sell something

3.2 Better ... or worse?

- Discuss progress and society
- Evaluate costs and benefits

P – stress-shift words
V – verb–noun collocations
G – negative inversion
S – reading to determine costs and benefits

LISTENING

A SPEAK Work in groups. Do you think life is generally getting better or worse for your generation?

3.3 **B LISTEN FOR MAIN IDEA** Listen to the first part of a radio show. Match the people (1–5) with the opinions (a–e).

1 Bob d
2 Mary b
3 James e
4 Callum a
5 Sonia c

a I'm more aware of bad things happening than I was.
b The earlier generation didn't have the same financial worries as we do.
c Everything was better when I was younger.
d Young people were more polite in the past.
e I feel bad when I compare myself with others.

C SPEAK Work in pairs and discuss the questions.

1 Do you agree with the interviewees' opinions?
2 What are some possible explanations for their opinions?

3.4 **D LISTEN FOR GIST** Listen to the second part of the radio show. Match the opinions (a–e) in Exercise B with the concepts (1–5).

1 the inequality paradox e
2 the reminiscence bump c
3 the them-and-us delusion d
4 the invisible struggle phenomenon b
5 the window-on-the-world effect a

3.4 **E LISTEN FOR DETAIL** Listen to the second part again. Are these sentences true (T) or false (F)? Correct the false sentences.

1 Professor Martinelli believes that life is getting better ~~everywhere.~~ for the average person T / (F)
2 Declinism ~~proves that things really~~ is a feeling that things are getting worse. T / (F)
3 When average levels of well-being improve, it can lead to a rise in declinism. (T) / F
4 People usually have nostalgia for their youth. (T) / F
5 We tend to focus on ~~good~~ bad behavior in groups that we don't belong to. T / (F)
6 Professor Martinelli's parents never worried about financial problems. She didn't notice them worry. T / (F)
7 Professor Martinelli is optimistic that people will try to prevent global tragedies. (T) / F

F SPEAK Work in pairs. Discuss the questions.

1 What are your experiences of the five concepts from the radio show?
2 Are you generally optimistic or pessimistic about the near future?

LEAD-IN

Books closed. Elicit examples of how the world is better or worse than 30 years ago.

AUDIO SCRIPT

3.3

Listening, Exercise B

P: Hello, and welcome to *The Progress Show*. According to a recent survey, despite amazing progress in technology and sharp increases in living standards, many of us believe our quality of life has actually decreased! So this week, I interviewed some people in the street about their lives. I asked them, would you say the world is generally getting better or worse? Let's hear a few extracts from those interviews. So Bob, would you say the world is getting better or worse?

B: Worse, definitely. When I was a teenager, we always showed respect for older people. For example, no sooner had an older person gotten on the bus than we all stood up to offer the person a seat. I was on a bus the other day, and it was full of teenagers, but not one person offered me a seat. Only after they'd all gotten off the bus could I finally sit down.

P: So Mary, what's your view?

M: I'd say it's getting worse for people of my age. People of my parents' age had it much easier. There was plenty of work for everybody, and apartments and houses were much cheaper. But everyone of my age seems to be struggling for money. No way could I ever afford an apartment. It's not fair!

P: James, what do you think?

J: I feel like I'm going backwards sometimes. I mean, when I was younger, life was simple. None of our neighbors had much money, and neither did we. But we didn't need much, so we were content just to get on with life. But these days, if you don't post endless selfies of your perfect lifestyle on social media, you feel like a reject from society. It's very frustrating and stressful.

P: Callum, what's your take on this?

C: On balance, it's probably getting worse. You see such terrible things on TV all the time – crime, wars, diseases! I don't remember anything like that from my childhood. Mind you, I didn't watch much TV when I was a kid and I certainly didn't read any newspapers.

P: Sonia, how about you?

S: Worse, much worse. I remember when I was in my early 20s, life was wonderful. Not only did I have great friends, but we also did cool things all the time ... and the sun always seemed to be shining. Nowadays, life's just work, work, work ... and the weather's always terrible, too!

3.4

Listening, Exercise D

Pre: Let's turn now to my guest, Professor Nila Martinelli, an expert in psychology. Professor, is the world really getting worse?

Pro: No, not at all. However you choose to measure people's
Ex E Q1 well-being, life for the average person is getting better. But the key word there is 'average'. By no means am I suggesting that life is wonderful for everyone everywhere. But the vast majority of the world's population really is better off, year after year.

Pre: OK, so why do so many people say the opposite?

Pro: Well, it's all due to a psychological process called declinism,
Ex E Q2 which is a feeling that things are declining, or getting worse. Declinism has a number of separate causes, including something called the inequality paradox. Let me give you an example. Say you live in a community where everybody has terrible healthcare and education, and so on, but overall
Ex E Q3 people just accept that life is hard. But now imagine that 20% of the people suddenly become a lot better off, with comfortable lifestyles and so on. Those 20% push the average up, so according to statistics, the population seems better off.
Ex E Q3 But in fact the remaining 80% feel much worse than before, because they're now aware of what they're missing.

Pre: Ah. That makes sense.

Pro: Another reason is the so-called reminiscence bump. Scientists have conducted plenty of research on this subject which shows that we build up our strongest
Ex E Q4 memories in our late teens and early 20s. Our memories of early adulthood stay with us forever. This is why so many people are nostalgic for that time in their life.

Pre: Oh ... so it's almost as if we rewrite the events in our memories in order to perfect the picture of our younger days!

Pro: Exactly! One of my favorite phenomena is something I call the them-and-us delusion. If you were a well-behaved child, you're likely to remember that most other kids of your age were similarly well-behaved. But that's probably because you didn't notice their bad behavior at the time. Or you've simply erased their negative attributes and bad conduct
Ex E Q5 from your memory. But when you look at a group of people from the outside, what do you notice most? The noisiest, worst-behaved ones. That explains why so many people think that kids today are worse than their own generations.

Pre: Yeah, I suppose you're right. I don't remember much about my childhood!

Pro: No – and that's normal. Children simply fail to notice things
Ex E Q6 that are obvious to adults. When I was a child, never in a million years did it occur to me that my parents were worried about money or job insecurity or whatever. But that doesn't mean they never talked about those things. This is something that we might call the invisible struggle phenomenon: we don't see the problems that other people face, so we think we're the only ones with such problems. We tend to attribute other people's success to luck and we overlook all the problems they've struggled with. And of course that's a major source of inter-generational conflict: young adults always suspect that earlier generations had it much easier!

Pre: Ah. I see what you mean.

Pro: There's one last aspect of declinism, and it's called the window-on-the-world effect. It arises when people become aware of the terrible things that happen around the world. Centuries ago, people were blissfully unaware of wars and diseases in distant countries. But nowadays, we see such things on a daily basis on the news, on social media and so on. So it's not that terrible events are necessarily becoming more frequent, but rather that we're aware of those events.
Ex E Q7 And for me, the fact that more and more people care about global tragedies makes it more likely that we'll do something about them. And that's my main reason for optimism that the world really is getting better, and will continue to do so.

Pre: Hmm ... Professor Nila Martinelli, thanks very much for joining us.

LISTENING

3.3; 3.4 **A–F** Put students into pairs to complete the exercises.

PRONUNCIATION

3.5; 3.6 **A–C** Put students into pairs to complete the exercises.

GRAMMAR

A–D Direct students to the **Grammar Hub** (see below). Use the **Grammar Worksheet** on page W14 for extra practice.

SPEAKING

A Put students into A/B pairs and direct Students B to the **Communication Hub** (see TB121) and Students A to the information at the bottom of page 31.

GRAMMAR HUB

3.2 Negative inversion

- We use negative inversion when we want to emphasize a negative element of a sentence. We place the negative element at the beginning and we invert (= swap over) the subject and auxiliary verb.

  I have never seen such waste in my life. = ***Never have I seen** such waste in my life.*

  I'm not saying we need to leave now. = ***By no means am I saying** we need to leave now.*

  ***No way could I ever drive** a gas-powered car again.*
- We add *do*, *does* or *did* in inverted clauses when there is no auxiliary verb.

  She never received an apology. = *Never **did** she receive an apology.*
- We use *than* after the phrase *no sooner*.

  *No sooner had she written the document **than** her computer crashed.*
- Inversion is often used with the structure *not only … but also*.

  Not only did I meet the mayor, but I also met the governor.
- Some words and phrases change in inversions, and negative verbs become positive.

  ***Nobody** told me about that once.* → *Not once did **anybody** tell me about that.*

  *You **must not** say that under **any** circumstances.* → *Under **no** circumstances **must** you say that.*

  ***That's not** the only solution by **any** means.* → *By **no** means **is that** the only solution.*
- There are also some inversions which do not contain negative words and phrases. These include sentences which start with *only* for time expressions, such as *Only after*, *Only when*, *Only once*, *Only if*, *Only by*, *Only rarely*, and *Rarely*, *Hardly* and *Barely*.

  Only by reading the instructions three times did I understand what to do.

Be careful!

- With some inversions, such as *No sooner … than*, *Not only*, *Hardly*, etc, it's the first verb and the subject which inverts.

  *Not only **was he late**, he was also unprepared.*

  *Hardly **had we sat down** when the fire alarm went off.*
- With other inversions, such as *Only after*, *Not until*, etc, it's the verb in the main clause which inverts.

  *Only after I'd arrived **did I realize** I'd gotten the day wrong.*

  *Not until he'd spent hours online **did he find** a suitable photo.*

- We don't use inversion when the negative word or phrase is the subject.

  None of my colleagues take public transportation.

  NOT ~~None of my colleagues do take public transportation.~~
- The verb and subject invert after *neither* and *nor*.

  *None of their staff knew the answer, and **neither did we**.*

  *I haven't told anyone, and **nor has Jake**.*

3.2 Negative inversion

A Rewrite the sentences (1–6) using inversion and the words given.

1 Nobody asked me if I passed my driving test.
Not once did anybody/anyone ask me if I passed my driving test.

2 I'd just arrived home when they called me back to the office.
No sooner had I arrived home than they called me back to the office.

3 We seldom see players with such natural ability.
Rarely do we see players with such natural ability.

4 He is really smart and incredibly funny.
Not only is he really smart (but) he's also incredibly funny.

5 Tina realized her purse had been stolen when she went to pay her bill.
Only when Tina went to pay her bill did she realize her purse had been stolen.

6 You must not open that door.
Under no circumstances must/should you open that door.

B Write one word in each blank.

Anna was in charge of organizing her company's annual conference. She had met the manager a week before to make the plans, and no [1] sooner had they sat down to talk than the manager was called away. She waited forty-five minutes, and [2] not until she got up to leave did the manager re-appear. On the day of the conference, [3] by no means did everything go according to plan. Not [4] only was the turnout low, but she [5] also had trouble with the conference venue. [6] Never in a million years would she have thought things could go so wrong.

➤ Go back to page 31.

PRONUNCIATION
Stress-shift words

A 3.5 **Listen to the sentences. Underline the stressed syllables in the words in bold.**

1 Despite amazing **progress** in technology and sharp **increases** in living standards, many of us believe our quality of life has actually **decreased**!
2 Let's hear a few **extracts** from those interviews.
3 You feel like a **reject** from society.
4 It's almost as if we **rewrite** the events in our memories.
5 You've simply erased their negative **attributes** and bad **conduct** from your memory.
6 We tend to **attribute** other people's success to luck.
7 That's a major source of inter-generational **conflict**: young adults always **suspect** that earlier generations had it much easier!

B 3.6 **Underline the stressed syllables in the words in bold. Then listen and check.**

1 Why are you always such a **rebel**? Why do you always **rebel** against everything I say?
2 I didn't think I'd like Thai food, but now I'm a **convert**. Your cooking has **converted** me!
3 You need to install an **upgrade** for your computer. When did you last **upgrade** it?
4 I deal with **imports** and **exports** in my job: I **import** raw materials and **export** finished products to customers.
5 I **frequent** this café during the summer, but I'm not really a **frequent** visitor during the rest of the year.

C **Practice saying the sentences with the correct stress.**

GRAMMAR
Negative inversion

A **Complete the extracts from the radio show with one word.**

1 No sooner _had_ an older person gotten on the bus than we all stood up.
2 Only after they'd all gotten off the bus _could_ **I finally sit down.**
3 **No way could I** _ever_ **afford an apartment.**
4 None of our neighbors had much money, and neither _did_ **we.**
5 Not _only_ **did I have great friends**, but we also did cool things all the time.
6 By no means _am_ **I suggesting** that life is wonderful for everybody everywhere.
7 _Never_ in a million years **did it occur to me** that my parents were worried about money.

B **WORK IT OUT** **Match the sentences (1–7) in Exercise A with the rules (a–d) in the box.**

Negative inversion

When we want to emphasize a negative element of a sentence (e.g. *never*), we can move it to the beginning and swap the subject and auxiliary verb. This process is called inversion.

a When there is no auxiliary verb, we add *do/does/did*. _4, 5, 7_
b Inversion with *could* is common after phrases like *only after* and *no way*. _2, 3_
c Inversion is very common in the structure *not only … but also*. _5_
d After *no sooner*, we need a *than*-clause. _1_

We don't use inversion when a negative word/phrase is the subject: *Not one person offered me a seat.* (NOT: ~~did offer~~)

C Go to the **Grammar Hub** on **page 126**.

D **Complete the sentences so they are true for you.**

1 Under no circumstances would I …
2 Only rarely do I …
3 Not only do I think …

SPEAKING

A **PREPARE** **Work in pairs. Imagine you are on a radio interview about progress. Student A – read the information below. Student B – go to the Communication Hub on page 154.**

B **SPEAK** **Role-play your interview.**

Student A

You're a radio interviewer. You believe that while people complain about the world today, overall it is actually getting better. Interview Student B about progress. Also give your view on the subject.

Discuss the following areas.

- the impact of technology
- community
- quality of life
- cost of living
- employment
- the environment

READING

A PREDICT Work in pairs. Discuss the questions.

1 Look at the pictures and title of the article. What do you think 'voluntourism' might be?

2 What do you think attracts people to these kinds of activities?

3 Why might some voluntary work do more harm than good?

B SKIM Read *Voluntourism: more harm than good?* quickly and check your ideas in Exercise A.

C READ FOR COSTS AND BENEFITS Work in pairs. What are the deep costs and benefits of voluntourism? Use the information in the box to help you.

Reading to determine costs and benefits

When you read a for-and-against, or pro and con, article, it's useful to distinguish between **surface-level** costs/benefits (e.g. obvious, short-term or unimportant ones) and **deep** costs/benefits (e.g. hidden, long-term or highly important ones). When deciding whether you agree with the writer's opinion, focus mainly on the deep costs and benefits.

VOLUNTOURISM

more harm than good?

When Pippa Biddle was a teenager, she went on a school trip to Tanzania, where she and her classmates were tasked with building a library for an orphanage. Ex D Q2 Lacking even basic construction skills, they did their best and, remarkably, over the course of a week, the building started to take shape. Only later did Pippa learn the truth: every night, Ex D Q2 a group of professional builders had been carefully undoing and redoing the teenagers' work in order to make the construction structurally sound. The whole project was an illusion: Ex D Q1 the true purpose wasn't to get help on the building project, but to make the teenagers feel good about themselves.

Ex B Q1 Welcome to the world of voluntourism, where volunteering meets tourism. Unlike true volunteering, this is paid work – but it's the worker who pays for the privilege. On the surface, voluntourism is a win–win situation. Ex B Q2 The voluntourist seizes an opportunity to travel to an exotic country and work with real people in authentic locations, while the recipients get free help. But the reality, as Pippa's story brings home to us, is somewhat more complicated.

Ex C Cost The main criticism of voluntourism is that it perpetuates the myth that people in some countries need help from wise and generous benefactors in richer countries. The reality, of course, is that these countries have plenty of kind-hearted experts of their own. But of course, most voluntourists aren't even experts: they're typically students looking for a quick adventure, with no valuable skills to offer. At best, their input is frequently a waste of time. Ex C Cost At worst, it could do more harm than good, as with Pippa's building experience.

Ex C Cost Even worse are stories of fake projects created merely to keep the volunteers busy, regardless of any inherent local need. For example, there are English-language schools in remote communities where the locals neither want nor need to study English.

It's hard to avoid the conclusion that voluntourism is nothing more than an ego-trip: a chance to pretend you're making the world a better place, so you can wow your friends back home with tales of your generosity, your suffering and your profound experience of 'finding yourself'.

But there's another side to volunteerism. While many people do sign up with naïve expectations, they frequently emerge from their experiences with a far deeper understanding. On their return home, they can spread a more positive and realistic image of the countries they visit, and counter rather than perpetuate stereotypes. Ex C Benefit Finally, many voluntourists go on to become committed life-long volunteers, Ex C Benefit with their new-found habit of helping others, whether globally or in their own communities.

It's also an oversimplification to claim that voluntourism is always harmful to local communities. Highly-skilled volunteers like doctors, scientists and engineers can indeed bring real benefits. Ex C Benefit The key is to do so in a spirit of cooperation and mutual respect with local experts, rather than following the 'watch me and learn' approach. Many voluntourism agencies can have a genuinely positive impact both on the volunteers and the communities they serve. Ex C Benefit

So if you're considering signing up as a voluntourist, seize the initiative and do some research beforehand. Be honest and realistic about your skills and expectations. Above all, never forget that the main beneficiary of your voluntourism adventure will probably be you. With the right mindset, this could well be the most important experience of your life. Ex D Q3

READING

A Draw students' attention to the pictures and elicit what they think is happening. Put them into pairs to discuss the questions. Get some feedback, but don't confirm or reject any of their suggestions at this stage.

Suggested answers

1 *A combination of volunteering (e.g. to help a charity) and tourism (e.g. traveling to interesting places).*

2 *It gives them a chance to travel to interesting places and help other people at the same time.*

B Tell students to read the article about voluntourism quickly to check their ideas. Get brief feedback and don't go into too much depth at this stage.

C Point out the information in the box about *Reading to determine costs and benefits*, and check students understand the difference between surface-level and deep costs and benefits. Then tell students to read again and to decide, in pairs, what the article claims the deep costs and benefits of voluntourism are. In feedback, ask students to justify their answers.

Deep costs:
perpetuates the myth that people in poor countries need help; does more harm than good; fake projects

Deep benefits:
spread a more positive and realistic image; many voluntourists go on to become committed life-long volunteers; highly-skilled volunteers … can indeed bring real benefits; a genuinely positive impact both on the volunteers and the communities they serve

METHODOLOGY HUB by Jim Scrivener

The importance of skills work

Don't underestimate the importance of skills work. Not every lesson needs to teach new words or new grammar. Lessons also need to be planned to give students opportunities to practice and improve their language skills. Skills work is not something to add in at the end of a five-year course in English. There is no need to wait for extensive knowledge before daring to embark on listening and speaking work. On the contrary, it is something so essential that it needs to be at the heart of a course from the start. Even a beginner with one day's English will be able to practice speaking and listening usefully.

METHODOLOGY HUB by Christine Nuttall

Equipping students for the future

Conscious development of reading skills is important because we are trying to equip students for the future. It is impossible to familiarize them with every text they will ever want to read; but what we can do is give them techniques for approaching texts of various kinds, to be used for various purposes. That is the essence of teaching reading.

Teaching students just how to read Text A is not teaching them how to read. However, the generalized skills of reading can only be acquired through practicing the specific skills required for reading Text A, Text B and so on. One of our responsibilities is to make sure that the bridge is built between the specific and the general. And one way of helping students to generalize their skills is to make sure that they read a lot and have a lot of practice in using the skills with varied materials.

METHODOLOGY HUB by Jim Scrivener

Reading for detail

A lot of in-class reading work has traditionally been 'reading for detail' – or 'intensive reading', i.e. reading texts closely and carefully with the intention of gaining an understanding of as much detail as possible. This is usually so that the student can answer comprehension questions (e.g. *Why did the three men go into the office?*). This is typically a stop/start kind of reading, involving going back over small pieces of the same text a number of times to find out more and more about it, making sure that the words have been correctly interpreted. This is how a competent language user might read an instruction manual for a piece of ready-to-assemble furniture or a brochure with guidelines on whether they have to pay income tax or not. It's not the way she would typically read a chapter from a novel or a magazine article, although, in classrooms, it is usually how students are asked to process such material (with true/false and other comprehension questions to check if they can pick up specific points).

In everyday life, we tend to do much more extensive reading, i.e. fluent, faster reading, usually of longer texts, for pleasure, entertainment and general understanding, but without such careful attention to the details. When we don't understand words or small sections, we usually just keep going, maybe only coming back when there has been a major breakdown in our understanding.

There is certainly a place for intensive reading in class, helping students to uncover and accurately understand details in a text – but this is by no means the only strategy that a good reader needs. Being able to read fast and fluently is also very important.

D Students read the article once again, if necessary, and then discuss the questions in pairs. When giving feedback, encourage students to expand on their answers and to suggest alternatives if they disagree with each other.

E Put students into groups to discuss the questions. Elicit some answers, and ask if anyone in the class has ever done anything like this before and, if so, what they thought of their experience and of the article. Ask students to justify why they would or wouldn't like to try something like this.

VOCABULARY

A Point out the information about *Verb–noun collocations* in the box, and stress that most of these are formed with very common verbs. Explain the task, and make it clear that although the exact sentences don't appear in the text, the collocations do.

B Direct students to the **Vocabulary Hub** (see TB121).

C Put students into pairs to discuss if they agree with the sentences in Exercise A. In feedback, ask students to explain their opinions, and encourage them to agree or disagree with each other. Use the **Vocabulary Worksheet** on page W15 for extra practice.

SPEAKING HUB

A Explain that students are going to introduce a voluntourism project in their community. Give an example of your own of a project you could introduce, and explain what the voluntourists' role would be. Put students into pairs to think of their own idea.

B Students make a list of the surface-level and deep costs. To check students remember what these are, elicit some ideas for the example project you gave in Exercise A. Monitor to help or prompt where necessary.

C First, elicit example answers about your project again. Then ask the pairs to discuss the questions.

D Ask each pair to present their ideas to the class. Tell the others to listen carefully, and encourage them to ask questions at the end of each presentation. At the end, take a vote to see which idea the class think would be most beneficial to the world. Finish with feedback on students' use of language in the activity.

Extra activity

To extend the activity, either find some examples yourself of real voluntourism projects, or ask students to find some. Students can then work in groups to discuss which projects they think are most beneficial to the world and which, if any, they would like to participate in and why.

METHODOLOGY HUB by Scott Thornbury

Collocation

If two words collocate, they frequently occur together. The relation between the words may be grammatical or lexical. One example of a grammatical relationship is when certain verbs collocate with particular prepositions, such as *depend on*, *account for* and *abstain from*. Another is when a verb, like *make*, *take* or *do*, collocates with a noun, as in *make an arrangement*, *take advantage*, *do the dishes*. Lexical collocations are when two content words regularly co-occur, as in *a broad hint*, *a narrow escape* (but not *a wide hint* or *a tight escape*). The strength of the collocation can vary: *a broad street* and *a narrow path* are weak collocations, since both of the elements can co-occur with a lot of other words: *a broad river* and *a busy street*, etc. *Broad hint* and *narrow escape* are stronger. Stronger still are combinations where one element rarely occurs without the other, as in *moot point*, *slim pickings* and *scot free*. Strongest of all are those where both elements never or rarely occur without the other, such as *wreak havoc* and *spick and span*. These have acquired the frozen status of fixed expressions.

Unsurprisingly, learners lack the intuition as to which words go with which, and this accounts for many errors, such as *You can completely enjoy it* (instead of *thoroughly*), *On Saturday, we made shopping* (instead of *went*) and *We went the incorrect way* (instead of *wrong*). Using texts to highlight particular collocations and teaching new words in association with their most frequent collocations are two ways of approaching the problem. These days, learners' dictionaries also include useful collocational information.

There are also many online sites that are linked to corpora, and which allow the user to check the collocations of a word, usually showing the strength of the collocation in the form of a mutual information (MI) score.

The term **colligation** describes a word's grammatical collocations, that is, the grammatical structures with which it occurs. For example, the verb *to base* is used in passive voice constructions much more often than in active ones: *The movie is based on the stage play*. Likewise, the verb *to budge* is much more common in negative contexts than in affirmative ones, and with modal verbs rather than on its own: *the door wouldn't budge; I can't budge it.*

METHODOLOGY HUB by Christine Nuttall

Active, receptive and throwaway vocabulary

Not all words are equally important. A primary attack skill is identifying the words that can be ignored, so that the other words that really stand in the way of comprehension can be tackled by some of the strategies described below. If you examine your own L1 vocabulary, you will find two categories of known words: an ***active*** vocabulary of words you know well enough to use yourself, and a ***receptive*** vocabulary of words you recognize and can respond to, but cannot confidently use. This is equally true of a foreign language. It is important for students to become aware of this, perhaps through considering their own L1 vocabulary, and to recognize that receptive vocabulary becomes available for active use naturally, if it is important, by being frequently encountered in context. This may make their attitude to new words more relaxed. But there is also a third category of words that students will meet once they move on to unsimplified material; these I label ***throwaway*** vocabulary. Not all the words we meet are worth learning, even to the receptive level. Students with a vocabulary of, say, 3,000 words cannot afford to clutter up their minds trying to learn words like *boost* or *epicene*. Instead, they must learn to ignore what is not important for their immediate purpose.

Of course no word is throwaway of itself; it all depends on the context, the student's level and reasons for reading. Perhaps an electrical engineer would find *boost* an essential item; perhaps for a specific text, *epicene* would have to be understood, but that does not make it worth learning for recall.

D READ FOR DETAIL Work in pairs. Read the article again and discuss the questions.

1 Why did the builders work at night? to create the illusion that the teenagers were doing all the work
2 How did Pippa's building experience 'do more harm than good'? inferred: her work had been pointless; it was potentially dangerous since they had no experience
3 What does the writer mean by 'the right mindset' in the last paragraph? your attitude or outlook will affect how you benefit from the experience

E SPEAK Work in groups. Do you think voluntourism does more harm than good? Would you consider doing it yourself?

VOCABULARY

Verb–noun collocations

A Choose a verb to complete each pair of verb–noun collocations. Then decide on the best collocation to complete each sentence. Use the information in the box to help you.

> **Verb–noun collocations**
>
> Verb–noun collocations are a good way to build vocabulary. Sometimes these include advanced verbs (e.g. *perpetuate*), but mostly they include very common verbs (e.g. *make, do, take*). Try to underline these as you read in English.

1 Unless you have valuable work experience you'll usually ____do____ ~~*your best*~~ / *more harm than good*.
2 Volunteer organizations should always ____take____ the *time* / ~~*shape*~~ to train volunteers before a project.
3 A trained English teacher can ____bring____ *benefits* / ~~*home*~~ to a host community.
4 It's vital that voluntourists ____take____ ~~*the responsibility*~~ / *the opportunity* to understand their host community before and during their visit.
5 Volunteer organizations should not ____perpetuate____ the *myth* / ~~*problem*~~ that their projects are just extended vacations.

B Go to the **Vocabulary Hub** on **page 143**.

C SPEAK Work in pairs. Do you agree with sentences 1–5 in Exercise A? Why/Why not?

SPEAKING HUB

A PREPARE Work in pairs. Imagine you are going to volunteer in another country. Choose one of the following voluntary projects or use your own idea.

- working at an animal sanctuary
- planting trees
- teaching children
- cleaning up trash

B PLAN Create a list of surface-level and deep costs and benefits for:

- you and your partner
- who you are helping
- the world in general.

C DISCUSS Discuss whether the benefits outweigh the costs. How could the costs be reduced? How could the benefits be increased?

D PRESENT Present your plans to the class. Whose ideas would have the best chance of making the world a better place?

Glossary

beneficiary (n) someone who gets an advantage from a situation
illusion (n) a false or wrong belief or idea
mindset (n) a way of thinking about things
orphan (n) a child whose parents have died
perpetuate (v) to make something such as a situation or process continue, especially one that is wrong, unfair or dangerous
profound (adj) used about very strong feelings
recipient (n) someone who receives something

- Discuss progress and society
- Evaluate costs and benefits

3.3 Sustainability

Ⓐ– the 'rule of three' Ⓢ– maintaining a conversation

Seaweed farming

A Work in small groups. What is being shown in each picture (a–e)? suggested answers

B Watch the video. Check your ideas to Exercise A and number pictures a–e in the order they appear.

a 3 There is a man standing up rowing a boat full of seaweed.

b 1 A man in a black T-shirt and shorts snorkeling is picking seaweed from the seabed.

c 4 There is seaweed laid on the ground to dry. The sea, fishing boats and island are in the background.

d 2 A man in the water is holding up the seaweed to show viewers.

e 5 There is a group of young children and white sacks of seaweed. In the background there are lots of boats on the water.

C Watch the video again. Answer the questions.

1. What have scientists discovered about seaweed? how to convert seaweed into ethanol
2. What can seaweed help us do? resolve some of our most pressing global issues
3. What are the three countries mentioned in the video? Hong Kong, China and Denmark
4. Is the presenter's tone generally positive, negative or neutral? positive

Glossary

allotment (n) a small piece of land in town you can rent and use for growing vegetables
harvest (v) to pick and collect crops or plants
seaweed (n) a green or brown plant that grows in the sea

AUTHENTIC ENGLISH

A Work in pairs. Read the sentence from the video and the information in the box. What three things doesn't seaweed need? land, fertilizers, fresh water

This doesn't need lots of land space to grow it, it doesn't need awful artificial fertilizers, it doesn't need lots of fresh water.

The 'rule of three'

The 'rule of three' is a rhetorical device we use to express concepts more completely, emphasize our points and increase the memorability of our message. In the 'rule of three', we frequently repeat the same grammatical construction.

B Work in pairs. Complete the sentences using your own ideas and the 'rule of three'.

1. To succeed in life, you need to work hard, you need *to have passion* and you need *to have a role model*.
2. I'm ready to start the day. My face is washed, my teeth are brushed and my hair is combed.
3. Maria was the ideal employee – she was always on time, she always worked hard and she always helped her workmates.
4. The current government has ruined the economy, it has ruined the education system and it has ruined the health system.
5. I told the sales clerk I wanted to exchange the item, to obtain a refund or to speak to the manager.
6. I know what you said. You know what you said. The whole class knows what you said.

C Compare your sentences with another pair.

D Work in small groups. Write sentences with the 'rule of three' to say what you need to do to learn a language successfully.

Fueling the future

SAM MALCOLM AMANDA HARRY EMILY

A Work in pairs. Discuss the questions.

1 Do you prefer to use public transportation or travel by car? Why?

2 What do you think about policies that ban or limit cars in city centers?

B Watch the video. Are these statements true (T) or false (F)? Correct the false sentences.

1 Malcolm has recently achieved a long-held ambition. (T) / F

2 Amanda understands the appeal of owning a sports car. Amanda doesn't understand the appeal of owning a sports car. T / (F)

3 Malcolm believes speed is the main positive of car ownership. Malcolm believes freedom and the open road are the main positives. T / (F)

4 Amanda says that ~~all new vehicles~~ will be banned from the UK by 2040. the sale of new gas vehicles T / (F)

5 Amanda thinks that other feasible options besides gas vehicles currently exist. (T) / F

6 Harry thinks alternative fuels will be the norm in the distant future. (T) / F

7 Malcolm is going to let Amanda test drive his car. He says 'not a chance'. T / (F)

SPEAKING SKILL

A Watch the video again. Complete the sentences (1–6) from the video.

1 ___What do you think about___ coming out for a look at my new wheels? inviting to speak/opinion

2 I mean we don't really need them in the city. ___Am I right___? asking for agreement

3 ___What's your view___ Harry? You're a cool young guy … you must like sports cars. inviting opinion

4 Just the other day we were discussing alternative fuels, ___weren't we___? request agreement

5 That kind of thing, must be a long way off though, ___mustn't it___? request agreement

6 ___What's up___ Malcolm? inviting to speak/opinion

B Work in pairs. Look at your answers in Exercise A. What are the speakers doing in each sentence? See Ex A for answers

1 Malcolm is asking Amanda to give her opinion.

Maintaining a conversation

Inviting people to give their opinion or speak

Ask a direct question (*Would you like to say something here, Andy?*) or invite someone to speak using a statement (*You haven't said anything yet, Maria.*)

Noticing changes in attitude

Respond to body language and facial expressions by asking questions or making statements. (*I can tell you don't agree with me.*)

Question tags

Add these to a statement to make it a question or to request agreement. (*I think we all pretty much agree on this, don't we?*)

Asking questions to get agreement

Ask people directly to agree with you in order to move conversations along. (*Am I right in thinking that's true?*)

C Work in pairs. Choose one of the topics below and try to maintain a conversation for four minutes without any long pauses.

- the environment
- a documentary you watched recently
- public transportation in your country

SPEAKING HUB

A **PREPARE** Work in a small group. Think about the pros and cons of the sources of energy below.

- wind power
- tidal power
- fossil fuels
- nuclear power
- solar power

B **PLAN** You are going to discuss which of the energies would be the best for achieving a sustainable future with another group. Plan how you are going to achieve agreement within your group and get all the members of the group to give their opinion.

A: What's your opinion?

B: Tidal power is too expensive compared to other renewable sources.

C **DISCUSS** Join with another group to discuss the pros and cons of the sources of energy.

D **REFLECT** As a class decide which arguments were the most convincing and which of the energy sources are necessary for a sustainable future.

Discuss renewable energy

➤ Turn to page 158 to learn how to write a persuasive email about sustainability.

3.3 Sustainability

Seaweed farming

A Draw students' attention to the pictures, and put them into pairs to discuss what they think is happening in each one. Get some feedback, but don't confirm or reject any suggestions yet.

B ▶ Students watch the video to check their ideas, and number the pictures in the order they appear. Point out the glossary before playing the video and check for understanding.

C ▶ Put students into pairs to try to answer the questions from memory. Then play the video again for them to watch and check.

AUTHENTIC ENGLISH

A Point out the example sentence from the video and the information in the box about *The 'rule of three'*. Ask students if they have this rhetorical device or anything similar in their language(s).

B Go through the example with the class, and make sure they notice how the same grammatical structure is repeated each time. Put students into pairs to complete the other sentences.

C Combine pairs to compare answers. In feedback, accept any answers that make sense and sound authentic, as long as they use the same structure three times.

D Give an example of your own, then put students into small groups to think of more. Get feedback and write on the board some of the best sentences, correcting or reformulating language if necessary. Ask students if they agree with the other groups' ideas.

Fueling the future

A Put students into pairs to discuss the question. Elicit some ideas from the class to see how similar or different students' opinions are. Give your own opinion, too.

B ▶ Allow students time to read the sentences before playing the video. Students watch the video and do the task. Let them compare in pairs before feedback. In feedback, elicit corrections for the false sentences. You can find the **video script** for *Fueling the future* on the Teacher's Resource Center.

SPEAKING SKILL

A ▶ Tell students to try to complete the sentences from memory. Then play the video again for them to watch and check.

B Point out the example and the information in the box about *Maintaining a conversation*. Ask students if they use similar strategies when speaking in their own language(s). Put students into pairs to decide what the speaker is doing in each sentence.

C Choose a stronger student and briefly (not for the full four minutes) demonstrate the task, using some of the strategies from Exercise B. Then put students into pairs to try to maintain a conversation for four minutes about one of the topics. Monitor attentively, then give feedback on how well students managed the task. You could ask any particularly successful groups to perform their conversation for the class.

SPEAKING HUB

A Elicit some examples of pros and cons for one of the energy types, then put students into small groups to think of ideas for the rest.

B Explain that students are going to try to reach a whole-class consensus on the best form of renewable energy. Give groups time to think about how they could achieve this. Monitor to help or prompt if needed as they do this.

C Combine groups to discuss the issue and try to reach an agreement. If they manage this quickly, re-group students to see if new groups can come to the same consensus.

> **Extra activity**
> As students have been discussing alternative energy, brainstorm other alternatives (e.g. *alternative medicine*, *music*, *comedy*, *education*, *travel*, etc) and write these on the board. Elicit a few pros and cons for each one, then put students into small groups to discuss what they think of them and why.

▶ VIDEO SCRIPT

Seaweed farming
S = Simon Reeve W = Wayan C = Child
SV = Simon voiceover

S: I'd come to this far corner of the Indian Ocean to learn about an unlikely treasure of the seas. There's seaweed tied onto bits of rope attached to the seabed. It's like an underwater allotment. Captain, what do we need to do? What work needs to be done that I can help with?

W: OK?

S: OK. Let's go, I'll help.

C: OK!

S: Wayan and the other islanders here grow edible seaweed and it's a pretty simple process. Seaweed cuttings are tied onto a line of string. They grow by using sunlight for energy and by absorbing nutrients
Ex C Q4 from the sea as food. This doesn't need lots of land space to grow it, it doesn't need awful artificial fertilizers, it doesn't need lots of fresh water. It just grows in the sea. Seaweed is amazing! Aah!

W: Thank you, Simon.

Ex C Q4 **S:** This seaweed is something of a wonder crop and many experts think we need to be eating a lot more of it because it's so easy to grow and it's a good source of vitamins, minerals and protein.
Ex C Q1 Perhaps most excitingly of all, scientists have now worked out how to convert seaweed into ethanol, which can be used as an alternative to petrol. It has
Ex C Q2 enormous potential. Seaweed could actually help us to resolve some of our most pressing global issues. You're already using seaweed extract in dozens of products ranging from ice cream to cheese even in your toothpaste. The seaweed trade is already worth billions of pounds every year but it's going to get a lot bigger.
Ex C Q3 Wayan's seaweed is sold around the world to China, Hong Kong and as far afield as Denmark. It's a good business to be in.

SV: It's been brilliant since day one. Now we can pay for our children's clothes. We can eat. We're very happy.

Ex C Q4 **S:** Family's happy, missus is happy, children are being educated. Everybody's doing well out of it.

3 Writing

Write a persuasive email

W– persuasive techniques

A SPEAK Read the email. Who is the writer? Who is he writing to? Why? Lakeside resident; other residents; to get their support

To: Lakeside residential estate (group)
From: Daniel Hernandez
Subject: Road resurfacing

Dear all

Ex C 2, Ex C 1, Ex C 1, Ex C 1, Ex C 4 **a** As you know, the internal roads in our neighborhood are in dreadful condition. Not only does this look ugly, but it also damages our cars. Furthermore, one of our loved ones may be injured by tripping on the uneven surface.

Ex C 2 **b** With that in mind, the housing association has set aside funds to resurface the roads. As I'm sure you remember, the roads were last resurfaced five years ago. One option is simply to use the same cheap materials again (and in five years, the surface will have deteriorated again).

Ex C 5 **c** I would like to propose an alternative: self-repairing concrete. Thanks to cutting-edge technology, self-repairing concrete is infused with billions of tiny limestone-producing bacteria, *Bacillus pseudofirmus*. While sealed in concrete, these bacteria remain inert, but when exposed to air they multiply rapidly. No sooner does a crack appear in the concrete than millions of these bacteria will wake up and plug the crack.

Ex C 2, Ex C 6, Ex C 3, Ex C 4, Ex C 2 **d** As you can imagine, although self-repairing concrete is somewhat expensive, it will save us money in the long run (see attached calculations). More importantly, if one serious accident can be prevented over the next five years, I'm sure you'll agree it will have been worth the extra cost.

Ex C 2 **e** I know you are all smart people, so let's make the smart decision. Please support my proposal at our next housing association meeting.

Best regards

Daniel

B Read the email again. Match the questions (1–5) with the paragraphs (a–e). Then discuss the questions in pairs.

1 What is a potential objection and how can it be overcome? d
2 What is the most likely solution and what's wrong with it? b
3 What action does the reader need to take? e
4 What is the problem and why should the reader care? a
5 What's an alternative solution and why is it better? c

C Underline examples of each technique in Daniel's email. Use the information in the box to help you.

Persuasive techniques

1 Use words like *we*, *our* and *let's* to build a connection with the readers.
2 Flatter your readers by claiming they're intelligent and knowledgeable.
3 Provide facts and figures to support your claims, in an attachment if appropriate.
4 Use emotive language and imagery to appeal to your readers' fear of loss, damage or injury.
5 Explain technical issues in simple language, but include some impressive technical terms.
6 Use *although* or *while* to link weaknesses with strengths.

D Work in pairs. Use the techniques in Exercise C to make these email extracts more persuasive.

1 Your biggest problem is that you spend too much money on electricity.
2 Please support me so I can solve this problem for you.
3 The road surface is so bad that delivery drivers may refuse to drive into our neighborhood.
4 I admit this solution will be extremely disruptive during the building work.

WRITING

A PREPARE Work in groups. You are going to write a persuasive email about sustainability, smart materials or voluntourism. Generate a list of ideas. Use the following questions to help you:

1 What problem are you trying to solve?
2 Who do you need to persuade?
3 What do you want your reader to do?

B PLAN Plan a five-paragraph email. You can use the five questions from Exercise B to help you.

C WRITE Write your email, using techniques from this lesson.

D REVIEW Exchange your email with a partner. Do you use similar techniques? Comment on how the email could be made more persuasive and underline any mistakes.

E EDIT Read your partner's comments. Rewrite any parts you think should change.

158 WRITING

Suggested answers

1 *Our biggest problem is that we spend too much money on electricity.*
2 *Let's solve this problem together.*
3 *The road surface is so bad that ambulance drivers may refuse to drive into our neighborhood in an emergency, or the fire department may be unable to drive in to fight a fire.*
4 *Although this solution may be rather disruptive during the building work, I'm sure you'll agree it will be worth it in the end.*

Refer students to this email as a model for the writing task.

Remind students to use persuasive techniques from the box as they write.

WRITING

A Ask students to read the email and answer the questions with a partner.

He is a resident of a neighborhood called 'Lakeside', and possibly a member of the neighborhood's housing association. He's writing to the other residents of the neighborhood to persuade them to vote for his proposal at their next meeting.

B Tell students to read the email again and to match the questions with the paragraphs. Get feedback, then put students back into pairs to discuss the questions.

C Remind students that Daniel wrote the email to persuade his neighbors to vote for his proposal, then point out the information in the box about *Persuasive techniques*. Elicit the first one from the class, then ask students to find examples of the other techniques in the email.

D Do the first one as an example with the class, then put students into pairs to rewrite the sentences using persuasive techniques.

WRITING TASK

A Explain that students are going to write their own persuasive email. Put them into small groups to think of ideas.

B Students plan their email, with each paragraph addressing one of the questions from Exercise B.

C Remind students about the persuasive techniques from earlier, and tell them to write their email in full. This can be set as homework if there isn't enough time to do it in class.

D Students swap emails with a partner. Ask them to read their partner's emails and to give each other feedback on how persuasive they are and on other language issues.

E Tell students to give the emails back and read their partner's comments. Give them time to make any necessary changes. Get some feedback, asking pairs how similar or different their emails were and whose they think was more successful.

Unit 3 Review

VOCABULARY

A Complete the brochure with the words in the box. There are two extra words that you do not need to use.

accumulate biodegradable consume depletion emissions exploitation neutral offset renewable

Want to live a more sustainable life?

Here's how.

1 Stop buying products wrapped in plastic, which ___accumulates___ in the oceans. Choose products that use ___biodegradable___ packaging instead.

2 Cut down on the energy you ___consume___, and use solar power, wind power or other ___renewable___ energy sources if possible.

3 Reduce your ___emissions___ of greenhouse gases by walking or biking instead of driving.

4 Become carbon-___neutral___ by planting trees to ___offset___ the carbon you generate.

B Complete the sentences with the correct form of the word in parentheses.

1 They want to ___enlarge___ (*large*) our college by adding a new building.
2 The dirty water is ___purified___ (*pure*) before being released into the sea.
3 If your dinner's cold, you can ___warm___ (*warm*) it up in the microwave.
4 They're ___strengthening___ (*strong*) the old bridge before it falls down.
5 We didn't bother to ___formalize___ (*formal*) our agreement – we trust each other.
6 Some screws are loose on this table. Can you ___tighten___ (*tight*) them up?
7 We were winning six-five, but the other team ___(has) equalized___ (*equal*) in the last minute.

C Complete the conversation with one verb in each space.

A: I want to [1] ___make___ the world a better place, but I don't know how. Could you [2] ___point___ me in the right direction?
B: The only thing that [3] ___comes___ to mind is voluntourism.
A: Good idea! I'll go for it.
B: Well, please don't [4] ___take___ this personally, but you don't really have any skills to offer. They have strict rules about who they accept.
A: Really? Maybe they'll [5] ___make___ an exception for me.
B: No, I think you need to [6] ___take___ the time to research it carefully so you don't end up [7] ___doing___ more harm than good.
A: OK, thanks for the advice. I'll try to [8] ___take___ it on board.

GRAMMAR

A Find and correct the mistakes in four of the sentences.

1 Fifty years from now, the world will have ~~been changing~~ changed completely.
2 My life's about ~~getting~~ to get a lot more complicated.
3 We'll be seeing a lot more of each other when we're neighbors. Correct
4 Call me again at ten – I might have finished by then. Correct
5 I'm on the verge of resigning from my job. Correct
6 Your eyes will hurt after ~~you'll~~ you have been studying all night.
7 Prices ~~setting~~ are set to fall by 10% over the next year.

B Reorder the words to make sentences. The first word is given in bold.

1 **By** / you / do / I / should / means / believe / no / resign
By no means do I believe you should resign.
2 **Under** / be / opened / may / circumstances / no / this box
Under no circumstances may this box be opened.
3 **Not** / did / thanked / all the work / you / have / me / once / for / I
Not once have you thanked me for all the work I did.
4 **Only** / the waiter / our food / three times / we / bring / complained / had / after / did Only after we had complained three times did the waiter bring our food.
5 **No** / the laundry / started / had / than / put out / sooner / it / I / to rain No sooner had I put out the laundry than it started to rain.
6 **No** / to college / ever / going back / I / way / consider / would
No way would I ever consider going back to college.
7 **Not** / this hard / since / worked / students / we / have / I / were
Not since we were students have I worked this hard.

Future choices at the Istituto Italiano Di Tecnologia, Genoa.

Intelligence (n) the ability to understand and think about things and to gain and use knowledge.
Synonyms: intuition (n), intellect (n)

Socrates means that an intelligent person realizes that it is impossible to know everything.

Socrates (470 BCE–399 BCE) was a classical Greek philosopher and teacher to Plato. Along with Aristotle, he is considered to be one of the fathers of Western philosophy.

OBJECTIVES

- discuss improving the brain
- talk about future technology
- talk about regrets
- discuss intelligence
- recount events
- write a report

Work with a partner. Discuss the questions.

1 Look at the picture. How is it connected to the topic of intelligence?
2 Read the quote. What do you think Socrates means? Do you agree?
3 Would you rather be very intelligent, very strong or very attractive? Why?

INTELLIGENCE 37

OBJECTIVES

Read the unit objectives to the class.

UNIT OPENER QUESTIONS

1 Put students into pairs to look at the picture and discuss the question. In feedback, ask students if they think there are different kinds of intelligence, and if so, what they are.

2 Put students back into pairs to discuss the question. In feedback, find out how similar their opinions are. Elicit examples of situations the quote could be applied to.

3 Elicit some examples of the advantages of being very strong, very intelligent or very attractive. Put students back into pairs to discuss the questions. In feedback, encourage students to expand on their opinions and to agree and disagree with each other. Record any useful language that comes up on the board.

WORKSHEETS

Lesson 4.1 Brain training

Vocabulary: Conceptual metaphors (W16)

Grammar: Conditionals without *if* (W17)

Lesson 4.2 Thinking and thought

Vocabulary: Science and research (W18)

Grammar: Wishes and regrets (W19)

Vocabulary: Thinking (W20)

4.1 Brain training

- Discuss improving the brain
- Talk about future technology

G conditionals without *if* **V** conceptual metaphors **P** adding information **S** identifying logical fallacies

LISTENING

A Work in pairs. Look at the brain teaser below. Do you know the answer? Go to the Communication Hub on page 149 for more brain teasers. David

TODAY'S BRAIN TEASER

David's mother had three children.

The first one was named April.

The second one was named May.

What was the name of the third child?

4.1 **B LISTEN FOR GIST** Listen to a radio discussion about ways to increase your brain power. What four methods of boosting brain power are discussed?

1 playing games (brain-training games or video games)

2 exercise

3 food

4 resting your brain / daydreaming / meditation

4.2 **C LISTEN AND IDENTIFY** Listen to three extracts from the radio discussion. Whose argument is weaker in each extract? Which type of logical fallacy (a–c) from the box have they used?

Identifying logical fallacies

a **Generalization:** drawing a conclusion about a large group from a very small amount of data.

b **Anecdotal evidence:** using non-scientific personal experience as proof for something.

c **False cause:** claiming a relationship exists between two things when there is no evidence to support this.

1 *Dr. Carter / Amanda* a

2 *Dr. Carter / Amanda* b

3 *Dr. Carter / Amanda* c

D SPEAK Work in pairs and discuss the questions.

1 Which of the methods that the speakers discussed do you think can really boost people's brainpower?

2 Do you agree with what Dr. Carter said about Sudoku?

3 Why do you think findings have been inconclusive on some methods?

PRONUNCIATION

Adding information

A Underline the part(s) of these sentences that provide additional information about something.

1 To answer the question, I'm joined today by two experts, Dr. Ramona Carter, a leading neuroscientist, and Amanda Saraha, a life coach and the author of *How to be smarter*.

2 So for example, if you do a lot of Sudoku, the math puzzle where you write the numbers in boxes, it's most likely that you will just become better at playing that game.

3 Recently, we've seen a lot of media stories about super foods, food that you should eat to boost your brain power.

4.3 **B** Listen to the sentences in Exercise A. Draw arrows where the intonation rises or falls. See Ex A for answers

C SPEAK Work in pairs. Give additional information about the underlined words.

1 I like to do some exercise, such as going for a run, before I start work in the mornings. (give more detail)

2 My friend, now in his 70s, is definitely one of the smartest people I know. (give more detail)

3 I try to do some meditation, an exercise where I concentrate on my breathing, because it helps me relax. (define the word)

4.1 Brain training

LEAD-IN

Books closed. Ask students to think of the most intelligent person they know. Put them into pairs to tell each other about this person.

LISTENING

A Direct students to the **Communication Hub** (see TB121).

4.1; 4.2 **B–C** Introduce the recording as a radio discussion in the first stage, then play it to students at each stage. Give feedback and check answers as a class after students complete each exercise.

1 *a: Generalization: Amanda claims that video games can be helpful but only uses one study to support her argument.*
2 *b: Anecdotal evidence: Amanda says she knows people whose diet has made them smarter. This is not a strong argument.*
3 *c: False cause: Amanda claims that high achievers are smart because they exercise but doesn't provide any evidence.*

D Put students into pairs to discuss the questions.

PRONUNCIATION

4.3 **A–C** Give feedback and check answers as a class.

AUDIO SCRIPT

4.1

Listening, Exercise B
H = Host Dr = Dr. Carter A = Amanda

H: On this week's episode of *Ask an Expert*, we're talking about boosting your brain power. These days, many products claim to make you smarter. But is it really possible? To answer the question, I'm joined today by two experts: Dr. Ramona Carter, a leading neuroscientist, and Amanda Saraha, a life coach and the author of *How to be smarter*. Thank you for joining me.
A: Thanks, John.
Dr: Thank you, John.
H: So first up, Amanda, the big question. Can people really make themselves smarter?
A: The short answer is yes, John. But the first step may actually be believing it's possible. Researchers have shown that when a group of students are told it's possible to become more intelligent, they can retain more of what they learn.
Ex B Q1 **H:** Dr. Carter, do you agree? One way that's very popular is braintraining games.
Dr: I have to admit, I love them. But I'm skeptical about whether they have any long-term effects. The problem is that the effects are probably not transferable. So, for example, if you do a lot of Sudoku, the math puzzle where you write the numbers in boxes, it's most likely that you will just become better at playing that game.
A team from Cambridge actually tried to shed some light on the impact of braintraining games. They had thousands of participants, so this was a big study doing braintraining activities for at least ten minutes a day, three times a week for six weeks. They tested them before and after. And the results showed no improvements in their test scores. In other words, their study showed that brain training didn't actually work.
A: Actually, if you don't mind me saying, that was just one study. Another study looked at older people playing a game that involved multi-tasking – they had to drive a car and look out for specific symbols as they drove. In this study, the participants showed that not only did they get better at the game, but that they also improved their attention and working memory.
Dr: Yes, you're right. But it's worth noting that this study specifically involved a video game rather than a typical braintraining game. Playing video games may affect our cognitive abilities according to research. But these kinds of games may prove to be more beneficial than dedicated brain-training games.
H: So overall the findings about playing games are a little inconclusive right now. So, what else can we do to boost our brain power?
A: There are actually a lot of things you can do. For example, have you ever wondered why so many high achievers boast about starting the day with a workout?
Ex B Q2 I strongly believe that the exercise they are doing makes them smarter and more competitive.
Dr: Well … I'd be cautious about making a direct link between high achievement and exercise, but there is a pretty clear consensus that exercise is good for the brain. Some scientists believe that exercise can help to promote the growth and formation of neurons in the hippocampus – so, as I mentioned before, if we retain the new cells that our body produces, it could affect our ability to think and remember.
Ex B Q3 **H:** Hmm … Is food another factor? Recently, we've seen a lot of media stories about super foods, food that you should eat to boost your brain power – fatty fish, blueberries, even chocolate. Is this true, Dr. Carter?
Dr: Um, the research is actually fairly inconclusive. Some studies have shown that eating a healthy diet has an impact on thinking ability, but claims that particular foods can impact your intelligence are mostly exaggerated or misleading.
H: Do you agree, Amanda?
A: As Dr. Carter says, we may still be in the dark about the science behind it, but I personally believe that the food we eat has a huge effect on every aspect of our lives. I know a lot of people who strongly believe that changing their diet has made them smarter.
H: OK. So maybe I do need to rethink my lunch choices. And is there anything else we can do to boost our intelligence, Amanda?
Ex B Q4 **A:** Well, we haven't talked about this yet, but it's actually really important to take some time out and unplug for a while. You need to disconnect from your phone and your computer and let your mind wander.
Dr: I completely agree with this. Getting enough sleep, taking some time to rest, sitting quietly or meditating has a big impact on reducing stress and anxiety, and it also helps you think. There are studies that back this up – they have shown that students who daydream do better on standardized tests than those who remain completely focused on a task.
H: So, resting can boost your brain power? That's good to know!

4.1 Brain training

VOCABULARY

A Point out the information in the box about *Conceptual metaphors.* Elicit the first one as an example, then tell students to match the other example sentences to the related metaphor.

B Tell students to look at the sentences from the radio discussion, and elicit that the underlined words are all connected by the same conceptual metaphor. Put them into pairs to decide what the metaphor is and what exactly each word or phrase means in these sentences.

C Ask students to identify the metaphor in each sentence. Do the first one as an example if necessary. Then put students into pairs to discuss the questions. Use the **Vocabulary Worksheet** on page W16 for extra practice.

SPEAKING

A Tell students to read the ads and to think about which products they would or wouldn't try. Put them into pairs to briefly compare ideas.

B Put students into groups to decide which service they're going to try to sell. Let them write some notes. Monitor as they do this to help or prompt if necessary. As each group presents their product to the class, tell the other groups to listen carefully and encourage them to ask questions at the end of each one.

C Put students into pairs to discuss the questions. In feedback, encourage students to expand on their answers.

Extra activity

Put students into small groups and tell them to design an intelligence test for another group. Tell students they can test any type of intelligence they like. Monitor to help if needed. Groups can then carry out the tests. In feedback, ask students what they thought of each other's tests. Which was the best in terms of really testing intelligence? Did any of them prove who the most intelligent students are?

METHODOLOGY HUB by Scott Thornbury

Metaphor

A metaphor is a figure of speech where one thing is stated in terms of another. For example, in the sentence *The teacher blew her top*, the teacher's anger is described as if it were literally a volcanic explosion. While metaphor tends to be associated with literary language (as in *The moon was a ghostly galleon, tossed upon cloudy seas*), a great deal of day-to-day language use is also metaphoric. In fact, some scholars, in the field of cognitive linguistics, have suggested that the fundamental roots of language are figurative rather than literal, and that metaphors structure the way we think about – and perceive – the world. Metaphors of this type are called cognitive metaphors. Thus, when I say *I look <u>forward</u> to hearing from you*, or *Picasso was ahead of his time*, we are (unwittingly) construing time as if the future was physically in front of us. Likewise, directional terms can express improvement (*Things are looking <u>up</u>*) or its opposite (*Why are you so <u>down</u>?*). Knowing how the way that spatial language is used metaphorically may help learners make sense of phrasal verbs, and the way prepositions are used in time expressions, such as *<u>in</u> January, <u>at</u> 10 o'clock and <u>on</u> the 4th of July.* A lot of formulaic language is also metaphoric in origin, as in these weather collocations: *a stormy relationship, a sunny disposition, thunderous applause, an icy smile.*

Grammatical metaphor is the term used to describe the way in which concepts that are normally expressed in one grammatical form (such as verbs) are expressed in another (such as nouns). For example, in the sentence *Using fossil fuels is destroying the ozone layer*, the words *using* and *destroying* are verbs expressing processes. In more formal language, such as in academic or technical writing, these verbal processes are frequently turned into 'things' through the use of nouns: *The use of fossil fuels is causing the destruction of the ozone layer*. Because *use* and *destruction* are not really things, but processes, this operation (also called nominalization) is considered metaphorical.

Typically, metaphorical language thinly masks a particular ideology or mindset. In our own field, terms like input, output and feedback are used unquestioningly, implying that language learning is a form of information processing. So ingrained do these metaphors become that it becomes hard to think 'out of the box' (another metaphor). Major theoretical advances usually come about because someone 'discovers' a new metaphor. The metaphor of scaffolding, for example, which is central to sociocultural learning theory, challenges the input–output metaphor of information processing theory.

TEACHING IDEA by David Seymour and Maria Popova

Similes

Highlight that similes are also a type of metaphor.

In small groups, think of a short anecdote leading up to one of these similes. (Allocate one to each group, randomly chosen, without the other groups hearing. While they are working, write the similes on the board.) Read your anecdote to the class and see if they can guess which simile completes it.

> The next day, he felt like death warmed up. I felt like a fish out of water. Well, you know me: I'm like a rolling stone. Oh well: like father, like son I suppose. It was like getting blood out of a stone. He was like a bull in a china shop.

TEACHING IDEA by David Seymour and Maria Popova

Time flies

Highlight that many sayings, for example, sayings related to time, involve metaphors.

In small groups, discuss and explain these sayings. Do you agree or disagree with them?

> Time is a great healer. Time is money. Time waits for no one. Tomorrow never comes. Time flies when you're having fun. You cannot save time; you can only spend it. What goes around, comes around. Tomorrow is another country.

VOCABULARY

Conceptual metaphors

A Match the sentences (1–6) with the related conceptual metaphor (a–c). Use the information in the box to help you.

> **Conceptual metaphors**
>
> Conceptual metaphors help us to talk about abstract or complex ideas by comparing them with something else. For example, life is frequently compared with a journey, such as in sentences like this:
>
> *She had reached a crossroads. Should she go to college or continue with her job?* (= reached a point when she needed to make an important decision about her life)

1 I spent an hour doing Sudoku. c
2 She shot down my arguments. b
3 He has a really fiery temper. a
4 After I had cooled down, I apologized. a
5 I've invested a lot of time in brain training. c
6 I couldn't defend my position. b

a anger = heat
b argument = war
c time = money

B Read three sentences from the radio show. What do the underlined words and phrases mean?

1 Of course, everyone would like to be more intelligent, but is it really possible? And if so, how can we make ourselves brighter? more intelligent
2 A team from Cambridge actually tried to shed some light on the impact of brain training games. explain it, provide some knowledge about it
3 As Dr. Carter says, we may still be in the dark about the science behind it, but I personally believe that the food we eat has a huge effect on every aspect of our lives. don't have the knowledge

C SPEAK Identify the conceptual metaphor being used in the questions. Then discuss the questions in pairs. metaphors labeled as per Ex A

1 Do you think brain training is a waste of time? c
2 What's a good strategy to convince people to buy brain-training products? b
3 Do you think intelligent people are usually more hot-tempered? a
4 Are you able to stay cool in an argument? a

SPEAKING

A Look at the advertisements. Which products would you try? Which would you avoid? Why?

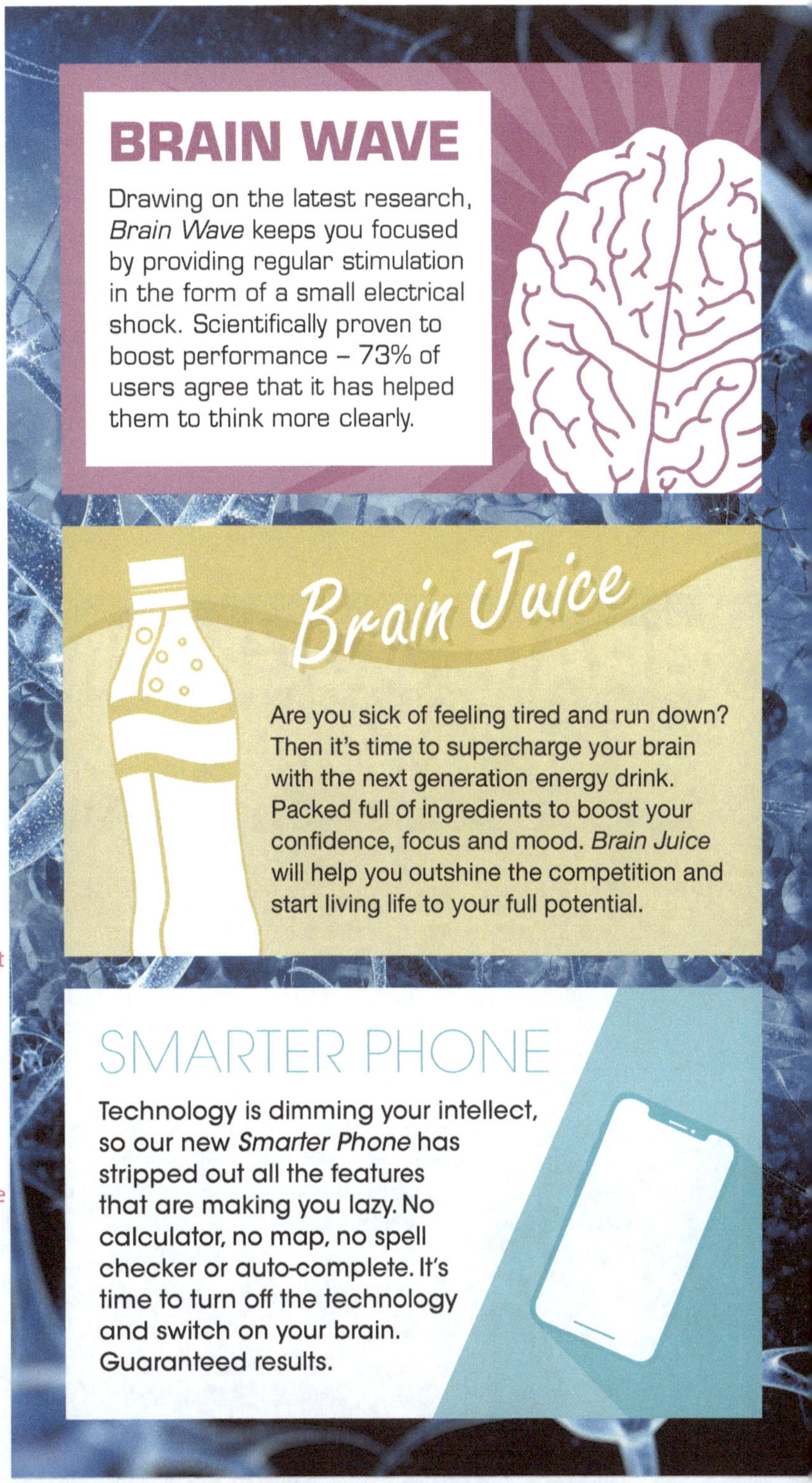

B PRESENT Work in groups. Think of a product or service that you could sell to people who wanted to boost their brain power. Present the product to the class. Which product is the most popular?

C DISCUSS Work in pairs and discuss the questions.

1 Do you believe that it's really possible to make yourself smarter?
2 Should companies be allowed to sell products like the ones in Exercise A? Why/Why not?

READING

A SPEAK Work in pairs. If you could significantly boost your intelligence overnight, would you do it? Why/Why not?

B PREDICT Work in pairs. Look at *Brain augmentation: The key to super intelligence*. In your own words, explain to your partner what you think the article is about.

C READ FOR MAIN IDEA Read the article and complete the table.

	Method of augmentation	Examples of benefits
1	Interfacing with the brain	Recording, storing and sharing information
2	Stimulating the brain	Repairing brains and improving their function and capabilities
3	Enhancing the brain with implants	Helping us learn faster, enhancing our memories, and providing us with a cognitive boost

D READ FOR DETAIL Read the article again and answer the questions.

1 When do scientists predict highly sophisticated robots will be a common sight?

2 How has technology been used to help blind people?

3 What did scientists learn from the research with epilepsy patients?

4 What potential dangers of brain augmentation does the article mention?

E SPEAK Work in pairs and discuss the questions.

1 What was the most surprising thing that you learned from the article?

2 Do you think that the government should control this kind of augmentation?

BRAIN AUGMENTATION:

The key to super intelligence

How far would you go to enhance your own intelligence? Would you implant a chip into your brain? For many scientists around the world, the answer appears to be *yes*. Brain augmentation, enhancing the intelligence of human Ex D Q1 brains with implants, is a growing area of interest as some predict that super-intelligent cyborgs will be a normal part of everyday life within the next 10 to 20 years.

In fact, experts believe that there are three main approaches Ex C Q1–3 to brain augmentation: interfacing with the brain, stimulating the brain and enhancing the brain with implants.

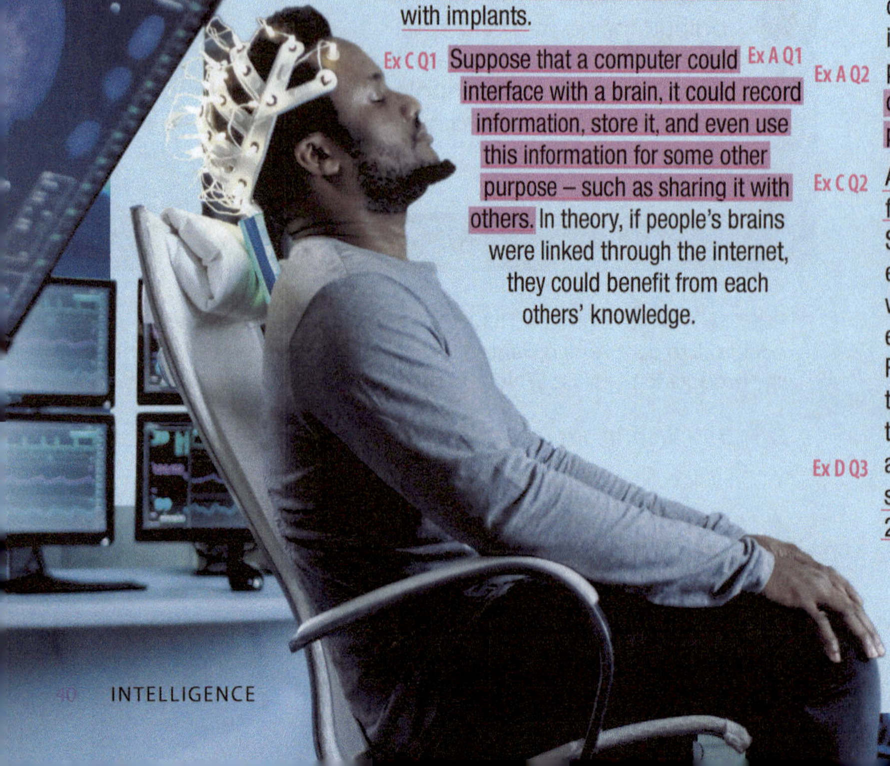

Ex C Q1 Suppose that a computer could Ex A Q1 interface with a brain, it could record information, store it, and even use this information for some other purpose – such as sharing it with others. In theory, if people's brains were linked through the internet, they could benefit from each others' knowledge.

Another way of augmenting the brain is by stimulating it in some way – typically with electricity. One goal of stimulation is to produce artificial sensations, such as Ex C Q2 the sensation of touch or vision. In this case, the main motivation comes from a desire to help repair the brains of people with neurological conditions. For example, in Ex D Q2 the last couple of years, scientists from *Second Sight* have been able to partially restore the sight of some blind people by implanting a chip into their retinas that sends signals to the brain from a camera. Although these people cannot see, the stimulation of the brain creates pictures in their mind. Right now these are just black and white, Ex A Q2 pixelated images, but assuming that the technology continues to improve, this could be the beginning of a permanent cure for blindness.

Ex C Q2 Another goal of stimulating the brain is to improve its function and its capabilities. A recent study led by Dong Song of the University of Southern California looked at the effects of stimulating the brain on memory. Researchers worked with twenty volunteers who were having electrodes implanted into their brains to treat epilepsy. Researchers examined the effects of stimulating the brain through these electrodes during tests that involved either the volunteers' short-term memory or working memory Ex D Q3 and found that the right kind of stimulation improved short-term memory by 15% and working memory by 25%. Interestingly, unless the right kind of stimulation was provided, the volunteers' memory was actually worse. So, there is clearly a lot of work to be done to understand the right kind of stimulation to provide.

4.1 Brain training

READING

A Put students into pairs to discuss the question and to think about reasons to justify their answers. In feedback, ask a student to explain what their partner's opinion was.

B Tell students to cover the article below the title to make sure they don't read the article yet. Put them into pairs to discuss what they think it will be about. Get some feedback, but don't confirm or reject any answers yet.

C Students read the text and complete the table. Set a time limit and stress that they don't need to read in too much detail to do this, but reassure them that they will have a chance to read it more carefully later. Point out the glossary, but emphasize that they should not worry about unfamiliar vocabulary at this stage.

D Ask students to read the text again and to answer the questions. If some students finish quickly, check their answers and if they're correct, tell them to prepare to lead feedback. In feedback, the fast finishers can then elicit answers from the other students, asking where exactly in the text the answers can be found. Keep a low profile here and let the students take the lead. At the end, give any extra feedback required to make sure all students understand the key points from the article and any new vocabulary that caused problems while reading.

1 *Within the next 10 to 20 years.*
2 *By implanting a chip into their retinas that connects to a camera, pictures can be sent to the brain.*
3 *They learned that the right kind of stimulation could boost memory.*
4 *It may change people's personalities and people with implants may be vulnerable to being hacked.*

E Put students into pairs to discuss the questions. In feedback, encourage plenty of agreement and disagreement if students have strong or differing opinions.

TEACHING IDEA by David Seymour and Maria Popova

Information technology

Use this activity to extend the theme of technology.

Discuss the questions in groups.

What are the greatest changes brought about by computers? Do you think there will ever be intelligent computers, i.e. computers that can learn?

In groups, list the advantages and disadvantages of modern technologies, e.g. *International telephone calls are very cheap. Working on computers all day is bad for your health.*

In groups, imagine a world without computers. How would it affect your day-to-day life? Make a list of five inconveniences, e.g. *I'd have to go to the library to get information rather than look on the internet.*

METHODOLOGY HUB by Scott Thornbury

While-reading and while-listening tasks

Giving learners something to do while reading or listening can help make sense of a text and ease the load, but only as long as the task is well suited to the text type. For example, if the text has a fixed sequence, as is the case of a narrative or a set of instructions, learners can be asked to put pictures in order as they read or listen. A sequencing task is not appropriate, however, for a text that presents information non-sequentially, as in many encyclopedia entries, for example. In this case, filling in details on a grid may be the best way of helping learners make sense of such texts. It's important to note that grid-filling tasks, or sequencing tasks, are not intended as a test of reader's comprehension so much as a framework to help them organize their developing understanding of the text. In this sense, such tasks are not so much comprehension tasks as comprehending tasks.

METHODOLOGY HUB by Christine Nuttall

Bottom-up processing

These are complementary ways of processing a text. They are both used whenever we read; sometimes one predominates, sometimes the other, but both are needed. And, though normally unconscious processes, both can be adopted as conscious strategies by a reader approaching a difficult text.

The bottom-up approach

In bottom-up processing, the reader builds up a meaning from the black marks on the page: recognizing letters and words, working out sentence structure. We can make conscious use of it when an initial reading leaves us confused. Perhaps we cannot believe that the apparent message is what the writer intended; this can happen if our world knowledge is inadequate, or the writer's point of view is very different from our own. In that case, we must scrutinize the vocabulary and syntax to make sure we have grasped the plain sense correctly. Thus bottom-up processing can be used as a corrective to 'tunnel vision' (seeing things only from our limited point of view).

Our image of bottom-up processing might be a scientist with a magnifying glass examining the ecology of a transect – a tiny part of the landscape the eagle surveys. The scientist develops a detailed understanding of that one little area (which might represent a sentence in the text); but full understanding only comes if this is combined with knowledge of adjacent areas and the wider terrain, so that their effects on one another can be recognized. In other words, the bottom-up and top-down approaches are used to complement each other.

4.1 Brain training

GRAMMAR

A Elicit the first one as an example to demonstrate how the sentences can be found in the text.

B Elicit that the alternatives to *if* used in the article all give it a more formal style, before students complete the rules.

C Direct students to the **Grammar Hub** (see below).

D Elicit the first one as an example, before students complete the other sentences with their own ideas.

E Put students into pairs to compare sentences. Use the **Grammar Worksheet** on page W17 for extra practice.

SPEAKING HUB

Put students into pairs, at first, AA and BB. Direct students to the **Communication Hub** (see TB121). In their pairs, they read the situations and discuss what they would do. Then re-pair students into AB pairs (make sure they realize that they have read about different situations). Tell them to explain their situations to each other and to discuss what they would do. Do they have the same opinions? Get class feedback and encourage students to expand on their answers. Finish with feedback on students' use of language during the activity, especially how well they used conditionals.

GRAMMAR HUB

4.1 Conditionals without *if*

We can use inversions to replace the word *if* in some conditional sentences.

- In first conditional sentences, we can use *should* to replace *if*.

  Should you have any questions, please don't hesitate to call. (= If you have … OR If you should have …)
- In second conditional sentences, we can use *were* to replace *if*.

  Were it banned, there would be an outcry. (= If it were banned…)
  Were I to do the quiz, I'm sure I would win! (= If I were to do …)
- In third conditional sentences, we can use *had* to replace *if*. This use of inversion is more common in formal language.

  Had he used a brain training game, he would have remembered more. (= If he had used …)
- We can also sometimes use verbs, *-ing*, past participles and the imperative in place of *if*.

Imagine / Suppose (that)	**Suppose** (that) I had a chip in my brain, would I be smarter?
Assuming / Supposing / Presuming / Providing (that)	**Assuming** (that) you complete the experiment, will you have all the data?
	Providing (that) we didn't make any mistakes, the results should be correct.
Provided (that)	**Provided** (that) you believe in yourself, you will definitely succeed.
Imperative … , and	**Read** more books, **and** you will improve your memory.

Be careful!

- With the imperative and *Imagine/Suppose (that)*, you cannot swap the clauses around.

  Imagine you were offered a brain implant, would you want it?
  NOT ~~Would you want a brain implant imagine you were offered it?~~

4.1 Conditionals without *if*

A Complete each second sentence so it means the same as the one before it.

1. If I had dropped my coffee on her carpet, I would have felt embarrassed!
   Had I dropped my coffee on her carpet, I would have felt embarrassed!
2. If brain implants were available to everyone, I would definitely get one!
   Should brain implants be / become available to everyone, I would definitely get one!
3. If you practiced Sudoku puzzles more, you would get better at them.
   Were you to practice Sudoku puzzles more, you would get better at them.
4. If you become dizzy after taking the medication, please contact your doctor.
   Should you become dizzy after taking the medication, please contact your doctor.

B Choose the correct options to complete the sentences.

1. *Imagine / Imagining* that you met Elon Musk, what would you say to him?
2. *Suppose / Providing* that we didn't make any errors during the experiment, the data should be correct.
3. *Look / Suppose we look* at the problem from a different angle, we might be able to find a solution.
4. *Imagine / Assuming* that she told us the truth, I think we can conclude that she's innocent.
5. *Supposing / Provided* all the participants had been men, would that have made a difference to the results?
6. *Conducting / Conduct* more research, and you will have a clearer picture.

C Complete the sentences with the correct form of the verbs in parentheses.

1. Act (*act*) confidently, and you will never again feel embarrassed.
2. Suppose you arrived (*arrive*) late for an exam, what would you do?
3. Provided that you think before you speak, you won't say / will not say (*not say*) anything silly.
4. Were I to say (*say*) the wrong thing, I would apologize.
5. Assuming you proved / could prove / had proven (*prove*) he was cheating, would you tell the examiner?
6. Should AI become a reality, we would need (*need*) to improve human intelligence.
7. Had I known / If I had known / If I'd known (*I know*) that the research was unethical, I would never have taken part in it.
8. Unless the government increases (*increase*) funding for the program, the researchers will never be able to complete their study.

➤ Go back to page 41.

GRAMMAR

Conditionals without *if*

A Underline conditional sentences in the article with the same meaning as sentences (1–6).

1 If a computer could connect to a brain, it could download information and make it available to others. (Paragraph 3)

2 If the technology gets better, it could lead to a cure for blindness. (Paragraph 4)

3 If robots decided to fight against humans, we would have to be smart enough to take them on. (Paragraph 6)

4 If people created successful brain-augmentation implants, we would need to think about the moral implications. (Paragraph 7)

5 If you ask many people about what's happening right now, they will tell you they don't know anything about it. (Paragraph 8)

6 If the government had not allowed this work into augmentation, we would not be developing innovations to assist people with vision problems. (Paragraph 8)

The final approach to augmentation is the most radical, because it involves merging man and machine. The biggest impact is likely to be from implanting a chip into your brain. Bryan Johnson, founder and CEO of neuroscience company Kernel, believes that these chips could be used to help us learn faster, enhance our memories, and provide us with a cognitive boost. *Space X* and *Tesla* are also working on technology to boost the human brain through the company Neuralink. One concern raised is that humans are able to enhance their intelligence, because, should AI turn against humans in the future, we would need to be smart enough to fight back. Ex C Q2 Ex D Q4 Ex A Q3

Of course, were brain-boosting implants to be successfully developed, they would raise several difficult ethical questions. Would changing people's brains change their personalities? If someone had an implant fitted, would they be at risk of being hacked? Could these super intelligent cyborgs be a danger to the rest of us? Ex A Q4 Ex D Q4

Ask many people about what's happening right now in this field and they will tell you they are completely in the dark. Unfortunately that includes the government, who many feel should be doing more to regulate the technology and ensure that it really is safe. However, had the government banned this kind of research, the technology to help blind people would not be under development. Ex A Q5 Ex A Q6

B Choose the correct words to complete the rules (a–c). Then look at the example sentences you found in Exercise A to complete the rules (d–f).

Conditionals without *if*

We can use inversions to talk about hypothetical situations in formal or literary English:

a *Had*: We use *had* + subject + ***infinitive*** / ***past participle*** / ***base form***.

b *Should*: We use *should* + subject + ***infinitive*** / ***past participle*** / ***base form***.

c *Were*: We use *were* + subject + ***infinitive*** / ***past participle*** / ***base form***.

We can use other words instead of *if*:

d Verbs: *imagine*, suppose

e Present participles: assuming, *presuming, providing, supposing*

- Past participles: *provided*

f We can also make a conditional sentence by starting with an imperative and joining the clauses with and.

C Go to the Grammar Hub on page 128.

D Change the start of these sentences to make conditionals without *if*. Complete the sentences with your own opinions.

1 If people were able to upload information into their brains, … Suppose people were able to upload information into their brains, …

2 If we ignore the potential danger of AI, … Ignore the potential danger of AI and …

3 If brain implants were only affordable for the super-rich, … Should brain implants only be affordable for the super-rich, …

4 If I were to be offered a brain-boosting implant, … Were I to be offered a brain boosting implant, …

E Compare your sentences with your partner. Do you agree with your partner's opinions?

SPEAKING HUB

Work in pairs. Student A – go to the Communication Hub on page 150. Student B – go to the Communication Hub on page 152. Describe the situations to your partner. Discuss what you would do.

Glossary

cyborg (n) a creature in science fiction stories that is part human and part machine

electrode (n) a small metal or carbon object inside an electrical cell or a battery that electricity flows through. There are two electrodes, one positive and one negative.

neurological (adj) relating to your nervous system or to the diseases that affect it

retina (n) the part at the back of your eye that sends light signals to your brain, where they are changed into images

- Discuss improving the brain
- Talk about future technology

4.2 Thinking and thought

- Talk about regrets
- Discuss intelligence

G – wishes and regrets
P – adding information or changing the topic
V – science and research; thinking
S – identifying different writing styles

READING

A SPEAK Read *No need to be embarrassed?* Discuss the following questions.

1. Have any of the situations described happened to you?
2. Which stories do you think are the most and least embarrassing?

B Read *The positive side of embarrassment*. What do scientists think is the purpose of embarrassment?
to help identify those likely to cooperate with the group

C READ TO IDENTIFY Who is each text written for? What is the purpose of each text?

Text 1 General readers: to entertain and reassure

Text 2 Students/academics: present findings about the purpose of embarrassment

D Read both texts again. Find examples of the writing styles (a–e) in the box. Use the information in the box to help you.

Identifying different writing styles

Texts written for a general audience usually use:

- **a** shorter, simpler sentences (including sentences that start with *and*, *but* and *so*)
- **b** idiomatic language (contractions, phrasal verbs, idioms).

Academic papers and articles:

- **c** are objective not personal (no *I*, *you* or *we*, no emotional adjectives)
- **d** use longer, more complex sentences
- **e** use formal language (no contractions or phrasal verbs, but academic vocabulary).

E SPEAK Work in pairs. Do you agree that displaying embarrassment can make a positive impression on others?

NO NEED TO BE EMBARRASSED?

Glossary

buddy (n) (American English) friend
consolation (n) something that makes you feel less unhappy or disappointed
cringeworthy (adj) something that makes you feel embarrassed or ashamed

Psychologists believe that embarrassment should actually be viewed as a positive thing. When we blush or stammer in embarrassment, we are showing that we know that we shouldn't have said or done something and that we don't
Ex B **normally do this kind of thing. In other words, showing we are embarrassed is a kind of non-verbal apology.**

Well that's all well and good, but when you're caught red-faced, I don't think that would
Ex D b be any consolation. In light of this research, I thought I'd do some of my own. Now I'm no stranger to embarrassment, but a quick survey revealed embarrassing work stories far worse than mine. Here are some of your most cringeworthy moments.

"Can you even begin to imagine what it's like to walk into a glass door at full speed? Must be painful, right? Now add to that the mortification that it was in front of your new boss. If I hadn't been trying to impress her with my walking-while-emailing skills –
Ex D a like I was a hot-shot political aide on a TV show – I might have noticed the door. But the humiliation doesn't stop there. All of my co-workers were sitting around a conference table
Ex D a on the other side of that glass door. I would have loved to make a good impression. But all I
Ex D b ended up with was wounded pride ... and a broken nose."

"Generally speaking I'm a pretty confident person. I'm great at putting people at ease and keeping conversation going. I just wish I wasn't so absent-minded. Over the years it has caused me infinite amounts of awkwardness. But never more so than just last month. An important client was flying in from Vancouver for an even more important
Ex D a meeting. So I offered to pick him up from the airport. The only problem was by the time he came through the arrivals gate, I had completely forgotten where I'd parked my car. We spent the next two hours wandering aimlessly around various parking lots in the pouring rain. I wish I'd never offered to give him a ride ... and I bet he does, too!"

"This happened five years ago but to this very day the memory still haunts me! The CEO where I used to work sent a (very smug) company-wide email congratulating *himself* on record profit margins. In response I wrote a very rude message making fun of the CEO to my office buddy ... or so I thought. If only I hadn't been in such a rush to have lunch, I might have noticed that I had hit *reply to all* instead of *reply* ... those two little words make a huge difference. My email was sent to every employee in London and Boston. It was only when I came back from lunch and everyone was snickering that it
Ex D b clicked what had happened. I just wanted the ground to swallow me up."

4.2 Thinking and thought

LEAD-IN

Books closed. Give an example of a time you were embarrassed, explaining what happened in as much detail as you can. Put students into pairs to think of embarrassing situations, either that have happened to them or people they know or just from their imagination. Get some feedback on the most interesting ideas, and find out if students find the same kind of things embarrassing.

READING

A Ask students to read the text and to answer the questions. Let students compare answers briefly in pairs before checking as a whole class.

B Tell students to read the second article and to answer the question. Stage feedback as you did for Exercise A.

C Tell students to look back through the two texts again if they need to, and then to discuss the questions in pairs. In feedback, again elicit examples from the text to support students' answers.

D Go through the information in the box about *Identifying different writing styles*, and elicit examples of the first one as a class. Then tell students to look through the two texts once again to find more examples of the different styles.

E Put students into pairs to discuss the questions. In feedback, encourage students to expand on their stories and to react to each other's.

Extra activity

Ask students to research two short texts or extracts on a different topic. These don't necessarily have to be related to psychology or thinking but you can give them the following examples to help: dreams, attitudes, personality types, leadership, memory, problem-solving, attention.

One text should be an informal text (e.g., an online magazine article). The other should be an academic text in a formal style. However, they should avoid long journal articles, using abstracts or extracts from popular science articles instead. Students should look for examples of formal/informal writing styles (a–e) in the texts.

Students should bring the texts to the next class, ideally removing any information about the sources. Put students into groups and distribute the texts. For each text, the students should discuss:

- who the text is written for
- the purpose of the text
- examples of formal and informal writing styles.

METHODOLOGY HUB by Christine Nuttall

Rhetorical structure

Coherence depends partly on how sentences are sequenced and on the value that each has; each sentence takes its value from the others and in turn it helps to give value to them. This complex network of relationships and the way that the underlying ideas are organized within a text is its *rhetorical structure*. It is built with the *rhetorical acts* (=values: explaining, describing, defining, etc) performed by the sentences in the text: not the words and grammar, but the way the sentences are used.

To understand more clearly what is meant by *rhetorical structure*, we need to think about the *topic* of the text, the writer's *purpose* in writing it and the *audience* she had in mind. If we ask what the topic is, we expect answers like 'The threat to privacy created by computers'. If we ask about the writer's purpose, we may be told 'she's telling a story' or 'They are trying to convince us that their views are correct'. If we ask about the intended audience (target readers), we will learn that the text is directed at schoolchildren, or laymen, or academics, and so on.

Once you know the topic, purpose and target readers, you can go on to ask how the writer approaches her objective. Answering the question involves tracing the rhetorical development of the text. You would not expect a children's story to have the same sort of structure as a college physics textbook. Equally, two physics textbooks are likely to be similar in structure. Readers need to know that choice is possible, and to be able to recognize how a text is organized, since this can help them (through top-down processing) to reach an interpretation.

METHODOLOGY HUB by Scott Thornbury

Style

Style is a (usually deliberate) choice of a particular way of saying or writing something. There is typically more than one way of conveying the same message. The choice is determined by:

1. specific contextual factors, such as the degree of formality that is required, or the conventions associated with a particular field or profession, such as the law
2. a particular effect – typically aesthetic – that the person wants to achieve.

The first kind of variability is usually called register, while the second is called style (although sometimes this distinction is collapsed). The study of style is called stylistics.

An example of language being used to create a particular effect is this Valentine's Day message:

To Wee Pig from Big Pig. Grunt Grunt!

Here the writer has chosen a style associated with children's literature. Style choices affect both grammar and vocabulary. Words that are used only in certain styles are usually identified as such in dictionaries. Styles include literary, old-fashioned, humorous and medical. For example, *allusion* (literary), *malarkey* (informal, humorous) and *dilly-dally* (old-fashioned).

4.2 Thinking and thought

VOCABULARY

A–C Direct students to the **Vocabulary Hub** (see TB121). Use the **Vocabulary Worksheet** on page W18 for extra practice.

GRAMMAR

A–C Direct students to the **Grammar Hub** (see below). Use the **Grammar Worksheet** on page W19 for extra practice.

SPEAKING

A Ask students to think of something they regret, either from the list on page 150 or something different. Give them some time to think about what they want to say.

B Make sure students aren't with the same partner they had at the start. Tell them to share their stories and listen carefully.

GRAMMAR HUB

4.2 Wishes and regrets

wish / if only + simple past/progressive	to wish that the present was different	**I wish / If only I didn't blush** so easily.
wish / if only + *could/would*		**I wish / If only I could stop** stammering. **I wish / If only you would speak** more clearly.
wish / if only + past perfect simple/progressive	to wish that the past was different	**I wish / If only I had participated** in the study.
wish / if only + *could have* + past participle		**I wish / If only I could have participated** in the study.
ought (not) to / should (not) have + past participle *ought (not) to / should (not) have been* + *-ing*		**I shouldn't have gazed** at the floor all the time!

- *If only* often sounds more dramatic or emphatic than *wish*. It can be used about other people, but usually suggests the speaker's opinion.
  If only David had known the answer! (= I wish David had known the answer!)
- To be more formal, we use *were* instead of *was* after *I/he/she/it*.
  *If only I **were** more confident.*
  *He wishes he **were** more confident.*
- When you want to talk about your own wishes, use *could* instead of *would*.
  *I wish I **could** speak Chinese. NOT ~~I wish I would speak Chinese.~~*
- We can also use *ought to have* + past participle to talk about things that were ideal or desired in the past.
  *They **ought to have managed** the meeting better.*
- We can use *would love to have* + past participle to talk about regrets.
  *I **would love to have had** enough time to explain my views. (= I didn't have enough time and that's a shame.)*
- We can also use *if* + past perfect simple + modal verbs (subordinate clause) and modal verb + *have* + past participle to talk about imagined situations in the past with regret.
  ***I could have learned** more, **if I had prepared** for the classes.*

4.2 Wishes and regrets

A Choose the correct options to complete the sentences.

1 I wish I had made a better first impression. = I *made* / *didn't make* a good impression.
2 I wish I could understand what the lecturer was saying. = I *understand* / *don't understand*.
3 You shouldn't have been so clumsy! = You *were* / *weren't* clumsy.
4 Helena wishes her new boss was more friendly. = Her new boss *is* / *isn't* friendly.
5 I would love to have taken part in the experiment. = I *took* / *didn't take* part.
6 You ought not to have worn that eccentric outfit. = You *wore* / *didn't wear* an eccentric outfit.
7 If only I didn't feel so socially awkward. = I *feel* / *don't feel* socially awkward.
8 If only he could express himself more clearly. = He *is* / *isn't* able to express himself clearly.

B Complete the sentences with the correct form of the verbs in parentheses.

1 I wish I __had prepared__ (*prepare*) more thoroughly for my interview yesterday.
2 If only I __knew__ (*know*) whether or not I got the job!
3 I wish I __could have gotten__ (*can / get*) her autograph but I wasn't brave enough.
4 If only I __hadn't said__ (*not / say*) that I'm disorganized!
5 I wish I __could think__ (*can / think*) clearly under pressure but I get so stressed.
6 I wish I __didn't have to__ (*not / have to*) go through job interviews!

C Correct the mistakes in each sentence.

1 You shouldn't have ~~copy~~ copied your essay from the internet.
2 The girls wish they ~~was~~ were on vacation.
3 You could ~~had~~ have told me the truth – I would have believed you!
4 I would love to ~~had~~ have taken part in the research.
5 The scientists ought to have ~~make~~ made their findings public.
6 Gemma ~~doesn't wish she was~~ wishes she wasn't so shy.
7 If only I ~~hadn't~~ didn't get embarrassed with new people.
8 I could have done better, if I ~~haven't~~ hadn't been so nervous.

➤ Go back to page 43.

The positive side of embarrassment

The outward signs of embarrassment are well known, and include blushing, gazing downward, turning away and face touching. However, researchers have been attempting to identify the evolutionary purpose of embarrassment.

Several researchers have postulated that embarrassment may Ex B help to signal whether humans are willing to develop long-term bonds with each other. For example, Lewis (2008) believes that embarrassment is when individuals make a negative evaluation of their actions, thoughts or feelings because they feel they have not behaved according to social standards.

Feinberg, Willer, Keltner and Dacher (2012) **hypothesised** that Ex D e embarrassment served several important social functions and **conducted** several **experiments** to test this hypothesis. Ex D e

In one experiment, **participants** were asked to tell an embarrassing story and then complete a questionnaire that looked at their tendency to be kind. The **findings** indicated that Ex D e people who showed more embarrassment were more likely to be kinder people. The researchers **concluded** that these people were more 'pro-social' – that is they wanted to be part of the Ex D d group and not behave in a way that was counter to the social **norms** of the group.

In another experiment, participants witnessed an interaction between a researcher and someone that they thought was another participant (but was actually an actor). The researcher praised the fake participant's performance on a test, and the fake participant either expressed embarrassment or pride. The participants who saw the actor look embarrassed were more likely to think he was trustworthy and want to interact with him. This experiment **demonstrated** that people are more Ex B likely to have a positive perception of someone who shows embarrassment. The researchers **speculated** that this was because this person is showing a desire to fit in with the group.

From examining the findings of studies such as these, it appears that the evolutionary purpose of Ex B embarrassment was to help identify individuals who would be likely Ex D d to cooperate with the group. So although embarrassment is widely thought of as a negative emotion, displaying embarrassment most likely makes a positive impression on others.

VOCABULARY
Science and research

A Match the words in bold from the second text with the meanings (1–9).

1. do (an experiment, a study) conduct
2. standard behavior norms
3. suggest a theory hypothesize
4. guess speculate
5. people taking part in a study or experiment participants
6. results findings
7. test experiment
8. decide conclude
9. show demonstrate

B Go to the **Vocabulary Hub** on **page 143**.

C **SPEAK** Work in pairs and discuss the questions.

1. Would you like to be a participant in a psychology study?
2. Think of an experiment you've heard about. What did it hypothesize? What were the findings?
3. Is it ethical to conduct a study where you make people feel embarrassed?

GRAMMAR
Wishes and regrets

A **WORK IT OUT** Look at the underlined sentences in *No need to be embarrassed?* Then choose the correct words to complete the rules.

Wishes and regrets

1. We use *wish* or *if only* + simple ***present / past*** to wish that the present was different.
2. We use *wish* or *if only* + ***present / past*** perfect to wish that the past was different.
3. We can use *should (not)* or *ought (not) to* + *have* + *past participle* or *been* + ***present / past*** participle to talk about regrets.
4. We can use *would* + *love* or *prefer* or *hate* + ***to have / have*** + *(not)* past participle to talk about regrets.

B Go to the **Grammar Hub** on **page 128**.

C Complete the sentences so they are true for you.

1. If only I could …
2. I wish I were …
3. I would have loved to …

SPEAKING

A **PREPARE** Think of a time when you did something you regret. You can use the list of ideas on **page 150** of the **Communication Hub** or your own ideas. What happened? What do you wish had happened differently?

B **DISCUSS** Tell your partner about what happened. Listen to your partner and ask questions.

LISTENING

A SPEAK Work in pairs. Look at the pictures. Discuss which of the following gives people the biggest advantage in life. Give reasons for your choice.

- Money
- Intelligence
- Supportive family
- Good health

B LISTEN FOR MAIN IDEA You are going to listen to part of a debate about whether being highly intelligent gives people an advantage in life. What are the speaker's three main points?

4.4

1 Highly intelligent people lack common sense.
2 They find it difficult to socialize.
3 They feel under pressure to live up to expectations.

C LISTEN FOR SPECIFIC INFORMATION Listen again and answer the questions.

4.4

1 What is the 'nutty professor' stereotype?
2 What mistakes do intelligent people frequently make at social events?
3 What do intelligent people sometimes do to preserve their reputation?

D SPEAK Work in pairs. Can you think of any counter-arguments or challenges to the three points in Exercise B? Present them to your partner. Use the phrases below to help you.

> First of all, the speaker claimed that … but …
> In addition, the speaker stated that …
> The speaker also mentioned the fact that …

E SPEAK Work in pairs and discuss the questions.

1 Do you know any intelligent people who behave in the ways that the speaker described?
2 Do you think the speaker has a convincing argument? Why/Why not?
3 The speaker says that intelligence and happiness don't necessarily come together. Do you agree?

VOCABULARY
Thinking

A Complete the questions (1–8) with the correct form of a word or phrase in the box.

> absent-minded common sense curious eccentric eureka moment overthink troubleshoot wishful thinking

1 Are you good at troubleshooting or do you find it difficult to find and fix problems and faults?
2 Do you sometimes think about the same thing over and over again? Are you overthinking things?
3 Do you solve problems with sudden bursts of inspiration, like a eureka moment?
4 Do you like to take things apart? Are you curious about how things work?
5 Do you make time in the day to organize work? Or does it seem like wishful thinking ________ to sit down and plan things?
6 Do you forget where you leave things? Are you absent-minded?
7 Are you a practical person? Or do you lack common sense?
8 Would you describe yourself as fairly conventional and similar to most people? Or are you a little eccentric?

B Go to the **Vocabulary Hub** on **page 144.**

C SPEAK Work in pairs. Ask and answer the questions in Exercise A. Then decide if your partner is a genius.

4.2 Thinking and thought

LISTENING

A With books closed, elicit advantages that people have in life that help them become successful. Tell students to open their books and draw their attention to the pictures and the ideas in Exercise A. Put them into pairs to discuss the question. In feedback, encourage students to support their opinions with examples.

4.4 **B** Explain to students that they're going to listen to a speech from a debate about whether intelligence gives people an advantage in life. Tell them to listen and to complete the task. Let students compare in pairs before feedback, and keep feedback brief at this stage.

4.4 **C** Put students into pairs to try to answer the questions from memory. Play the recording again for students to listen and check, and let them compare in pairs again before feedback.

1 *An intelligent person who is absent-minded and lacks common sense.*
2 *They try to discuss the wrong topics, they correct people's mistakes, and they try to start debates. They are very self-conscious.*
3 *They don't ask questions and they try to skip the basics when they learn something new.*

D Elicit one example, then put students into pairs to think of and present more ideas. Get feedback on some ideas and encourage students to agree or disagree with each other. Give feedback on use of language here, too.

E Put students into pairs to discuss the questions. In feedback, encourage further debate if students have differing opinions.

VOCABULARY

A Do the first one as an example with the class, then put students into pairs to complete the questions. In feedback, further check understanding with extra examples where necessary. Practice pronunciation of tricky words, e.g. *curious*, *eccentric* and *eureka*.

B Direct students to the **Vocabulary Hub** (see TB121).

C Put students into pairs to ask and answer the questions from Exercise A. Tell them to think about what they heard in the listening to help them decide if they think their partner is a genius. In feedback, ask students if they think their partner is a genius and why, or why not.

Use the **Vocabulary Worksheet** on page W20 for extra practice.

AUDIO SCRIPT

4.4

Listening, Exercise B
C = Chair E = Ella

C: So the motion is: 'Intelligence gives people the greatest advantage in life.' Now I look to Ella to open the case against the motion.

E: Thank you very much. It's an honor to speak against the motion tonight. Right, it's easy to see why so many people believe being intelligent makes your life better. After all, we see intelligent people thriving at school. We see them getting into the college courses they want. We see them graduating with good academic certifications. And on top of that, we see the importance the world gives to certifications.

So, it may seem strange for me to stand here and argue that intelligent people aren't necessarily at an advantage in life. However, that is exactly what I'll do. In fact, there are several clear disadvantages in having a superior intellect.

Ex B Q1 Let's start with a lack of common sense. And let's talk about a chess champion. Not just any chess champion, but a chess champion that was also a child chess prodigy. She must be smart, right? Well, talk to her mother. According to her, she frequently locks
Ex C Q1 her car keys inside her car. The 'nutty professor' – smart but absent-minded and eccentric – is a common stereotype of highly intelligent people. Some scientists believe that geniuses' brains are wired differently. While highly intelligent people are curious about complex puzzles and are able to troubleshoot, they can't deal with more mundane tasks. So Ms. Chess Champion could beat 15 chess players in a row … but she can't drive herself home.

Ex B Q2 Another problem faced by intelligent people is an inability to socialize. We've all known that friend at school or college. They're ready to answer in the physics class, they ask the lecturer countless questions and their voice drowns out everybody else's in the seminar. Then you take them to a party. Suddenly it seems like wishful thinking that anyone will talk to them again. Ever. Probably because they're still talking about physics. There are a few reasons why highly intelligent people are thought of as socially awkward. First, they find small talk
Ex C Q2 tedious. You find them correcting other people's mistakes or trying to engage in a passionate debate at a casual social event. Second, they are incredibly
Ex C Q2 self-conscious. This means they tend to overthink things and appear awkward.
Ex B Q3 And finally, there's the burden of expectation. You have a reputation to protect. If everyone thinks you're a genius, they expect you to be successful and make an impact in the world. Sometimes the pressure is
Ex C Q3 just too much. Highly intelligent people can end up dropping out of education altogether and trying to hide their intellect to fit in. Or they're afraid to look
Ex C Q3 stupid. So they avoid asking questions when they need to, or they try to skip the basics when they learn something new, which, of course, only creates problems down the line.

In summary, if you think that being smart means lounging in a bath tub waiting for a eureka moment, then think again. There are a lot of downsides to intelligence. Geniuses can lack common sense, find it difficult to socialize, and feel pressure to live up to expectations. I've always said myself that intelligence and happiness don't necessarily go together. This is no surprise to people who lock their keys in their car, don't have any friends to drive them and are too scared to ask. In fact, being highly intelligent makes life more not less difficult.

4.2 Thinking and thought

PRONUNCIATION

4.5 **A** Tell students to listen to the beginning of the debate again and to mark the intonation. If students seem unsure of what this means, stop the recording after the first one and elicit the answer as an example. Then model this yourself, exaggerating slightly if necessary so it's clear. Let students compare in pairs before feedback, saying the sentences aloud to help them remember or decide what the intonation was like.

B Model the first dialogue with a stronger student, and try to continue the conversation for as long as you can. Put students into pairs to do the same. In feedback, ask some pairs to perform one of their conversations. Tell the other students to listen carefully and comment on the use of intonation.

SPEAKING HUB

A Split the class into an even number of groups. Tell half of the groups that they are going to argue for the motion and half that they are going to argue against it. Go through the order of presentations with the class.

B Ask students to decide on their roles, i.e. who is going to present their group's arguments and who is going to challenge the other group's arguments. Tell students presenting to plan their arguments. Those challenging the other presentation should anticipate the arguments they think the other team will make, and prepare counter-arguments. Elicit an example for each side of the argument to model how they could do this before students work in groups to plan more. Monitor to help and prompt if necessary.

C Combine groups so that one arguing for the motion joins one arguing against. Remind them of the order of presentations, and tell them to have the debate.

D Tell the students to stay in their groups and to discuss the questions. In feedback, find out why they thought the debate was or wasn't successful and whose arguments were the most convincing and why. Finish with feedback on students' use of language during the debate, focusing on how successfully they organized their arguments as well as structures and vocabulary.

Extra activity

After finding out if students really believe that highly intelligent people should be educated separately, elicit other types of people who should stand out from the crowd, e.g. *extremely attractive people*, *people with exceptional athletic ability*, *very talented musicians*, etc. Put students into pairs to discuss what, if any, specialist attention these people should receive.

METHODOLOGY HUB by Jim Scrivener

Intonation

Intonation is sometimes referred to as the 'music' of the language, and we use it as a kind of oral equivalent of written punctuation. It is closely connected to prominence, for the main movement of intonation begins at the tonic syllable. This movement can be upwards (a rise), downwards (a fall), a rise with a fall (a rise-fall), a fall with a rise (a fall-rise) or flat. Intonation has a definite effect on meaning and also gives us information about the speaker's attitude.

It is hard to teach intonation systematically because, although there are some common patterns, there are few clear rules, and many people with an 'unmusical' ear find it hard to recognize or categorize intonation patterns. It is, however, so important that it is essential to include work on intonation in most courses. Many learners speak English with a flat intonation, which can sound boring, bored or uninterested. Using wrong intonation can also give offense.

TEACHING IDEA by David Seymour and Maria Popova

Balloon debate

Use this activity to extend the themes of intelligence and debating.

(Elicit the names of two people known historically for their intelligence. Then draw a picture of a balloon on the board, with someone jumping out of it.)

Work in two groups. (Allocate one of the important people to each group.) The balloon has a leak and it can only carry one person. Convince me that your person should be the one to survive. Why is he/she more useful to the human race than the other person? Discuss your arguments and take turns to present them. I'll decide who has to jump.

Work in groups of five for another balloon debate. Each choose a famous person and prepare the reasons why you should stay and the others should jump. When you have finished, vote for the winner.

(Variation: This can be played with professions instead of individuals, e.g. *lawyer*, *doctor*.)

METHODOLOGY HUB by Scott Thornbury

Agreeing/disagreeing

The functions of agreeing and disagreeing are ways of responding to statements of opinion and to suggestions. They are commonly realized lexically, most literally by the verbs *agree* and *disagree*, as in *Yes, I agree (with you)* or *I (totally) disagree*. Other agreement expressions include *You're right*; *Good idea*; *I know*; and *I think so (too)*. Strong agreement can be expressed by *absolutely* and *exactly*. Mild agreement, on the other hand, is usually signaled by verbs like *suppose* and *guess*, as in *I suppose so*; *I guess that's true*, or with modal verbs, as in *That may be true*; *You could be right*.

Disagreeing with someone poses a threat to their face (politeness), so it is usually softened (or mitigated) by the use of discourse markers such as *Yes, but …* or *I see your point, but …* (hedging) – usually an indication that the speaker does not agree at all!

Teaching learners a set of expressions for agreeing and disagreeing is particularly useful as preparation for discussions and debates. These expressions can be displayed on the classroom wall for ready reference.

PRONUNCIATION

Adding information or changing the topic

4.5 **A** Listen again to the beginning of the debate. Draw arrows to show whether the intonation is rising (↗), falling (↘) or fall-rising (↘↗) at the end of the underlined words/phrases.

> Thank you very much. It's an honor to speak against the motion tonight. [1]____, (↘) it's easy to see why so many people believe being intelligent makes your life better. [2]<u>After all</u>, (↘↗) we see intelligent people thriving at school. We see them getting into the colleges they want. We see them graduating with good academic certifications. And [3]<u>on top of that</u>, (↘↗) we see the importance the world gives to certifications.
>
> So, it may seem strange for me to stand here and argue that intelligent people aren't necessarily at an advantage in life. [4]<u>However</u>, (↘) that is exactly what I'll do. [5]<u>In fact</u>, (↘↗) there are several clear disadvantages in having a superior intellect.

B SPEAK Work in pairs. Read the dialogues, focusing on the intonation of the underlined words and phrases. Then continue them with your own ideas.

1 **A:** I read that highly-intelligent people frequently like to spend time alone.
B: <u>On top of that</u>, they find it really hard to make friends.

2 **A:** Are you going to watch the debate on intelligence on TV tonight?
B: Yes, I'm planning to. <u>By the way</u>, do you want to go to a debate?

3 **A:** Einstein has been voted the most intelligent person ever.
B: Really? <u>Incidentally</u>, how did you do on your exam?

SPEAKING HUB

A PREPARE Work in groups. Read the motion below and decide whether you will argue for or against it.

Motion: Highly intelligent people should be educated separately.

Order of debate

1 Presentation in support of the motion.
2 Challenge to this presentation.
3 Presentation against the motion.
4 Challenge to this presentation.

B PLAN Decide on the roles each team member will have. Brainstorm arguments to support your position. Try to anticipate the arguments the other team will make, and prepare counter-arguments to them.

C DISCUSS Hold the debate. Follow the order given in Exercise A.

D REFLECT Discuss the following questions:

- How successful was the debate?
- What was your real opinion about the motion?
- Is it difficult to argue for a point of view you don't really agree with?

- Talk about regrets
- Discuss intelligence

Café Hub

4.3 Life-changing tech

A– *straight out of* S– recounting events

Sound and vision

A Work in pairs. Look at pictures a and b and discuss the questions.

1 In picture a, is each half of the circle the same shade of red?

2 In picture b, are the rectangles the same shade of blue?

Turn to **page 154** to check your answers.

B 4.6 Listen to two short pieces of music. What colors do they make you think of? Why? Turn to page 153 to check your answers.

C Watch the video about an artist. Complete the sentence with the best option.

Neil Haribsson has …

1 partial color blindness in which it is difficult to distinguish between blue and yellow, violet and red, and blue and green.

2 slight color blindness in which it is difficult to distinguish between red, green, brown and orange.

(3) total color blindness in which colors are seen as black and white.

Glossary

implant (v) to put an organ, group of cells, or device into the body in a medical operation

sensor (n) a piece of equipment that reacts to physical changes such as the amount of heat or light that exists somewhere

skull (n) the bony case which contains the brain

D Watch the video again. Complete the summary.

Neil Harbisson, an [1] artist, has never been able to see color. He was [2] curious about color because people always refer to it. He wanted to be able to [3] sense color rather than to alter his sight. A team of doctors and [4] engineers helped him create an electronic device. This is made up of a color sensor and a [5] chip. The sensor picks up [6] light frequencies and the chip [7] transforms the frequency into a sound. Each color creates a different [8] note.

AUTHENTIC ENGLISH

A Read the sentence from the video and the information in the box. Why do you think Neil's electronic device is compared to something from science fiction?

Because it uses technology that would seem new to most people and like something from a sci-fi movie/novel.

With the help of a team of engineers and doctors he created something ***straight out of*** *science fiction.*

straight out of

You use *straight out of* to say that something is similar in type to something else. This structure is frequently used to compare the thing we are describing to an imagined or fictional scenario.

B Work in pairs. Complete the sentences in an interesting way.

1 The scenery in Ireland is stunning – straight out of a travel brochure.

2 The band is really like *The Beatles*. They sound like something straight out of the 60s.

3 Himari saw snow for the first time that winter. It was like something straight out of a fairy tale.

4 The town has spectacular old buildings, a beautiful lake and no roads. It's straight out of a postcard.

5 My bag had been stolen, it was pouring rain and I couldn't speak the language. It was straight out of a nightmare.

6 The climb to the summit was long and difficult. It was like something straight out of a disaster movie.

C Join with another pair. Compare your answers to Exercise B.

Hearing colors

A Work in pairs. Discuss the following questions.

1 What gadgets or devices do you use?
2 Are there any new gadgets or devices you want to buy?
3 Have you ever been to a technology fair or exhibition? Why/Why not?

B Watch the video. Are these sentences true (T), false (F) or not given (NG)?

1 Harry is out sick from work. T / F / (NG)
2 The café was very busy in the morning. (T) / F / NG
3 Emily was about to leave the Tech Fair when a woman approached her. (T) / F / NG
4 The device looked like ~~headphones.~~ a microphone on a headband T / (F) / NG
5 The first thing that Emily saw on the screen was ~~a red square.~~ the woman T / (F) / NG
6 Emily agrees that Sam should go to the Tech Fair. (T) / F / NG

SPEAKING SKILL

A Work in pairs. Put the following sentences from the video in the order they are spoken.

[2] Well, I was at this big Health Tech Fair earlier today, right?
[4] But hang on, I'll get to that.
[1] Tell me about it. I've had rather a strange one myself.
[6] [The woman] asked me to step inside a large box. So I did.
[3] [I'm] thinking about heading out when all of the sudden, this woman stops me.
[8] Overall it was a strange but unforgettable experience.
[5] I was just about to ask her what it was when she slammed the door on me!
[7] So I'm standing there saying 'Excuse me … what's going on' and thinking what on earth have I got myself into.

B Match the sentences from the video (1–8) with the strategies (a–d) in the box.

Recounting events

We frequently recount events. To do this effectively we use a number of strategies.

a signaling the start of a story. For example, 1
b giving the background to a story. For example, 2
c evaluating parts of a story. For example, 7, 8
d sequencing events in a story. For example, 3, 4, 5, 6

SPEAKING HUB

A PLAN You are going to tell an interesting anecdote to a partner. You can choose one of the following topics or use your own idea.

- a strange coincidence
- a great event
- an unforgettable trip

B PREPARE Write notes on how you are going to sequence the events in your anecdote.

C DISCUSS Work in pairs. Tell your anecdote. Change roles.

So I'm thinking to myself this is like something straight out of a Hollywood movie.

D REFLECT Work with a new partner and retell them your previous partner's anecdote.

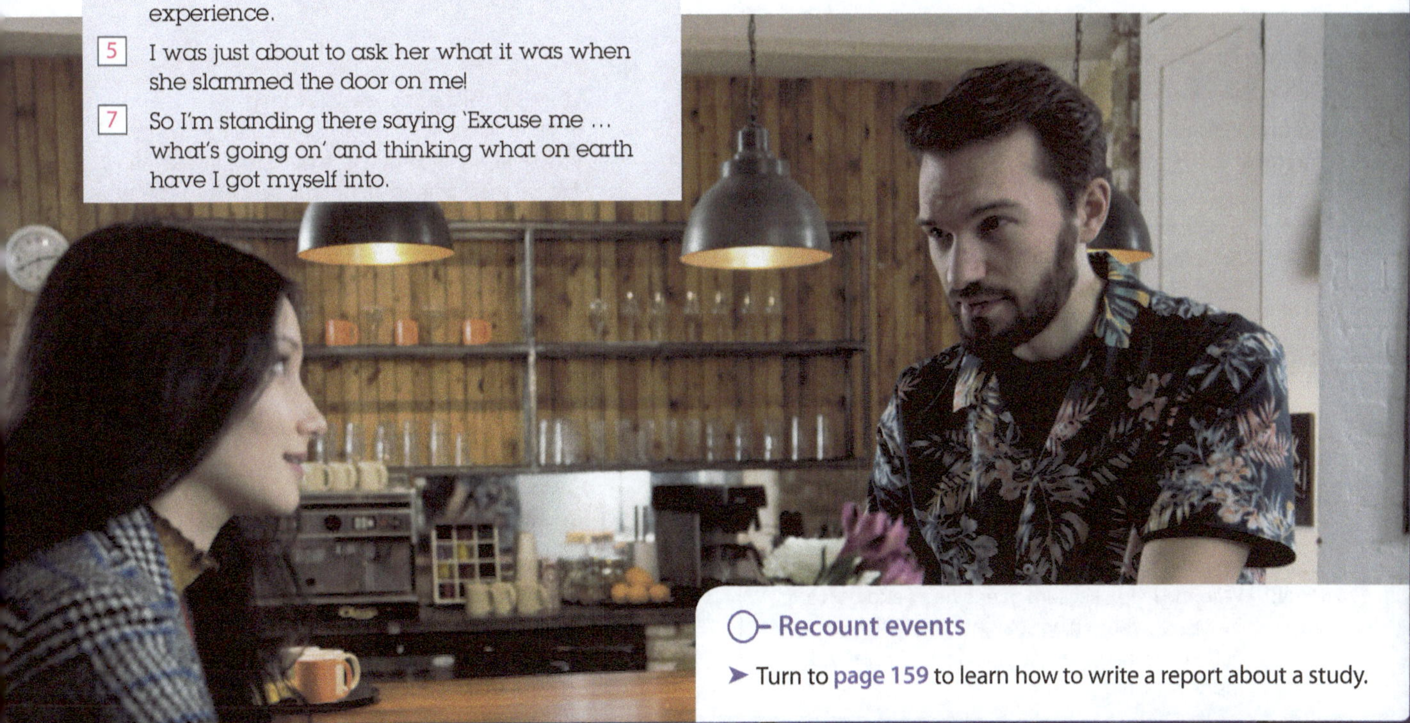

Recount events

➤ Turn to page 159 to learn how to write a report about a study.

4.3 Life-changing tech

Sound and vision

A Put students into pairs to look at the pictures and to discuss the questions. After they have, direct them to the **Communication Hub** (see TB121) to check their answers. Get some feedback on how students feel about these answers.

4.6 **B** Tell students to listen to the music and to discuss the questions. Direct them to the **Communication Hub** (see TB121) to check, and again get feedback on their reactions.

C ▶ Explain that students are going to watch a video about an artist. Go through the glossary and check for understanding, then play the video for students to watch and answer the question. Let them compare answers in pairs before feedback, but keep this brief at this stage.

D ▶ Tell students to try to complete the summary from memory. Then play the video again for them to watch and check.

AUTHENTIC ENGLISH

A Go through the information in the box about the phrase *straight out of*, and give some other examples. Ask students to think about how they would say that in their language. Then put them into pairs to discuss the question.

B Go through the example, then put students into pairs to complete the other sentences.

C Combine the pairs with another pair to compare ideas. In feedback, ask students to explain why they completed the sentences in the way they did.

Hearing colors

A Put students into pairs to discuss the questions. In feedback, ask students to expand on their answers to generate as much interest as you can in the topic.

B ▶ Tell students to watch the video and to answer the questions. Make sure they realize that there is a *Not given* option, as well as *True* or *False*. Point out that the answer is *Not given* if the information doesn't appear in the video, so there is no way of knowing whether the sentence is true or false. Contrast this with *False*, where there is clear evidence to show that it is not true. You can find the **video script** for *Hearing colors* on the Teacher's Resource Center.

SPEAKING SKILL

A Put students into pairs to put the sentences in order. If they find this difficult, play the video again for them to watch and check.

B Point out the information in the box about *Recounting events*. Do the first one as an example, then tell students to match the sentences from Exercise A with the strategies in the box. In feedback, ask students if they use similar strategies when telling stories in their language.

SPEAKING HUB

A Tell students to decide what anecdote they're going to tell, either using one of the suggestions or their own idea.

B Tell students to refer to the *Recounting events* strategies to help them write notes about how they will sequence the story. Monitor to help or prompt if necessary, and make sure students are only writing notes and not writing out the story word for word.

C Put students into pairs to tell each other their anecdotes. Encourage them to listen carefully, to respond appropriately and to ask questions to ensure they fully understand all the details of their partner's story.

D Re-pair students and ask them to tell their new partner their previous partner's story, in as much detail as possible. In feedback, ask a few students which of the stories they heard was the most interesting, and why. Finish with feedback on students' use of language during the activity.

Extra activity

This activity could also be used before students watch the video *Hearing colors*. Elicit common objects or possessions that most people have, e.g. *a car*, *a phone*, *a bag*, etc. Ask students to discuss what color they prefer these things to be and why. Get feedback to find out how similar students' opinions are, and encourage further explanation or discussion if any surprising answers come up. If this activity is used at the end of the lesson, you can provide further practice of techniques for recounting events, by asking students to tell an anecdote related to a common object or a possession.

▶ VIDEO SCRIPT

Sound and vision
N = Narrator NH = Neil Harbisson

N: New York City. And this is Neil Harbisson. He has never seen color. (Ex C) Born with a condition called achromatopsia, he only sees a world of black and white. (Ex D Q1) But despite this limitation, Neil became an artist and in 2004 began an incredible journey to bring him closer to the world of color.

NH: There's lots of red things – very F street. This is more F-sharp. The woman sounded very high-pitch E. (Ex D Q2) I was always curious about color 'cause everyone is using it in daily life. They're mentioning it every single day, so (Ex D Q3) I was interested in sensing color, not because I wanted to change my sight, but because I wanted to have this element of color in my life.

(Ex D Q4) **N:** With the help of a team of engineers and doctors, he created something straight out of science fiction. Neil had an electronic device implanted inside his skull.

(Ex D Q5) **NH:** So this is a color sensor, it picks up light frequencies; it sends the light frequency to a chip (Ex D Q6) and then the chip transforms the light frequency into a real vibration that … that moves inside the skull, so the vibration in my skull becomes a sound (Ex D Q7) in my inner ear and each color has a different vibration so it creates a different note. So now the antenna is picking up the light frequencies of this color. People can see the light frequencies and they say it's blue. I can say it's blue because the light frequencies are being converted into a vibration in my skull. In the same way that people can see this frequency, I can sense it through vibrations in my head. (Ex D Q8) So, for example, red is very low, it's an F, then blue sounds C-sharp and the green sounds A, so when I look at this wall I hear lots of music, so it's a musical wall and there's lots of sound coming out of these colors.

4 Writing — Write a report

W — hedging

A Study the list of twenty words for one minute. Then try to write them all down.

experiment brilliant eccentric participant professor memory argument common sense fashion metaphor trend brainpower website conclusion project world-famous iconic obstacle self-portrait inspiration

B Work in groups. Compare the words that you remembered. Which words did most people remember?

C Read the report. Which words did the study find were more likely to be recalled? Why were these words more likely to be recalled?

INVESTIGATING SHORT-TERM AND LONG-TERM MEMORY

Introduction

This report describes an experiment to replicate the results of an earlier study. Murdock (1962) investigated the concepts of short-term and long-term memory by getting students to memorize a list of words. He found that students were more likely to recall the words at the beginning and end of the list. [a]He concluded that this **may** be because the words from the beginning of the list were stored in the long-term memory, whereas the words at the end of the list were stored in the short-term memory.

Methods

Thirty participants (16 men and 14 women) were asked to look at a list of 20 words for a minute. They were then asked to try to recall the words.

The words that participants wrote down were analyzed to see which words were recalled the most and if the position of the word in the list affected the students' ability to recall the word.

Results

The results confirmed Murdock's findings and showed that students were more likely to recall words from the beginning and end of the list.

Discussion

Murdock suggested that students studied the words at the beginning of the list more carefully, maybe by saying the words out loud. [b]**He believed that** this meant that the words had been processed enough to enter the long-term memory. [c]The words at the end of the list were the words students had just looked at, so these were **likely** to be stored in the short-term memory. [d]This study replicated Murdock's findings and **suggests** that his theory may be correct.

Conclusion

It can be concluded that when given information as a list, we are more likely to recall items from the beginning and end of the list.

D Look at the report again and match the report headings with the descriptions (1–5).

1. Analysis of the meaning of the findings Discussion
2. Description of participants and what was done Methods
3. The findings Results
4. A summary of the outcome Conclusion
5. An overview and background information Introduction

E Match the rules with the four sentences (a–d) in the report.

Hedging

In a scientific report unless something is a well-established fact, we should use hedging to make our claims less strong and less open to criticism. Use:

1. auxiliary verbs such as *may, might* and *could*: a
2. adverbs such as *probably, possibly* and *likely*: c
3. verbs that that allow for some doubt, such as *seem, appear, suggest, indicate*: d
4. introductory phrases to qualify, such as *We believe, We understand, In our view*: b

WRITING

A PREPARE Read about a similar experiment. Imagine you have recently replicated this experiment.

B WRITE Write a full report about it.

Glanzer and Cunitz (1966) did a similar experiment to Murdock, but they had two different groups. One group received the test immediately after looking at the words. The other group had a 30-second delay before they did the test and had to count backwards in threes from 99 during the delay. The results showed that although participants could recall the words from the start of the list, they could not recall the words from the end of the list. Glanzer and Cunitz concluded that this was because these words were no longer in participants' short-term memories because of the delay and the distraction.

References

Glanzer, M, & Cunitz, A R (1966) 'Two storage mechanisms in free recall' *Journal of Verbal Learning and Verbal Behavior*, 5(4), 351–360.

Answers

Words at the start of the list; they have been processed long enough to be stored in long-term memory

Refer students to this report as a model for the writing task.

Remind students to use hedging in their report.

WRITING

A Give students one minute to study the list of words and to remember as many as they can. After one minute, tell students to cover the list and to write down as many as they can remember.

B Put students into small groups to compare what they wrote down and to find out who remembered the most. In feedback, ask students how they remembered the words and which words they found easier or more difficult to remember.

C Tell students to read the report and to answer the questions.

The words from the beginning and end of the list were more likely to be recalled. The words from the beginning of the list had probably been stored in the long-term memory, whereas the words at the end of the list had probably been stored in the short-memory.

D Elicit the first one as an example, then tell students to read the report again and to match the descriptions to the headings.

E Point out the underlined sentences in the report and the information about *Hedging* in the box, and check students understand what is meant by hedging. Tell students to match the underlined sentences to the four methods of hedging. In feedback, ask if students use similar techniques when writing in their own language.

WRITING TASK

A Tell students to read about the experiment, and to imagine that they have recently replicated it. Get feedback to check they understand the details of the experiment.

B Explain that students are going to write a report about the experiment. Remind them about the structure of the report they read earlier, and tell them to use the same headings. Encourage them to use hedging techniques where appropriate, too. Monitor to help and prompt as students write their reports. When they have finished, tell them to swap reports with a partner and to read each other's. Encourage them to give each other feedback on how clear and effective the reports are.

Unit 4 Review

VOCABULARY

A Identify the conceptual metaphor in each sentence. Do you agree with the sentences?

1. If you're not learning something, you're wasting your time. time = money
2. Don't show that you're bright or people will expect big things. light = intelligence or knowledge
3. Always keep moving, but never go backwards. life = a journey
4. Invest in your friendships above all else. time = money
5. If you want to win an argument, attack first and attack hard. argument = war
6. Keep people in the dark about your goals until you succeed. light = intelligence or knowledge

B Replace the underlined words in the article with the words in the box. You may need to change the tense of the words.

conclude conduct demonstrate experiment findings hypothesize participants speculate the norm

Pavlovian responses

One of the most famous psychological [1]studies (experiments) was [2]done (conducted) by Ivan Pavlov, where the [3]subjects (participants) were dogs. Pavlov observed that all dogs naturally salivated whenever they saw food, so he [4]decided (concluded) this was not a behavior they had to learn.

However, he noticed that his dogs also salivated when his assistant, who frequently fed the dogs, walked into the room. Pavlov [5]guessed (speculated) that the dogs had learned to associate his assistant with food.

He [6]theorized (hypothesized) that the dogs could learn to associate a stimulus with food and would salivate when exposed to this stimulus even when no food was present. He rang a bell whenever he fed his dogs, so that this became [7]typical (the norm) for them.

After several sessions, he rang the bell when no food was present and his dogs salivated. His [8]results (findings) [9]showed (demonstrated) that dogs could learn an automatic response to a stimulus.

C Match the sentences (1–8) with the sentences (a–h) that have the same meanings.

1. You're great at troubleshooting. h
2. You frequently overthink things. f
3. You can be a little absent-minded. d
4. You have no common sense. g
5. You're a little eccentric. a
6. You frequently engage in wishful thinking. e
7. You're naturally curious about everything. c
8. You frequently have eureka moments. b

a You don't have conventional tastes.
b You have sudden instances of inspiration.
c You like learning about things and how they work.
d You are pretty forgetful.
e You're not always realistic when you think about future events or situations.
f You have a tendency to spend too much time considering an issue.
g You don't understand how to do basic things.
h You're good at analyzing and solving problems.

GRAMMAR

A Rewrite the beginning of the sentences using the words in parentheses. Then complete the sentences with your own ideas.

1. If all vehicles were automated … (*Were*)
   Were all vehicles automated, there would be a lot fewer traffic accidents.
2. If companies started selling robots to do the housework … (*Should*) Should companies start selling robots to do the housework, they would be very popular.
3. If schools employed robot teachers … (*Imagine*)
   Imagine if robot teachers were employed at schools and students didn't learn how to interact with people.
4. If humans could marry robots … (*Supposing*)
   Supposing humans could marry robots, it could lead to a decrease in the population.
5. If factories hadn't started using robots … (*Had*)
   Had factories not started using robots, there would be more jobs available.
6. If robots develop conscious thought … (*Suppose*)
   Suppose robots develop conscious thought, they could decide to disobey their makers.

B Choose the correct words to complete the sentences.

1. Jim wishes he *is* / *were* better at sports.
2. If only I *can* / *could* speak three languages.
3. She would love *have* / *to have* a better memory.
4. Tina and Bill wish they *could save* / *had saved* more money as they can't afford their mortgage this month.
5. We should *not eat* / *not have eaten* so much junk food when we were younger.
6. If only I *have* / *had* traveled more.
7. My brother ought to *spend* / *have spent* more time with our parents while they were visiting.
8. I wish I *can* / *could* cook.

Generation games – a grandma and granddaughter play.

Game (n) an activity that you do for fun that has rules and that you can win or lose.
Examples: *board game* (n), *card game* (n), *computer game* (n)

Benjamin Franklin means that games are important at all stages of life and play an important part in keeping us feeling young and full of life.

Benjamin Franklin (1706–1790) was one of the founding fathers of the United States, as well as being an author, politician and scientist, among other things.

OBJECTIVES

- discuss problem-solving tasks
- discuss gaming and game design
- identify generalizations
- discuss ideas for solving a challenge
- plan a fundraising event
- write a formal report

Work with a partner. Discuss the questions.

1 Look at the picture and read the quote. Why do you think people stop playing games? How does this make us 'grow old'?

2 What games did you like when you were younger? Did you stop playing these games? Why?

3 What games do you like now? Will you keep playing these games when you are older? Will you start any new games?

GAMES 49

OBJECTIVES

Read the unit objectives to the class.

UNIT OPENER QUESTIONS

1 Focus students on the photo, and elicit what they can see. Put them into pairs to discuss the questions. In feedback, elicit different possible interpretations of the game and a range of possible interpretations of the quote, as well as situations it could be applied to.

2 Elicit or give an example before students discuss the questions in pairs. In feedback, write on the board any useful language that comes up, especially types of game (e.g. *board game*, *card game*).

3 Give an example of your own again, then put students back into pairs to discuss the questions. In feedback, encourage students to expand on their answers and give reasons for them.

WORKSHEETS

Lesson 5.1 21st century games

Grammar: The passive voice (W21)

Vocabulary: Competition and cooperation (W21)

Lesson 5.2 Serious gaming

Vocabulary: Reporting verbs (W22)

Grammar: Passive reporting structures (W23)

Vocabulary: Motivation and manipulation (W23)

5.1 21st century games

- Discuss problem-solving tasks
- Discuss gaming and game design

G the passive voice **V** competition and cooperation **P** expressing disbelief **S** understanding colloquial asides

LISTENING

A SPEAK Read about escape rooms. Do they exist in your country? Are they popular? Why/Why not?

5.1 **B LISTEN FOR GIST** Listen to a conversation between three friends, Lin, Joe and Olga, in an escape room. The conversation is in three parts. Answer the same three questions after each part.

1 Which objects from the pictures did they mention for the first time?
2 Which problem(s) are they trying to solve in this part?
3 What do you think will happen next?

ESCAPE ROOMS

An escape room is a game where a group of people try to escape from a locked room, for example by finding hidden objects, solving clues and working as a team. The idea came from TV shows and computer games with similar problem-solving activities. Escape rooms started in Japan in 2007 and quickly spread around the world. They are popular with children (as venues for birthday parties) and adults (for team-building exercises). There are now over 2,800 escape room venues worldwide.

5.1 **C LISTEN FOR DETAIL** Listen to the whole conversation again. Choose the correct options (a, b or c) to answer the questions.

1 Apart from the metal bar, why can't they get the key out?
   a The cylinder is too deep to reach the bottom.
   b They're worried about breaking the cylinder.
   c The cylinder is too narrow for their arms.
2 How many of the friends have read the instructions?
   a one
   b two
   c three
3 Why can't they use the vase to transfer the oil?
   a It's full of water.
   b It's too big.
   c It can't be moved.
4 Why didn't they notice the message before?
   a The room was too bright.
   b They didn't look in the right direction.
   c They couldn't open the drawer.
5 Why does Joe want to keep playing?
   a He's having too much fun.
   b He's sure they've found all the clues.
   c He thinks people will laugh at him.
6 Why was the towel necessary?
   a Because they needed an accurate measurement.
   b Because the ball was too slippery to hold.
   c Because they needed to weigh it on the scale.

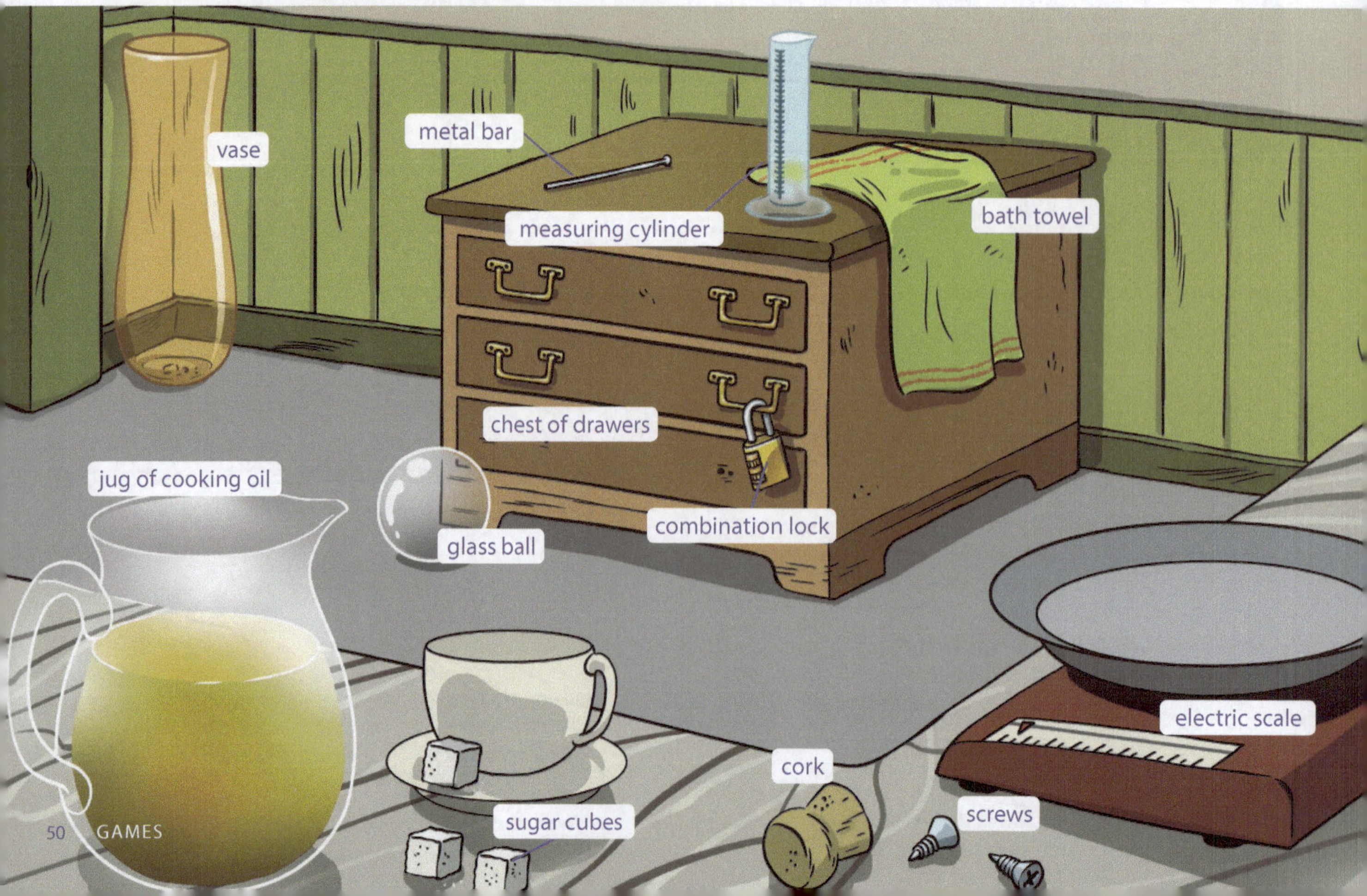

5.1 21st century games

LEAD-IN

Put students into pairs to discuss what they think *escape room* means.

LISTENING

5.1 **A–D** Put students into pairs to complete the exercises.

B Answers

1 *Part 1: measuring cylinder, metal bar, combination lock, cork; Part 2: vase, jug of cooking oil, chest of drawers, electric scale, bath towel, sugar cubes; Part 3: screws, glass ball*

2 *Part 1: get the key out of the measuring cylinder. Problem: bar across the top with lock, cylinder attached to wall.*
Part 2: how to fill the measuring cylinder with water/oil, get the oil out of the jug, open the third drawer, use the sugar cubes. Problem: jug is fixed to the shelf and the vase is too big.
Part 3: how to open the drawer, work out the lock, transfer the oil.

AUDIO SCRIPT

5.1

Listening, Exercise B
J = Joe O = Olga L = Lin

Part 1

J: OK, so we've been locked in. So where's the key?
Ex B Q1 **L:** Found it! It's at the bottom of this measuring cylinder.
J: Really?! That was easy!
Ex B Q1 Ex B Q2 **L:** Yeah, but there's a metal bar across the top with a combination lock attached to it. No way will we get that big key through this narrow gap.
O: So we need to figure out the combination to remove the bar, right?
Ex C Q1 **L:** Exactly. But even if we could do that, my arm's nowhere near long enough to reach the key at the bottom.
O: Can you tip it upside down?
L: Nah, it's attached to the wall. It can't be moved.
J: Try pulling it really hard.
O: Seriously?! That's cheating! Anyway, we'll get thrown out if anything gets broken! According to the instructions, we're not allowed to use force to move things!
Ex C Q2 **J:** I don't remember being given any instructions.
O: We were asked to sign a form at the front desk. Those were the instructions, Joe!
J: Ah, I wondered what that form was.
Ex C Q2 **L:** Didn't you read it?!
J: Uh, sorry. I just signed it.
L: Unbelievable! Anyway, there are microphones all over the place, so we're probably being listened to right now!
J: OK, so we need to get the key out of the cylinder without touching it. But that's impossible.
Ex B Q1 **O:** Not necessarily. Look. There's a cork attached to the key.

Part 2

Ex B Q2 **O:** I think the cylinder needs to be filled with water. Then the cork will float to the top, lifting the key with it.
Ex B Q1 **L:** Well, there's some water in this big vase, but nowhere near enough to fill that measuring cylinder.
J: What about this cooking oil? Do you think the cork will float on oil?
O: Absolutely. Bring it over here.
Ex B Q2 **J:** Hmm, I can't. The jug's attached to the shelf.
L: Typical! Could we use the vase to transfer the oil?
Ex C Q3 Ex B Q1 Ex B Q1 **O:** No. It needs to be something small enough to fit inside the jug and scoop out the oil. There must be a cup hidden somewhere. What's in that chest of drawers, Lin?
Ex B Q1 Ex B Q2 **L:** Let's take a look. An electric scale, a bath towel and, hmm, there's no handle on the bottom drawer. I can't open it. Any ideas?
J: Uh, maybe it'll open if we press that switch on the wall.
L: It's just a light switch, Joe! It won't … Oh amazing! You just turned all the lights off! Excellent!
Ex C Q4 **J:** Wait! I did it! Look up! There's a secret message on the ceiling! It must have been written in flourescent paint – it's only visible in the dark. But it's just one word: sugar.
Ex B Q1 **O:** Really? There are some sugar cubes on the shelf, but how does that help us?

Part 3

L: This is ridiculous. We've been stuck in here for almost an hour. We should've been given more clues. Should we give up?
Ex C Q5 **J:** Give up?! No way! I told all my friends I'm great at puzzles. If we give up now, I'll be made fun of for weeks. There must be a clue somewhere – something we're missing.
O: I've figured it out! Something must have been hidden inside those sugar cubes! We need to dissolve them in water!
J: Yesss! There's some water in that vase.
O: Great! They're dissolving. And I was right. There's something there. What is it? Something metal?
Ex B Q1 Aha! Two screws!
L: Screws? What are we supposed to do with them?
Ex B Q2 **O:** We can screw them into the holes in the drawer and use them to pull it open. Just a second.
Ex B Q1 **J:** You did it! You've found the cup! We're free!
Ex B Q2 **L:** Are you joking?! We still need to remove the metal bar from the cylinder, which means working out the combination to that lock.
J: Oh yeah, I forgot.
L: Joe! We have two minutes left! Think of something!
J: Stop yelling at me! I can't think when I'm being yelled at!
Ex B Q2 **O:** I suppose at least we can transfer the oil to the cylinder while we're thinking. Pass me the cup. Thanks. Ooh! There's something in the jug!
L: Yeah right! There's nothing there besides the oil. You need to get your eyes tested! Oh!
Ex B Q1 **O:** I was right! A glass ball. Maybe we're supposed to weigh it.
J: Great! But it's covered in oil, and so are you! Be careful not to drop it!
Ex C Q6 **O:** Aha, that's what the towel's for! We need to clean the oil off it first!
L: OK, but hurry up! We only have 60 seconds!
O: Calm down! OK, it weighs one kilogram 327 grams. Try that combination, Joe! One three two seven.
J: One, three, two, seven. Yes! It worked. Quick, bring the oil over! How much time do we have?
L: Forty-five seconds! Come on! Hurry up!

5.1 21st century games

GRAMMAR

A Make sure students realize that the sentences are all from the conversation they listened to. Go through the example, then tell students to complete the second sentences so that they are in the passive voice while having the same meaning as the first. In feedback, elicit what effect the use of the passive voice in the second sentence has, and why it might be used rather than the active.

B Explain that the sentences are all complex forms of the passive voice. Point out the information in the box about *The passive voice*, and tell students to match the sentences with the rules.

C Direct students to the **Grammar Hub** (see below and TB53).

D Do an example for the first one with a stronger student, then put students into pairs to ask and answer questions about the topics. Use the **Grammar Worksheet** on page W21 for extra practice.

PRONUNCIATION

5.2 **A** Tell students to try to match the extracts with the responses, then play the recording for them to listen and check.

5.3 **B** Students listen to the pairs of sentences and do the task. Get feedback, then tell students to practice saying the sentences. Model the first pair yourself, exaggerating slightly to make sure students all attempt the practice wholeheartedly.

C Go through the example, then give your own and encourage students to respond with disbelief, using some of the phrases from Exercise A. Students then practice in pairs.

SPEAKING

Elicit some ideas from the class, and express disbelief at their suggestions. Then put students into small groups to do more. Get feedback on the most imaginative ideas, and comment on students' use of language during the activity.

Extra activity

Give each student a small piece of paper, and tell them to write something strange but true about themselves on it, e.g. *I used to play the trumpet*. Tell them it should be something their classmates don't know about, and not to show it to anyone else. Collect the pieces of paper and redistribute to other students, making sure that no one has their own. Students then move around the room and ask each other if the fact on their piece of paper applies to them, e.g. *Did you use to play the trumpet?* Whenever they are asked, students should say that the fact is true for them and try to answer as convincingly as possible. Students ask further questions to check details of the stories, expressing disbelief where appropriate.

When everyone has spoken to everyone else, get the class together again. Each student can say who they think wrote the fact on their piece of paper, and find out if they are correct. Encourage students to ask each other more questions to find out more information about the true stories once the real writers have been revealed. Since this activity could take a long time, this could be done in smaller groups if necessary.

GRAMMAR HUB

5.1 The passive voice

	Passive voice
make sb do sth	We **were made to wait** for over an hour.
Passive voice with *-ing*	I hate **being kept** waiting.
Passive voice with infinitive	He would like **to be given** the chance to retake the test.
get passive voice (informal)	They **got thrown** off the course.
Causative *have* and *get*	I need to **have** my phone **serviced.**

- Remember that we use the passive voice when we don't say who or what causes the action (usually because the person or thing is not known, not important or not obvious).

  *We **were made to take** the exam again.* NOT ~~*We were made by the examination board to take the exam again.*~~

- We use *by* when we know who does/did an action and we want to mention it.

  *I don't mind being told **by my boss** to work late but I don't like it when I have to cover for other people.*

- We can use an infinitive or *-ing* passive voice form, depending on the verb or construction that comes before it. Some verbs can be followed by an infinitive or *-ing* with no or little change in meaning. Prepositions are always followed by *-ing*.

  *We arranged **to be** paid in cash.*
  *I appreciated **being** told about the delay.*
  *The child loved **to be** / **being** thrown up in the air.*
  *Johnny never talks about **being** thrown out of college.*

- We use the causative (in any tense) when someone does something for us, or when we are victims of a crime or accident. The causative with *have* is more formal than the causative with *get*.

  *I **got** my hair cut.* OR *I **had** my wallet stolen on the train.*

- We can use *get* + object + past participle when we talk about causing something to happen or be done by somebody else.

  She is popular because she gets things done.
  They are angry because they are not getting their packages delivered on time.

- We can also use *get* + object + *-ing* to talk about causing someone or something to do something.

  The book on game theory got Susan thinking.

Be careful!

- In both the *get* passive voice and the causative, *get* is usually less formal than *have*. Don't use it in formal situations.

  The letter asked us when we had had the house built. NOT ~~*The letter asked us when we had got the house built.*~~

D SPEAK Work in pairs and discuss the questions.

1 How could they have escaped more quickly?
2 Do you think you would have solved all the puzzles?
3 How long would it have taken you to escape from the room?

GRAMMAR
The passive voice

A Look at these sentences from the conversation. Complete the second sentence so that it is in the passive voice.

1 OK, so they've locked us in.
OK, so, *we've been locked in.*
2 Somebody's probably listening to us right now!
We're probably being listened to right now!
3 Somebody must have written it in fluorescent paint.
It must have been written in fluorescent paint.
4 They should have given us more clues.
We should have been given more clues.
5 If we give up now, my friends will make fun of me for weeks.
If we give up now, I'll be made fun of for weeks.
6 I can't think when somebody's shouting at me!
I can't think when I'm being yelled at!

B Match the sentences (1–5) with the rules (a–d).

The passive voice

a In the structure *make sb do sth*, you need to add *to* in the passive voice (e.g. 3).
b You can make the passive voice from *-ing* forms (e.g. 2) and infinitives (e.g. 4).
c The *get*-passive voice (*get* + past participle) is somewhat informal. Use it to describe unexpected/unwanted events (e.g. 1). It's also useful for distinguishing actions (e.g. *to get married*) from states (e.g. *to be married*).
d Use the causative passive voice (*have/get* + something + past participle) to focus on the person who organizes/pays for a service (e.g. 5) or is the victim of a crime (e.g. *I had my car stolen*).

1 We'll get thrown out if anything gets broken!
2 I don't remember being given any instructions.
3 We were made to sign a form at the front desk.
4 I think the cylinder needs to be filled with water.
5 You need to get your eyes tested!

C Go to the **Grammar Hub** on **page 130**.

D SPEAK Work in pairs. Ask and answer questions about these topics.

- a way you like/don't like being treated
- a time when you were made to do something
- something you've had done recently/you need to get done soon
- a time when you got lost/stuck/delayed, etc

A: I hate being treated like a child.
B: Really? When do you get treated like that? Who by?

PRONUNCIATION
Expressing disbelief

5.2 **A** Match the extracts from the conversation (1–7) with the responses (a–g). Then listen to check.

1 It's at the bottom of this measuring cylinder. f
2 Try pulling it really hard. d
3 I wondered what that form was. b
4 Should we give up? c
5 Something metal? Aha! Two screws. a
6 You did it! We're free! g
7 There's something in the jug! e

a Screws? What are we supposed to do with them?
b Didn't you read it?
c Give up? No way!
d Seriously? That's cheating!
e Yeah right! There's nothing there apart from the oil.
f Really? That was easy!
g Are you joking? We still need to remove the metal bar.

5.3 **B** Listen and decide in which sentence (a or b) the speaker is expressing disbelief.

1 b 2 a 3 a 4 b

C SPEAK Work in pairs. Take turns to talk about something surprising you did this month. Express disbelief at your partner's statements.

A: I volunteered to teach in India.
B: Really? India? No way!

SPEAKING

DISCUSS Work in small groups. Imagine the room you're in now is an escape room. What clues might help you to escape? Where might those clues be hidden? Express disbelief at each other's suggestions.

READING

A SKIM Look at the picture and the title of the blog post. What do you think urban games are? Skim the blog post to check.

B READ FOR GIST Read the blog post. Which game (a–d) …

1 isn't only played in cities? b
2 teaches you about a place while you play? d
3 has more viewers than live players? a
4 has players who stand out from the crowd? c
5 can be confusing to play? a
6 takes advantage of a weakness in technology? b

a Hidden Bonds
b Geocaching
c Pac Manhattan
d Poznan Beyond Time

URBAN GAMES TURN CITIES INTO PLAYGROUNDS

Glossary

encapsulate (v) to express something in a short clear form that gives the most important facts or ideas

gobble (v) to eat something quickly and usually noisily

It's 6 am and I'm sitting on Trafalgar Square, feeling apprehensive. [1]What on Earth have I let myself in for? The square is virtually empty but I have the distinct feeling I'm being watched by thousands of curious eyes. I receive an SMS: 'Follow the man with the striped umbrella. Don't let him see you.' I spot the man in the distance, jump to my feet and set off in hot pursuit, heart pounding.

I'm playing *Hidden Bonds*, one of the new generation of urban games that are taking off in cities around the world. Urban games encapsulate the best elements of computer games and transfer them to the real world, adding social and physical dimensions to activities that would otherwise involve sitting alone for hours in a darkened room – [2]something I'm all too familiar with!

Urban games originated from a game called *Geocaching*, which uses GPS devices to create virtual treasure hunts. Players are given the GPS coordinates of special boxes called caches, which could be hidden anywhere in the world. (Ex B Q1) Part of the challenge comes from the limitations of GPS, which is only accurate to within a dozen or so meters, so you need to use your eyes. (Ex B Q6) After locating a cache, you win the prize inside – but you must replace it with an appropriate prize for the next player. [3]Sounds amazing, right? … If you're into trudging around muddy fields disoriented and in the middle of nowhere! (Ex B Q1)

One of the best-known modern urban games is *Pac Manhattan*, a version of the arcade game *Pac Man*, played out on the bustling, grid-like streets of New York. [4]How cool is that? Players dressed up as brightly-colored characters from the game race around city blocks, gobbling up virtual 'dots' as they go (Ex B Q4) – and trying to **outmaneuver rival** players to avoid being caught.

Luckily, some urban games are played at a more moderate pace. Visitors to Poznan in Poland can choose from a range of treasure-hunt games to explore the city, while solving clues about the city's cultural heritage and history. (Ex B Q2) For example, in *Poznan Beyond Time*, players embark on a time-traveling adventure to save the world. All you need is a printed game sheet … and some good walking shoes – [5]as I learned through experience!

Then there are games played out for an online audience – which brings me back to *Hidden Bonds*. It's fairly complicated, (Ex B Q5) but in a nutshell, there are four teams, each represented by five 'agents' on the streets of London. The objective is to **cooperate** with your **allies** to **overcome** rival agents, by sending a Bluetooth message to their phone before they can send one to yours. Problem is, the agents have no idea who the other agents are and who's just a normal passer-by, which can lead to some embarrassing moments, (Ex B Q5) [6]I can tell you! The agents receive instructions on their cell phones from 'spymasters', who **coordinate** the players' movements based on the votes of hundreds of 'team members' watching the game live online. (Ex B Q3) The team with the last remaining agent **prevails.**

At a rough estimate, I'd say I've played *Hidden Bonds* as an online team member about 50 times – [7]yeah, sad, I know. **Collaborating** with hundreds of strangers is surprisingly satisfying, but playing live is altogether more exhilarating, especially when you come face-to-face with a rival agent. I managed to catch four opponents before getting caught myself mid-afternoon. Only later did I realize that I'd walked over 20 kilometers in the process! [8]Pretty impressive, right? I'd do it again tomorrow if I could, but there's a seven-month waiting list to participate again as an agent. [9]Just my luck, huh?

5.1 21st century games

READING

A Focus students on the pictures and elicit what they can see. Put them into pairs to discuss the question. Then tell students to read the text quickly to find out.

B Set a time limit and tell students to read quickly to match the games to the sentences.

C Go through the information in the box and the first example in the blog post to ensure students are clear what an *aside* is.

D Put students into pairs to discuss the questions. In feedback, encourage students to expand on their answers.

METHODOLOGY HUB by Scott Thornbury

Genres

A genre is any type of spoken or written discourse which is used and recognized by members of a particular culture or subculture. As a genre becomes established, it acquires a conventionalized structure and, usually, a characteristic vocabulary and grammar. Examples of written genres are news reports, academic papers and magazine horoscopes. Spoken genres include sports commentaries, answer phone messages and business presentations. The specialized nature of many genres can make them difficult for non-members of the 'in-group' to understand. For example, the following is an instance of a genre that botanists would recognize as being a *botanical description*:

> **Corncockle.** *Agrostemma githago* L., plant, gray with shaggy hairs, 30–100cm; lvs opposite, linear; sepals 5, united into a bell-shaped tube, with long spreading lobes; corolla purple, 3–5cm wide, much exceeded by the free calyx teeth; seeds poisonous! Fl.6–7. Cornfields; formerly widespread, but now rare due to efficient seed cleaning. Almost all of Europe. Protected!
>
> Schauer, T. *A Field Guide to the Wild Flowers of Britain and Europe*. (Collins, 1992) p.62.

The specialized vocabulary, the long noun phrases, the use of abbreviations and ellipsis – as well as the way the information is sequenced and punctuated – are generic features of this type of text. They are also consistent with the text's function, which is 'to describe for the purposes of identification'. (Imagine how different the text would be if it were a poem about the corncockle, or the instructions on a packet of corncockle seeds.) Anyone wishing to become a member of the discourse community that uses this genre (i.e. botanists) will need to know how to interpret – and maybe even how to reproduce – these generic features. This will involve choices at the macro level, that is, the overall organization, and the micro level: the specific grammatical and lexical features.

There are several schools of genre theory, the most influential being that associated with systemic functional linguistics (SFL). SFL distinguishes between genre and register – a distinction that is typically ignored or conflated in other schools of textual analysis. Practitioners of genre analysis investigate not only the formal features of genres, but they also attempt to relate these to their social contexts and purposes. The fact that genre knowledge provides 'entry' into a culture supports the case for the teaching of specific genres, especially in English for specific purposes and English as a second language contexts.

GRAMMAR HUB

5.1 The passive voice

A Find the mistakes and correct them. Some sentences are correct.

1 I was made to fill in pages of details on the form. Correct
2 I dislike ~~to be~~ being spoken to as if I don't understand anything.
3 He looks forward to ~~be~~ being spoiled when he visits his family.
4 In my school, we used to get told off for the slightest things. Correct
5 You look different – have you had your hair done? Correct
6 Do you know what we were ~~made do~~ made to do in the intelligence test?

B Complete the sentences with the correct *-ing* or infinitive passive voice form of the verb in parentheses.

1 I miss being able to spend summer vacation days on the beach. (*be able to*)
2 Justine begged to be forgiven for the things she'd said in anger. (*forgive*)
3 The taller kids tended to be chosen for basketball, regardless of their ability. (*choose*)
4 The manager wouldn't tolerate being disagreed with. (*disagree*)
5 Paul didn't mention being stopped by the police – do you think he's hiding something? (*stop*)
6 He couldn't remember being lifted onto an elephant, although he had the photo to prove it had happened. (*lift*)

C Complete the sentences in the passive voice or causative form.

1 Active: They made him sign the document.
Passive: He was made to sign the document.
2 Active: If you're not careful, they'll throw you out.
Passive: If you're not careful, you'll get/be thrown out.
3 Active: I'd like to know how much it costs for you to clean my car professionally.
Causative: I'd like to know how much it costs to get/have my car cleaned professionally.
4 Active: How on earth are we going to find someone to repair that window on a Sunday?
Causative: How on earth are we going to get that window repaired on a Sunday?
5 Active: I'm sure they didn't tell me to be here half an hour early.
Passive: I don't remember being/getting told to be here half an hour early.
6 Active: Someone will steal your car if you leave it there.
Causative: You'll get your car stolen if you leave it there.

➤ Go back to page 51.

5.1 21st century games

VOCABULARY

A Point out the words in bold in the text, and tell students to match them to the definitions. Elicit the first one as an example, demonstrating how to use the context to work out and check the meaning. Put students into pairs to do the rest. In feedback, be ready with extra examples to help fully clarify the meaning if necessary. Practice pronunciation of some items (e.g. *opponents*, *allies*, *cooperate*, *coordinate*) where necessary.

B Direct students to the **Vocabulary Hub** (see TB121).

C Give your own opinion as an example, then put students into groups to discuss the questions. In feedback, elicit as many examples as you can and ask students to expand on their answers. Write on the board useful language that comes up, and give feedback on students' use of language, praising successes and correcting errors. Use the **Vocabulary Worksheet** on page W21 for extra practice.

SPEAKING HUB

A Put students into pairs and tell them they're going to plan an urban game. Tell them they can use ideas from the blog post or their own ideas. Tell them to make notes, and monitor to help or prompt if necessary.

B Combine pairs to present their games to each other. Tell them to listen carefully and to ask questions about how exactly the game works and any other details they'd like to know.

C Tell the groups to decide which one of the games to develop more fully. Tell them to write down rules and step-by-step instructions. Again, monitor to help or prompt where needed.

D Tell each group to present their game to the class. Encourage the other students to ask questions at the end of each presentation. Then put students back into their groups to decide which of the other games they would most like to play. In feedback, find out which game was the most popular and why. Finish with feedback on students' use of language during the activity.

Extra activity

Elicit examples of other kinds of games that could be invented, e.g. *rural games*, *office games*, *living room games*, *grocery store games*. Put students into pairs to think of an example of some of the categories, which could be either serious or ridiculous. Get feedback and find out if anyone thinks any of the games could work.

METHODOLOGY HUB by Scott Thornbury

TAVI vs TALO

Some texts' primary purpose is not to inform or entertain us but rather to display features of the language that have been pre-selected for teaching purposes. When the aim is solely language display, then texts don't need to be true or interesting.

But there is the other – skills development – reason for reading or listening to texts in the classroom. Learners need to become more efficient listeners and readers in their second language. Part of being an efficient reader/listener is having the capacity to extract information from a text, especially the information you need or are interested in. It follows that listeners need to hone their reading and listening skills by using texts that are truly informative and where the information is of a type that learners may be motivated to seek out. Hence, not only should learners be exposed to texts designed to display pre-selection language features, that is, *texts as linguistic objects*, or TALOs, but they should also learn to cope with *texts as vehicles for information*, or TAVIs.

For the first purpose, i.e. TALO, it used to be thought that contrived texts would do. We now know that these kinds of texts tend not to be sufficiently representative of language 'as it is really used'. For the second purpose, i.e. TAVI, authentic texts were felt to offer the best training for real-life text processing. However, authentic texts, as we have seen, are typically too difficult for learners to deal with, and rather than developing fluent reading or listening, they may actually inhibit it.

The solution? Combine the two purposes in one text. The text can be simplified – in the interests of intelligibility – but also informative. Moreover, it can be re-worked to include pre-selected language items. Or, better, it can be chosen because it already includes pre-selected language items. And the tasks that accompany the text can focus on both its contents (i.e. TAVI-type tasks) and its linguistic forms (TALO-type tasks).

METHODOLOGY HUB by Scott Thornbury

Discussion

Discussions and debates provide learners with opportunities to interact freely and spontaneously, to cope with unpredictability and to voice opinions using language that is both complex and fluent. They are generally more structured than conversation, and involve arguing for or against a particular point of view. For this reason, there is always the risk that they might get out of hand, that learners might feel unduly constrained by the target language and revert to their first language, or that certain learners will dominate while others remain silent. Here are some ways of minimizing these risks:

- To start with, focus on the specific rather than the general. For example, rather than start a general discussion on the topic of drug use in sports, give learners a short news item describing a particular case.
- Allow learners time in advance of an open-class discussion to formulate their point of view, to access vocabulary (using dictionaries, for example) and to compare opinions (in pairs or small groups).
- Appoint a chairperson, whose job it is to allocate turns and ensure all learners participate.
- Establish some ground rules, such as:
    - Only one person can speak at a time.
    - Ask permission to speak.
    - Use people's names (not *She/You said …* but *Marta said …*), etc.
- Equip learners with a repertoire of expressions for voicing strong agreement, strong disagreement and all the shades of opinion in between (agreeing/disagreeing; opinion, giving and asking for). These could be made available on posters around the room.
- Take advantage of discussions that emerge spontaneously, as a result of something that someone says or from the textbook, for example. The best discussions are often those that happen naturally.

C UNDERSTAND ASIDES Look at the asides (1–9) underlined in the blog post. Then answer the questions (a–f). Use the information in the box to help you.

Understanding colloquial asides

Colloquial asides are informal phrases that comment on other information in the text (e.g. *Not bad, huh?*). They frequently take the form of questions or exclamations and they make a text feel more chatty, personal and friendly.

Asides can reveal the writer's personality and attitudes. However, watch out for irony, where the writer means the opposite of what they've written.

Which aside(s) …

- **a** express(es) genuine enthusiasm? 4 8
- **b** is/are likely to be irony? 3
- **c** suggest(s) the writer feels guilty about their lifestyle? 2 7
- **d** show(s) how the writer felt at the beginning? 1
- **e** suggest(s) the writer frequently describes frustrations in their blog posts? 9
- **f** hint(s) at problems the writer experienced while playing? 5 6

D SPEAK Work in pairs and discuss the questions.

1. Which games from the blog post would you like to play? Why?
2. Which would you not want to play? Why?
3. Can you think of any dangers or weaknesses of urban games?
4. Why do you think games like this have become more popular?

VOCABULARY
Competition and cooperation

A Match the words in bold in the blog post with the definitions.

1. collaborating (v) working in partnership
2. allies (n) people on the same side as you
3. prevails (v) wins (e.g. after a long contest)
4. coordinate (v) organize people working together
5. overcome (v) beat another player or solve a problem
6. rival (n) a person competing against you
7. cooperate (v) help/support others

B Go to the Vocabulary Hub on page 144.

C SPEAK Work in groups and discuss the questions.

1. Do you prefer games that involve overcoming rivals or cooperating with allies? Think of examples.
2. Think of examples of sports or games where you have to outsmart, outmaneuver, outplay or outrun your opponents.

SPEAKING HUB

A PLAN Work in pairs. Create an urban game for your town/city. Use ideas from the blog post and your own ideas.

B DISCUSS Present your ideas to another pair. Ask and answer questions about how your game ideas will work in practice.

C PREPARE Choose one game idea to develop more fully as a group. Write some simple rules or instructions for your game.

D PRESENT Present your ideas to the class. Which games would you most like to play? Why?

- Discuss problem-solving tasks
- Discuss gaming and game design

5.2 Serious gaming

- Identify generalizations
- Discuss ideas for solving a challenge

G – passive reporting structures
P – *-ate* words
V – reporting verbs; motivation and manipulation
S – distinguishing generalizations from preferred solutions

LISTENING

A SPEAK Work in pairs. Read *The Food Truck problem*. Discuss two or three possible solutions.

B Work in small groups. You are going to think of a solution for three more puzzles. Go to the **Communication Hub** on **page 151**.

5.4 **C LISTEN FOR SOLUTIONS** Listen to the presentation on Game Theory. What are the correct answers to the puzzles? Use the information in the box to help you.

Distinguishing generalizations from preferred solutions

A speaker frequently presents his or her preferred solution to a problem or puzzle, alongside obvious but problematic solutions or generalizations. Frequently, the generalization is discussed first, before the speaker's preferred solution.

Use the following techniques to distinguish the preferred solution.

- Pay attention to the order in which the speaker presents solutions. Preferred solutions may be presented later.
- Listen for phrases that signal a generalization (e.g. *it seems obvious, you might expect, according to conventional wisdom*).
- Listen for solutions presented with questioning intonation. This may indicate the speaker does not believe this is the correct answer.
- Listen for attitude words like adverbs which can show that the speaker has a skeptical or cautious attitude to a solution (e.g. *presumably, allegedly*).

5.4 **D LISTEN FOR DETAIL** Listen again. Are these sentences true (T) or false (F)? Correct the false sentences.

1 In puzzle A neither participant is likely to win any money. (T) / F
2 Game Theory uses ~~scientific~~ mathematical models to find solutions. T / (F)
3 The favorite in talent shows ~~is rarely eliminated~~ has reportedly been eliminated many times in reality. T / (F)
4 The food truck owner in C has no good reason to move. (T) / F
5 The new network would ~~double the amount of~~ have twice as much traffic. T / (F)

PRONUNCIATION

-ate words

5.5 **A** The suffix *-ate* has two pronunciations. Listen to the extracts from the presentation on Game Theory. Complete the table with the words in the box.

accurate appropriate complicated cooperate eliminated fascinating

/eɪt/	/ət/
cooperate	accurate
complicated	appropriate
fascinating	
eliminated	

B SPEAK Work in groups . Discuss the following questions.

- Do you prefer games where you have to cooperate with others rather than compete individually?
- What is the most fascinating sporting event you've ever watched?
- Do you prefer playing simple or complicated games?

PUZZLE C:
THE FOOD TRUCK PROBLEM

You decide to open a food truck business.
There's already one other food truck in town, which always parks in the town center (point C).
Where's the best place to park your food truck? You can negotiate with the other food truck owner, if you wish.

5.2 Serious gaming

LEAD-IN

Books closed. Elicit different types of puzzle (e.g. *jigsaw puzzle, crossword, Sudoku, riddles, logic puzzles*), and write them on the board. Put students into pairs to discuss if they like doing these, if they're good at them and if they think puzzles are a useful way to spend time.

LISTENING

A Put the students into pairs and tell them to read *The Food Truck problem* puzzle. Tell them to discuss their solutions, and in feedback encourage students to explain their answers and to agree with or challenge each other's ideas, but don't give the correct answer yet.

B Put students into small groups and direct them to the **Communication Hub** (see TB121). Tell them to discuss solutions to the puzzles. In feedback, again encourage students to explain their answers and to agree or disagree with each other. Again, don't give the correct answers yet.

5.4 **C** Tell students they're going to listen to a presentation about game theory. Explain that they will hear the answers to the puzzles in the presentation, and point out the information in the box about *Distinguishing generalizations from preferred solutions*. Ask students to read that, then to listen and check the answers to the puzzles.

Puzzle A: Play once: TAKE the money. Play many times: one of the best strategies is to SHARE first, then copy your opponent's previous move (but it isn't always the best).

Puzzle B: your favorite contestant

Puzzle C: Point C

Puzzle D: Nowhere. A new road would make the problems worse.

5.4 **D** Put students into pairs to try to remember if the sentences are true or false. Then play the recording again for them to listen and check. In feedback, elicit why the sentences are true or false.

PRONUNCIATION

5.5 **A** Point out the box and model the two different pronunciations of the suffix *-ate*. Tell students to listen to the extracts from the presentation and to complete the table. In feedback, practice pronunciation of the words. You can also mention that some words ending in *-ate* will have different pronunciations depending on whether they are verbs or nouns (e.g. *estimate*).

B Put students into small groups to discuss the questions. In feedback, ask students to expand on their answers.

AUDIO SCRIPT

5.4

Listening, Exercise C
P = Presenter

P: So? What did you make of puzzle A – the Take or Share game? The fairest outcome would be for both of you to choose SHARE, and to win $500 each. Sadly, it's more complicated than that. By choosing that option, you're risking losing everything. (Ex C) It turns out that the best strategy in a one-round game is to be selfish, because you have a 50/50 chance of winning $1,000, which is better than a 50/50 chance of winning $500. The problem is, your opponent can be assumed to be having the same thoughts, so (Ex D Q1) you'll both probably end up with nothing anyway!

This example comes from (Ex D Q2) Game Theory, which involves using mathematical models to solve problems where your choices affect – and are affected by – other people's choices. It allows for more accurate predictions and estimates.

Coming back to puzzle A, things get really fascinating over several rounds, because now you can reward your partner's kindness, or punish his or her selfishness. For example, if you share the money in the first round, you're implying that you're willing to cooperate. (Ex C) It turns out that one of the best approaches over several rounds is to share in round 1 and then spend the rest of the game copying your opponent's previous move. However, it's important to acknowledge that this strategy doesn't always work.

Let's turn to puzzle B – the Talent Show Dilemma. If there's a clear favorite, you might conclude that voting for her would be a waste of your precious vote, because she's expected to win by a landslide anyway. Supposedly then the most appropriate solution is to vote for your second favorite contestant, to make the final more interesting. But if everyone follows the same strategy, no one will vote for the favorite, and she'll be eliminated! (Ex D Q3) This type of thing is reported to have happened many times in real life – not just in talent shows, but also in important elections. (Ex C) So in such situations, I'd urge you to resist the temptation to vote tactically, and to vote for your own favorite.

What about puzzle C – the Food Truck problem? The answer seems obvious, right? You should put your truck at point B and instruct the other truck to move to point D – or vice versa. That way, you serve half the town each, and all the town's residents have one food truck fairly close. (Ex D Q4) Wonderful, except that the other owner has no incentive to move her truck from point C. If you park at point B, she can simply assert that she's staying in her prime spot in the town center, and end up with three-quarters of the town's customers. (Ex C) The only way for you to get 50% is to park right next to her at point C! Even if a hundred new food trucks arrived, they'd each be better off by clustering together in a single point.

Finally, what about puzzle D – the road network? To reduce congestion, we need to build a new fast road between Smallton and Littlemarket, right? It's common sense, isn't it? But let's check. In the original network, there are two routes between the two big towns, so half the traffic is likely to choose each route. But in the new 'improved' network, there's now one obvious route that everyone's going to choose. (Ex C, Ex D Q5) So it'll have almost twice as much traffic as either of the old routes, and the whole network will have much worse congestion than before!

5.2 Serious gaming

VOCABULARY

A Make sure students realize that all the sentences come from the presentation about game theory. Tell them to replace the underlined phrases with a verb from the box with the same meaning. In feedback, give more examples where necessary to consolidate understanding of the meaning of the verbs, and practice pronunciation where necessary, too.

B Direct students to the **Vocabulary Hub** (see TB121).

C–D Give one or two examples of your own, then ask students to complete the sentences with their own ideas. Put them into pairs to discuss their answers. Then change pairs so students can report to a new partner what their previous partner told them. In feedback, ask students to share with the class some of the most interesting answers they heard and give feedback on their use of reporting verbs. Use the **Vocabulary Worksheet** on page W22 for extra practice.

GRAMMAR

A Elicit the first one as an example, then tell students to work on the rest. Encourage them to work in pairs on this.

B Students use the sentences from Exercise A to help them complete the rules.

C Direct students to the **Grammar Hub** (see below and TB56).

D Put students into pairs to discuss the questions. In feedback, allow students to suggest various answers. Use the **Grammar Worksheet** on page W23 for extra practice.

1 *When we don't know or don't care who said or thought something; when we're reporting the speech or thoughts of people in general.*

2 *Rumors are spread by a lot of people, so it doesn't make sense to say that a particular person did it.*

3 *It's shorter than the version with it + passive reporting verb + that clause. The human subject (rather than impersonal it) also makes it less formal.*

SPEAKING

Go through the example with the class, then put students into pairs to think of more. In feedback, write on the board good sentences that come up, and comment on how successfully students have used passive reporting structures.

Extra activity

Elicit some recent events in the news, and ask how students could report them using the structures from this lesson. Put students into pairs to think of another topical person and event and to write some sentences about it using passive report structures. Instruct students not to say who the person or what the event is. When they have finished, put pairs into larger groups to read their sentences to each other. Tell students to listen carefully and to decide who or what is being described.

GRAMMAR HUB

5.2 Passive voice reporting structures

- Some verbs, such as *allege*, *assume*, *believe*, *expect*, *know*, *say*, *report*, *rumor*, *suppose*, *understand*, are often used in the passive voice as reporting verbs. The verb *rumor* can only be used in this way.
- We frequently use the impersonal *it* with these verbs.

  It is rumored that the President will announce her resignation today. (= There is a rumor that ...)
- With an impersonal *it* passive voice, we can follow the reporting verb with either an infinitive or *that*.

  *It is understood **to be** a complicated situation.*

  *It is understood **that** the situation is complicated.*
- With a personal reporting structure, beginning with *I/you/he/she/it/we/they*, we use the past participle of the reporting verb, followed by infinitive.

infinitive	He **is known to be** a thief.
progressive infinitive	She **is thought to be planning** a comeback.
perfect infinitive	They **are rumored to have started** a secret mission.
perfect progressive infinitive	They **are believed to have been watching** us.

- We can sometimes use modal verbs before the reporting verb.

  It can be assumed that the business is still profitable.
- In both personal and impersonal constructions, we can use the reporting verb in the past if we are referring to something people *expected/knew/thought*, etc. However, if the action was done in the past, and we are reporting it now, the verbs must reflect this.

  *He **was** known to be hiding.*

  *It **was** thought that they **had failed**.*

  *He **is** understood to **have made** contact.*

  *It **is** believed that he **discovered** America.*

Be careful!

- Do not use *that* in a personal passive voice (one that begins with *I/You/He/She*, etc).

  He is rumored to be planning to make cuts. NOT ~~*He is rumored that he is planning to make cuts.*~~

VOCABULARY

Reporting verbs

A **Replace the underlined words in each sentence with the correct form of the verbs in the box.**

acknowledge assert conclude imply instruct urge

1 If you share the money, you're <u>saying indirectly</u> [implying] that you're willing to cooperate.
2 It's important to <u>say (although it makes my argument weaker)</u> [acknowledge] that this strategy doesn't always work.
3 You might <u>decide after thinking carefully</u> [conclude] that voting for her would be a waste.
4 So I'd <u>strongly advise</u> [urge] you to resist the temptation to vote tactically.
5 You should <u>give instructions to</u> [instruct] the other truck to move to point D.
6 She can simply <u>state as a fact</u> [assert] that she's staying in her prime spot.

B Go to the **Vocabulary Hub** on **page 144**.

C **SPEAK** **Complete the sentences with your own ideas. Then discuss your sentences with a partner.**

- I firmly believe that …
- I'm not sure whether …
- I'm great at …
- Maybe if I'd done … I might not have …
- You really must …

D **Swap partners and report what your previous partner said using reporting verbs.**

GRAMMAR

Passive reporting structures

A **Complete the sentences so they mean the same as the passive voice sentences with *It*.**

1 It can be assumed that your opponent is having the same thoughts.
Your opponent can be ___assumed to be___ having the same thoughts.
2 It is said that Game Theory is one of the hardest branches of mathematics.
Game Theory is ___said to be___ one of the hardest branches of mathematics.
3 It's rumored that sports coaches have been experimenting with Game Theory.
Sports coaches ___are rumored to___ have been experimenting with Game Theory.
4 It's expected that she'll win by a landslide.
___She's expected___ to win by a landslide.
5 It's reported that this type of thing has happened many times in real life.
This type of thing ___is reported to have___ happened many times in real life.

B **WORK IT OUT** **Complete the rules about passive reporting structures with information from Exercise A.**

Passive reporting structures

Reporting verbs can be used with passive voice structures when we want to introduce a widely held opinion or fact. There are two main ways of doing this.

- ___*It*___ + passive voice + ___*that*___ clause
- ___*It*___ + passive voice + infinitive

Some verbs commonly used with these structures are: ___*assume*___, ___*expect*___, ___*report*___, ___*rumor*___ and ___*say*___.

C Go to the **Grammar Hub** on **page 130**.

D **SPEAK** **Work in pairs and discuss the questions.**

1 When is it useful to use the passive voice to report speech/thoughts?
2 Why do you think 'to rumor' has no active voice form?
3 What's the advantage of using the structure with an infinitive?

SPEAKING

DISCUSS **Work in pairs to think of examples of how Game Theory might be used in sports, business, etc. Use the structure with an infinitive to report generalizations, expectations and assumptions.**

The best time to make an investment is assumed to be when the price is low, but if everyone has the same idea at the same time, then …

READING

A SPEAK What tricks do smartphone games use to keep people playing again and again? Try to think of other situations where these tricks are used.

B SKIM Read *Gamification: treading the line between motivation and manipulation*. Are any situations from Exercise A mentioned?

C READ FOR DETAIL Read the article again. According to the article, are these sentences true (T) or false (F)? Correct the false sentences.

1. Many companies are ~~not yet aware of the potential of~~ [already tapping into] gamification. T / (F)
2. Virtual prizes can still be highly motivating. (T) / F
3. The majority of people ~~are aware~~ [probably didn't realize] that gamification has been used on them at some point. T / (F)
4. The major benefit of gamification for charities is that it ~~increases financial donations.~~ [fosters a sense of community.] T / (F)
5. Gamification is used to help people recover from injuries. (T) / F
6. ~~A brand new~~ [An] interactive show ~~is being~~ [was] developed by a production company. T / (F)
7. Gamification sometimes encourages people to behave in a way that isn't right. (T) / F
8. The personality of workers may affect how motivating gamification techniques are. (T) / F

D Work in pairs. Look at the two quotes from Christabel Maware and Lisa Tanaka in the article. Which speaker do you agree with most? Why?

VOCABULARY

Motivation and manipulation

A Match numbers (1–7) with letters (a–g) to form full sentences. Then check by looking for the underlined phrases in the article.

1. As a result of marketing tricks, customers **went** e
2. Getting into the college **spurred** c
3. People don't mind working hard if you can **tap** g
4. If people know *why* they're doing something, they'll be more **inclined** … a
5. Gamification can make people **act against** … f
6. We offered virtual prizes to **coax** … b
7. The online store is designed to **steer** people … d

a. to spend time doing it properly.
b. people **into** giving us their data.
c. **me on** to study harder for the exams.
d. **toward** the most expensive products.
e. **nuts for** the new product.
f. **their best interests**.
g. **into** their natural desire to do a good job.

B Look at the complete sentences in Exercise A. Decide whether the phrases in bold are related to motivation or manipulation. Motivation: 2, 3, 4; Manipulation: 1, 5, 6, 7

C Go to the **Vocabulary Hub** on **page 145**.

D SPEAK Work in pairs. Think of examples from your own experience of each verb in Exercise A. Tell your partner your examples.

My friend tried to coax me into editing her dissertation for her.

SPEAKING HUB

A PREPARE Work in small groups. Choose one of the following challenges, or a similar idea, to solve with your group.

- How to motivate children to read/write more
- How to encourage people to pick up trash

B PLAN Discuss ideas for solving your challenge, using Game Theory and/or gamification techniques.

C PRESENT Present your challenge and solution to the class. Ask and answer questions about how it will work in practice.

D REFLECT Discuss with the class. Which solutions have a chance of becoming popular? Could they make money?

5.2 Serious gaming

READING

A Ask students what smartphone games they know, and if they play them. Elicit one example of a trick they use and another situation where this trick is used, e.g. *in advertising campaigns or TV series*. Put students into pairs to think of more examples.

Suggested answers

Tricks: Targets; points; competitions; reminders; ads; rewards

Other situations: buying particular products and services; eating healthily; keeping active; learning a language / a new skill; posting updates on social media; visiting new places (e.g. restaurants, museums); working harder in your job

B Instruct students to read the article and to check how many of the suggestions on the board are mentioned. Tell them to read quickly at this stage, and let them compare in pairs before feedback.

to get people to use stairs at subway stations; to encourage good habits in school classrooms; for charities to retain and build membership; to encourage physical activity in general/specialized healthcare; to make television shows more appealing; in business to improve employee performance

C Students decide if the sentences are true or false, correcting the false ones.

D Put students into pairs to discuss the question. In feedback, ask students to explain their opinions.

VOCABULARY

A Make sure students realize that the sentences are all from the article, but ask them not to look at the text as they match the sentence halves.

B Elicit the first one as an example, and check students understand what is meant by *motivation* and *manipulation*. Tell students to categorize the other sentences.

C Direct students to the **Vocabulary Hub** (see TB121).

D Go through the example, and give another of your own. Then put students into pairs to think of more examples. Use the **Vocabulary Worksheet** on page W23 for extra practice.

Extra activity

Encourage students to research one article on the theme of manipulation and one article on the theme of motivation online.

If they find examples of the phrases from the lesson, they can add these in the text with blanks (i.e. by copying it into a word processor and removing the phrase or part of the phrase). They should also underline any other useful vocabulary related to motivation or manipulation they find.

Ask students to bring their texts to class. Put them into small groups to see if they can complete any answer blanks. Each group should also sort any new phrases from answer blanks into vocabulary related to manipulation or motivation.

GRAMMAR HUB

5.2 Passive reporting structures

A Choose the correct options to complete the sentences.

1. We are supposed *to be* / *to be being* there at nine o'clock.
2. It is rumored *to be* / *that* the company is having difficulty.
3. Two members of staff are alleged to *transfer* / *have transferred* money into private accounts.
4. It *is* / *was* originally thought that they were related.
5. They are believed to *plan* / *be planning* a trip overseas.
6. The police are known to *be* / *have been* following him recently.
7. It was thought that there *was* / *to be* a secret tunnel, but nothing has been found.
8. On her first day, *it* / *she* was expected to write three reports.

B Complete the text with a suitable form of the verbs in the box.

announce discuss focus look make plan

Director disputes

Home Articles About us Contact

Following tomorrow's meeting, Collins is expected [1] to announce his resignation. The company is thought [2] to to be planning to specialize in the near future. They are expected [3] to focus on only one product, and Collins is known [4] to have made his objections to this very clear on several occasions in the past. Although Collins is understood [5] to have been discussing / to have discussed the situation with top management for several weeks, the company is now rumored [6] to be looking for a way to force him out.

C Rewrite the sentences using both personal and impersonal passive voice structures. Use the reporting verb in bold.

1. People **believe** he is very rich.
   He is believed to be very rich.
   It is believed (that) he is very rich.
2. Some people **report** that he was awarded over one million dollars.
   He is reported to have been awarded over one million dollars.
   It is reported that he was / has been awarded over one million dollars.
3. They **say** she knows her subject inside out.
   She is said to know her subject inside out.
   It is said (that) she knows her subject inside out.
4. Critics **claim** that the game's story is too complex.
   The game's story is claimed to be too complex.
   It is claimed that the game's story is too complex.
5. Many **think** that it is a complex problem.
   The problem is thought to be complex.
   It is thought (that) the problem is complex.
6. People **assume** she is shy but she's just quiet.
   She is assumed to be shy but she's just quiet.
   It is assumed (that) she is shy but she's just quiet.

➤ Go back to page 55.

5.2 Serious gaming

SPEAKING HUB

A Put students into small groups and tell them to choose one of the challenges or one of their own.

B Students stay in their groups and discuss ideas for solving their challenge. Elicit or remind students about game theory and gamification techniques, and tell them to make use of these in their solution. Monitor to help or prompt if necessary.

C Each group presents their idea to the class. Tell the other students to listen carefully and to ask questions at the end of each presentation.

D Ask students first to discuss the questions in their groups, then open it up to a whole-class discussion. Encourage students to expand on and explain their opinions. Does the class agree on the most promising idea? Finish with feedback on students' use of language during the activity.

Extra activity
Elicit some of the ways that the article about gamification claimed that technology will influence the future of entertainment. Put students into pairs to make more predictions about the future of entertainment, which could be serious or humorous. Get feedback on students' different ideas.

METHODOLOGY HUB by Scott Thornbury

Ways of organizing discussions

- Pyramid discussions:
  Learners have to reach an agreement, in pairs, about an issue. This could be by modifying a statement (e.g. *Children should never be yelled at*) so they both agree on it, or by ranking a list of items (e.g. qualities of a good friend) in the order they think are most important. They then form groups of four, then eight, and then sixteen, etc, each time repeating the process.
- Balloon debate:
  Learners represent different jobs or famous people (alive or dead) in a hot-air balloon. One member of the group must be sacrificed to save the sinking balloon, so each has to argue why they should be spared.
- Formal debate:
  Learners form teams and each team alternates to argue for a motion (e.g. *Homework should be banned*) and to rebut the arguments of the opposing team. Other learners form the audience and vote for the winning team.

Discussions can also take place online, and discussion boards are key features in most learning management systems. Contributions to online discussions are typically written, i.e. keyed in, rather than spoken. They can take place in real time (synchronously) but more often they occur asynchronously: participants post their responses to the discussion question, revisiting the discussion over a fixed time period to read and respond to the posts of other students.

Online discussions work best when there is a clear task to which everyone must contribute, and an outcome. For example:

Post a picture of a person you admire, and tell us why he or she is important to you. Comment on the choices of your classmates. Then decide what three values all the class thinks are really important.

METHODOLOGY HUB by Jim Scrivener

Approaches to speaking

How to organize learners in speaking tasks

Getting the physical arrangements right is typically a big part of getting a speaking activity to work well. That may seem an obvious enough comment, but it's interesting how frequently teachers set up a group speaking activity and then, for example, leave students sitting in shoulder-to-shoulder lines. It's hard to talk to someone you can't make eye contact with (though sometimes you may want to play around with this idea, for example, deliberately keeping students apart when practicing 'phone calls').

Learners usually need to be able to:

- make eye contact with those they are speaking to;
- hear clearly what the other person/people are saying;
- be reasonably close together.

Different variations of seating/standing arrangements can be useful. Plan the arrangement carefully to match the requirements of the specific activity; for example, you may want an arrangement that allows students to talk secretly without other teams overhearing (e.g. making plans for a confrontational 'public inquiry' meeting to be held later in the lesson).

Devising a discussion activity

The subject is 'pop festivals'. Devise a discussion activity suitable for a range of levels.

Commentary

One possible idea: in groups, plan a pop festival for our town. Who should be invited to play? Where would it be? What problems might there be? How will we keep the locals happy? Finally, design an advertisement poster to include important information and encourage visitors to come. At the end, the separate groups pin up their posters around the walls and visit each other's. In the role of potential visitors and festival organizers, they ask and answer questions.

METHODOLOGY HUB by Scott Thornbury

Gamification

What motivates the players of most computer games is the challenge to earn points (or badges) and to accumulate enough to advance to the next level. Importing the same principle into the design of classroom and online activities is called gamification. This might be as simple as rewarding good written work with points or creating a class 'leaderboard' (i.e. a chart showing the names of the students and the number of points they have earned); similarly, a points-and-levels feature might be integrated into the design of vocabulary learning apps. Critics of gamification argue that it promotes a somewhat behaviorist view of learning, and that earning badges is no substitute for getting personalized feedback. On the other hand, by taking some of the drudgery out of the more mechanical aspects of language learning – such as memorizing vocabulary – it may motivate otherwise lazy learners.

GAMIFICATION

treading the line between MOTIVATION and MANIPULATION

Hitting the treadmill before work, ploughing through deadlines, and finding time to study in the evenings. Maybe these aren't the sort of activities you'd necessarily associate with fun. Yet a glut of apps, websites and online communities that place game-like experiences right at the center of motivation might give you pause for thought. None of this is news for many commercial Ex C Q1 and public organizations which are already **tapping into** gamification – the application of elements from gameplay psychology to everyday tasks.

Gamification is about more than creating new games for non-gaming contexts. At its heart lies an understanding of the powerful principles that underlie gameplay, the elements that make it so compelling to so many: gratification, competition and rewards. Games increase engagement. Giving people rewards even virtual ones Ex C Q2 releases dopamine, the feel-good hormone. This leads them to associate that activity or behavior with positive emotions. And that's frequently enough to **spur them on** to repeat it.

The applications of this are diverse: **steering commuters toward** the stairs over the escalator on the Odenplan subway in Sweden by turning them into a giant piano staircase or promoting good learning habits and classroom behavior by giving students 'experience points'. It's highly likely you've experienced gamification yourself, although Ex C Q3 you probably didn't realize it.

So how can this benefit us? Gamification has made inroads into both the not-for-profit and health sectors. For charities, its greatest potential lies not in fundraising Ex C Q4 but in fostering a sense of community. If volunteers feel part of an engaged community, they are more **inclined to** stay. Furthermore, they can be incentivized to recruit others or blog about a cause through rewards.

Gamification can also be integrated directly into grassroots campaigning. Hopelab's Zamzee, a physical activity program for families, uses child engagement with technology to improve health. It guides younger users toward doing more physical activity through an activity sensor and a 'physical points' reward system. More Ex C Q5 specialized healthcare like physical rehabilitation is using and trialing similar approaches. The Medical Interactive Recovery System (Mira) uses a camera to track a patient's physiotherapy movements and translate them into actions within a video game.

Glossary

crave (v) to want something very much and in a way that is very hard to control
incentivize (v) to give someone a reason for wanting to do something
grassroots (adj) relating to or involving ordinary people, especially in politics
plough (v) to finish something that takes a long time and is difficult or boring
recognition (n) praise, respect or admiration

As well as bringing fun to areas where it might be wanting, gamification promises to take fun to the next level in traditional entertainment. Younger and more technologically-savvy viewers may crave an immersive experience, being able to participate in a TV show rather than simply view it. Well, now they can have both their needs for compelling stories and recognition or rewards for their gaming achievements, met at the same time. For example, the popular sci-fi TV show, *Defiance*, by Ex C Universal Cable Productions, allowed viewers to shape Q6 the plot of television episodes through their actions in an accompanying game.

Some are cautious about gamification, precisely because of its power and how widely it is being used. 'If it can help change our behavior, it can also manipulate us to Ex C **act against** our best interests', warns technology lecturer Q7 and game designer Christabel Maware. 'I can see it being used very cynically to exploit consumers and employees.' Some companies and organizations have already been Ex C called out. For example, a ride-sharing app was criticized Q7 for supposedly encouraging drivers to drive further without breaks.

And even where gamification is encouraging 'healthy' competition or making a mundane but necessary work task more appealing, there are concerns around work freedom and surveillance. While leader boards and badges can keep us motivated, having our performance and potentially complex interactions monitored, graded and immediately reported back on by machines sounds more dystopian. 'Simply, not everyone is going to **go nuts** Ex C **for** badges at work', says a Recruitment Manager for Q8 AdTech Analytics. For workers who are more introverted or prefer to work privately, this kind of surveillance might be unwelcome and demotivating.

As Lisa Tanaka, founder and CEO of creative agency Gamified International puts it, 'On balance gamification can bring some very positive benefits to many sectors. This stuff works, our brains really are hard-wired for rewards and fun is addictive. We're already being **coaxed into** doing all kinds of things. But with such a powerful tool, there's a pressing need now for companies to be socially responsible in how they use it.'

- Identify generalizations
- Discuss ideas for solving a challenge

Café Hub

5.3 Win or lose

A– *ellipsis* S– building relationships

Would you risk it?

A Work in pairs. What do you think is happening in the pictures (a and b) from the video?

B 00.00–01.00 Watch the first part of a video about an experiment. Answer the questions.

1 What happens if the coin lands on heads?
The person wins £10.
2 What happens if the coin lands on tails?
The person doesn't win any more money.

Glossary

flip (v) to turn over quickly or to make something turn over
heads (n) the side of a coin that has a picture of a head on it
scenario (n) a situation that could possibly happen
tails (n) the side of a coin that does not have a picture of a person on it

C 01.00–01.30 Watch the second part of the video. Choose the best option (a, b or c) to complete the sentence.

In this situation most people …

a take a risk and maybe win an extra ten pounds or nothing.
(b) choose the safe option and take fifteen pounds.
c risk it for the chance to win an extra five pounds.

D 01.30–02.20 Work in pairs. Watch the third part of the video and complete the sentences with the correct option.

1 In the second scenario you are given *ten* / *twenty* pounds.
2 You have to choose to accept a safe loss of *five* / *ten* pounds or take a risk.
3 You flip a coin. If it comes up heads, you don't lose anything, but if it comes up tails, you lose *five* / *ten* pounds.

E 02.20–03.27 Watch the last part of the video. What do most people do in the second scenario? Why?
Most people take a risk. Professor Paul Dolan explains that the pain of losing £10 feels greater than the joy of finding £10. You would have to find £20 to offset the pain that you feel by losing £10.

AUTHENTIC ENGLISH

A Work in pairs. Read the sentence from the video and the information in the box. What word has been left out of the sentence?

Would you choose the safe option and get an extra five pounds or take a risk and maybe win an extra ten ^pounds *or nothing?*

Ellipsis

Ellipsis is the practice of leaving a word or words out of a sentence when they are not necessary for understanding it. In spoken English, unstressed words are frequently left out at the beginning of sentences if the meaning remains clear.

B Work in pairs. Match the questions (1–6) with the replies (a–f). Then cross out any words which can be omitted from each question and reply.

1 ~~Did you~~ enjoy your vacation? f
2 ~~Are you~~ ready yet? a
3 ~~Is~~ your dad any better? c
4 ~~Are~~ you coming out ~~with us tonight~~? e
5 ~~Did you have~~ any luck with the tickets ~~for the Beyoncé concert~~? d
6 ~~I'm sorry, are~~ you talking to me? b

a ~~I'm~~ almost ready. ~~I'm~~ just putting on my makeup.
b ~~Yes, I~~ was asking if you're doing anything nice on the weekend.
c Yes, thanks. ~~He~~ should be out on the weekend.
d No, ~~they were~~ all sold out. ~~It's a~~ shame, really.
e ~~I'm afraid, I~~ can't. ~~I~~ have to work late.
f ~~It was~~ absolutely amazing! Just got back, actually.

C Work in pairs. Take it turns to ask each other short questions from Exercise B and reply with your own short answers.

How sure are you?

SAM MALCOLM AMANDA HARRY EMILY

A Work in pairs. Look at the picture.

1 What board games are popular in your country?

2 Do you ever play them?

B Watch the video. Answer the questions.

1 If Sam and Amanda go in a counter-clockwise direction, which category do they land on? Entertainment

2 Why does Amanda think Geography is the better option? She thinks it's better to get your bad subjects out of the way earlier.

3 How does Sam feel about Amanda's strategy? disagrees

4 How does Malcolm indicate the correct answer to Sam and Amanda? He rustles his newspaper and coughs.

5 How does Amanda suggest making the game more interesting? miss two turns for right answer, two extra turns if wrong

6 Why doesn't Emily want to take the risk? thinks Malcolm doesn't know much about sports

7 What's the question Emily and Harry have to answer? Which footballer/soccer player won the Ballon d'Or in 2017?

8 What's Malcolm's answer? Is he correct? Messi. No.

SPEAKING SKILL

A Work in pairs. Look at the underlined expression from the video and answer the questions.

1 What is Harry doing? signaling agreement with what Sam has said

2 Why do we do this when we're speaking? to indicate that we agree with what another person says

Sam:	Don't you think it's better to play it safe and go for your strongest categories first ... you know ... try and build up a lead?
Harry:	<u>That sounds like a solid strategy to me</u>.

B Look at the information in the box. Decide which strategy (a or b) is being used in the exchanges (1–4) from the video.

Building relationships

We can build relationships using the following strategies.

a Agreeing with the other person by adding on to what they have said.

b Relating to what the other person has said by evaluating or commenting.

1	**Sam:**	I'm thinking we should go for Geography.
	Amanda:	Totally ... I absolutely hate Geography ... it's better to try and get it out of the way earlier. a
2	**Emily:**	Ah, good – this is quite hard, I think.
	Sam:	That is quite tricky. a
3	**Sam:**	OK, it can only be one of two countries ...
	Amanda:	... either Finland or Norway. b
4	**Emily:**	I mean sport hardly looks like it would be Malcolm's strongest category. b
	Harry:	I guess not but he is smart.

C Work in small groups. Give your opinions on one of the following topics. Use the strategies from Exercise B to build a positive rapport.

- your favorite board game
- your favorite type of movie
- your favorite type of book

SPEAKING HUB

A PLAN Work in small groups. You are going to plan a fundraising event for a local charity. Decide on one of the following.

a dinner   a board game evening   a yoga class
a bake off   a fashion show   a quiz

B PREPARE Individually think about the preparations for the event. Consider the following points.

- space
- logistics
- timing
- cost

C PRESENT Work in small groups. Decide on a course of action for the event. Try to build up positive relationships and create a consensus.

A: We could hold a banquet dinner at the town hall.

B: Great idea! It could go on all evening.

Plan a fundraising event

➤ Turn to page 160 to learn how to write a formal report about gamification.

5.3 Win or lose

Would you risk it?

A–E ▶ 00:00–3:27 Allow students to compare answers in pairs after each exercise, before checking understanding as a class.

AUTHENTIC ENGLISH

A Go through the information in the box about *Ellipsis* and give some more examples. Then put students into pairs, and tell them to read the sentence from the video and to answer the question.

B Elicit the first one as an example, then tell students to stay in the same pairs and to match the questions with the replies, crossing out any words that can be omitted.

C Ask a student to ask you one of the questions, then reply with your own answer. Then ask a question to a stronger student for them to answer with their own idea. Put students into pairs to do the same together with the questions from Exercise B.

How sure are you?

A Focus students on the pictures, then put them into pairs to discuss the questions.

B ▶ Tell students to watch the video and to answer the questions. Let them compare in pairs before feedback. You can find the **video script** for *Win or lose* on the Teacher's Resource Center.

SPEAKING SKILL

A–C Model with a stronger student before the class discuss the topics in small groups.

SPEAKING HUB

A Put students into groups and ask them to choose one of the events.

B Tell students to work individually to think and make notes about the points. Monitor and help with language if needed.

C Put students back into their groups for them to present their ideas to each other.

▶ VIDEO SCRIPT

Would you risk it?
J = Journalist F1 = Female 1 N = Narrator
F2 = Female 2 F3 = Female 3 M1 = Male 1
F4 = Female 4 F5 = Female 5 F6 = Female 6
P = Professor Paul Dolan

J: Excuse me, guys. Can you spare two minutes to help us with a little experiment where you have to try and win as much money as you can? OK?
F1: OK.
J: OK. In my hands here, I have £20. OK?
N: Here are two scenarios …
J: And I'm going to give you 10.
N: In the first case, you're given £10.
J: That's now yours. Put it in your pocket, take it away. Spend it on a drink on the South Bank later.
F2: OK, OK.
J: OK.
F1: OK.
N: Then you have to make a choice about how much more you could gain.
J: You can either take the safe option, in which case I give you an additional 5, or you can take a risk. If you
Ex B Q1 take a risk, I'm going to flip this coin, and if it
Ex B Q2 comes up heads, you win 10, but if it comes up tails, you're not going to win any more.
N: Would you choose the safe option and get an extra £5, or take a risk and maybe win an extra 10 or nothing?
J: Which is it going to be?
F3: I'd go safe.
J: Safe 5?
F3: Yeah.
M1: Take 5.
J: Take 5?
M1: Yeah, man.
J: Sure? There we go.
Ex C **N:** Most people presented with this choice go for the certainty of the extra fiver.
M1: Thank you very much.
J: All right. Told you it was easy.
N: In a winning frame of mind, people are naturally rather cautious.
J: That's yours, too.
F1: That was it?
J: That was it.
F1: Really?
J: Yes.
F1: Eh?
N: But what about losing? Are we similarly cautious when faced with a potential loss?
J: In my hands, I've got £20. I'm going to give that to you – that's now yours.
F4: OK.
J: You can put it in your handbag.
Ex D Q1 **N:** This time, you're given £20 and again you must make
Ex D Q2 a choice – would you choose to accept a safe loss of £5 or would you take a risk?
J: If you take a risk, I'm going to flip this coin, if it comes
Ex D Q3 up heads, you don't lose anything, but if it comes up tails, then you lose £10.
N: In fact, it's exactly the same outcome. In both cases, you face a choice between ending up with a certain £15 and tossing a coin to get either 10 or 20.
F5: I will risk losing 10, I think.
J: OK.
N: But the crucial surprise here is that when the choice is framed in terms of a loss, most people take a risk.
F6: Take a risk.
J: Take a risk? OK?
F4: I'll risk it.
J: You'll risk it? OK.
N: Our slow system two could probably work out that the outcome is the same in both cases.
J: And that's heads. You win.
N: But it's too limited and too lazy.
J: That's the easiest £20 you'll ever make.
N: Instead, fast system one makes a rough guess based on change.
J: And that's all there is to it. Thank you very much.
F2: Oh no!
N: And system one doesn't like losing.
F2: Thank you very much!
Ex E **P:** If you were to lose £10 in the street today and then find £10 tomorrow, you would be financially unchanged but actually we respond to changes so the pain of the loss of £10 looms much larger – it feels more painful. In fact, you'd probably have to find £20 to offset the pain that you feel by losing 10.

5 Writing

Write a formal report

W using depersonalization

A Read the report and answer the questions.

1 Who commissioned the report? Why?
2 What worked well in the two case studies? What went wrong?
3 Which elements does the writer recommend copying? What would the writer change?

Using games to attract tourists to Littlemarket

Background
At a recent meeting of the Littlemarket Tourism Board, [1]it was proposed that an investigation should be conducted into the use of urban gaming and gamification to attract tourists. This report summarizes the research and provides a series of recommendations.

Case study 1: Bighampton
Two years ago, the tourism board in Bighampton launched a series of treasure-hunt worksheets for tourists, which [2]were reported to be enjoyable by 55% of participants. However, they were found to be too easy by 25%. The games were moderately successful in attracting tourists to some lesser known attractions, but the overall impact on tourist numbers was minimal (a 1.5% rise).

Case study 2: Smallton
Last year, the Smallton Tourism Board developed an app to gamify tourists' experience of the town. Badges could be won for visiting particular cafés, museums and other attractions. [3]In spite of widespread frustration with technical problems, the results were impressive, with some cafés and restaurants reporting an 80% increase in sales. [4]It remains to be seen how successful the app has been at boosting overall tourist numbers, but initial indications are positive.

Recommendations
[5]It would be relatively cheap and simple to develop a series of printable treasure hunt maps. Ideally, a range of levels (beginner to expert) would be offered. However, [6]it would be necessary to invest significantly in marketing [7]to raise awareness of the games. [8]It would also make sense to use the gamification techniques from Smallton's experiment to encourage tourists to spend more money. Unlike Smallton, we should involve local businesses in the costs of developing and promoting our games.

The costs of developing an app are currently beyond our budget, so I recommend gaining experience first with a cheaper, low-tech solution and then, if appropriate, upgrading to a sophisticated technical solution in two to three years.

B Complete the examples with the extracts (1–7) from the report.

Using depersonalization

Depersonalization involves removing people from your writing to make it more formal. Depersonalization techniques include:

a *it* + *be* + adjective + infinitive: *we could cheaply and easily* → 5 ; *we'd need to* → 6
b preposition + noun: *Although many people got frustrated* → 3
c changing verbs into nouns or adjectives: *55% of participants said they had enjoyed* → 2 ; *to inform people about* → 7
d the passive voice: *somebody proposed that* → 1
e other impersonal phrases: *We still don't know* → 4 ; *we should also* → 8

WRITING

A PREPARE Work in groups. You have been asked to write a report for a language school about using games to attract new students and improve language skills. Discuss how escape rooms, urban games, game theory or gamification could help your language school.

B PLAN Imagine two or three case studies involving other language schools. Write notes about each case study in your plan.

C WRITE Write your report. Use depersonalization techniques to make it suitably formal.

D REVIEW Exchange your report with a partner. Do you use similar techniques? Comment on how your partner has used depersonalization.

E EDIT Read your partner's comments. Rewrite any parts you think should change.

160 WRITING

Answer

It was commissioned by the Littlemarket Tourism Board to investigate how to use urban gaming and gamification to attract new tourists.

Answers

Case study 1:
What worked well? 55% liked the treasure hunts; increased visitor numbers at some lesser known attractions.
What went wrong? 25% found the treasure hunts too easy; minimal overall impact on tourist numbers.

Case study 2:
What worked well? Impressive results for participating businesses.
What went wrong? Frustration with technical problems.

Answers

Case study 1:
Copy: Printable treasure hunts
Change: Offer a range of levels; invest more in marketing.

Case study 2:
Copy: Gamification techniques; develop an app (but in two to three years).
Change: Involve local businesses in the costs.

WRITING

A Students read the report and answer the questions.

B Focus students on the information in the box about *Using depersonalization*, and tell them that the underlined phrases in the report are examples of the techniques in the box. Tell students to match them. In feedback, make sure students appreciate that this is a technique to use in formal writing.

WRITING TASK

A Explain the task, then put students into groups to think of ideas. Get some class feedback, and write on the board any useful language that comes up or that students need.

B Tell students to work individually to imagine and make notes about the case studies. Monitor to prompt or to help with language if needed.

C Tell students to write their report. Remind them to refer to the report they read earlier as a guide on how to structure their report, and encourage them to use some of the depersonalization techniques as well.

D Tell students to swap reports with a partner and to read each other's. Tell them to give each other written feedback on how clear and effective the reports are and also on how well they have used depersonalization.

E Tell students to swap back and to read their partner's comments. Tell them to make any changes they think necessary after reading the feedback.

Unit 5 Review

VOCABULARY

A Complete the instructions with the correct form of a word in the box.

ally collaborate cooperate coordinate overcome prevail rival

Bike clash

The game involves outmaneuvering players on [1] rival teams by racing around the city on bikes. Each team has four players, who [2] collaborate with each other, and a 'boss', who [3] coordinates their movements. By [4] cooperating with their [5] allies, players solve puzzles to identify the times and locations of 'clashes', where they try to [6] overcome their rivals. When a clash begins, the team with the most players wins a 'trophy'. Any teams that have been outnumbered lose a player. At the end, the team with the most trophies [7] prevails.

B Choose the correct word to complete each sentence.

1 Stores are laid out to ***discourage / steer / trigger*** customers toward expensive items.
2 Salespeople try to manipulate us by ***coaxing / dissuading / exploiting*** us into spending more than we intended.
3 Loyalty cards can make people ***act / spur / tempt*** against their best interests.
4 My sister ***spurred / influenced / dissuaded*** me on to enter the race.
5 I wasn't ***exploited / inclined / influenced*** to go, but you've persuaded me.
6 Advertising can ***tap / tempt / influence*** into people's emotional needs.

C Complete the definitions with the words in the box.

discourage dissuade exploit influence manipulate motivate tempt trigger

1 If you motivate somebody, you encourage them to want to do something.
2 If you manipulate somebody, you use tricks to convince them do something.
3 If you dissuade somebody from doing something, you persuade them not to do it.
4 If you discourage somebody from doing something, you encourage them not to do it.
5 If you exploit somebody, you take advantage of their kindness or naivety.
6 If you tempt somebody, you offer them something that's hard to resist.
7 If you influence somebody's behavior, you change it, maybe without the person noticing.
8 If your actions trigger a response, they cause it to happen automatically.

GRAMMAR

A Rewrite the sentences so they start or end with the words in parentheses.

1 Somebody must have moved my car. (*my*)
My car must have been moved.
2 You can always rely on Leo. (*Leo*)
Leo can always be relied on.
3 I'm worried about somebody seeing me. (*seen*)
I'm worried about being seen.
4 They made us leave our phones outside. (*we*)
We were made to leave our phones outside.
5 Somebody's going to fix my car. (*I'm*)
I'm going to have/get my car fixed.
6 It was nice of them to invite us. (*invited*)
It was nice to be / have been invited.
7 How did somebody break the vase? (*broken*)
How did the vase get broken?

B Put the words into the correct order to make sentences.

1 good / considered / my proposal / be / to / enough / wasn't
My proposal wasn't considered to be good enough / My proposal wasn't good enough to be considered.
2 to / anyone / to the party / expected / hardly / was / come
Hardly anyone was expected to come to the party.
3 have / reported / is / hundreds of complaints / received / to / the company
The company is reported to have received hundreds of complaints.
4 going / at / been / alleged / have / the time / to / the driver / is / too fast
The driver is alleged to have been going too fast at the time.
5 planning / is / a new hospital / to build / rumored / to / the city council / be
The city council is rumored to be planning to build a new hospital.
6 been / the kidnappers / have / is / the letter / by / to / believed / written
The letter is believed to have been written by the kidnappers.

6 DISCOVERIES

Unearthing the past in Huara Rajada, Northern Peru

Discoveries (n) something that is found or something new that is learned.
Synonyms: breakthrough (n), unearthing (n)

Marcel Proust means that we can learn more by changing our perspective and looking at what we already know in a different way, rather than by traveling to new places.

Marcel Proust (1871–1922) was a French novelist, best known for *In Search of Lost Time*, where this quote comes from.

OBJECTIVES

- speculate and make deductions about the past
- plan an amazing journey
- discuss rewarding jobs
- give a presentation about someone you admire
- plan and perform an interview
- write an expository essay

Work with a partner. Discuss the questions.

1 Look at the picture. What do discoveries like this tell us? Are they important? Why/Why not?
2 Read the quote. What does Proust mean? Do you agree?
3 What do you think has been the greatest discovery ever? Give reasons for your answer.

DISCOVERIES 61

OBJECTIVES

Read the unit objectives to the class.

UNIT OPENER QUESTIONS

1 Focus students on the picture and elicit what it shows. Put them back into pairs to discuss the question before some whole-class feedback.

2 Put students into pairs to discuss the quote. In feedback, elicit examples of situations this could apply to.

3 Elicit an example of an important discovery, then put students into small groups to think of more. Get feedback and write their ideas on the board. Put students back into their groups to try to agree on which is the most important and why. In feedback, encourage students to justify their opinions and to agree or disagree with each other. Write on the board useful language as it comes up.

WORKSHEETS

Lesson 6.1 Challenging journeys

Vocabulary: Journeys and adventures (W24)

Grammar: Past modals of speculation and deduction (W25)

Vocabulary: Three-part phrasal verbs (W26)

Lesson 6.2 Inquisitive minds

Grammar: *-ing* and infinitive forms (W27)

Vocabulary: Binomial expressions (W28)

- Speculate and make deductions about the past
- Plan an amazing journey

V – journeys and adventures; three-part phrasal verbs
P – showing your attitude
G – past modals of speculation and deduction
S – prediction strategies for reading

READING

A SPEAK Work in pairs. Do you know any famous explorers? What did they do?

B PREDICT Look at the title and the pictures in the article. Read the information in the box and answer questions a and b.

Prediction strategies for reading

Use the prediction cycle to help you predict the content of a text:

- Make predictions about the content of the text.
  - **a** What information will be included?
  - **b** What questions will it answer?
- Read part of the text to find out if your predictions were correct or not.
  - **c** Were your predictions correct?
  - **d** What information supported or challenged your predictions?

C SKIM Read *The disappearance of Percy Fawcett*. Answer questions c and d in the box in Exercise B.

D READ FOR DETAIL Complete the table with evidence for and against each theory in the article.

	For
1	Kalapalos tribe saw them walking into the territory of a dangerous tribe.
2	Opinion of former traveling companion.
3	Fawcett's papers; archaeologists found evidence of similar cities.
	Against
1	No bones were found.
2	
3	Left behind wife and children.

E SPEAK Work in groups. Which theory do you think is the most likely explanation for what happened? Why?

THE DISAPPEARANCE OF

PERCY FAWCETT

In the age of **long-haul** flights and travel **off the beaten path**, many now consider themselves seasoned **globetrotters**. However, there was a time when traveling to the far corners of the world was both dangerous and rare.

This was true in January 1925 when accomplished British explorer Percy Fawcett **embarked on** his latest expedition, hoping to find an ancient city in the jungle, the Lost City of Z.

Despite previous failed attempts to find it, he was still convinced that a large city that was 'more ancient than the oldest Egyptian discoveries' lay **at the heart of** the Amazon. On April 20th, his group departed from the Brazilian city of Cuiabá and headed for the jungle.

On May 29th, Fawcett sent a letter to his wife telling her that they were about to enter **uncharted territory**. They were never heard from again.

So what happened to Fawcett and his party? This remains one of the world's greatest unsolved mysteries and has inspired a lot of speculation. Here are three possible explanations.

1 THEY WERE KILLED BY INDIGENOUS PEOPLE

Some people believe that Fawcett and his companions must have been killed by an indigenous tribe. While journalist David Grann was retracing Fawcett's journey in 2005, he met with a tribe called the Kalapalo. They told him that they had heard stories from their grandparents about explorers coming to their territory and ignoring warnings not to walk through territory belonging to another tribe because this tribe was hostile to intruders. The Kalapalo tribe believe that it is highly likely Fawcett and his companions were killed by this other tribe. However, no bones have ever been found. Ex D Q1

6.1 Challenging journeys

LEAD-IN

Books closed. Write the word *explore* on the board, and put students into pairs to discuss what it means to them. Get some feedback, then elicit an example somewhere of something that hasn't yet been explored, e.g. *the bottom of the ocean* or *the full potential of the human brain*. Put them into pairs to think of more examples. Get feedback on the most interesting ideas.

READING

A Elicit an example, then put students into pairs to discuss the questions. Get feedback, and encourage students to expand on their answers if others haven't heard about the explorers before.

B Ask students to cover the article (e.g. with a phone, book or pencil case) so that they can see the title above and the pictures below, but not the main text. Point out the box about *Prediction strategies for reading*, and go through the information. Put students into pairs to make predictions for questions a and b. Get some feedback, but don't confirm or reject any ideas here.

C Set a time limit and tell students to uncover the text, to read it quickly and to answer questions c and d from the box in Exercise B. Keep feedback brief at this stage.

D Tell students to read the three possible explanations again, more carefully this time, and to complete the table with the evidence for and against each given in the article. Put them into pairs to compare their answers, and in feedback ask students to refer to the text to support their answers.

E Put students into groups to discuss the question. In feedback, encourage students to justify their answers.

Extra activity

Ask students to research two or three more sources online with information on Fawcett's disappearance. They should read for:

- other possible theories explaining the disappearance
- the evidence for or against these theories.

METHODOLOGY HUB by Christine Nuttall

Text attack skill: Prediction

Prediction relates to the text as a sequenced development of thought. Prediction is possible because writers organize their ideas, because people tend to think in similar ways, and because certain kinds of text (e.g. fairy tales, recipes) have predictable structures with which experienced readers become familiar.

The ability to predict is both an aid to understanding and a sign of it. If you understand a text, you can say with a fair chance of success what is likely to come next and what is not: you can predict *because* you understand. The extent to which you can use prediction in order to understand is *less clear*, but it is a principle of learning that new information is more easily assimilated if it can be fitted into an existing framework of ideas. Thus, if you can frame the kind of thoughts the writer is likely to put forward next, it will typically help you to understand the text, even if you predicted incorrectly.

Some kinds of text lend themselves more to prediction than others. Fiction is usually difficult at the micro level (i.e. guessing what the next sentence or paragraph will contain) but enjoyable at the macro level, because a good writer foreshadows the story in the way she writes.

Other kinds of text, particularly those with easily identifiable patterns of organization, lend themselves more readily to prediction at the micro level. In a discursive text, for instance, it is usually possible to recognize the point at which the writer will introduce an opposing argument. Similarly, if a student learns the way standard scientific articles in his field are organized, he will be able to predict the pattern of a new article, which should help him to interpret it.

Prediction begins to form the moment we read the title and form expectations of what the text will contain. Even false expectations start us thinking about the topic and make us actively involved. Prediction need not be 'successful' to be useful.

Predictions can be formulated as questions which you think the text may answer. This gives an added purpose to reading: to see which of your questions are in fact dealt with, and what answers are offered. The clearer the purpose, the more likely you are to understand.

TEACHING IDEA by Jim Scrivener

Budgets

Use these activities to extend the theme of adventure, exploration and travel.

In small groups, you are going on vacation together. I'll give each group a budget. You must agree on the details of your vacation, e.g. destination, transportation, food, accommodation and entertainment. You must keep to your budget. (For the poorest group, estimate how much they'll need for a hitch-hiking and camping trip, for example. For the richest group, make sure that they have more than they could possibly spend.)

Now imagine you are on your vacation and write a postcard. Now imagine you are back from your vacation. Compare your experiences with those of a student from another group.

TEACHING IDEA by Jim Scrivener

Adventure vacations

Work in groups of four. Imagine you have each just gotten back from a different adventure vacation. Here are the four vacations; decide where you went and tell each other what you did and saw.

the Amazon, the Himalayas, Siberia, the Sahara

If you have been on an adventure vacation, e.g. whitewater rafting, tell your group about it.

6.1 Challenging journeys

VOCABULARY

A Point out the words in bold in the article, and tell students to match them to the definitions. Elicit the first one as an example, and demonstrate how to use the context to work out the meaning by checking if the definition makes sense in the sentence. Put students into pairs to do the rest. In feedback, provide more examples to fully clarify the meaning of the vocabulary if necessary, and practice pronunciation of some items (e.g. *long haul*, *impenetrable*).

B Direct students to the **Vocabulary Hub** (see TB121).

C Give an example of your own, then put students into pairs to discuss the question. In feedback, find out who has been on the most adventurous journey. Ask other students if that kind of thing appeals to them, and why or why not. Use the **Vocabulary Worksheet** on page W24 for extra practice.

GRAMMAR

A Focus students on the underlined sentences in the article, and elicit that they are all about past situations where what happened is not known for sure. Elicit the first one as an example, then put students into pairs to complete the rules, referring to the examples in the text to help them.

B Direct students to the **Grammar Hub** (see below and TB64).

C Elicit the first one as an example, then put students into pairs to discuss the other theories. In feedback, encourage different answers and clarify how the meaning changes depending on which structure students chose to use. Use the **Grammar Worksheet** on page W25 for extra practice.

SPEAKING

A Put students into an even number of small groups. Direct groups to the **Communication Hub** (see TB121). Tell them to read about the mysteries and to discuss possible explanations. Monitor to help and prompt if needed.

B Put students into new pairs, so someone from group A is working with someone from group B. Tell them to explain the mystery they read about to each other and to give their explanation. Encourage students to listen to each other carefully, to ask questions if they don't understand any part of the mystery and to say whether or not they agree with their partner's explanation. If they don't, they should suggest an alternative. In feedback, try to reach a class consensus on the most likely explanation for each mystery. Finish with feedback on students' use of language during the task, especially on their use of the past modal structures.

Extra activity

Give another example of an unexplained mystery of your own, then put students into small groups to discuss any others they have heard about. Ask students to select a mystery (either the one you gave or their own). If appropriate, allow them time to do research on their phones or computers to check details. Then ask them to agree on the most likely explanation in their group. In whole-class feedback, allow the groups to introduce their mysteries and explanations. Encourage the rest of the class to ask questions and give their opinion.

GRAMMAR HUB

6.1 Past modals of speculation and deduction

- We use *must* + *have* + past participle for things we believe logically happened.

  *It's a huge book, so it **must have taken** her a long time to research and write.*

- We use *could/might/may well* + *have* + past participle for things we believe likely happened.

  *They're still not sure what caused the fire but it **may well have been started** deliberately.*

- We use *could/might/may* + *have* + past participle for things we think possibly happened.

  *The plane **might have crashed** in the mountains but they never found the wreckage.*

- We use *can't/couldn't* + *have* + past participle to say something was not logically possible.

  *They **couldn't have built** this massive fort in just a week.*

Be careful!

- Although *could/might/may have* + past participle all mean the same thing, *might/may not have* expresses possibility, whereas *couldn't have* expresses certainty.

  It's possible that Aled didn't see the email. = Aled may/might not have seen the email. NOT ~~Aled couldn't have seen the email.~~

- We can use phrases that start with *There is* + *a/an/the* + adjective + noun + (*that*) to speculate, with adjectives such as *distinct*, *fair*, *high*, *remote*, *slim* and *slight*, and nouns such as *chance*, *likelihood* and *possibility*.

  ***There is a distinct possibility that** he picked up the illness while in the jungle.*

- We can also use phrases that start with *It is* + adverb + adjective + (*that*) to speculate, with adverbs such as *extremely*, *highly*, *reasonably and somewhat* and adjectives such as *likely* and *possible*.

  ***It's extremely possible that** rival explorers sabotaged their plans.*

2 THEY DIED OF NATURAL CAUSES: EXHAUSTION, STARVATION OR ILLNESS

According to Henry Costin, a man who accompanied Fawcett on several of his previous expeditions, Fawcett was always friendly and respectful toward the tribes he met, so he couldn't have been killed by them.

Costin believed that there was a distinct possibility, given the scale of the expedition and the **impenetrable** terrain, that Fawcett and his companions died from exhaustion, or lack of food when their **provisions** ran out. Alternatively, given that several explorers at the time died from tropical diseases, they may well have succumbed to illness in the jungle.

3 THEY STAYED IN THE JUNGLE

After studying Fawcett's private papers, television director Misha Williams came up with an alternative theory. She believed that Fawcett had become disillusioned with life in Europe and may have decided to establish a commune in the jungle and live a simpler life.

However, many people point out that this theory doesn't make a lot of sense, because Fawcett had a wife and two children, so he couldn't have deliberately abandoned them. Similarly, he could have found the Lost City of Z and decided to stay. In recent years, archaeological discoveries have shown that Fawcett might have been right after all.

Researchers have found the ruins of huge cities in the Amazon that may well have been home to thousands of people. Did he finally find what he was looking for?

Glossary

disillusioned (adj) disappointed because you have discovered that someone or something is not as good as you had believed

starvation (n) a situation in which a person or animal suffers or dies because they do not have enough to eat

succumb (v) to become very sick or to die from a disease

intruder (n) someone who enters a place where he or she is not allowed to go

retrace (v) to go along the same path or route that someone else has gone along previously

seasoned (adj) experienced in a particular activity or job

VOCABULARY

Journeys and adventures

A Scan the article again. Complete the definitions with the words in bold.

1. provisions (n) supply of food, drink, equipment, etc for a journey
2. impenetrable (adj) impossible to move through or enter
3. embark on (v) begin
4. uncharted territory (n phr) places not covered by maps
5. at the heart of (n) middle of
6. globetrotters (n) frequent international travelers
7. long-haul (adj) long distance
8. off the beaten path (phr) away from frequently visited places

B Go to the **Vocabulary Hub** on page 145.

C SPEAK Work in pairs. Tell your partner about an adventurous journey you've been on or heard about.

GRAMMAR

Past modals of speculation and deduction

A Look at the underlined sentences in the article. Complete the rules with the words in the box.

adjective adverb can't/couldn't could/might/may may well must

Past modals of speculation and deduction

1. We use *must* + *have* + past participle for things we believe logically happened.
2. We use *may well* + *have* + past participle for things we think are likely to have happened.
3. We use *could/might/may* + *have* + past participle for things we think possibly happened.
4. We use *can't/couldn't* + *have* + past participle to say something was not logically possible.
5. We can use phrases that start with *There's a/an* + adjective + noun + (*that*) … to speculate.
6. We can use phrases that start with *It's* + adverb + adjective (*that*) … to speculate.

B Go to the **Grammar Hub** on page 132.

C SPEAK Work in pairs. Discuss these theories about Percy Fawcett's disappearance.

1. They were attacked by wild animals.
2. Rival explorers killed them.
3. They were killed by a natural disaster.
4. They decided to join one of the tribes.

SPEAKING

A DISCUSS Work in small groups. Group A – go to the **Communication Hub** on page 153. Group B – go to the **Communication Hub** on page 155.

B PRESENT Work with someone from the other group. Tell him or her about the historical mystery you read about.

VOCABULARY

Three-part phrasal verbs

A Work in pairs. Read *Seven reasons to go traveling*. Discuss which you think is the best reason to go traveling.

B Find nine three-part phrasal verbs in the article. Use the information in the box to help you.

1. are up for
2. come up against
3. find out about
4. brush up on
5. get away from
6. keep (yourself) away from
7. switch off from
8. look back on
9. get around to

Three-part phrasal verbs

Phrasal verbs are common in informal English.

Most phrasal verbs only have two parts (for example, *sit down, turn up*). However, there are also three-part phrasal verbs which contain a verb + a particle + a preposition (for example, *look up to*).

C Choose the correct options to complete the rules. Use the examples in Exercise B to help you decide.

1. Most three-part phrasal verbs are *separable* / *inseparable*.
2. The particle and the preposition *can* / *can't* be separated.
3. Some three-part phrasal verbs can take an object after the *verb* / *particle*.

D Complete the sentences with a three-part phrasal verb from Exercise B. Use the hint in parentheses to help you.

1. It's important to find out about (*research*) a place before you visit it.
2. If you come up against (*experience*) problems on a trip, it makes it more of an adventure.
3. Getting away from (*moving away from*) the crowds is more interesting than going sightseeing.
4. I don't think I would be up for (*be interested in*) traveling to another country by myself.
5. I look back on (*remember*) my childhood vacations with fondness.
6. Travel is a great way to help people to switch off from (*stop thinking about*) work or study.
7. You should always brush up on (*review and practice*) your language skills before a trip.
8. You should always pack in advance rather than only getting around to (*eventually do*) it the night before you leave.

E Work in pairs. Discuss whether you agree or disagree with the sentences in Exercise D.

F **SPEAK** Work in small groups. Which reasons from the article do you think are the most worthwhile? Why? Think of three more reasons to go traveling.

Seven reasons TO GO TRAVELING

Ex B **1** Because you are up for an adventure. Challenge yourself with something that pushes you outside your comfort zone.
Ex B See how you react when you come up against obstacles.

Ex B **2** Because you want to find out about the world. You can read about different countries and cultures, but nothing compares to being there and seeing it for yourself.

3 Because you want to learn the language.
Ex B If you really want to brush up on your language skills, you need to travel to where the language is spoken.

4 Because you want to learn about yourself. Getting away from home and work means you have Ex B
time to reflect on your life and decide if you want to make any changes.

5 Because you need to recharge your batteries. If you find it hard to keep yourself away from work, traveling Ex B
can help you switch off from all the things you need to Ex B
do and get some well-earned rest.

6 Because you want to celebrate a special occasion with friends or family. Travel can create precious memories that you can look back on together. Ex B

7 Because you always wanted to. Don't keep putting it off or you'll never get around to it! Ex B

6.1 Challenging journeys

VOCABULARY

A Books closed. Explain that students are going to read an article entitled *Seven reasons to go traveling*. Elicit an idea for one of the reasons that might be given, then put students into pairs to predict more. Get feedback, then tell students to open their books and to read the article to see how similar their ideas are to those in the text. When they have read the article, put them back into pairs to discuss which reason they think is the best.

B Go through the information in the box about *Three-part phrasal verbs*, and tell students that there are nine examples in the article. Elicit the first one as an example, then tell students to find and underline the others. In feedback, use examples to clarify the meaning of the phrasal verbs where necessary, and model and practice pronunciation, making sure students notice that the main stress falls on the first particle.

C Tell students to look again at how the phrasal verbs are used in the article to help them complete the rules. In feedback, refer to the examples from the text to make sure all students understand the rules.

D Do the first one as an example with the class, then put students into pairs to complete the other sentences.

E Tell students to discuss in pairs whether they agree or disagree with the sentences in Exercise D. In feedback, encourage students to expand on their answers and to ask each other further questions.

F Divide the class into small groups and explain the task. Monitor as students discuss their reasons, and help out with further ideas where necessary. After the activity, elicit a different reason for traveling from each group. Use the **Vocabulary Worksheet** on page W26 for extra practice.

TEACHING IDEA by Jim Scrivener

Finding interesting collocations

Use this activity to review phrasal verbs.

Choose an interesting set of suitable phrasal verbs (*give up, get over, look up, blow up*). Ask students to think of a funny or unexpected collocation for each one (*give up mountain climbing*) and then use it in an amusing sentence (*My 80-year-old grandma finally gave up mountain climbing last summer*).

TEACHING IDEA by Jim Scrivener

Phrasal verb story

Use this activity to review phrasal verbs generally, or adjust it to make your examples three-part phrasal verbs.

Dictate a list of about ten phrasal verbs (*get up, put on, turn on, drop in, give back*). Ask students to work together to create a story using as many of the verbs as they can. To make it harder, you could ask them to use the verbs in exactly the order dictated.

GRAMMAR HUB

6.1 Past modals of speculation and deduction

A Find and correct mistakes in some of the sentences.

1 You ~~may~~ must have been exhausted after such a long trip.
2 She must be lying. She ~~might not~~ couldn't/can't have traveled all that distance in one day. It's impossible!
3 They could have taken a wrong turning, but it's hard to tell at this stage. Correct
4 He ~~must well~~ may/could/might well / must have taken his bike with him as he loves biking.
5 Janessa couldn't possibly have climbed Mt. Kilimanjaro with a broken ankle. Correct
6 She ~~can't~~ must have been a globetrotter in her youth because she has souvenirs from all around the world.
7 Jonathan ~~must~~ may/might not have gotten our message. I suppose we'll only find out when we hear from him.
8 They must have already left because their room is empty and their bags are gone. Correct

B Choose the correct options to complete the sentences.

1 There is ***a distinct possibility*** / *extremely possible* that they checked in under a false name.
2 It is *a slim chance* / ***somewhat likely*** that the courier company had the wrong address.
3 There's *highly possible* / ***a remote chance*** that the Sphinx was carved more than 10,000 years ago.
4 There isn't ***the slightest possibility*** / *highly unlikely* that anyone survived that plane crash.
5 It's not *a distinct likelihood* / ***completely impossible*** that she made her way out of the cave alive.
6 There's *somewhat possible* / ***a reasonable chance*** that Geoff kept copies of all the correspondence.

C Complete the text with the words in the box.

couldn't it might must there well

Cabeza de Vaca may [1] ___well___ have been one of the luckiest and unluckiest explorers ever. Of the 600 men on his 1527 expedition to the Americas, he was one of only four to survive. While they probably imagined a difficult journey, they [2] ___couldn't___ have known the misfortune that awaited them. They risked it because [3] ___there___ was a possibility of finding gold. Before they even set foot on land, 100 men deserted. They [4] ___must___ have been too exhausted to continue.

Shortly before reaching the coast, a hurricane killed 60 more. On land, the Apalachee people they encountered weren't very hospitable. [5] ___It___ is likely they sensed the explorers' ill intentions. The Spanish tried to escape, and they [6] ___might___ have been successful except for another hurricane! More men died, the natives in Texas enslaved them, and it was ten years before Cabeza de Vaca and his last three men were finally free.

➤ Go back to page 63.

6.1 Challenging journeys

LISTENING

6.1 A–D Put students into pairs to complete the exercises.

PRONUNCIATION

6.2; 6.3 A–C Put students into pairs to complete the exercises.

SPEAKING HUB

A Put students into small groups and instruct the task.

B Tell each group to present their idea to the class.

C Tell each group to agree on which idea was the most interesting. Of course, they can't choose their own!

AUDIO SCRIPT

6.1

Listening, Exercise B
P = Presenter K = Kyle

P: Today, we're talking about unusual travel challenges. Forget remote beaches and idyllic islands or precarious mountain treks and volcano hiking. None of that is enough to impress anybody these days. If you really want to stand out from the crowd, you need a travel challenge. At least that's what travel journalist Kyle Chen, who's been following this trend closely, is here to tell us today. Welcome to the show, Kyle.

K: Thanks for having me, Jo.

P: So … first of all, what exactly is a travel challenge?

Ex B Q1 **K:** Well, basically, it's traveling with a goal or some sort of self-imposed restriction – or both in some cases.

P: OK. Can you give us some examples?

K: Sure. So you can limit yourself to a particular method of transportation, you can visit locations with a theme, or you can choose a particular route.

P: Actually, that sounds kind of fun. But why do you think these kinds of challenges are so popular all of a sudden?

K: Different reasons I guess. Well, in general, I think people want to be different. Perhaps they want to have a goal to make their trip more interesting. And,
Ex B Q3 I think for some of them, they want to share their adventure. Or maybe they're doing something for charity, or hoping to write a book.

P: So, can you tell us about some interesting challenges that people have done?

Ex B Q2 **K:** OK. Well, this was a pretty ambitious one. A guy named Adam Leyton challenged himself to visit
Ex C Q1 as many countries as possible in 24 hours using public transportation.

P: Woah! I'm guessing you can't visit that many countries in 24 hours, though?

Ex C Q2 **K:** Well, amazingly, he visited 12.

Ex C Q2 **P:** Twelve countries in a day!

K: Right. It wasn't an easy 24 hours by the sounds of it either. He came up against a few challenges. He had no time to sleep, on the whole, except for a couple of hours on a night train. But he had to wake up, and get off and on the train, to set foot in Czechia. He had to jog to the border
Ex C Q3 with Hungary and only had 22 minutes to get from there to the Austrian border.

P: That's sounds pretty … intense. What gave him the idea to take on the challenge?

K: Supposedly, he wanted to break a record but he also
Ex C Q4 wanted to raise $900 for charity.

P: Hmm … it does sound like an incredible trip.
Ex B Q4 But … the fact is, you need some spare time to plan a challenge like that. What are some other challenges you've come across?

Ex B Q2 **K:** Well, one of my favorite challenges is a guy named Dixe Wills. He decided he was going to visit places in Great Britain, except he was only going to visit places that started with the letter Z. And he was going to visit all of them.

Ex C Q5 **P:** How many places is that?

K: There are 41 apparently! He wrote a book about it called *The Z-to-Z of Great Britain*. It's a great book, actually. It's about all these obscure places you might never have heard of – small farms in the middle of nowhere, a rock on the Isles of Scilly.

P: Hmm. That sounds like an interesting read. What else have people done?

Ex B Q2 **K:** Well, another really quirky one is Daniel Tunnard, a British man who lives in Buenos Aires. He decided to
Ex C Q6 ride all of the 140 bus lines in the city.

P: One hundred and forty bus lines? Why?

K: It's a travel challenge. It took him about six months. Remarkably, he was sometimes traveling for
Ex C Q7 14 hours at a time.

P: OK. That actually doesn't sound like fun to me.

Ex B Q5 **K:** Hmm … me neither. But you have to admire his dedication. He set himself a goal and then he went through with it, taking three bus routes a day. He also blogged about his experiences – in English and Spanish – and he published a book about them. It's actually a really fascinating read.

P: Good for him. So how do these people fund their trips, on the whole?

K: Well, I think most of the examples I gave were self-funded. Mind you, traveling on the buses was actually very cheap. I think it cost about
Ex C Q8 $55 altogether.

P: Right, got you.

K: However, some people ask for donations through crowdfunding sites like GoFundMe.

P: Isn't that a little … bold? Surely, you should pay for your own adventures.

K: I think it's OK. The idea is that if people enjoy reading your blog or looking at your photos, they can make a small donation. People don't have to give anything unless they want to.

P: And what would your advice be for someone thinking about trying a travel challenge?

K: OK, first, it's super important to be realistic about what you can do. Think about your budget. Think about how much time you can spare. Think about
Ex B Q6 what you would be comfortable doing. The most important thing is to enjoy yourself. You don't have to travel far to have an adventure.

LISTENING

A PREDICT Work in pairs. You are going to listen to a discussion about travel challenges on a radio program. What do you think a travel challenge is?

6.1 **B LISTEN FOR GIST** Listen to the radio program. Answer the following questions.

1 What is a travel challenge?
Traveling with a goal or some self-imposed restriction

2 How many examples of travel challenges does Kyle give?
Three

3 What reasons other than to be different does Kyle give for people doing these challenges?
To share their adventure, to do something for charity or to write a book

4 What does the presenter think you need to do a trip like Adam Leyton's?
Time to plan

5 What does Kyle admire about Daniel Tunnard?
His dedication

6 What is Kyle's most vital piece of advice for someone doing a travel challenge?
Enjoy yourself

6.1 **C LISTEN FOR DETAIL** Listen again. What is the significance of the following numbers?

1 24	hours	5 41	places
2 12	countries	6 140	bus lines (in Buenos Aires)
3 22	minutes	7 14	hours
4 900	dollars	8 55	dollars

D SPEAK Work in pairs. Discuss the questions.

1 Do you agree that these kinds of travel challenges are becoming more popular?
2 Which of the three travel challenges sounds the most interesting to you?
3 Would you donate money to help someone pay for his or her trip?
4 Would you rather go on a normal vacation or try a travel challenge?

PRONUNCIATION
Showing your attitude

6.2 **A** Listen to these extracts from the radio program. Match each extract (1–4) with the speaker's attitudes to what they say (a–d).

a certain that what they say is true 4
b believes what they say is a generalization or approximation 1
c believes that what they say is an important point 3
d unsure that something is true 2

6.3 **B** Work in pairs. Draw arrows to predict whether the intonation rises (↗), falls (↘) or fall-rises (↘↗) on the underlined attitude words. Then listen to check.

1 Allegedly, (↘↗) you need to be very careful backpacking in some areas of that country.
2 On the whole, (↘↗) I think it's better to travel alone than with a group of friends.
3 The question is, (↘↗) do you have the luxury of taking time out from work.
4 Surely, (↘) it can't be that much fun visiting a lot of countries in a short span of time.

C SPEAK Work in pairs. Discuss the questions using words, phrases and intonation to show your attitude.

1 Which countries would you like to visit and why?
2 Should people travel more within their own countries before they go to another country?
3 Do you think taking time out to go traveling can help your career?

SPEAKING HUB

A PREPARE Work in small groups. You have entered a competition to win sponsorship for a trip to another country. To win, you must come up with an original travel challenge. Think of an idea to enter into the competition and prepare to present this idea to your class. Think about:

- how you will travel.
- where you will travel.
- what your goal will be.
- what the budget will be.
- how you will publicize the trip.

B PRESENT Present your idea to the class. Listen to the other groups' ideas.

C DISCUSS Vote on the most interesting idea.

- Speculate and make deductions about the past
- Plan an amazing journey

6.2 Inquisitive minds

- Discuss rewarding jobs
- Give a presentation about someone you admire

G – *-ing* and infinitive forms
V – binomial expressions
P – pauses and pitch in presentations
S – writing notes while listening

READING

A SPEAK Work in pairs. Rank the following qualities in order of how important they are in journalism. Give reasons for your answer.

___ passion ___ courage
___ curiosity ___ determination
___ integrity

B READ FOR MAIN IDEA Read *Chase down your story*. What is the purpose of the article?

1 To give advice to journalism students.
(2) To share life lessons which the writer has learned from journalism.
3 To evaluate the importance of journalism in the 21st century.

C READ FOR DETAIL Read the article again. Match the questions (1–6) with the sections (a–d). Sections may be chosen more than once.

Which section of the article …

1 acknowledges a misconception the writer had? c
2 highlights the difference between news in the past compared to now? d
3 mentions an event which changed the writer's approach to learning? b
4 describes a characteristic which the writer admires? d
5 emphasizes the importance of personal experience? c
6 mentions discovering lessons by accident when looking for help? a

D SPEAK Work in pairs. Discuss the questions.

1 Which do you think is the most useful piece of advice? Which do you think is the least useful? Why?
2 Have you ever learned anything from work or study that you could apply to your personal life?

Chase down your story

a Finding stories

Ever wondered how journalists find the stories worth telling? Over my first year at a bona fide national newspaper, I learned the hard way that getting the 'scoop' – being the first to report an exciting or important newsworthy story – was easier said than done. So I asked some of my more experienced colleagues to pass on their tricks of the trade.
Ex C Q6 But what I soon discovered was that their advice could be applied not only to my job, but also to my personal life.

b Be curious

As journalists, we're paid to be curious. The number one suggestion I got was to have an inquisitive mind: figure out what matters, and which stories will inspire, move or make us laugh. It is not enough to report facts these days. But if something sparks your curiosity, the chances are other people will be interested, too.

Ex C Q3 There was the time I met a woman who mentioned she was thinking about moving to a remote Pacific island for a year. A whole year away from family, friends … the internet! I had so many questions – and it was no surprise it made a great story, too.

In every conversation I have now, I think about what I can ask and what I can learn. Everybody has something they can teach you. It also helps to ask yourself questions about your own life: Why am I doing what I'm doing? What do I hope to achieve?

c Local is global

Writers have a great imagination. But, as I learned from my colleagues, that can sometimes have a downside. It can keep us looking toward the horizon, craving uncharted
Ex C Q1 territory. Fresh out of college, I pictured myself jetting off to parts unknown to break the next big story. While there is much to be said for this, articles don't need to be exotic
Ex C Q1 or even big news to catch a reader's attention. More often than not, we find that we write best when we write what
Ex C Q5 we know. This second lesson is possibly one of the hardest to learn as a new writer.

6.2 Inquisitive minds

LEAD-IN

Books closed. Write the word *story* on the board and elicit collocations (e.g. *a news story, a children's story, a success story*). Put students into pairs to think of examples of each type of story.

READING

A Explain the task, then put students into pairs to rank the qualities. In feedback, encourage students to explain their opinions and expand on their answers.

B Set a time limit and tell students to read the article quickly, just to decide what the main purpose of it is. Stress that they only need to skim in order to do this, and remind them that this strategy is important to help increase reading speed. Point out the glossary, but tell students not to worry about any other unknown vocabulary at this stage.

C Tell students to read the article again, more carefully this time, and to match the questions to the sections. Encourage them to underline the parts of the article where they find the information. Let students compare in pairs before feedback. If some pairs finish more quickly than others, change partners from the fast finishing pairs so they can compare again with a new partner while the other students have a little more time to try to finish. In feedback, ask students to refer to the text to justify their answers. Clarify any difficult lexis that comes up in these sections.

D Put students into pairs to discuss the questions. In feedback, encourage students to explain their opinions and to agree and disagree with each other for question 1. For question 2, try to get students to share life lessons learned in a range of different situations.

Extra activity

The lesson could be extended into extra speaking or writing practice. Give students more time to brainstorm important lessons they have learned from work and school and how these can be applied to life generally. Then tell the students that they are going to be interviewed about their life tips or advice.

Put students into pairs and ask one student to play a journalist while the other student is the interviewee. The journalist should interview the other student to find out about their life lessons from work/school. Journalists should listen to the interviewee's recommendations, write notes and ask follow-up questions. Monitor as students speak and help as necessary. When students have finished, ask them to swap roles. In whole-class feedback, ask students to report back on the most interesting life lessons they heard.

Alternatively, after students have brainstormed life lessons, they could write a short article for homework or in their own time entitled 'What I have learned from …'. They should include four life lessons and a personal example for each.

METHODOLOGY HUB by Christine Nuttall

Organization of paragraphs into texts

To make students aware that rhetorical organization exists, and is useful, it is probably easier to begin with the organization of paragraphs into texts (rather than of sentences into paragraphs, which we will deal with later).

1 Supply a text several paragraphs long, with one paragraph omitted. Supply the omitted paragraph separately.
Task: To decide where in the text the omitted paragraph fits.
Note: This can be made easy or difficult by choosing a text with a very clear sequence or one with a looser structure.

2 Supply a text several paragraphs long with the opening or concluding paragraph omitted. Supply separately several possible opening or concluding paragraphs, including the original one.
Task: To decide which paragraph best fits the text.
Note: This entails working out the purpose of the text, in the case of the opening paragraph; and the conclusion it reaches, in the case of the concluding one. If you choose paragraphs that differ in style, the exercise will be easier, but for the wrong reasons: the idea is to get students to trace the sequence of thought.

3 Supply a text several paragraphs long with the key (topic) sentence of each paragraph replaced by a blank. Supply separately a set of sentences including the omitted topic sentences (with others as distractors for advanced students).
Task: To decide which sentence fits into which paragraph.
Note: The topic sentences, if they were arranged in the correct sequence, should provide a skeletal summary of the text organization. So to concentrate on them should make the student aware of the organization.

4 Supply a text several paragraphs long with one paragraph in the wrong place (e.g. original paragraph 2 is moved to a later position in the text).
Task: To decide which paragraph is out of place and where it should be.

5 Supply a text, several paragraphs long, with the paragraphs arranged in random order. Or cut up the text so that each paragraph is on a separate piece of paper or card: this method is more fun to use and is particularly suitable for group work. Keep each set of paragraphs in a labeled envelope.
Task: To arrange the paragraphs to make a coherent text.

6 This is a variation of 3 and 5 combined. Supply the paragraphs of text, arranged in random order, with the topic sentences removed and replaced by blanks. Supply the topic sentences, arranged in the correct sequence, to provide a skeletal summary of the text.
Task: To match the paragraphs with the topic sentences and produce a coherent text.
Note: If you number the paragraphs and sentences (in random order of course), you can prepare an answer sheet giving the correct sequence of numbers. Alternatively you can supply the full original text, as for all these exercises.

6.2 Inquisitive minds

GRAMMAR

A–C Put students into pairs to complete the exercises and check answers.

D Direct students to the **Grammar Hub** (see below). Use the **Grammar Worksheet** on page W27 for extra practice.

SPEAKING

Focus students on the pictures and elicit what they show. Put students into pairs to discuss the questions. When they have finished, tell all Students B to stand up and join the next Student A, making new pairs. Tell them to repeat the task, but this time with Student B comparing the pictures and Student A giving their opinion.

GRAMMAR HUB

6.2 *-ing* and infinitive forms

- We use *-ing* after a preposition.

  She praised the journalist ***for exposing*** *the injustice.*
  They're not interested ***in finding*** *out the truth.*
- We also use *-ing* after expressions such as *It's no good…, It's not worth…, There's no point (in)…* and *…have a good time/difficulty/fun/problems… .*

  It's ***not worth publishing*** *the article if it will get you fired.*
  There's ***no point (in) helping*** *people who are ungrateful.*
  You'll ***have difficulty justifying*** *that answer.*
- We use an infinitive after adjectives, nouns, quantifiers and the word *time*.

  She's ***eager to get*** *started on her work.*
  They urged ***people to take*** *shelter in the new facility.*
  The report is lengthy, and there's ***too much to read*** *in one night.*
  Let's pick a good ***time to review*** *the materials.*

Be careful!

- We use an infinitive after the word *time*, but after the phrase *have a good/great time…*, we use *-ing*.

  It's time to make a decision. NOT ~~It's time making a decision.~~
  We had a great time painting the wall. NOT ~~We had a great time to paint the wall.~~

- Some verbs can be followed by *-ing* (e.g. *appreciate, suggest*) and some can be followed by infinitive (e.g. *attempt, manage*). Some can be followed by *either, usually* with a change of meaning (e.g. *remember, stop, try*).

  Why don't you ***try doing*** *some research online? (= experiment)*
  I ***tried to get*** *in touch with Jan but couldn't find her anywhere. (= attempt)*
- We can use *-ing* or base form after the object of sense verbs like hear, see, etc. The base form emphasizes a complete action that is seen or heard, while the *-ing* emphasizes an ongoing activity.

  I ***saw her drinking*** *the coffee. (= The action was in progress. I didn't see her finish the coffee.)*
  I ***saw her drink*** *the coffee. (= The action was completed. I saw her finish the coffee.)*

6.2 *-ing* and infinitive forms

A Choose the correct options to complete the sentences.

1 It's no good ___ him for information. He doesn't give anything away.
   a to ask   (b) asking
2 It's time ___ our invention to the test!
   a putting   (b) to put
3 Despite putting his heart and soul into the project, he had a hard time ___ it.
   a to finish   (b) finishing
4 Even though the city has money, they have little ___ to those in need.
   (a) to give   b giving
5 It's correct ___ that her life was a true rags-to-riches story.
   a saying   (b) to say
6 I'm not very interested in ___ a meeting on a Saturday.
   a to arrange   (b) arranging
7 The police didn't have enough evidence ___ the crime.
   (a) to solve   b solving
8 Jason found it harder ___ with his colleagues after the disagreement.
   (a) to work   b working

B Write the correct form of the verb in parentheses.

1 Justin was disciplined for not finishing (*finish*) his assignment.
2 She brought food for the picnic, but there wasn't enough to go (*go*) around.
3 It's not worth doing (*do*) such hard work for so little money.
4 I'm sorry, but this is a bad time to discuss (*discuss*) this topic.
5 Is she having difficulty adjusting (*adjust*) to her new life?
6 They advised him on investing (*invest*) in new business ventures.
7 There are many ideas here to help (*help*) you get started on the project.
8 Your plan failed miserably. Have fun explaining (*explain*) that to the boss!
9 I saw them steal (*steal*) the bike. I witnessed the whole thing from start to finish.

➤ Go back to page 67.

GRAMMAR
-ing and infinitive forms

A Choose the correct form of the verbs to complete the sentences.

1 She was thinking about ***moving*** / ***to move*** to a remote Pacific island for a year.

2 It is time to acknowledge how vital it is ***staying*** / ***to stay*** on course.

3 It's all too easy for details ***slipping*** / ***to slip*** through the cracks.

4 Articles don't need to be exotic ***catching*** / ***to catch*** a reader's attention.

5 It is not enough ***reporting*** / ***to report*** facts these days.

6 Ever wondered how journalists find the stories worth ***telling*** / ***to tell***?

B Scan the article again and check your answers to Exercise A.

Most of the greatest reporters have cut their teeth reporting on local news, whether that's uncovering home-grown corruption and injustice or just telling human-interest stories. What I've come to realize is that these stories often have a global reach because we have the same emotions, interests and concerns the world over. This has led me to believe – that Ex C Q5 while we must not be inward looking – appreciating what is right in front of us can be just as rewarding as looking further afield.

d *Follow up*

We are living in a world that is always on, where consumers can access massive amounts of content and expect instant gratification. In comparison to Ex C Q2 only five or ten years ago, we are so concerned with the beginning of the story that the middle and end have fallen by the wayside. It's all too easy for details to slip through the cracks and for stories, which should be huge, to be all but forgotten by the next news cycle.

And here lies the last tip, get to the conclusion of your story. Don't get distracted. Many of the finest Ex C Q4 journalists in history were renowned for their tenacity – their innate ability to chase down the facts in the face of seemingly indomitable odds.

This is a quality to aspire to in life. It is time to acknowledge how vital it is to stay on course, not to allow yourself to be side-tracked by modern distractions and the illusion of endless choice. See things through to their conclusion: whether that's the project you're working on or the sport you're learning. And it applies to people too – valuing and caring for the friends and networks you have is as important as growing them.

Glossary

cut your teeth on (phr) to get your first experience in a particular job by doing something

tenacity (n) the behavior of being very determined and unwilling to stop when trying to achieve something

C Match the examples in Exercise A to the rules in the box.

***-ing* and infinitive forms**

We use the *-ing* form:

a after prepositions 1

b after expressions such as *it's no good …, it's not worth …, there's no point in …, have a good time/difficulty/fun/problems …* 6

We use the infinitive:

c after adjectives 4

d after nouns 3

e after quantifiers 5

f after the word *time* 2

D Go to the **Grammar Hub** on **page 132**.

SPEAKING

Work in pairs. Look at the pictures of people with different jobs below.

Student A: Compare the two pictures. Say what qualities and skills people need for these jobs and why people choose to do these jobs.

Student B: Which job would you most like to do and why?

LISTENING

A PREDICT Work in pairs. Look at the infographic of events in a famous inventor's life. Can you guess who it is? Garrett Morgan

B Read the information in the box and look at the notes table.

> **Writing notes while listening**
>
> When you need to take effective notes, you can use the Cornell system. It involves the following five stages:
>
> **Stage 1 Notes:** Write notes in the note-taking column. Focus on main ideas. Use bullet points and abbreviations.
>
> **Stage 2 Questions:** Write questions about your notes in the column on the left. (e.g. *Is this still true today?*, *What does inhalation mean?*)
>
> **Stage 3 Summarize:** Read your notes and questions. Then write a summary of what you learned.
>
> **Stage 4 Reflect:** Think about what you have written. (e.g. *Overall, do you agree with the speaker?*)
>
> **Stage 5 Review and recall:** Review your notes. Cover the second column and answer the questions in the first.

6.4 **C LISTEN TO WRITE NOTES** Listen to a presentation about an inventor. Follow the method in Stage 1 in the box. Write notes in the table as you listen.

Questions	Notes
Summary	

D REFLECT Read your notes. Follow Stage 2 in the box. Write questions in the table.

E SUMMARIZE Follow Stage 3 from the box. Write a summary of your notes in the table. Use the questions in the box to help you.

F REVIEW Compare your notes and questions with your partner. Are they similar? Can your partner answer any of your questions?

G SPEAK Work in pairs. If you were an inventor what type of invention would you focus on?

- inventions that save lives
- everyday products that fix common problems
- niche products for rich people

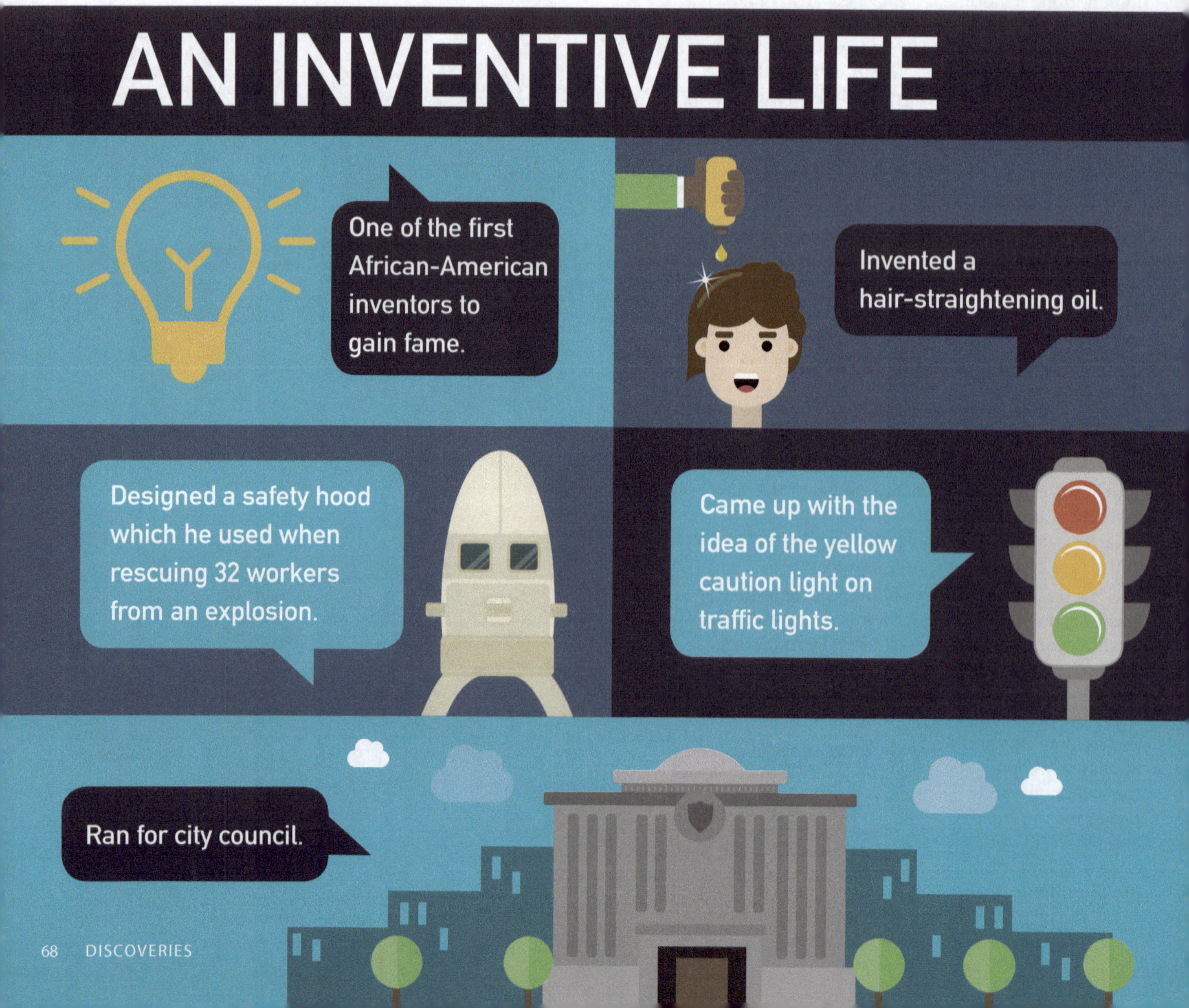

6.2 Inquisitive minds

LISTENING

A Put students into pairs to look at the infographic and to try to guess who the inventor is. Get some feedback, but don't confirm or reject any answers yet.

B Tell students they're going to listen to a presentation about an inventor and to write notes about it. Tell them to read the information in the box about *Taking notes while listening*, to look at the table in Exercise C and to think about how they could apply the system described.

6.4 **C** Students listen to the presentation and write notes in the appropriate section of the table, following the method described in Stage 1 of Exercise B.

Suggested answer

Questions

What else did Morgan invent?

What parts of his life do I want to research further?

Notes

Garrett Morgan

Bio

- inventor, entrepreneur
- 1877 -1963
- African American

Achievements

- Hair straightener made him financially secure
- Gas mask saved people in tunnel, sold to police and fire dept.
- Traffic light used all over country, saved 1,000s of lives
- Admired for his community spirit

Summary

Garrett Morgan was a prolific inventor, saved lives and helped the community. I'd like to find out more about his earlier life and less-known inventions.

D Instruct students to read their notes and to write questions to go with them, following the method from Stage 2 in Exercise B. Do an example for this by asking one student for the first piece of information they have in their notes and eliciting a question this could be answer to.

E Tell students to write a summary of their notes, following Stage 3 from the box. Monitor to help and prompt if needed. Then tell students to compare summaries with their partner to see how similar they are.

F Put students into pairs to compare their notes and questions and to see if they can answer all of each other's questions. In feedback, find out how similar the pairs' notes were and if there was any information that only a few students wrote down.

G Tell students to discuss the question in pairs and to reach an agreement on the most interesting thing. In feedback, encourage students to justify their answers. Does the whole class agree on what the most interesting thing is?

Extra activity

You can extend the discussion by asking students to think of other famous people (not necessarily inventors) who have discovered or created something important. Add the following to the board to give them some ideas: *explorers*, *scientists*, *business entrepreneurs*, *mathematicians*. Students can discuss the people in pairs or groups to decide on the most important.

AUDIO SCRIPT

6.4

Listening, Exercise C
P = Presenter

P: Today, I'd like to talk about someone who I particularly admire. In my opinion, he's far and away one of America's greatest inventors. His innovations have fixed everyday problems but also probably saved thousands of lives. In addition, he was one of the first African-American inventors to gain public recognition for his work. His name was Garrett Morgan and he was a prolific inventor and entrepreneur who lived between 1877 and 1963. And while you may not all know his name, you're likely to have experienced his innovations.

One of Morgan's early successes was actually an accident. He was repairing a sewing machine in his store when he noticed that some oil he was using had straightened the hairs on a cloth. Realizing that he might be on to something, he decided to test the oils on something bigger. So he borrowed his neighbor's dog and used the oils to straighten its hair. It worked. So well, in fact, that his neighbor didn't recognize his own dog and tried to chase it away. Morgan bottled his new invention, labeled it 'G.A. Morgan's Hair Refiner' and he was soon selling it far and wide.

His second big success, a safety hood, turned him from an innovator into a hero. Morgan had noticed how smoke inhalation made the work of firefighters both difficult and dangerous. His solution was a hood worn over the head with two tubes that extended to the ground, where the air was breathable. He soon had an opportunity to test out his invention. An explosion in a tunnel near his home trapped 32 workers underground with smoke, dust and poisonous gases. With emergency services unable to enter the tunnel, it was truly a life-or-death situation. Morgan and his brother Frank raced to the scene and went in side by side, each wearing one of Morgan's safety hoods. It was a tense moment, but they soon re-emerged safe and sound with survivors. Morgan's fame began to spread slowly but surely, with his device being used by fire and police departments across the country.

Another of Morgan's life-saving inventions was an improved version of the traffic light. By and large, in the early 1920s, American roads were dangerous places. They were filled with horses, carriages and wagons – and increasingly, the newly invented automobile. On top of this, there were only two traffic signals – stop or go. Time after time, there were stories of injuries and fatalities in traffic accidents. One day, Morgan and his family saw such an accident – a collision between a car and a horse-drawn carriage at a busy intersection. The driver of the car was knocked unconscious, a little girl was thrown from the carriage, and the horse had to be put down. Determined that accidents like that shouldn't happen, Morgan's innovation was to add a third light – a 'caution' light. This gave vehicles that had entered the intersection enough time to get out before the signal changed to 'go'. Morgan sold the patent to the General Electric Motor Company, which installed the new traffic lights in cities all over the country. As a result, roads became safer and many lives were saved.

So why is Morgan so widely admired? Not only did his inventions save the lives of millions, but he also put his heart and soul into the community, even running for the city council. So while his life was a classic rags-to-riches story, it was also the story of a man who took a leadership role and truly cared about others.

6.2 Inquisitive minds

VOCABULARY

A Go through the information in the box about *Binomial expressions*, then explain that all the sentences below come from the listening and contain a binomial expression. Elicit the first one as an example, then put students into pairs to match the other expressions to their meanings. In feedback, check understanding where necessary with more examples. Ask students if they use similar expressions in their language, and if any of these binomial expressions can be translated literally, keeping the same meaning.

B Direct students to the **Vocabulary Hub** (see TB121).

C Give your own example, then tell students to complete the sentences with their own ideas. Put students into pairs to compare ideas. In feedback, ask students to expand on their answers and to ask each other further questions. Use the **Vocabulary Worksheet** on page W28 for extra practice.

PRONUNCIATION

6.5 **A** Instruct the task. Play the recording and stop after the first sentence. Elicit where the pause was to ensure all students understand the task and noticed the pause. Then play the rest of the recording. Let students compare with a partner before feedback.

B Put students into pairs and direct them to the **Audio script** on page 172. Tell them to practice reading the presentation, remembering to pay attention to pauses and pitch. Give feedback on how well they did this, and ask any students who did it particularly well to read part of the presentation to the class.

SPEAKING HUB

A Explain that students are going to give a presentation about someone they admire who made a big difference to the world. Tell them to use the suggestions given to help them choose someone.

B Students write their presentation, using the suggestions for ideas on what to include. Monitor to help and prompt if necessary. Tell fast finishers to think about where there will be pauses or changes in the pitch in their presentation and to mark them.

C Tell students to give their presentation, either to the whole class or in groups if the class is very large. Students should listen carefully and make a note of any questions they would like to ask about the person.

D Put students into groups to discuss which people they would like to know more about. In feedback, give students an opportunity to ask each other further questions. Finish with feedback on students' use of language in the activity.

Extra activity

Give or elicit an example of something that hasn't been invented yet but should be. This could be something realistic and practical or something more fantastical. Put students into groups to think of more ideas. In feedback, ask students to explain their answers. Encourage others to say whether or not they think it would be a good idea, and if they think it will ever be invented.

METHODOLOGY HUB by Christine Nuttall

Careful colloquial speech

This style contains all types of simplification to a moderate degree. Words remain closer to their dictionary pronunciation than with rapid colloquial speech. This style is likely to be used in a formal setting, the speaker shaping utterances more carefully, deliberately and slowly. (An internationally available example of careful colloquial RP is that of newscasters and announcers on the BBC World Service).

I suggest that careful colloquial speech is useful as a target for learners to aim at speaking, as it is clear, easy to listen to and widely understood. (There are many situations throughout the world where it may be more useful to use the local variety of English as the learning model.)

METHODOLOGY HUB by Jim Scrivener

Lexis, vocabulary and grammar: a summary

- Vocabulary typically refers mainly to single words (e.g. dog, green, wash) and sometimes to very tightly linked two- or three-word combinations (e.g. stock market, compact disc, sky blue, go off).
- The concept of lexis is bigger. It refers to our 'internal database' of words and complete 'ready-made' fixed / semi-fixed / typical combinations of words that we can recall and use quite quickly without having to construct new phrases and sentences word by word from scratch using our knowledge of grammar. Lexis includes:
  - **a** traditional single-word vocabulary items;
  - **b** common 'going-together patterns' of words (e.g. blond hair, traffic jam). These frequent combinations are known as collocations;
  - **c** longer combinations of words that are typically used together as if they were a single item (e.g. someone you can talk to, on-the-spot decisions, I'd rather not say). These longer combinations (which a few years ago would probably not have been considered as anything remotely related to vocabulary) are commonly referred to as chunks or sometimes as multiword items. (Categories (b) and (c) are both classed as lexical items.)
- Grammar refers to the generalizable patterns of the language and to our ability to construct new phrases and sentences out of word combinations and grammatical features (verb endings, etc) to express a precise (and probably unique) meaning.

We could argue that collocations and chunks occupy an intermediate zone between vocabulary and grammar.

VOCABULARY

Binomial expressions

A Match the binomials in bold (1–10) with their definitions (a–j). Use the information in the box to help you.

Binomial expressions

A binomial expression is two words (nouns, verbs, adjectives or adverbs) joined by words like *and*, *or*, *but*, *by* and *to*.

The two words can:

- be antonyms (*give and take*)
- be synonyms (*peace and quiet*)
- use the same word twice (*back to back*)
- use words that start with the same sound (*black and blue*)
- use words that sound similar (*here and there*).

When a binomial expression is a compound adjective used before a noun it is generally hyphenated (a *happy-go-lucky* person).

1 In my opinion, he's **far and away** one of America's greatest inventors. d
2 He was soon selling it **far and wide**. h
3 It was truly a **life-or-death** situation. i
4 Morgan and his brother Frank raced to the scene and went in **side by side**. e
5 They soon re-emerged **safe and sound** with survivors. g
6 Morgan's fame began to spread **slowly but surely**. j
7 **By and large**, in the early 1920s, American roads were dangerous places. a
8 **Time after time** there were stories of injuries and fatalities in traffic accidents. c
9 But he also put his **heart and soul** into the community. b
10 While his life was a classic **rags-to-riches** story. f

a generally
b all of one's energy and passion
c repeatedly
d by a very large amount
e next to each other
f from poor to wealthy
g unharmed and not in danger
h in many different places
i potentially fatal
j gradually

B Go to the **Vocabulary Hub** on **page 145**.

C SPEAK Work in pairs. Complete the sentences with your own ideas. Then share your ideas with your partner.

1 ______________________ is **far and away** the greatest invention.
2 I always put my **heart and soul** into ______________________.
3 When I was younger, I couldn't ______________________. Then **slowly but surely**, I learned how.

PRONUNCIATION

Pauses and pitch in presentations

6.5 **A** Listen to the first part of the presentation again and mark any pauses with (/).

Today,/ I'd like to talk about someone who I particularly admire./ In my opinion,/ he's far and away one of America's greatest inventors./ His innovations have fixed everyday problems/ but also probably saved thousands of lives./ In addition,/ he was one of the first African-American inventors to gain public recognition for his work./ His name was Garrett Morgan/ and he was a prolific inventor and entrepreneur/ who lived between 1877 and 1963. And while you may not all know his name,/ you're likely to have experienced his innovations./

One of Morgan's early successes was actually an accident./ He was repairing a sewing machine in his store/ when he noticed that some oil he was using had straightened the hairs on a cloth.

B Work in pairs. Turn to the **audio script** on **page 172** and practice reading the presentation about Garrett Morgan. Focus on pauses and pitch.

SPEAKING HUB

A THINK You are going to give a presentation about someone you admire. Choose someone who made a big difference to the world by:

- leading social change
- challenging the status quo
- inventing or discovering something important.

B PREPARE Write a short presentation to tell your classmates about this person. Focus on:

- the life of the person you are talking about
- the main achievements of the person you are talking about
- a big problem the person solved.

C PRESENT Give your presentation.

D DISCUSS Listen to your classmates' presentations. Which of the people do you want to learn more about? Why?

Discuss rewarding jobs
Give a presentation about someone you admire

Café Hub

6.3 World of knowledge

Ⓐ– engaging listeners Ⓢ– conducting an interview

▶ Connecting with nature

a

b

c

A Work in pairs. Look at the pictures (a–c) and discuss these questions.

1 What are they?

2 How might they be connected?

B ▶ Watch the video. Check your answers to Exercise A.

Glossary

assemble (v) to build something by joining parts together
countless (adj) very many
tangled (adj) twisted into an untidy mass
vaporize (v) to turn from a solid or liquid state into gas

C ▶ Watch the video again. Are the sentences true (T) or false (F) according to the video? Correct the false sentences.

1 An oak tree is made up of only carbon, nitrogen, oxygen and hydrogen. and a few other things — T / (F)

2 The carbon atom in the acorn was created inside a star billions of years ago. — (T) / F

3 The carbon atom in the acorn has formed part of the earth for ~~two~~ billion years. four and a half — T / (F)

4 The carbon atom in the acorn got into some ancient oak tree through the action of photosynthesis. — (T) / F

5 In billions of years, when the sun dies and the earth is vaporized, all atoms will ~~die~~. be thrown back into space — T / (F)

D ▶ Watch the video again. Complete the sentences.

1 When atoms react and ___combine___ they make up everything in the Universe.

2 Many different types of plants, trees and animals make up the ___ecosystem___ of a forest.

3 When you understand that everything is made of atoms, a forest doesn't seem like such a ___complicated/complex___ place.

4 An atom in an acorn has spent many years in ___rocks___.

5 Life is only a ___temporary___ home of the atoms that make up the universe.

AUTHENTIC ENGLISH

A Work in pairs. Read the sentence from the video and the information in the box. Which device has been used to engage listeners? Summarizing information

So life is just a temporary home for the immortal elements that build up the universe.

Engaging listeners

Brian Cox is a very engaging speaker. He uses a number of strategies to engage listeners.

- Summarizing information, for example, *So, when you look at it like that it's really not that complicated at all.*
- Repetition of certain words such as *billions* to emphasize a point.
- Dynamic words such as *thrown back out* and *vaporize*.

B Go to the transcript on page 154. Underline examples of the strategies from the box that Brian Cox uses to engage listeners.

C Write a short speech on a topic that you're passionate about. Use strategies to engage your listeners.

D Work in pairs. Read your speech to your partner. Try to be as engaging and passionate as possible.

Getting answers

A Work in pairs. Discuss the questions.

1 Do you ever watch documentaries about science? Why/Why not?

2 Should we try to make science more accessible than it is now?

3 Are there any cons to simplifying science for a wider audience?

B Watch the video. Were any of the things you discussed in Exercise A mentioned?

C Watch the video again. Complete the sentences with one to three words.

1 Amanda is interviewing Veronica about her (new) book.

2 Malcolm tells Sam that Veronica is one of the country's best-known physicists.

3 Veronica says she saw Brian Cox give a lecture

4 Since being inspired by Brian Cox, Veronica has been making documentaries.

5 Malcolm comments that Veronica's book is at the top of the bestseller chart.

SPEAKING SKILL

A Work in pairs. Complete the line from the video. Why has Amanda asked her question in this way?

Professor Matos, how would you respond to accusations that your book is under-researched?

Amanda is asking a question in an indirect, tactful way because the subject is delicate.

SAM MALCOLM AMANDA HARRY EMILY

B Look at the information in the box. Match the questions (1–5) with the types (a–e).

Conducting an interview

a **Direct questions** are asked in order to make a point about a situation or to point out something for consideration. For example, 4

b **Indirect questions** are used when we want to be more polite. We use an introductory phrase followed by the question itself in a positive sentence structure. For example, 3

c **Negative questions** can ask for confirmation of our opinions or make invitations or suggestions. For example, 1

d **Tag questions** can either be 'real' questions where we want to know the answer or simply ask for agreement when we already know the answer. For example, 2

e **Rhetorical questions** are often statements given in question format in order to make a point about a situation. For example, 5

1 Why don't you go over and introduce yourself?

2 It builds on some of the theories set out by Professor Brian Cox, doesn't it?

3 I hope you don't mind me asking, why did you decide to write a book?

4 Can I quote you on that?

5 Did I dumb down the science a little for the masses?

C Work in pairs. Think of one more example for each of the question types (1–5) in Exercise B.

SPEAKING HUB

A PLAN Work in pairs. Student A: Imagine you are a journalist for a website. Look at the bullet points and prepare a list of questions to ask Veronica Matos.

Student B: Imagine you are Veronica Matos. You are going to be interviewed. Plan what you are going to say using the bullet points.

- when you first became interested in science
- your book
- your future career plans
- advice to young people

B DISCUSS Work in pairs. Perform your role-play.

A: What advice would you give to teenagers who want a career in science?

B: Decide early which area of science you want to work in. There are hundreds and hundreds of different career paths.

Plan and perform an interview

➤ Turn to page 161 to learn how to write an expository essay about space exploration.

6.3 World of knowledge

Connecting with nature

A Focus students on the pictures and put them into pairs to discuss the questions. In feedback, encourage students to give different suggestions, and don't confirm or reject any yet.

B ▶ **Suggested answers**

1 *a supernova, a person breathing in a wood on a cold winter morning, an oak tree*

2 *A carbon atom in an acorn was created in a star and got thrown out into the universe in a supernova explosion. It could have been breathed out by a person who walked through the woods hundreds of years ago. It got into some ancient oak tree through the action of photosynthesis.*

C ▶ Put students into pairs to decide if the sentences are true or false and to correct the false ones. Play the video again for students to check.

D ▶ Put students into pairs to try to complete the sentences. Then play the video for them to check.

AUTHENTIC ENGLISH

A Go through the information in the box about *Engaging listeners*. Then put students into pairs to discuss the question.

B Direct students to the transcript on page 154. Elicit an example, then tell students to find and underline more devices.

C Tell students they're going to make a short speech about a topic they're passionate about. Give them some time to choose a topic and prepare what they want to say. Remind them to use the devices from the box. Monitor to help and prompt.

D Put students into pairs to read their speeches to each other. Tell students to listen carefully to their partner's speech and to ask questions at the end, as well as giving feedback about how engaging it was. Finish with whole-class feedback.

Getting answers

A Focus students on the picture and put them into pairs to discuss the questions. Get some feedback but don't confirm or reject any answers at this stage.

B ▶ Students watch the video and check their answers.

C ▶ Put students into pairs to try to complete the sentences from memory. Then play the video again for them to watch and check. You can find the **video script** for *Getting answers* on the Teacher's Resource Center.

SPEAKING SKILL

A Put students into pairs to read and complete the line from the video and to answer the question. In feedback, ask if students use indirect questions like this in their language. This should lead smoothly into Exercise B.

B Go through the information in the box about *Conducting an interview*, and tell students to match the five types of question to the five example questions from the video.

C Put students into pairs to think of another example for each of the question types in Exercise B. In feedback, elicit and write on the board a range of students' questions.

SPEAKING HUB

A Put students into AA and BB pairs, so they have the same role as their partner. Instruct the role play and let them prepare together. Monitor to help with ideas or language if needed.

B Re-pair students into AB pairs to perform the role play. Monitor attentively to hear how well students manage this. In feedback, choose some of the more confident and successful pairs to perform their role plays to the class. Tell the other students to listen carefully and to give feedback at the end. Finish with feedback on students' use of language during the activity.

Extra activity

Give your own example, then put students into pairs to discuss who they would most like to interview and what they would ask them. Get whole-class feedback on the range of students' choices, and encourage them to expand on their answers and ask each other further questions.

▶ VIDEO SCRIPT

Connecting with nature
B = Brian Cox

B: Hydrogen atoms, carbon atoms, oxygen and sulphur atoms – these basic building blocks react and combine to make everything. A woodland is a complex place – there are oak trees and grass and mosses and ferns and countless animals and plants all living together in a tangled ecosystem. But there's a simpler level of description – everything is made of
Ex C Q1 atoms. So an oak tree is really just carbon, nitrogen, oxygen and hydrogen and a few other bits mixed together. So, when you look at it like that, it's really not that complicated at all.

The atoms that make up this woodland have been on an extraordinary journey to get here. Think of a carbon
Ex C Q2 atom in this acorn. It was assembled in the heart of a star billions of years ago out of protons that were
Ex C Q3 built just after the Big Bang. It got thrown out into the universe in a supernova explosion, collapsed as part of a dust cloud to form the sun and then the Earth four and a half billion years ago. It will have spent a lot of time in rocks. It was probably part of some of the first living things on Earth. It would have got breathed out as carbon dioxide by someone that walked
Ex C Q4 through this wood 400 years ago. It will have got into some ancient oak tree through the action of photosynthesis, constructed into this acorn, fallen down to the ground, and there it is. It's got a history that goes back billions of years. In fact, a history in terms of the building blocks of carbon, the protons,
Ex C Q5 that goes back right to the origin of the universe. And in billions of years' time, when the sun dies and the Earth is vaporized, they'll be thrown back out into space and probably condensed into a new world billions of years in the future.

So life is just a temporary home for the immortal elements that build up the universe.

6 Writing
Write an expository essay

structuring an expository essay

A SPEAK Work in pairs. Read the essay prompt and brainstorm possible answers.

What are the benefits of deep-sea exploration?

B Read the essay. What benefits does the writer mention? What evidence or examples does the writer give for each benefit?

The benefits of DEEP-SEA EXPLORATION

Did you know that humans have only explored 5% of the world's oceans? This means there is clearly a lot left to be discovered. There are benefits of deep-sea exploration, such as learning more about climate change, addressing the problems of food shortage, and finding cures for diseases.

First, deep-sea exploration is providing vital information about climate change. For example, researchers have been observing how rising temperatures affect the movements of sea creatures. In addition, some studies have found that the sea is able to absorb carbon from the atmosphere.

Second, exploration of the seas will help governments ensure there is enough food for everyone in the future. According to the UN Food and Agriculture Organization, fish stocks are already getting low. However, improvements to fish farming methods will allow countries to support sustainable fishing.

Finally, exploring the seas is leading to advances in medicine to help fight disease. For example, medicines have already been discovered to help with chronic pain, asthma and even cancer. Many scientists believe we are much more likely to discover new medicines in the sea than on land.

In summary, there are many benefits to deep-sea exploration. It can help scientists to understand climate change better as they try to prevent it. It can also help people to ensure the ocean remains a valuable source of food. In addition, discovering new species of plant and animal could lead to the development of new medicines. People have already discovered a lot from just 5% of the ocean. Imagine what they could find in the other 95%.

C Read the essay again and answer the questions. Use the information in the box to help you.

Structuring an expository essay

The typical structure of an expository essay is:

- **Introduction:** Includes a 'hook' to get readers' attention, background information and the thesis statement, which states what the essay will describe or explain
- **Body paragraph one:** Describes or explains the first point
- **Body paragraph two:** Describes or explains the second point
- **Body paragraph three:** Describes or explains the third point
- **Conclusion:** Summarizes the points that were made and leaves the reader with a 'final thought'.

1 Which sentence is the hook? How does the writer get the reader's attention?
2 Which sentence is the thesis statement? What do you notice about the order of the points in the thesis statement?
3 The first sentence of each paragraph is called a topic sentence. What information is included in this sentence?
4 What kind of information is included in each paragraph to support the idea introduced in the topic sentence?
5 The conclusion contains a summary of the points made in the essay. What do you notice about the order of the points in the summary?

WRITING

A PREPARE Work in groups. Read the essay prompt in Exercise A again. Come up with ideas and make a list of possible benefits.

B PLAN Choose the best ideas and organize them into paragraphs.

C WRITE Use your plan to write an expository essay. Write approximately 250 words.

D REVIEW Work in pairs. Edit your partner's essay. Check:

- spelling and punctuation
- use of language
- clarity of the structure

WRITING 161

Answers

Benefit: *vital information about climate change.* Evidence/examples: *rising temperatures affect movements of sea creatures; the sea is able to absorb carbon from the atmosphere.*
Benefit: *helps ensure food supplies in the future.* Evidence/example: *improvements to fish farming methods will allow countries to support sustainable fishing.*
Benefit: *leads to advances in medicine.* Evidence/examples: *medicines have already been discovered to help with chronic pain, asthma and cancer. Scientists believe we are more likely to discover new medicines in the sea than on land.*

Answers

1 *The first sentence. The writer uses a surprising fact.*
2 *The last sentence of the introduction. The order of the points matches the order they are covered in the essay.*
3 *It includes a transitional expression, the topic of the essay, and what this paragraph is going to say about that topic.*
4 *Supporting information: examples or references to studies or reports.*
5 *The order matches the order they were discussed in the essay.*

WRITING

A Elicit an example, then put students into pairs to think of more ideas. In feedback, write on the board any useful language that comes up.

B Tell students to read the essay and to answer the questions. Put them into pairs to compare answers before feedback.

C Go through the information in the box about *Structuring an expository essay*. Tell students to use this to help them as they read the essay again to answer the questions. Again, let them compare with a partner before feedback.

WRITING TASK

A Put students into small groups to brainstorm ideas. Get some whole-class feedback and write on the board useful language.

B Tell students to work individually to select the ideas they want to include and to organize them into paragraphs. Remind them to refer to the box from earlier for guidance on structuring the essay.

C Students write the essay, either in class or as homework if there isn't enough time.

D Ask students to swap their essays with a partner. Tell them to read each other's essays and to edit them, thinking about the points given. They then swap back and discuss how they feel about their partner's editing. In feedback, ask students to share what they liked about their partner's essays and how their partner helped them improve their own.

Unit 6 Review

VOCABULARY

A Choose the correct words to complete the sentences.

1. Airlines keep introducing new long-haul flights to tempt today's *globetrotters* / *distance travelers*.
2. You *embargo* / *embark* from Santiago, Chile, to fly direct to Easter Island.
3. Fourteen of the world's highest *summits* / *culminations* are in the Himalayas.
4. It takes several hours of trekking through *ragged terraces* / *impenetrable terrain* to reach Waimea.
5. Manaus is the closest city to the *heart* / *heat* of the Amazon.
6. Siberia still has a lot of *unchartered* / *uncharted* territory.
7. You can quickly get off the beaten *path* / *road* in the outback in Australia.

B Complete the three-part phrasal verbs with the correct preposition.

1. I use language learning apps to **brush up** __on__ my vocabulary.
2. I'd like to **find out** __about__ volunteering.
3. Playing video games helps me **switch off** __from__ the stress of the day.
4. I frequently **look back** __on__ the vacations I took with my parents as a child.
5. I keep meaning to visit my grandparents, but I never **get around** __to__ it.
6. I **am up** __for__ a camping trip.
7. Whenever I suggest somewhere to go, my family **come up** __with__ objections.
8. I don't like staycations. I want to **get away** __from__ the area where I live for a vacation.

C Match numbers (1–10) to letters (a–j) to form full sentences.

1. I looked far and d
2. She amazes me time after f
3. Slowly but a
4. She's far and g
5. He always puts his heart and c
6. They always work side by h
7. It was a matter of life j
8. It's a real rags-to- b
9. By and e
10. She returned safe and i

a surely he taught himself how to do it.
b riches story, because he was born into a very poor family.
c soul into everything he does.
d wide, but I couldn't find it.
e large, I don't read biographies, but his story was fascinating.
f time with her ideas.
g away the most important scientist working today.
h side, which is really sweet.
i sound from her adventures.
j or death at one point, but he survived.

GRAMMAR

A Complete the text using *can't have, could have, couldn't have, may/might well have, might have, must have* and the verbs in parentheses.

In 1900, three men mysteriously disappeared from the lighthouse where they were working on a remote island in Scotland. Initially, newspapers contained implausible explanations such as that they [1] __could/might/may have been__ (*kill*) killed by ghosts or they [2] __could/might/may have been__ (*capture*) captured by foreign spies. However, a later investigation concluded that they [3] __couldn't/can't have been__ (*not abduct*) abducted, because there were no signs of a struggle.

The investigation found a lot of damage had been done to one of the landing stages and that the kind of damage indicated that this [4] __might/must have been/ might well have been__ (*cause*) caused by large waves during a storm. Therefore, it's possible that the men were securing boxes on the landing stage in bad weather and the investigators believed that they [5] __might/might well have been__ (*sweep*) swept into the sea by strong waves. Normally, one man should have stayed behind to man the lighthouse, but he [6] __could/might/may have gone__ (*go*) to the landing stage to warn his colleagues of the approaching waves.

B Choose the correct words to complete the sentences. Then decide if you agree or disagree with each sentence.

1. In my country, schools have problems *encouraging* / *to encourage* children to study science.
2. It's not worth *studying* / *to study* the arts at school because it's not useful for work.
3. It's impossible *making* / *to make* history interesting for school children.
4. It's time *introducing* / *to introduce* more practical subjects into the school curriculum.
5. Schools need to teach computer programming *helping* / *to help* students get jobs in the future.

Stepping over the abyss in Mondsee, Austria

Extremes (n) an opinion or way of behaving that is as different from another as it is possible to be.
Synonyms: opposite (n), reverse (n)

Mark Twain means that everyone feels fear, but a courageous person can overcome this and do what needs to be done.

Mark Twain (1835–1910) was an American writer best known for his novels *The Adventures of Tom Sawyer* and *Adventures of Huckleberry Finn*.

OBJECTIVES

- describe reactions to extreme experiences
- describe extreme situations and achievements
- discuss extreme jobs
- deal with difficult interview questions
- tell a story about an exciting journey
- write a cover letter

Work with a partner. Discuss the questions.

1 Look at the picture. Why do people put themselves in extreme situations? When do you think this is a positive thing? When is it negative?

2 Look at the quote. How can we resist fear? Is it possible to master fear? Think of examples.

3 Do you prefer extreme experiences or safe/predictable ones? Why? What does it depend on?

EXTREMES 73

OBJECTIVES

Read the unit objectives to the class.

UNIT OPENER QUESTIONS

1 Focus students on the picture and ask if any of them have ever done anything like this. Put them into pairs to discuss the questions, then again get feedback on the range of opinions or experiences in the class.

2 Focus students on the quote and elicit what it means. Elicit an example of how we can master fear, then put students into pairs to discuss the questions. In feedback, elicit more examples and find out how similar students' opinions are.

3 Elicit some examples of safe/predictable experiences, then put students into pairs to discuss the question. In feedback, write on the board any useful language that comes up.

WORKSHEETS

Lesson 7.1 Beyond the limits

Grammar: *it* clefting (W29)

Vocabulary: Feelings (W30)

Lesson 7.2 Extreme jobs

Vocabulary: Polysemy (W31)

Grammar: *what* clefting and *all* clefting (W32)

Vocabulary: Intensifiers (W33)

7.1 Beyond the limits

- Describe reactions to extreme experiences
- Describe extreme situations and achievements

G – *it* clefting **V** – feelings **P** – intonation in question tags **S** – identifying causation

READING

A PREDICT Work in pairs. Look at the picture. Discuss the questions.

1 What do you think the story is going to be about?

2 Have you ever been somewhere like this? If so, how did you feel? If not, how do you think you would feel?

3 Why do you think some people choose to put themselves in dangerous situations?

B SKIM Read *Into the abyss*. What different emotions does the writer go through on her journey? Were any the same as your answers to Exercise A? tentative/nervous, calm, panic, focused, between dread and calm, exhilaration, melancholy

C READ FOR DETAIL Read *Into the abyss again*. Six sentences have been removed from the story. Choose from the sentences (a–g) the one which fits each blank. There is one extra sentence which you do not need to use.

a It was his lack of words that finally allowed me to shake off the morning's nerves.

b It was myself who I was really trying to convince.

c It was that murky half-light, before the night gives in to the dawn, which I now watched.

d It is hard to describe moments like these.

e It is in situations like this that it occurs to me how often I put my life in the hands of complete strangers.

f It was reaching the summit that was my ultimate goal.

g It was just as Batsal disappeared over a rise that I lost my footing.

D INFER MEANING Work in pairs. Decide which of the words in bold from the story match the meanings (1–5).

1 dread (n) fear of something bad that might happen or that is going to happen

2 melancholy (n) a feeling of sadness and of being without hope

3 exhilaration (n) a feeling of extreme excitement and happiness

4 companionable (adj) relaxed and pleasant because shared with friends or friendly people

5 dour (adj) very serious, and not smiling or friendly

E SPEAK Work in groups. Think of a time when you felt one of the emotions from Exercise D. Tell your group about your experience. Mention the following points.

- when you felt this way
- the reason(s) for feeling the emotion

GRAMMAR

it clefting

A Find a sentence in Reading Exercise C that means the same as the one below. What is different about the version in the article? What is the focus in each sentence? Use the information in the box to help you.

I was really trying to convince myself.

> ***it* clefting**
>
> We can use *it* clefting to focus attention on part of a sentence (e.g. the subject, an object, a time clause, a *because*-clause, infinitive, etc).
>
> *My ultimate goal was reaching the summit.* → *It was reaching the summit that was my ultimate goal.*

B Rewrite the remaining sentences in Reading Exercise C so they don't use *it* clefting.

a His lack of words finally allowed me to shake off …

b *I was really trying to convince myself.*

c I watched that murky half-light before …

d Moments like this are hard to describe.

e In situations like this it occurs to me how often I put my life in …

f *My ultimate goal was reaching the summit.*

g Just as Bastal disappeared over a rise I lost my footing.

C Go to the **Grammar Hub** on **page 134**.

D SPEAK Work in pairs and complete the sentences so they are true for you.

1 It was because I wanted to … that I …

2 It's not … that's important …

3 It wasn't until …

SPEAKING

DISCUSS Work in pairs. Can you think of a time when you felt a mix of emotions? Use the questions to help you.

1 What was the situation?

2 How did you feel?

3 What happened?

7.1 Beyond the limits

LEAD-IN

Books closed. Ask students to think of the most difficult thing they have ever done. Give your own example, explaining what it was, why it was difficult, if you managed to do it successfully and how you felt afterwards. Put students into pairs to tell each other about their experiences. In feedback, find out if students talked about similar or very different situations. Write on the board any useful language that comes up here.

READING

A Focus students on the picture and elicit their immediate reaction to it. Then put them into pairs to discuss the questions. In feedback, write on the board useful language that comes up to describe emotions.

B Set a time limit and encourage students to read quickly to identify the emotions. Stress that students don't need to read and understand every word in order to do this, but reassure them that there will be an opportunity to read in more depth later. Stick to your set time limit, and let students compare answers in pairs before feedback. Keep this feedback brief at this stage.

C Tell students to read the article again, more closely this time, and to choose which sentences fit into the blanks. Let them compare with a partner before feedback.

D Draw students' attention to the words in bold in the text and explain the task. Elicit the first one as an example, and demonstrate how to use the context provided by the article to work out or check meaning of the words. Put students into pairs to do the rest. In feedback, clarify the meaning of the words or phrases with more examples if necessary.

E Put students into small groups to discuss the questions. In feedback, ask students to expand on their answers with examples from their own experience if possible.

GRAMMAR

A Ask students to look back at the six sentences.

The writer is emphasizing a contrast between 'my climbing partner' and 'myself'.

B–D Direct students to the **Grammar Hub** (see TB75). Use the **Grammar Worksheet** on page W29 for extra practice.

SPEAKING

Give an example of your own, before they discuss their experiences.

TEACHING IDEA by David Seymour and Maria Popova

Sporting extremes

Use this activity to extend the theme of extreme hobbies.

In groups, imagine you have just won a major international competition in your extreme sport. Write a script for a television interview. Choose two of you to read it out to the class. In groups, invent a new extreme sport, e.g. *It's played with a bean bag and a sock. The contestants are blindfolded …* Which group's sport do you think should be included in the next Olympic Games?

METHODOLOGY HUB by Scott Thornbury

Cleft sentence

In order to foreground one element in a sentence in relation to others, the sentence can be split in two: the result is a cleft sentence. For example, the sentence *Dorothy gave Toto a bone* can be rearranged in at least three ways – depending on the emphasis required – using two verbs instead of the original one:

1 It was Dorothy who gave Toto a bone.

2 It was Toto who Dorothy gave a bone to.

3 It was a bone that Dorothy gave Toto.

In each case, the information that is being emphasized is the noun phrase which follows the first verb in the sentence (in this case, *was*). This follows the principle of end-focus, when new (and therefore important) information goes into the predicate – that is, the part of the sentence after the main verb. This is reflected in the fact that the main stress in a cleft sentence is on the head of the noun phrase after the main verb: *It was DOROTHY who gave Toto a bone.* In order to focus on the action, rather than the agents, a fourth organization is also possible (sometimes called a pseudo-cleft sentence):

4 What Dorothy did was give Toto a bone.

It's important to remember that these arrangements are not arbitrary but respond to the demands of the context. For example, only one of sentences 1–3 logically completes this text:

People said that I gave Toto a bone. They are wrong. It was Dorothy who gave Toto a bone.

METHODOLOGY HUB by Christine Nuttall

Text attack skill: recognizing implications and making inferences

Inference can usually be used to reconstruct the writer's unstated presuppositions. It can also be used for a different purpose: when the writer expects the reader to draw certain unstated conclusions from facts, points in an argument, etc. In this case, the reader has all the evidence required, but is expected to take the final steps himself. In practice the division between these uses of inference is not always clear.

In order to infer, we make use of common sense, powers of reasoning, knowledge of the world and schemata; our schema of what constitutes a good hiding place, for instance, or our schema of the concept 'city', which surely includes the presence of many cars.

The presuppositions the writer makes, and the inferences she expects us to draw, affect our interpretation of the value of a sentence.

Inference is therefore an essential skill, but a tricky one, because it is usually not clear how much the writer expects us to infer. Consider this example:

The second of these statements is demonstrably untrue.

Are we to infer that the first statement is true? Or just that the writer cannot disprove it? We need to be alert to the ambiguity so that we can go back and correct the inference if necessary. Similarly:

The treatment was later withdrawn. Next day, the patient died.

The sequence of sentences suggests, but does not assert, that the withdrawal of treatment caused the death. This kind of doubt is of use to writers who wish to equivocate – to imply something they know to be untrue, without actually lying. (This is a form of innuendo; the political context springs to mind.)

GRAMMAR HUB

7.1 *it* clefting

- We can use the structure *It* + *is/was* + 'focus' + defining adjective clause to focus on a particular piece of information in a sentence. This focus could be:

a person/people	It was **Tenzing Norgay and Edmund Hillary** who first reached the summit of Mount Everest.
a time	It was **1953** when Sir John Hunt successfully led the expedition to reach the summit of Mount Everest.
a place	It is **Mount Everest** which has always captured people's imaginations.
a thing or idea	It was **the challenge of the climb** which inspired generations of climbers.
a clause with *because*	It was **because he had almost reached the summit one year previously** that Tenzing Norgay was hired for the expedition.
a clause with infinitive	It was **to show his respect for the people of Nepal** that Sir Hunt asked Tenzing to make the final climb to the summit.
a clause with *until*	It wasn't **until years later that Tenzing revealed** which climber had first stepped onto the summit of Mount Everest.

Be careful!

- In sentences like this, we usually leave out the second defining adjective clause to avoid repeating the same information.

It wasn't John Hunt who first climbed Everest – it was Edmund Hillary.
NOT ~~It wasn't John Hunt who first climbed Everest – it was Edmund Hillary who first climbed Everest.~~

7.1 *it* clefting

A Write one word in each blank to complete the responses.

1 Did you know that Jack was going to come with us?
No, it ___was___ a surprise that he decided to come.

2 What time did Antonio arrive home?
It was seven o'clock ___when___ I heard his key in the lock.

3 Was he worried about the cost of fixing his laptop?
No, it was losing all his work ___that/which___ he was more worried about.

4 You've met my sister, haven't you?
No, it was your brother ___who/that___ I met.

5 Did you recognize Stella right away?
No, it wasn't ___until___ somebody introduced us that I realized it was her!

B Read the questions. Use *it* clefting and the information in parentheses to complete the answers.

1 What first got you interested in rock climbing? (*my friend Seb*)
___It was my friend Seb who/that___ first got me interested in the sport.

2 What do you think attracts people to Yosemite? (*the idea of being in the wilderness*)
I think ___it is/it's the idea of being in the wilderness which/that___ attracts so many people to go there.

3 When did you set out to climb the Half Dome? (*early in the morning*)
___It was early in the morning when___ we set out.

4 When did you realize how high the Half Dome is? (*only when I reached the top*)
___It was only when I reached the top that___ I realized how high up it is!

C Complete the second sentence so that it has a similar meaning to the first sentence, using the word given. Write between two and five words.

1 Susan wasn't hysterical, Jane was.
WAS
It ___was Jane who/that was___ hysterical, not Susan.

2 Not until after we were rescued did I realize the danger we had been in.
UNTIL
It ___wasn't until after we___ were rescued that I realized the danger we had been in.

3 We took part in the charity walk because we wanted to raise money.
IT
___It was to raise___ money that we took part in the charity walk.

4 What caused her to fail the interview was her over-confidence.
WAS
It ___was her over-confidence which/that___ caused her to fail the interview.

5 I believe yoga will help you to relax.
THAT
It ___is my belief that___ yoga will help you to relax.

6 Somebody else upset Mzia, not you.
YOU
It ___wasn't you who/that / was somebody else who/that___ upset Mzia.

➤ Go back to page 74.

INTO THE ABYSS

[1] c I had arrived early at the café and now sat waiting at a formica table, tentatively sipping the strongest coffee Ex B I had ever tasted. The bitterness was cloying, my hands shaking, but a 6 am start meant that rocket fuel was what I needed. The front door burst open, my coffee spilling Ex B across the table. The light struggling through the smeared glass door was blocked out by the silhouette of a man. He paused there in the doorway for a second. Though I couldn't see his face, I knew he was watching me.

He crossed the café in two strides. A weathered face forced itself into a half smile. 'Carla?' 'Yes. Batsal?'. A curt nod and then, 'If we are going, we go now, before the weather turns.'

I shouldered my pack and we set off down the pot-holed street beneath the shuttered-up houses and the tangle of electricity cables dangling menacingly low above us. 'Where is everyone?' He gestured a few meters ahead where a teenage boy was struggling to kick-start a motorcycle, way past its prime, into life. The boy, who was almost certainly Batsal's son, glanced at me shyly and stepped aside as his father took hold of the motorcycle. With a swift movement the engine roared. Batsal jerked his head at the seat behind him.

We were off. Hurtling down the road and then out toward the distant mountains. [2] e I've been conned, ripped off and outright robbed during my travels even by friendly-faced guides. Batsal was different though … I found his **dour** demeanor weirdly reassuring. [3] a Ex B

Maybe I was feeling too calm as we set off on foot up Ex B a narrow trail. My mind didn't dwell on the terrifying exposure of the route or the crevasses that seemed to plunge down into the depths of the earth. Instead I let my gaze calmly return to the untouched snow of the Ex B peaks which glistened in the low sun. We climbed in **companionable** silence for an hour or so. Up and over some boulders the size of cars.

[4] g A small lapse in concentration. I found myself on my back skidding toward the edge. The boulder felt smooth. I watched in panic as my hands and feet Ex B flailed, trying to get ahold of something, anything. My legs were disappearing into the abyss. I thought of my family. Then time slowed, my focus narrowed and I gripped the rock. As I held on I found myself in a place I'd never been, somewhere between **dread** and calm. Ex B

A searing pain jolted through me as I was yanked by my arm. I twisted my neck to see Batsal retreating up the boulder, dragging me behind him like a rag doll. He pulled me to my feet. The question in his eyes. 'I can continue on,' I replied. [5] b And my shoulder throbbed in protest.

We scrambled upward for five more hours over loose shale. The air was thinning out – every breath was labored. But something of that strange calmness Ex B remained. When we reached a ledge, we stopped. I looked again over at the peaks that seemed no closer than they had at sunrise. 'OK, but let me see it more fully before we turn back.' With one last effort I pulled myself up onto the ridge above the ledge and looked out over the perfect vista. [6] d The sheer **exhilaration** Ex B but also **melancholy** of a journey's end. After ten minutes, we began our descent. My heart thumping. Ex B

Glossary

gesture (v) a movement that communicates a feeling or instruction

skid (v) to slide across the ground in an uncontrolled way

weathered (adj) appearance changed because of the effects of wind, rain, etc

VOCABULARY

Feelings

A **Match the quotes (1–10) with the adjectives in the box. How do the people feel?**

courageous	devastated	disgusted	frustrated	grumpy
humbled	hysterical	indifferent	resilient	superior

1 'I feel bad because there's nothing I can do about my situation.' frustrated

2 'I was overwhelmed by our local community's kindness and generosity.' humbled

3 'I lost control of my emotions and started shaking and crying.' hysterical

4 'I feel terrible because I've lost all hope.' devastated

5 'When I'm in a bad mood, I'm not very nice to other people.' grumpy

6 'You can do what you like. I really don't mind.' indifferent

7 'When other people do stupid things, it makes me feel better about myself!' superior

8 'I know it's dangerous, but I won't let my fear stop me.' courageous

9 'When things go wrong, I just have to pick myself up and continue on.' resilient

10 'I'm so angry! It makes me feel sick.' disgusted

B Go to the **Vocabulary Hub** on **page 146**.

C **SPEAK** **Work in pairs. Think of examples of situations where people feel the ten emotions in Exercise A. Share your ideas with the class.**

LISTENING

A **SPEAK** **Work in pairs and discuss the questions.**

1 What morning TV shows are there in your country?

2 What type of news stories are discussed on them?

B **LISTEN FOR SPECIFIC INFORMATION** **Listen to part of a TV show, *The Breakfast Show*. Decide if the statements are true (T), false (F) or not given (NG).**

7.1

1 Arjun didn't see the accident happening. T

2 The other driver ~~helped Arjun to move the car.~~ pulled the bicyclist free F

3 The car that Arjun lifted weighed over 1,500 kg. NG

4 Professor Ivănescu thinks Arjun has extremely unusual powers. Arjun just lifted part of the car. F

5 Tony (the announcer) doesn't think he'd ever be able to lift the car. T

6 Arjun used hysterical strength. T

7 Whenever our muscles hurt, it means we're damaging them. you could push yourself farther F

8 The bicyclist ~~suffered permanent injuries.~~ made a full recovery F

C **LISTEN FOR CAUSATION** **Listen again. Which pairs of events are examples of correlation (a)? Which are examples of causation (b)? Use the information in the box to help you.**

7.1

Identifying causation

It's important to distinguish between ***correlation*** (= two or more things happen at about the same time) and ***causation*** (= one thing causes another thing to happen).
Common ways of signaling causation include:

- linking expressions (e.g. *as a result of, due to, thanks to, that's why*).
- conditionals (e.g. *If X hadn't happened, Y might not have happened*).
- past perfect in time clauses (e.g. *After I'd done X, Y happened*) rather than simple past (e.g. *After I did X, Y happened*).

1 Arjun wasn't paying attention to the other vehicles. The car ran over a bicycle. (a) / b

2 The driver freed the bicyclist. Arjun put the car down. a / (b)

3 They used a cell phone. A spark caused the car to explode. (a) / b

4 Arjun was brave. The bicyclist wasn't seriously injured. a / (b)

5 Arjun's back hurts now. He lifted the car. (a) / b

6 Tony was unable to lift the car. His muscles hurt. a / (b)

7 The adrenaline wore off. Arjun felt extreme pain. a / (b)

8 Athletes feel stressed. They can break world records. a / (b)

9 The bicyclist survived. She spent a few weeks in the hospital. (a) / b

D **SPEAK** **Work in groups. Discuss the questions.**

1 How do you think you would react in an extreme situation like the one Arjun described?

2 Have you heard of any examples of people doing amazing things in extreme situations? What happened?

7.1 Beyond the limits

VOCABULARY

A Elicit the first one as an example, then put students into pairs to match the other adjectives to the quotes. In feedback, give more examples to fully clarify meaning and, where necessary, practice pronunciation.

B Direct students to the **Vocabulary Hub** (see TB121).

C Give your own example, then put students into pairs to think of examples for the adjectives. In feedback, elicit plenty of different ideas, including any personal examples students want to share. Use the **Vocabulary Worksheet** on page W30 for extra practice.

LISTENING

A Put students into pairs to discuss the questions. In feedback, encourage students to give different answers but don't confirm or reject any at this stage.

7.1 **B** Tell students they're going to listen to a part of a TV show. Give them time to read the sentences before they listen, and make sure they realize that there is a *Not given* option as well as *True* or *False*. After listening, let students compare answers in pairs. In feedback, ask students to support their answers by saying exactly what they remember hearing in the show. (See Audio script below and TB77)

7.1 **C** Go through the information in the box about *Identifying causation*, then put students into pairs to try to answer the questions from memory. Play the recording again for them to listen and check. In feedback, ask students to explain why exactly the events are examples of causation or correlation.

1 *It was a different car that ran over the bicyclist.*
2 *'As soon as she'd freed the bicyclist, I put the car down again.' The use of past perfect after 'as soon as' (rather than simple past, which is also possible here) strongly suggests a cause-effect relationship.*
3 *There's no suggestion that the cell phone caused the explosion. They carried the bicyclist 'to safety' before calling the ambulance, which suggests they were some distance away from the car.*
4 *'There's no doubt that the bicyclist escaped serious injury thanks to Arjun's heroic actions.'*
5 *Arjun says that he's had a bad back for several months, but we don't know whether it started hurting before, during or after the accident.*
6 *'I was in too much pain to lift the car.' Structures with 'too' or 'not enough' + 'to' + base form show a clear cause-effect relationship.*
7 *'He didn't notice the pain until the adrenaline had worn off.' The use of past perfect after 'until' strongly suggests a cause-effect relationship.*
8 *'But in high-stress situations, …, it's often possible to go much higher. That's why so many world records are broken at such events.'*
9 *'… after a few weeks in the hospital, she said if it hadn't been for my actions, she might not be alive today.' In other words, she survived as a result of Arjun's actions. We don't know whether her stay in the hospital also saved her life.*

D Put students into groups to discuss the questions. In feedback, ask students to expand on their answers, especially if they or anyone they know have been in a similar situation.

AUDIO SCRIPT

7.1

Listening, Exercise B
A = Arjun C = Catina T = Tony

T: Welcome back to *The Breakfast Show* with me, Tony Scott. Now I'd like you to meet a real-life superhero, Arjun Prasad. Good morning, Arjun. What's your story?

A: Good morning. Well, I was driving home from work about three months ago, not really paying attention to the other vehicles, when suddenly I heard a loud bang from the road behind me. I looked in my mirror and saw a car had run over a bicycle. The bicyclist was still trapped under the car, which was leaking fuel onto the road. (Ex B Q1)

T: Sounds terrifying! So the car could have exploded at any second, couldn't it?

Ex B Q2 **A:** Exactly. So I ran over and lifted up the car while the other driver pulled the bicyclist free. As soon as she'd freed the bicyclist, I put the car down again. Then together we carried her to safety and called an ambulance. And we were just in time – the car exploded a few seconds later. A spark must have caused the fuel to catch fire.

T: My goodness! Now, you said you lifted up the car. But that's incredible. I mean, you're a big guy, aren't you? But a car!

A: Yeah. It's weird, isn't it?

T: It certainly is. This seems like a good point to introduce my second guest, Catina Ivănescu, a professor of kinesiology. Catina, how is it possible for a person to lift a car? I mean, a car weighs, what, a metric ton and a half, doesn't it?

C: Good morning. Yes, a typical family car weighs between 1,500 and 2,000 kilograms. The world record for weight-lifting is just over 500 kilograms.

T: Are you saying that Arjun lifted over three times the world record?

Ex B Q4 **C:** No, not at all. If he'd lifted the car above his head, that would have been a superhuman feat. But in fact Arjun just lifted part of the car a few centimeters off the ground. Three or even all four of the car's wheels were still on the ground, supporting most of the car's weight.

T: Right. So Arjun's achievement is nothing special, then?

C: Far from it! First of all, as Arjun said, it was an incredibly dangerous situation, with a high risk of an explosion at any second. So Arjun's actions were unquestionably courageous. There's no doubt that the bicyclist escaped serious injury thanks to Arjun's heroic actions. But in addition, it still takes exceptional strength to lift a car, even by a few centimeters.

T: OK. Let's conduct a little experiment now. We have here in the studio a car of the same model as the one you lifted, Arjun. Could you lift it for us now?

A: Uh, not really. I've had a bad back for several months, and the doctor advised me against doing any more heavy lifting.

PRONUNCIATION

7.2 **A** Explain that all the sentences are extracts from the TV show they listened to. Do the first one as an example. Don't immediately tell students that they need to use a question tag, but try to elicit this. Put them into pairs to do the rest, then play the recording for them to listen and check.

7.2 **B** Put them into pairs and encourage them to say the sentences out loud to help them decide what sounds right. Play the recording again for them to listen and check, and pause after each one for students to repeat.

C Go through the example, then put students into small groups to have similar conversations about the pictures. Monitor to see how well they do this, and in feedback invite some of the more successful groups to perform their discussion for the class.

Extra activity
As students practice the intonation of question tags in their groups, they can record themselves (e.g. on their smartphones if these are available and allowed). Encourage students to share their recordings to comment and check on their pronunciation in pairs.

SPEAKING HUB

A Put students into groups of three, and assign each person one of the roles. Give them time to decide on the details of the extreme abilities or achievements they're going to discuss.

B Tell students to practice their interviews. Ask them to improvise and not to script anything, but remind them about the adjectives and question tags from earlier in the lesson that they could try to use. Monitor to help or prompt if needed.

C Each group acts out their interview for the class. Tell the other students to listen carefully and to think about how believable and how entertaining the interviews are, and why.

D In whole-class feedback, ask students to explain which interviews they found the most believable and entertaining, and why. Finish with feedback on language use.

Extra activity
Elicit examples of super powers, either from well-known stories or from the students' own ideas. Put students into groups to discuss which of the super powers they would most like to have and why.

7.1 (continued)

T: Oh. That's a shame!
C: Why don't you lift it, Tony?
Ex B Q5 **T:** Me? Uh, OK. Wow! That's heavy! There's no way I could lift that!
C: Well, not here and now. But who knows? Maybe if you were in the situation Arjun found himself in, you might be able to. It's all about something called 'hysterical strength': the strength that you get in extreme situations.
Ex B Q6 **T:** So that's what helped Arjun, then, was it? Hysterical strength?
C: Exactly. Basically, we're all a lot stronger than we think we are. But when we push our muscles to the limit, it's really painful.
T: Yeah, I know. I was in too much pain to lift the car – it was agony!
C: But that pain is just our body's way of telling us to stop exerting ourselves before we break anything. We feel it when our muscles are operating at
Ex B Q7 around 60% of their potential. But, you could, theoretically, push yourself a lot farther without damaging your muscles.
T: OK. But surely it would hurt so much that you'd want to stop.
C: Exactly. But in a high-stress situation, your body is flooded with adrenaline, which blocks your body's pain sensors – but only temporarily. That's how Arjun was able to go way beyond 60% of his strength. He didn't notice the pain until the adrenaline had worn off.
A: Exactly. I literally didn't feel any pain at all until about an hour after the accident. And then every muscle in my body was in agony!
T: I'm sure. Uh, I'm just wondering, Catina. We can't harness this strength in everyday life, can we?
C: Well, world-class athletes are able to harness it to some extent. During training, they can often push themselves up to 80% of their potential. But in high-stress situations, such as when they're chasing an Olympic medal, it's often possible to go much higher. That's why so many world records are broken at such events, rather than in regular training sessions. The adrenaline blocks the pain, allowing you to go way beyond your normal limit.
T: Ah. OK, one last question, Arjun. What happened to the bicyclist?
Ex B Q8 **A:** She made a full recovery. When I met her last week, after a few weeks in hospital, she said if it hadn't been for my actions, she might not be alive today. But I don't feel like a hero – I'm just a normal guy, aren't I?
T: Well, I'm not so sure about that, Arjun! Anyway, let's have a break now, shall we? We'll be back very soon.

PRONUNCIATION

Intonation in question tags

7.2 **A** Complete the extracts from *The Breakfast Show* with the correct question tag. Then listen to check.

1 So the car could have exploded at any second, ___couldn't it___?
2 I mean, you're a big guy, ___aren't you___?
3 It's weird, ___isn't it___?
4 I mean, a car weighs, what, a ton and a half, ___doesn't it___?
5 So that's what helped Arjun, then, ___was it___?
6 We can't harness this strength in everyday life, ___can we___?
7 I'm just a normal guy, ___aren't I___?
8 Anyway, let's have a break now, ___shall we___?

7.2 **B** Listen again. Try to copy the intonation.

C SPEAK Work in small groups and discuss the extreme human abilities shown in pictures 1–5. Use question tags to ask questions, make suggestions, check assumptions and invite agreement.

Should we start with this one? It's bungee jumping, isn't it?

SPEAKING HUB

A PLAN You are going to conduct a daytime TV interview about examples of extreme achievements. Work in groups of three. Use pictures 1–5 to help you.

Student A: You are the **interviewee**. You can talk about a real experience from your life, or you can invent the details.

Student B: You are an **expert** (e.g. a college professor). You have been invited to explain Student A's abilities/achievements. You can use your real knowledge or invent details.

Student C: You are the **interviewer**. It's your job to make the interviewee and the expert feel comfortable, and to make the TV show entertaining for the audience at home.

B PRACTICE Practice your interview. Try to use the vocabulary, grammar and pronunciation from this lesson in your interviews.

C PRESENT Act out your interview for the class.

D REFLECT Which of the interviews was the most believable? Which was the most entertaining?

3

4

5

- Describe reactions to extreme experiences
- Describe extreme situations and achievements

7.2 Extreme jobs

- Discuss extreme jobs
- Deal with difficult interview questions

G – *what* clefting and *all* clefting
P – *any* and *really*
V – polysemy; intensifiers
S – understanding reference within texts

READING

A SPEAK Work in pairs. Look at the pictures. Why do people choose to work in such extreme places?

B READ FOR MAIN IDEA Read *Risky business*. Match the statements (1–6) with the workplaces (a–c).

1. It's dangerous if you go up too fast. c
2. The weather may prevent you from working. b
3. You'll need to work at least half a year. a
4. You'll earn a lot of money. c
5. It's hard to get a job there. a
6. It takes over a week to get home. c

a The Antarctic
b At extreme heights
c Under the ocean

C READ FOR REFERENCES What do the reference devices (1–10) in the article refer to? Use the information in the box to help you.

1. people in general (E)
2. a job in Antarctica (A)
3. people in general (E)
4. people (but not writer) (E)
5. being a window cleaner (C)
6. (more) than a being a window cleaner (A)
7. exception to conditions (A)
8. being a saturation diver (C)
9. saturation divers (C)
10. the fact that they're well-paid (C)

Understanding reference within texts

Reference devices (e.g. pronouns, articles, contrast linkers, comparatives) link different parts of a text.

Anaphoric reference: refers back to something mentioned earlier in the text.

Cataphoric reference: refers forward to something mentioned later in the text.

Exophoric reference: refers to things outside the text, e.g. *you* (the reader), *they* (people in general).

D SPEAK Work in pairs and discuss the questions. Do any of the jobs in the article appeal to you? Which would you hate?

RISKY BUSINESS

[1]They say over half of us are doing jobs that we don't care about, and a further 16% actively hate our jobs. If you're **sick** of the nine-to-five, here are some of the more extreme places where you can actually make a living.

ANTARCTICA

Unfortunately, it's not exactly easy – or cheap – to visit Antarctica as a tourist. So if you really want to go, what you should do is get a long-term job, not a summer or spring break job: no employer is going to pay your airfare if you're planning to stay for less than six months. Ex B Q3

There are scientific jobs for biologists, glaciologists, geologists, meteorologists, oceanologists, and so on. Trouble is, there's plenty of **competition** for them, with hundreds of applicants for each vacancy. Ex B Q5 Your best chance of **landing** [2]one is to be a well-qualified specialist already, ideally with a doctorate or two.

There are also a few support jobs for engineers, technicians, divers, radio operators, etc. Just be warned: you'll spend most of your time on the base, where you'll quickly get bored with the same faces every day. Due to the extreme weather, it's usually too dangerous (or too expensive) to venture out into the wilderness for some sightseeing.

AT EXTREME HEIGHTS

For [3]those of us who get dizzy at the thought of standing on a chair, the prospect of climbing up a radio mast, wind turbine or skyscraper is the stuff of our worst nightmares. But for [4]the lucky few who have no fear of heights, there are plenty of career opportunities.

[5]It's not especially glamorous, but the easiest way to make a career at heights is as a window cleaner. You can literally start at the bottom – all you'll need is a ladder and a bucket – and gradually work your way up to office blocks and skyscrapers.

A [6]more lucrative career for real-life 'high-climbers' is as a tower climber. These brave people spend their time 100 to 150 meters above the ground, inspecting cellular phone towers for damage, changing light bulbs, replacing cables, etc. One of the biggest challenges is that they need to work in all **conditions**, including the cold, the wind and the rain, all of which add to the level of danger. Ex B Q2 The [7]one exception is thunderstorms, which tower climbers steer well clear of.

7.2 Extreme jobs

LEAD-IN

Books closed. Give an example of your own, then put students into pairs to tell each other about an unusual job they or someone they know has had. Get feedback, and ask students to decide which job is the most unusual.

READING

A Focus students on the pictures and tell them that they show people at work. Elicit some ideas for what the jobs are, then put students into pairs to discuss the question. In feedback, encourage students to express a range of different opinions.

B Tell students they're going to find out exactly what the jobs in the pictures are, and why people choose to do them. Tell them to read the article and to match the statements to the workplaces. Put students into pairs to compare answers before feedback. In feedback, ask students to justify their answers with reference to the text.

C Go through the information in the box about *Understanding reference within texts*. Point out the underlined words in the article, and tell students that they are all examples of these reference devices. Elicit the first one as an example, then put students into pairs to decide what type of reference device each one is. Encourage them to read closely around each underlined word to help them fully understand its purpose in the text. In feedback, elicit as much detail as you can in the explanations to ensure all students understand the answers.

D Put students into pairs to discuss the questions. In feedback, ask students to explain their answers, and encourage them to agree or disagree with each other.

Extra activity

Give your own example, then put students into pairs to discuss what changes they would most like to make to their lives. Tell them they could think about their career, their home, their family and friends, their appearance or anything else. Encourage students to listen to their partner and to try to give them advice about what they should do.

METHODOLOGY HUB by Scott Thornbury

Reference

Reference is the relation between language forms and things in the real world (their referents). Some language is highly referential, in the sense that we can identify the particular person or thing that is referred to, as in *That towel belongs to me*, or *The White House is in Washington*. But, more often, words do not refer to specific things but to concepts. Thus, in *I need a new towel*, the referent of the word *towel* is not a specific towel that I can see and feel. Rather, it is a *generic* towel – the concept of a towel. My addressees understand me, not because there is a towel present in the context but because they share the concept of what a towel is. Learning a second language is largely the matching of new forms to existing concepts. But, of course, the process can be facilitated by using real things (realia) or pictures of them to represent the concepts we are teaching.

Reference also has a narrower sense and describes the relation between language forms and their referents in discourse.

Thus, in the exchange:

A: *Where's my towel?*

B: *I hung it on the line.*

the pronoun *it* refers back to *my towel*. This kind of reference is called anaphoric reference, meaning back reference. In the sentence *That's what I like, a nice dry towel*, the pronoun *that* refers forward in the discourse and is an instance of cataphoric reference (forward reference). Finally, the use of the definite article *the*, in *I hung it on the line*, is a kind of reference, too. But it is not a reference that has a referent in the discourse. The referent is in the shared world of speaker and addressee. (Compare it to *I hung it on a line*, which has no such shared referent.) Direct reference to the non-linguistic context is called exophoric reference. Deictic terms – like *this*, *that*, *here* and *there* – typically have exophoric reference.

Reference, using pronouns (such as *it*, *he* and *they*) and determiners (such as *this …*, *that …* and *the …*), contributes to the overall cohesion of spoken and written text.

7.2 Extreme jobs

VOCABULARY

A Go through the information in the box about *Polysemy* and tell students that the words in bold in the text are all examples of this. Elicit the first one as an example, demonstrating how students should read carefully and use the context to decide which definition is more appropriate in this case. Put students into pairs to do the others.

B Remind students that both definitions offered for each word in Exercise A are possible, depending on the context. Tell them to look back at the definitions and to answer the questions.

C Direct students to the **Vocabulary Hub** (see TB121). Use the **Vocabulary Worksheet** on page W31 for extra practice.

GRAMMAR

A Go through the information in the box about *what clefting* and *all clefting*, and tell students that there is an example of each in the article. Put them into pairs to find the examples and to complete the box. In feedback, make sure students understand how the sentences from the text have a more dramatic effect than the simpler sentences in the box.

B Direct students to the **Grammar Hub**. Use the **Grammar Worksheet** on page W32 for extra practice.

SPEAKING

Give an example, then put students into pairs to do the task together. Assign one student the role of someone who is thinking of applying for one of the jobs in the article and their partner the role of the person giving them advice. When they have finished, swap roles and tell the student thinking of applying for a job to choose a different one from their partner. In feedback, ask students what the best advice they received was, and if it changed their mind about whether or not they wanted the job. Finish with feedback on students' use of cleft structures during the activity.

GRAMMAR HUB

7.2 *what* clefting and *all* clefting

- We can use a *what* clause + *be* + second clause in order to emphasize the information in the second clause.

  With this structure, the information in the *what* clause is usually known or understood whereas the information in the second clause is usually new and therefore the main focus of the sentence.

  What Prianka wants is to escape the rat race.
  What they needed, after their walk in the snow, was a hot bath.
  What he decided to do was to change careers.
- To emphasize a verb in the second clause, we can use the structure: *what* clause with *do* + *be* + second clause. We can use the infinitive or the base form after the verb *be*.

  What he does is (to) climb cellular phone towers.
- We can use *All* instead of *What* at the beginning of the first clause. This emphasizes the idea of there being 'only one thing'.

  All you need to do in the interview is (to) act naturally. (= the only thing you need to do)
- It is also possible to use *Why, Where, How, When* to begin this kind of cleft sentence.

  Why he enjoys extreme sports is a mystery to me.

Be careful!

- The structure *what* clause + *be* + second clause is reversible.

  What he enjoys about his job is living in the wilderness. OR Living in the wilderness is what he enjoys about his job.
- The structure *what* clause with *do* + *be* + second clause is not reversible.

  What they did was move to the country. NOT ~~Move to the countryside was what they did.~~

7.2 *what* clefting and *all* clefting

A Reorder the words to make sentences.

1 about the winter / dislike / is / What / the long nights / I
What I dislike about the winter is the long nights.

2 I / want / a normal life / All / is
All I want is a normal life.

3 we're / a solution to our problems / to find / is / here / What
What we're here to find is a solution to our problems.

4 the last train / we missed / happened / that / What / was
What happened was that we missed the last train.

5 I / to ask you / did / All / a simple question / was
All I did was to ask you a simple question.

6 I / remember / All / is / really difficult / the questions / were / that
All I remember is that the questions were really difficult.

B Rewrite these sentences using *what* clefting or *all* clefting.

1 I've found that working underwater isn't as bad as it sounds.
What I've found is (that) working underwater isn't as bad as it sounds.

2 I'm only saying that you should think twice before moving to Antarctica.
All I'm saying is (that) you should think twice before moving to Antarctica.

3 I'm going to look for a job as a window cleaner.
What I'm going to do is look for a job as a window cleaner. / I'm going to look for is a job as a window cleaner.

4 I only asked for your opinion.
All I did was ask for your opinion. / I asked for was your opinion.

5 I bought a ladder and a bucket.
What I bought was a ladder and a bucket.

➤ Go back to page 79.

ON THE OCEAN FLOOR

[8]It's one of the most bizarre careers imaginable. [9]These people do construction, maintenance and demolition work 300 meters or more beneath the ocean's surface. To survive the extreme **pressure** at such depths, they spend weeks or months at a time living in tiny pressurized containers, either deep underwater or inside pressure tanks on board ships. Welcome to the world of the saturation diver.

Breathing pressurized air causes inert gases to dissolve in your blood and body tissues. If you were to release the pressure suddenly, by coming to the surface, the bubbles formed would quickly kill you. Ex B Q1 To avoid this, saturation divers spend several hours building up to the necessary pressure, saturating their bodies with inert gases. At the end of their work, they spend as much as eleven days de-pressurizing, before finally returning to normal life. Ex B Q6

Saturation divers carry out essential work for some of the world's richest businesses, so [10]it's no surprise to find that they're extremely well-paid. Ex B Q4 However, before sending off your **application**, you need to consider how you'd feel about spending months in a tiny metal container with your co-workers, constantly aware that the failure of a single pressure valve would mean certain death.

Glossary

lucrative (adj) bringing a lot of money
venture (v) to go somewhere unpleasant, dangerous or exciting

VOCABULARY
Polysemy

A Choose the correct definition of the words in bold from *Risky business*. Use the context in the article and the information in the box to help you.

Polysemy

Polysemy is where a word has two or more related meanings. Sometimes different meanings have different grammatical properties (e.g. countable/uncountable).

1 sick
- a feel unwell
- (b) bored or tired of something

2 competition
- (a) rivalry
- b a contest

3 to land
- a bring a plane down
- (b) get something you want

4 condition(s)
- (a) weather
- b an important part of a contract

5 pressure
- a a feeling of too much work
- (b) a 'pushing' force

6 application
- a a way of using something
- (b) a document stating why you want a job

B In which pair of meanings from Exercise A is one meaning countable and the other uncountable? In which pair is one meaning always plural? competition, condition(s)

C Go to the **Vocabulary Hub** on **page 146**.

GRAMMAR
what clefting and *all* clefting

A Complete the rules with examples from the article.

***what* clefting and *all* clefting**

Form: *what/all* + FIRST FOCUS + *is/was* + SECOND FOCUS

Example: *What you need to succeed is mental strength.*

We can use *what* clefting to focus attention on two different parts of a sentence by keeping them separate.

1 You should get a long-term job. → What you should do is get a long-term job.

All clefting has the extra meaning of *only*.

2 You'll only need a ladder and bucket. → All you'll need is a ladder and a bucket.

B Go to the **Grammar Hub** on **page 134**.

SPEAKING

DISCUSS Work in pairs. Think about the advantages and disadvantages of the jobs in the article. Your partner is planning to apply for one of the jobs. Give your partner advice using *what* clefting and *all* clefting.

LISTENING

A SPEAK Work in pairs. Have you ever had a stressful job interview? What happened?

B Read *Extreme job interviews*. Rank the questions in order from hardest to easiest (1–7).

7.3 **C LISTEN FOR DETAIL** Listen to a recruitment specialist giving advice about the questions below. For each question, write notes on the dos and don'ts for job interviewees.

7.4 **D LISTEN FOR GIST** Now listen to some extracts from an interview for a job as a marketing designer. Does Oscar (the interviewee) follow the recruitment specialist's advice for each question?

EXTREME job interviews

These days, recruiters are going to extremes to sort the best from the rest. The following questions, all taken from real job interviews, have no correct answer. But they are designed to show how you cope with stress and how creative you are. They might also reveal the real 'you' behind the business suit and the polished résumé.

- *What would you take with you to a desert island and why?*
- *If you could be any dinosaur, which dinosaur would you be?*
- *What's your biggest weakness?*
- *Name four uses for a stapler, without the staples.*
- *How many square meters of pizza are eaten in the US each year?*
- *What's the most interesting thing about you that we wouldn't learn from your résumé?*
- *How would your worst enemy describe you?*

7.4 **E LISTEN FOR DETAIL** Listen again. Choose the correct options (a, b or c) to answer the questions.

1 How would Oscar feel on a desert island?
   a lonely (b) inspired c upset

2 What would be Oscar's priority as a dinosaur?
   a pleasure b beauty (c) safety

3 How does Oscar feel at the end of each day?
   (a) relieved b disappointed c exhausted

4 Which one of the following is NOT mentioned as a use for a stapler?
   a tissue-holder b child's toy (c) doorstop

5 How many pizzas does Oscar think a typical American eats each year?
   (a) 12 b 144 c 300

6 How does Oscar feel about taking care of his brothers and sisters?
   a grateful b frustrated (c) proud

7 How does Oscar feel about people who don't like him?
   a grumpy (b) indifferent c superior

F SPEAK Work in pairs. Ask and answer the questions from *Extreme job interviews*.

LISTENING

A Give an example about yourself or someone you know, then put students into pairs to discuss the questions.

B Tell students to read about extreme job interviews, and then to rank the questions in order of how difficult they would find them to answer. Put students into pairs to compare.

7.3 **C** Tell students to write notes as they listen, and let them compare in pairs.

Suggested answers

- *Do focus on the image you want to convey about yourself; Don't pretend to be something you're not.*
- *Do justify your choice; Don't say obvious answers like 'T-Rex'.*
- *Do describe a weakness you've overcome; Don't claim to have no weaknesses.*
- *Do think beyond the obvious applications and explore the properties of the object; Don't say 'a paperweight'.*
- *Do work out a plan; Don't say any old number that pops into your head.*
- *Do remind the interviewer that you're a real person; Don't forget to bring your story back to how you're suitable for the job.*
- *Do say you don't have enemies, talk about weaknesses that are strengths and show you can see yourself through others' eyes; Don't leave it as 'I don't have enemies'.*

7.4 **D Suggested answers**

- *Yes. They are likely to be looking for someone creative rather than practical/sensible.*
- *Yes. He avoided the obvious answer and justified his choice.*
- *Yes. He described a past weakness and how he overcame it.*
- *Yes and no. The 'paperweight' answer was too obvious, but the other three were more creative.*
- *Yes (mostly). He made fair estimates and worked through a logical process. His answer was right on the edge of the target 'ballpark figures', but this is probably OK.*
- *Yes and no. He described something real and personal. He implied that he has skills that could be useful in business. However, he didn't explicitly show how his experiences are relevant to the job.*
- *Yes. He answered this question well, which is a missed opportunity.*

7.4 **E** Put students into pairs to try to answer the questions from memory. Then play the recording again for them to listen and check.

F Put students into pairs to ask and answer the questions together. Remind them to try to follow the recruitment specialist's advice. In feedback, ask students how well they think their partner answered the questions, and why.

AUDIO SCRIPT

7.3

Listening, Exercise C
RS = Recruitment specialist

RS: OK, so let's look at those questions now. Interviewers often use the 'desert island' question to determine what sort of person you are. A practical survivor type might take a knife or even a satellite phone. A more creative dreamer would take something original and fun. There's no correct answer – it depends what type of employee they're looking for. Just don't pretend to be something you're not. Focus instead on the image you want to convey about yourself. *(Ex C)*

Next, the 'dinosaur' question tests your ability to avoid obvious answers. Ninety percent of people say T. Rex, the first dinosaur they think of. But unless the employer is looking to recruit cold-blooded predators, T. Rex would be pretty unsuitable as a potential employee. Almost any other answer is much better – as long as you justify it. *(Ex C)*

The 'weakness' question is an old classic. Whatever you do, don't claim to have no weaknesses, or you'll come across as arrogant and lacking in self-awareness. A good trick is always to describe a weakness that you've overcome. *(Ex C)*

With the 'stapler' question, the key is to think beyond the obvious applications, and to explore the properties of the object in question. I wouldn't recommend saying 'a paperweight' – it's what everyone always says. *(Ex C)*

OK, so the 'pizza' question tests your ability to make estimates and work out a plan. So don't just say any old number that pops into your head. You don't need to produce an accurate answer – which would be about 150 million in this case. But of course it's better if you're in the right ballpark, which in this case would be between around 75 and 300 million. *(Ex C)*

Next, the 'not on your résumé question is a great opportunity to remind the interviewers that you're a real person, not some invented character whose life revolves around landing this particular job. It's fine to get personal, but don't forget to bring your story back to how you're suitable for the job. *(Ex C)*

Finally, for the 'worst enemy' question, it's always worth mentioning that you don't have any enemies. But resist the temptation to leave it there; talk about perceived weaknesses that are actually strengths. Demonstrate your ability to see yourself through others' eyes – a crucial skill for any employee. *(Ex C)*

7.4

Listening, Exercise D
I1 = Interviewer 1 O = Oscar I2 = Interviewer 2

I1: What would you take with you to a desert island and why?

O: Uh, a notebook and a pen. I find writing poetry immensely calming, so an extended stay on a desert island, without any other people to distract me, would really get my creative juices flowing. I'd be utterly devastated if I couldn't record my ideas on paper. *(Ex D; Ex E Q1)*

I2: Thank you. If you could be any dinosaur, which dinosaur would you be?

O: Oh, a pterodactyl, a flying dinosaur, soaring high above the plains. The views would be spectacular, and the sense of freedom would be really exhilarating. But much more importantly, compared to the ground, the sky would be a relatively good place for staying out of harm's way! *(Ex D; Ex E Q2)*

7.2 Extreme jobs

VOCABULARY

A Point out that all the sentences come from the interview they listened to. Elicit the first one as an example, then put students into pairs to do the rest. If students are unsure about the meaning of any of the intensifiers, avoid clarifying at this stage. Tell students that you will cover that next.

B Elicit the first one as an example, demonstrating how to use the context provided by the sentences to work out the meaning of the intensifiers. Put students into pairs to do the rest. In feedback, give further examples to clarify meaning where necessary, and practice pronunciation where needed, too.

C Direct students to the **Vocabulary Hub** (see TB121).

D Give one example of your own, using one of the intensifiers from Exercise A. Then put students into small groups to think of more advice. In feedback, comment on how well students have used the intensifiers, and write on the board any particularly good advice. Ask the class to decide which piece of advice is the best. Use the **Vocabulary Worksheet** on page W33 for extra practice.

PRONUNCIATION

7.5 **A** Put students into pairs and encourage them to read the sentences aloud to each other to help them decide whether the words *any* and *really* are stressed or unstressed. Then play the recording for students to listen and check. In feedback, check students understand that *any* is stressed to mean *it doesn't matter which one*, and *really* is stressed before extreme adjectives to mean *absolutely*.

7.6 **B** Play the recording for students to listen and identify where *any* or *really* is stressed. In feedback, elicit how the meaning changes when they are stressed or unstressed.

SPEAKING HUB

A Put students into groups of three to decide on the details of the job, and some suitable interview questions. Remind them about the kind of 'extreme' interview questions they heard about earlier, and encourage them to come up with similar questions for their interview. Monitor to help and prompt where necessary.

B Tell the groups to decide on what they would consider 'good' or 'bad' answers for their questions. Again, remind them about the recruitment specialist's advice they heard earlier.

C Put students into new pairs, so that they are working with someone from a different group, to conduct an interview. Make sure they explain what the job is before starting the interview. After both partners have interviewed each other and given feedback and advice, change pairs again so everyone is with someone from a different group and being interviewed for a different job. Again, tell students to explain what the job is, carry out the interview and give feedback and advice afterwards.

D Put students back into their original groups to talk about the different people they interviewed and to decide who should get the job. In feedback, ask each group to reveal who they want to offer the job to, and why. Finish with feedback on students' use of language during the activity.

Extra activity

Elicit well-known people, either alive or dead, and write their names on the board. Tell students to imagine they could ask one question to each of the people on the board. Put them into pairs to discuss what they would like to ask. In feedback, compare students' questions and find out how similar they are. Ask students what they think the answers to the questions would be.

7.4 (continued)

I1: OK. What's your biggest weakness?

Ex E Q2 **O:** Hmm, well I tend to be somewhat disorganized. When I was a student, I frequently missed deadlines. But then I learned some remarkably simple techniques, and I've improved noticeably since then. For example, I make a to-do list every day, and I can't have any rewards until I've cleared my list. It takes a lot of self-discipline, but it's so satisfying to know that, at long last, there's nothing hanging over you. (Ex E Q3)

I2: Thank you. Name four uses for a stapler, without the staples.

Ex D **O:** You could use it to pick up tissues without getting your hands dirty! You could also use it as a hammer for bashing things. I suppose you could also give it to a child as a toy – the child might have fun pressing it and listening to the noises. And I suppose you could also use it as a paperweight, to hold down papers when it's windy. (Ex E Q4)

I1: Hmm. How many square meters of pizza are eaten in the US each year?

O: A standard pizza is, what, 30 centimeters across? So you could easily fit nine inside a square meter. In fact, if you cut them up, there'd be room for possibly three more in the spaces, so, twelve. That's a year's supply for me. I'm not completely sure how typical I am – I guess some people would eat that many in a single month! But if we assume I'm not radically different from the average American, then we're looking at around one square meter per person per year. The US has around 300 million people, so that's my estimate: 300 million. (Ex E Q5; Ex D)

I1: Not bad. What's the most interesting thing about you that we wouldn't learn from your résumé?

O: Well, I have six younger brothers and sisters, who are all really adorable. I'm the oldest, so I've spent most of my life looking after them while my parents were working. It's been really challenging, because I never had any time to myself and it was practically impossible to study, but it's also incredibly rewarding when I see how far they've come. (Ex D; Ex E Q6)

I2: Great. How would your worst enemy describe you?

Ex D **O:** Hah! I'm not the sort of person who has outright enemies. It used to irritate me when people treated me badly, but I've learned that the best trick is to ignore them and move on! I know some people are jealous of what I've achieved and they think I'm lucky. But they haven't seen all the struggles I've been through. The people who matter know that I deserve any luck that has come my way. (Ex E Q7)

I1: OK, great. Thanks. That's the end of the interview.

VOCABULARY
Intensifiers

A Complete the sentences from the interview with intensifiers in the box. Sometimes more than one answer is possible.

altogether immensely noticeably outright practically radically relatively remarkably somewhat utterly

1 I find writing poetry immensely/remarkably calming.
2 I'd be utterly devastated if I couldn't record my ideas on paper.
3 Compared to the ground, the sky would be a relatively good place.
4 I tend to be somewhat/remarkably disorganized.
5 I learned some remarkably/relatively simple techniques, and I've improved noticeably/immensely since then.
6 I'm not altogether sure how typical I am.
7 I'm not radically/noticeably different from the average American …
8 It was usually practically impossible to study.
9 I'm not the sort of person who has outright enemies.

B Work in pairs. Complete the sentences with an intensifier from Exercise A.

1 immensely means 'to a huge extent'.
2 utterly is mainly used before negative adjectives and adverbs.
3 relatively means 'compared to other things'.
4 somewhat means 'a little'.
5 noticeably means 'so much that it's obvious or easy to see'.
6 altogether is frequently used in negative sentences, especially with 'sure'.
7 outright is often used before nouns with a negative meaning.
8 practically means 'not really 100%, but as good as 100%'.
9 radically is often used before 'different'.

C Go to the **Vocabulary Hub** on **page 146**.

D SPEAK Work in small groups. Offer advice for preparing for and coping with extreme job interviews. Use intensifiers in your advice.

PRONUNCIATION
any and *really*

A 7.5 Listen to the extracts from the recruitment specialist's advice. Underline *any* and *really* when they are stressed.

1 Almost any other answer is much better …
2 So don't just say any old number that pops into your head.
3 … on a desert island, without any other people …
4 … would really get my creative juices flowing.
5 … the sense of freedom would be really exhilarating.
6 It's been really challenging …

B 7.6 Listen and underline the sentence (a or b) in which *really* or *any* is stressed.

1 a The interview was really difficult.
b The interview was really impossible.
2 a Don't say anything!
b Don't say anything!
3 a Her house was really dirty.
b Her house was really dirty.
4 a Any questions can be answered.
b Any questions can be answered.

SPEAKING HUB

A PLAN Work in groups of three. You are going to interview several candidates for a job. First, decide what the job is, what exactly it involves and what sort of candidate you are looking for. Then plan four or five extreme questions for your interview. Use the ideas below or your own ideas.

- If you could be any …, what would you be?
- Name four uses for a …
- How many … could you fit inside this room?
- How would … describe you?

B PREPARE Discuss what would be a 'good' or 'bad' answer for each of your questions, bearing in mind the type of candidate you are looking for.

C INTERVIEW Interview two candidates from other groups. At the end of each interview, provide feedback on what the candidate did well/badly and give advice on how to improve.

D DISCUSS Work in your original groups to choose the best candidate for your job. Make sure you justify your choice. Share your decision and reasoning with the class.

- Discuss extreme jobs
- Deal with difficult interview questions

Café Hub

7.3 Push your limits

Ⓐ– fronting Ⓢ– changing and recycling topics

Driving on the edge

A Work in pairs. Look at the picture and discuss the questions.

1 Where do you think this is? The Peruvian Andes

2 What do you think it would be like to be a bus driver in these mountains? probably a very dangerous/stressful job

B Watch the video. Check your answers to Exercise A.

Glossary

abrasive (adj) having a rough surface
canyon (n) a long deep valley with steep sides made of rock
maze (n) a set of small streets, roads, paths, etc that it is easy to get lost in
slope (n) a surface or piece of land that has one end higher than the other end

C Watch the video again. Complete the sentences with between one and three words.

1 The mountains of Northern Peru consist of a network of ___steep slopes___, basic roads and deep canyons.

2 Glorioso is considered a ___hero___ among some of the villagers in Huancabamba.

3 The truck tires need to be changed after ten weeks because the roads here are so ___abrasive___.

4 Annually, over a ___thousand/1,000___ people die on the mountain roads of Peru.

5 The passengers on the bus are not ___in a rush___.

6 The secret to a long ___career___ as a Peruvian bus driver is to take your time.

AUTHENTIC ENGLISH

A Work in pairs. Read the information in the box. Complete the sentence from the video.

And that's ___the secret___ *to a long career as a Peruvian bus driver – taking the mountains at their own pace.*

Fronting

Fronting involves moving information to the front of a sentence, often to give it emphasis. It is often used in informal spoken English, for example, *Really good it was – best movie I've seen for ages.*

Whole clauses can be fronted, for example, *Why they decided to buy that house, I couldn't tell you.*

B Work in pairs. Rewrite the sentences to create emphasis. Begin each sentence with the underlined word.

1 I'll never know <u>why</u> Maria married Tony.
Why Maria married Tony, I'll never know.

2 He didn't know <u>whether</u> he'd gotten the job or not.
Whether he'd gotten the job or not, he didn't know.

3 I'll be there <u>in</u> about twenty minutes.
In about twenty minutes, I'll be there.

4 It cost me <u>three</u> hundred dollars.
Three hundred dollars it cost me.

5 I just don't know <u>how</u> you put up with your boss.
How you put up with your boss, I just don't know.

6 It started to snow <u>all</u> of a sudden.
All of a sudden, it started to snow.

7 It must have cost <u>an</u> absolute fortune.
An absolute fortune it must have cost.

8 An old woman sat quietly <u>in</u> the corner.
In the corner, an old woman sat quietly.

C Compare your sentences in Exercise B with another pair.

Hello from the Andes

SAM MALCOLM AMANDA HARRY EMILY

A Work in pairs. Discuss the questions.

1 Do you prefer traveling with other people or on your own? Why?

2 Do you know anybody who has visited many countries? What motivates them to travel?

B Watch the video. Who calls Sam and where are they?

Sam's cousin Fred, the Andes

C Watch the video again. Answer the questions.

1 Who did Fred meet by chance?

He bumped into his old friend Daniel.

2 What does Fred's meeting make Sam think of?

The time he was in Spain and bumped into a neighbor.

3 What does Fred say about the condition of the bus?

an old bus, might breakdown

4 What could Fred see when he looked out of the window?

a sheer drop

5 What did Fred find comforting?

The driver was very experienced.

6 What does Sam suggest doing when Fred returns?

going for dinner

SPEAKING SKILL

A What is the purpose of the phrases in bold in each of the examples from the video?

1 Sorry, not very good signal out here. **So where was I?** Oh yes … The speaker wants to go back to a previous topic.

2 **I tell you what** when you're back from the Andes, let's go out for dinner. The speaker wants to change the topic.

B Work in pairs. Underline the words and phrases which are used to change or recycle topics in the extracts below.

1 I had just arrived in Lima and guess who I ran into?

2 Well, funny you should ask. I had a bit of an adventure getting to my adventure.

3 That reminds me of the time when I was in Spain and bumped into my next door neighbor.

4 Well, yeah … made worse by the fact it was quite an old bus.

5 For sure … which brings me back to what I was saying … Daniel suggested I come with him on a trek.

Changing and recycling topics

We use many different set phrases to try to steer conversations toward the topics we wish to talk about.

We can use them to recycle a topic we were speaking about, for example, *as I was saying*. We can also use them to change topic, for example, *that's like the time when*.

SPEAKING HUB

A PREPARE Student A: you are going to describe your exciting journey to your partner. However, your partner is going to try to distract you and talk about himself/herself.

Student B: you are going to listen to your partner describing a journey. However, you are not very interested in what your partner has to say and you want to talk about yourself and your experiences.

B PRESENT Perform your conversation. Change roles.

A: Why I'd decided to drive through the wilderness alone, I couldn't tell you.

B: Speaking of which, I'm going camping in the wilderness next month.

C REFLECT Work in small groups. Perform and listen to each other's conversations again. Give feedback using the points below.

- use of language
- fluency
- pronunciation
- interaction

Tell a story about an exciting journey

➤ Turn to page 162 to learn how to write a cover letter for a dream job.

Driving on the edge

A Focus students on the picture and put them into pairs to discuss the questions. In feedback, encourage lots of different suggestions but don't confirm or reject any answers.

B ▶ Point out the glossary, then tell students to watch the video and to check their answers from Exercise A.

C ▶ Put students into pairs to try to complete the spaces from memory. Point out that they can use between one and three words for each space. Then play the video again for students to watch and check.

AUTHENTIC ENGLISH

A Go through the information in the box about *Fronting* then put students into pairs to try to complete the sentence from the video.

B Elicit the first one as an example, then put students back into pairs to rewrite the sentences, starting with the underlined word each time.

C Combine pairs to compare their sentences. In feedback, accept any sentences that make sense. Make sure students realize the effect created by rewriting the sentences; the emphasis makes them sound more dramatic and interesting.

Hello from the Andes

A Focus students on the picture, then put them into pairs to discuss the questions. Get some feedback, but don't confirm or reject any answers yet.

B ▶ Students watch the video to check their answers.

C ▶ Put students into pairs to try to answer the questions from memory. Then play the video again for them to watch and check. You can find the **video script** for *Hello from the Andes* on the Teacher's Resource Center.

SPEAKING SKILLS

A Focus students on the examples from the video, then put them into pairs to discuss the question.

B Elicit the first one as a whole-class example, then put students into pairs to do the rest.

SPEAKING HUB

A Put students into pairs and explain that they will both have a turn at being Student A, so they should both think about an exciting journey they have been on. When they have an idea of what they are going to talk about, remind them about the phrases for changing and recycling topics they saw earlier. Encourage them to use these when they are Student B, and make sure students realize that this is a light-hearted activity with an opportunity for humor. Tell students that when they are Student B, their goal is to prevent Student A from being able to tell their story, no matter how interesting it may sound.

B Assign roles and tell students to act out their conversations in pairs. When they have finished, tell them to change roles and have another conversation.

C Put students into larger groups, keeping the pairs from the previous stage together. Tell each pair to perform their conversation to their group. The other students listen carefully and should be prepared to give feedback at the end of each conversation, referring to the points listed. Finish with whole-class feedback on which conversations were the most successful and why.

Extra activity

Put students into pairs to talk about either the most interesting journey they've ever been on (without being distracted by their partner this time) or one that they would like to make. In feedback, find out how similar students' experiences or dreams are.

▶ VIDEO SCRIPT

Driving on the edge
N = Narrator

Ex C Q1 **N:** Northern Peru is a maze of steep slopes, deep canyons and rough tracks. They're only for the bold.
Ex C Q2 In Huancabamba, villagers rely on one man – some here call him a hero. Glorioso Albeneida has one of the world's most dangerous jobs – he's the bus driver. Glorioso has been behind the wheel for over 50 years. He started aged 14 driving trucks across the Andes.

It starts off easy enough – dropping a thousand meters in a series of switchbacks called the Horse Killer.
Ex C Q4 Every year, over a thousand lives are lost on Peru's mountain roads.
For Glorioso, it's just a normal day. He's been driving this
Ex C Q3 route for 12 years. Mountain roads are so abrasive his tires last only ten weeks.
But the really hard part is further down the valley. Not the place to meet oncoming traffic. For the
Ex C Q5 passengers, it's just the usual commute. Nobody's
Ex C Q6 in a rush … and that's the secret to a career as a Peruvian bus driver.

7 Writing — Write a cover letter

W — using power verbs

A Read the job advertisement.

Which skills and abilities:

1 will candidates need to prove from their certifications and experience? technical skills

2 will candidates try to show from their life experience and character? cope in conditions, follow instructions, team work

3 are useful but not essential? work in glaciology, geology, meteorology or oceanology

Research Technician – Antarctica

The **International Antarctic Research Station (IARS)** is recruiting a research technician. The job involves setting up and maintaining equipment for scientific experiments, collecting data and providing support as part of the IARS team.

No research skills are required but experience with work in glaciology, geology, meteorology or oceanology would be valuable. The main requirements are technical skills (including electrical and mechanical engineering). You will need to cope with extreme conditions (including severe weather, dangerous environments and hazardous materials), work as a reliable member of an international team and follow instructions accurately and intelligently.

Applications to: Dr. Adelia Ross, IARS

B Read the cover letter. Which skills and abilities from Exercise A does Francesca mention? What doesn't she mention?

Dear Dr. Ross,

I am writing to apply for the position of Research Technician at the IARS.

You will see on my résumé (attached) that I have six years' experience as a laboratory technician at an international energy company, where I investigated energy efficiency. During this time, I gained invaluable insights into real-life research, where quick thinking and creativity are just as valuable as patience and precision.

I have explored the Polar regions many times. Last summer, I successfully led an international expedition to a remote part of Greenland, where I demonstrated exceptional organizational skills, resilience in the face of extreme challenges and, above all, the ability to work on a team.

I look forward to the opportunity of an interview.

Best regards,

Francesca Matienzo

C Read the information about using power verbs to apply for a job. Add five power verbs from Francesca's letter to the list of examples.

Using power verbs

In résumé and cover letters, it's more powerful to use verbs to describe your achievements (*I managed the project*) rather than nouns (*I was the manager of …*) or adjectives (*I was responsible for …*).

Examples: *achieved, coordinated, designed, implemented, improved, negotiated, organized, persuaded, strengthened, updated,* investigated, gained, explored, led, demonstrated

D Make these extracts more powerful.

1 I was involved in negotiations to buy raw materials.
2 My manager agreed to my idea to switch suppliers.
3 I was in charge of a team of six.
4 Our old records were out of date, so I fixed them.
5 I did general office tasks, like answering the phone and checking emails.

WRITING

A PREPARE You are going to apply for your dream job or one of the jobs below. First, list the skills, abilities, experience and certifications required for the job.

- stunt performer
- zoo keeper
- safari or mountain guide
- astronaut

B PLAN Draft your cover letter, using Francesca's letter as a model.

C WRITE Make your letter more powerful by adding at least five power verbs.

D REVIEW Read some of your classmates' letters. Which letters would persuade you to invite the candidate for an interview? How could you improve the other letters?

162 WRITING

Suggested answers

1 I negotiated the purchase of raw materials.
2 I persuaded my manager to switch suppliers.
3 I led/managed a team of six.
4 I updated our records.
5 I coordinated communications with customers.

Suggested answers

She mentions her technical skills (as a lab technician), her ability to cope in extreme conditions, her ability to work well on a team and her creativity. She hints at her ability to follow instructions accurately and intelligently ('quick-thinking', 'patience and precision'), but this could be clearer.
She doesn't mention any experience of work in glaciology, geology, meteorology or oceanology. This might be covered in her résumé.

WRITING

A Students read the job ad and answer the questions. Let them compare in pairs before feedback.

B Tell students to read the cover letter and to answer the questions, again comparing with a partner before feedback.

C Go through the information in the box about *Using power verbs*. Instruct students to look back at the cover letter and to find five examples to add to the list.

D Elicit the first one as an example, then ask students to continue with the rest. In feedback, stress that there is more than one possible answer, but praise the sentences that sound the most powerful.

WRITING TASK

A Students think of their dream job or choose one of the examples given. Give them time to write notes about the skills, abilities, experience and certifications required.

B Ask students to think about how they meet the criteria for their chosen job, pointing out that they could base this on truth, or they could invent skills, abilities, experience and certifications if they prefer. Tell them to draft a cover letter, using Francesca's from earlier as a model to help them organize and structure it. This could be done as homework if there isn't time to do it in class.

C Tell students to look back at their draft and to add five power verbs in appropriate places.

D Tell students to pass their cover letters around and to read each other's. In feedback, ask students which letters they think would be likely to earn the writer an interview. Encourage them to suggest improvements to the letters where possible, too.

Unit 7 Review

VOCABULARY

A Match numbers (1–10) to letters (a–j) to form full sentences.

1 I'm frustrated because I e
2 I thought she was so courageous d
3 I became hysterical h
4 I always get grumpy a
5 I'm fairly resilient j
6 They were disgusted by i
7 As a child, I was indifferent b
8 I try to be humble c
9 I felt devastated about f
10 He acted superior g

a when I'm tired.
b to my classmates' bad behavior.
c about my success when I meet strangers.
d when she chased away the burglars.
e can't do anything to help.
f losing all that work.
g around the others, as if he were the best player.
h and couldn't calm down for a long time.
i the condition he left the apartment in.
j so I'm sure I'll get over this setback.

B Complete the sentences with the correct form of the words in the box. Use each word twice.

sick competition condition application

1 Unfortunately your application for the job hasn't been successful.
2 We can't go out in these conditions! We'll get wet!
3 I'm sick of his excuses. He's just lazy!
4 The product can be used in a number of ways – it has many applications.
5 I enter a lot of competitions but I never win.
6 There's a lot of competition for each place on the course.
7 I find an early night helps if you are feeling sick.
8 You can go out on condition that you're home by 10 pm.

C Put the lines (a–h) in order so that they form a paragraph.

4 **a** long periods – the world-record free-diver, Herbert Nitsch, can go an utterly
7 **b** dangerous changes of pressure. Nitsch's record of 253 meters was spoiled
2 **c** different from normal deep-sea diving, because the divers have practically
6 **d** easy compared to the challenge of coping with immensely
8 **e** somewhat by the medical problems he suffered as a result.
1 **f** Free diving is radically
5 **g** incredible nine minutes without breathing. But holding your breath is relatively
3 **h** no equipment. It involves holding your breath for remarkably

GRAMMAR

A Complete the sentences with words from the box. Each word can be used more than once.

is was until that not because who it

1 It was because I was scared that I decided not to climb the cliff.
2 It's not adrenaline that I'm looking for; it is/'s a sense of flow.
3 It wasn't until I reached the top that I realized how high the cliff was.
4 When I said 'Stop being stupid', it was not you I was talking to; it was James I was talking to.
5 It was at that moment that I realized I was no longer afraid.
6 It was to impress my friends that I tried to lift the car.
7 It's you that/who is causing most of the delays, not us!

B Find and correct the mistakes in five of the sentences.

1 All what I'm trying to say is you should be careful.
All I'm trying to say is you should be careful.
2 What you should avoid to do is to pretend you don't have any weaknesses.
What you should avoid doing is to pretend you don't have any weaknesses.
3 What I did was stretched my arms to calm my nerves.
What I did was stretch my arms to calm my nerves.
4 All I remember is staring out into the abyss and feeling sick.
Correct.
5 What happened next was that some people call an ambulance.
What happened next was that some people called an ambulance.
6 All they did was watch TV.
All they did is watch TV.

Sunset swimming washes away the day's cares.

Well-being (n) the satisfactory state that someone or something should be in, that involves such things as being happy, healthy, safe and having enough money. Synonyms: health (n), happiness (n)

Plato means that we should look at the bigger picture and not just at individual elements. This could be applied to the well-being of one person, of society in general or any other structure or organization.

Plato (428/427 BCE or 424/423 BCE–348/347 BCE) was an Ancient Greek philosopher. He was a student of Socrates and teacher of Aristotle, and along with them is considered to be a key figure in the development of Western philosophy.

OBJECTIVES

- discuss wellness treatments
- talk about health and technology
- talk about sports psychology
- discuss nutrition and fitness
- explain and give instructions about a process
- write a summary

Work with a partner. Discuss the questions.

1 Look at the picture. Do you often swim in lakes, rivers or the sea? How is it different from swimming in a pool?

2 Read the quote. What does Plato mean? Do you agree?

3 Do you think it's easy for people to stay healthy these days? Why/Why not?

WELL-BEING 85

OBJECTIVES

Read the unit objectives to the class.

UNIT OPENER QUESTIONS

1 Focus students on the picture and elicit how it makes them feel. Put them into pairs to discuss the questions. In feedback, ask students with particularly strong feelings to expand on and explain them.

2 Focus students on the quote and put them into pairs to discuss the questions. In feedback, elicit a range of possible interpretations of the quote and situations it could be applied to.

3 Elicit or give an example before students discuss the question in pairs. In feedback, write on the board any useful language that comes up.

WORKSHEETS

Lesson 8.1 Health and wellness

Vocabulary: Health problems (W34)

Grammar: Adjective clauses with complex relative pronouns (W35)

Lesson 8.2 Sports and wellness

Vocabulary: Idioms (W36)

Grammar: Pronouns and determiners (W37)

Vocabulary: Describing taste (W38)

8.1 Health and wellness

- Discuss wellness treatments
- Talk about health and technology

G adjective clauses with complex relative pronouns
P building suspense
V health problems
S identifying writers' opinions

VOCABULARY

Health problems

A **Work in pairs. Discuss the questions. Try to write down five words for each question.**

1. Name five parts of the body connected to the five senses.
2. Name five joints.
3. Name five parts of the body that people have more than two of.
4. Name five parts of the body that can be used as verbs.

B **Work in pairs. Match the words in bold in 1–9 with the definitions (a–i).**

1. **fracture** a rib/your leg d
2. **dislocate** your shoulder/thumb f
3. a **sore** throat/back e
4. **pull** a muscle i
5. **sprain** your ankle/your wrist b
6. **inflamed** joint/skin g
7. skin **rash** h
8. fast/slow **heart rate** c
9. high/low **blood pressure** a

a the force at which the blood flows through the body
b twist (a joint)
c the speed that your heart beats
d break or crack (a bone)
e painful
f force a joint out of its socket
g red and swollen
h red spots on the skin
i overstretch or tear

C Go to the **Vocabulary Hub** on **page 147**.

D **SPEAK** **Work in pairs. What can people do to avoid having the health problems in Exercise B? What can people do if they have these problems?**

READING

A **SPEAK** **Work in pairs. Have you ever tried any wellness treatments (e.g. a massage, a sauna, a spa)? Did you enjoy them? Did they have any lasting benefits?**

B **READ FOR MAIN IDEA** Read *From forest bathing to halotherapy*.

Which treatments are good for …

1 your lungs? halotherapy
2 your heart? carbon dioxide dry bath
3 reducing stress? forest bathing, So Sound lounger
4 your skin? forest bathing, halotherapy
5 insomnia? oxygen therapy

C **READ TO IDENTIFY OPINIONS** **Work in pairs. Read the article again and discuss the questions. Use the information in the box to help you.**

1. What is the writer's attitude to the things she is writing about? skeptical Find examples of three types of language which show her attitude.
2. What is the purpose of this article? Is it mainly written to inform, entertain or persuade? to entertain but also to inform

Identifying writers' opinions

Writers can choose particular words and phrases to show their opinion of a topic.

- Adverbs can show a positive attitude (*interestingly, surprisingly, intriguingly*), a negative attitude (*disappointingly, infuriatingly, predictably*) or a skeptical or cautious attitude (*supposedly, allegedly, presumably*).
- Different structures can be used to show writers believe something is true (*it is good for the heart*), they have a neutral stance about reported information (*it is said/thought to be good for the heart*) or they are uncertain or even skeptical (*it is supposed/meant/claimed to be good for the heart*).
- Writers can also use colloquial asides, including tag questions and rhetorical questions (*sounds fascinating, doesn't it?*) to comment on information. They can use humor, sarcasm and irony to show a skeptical attitude.

D **SPEAK** **Work in pairs. Do you agree with the writer's attitude to the treatments? Why/Why not?**

SPEAKING

DISCUSS **Work in groups. Discuss the questions.**

1. Why do some people prefer alternative treatments to conventional medicine?
2. Should doctors be allowed to recommend wellness treatments and alternative medicine?
3. Should companies be allowed to offer scientifically unproven wellness treatments?

8.1 Health and wellness

LEAD-IN

Books closed. Divide the board into two halves, and write the heading *a healthy lifestyle* on one side and *an unhealthy lifestyle* on the other. Elicit and write on the board one example of something you could write under each heading (e.g. *a balanced diet / junk food*). Then arrange the class into two teams, with each team standing in a line in front of one of the categories. Give the person at the front of each line a marker, and explain that when you tell them to start, they should add another word or phrase to their category, then give the marker to the next person in their team and go to the back of the line. Point out that this is a race, and the team who gets the most answers on the board in the time limit you set (e.g. three minutes) will be the winner. When time is up, go through the answers on the board, and ask students to explain any answers that need further clarification.

VOCABULARY

A Put students into pairs to do the task.

Suggested answers

1 *Eyes, ears, nose, tongue, fingers/skin*
2 *Knee, ankle, wrist, elbow, shoulder, knuckles, hips*
3 *Fingers, toes, teeth, hair, ribs, finger nails, toe nails, bones, veins, arteries, taste buds, moles, knuckles, eye lashes*
4 *to head (= to be in charge of a group or organization; to hit the ball with your head); to knee (= to hit someone with your knee); to stomach (= to put up with something); to hand (= to give something to someone); to eye (= to look at); to nose around (= to try to find out information about someone or something); to shoulder (= to take on a task)*

B Elicit the first one as an example, then put students back into pairs to do the rest.

C Direct students to the **Vocabulary Hub** (see TB121).

D Do the first one as an example, then put students into pairs to discuss the others. In feedback, encourage students to expand on their answers and refer to their own experience wherever possible. Use the **Vocabulary Worksheet** on page W34 for extra practice.

TEACHING IDEA by David Seymour and Maria Popova

Staying active

Use these activities to extend the theme of health and wellness.

Who in the class thinks they are very healthy? Are there any fitness fanatics? In groups, write ten pieces of advice for people who want to get in better shape.

Healthcare

In groups, discuss the ways in which healthcare has changed. Here are some topics.

Old and modern medicine: How have medical techniques improved? Nutrition: How has what we eat changed? Institutions: How have hospitals and mental health institutions changed?

TEACHING IDEA by David Seymour and Maria Popova

Project

Use these activities to extend the theme of health and wellness.

Look up the World Health Organization on the internet and find out about these things.

the latest information about a current health topic
the life expectancy for men and women in your country
your country's annual health expenditure

In class, work in groups and share the information you have found. (Some other issues that you might like to suggest for research are clean water and nutrition.)

METHODOLOGY HUB by Scott Thornbury

Opinions, giving and asking for

The language of asking for, giving and comparing opinions is useful not only in 'real life', but in the classroom context, too, especially where learners are encouraged to take part in discussions and debates. It is therefore helpful to have some common expressions of opinion displayed in the classroom, along with other useful classroom language. To ask for and state opinions, judgements, beliefs, etc, the following verbs are common:

think, believe, find, suppose, feel, assume and *imagine*:

A: What did you think of the movie?

B: I found it a little dull.

A: Who do you think will win?

B: I imagine Arsenal will.

Other common expressions for framing an opinion include: *in my opinion; if you ask me; it seems to me (that); to my mind; quite frankly;* and *to tell (you) the truth*. Comment clauses, beginning with *it*, are also used to introduce an opinion: *It seems to me that …; It worries me that …*

Opinions are often hedged so as to make them less assertive, e.g. by the use of expressions that reduce the force of an adjective: *I found it a little dull; It was rather long*. Verbs like *seem* and *appear* are also used to reduce the assertiveness of an opinion: *I don't know but she seemed a little distracted* (hedging).

To make opinions more emphatic, intensifying expressions are used: *He was definitely off side, without a doubt; I thought it was absolutely amazing*. More formal and particularly written ways of stating or reporting opinions can involve the use of the passive voice with verbs of cognition:

The house is believed to have been unoccupied at the time.

It is thought that the fire started in the basement.

To practice the language of opinion, the following topics are usually productive: movies, books, music, etc; sports and sports people; local, national and international politics, particularly topical issues; and moral issues, such as cloning or animal rights (discussion).

8.1 Health and wellness

READING

A Give an example of your own if you can (either about yourself or someone you know), then put students into pairs to discuss the questions. In feedback, encourage any students who have experience of or strong feelings about wellness treatments to share these.

B Set a time limit and tell students to read quickly to complete the task. Remind them that it's not necessary to understand every word at this point and that they will have an opportunity to read more closely later. When the time is up, let students compare in pairs before feedback.

C Go through the information in the box about *Identifying writers' opinions*, then tell students to use this to help them answer the questions. Tell students to compare in depth with a partner before feedback, and in feedback elicit as many specific examples from the text to support students' answers as possible.

D Put students into pairs to discuss the question. In feedback, encourage students to expand on their answers and to agree or disagree with each other.

SPEAKING

Put students into groups to discuss the questions. In feedback, encourage students to express a range of opinions and to ask each other further questions. Finish with feedback on students' use of language during the discussion.

Extra activity

Divide the class into two, and tell them that they are going to have a debate. Tell one half of the class that they're going to argue in favor of wellness treatments and alternative medicine being used more widely, and the other half that they are going to argue against this and in favor of the use of only conventional medicine. If you have a large class, subdivide the halves of the class into groups of three or four, and give them time to prepare their arguments. Monitor to help and prompt if needed. Then create new groups of four or six for students to debate against each other. Finish with feedback on who had the most convincing arguments and on students' use of language.

METHODOLOGY HUB by Scott Thornbury

Context and register

We have seen that the purpose of a text affects its production. Although not in ways that are always completely transparent. What other contextual factors determine the choice of language we make when we create a text? And can we relate these factors directly to specific formal features of the text?

Of all the possible components of the context that might impact on the language choices in text production, just three seem to be particularly significant:

- The what of the situation – what kind of social activity is going on, and about what sort of topic (what is called the field)
- The who of the situation – the participants, their relationship and so on (what is called the tenor)
- The how of the situation – the means by which the text is being created, e.g. email, fact-to-face talk, broadcast talk, written monologue and so on (what is called mode)

These three contextual dimensions – field, tenor and mode – determine what is called the register of the resulting text. That is to say, different configurations of these dimensions demand different kinds of choices at the level of grammar and vocabulary, and these choices create textual effects that we recognize as being appropriate to the context of the text's use. Thus, register of a teenage magazine allows for expressions that would be inappropriate in a children's encyclopedia or in academic correspondence, for example. By the same token, you would not expect expressions such as *are kindly requested to …*, *we would also be pleased if …*, on a teabag wrapper.

Let's look at an example of register at work: Here is an emailed response from a journal editor:

Dear Professor Thornbury,

It appears that we will be including your Forum commentary in the spring issue. I would greatly appreciate it if you could send a disk copy of your response for production purposes to my office at San Francisco State University. Please label the disk with the word processing program you are using.

Thank you in advance,

Sandra McKay

The field in which the text is situated is very generally academic publishing and accounts for the presence of words such as spring issue, disk copy, production purposes, word processing program.

The tenor is very formal, even frozen, influenced by the fact that neither of the participants have met, nor know much about each other's status. By addressing me as Professor Thornbury, the writer avoids causing any offence, in case I am indeed a professor (which I am not). The use of the highly indirect and modalized language (i.e. language using modal verbs such as *would*, *could*) is another way of creating a safe distance. The mode is email communication, usually a rather informal medium, but the writer uses the conventions of a formal letter, again, just to be on the safe side.

In my reply, while the field and mode remain the same, I seem to deliberately have adjusted the tenor, opting for a less formal wording, but still maintaining some of the conventions of a formal letter, e.g. in the address form and the closing:

Dear Sandra McKay,

I sent the disk off today. I hope it opens OK – let me know if there is any problem.

Thanking you for your interest.

Scott Thornbury

The response is startling in the degree to which the writer has picked up on the adjustment to the tenor:

Scott,

Thanks for sending me the disk.

Sandy Mckay

The text is much more in keeping with the informality of email communication (including uncorrected errors of punctuation). But, of course, it would not have been appropriate to have initiated the exchange in this style. Nor could the adjustment to the tenor have occurred had the writer not been sensitive to the signs I sent out in the previous email. This is a good example of how register is both jointly negotiated and in a constant state of flux. Needless to say this can present enormous difficulties to writers – such as learners of English – who are not familiar with the conventions or cannot easily recognize the subtle indicators of register adjustment.

FROM FOREST BATHING TO HALOTHERAPY: THE FIVE LATEST WELLNESS TRENDS

Know your 'sound lounger' from your carbon dioxide bath with our guide to the latest and not-so-greatest spa innovations.

'Wellness' is all the rage these days, but we've noticed that Ex C Q1 some therapies doing the rounds at hotel spas right now sound Ex C Q1 suspiciously basic. Surely oxygen therapy is just breathing, right? Decide for yourself, as we explore a few of the more interesting treatments we've spotted on spa menus around the world.

Forest bathing or 'going for a walk'

Forest bathing is based on the Japanese practice of *Shinrin-yoku*. That may sound like some sort of elaborately mystical ritual, but in fact involves simply 'being in the forest'. You might call it walking, or even Ex B Q3 sitting, in, you know, a forest. The practice is supposed to exercise Ex C Q1 the mind as well as reduce stress by bringing you back to nature. Possibly eager to jazz up the concept, The Mayflower Grace Hotel in Ex B Q4 Connecticut has put together a forest-bathing package that involves 90 minutes of skin-cleansing treatments, using plant-derived lactic acid and exfoliators made with peat enzymes and berries. Finally, Ex C Q1 a 'plant hydrosol ionizing mist' supposedly boosts your lymphatic system with a 'stimulating breeze'.

Carbon dioxide dry bath or 'sitting in a bag'

Ex C Q1 Does lying fully clothed on a bed while wrapped in a bag of carbon dioxide sound fun? Didn't think so, but in the Czech Republic it's all the rage. In the west of the country – an area known for its natural gas – you can have a large bag wrapped around you all the way from your toes to under your arms and watch it slowly inflate with CO_2. Ex B Q2 The treatment is meant to slow your heart rate, reduce your blood pressure and improve circulation, but this happens by the gas seeping into your clothes and skin – that thought would put most people's blood pressure up, not down.

So Sound lounger or 'napping and listening to music'

Yes, Tibetan singing bowl therapy has been around for centuries, but it's now been upgraded for the digital age. The So Sound lounger Ex B Q3 is meant to help you relax by, well, sitting in a lounger and listening to music. Revolutionary stuff. You're supposed to be able to take a 'therapeutic nap' while the lounger sends musical vibrations through your body … A little like an airport massage chair, maybe? Ex C Q1

Halotherapy or 'a salty room'

Halotherapy is actually a fancy name for salt therapy. In a natural setting, this treatment would mean sitting in a salt cave and breathing in the dry, salty air, Ex B Q1 which is supposed to be good for respiratory and skin Ex B Q4 conditions. Now hotels are replicating salt caves; the Windsor Arms Hotel in Toronto has created a room filled with salt and negative ions that has darkened ambient lighting to replicate natural salt caves found in Europe. Supposedly this also helps strengthen the immune system, among other health benefits.

Oxygen therapy or 'breathing'

Ex B Q5 Oxygen therapy is supposed to help with headaches, Ex C Q1 depression and sleep deprivation by – that's right – breathing oxygen. It involves being hooked up to a machine, sticking some tubes up your nose and, well, breathing.

Glossary

circulation (n) the continuous movement of blood around your body
lymphatic (adj) relating to the body's liquid lymph, or involved in moving lymph around your body
mystical (adj) relating to or involving mysterious religious or spiritual powers
nap (v) to sleep for a short period of time, usually during the day
ritual (n) a formal ceremony

LISTENING

A SPEAK **Work in pairs. Discuss the questions.**

1 Do you own any gadgets that monitor your health? If so, how often do you use them?

2 What are some of the benefits and drawbacks of these devices?

8.1 **B LISTEN FOR GIST** **Listen to a conversation between friends discussing technology to help you stay healthy and answer the questions.**

1 What kinds of health data can be provided by the devices they talk about? amount of activity done, amount of sleep, breathing, temperature, glucose levels in blood, heart rate

2 What four devices do they talk about?
a smart watch   a smart bottle
a smart swimsuit   a smart thermometer

8.1 **C LISTEN FOR DETAIL** **Listen again and answer the questions.**

1 Why are they talking about wellness technology? She is writing an article about it.

2 Why do Cheryl and Luke think that wellness technology is a good idea? can make people aware of health problems, give them the big picture, remind them to take medication

3 Why is Jake uncertain? thinks it is information overload; people can become obsessed about tracking

D DISCUSS **Work in pairs. Discuss the questions.**

1 Would you use any of the devices the speakers discussed? Why/Why not?

2 Do you think it's useful for people to collect data about their health?

GRAMMAR

Adjective clauses with complex relative pronouns

A **Read the extracts from the conversation. Underline the adjective clauses and circle the relative pronouns.**

1 Wellness technology is technology with which we can improve our health and well-being.

2 I've just read several news stories about people whose lives may have been saved because their smart watch alerted them to a problem.

3 I'm meeting the person [who is] writing the article with me for lunch today.

4 It's basically a thermometer which a smartphone can be attached to.

5 This device has an automated diagnosis feature where it checks the symptoms of the person to whom it's attached against a database.

8.1 Health and wellness

LISTENING

A Give an example of your own, then put students into pairs to discuss the questions. In feedback, write on the board any useful language that comes up.

8.1 **B** Tell students to listen to the conversation and to answer the questions. Let them compare with a partner before feedback.

8.1 **C** Tell students to work in pairs to try to answer the questions from memory. Then play the recording again for them to listen and check.

D Put students into pairs to discuss the questions. In feedback, ask students to expand on their answers and ask each other further questions, especially if any students already have experience of using any similar gadgets.

GRAMMAR

A Make sure students realize all the sentences come from the conversation they heard. Elicit the first one as an example, checking students understand the terminology of *adjective clause* and *relative pronoun*, then tell students to do the rest.

B Tell students to look at the sentences from Exercise A to help them complete the rules. In feedback, refer to these examples to make sure all students understand the uses of the adjective clauses.

C Do the first one as an example, referring back to the rules in Exercise B to remind students to think about them as they tackle the other questions.

D Put students into pairs to discuss the sentences. In feedback, encourage students to expand on their answers, especially for sentences where there are different opinions in the class.

E Direct students to the **Grammar Hub** (see TB89). Use the **Grammar Worksheet** on page W35 for extra practice.

AUDIO SCRIPT

8.1

Listening, Exercise B
C = Cheryl J = Jake L = Luke

L: Hey, Cheryl.
J: Hello, Cheryl. What you doing?
Ex B Q2 **C:** Oh, hey guys. Check out my brand new … smart watch! What do you think?
L: Cool. I've been meaning to get one of those. Is that turned on, Cheryl?
C: Um … maybe.
J: Smart watch eh? Hmm … not a hundred percent convinced about those. I mean if I want to check my email, I can just look at my phone.
Ex B Q1 **L:** Yeah, yeah … but you can use it whenever you exercise to monitor the amount of activity you do.
J: Didn't know you were so big on fitness Cheryl.
C: Yeah, sure. I mean … I do like to stay active … and … well, OK so … You'll never guess what … I've just been commissioned to write an article about wellness technology. (Ex C Q1)
L: Amazing!
J: Cool. Congratulations. But what's wellness technology?
C: Good question. So wellness technology is … technology with which we can improve our health and well-being.
J: Did you just read that somewhere?
C: Maybe. But you get the idea. There are a lot of other devices you can get to track things. Actually, you can monitor whatever you need
Ex B Q1 to keep an eye on: your breathing, temperature, glucose levels in your blood, amount of sleep, pretty much everything!
Ex C Q3 **J:** Yeah. And it sounds a little like information overload to me.
C: Well, yes and no. Sure more information doesn't
Ex C Q2 necessarily mean better health. But I've just read several news stories about people whose lives may have been saved because their smart watch alerted them to a problem. For example, on this smart
Ex B Q1 watch, take this handy … heart rate tracker.
L: Eighty-five beats per minute. Isn't that fairly high …
C: Not for me, Luke. No. And anyway I'm a little stressed. I'm meeting the person writing the article with me for lunch today. I'm supposed to share my ideas. But I think I'm out of new ideas!
Ex B Q2 **L:** Well, what about the smart swimsuit? Have you heard of that?
C: Hmm … tell me more.
L: Hang on – here it is. It's a swimsuit with a tracking tag embedded, so you can log your time and how far you swim. It will start tracking all that whenever you put the swimsuit on.
J: I don't know. What happened to just going for a
Ex C Q3 swim? People are obsessively tracking everything these days. Writing down everything they eat or do. It takes over your life – when really all you need to do is get some exercise and eat healthily.
L: But I don't think wellness technology is just about
Ex C Q2 fitness fads. For example, monitoring devices can help show your doctor the big picture so he or she will be more likely to pick up on any problems.
Ex B Q2 And it goes beyond just tracking. Like the smart pill bottle.
C: The smart pill what? Let me write this down.
L: It's a pill bottle for medication, like the Adhere Tech
Ex C Q2 bottle. It glows blue when it's time to take your medication. And … if you forget … it starts flashing red. It can also text you or email you to remind you to take medication.
J: OK, maybe that could be useful for my grandpa.
L: There are a few health devices like that now. I was also reading about this thermometer. It's basically a
Ex B Q2 thermometer which a smartphone can be attached to. Here it is. It says … this device has an automated diagnosis feature whereby it checks the symptoms of the person to whom it's attached against a database. I'll send you a link to the review. And look at this – this could be a great quote for your article. 'As tech gets smarter and people get smarter about tech, this could be the decade in which we revolutionize healthcare.'
C: Yeah. Yeah. I think that would work as a tagline. Great! Thanks, guys. One last question though. Is this thing really turned on?

8.1 Health and wellness

PRONUNCIATION

8.2 **A** If students seem unsure about what to do or what you mean by changing pitch, stop the recording after the first sentence and elicit the answer as an example. Then play the others and let students compare answers in pairs before feedback.

B Give an example of your own, then tell students to complete the sentences for themselves.

C Repeat your example from Exercise B, exaggerating slightly to make sure students notice the intonation and the way it built suspense. Then put students into pairs to share their sentences with each other. In feedback, ask students what the most interesting thing their partner told them was, and if the way their partner told it to them made it even more interesting.

SPEAKING HUB

A Put students into small groups to prepare their ideas.

B Students use their ideas from the previous stage to prepare a presentation. Again, monitor and help with language if needed.

C Tell each group to present their idea to the class. The other students should listen carefully and ask questions after each presentation. At the end, each group decides which idea to vote for – they can't vote for themselves! Tell one representative from each group to announce who they vote for and establish the winner. Ask students to explain what they liked about the idea they voted for. Finish with feedback on students' use of language during the activity.

GRAMMAR HUB

8.1 Adjective clauses with complex relative pronouns

- We use *whose* to add information about someone's possessions.

  I was happy to meet Georgia, ***whose*** *sister had helped me find a place to stay.*
- We use *whereby* to add information about a method (formal).

  They introduced a new system in the company ***whereby*** *everybody has a full induction on their first day.*
- We use *whom* to add information about a person where they are the object of the clause (formal).

  The people ***whom*** *I asked were all in favor of the plan.*
- In very formal English, we place the preposition (generally only with *whom*, *whose* and *which*) before the relative pronoun.

  The President, ***in whose*** *honor the event was being held, welcomed all the guests.*
  The person ***on whom*** *I depend the most ...*
  The place ***to which*** *I often return ...*
- In less formal English, we put the preposition at the end of the clause.

  Martin, ***whose house I was staying in****, was a very neat person.*
  The person ***(who)*** *I depend* ***on*** *the most ...*
  The place ***(which)*** *I often return* ***to*** *...*
- Formal constructions can use a variety of prepositions depending on meaning.

  The person ***in whom*** *I have the most confidence ...*
  The person ***to whom*** *I sent the letter ...*
  The person ***for whom*** *the money was being raised ...*

Be careful!

- The relative pronoun *whom* is very formal. We don't usually use it with a preposition at the end of the clause.

  The person to whom you gave the money ...
  NOT ~~The person whom you gave the money to ...~~

8.1 Adjective clauses with complex relative pronouns

A Choose the correct options to complete the sentences.

1 Do you know the name of the person to *who* / ***whom*** the letter must be addressed?
2 That's Melanie, ***whose*** / *who* mother is the manager of our company.
3 This is the cell phone ***which*** / *whereby* I am most interested in.
4 His father, ***to whom*** / *whom* he would often go for financial help, had refused to give him more money.
5 We need to find a solution ***whereby*** / *which* everyone will be happy.
6 The new grocery store will benefit the villagers, ***among whom*** / *for whom* there are a number of families without cars.

B Complete each sentence with a word or phrase from the box.

for whom | into which | into whose | whereby | whose | with which

1 A pedometer is a mechanical or digital device ___with which___ we count steps taken while walking.
2 The owner, ___into whose___ pocket the pedometer can be slipped, can then use it to calculate their distance traveled.
3 More recently, cell phones have started featuring fitness apps, ___into which___ pedometers or 'step counters' have been incorporated.
4 Some experts claim that people ___whose___ daily number of steps is lower than 10,000 should be concerned about their health and fitness.
5 Most fitness experts agree that any method ___whereby___ our steps can be counted is a useful one.
6 Pedometers make people ___for whom___ exercise is not a priority aware of their daily activity and motivate them to do more.

C Match the sentence beginnings (1–6) with the endings (a–f) to make sentences.

1 We reached an agreement ___d___
2 He was uncomfortable because it was a situation in ___f___
3 Paula is a person whose ___a___
4 This will be popular with the team, among ___e___
5 The explorer contracted an illness from ___b___
6 We still hadn't met Mr. Dawson, in whose ___c___

a mood never changes.
b which he never recovered.
c house we were all staying.
d whereby everyone was satisfied.
e whom any extra support is appreciated.
f which he had never been before.

➤ Go back to page 88.

B Complete the rules (1–6) with the words in the box and the example sentences from Exercise A. You may use the words in the box more than once.

informal formal whereby whom whose

Adjective clauses with complex relative pronouns

Advanced relative pronouns

1 Use ___whose___ to add information about someone's possessions.

2 Use ___whereby___ to add information about a method (mainly used in formal English).

3 Use ___whom___ to add information about a person where they are the object of the clause (mainly used in formal English).

Prepositions and relative pronouns

4 In ___informal___ English, prepositions usually come at the end of the adjective clause.
Example: ___sentence 4___

5 In ___formal___ English, prepositions come before the relative pronoun.
Examples: ___sentence 1___
and ___sentence 5___

Reduced adjective clauses

6 In ___informal___ English, we can often omit *who*, *that* or *which* in adjective clauses – and in adjective clauses that use *be*, we can leave out the pronoun + the part of *be*.
Example: ___sentence 3___

C Complete the sentences with the correct relative pronoun. Add a preposition if needed.

1 The device ___in which___ I'm most interested is something that helps me eat healthfully.

2 Wellness devices are the technology ___with which___ people will be able to extend their lives.

3 Companies need to develop security systems ___whereby___ it's impossible for hackers to gain access to users' private health data.

4 I don't understand people ___whose___ first thought when they are sick is to look up their symptoms online rather than go to the doctor.

5 The people ___for whom___ wellness technology will make the biggest difference are older people.

D SPEAK Work in pairs. Do you agree with the sentences in Exercise C?

E Go to the **Grammar Hub** on **page 136**.

PRONUNCIATION

Building suspense

A 8.2 Listen to the example sentences from the conversation. Underline the word where the speaker changes pitch.

1 So check out my brand new smart watch!

2 You'll never guess what … I've just been commissioned to write an article about wellness technology.

3 For example, on this smart watch take this handy heart rate tracker.

4 And if you forget, it starts flashing red.

B Complete the sentences so they are true for you.

1 The app I use most on my phone is …

2 The person I send most messages to is …

3 In one of the messages I received recently, someone said …

C Work in pairs. Present the information in Exercise B to your partner. Use pitch and pauses to build suspense.

SPEAKING HUB

A PLAN Work in groups. Imagine that you work for a technology start up. Your group needs to think of a health and wellness product idea and pitch it to potential investors. Discuss your ideas and think about the following questions.

- Will your idea help prevent health problems, encourage healthy behavior or help people who are already sick?
- What problem do people have that your idea could help to solve?
- Is your idea for a device, an app or a service?
- Who is the target market for your idea?
- How will you make it easy for users to use your product or service?
- What are the benefits for users of your product or service?

B PREPARE Prepare a presentation about your idea. Think of ways to sell the idea to your classmates.

C PRESENT Present your idea to the class. Then as a class, vote on the best idea.

- Discuss wellness treatments
- Talk about health and technology

8.2 Sports and wellness

- Talk about sports psychology
- Discuss nutrition and fitness

G pronouns and determiners
P pronunciation of idioms
V idioms; describing taste
S understanding speech with background noise

LISTENING

A SPEAK Work in pairs. Discuss the questions.

1 Do you know any players or teams that use a sports psychologist?

2 How do sports psychologists help athletes?

8.3 **B LISTEN FOR GIST** Listen to the first part of a podcast about sports psychology. What are the two training techniques the sports psychologist mentions? Positive thinking, self-talk

8.3 **C LISTEN FOR DETAIL** Listen again and answer the questions.

1 What example situation does Professor Rohan Kumar give for using therapy?

2 How do Professor Kumar's positive thinking techniques help athletes?

8.4 **D LISTEN WITH NOISE** Listen to the second part of the podcast. Some parts are fairly hard to hear because of background noise. Which two main sports psychology techniques does the interviewee use in her training sessions? Use the strategies in the box to help you.

1 helping team to get over fear of failure

2 learning what the best approach is for each player

Understanding speech with background noise

If there's a lot of background noise and you can't ask the speaker to repeat what he or she said:

- use the context of the situation to help you. Remember that you don't need to understand every word that is spoken to get the gist of what somebody is saying. Use your knowledge of the topic to help fill in the blanks.
- remember that speakers stress the most important words, so these words should be easier to hear. Use this information plus the context to help make intelligent guesses about what the people are saying.

8.4 **E LISTEN FOR DETAIL** Listen to the second part of the podcast again and answer the questions.

1 What problem had the soccer team been facing?

'going through a losing streak', losing games

2 What kind of coaching style does she say many players won't accept?

a coach shouting at the players

3 What kind of coaching style does Bill prefer?

He prefers a supportive style of coaching.

F SPEAK Work in pairs and discuss the questions.

1 Do you think sports psychologists are important?

2 Which techniques do you think would be most helpful for you when playing sports?

3 How difficult did you find it to understand what the speaker was saying when there was background noise?

VOCABULARY

Idioms

A Look at the three groups of idioms (1–12). Complete the headings for each group with the words in the box.

body sports food

Body idioms

1 My gut feeling is we'll lose the game.

2 Their striker was head and shoulders above the rest of us.

3 Keep an eye out for John – we're supposed to meet him at the stadium.

4 get cold feet

Food idioms

5 It wasn't a big problem, but he was really making a meal of it.

6 He says he knows Ronaldo, but you have to take what he says with a grain of salt.

7 What she said about coaching gave me food for thought.

8 not everyone's cup of tea

Sports idioms

9 The other athletes are really good. I think she's out of her league.

10 I can't win, so I think it's time to throw in the towel.

11 I thought I'd finished my part of the work, but then they suddenly moved the goal posts.

12 give it their best shot

B Put the underlined idioms below into the correct group in Exercise A. See 4, 8 and 12 in Ex A

- They have times when they doubt their abilities or get cold feet because they're anxious about competing.
- It's all about staying calm and focused, so they can give it their best shot.
- I need someone to nag me and tell me to up my game, but I know that's not everyone's cup of tea.

8.2 Sports and wellness

LEAD-IN

Books closed. Give students one minute to write down as many different sports as they can. When time is up, whoever has written the most is the winner. Elicit clarification of any sports that students haven't heard of. Then put students into pairs to discuss which sports they like or don't like and why. Get some feedback, and write on the board useful language related to sports that comes up.

LISTENING

A Put students into pairs to discuss the questions. In feedback, encourage students to explain their answers and give examples where possible.

8.3 **B** Tell students they're going to listen to a podcast about sports psychology, starting with just the first part. Play the recording, and let them compare briefly in pairs before feedback.

8.3 **C** Put students into pairs to try to answer the questions from memory. Then play the recording again for them to listen and check.

1 long-term injuries

2 They help the athlete visualize their performance; imagine doing the steps in the right way; stop worrying about problems they could have; visualize completing things successfully; think about smaller goals rather than get distracted by the big picture

8.4 **D** Tell students that there will be background noise in the second part of the podcast, making some parts hard to hear. Go through the information in the box about *Understanding speech with background noise*, then tell students to listen and answer the question. Again, let students compare in pairs before feedback.

8.4 **E** Put students into pairs to try to answer the questions from memory. Then play the recording again for them to listen and check.

F Put students into pairs to discuss the questions. In feedback, encourage students to expand on their answer and to agree or disagree with each other. For the question about background noise, remind students that they undoubtedly manage to do this when listening in their own language, and encourage them to try to transfer this skill into listening in English.

VOCABULARY

A Focus students on the underlined phrases, and elicit that they are idioms. Tell students to think about what the idioms in each group have in common and to complete the headings for what types of idioms each group contains. Tell students not to worry about the exact meanings of the idioms yet, as you'll come to that later. Note that the phrases "grain of salt" and "pinch of salt" are both used in American English, depending on the region.

B Focus on the three further idioms, and tell students to add one to each group from Exercise A.

AUDIO SCRIPT

8.3

Listening, Exercise B
L = Laura B = Bill R = Rohan J = Julie

L: Hello, everyone. This is *First Past the Post*, the sports performance podcast. My name is Laura Ford …

B: And I'm Bill Williams.

L: This week, we're talking about sports psychology. A lot of the big teams have sports psychologists these days. But what do they actually do? This week we set out to find out more.

B: First up, we spoke to Professor Rohan Kumar, a lecturer in sports psychology. Here's what we discussed …

L: So Rohan, could you explain what a sports psychologist does?

R: Certainly. Essentially, our job is to help athletes perform at the peak of their abilities. We do that by offering training and therapy. Training usually means things like encouraging positive thinking, whereas therapy could be supporting them with off-field issues – this is particularly important in the case of long-term injuries. (Ex C Q1)

L: You mentioned working on positive thinking. How exactly does that work?

R: Well, athletes, even elite athletes, suffer from the same fear of failure that we all do. They have times when they doubt their abilities or get cold feet because they're anxious about competing. Our job is to help athletes cope with these feelings, so they can perform to the best of their abilities.

L: So what kind of training do you do with them?

R: (Ex B) Well, I said before that positive thinking is important – but that doesn't just mean encouraging people to imagine winning a game or winning a trophy. (Ex C Q2) It's actually more about visualizing your performance, thinking about the individual steps that you need to take and imagining doing each one of those steps in exactly the right way. It's all about staying calm and focused, so they can give it their best shot.

L: So you encourage them to break things down into smaller goals?

R: (Ex C Q2) That's right. It helps people focus by thinking about these smaller goals rather than getting distracted by the big picture. (Ex B) We also work on self-talk, which means trying to get control of that little voice inside your head that says you're not good enough or that you're having a bad day. We train athletes to use positive self-talk to build self-confidence and self-belief – and if it's a team game, to talk out loud and encourage those same feelings in the rest of the team.

L: That's been really helpful. Thank you for your time, Rohan.

R: You're very welcome.

C Elicit the first one as an example, and demonstrate how to use the context provided by the whole sentence, not just the underlined idiom, to help work out the meaning. Then put students into pairs to do the rest. In feedback, use further examples to fully check understanding where necessary.

D Put students into pairs to discuss the questions. In feedback, ask students to expand on their answers and share their experiences and opinions fully. Do the same yourself. Use the **Vocabulary Worksheet** on page W36 for extra practice.

PRONUNCIATION

8.5 **A** Play the recording for students to listen and circle the prominent words. If students seem unsure what you mean by this, pause the recording after the first sentence and go through it as an example. Then play the rest, and let students compare in pairs before feedback.

B Give an example of your own for the first one, then tell the students to complete the advice with their own ideas. Monitor to help or prompt if needed.

C Put students into pairs to read their sentences to each other. Tell them to listen carefully to their partner's advice, to ask questions if they need clarification and then to say if they agree or disagree. In feedback, ask students to share the best or worst advice they heard. Comment on how well students pronounced the idioms during this feedback, too.

SPEAKING

A Tell students to read the list and think of their own order, then put them into groups to discuss their rankings and to try to agree on an order that they are all happy with. Open this up to the whole class in feedback, and try to reach a whole-class consensus.

B Put students back into groups to discuss the questions. Encourage them to think of as many reasons as they can for each question.

C Combine groups to share ideas. In feedback, find out how similar the different groups' ideas were. Finish with feedback on students' use of language during the activity.

Extra activity

Tell students to think of idioms they use in their own language. If the students speak different languages, put them into pairs to explain the idioms and their meaning to each other. Do the same idioms exist in different languages? If the students all speak the same language, tell them to think of idioms they use and to research if these can be translated directly into English or if there is a different idiom with the same meaning. Point out how direct translation is occasionally possible for idioms, but more often there is a different way of expressing the same idea, and sometimes an idiom is entirely unique to one language or one culture.

AUDIO SCRIPT

8.4

Listening, Exercise D
B = Bill J = Julie L = Laura

B: After Laura spoke to Professor Kumar, I spoke to Julie Matic, a sports psychologist working with a local soccer team. I should mention that Julie was speaking to me from a training session, so there's a little background noise during this interview. Julie, thank you for taking the time to talk with me today.

J: No problem.

B: So, can you tell me a little about your role with the team there?

Ex E Q1 **J:** Well, before I started here, the team had been going through a losing streak, so one of the first things I needed to do was to help the team get over their
Ex D Q1 fear of failure. I've been helping them to think about failure in a more positive way, so they don't dwell on the fact that they failed, but they try to learn from that experience, so that failure becomes a positive thing. Nobody can win every game, so it's not a disaster to lose – as long as you just think about what you can do differently next time.

B: What about working with individual players? What kinds of things do you focus on?

Ex D Q2 **J:** Well, the most important thing is to get to know the individuals, and encourage the manager to do the same, so that we can work out the best way to get the most out of each person. When people think about coaching, most people have a stereotypical
Ex E Q2 image of a coach shouting at the players, but that's very outdated because many players won't respond positively to that kind of coaching. Different players need different approaches – some people need a lot of guidance, some need a lot of praise, others need to feel trusted and important. It's important to talk to the players – to listen to them and find the right way to work with them.

L: Apologies again for the sound quality on that interview, but she said a lot of really interesting things. I completely agree that it's important to think about the right kind of coaching to suit individual players. I need someone to nag me and tell me to up my game, but I know that's not everyone's cup of tea.

B: Yeah, actually I find that kind of coaching ends up distracting me because I get so angry with the coach. It means I don't concentrate on the game
Ex E Q3 and I end up playing even worse! I prefer a more supportive approach.

L: Yeah, I can imagine that! So we also interviewed …

C Match the underlined idioms (1–12) in Exercise A with the meanings (a–l).

a something to think about carefully 7
b change the rules or goals 11
c watch for 3
d feel nervous 4
e make something seem more important or serious than it really is 5
f decide to give up 10
g lack the required ability or knowledge 9
h much better than 2
i be skeptical about something as it may not be accurate or true 6
j to have an instinctive feeling about 1
k try your hardest 12
l not something that everyone likes 8

D SPEAK Work in pairs and discuss the questions.

1 Do you usually have a gut feeling about who will win a sports game?
2 Have you ever felt out of your league playing a game or sport?
3 Do you keep an eye out for new trends in fitness and nutrition?
4 What kinds of sports are not your cup of tea?
5 Do you know anyone who is head and shoulders above the rest at a sport?

PRONUNCIATION

Pronunciation of idioms

8.5 **A** Listen to the sentences. Circle the prominent words in the underlined idioms.

1 I had a gut feeling.
2 It's time to throw in the towel.
3 He was really making a meal of it.
4 Keep an eye out for the others.
5 You have to take what she says with a grain of salt.

B Complete the advice for sports players with your own ideas.

1 If you feel that someone is out of your league, remember, …
2 If you have cold feet, …
3 You should always keep an eye out for …
4 If you want to give something your best shot, …
5 If your opponent is making a meal of something, …
6 Take it with a grain of salt if …

C Work in pairs. Read the sentences you wrote in Exercise B to your partner. Do you agree with your partner's advice?

SPEAKING

A Work in groups. Rank the following in order of how important they are for success in sports.

- coaching
- diet and nutrition
- insights from technology
- natural ability
- physical fitness
- sports psychology
- training facilities

B DISCUSS Work in groups and discuss the questions.

1 Could students benefit from using sports psychology techniques? How?
2 Could people at work benefit from using sports psychology techniques? How?

C Share your ideas with another group.

READING

A SPEAK Work in pairs. What kind of diet should an athlete have?

B SKIM Read *Should athletes go gluten-free?* about someone trying out a diet. Which foods did the writer eat? Which did the writer have to avoid?

C READ FOR DETAIL Read the article again and answer the questions.

1 Why did he decide to try this diet?
2 What problems did he experience?
3 What was his conclusion about the effectiveness of the diet?

D Work in pairs and discuss the questions.

1 Have you tried a gluten-free diet?
2 Would you like to try a gluten-free diet? Why/Why not?
3 Would might be the advantages and disadvantages?

Should athletes go *gluten-free*?

For those who are gluten intolerant, a diet that is gluten-free is a necessity rather than a choice. But there are some who may be motivated to try this diet for other reasons. When tennis player Novak Djokovic became world number one, he credited going gluten-free as the reason for his success. Some athletes have followed suit and switched to a gluten-free diet and some are already swearing by its effects. Ex C Q1 **So, I'm going gluten-free for two weeks to see if it makes me a better soccer player.**

Ex B **DAY 1** Going gluten-free means no bread and no cereal, so I had nice **tangy** grapefruit for breakfast. Then for lunch, I had a big salad Ex B full of nice **crisp** lettuce and **crunchy** carrots. I was briefly impressed Ex C Q2 by how healthy I was being. But then I worked out in the afternoon, and was suddenly ravenous.

DAY 2 I was overjoyed when I saw the gluten-free section of my local grocery store stuffed full of packets of bread, pasta, cakes, and cookies – all long lost friends! [1]I put several in my basket. Then I added some more packages just in case. At home, I made myself my first Ex C Q2 sandwich for two days. Disappointingly, the bread was incredibly dry and incredibly **bland**.

Ex B **DAY 3** [2]I'd been planning to have grapefruit some days and melon some days, but I was so hungry today that I had both. However, the grapefruit tasted **sour**, so I decided to try one of my gluten-free cupcakes instead. It didn't look that **appetizing** but it was actually Ex B pretty good – **moist**, unlike the bread, and with very sweet, **sticky** icing. Relieved that I had found some comfort food, I had two more before lunch.

DAY 4 A revelation! Maybe the gluten-free bread would be passable as Ex B toast? I spread a generous amount of honey on top. Maybe too much because it was a little **soggy** – but it actually tasted OK. A relief, because I didn't want a grapefruit or melon for breakfast again.

DAY 5 For variety, I decided to try some probiotic food – food rich in healthy bacteria that are said to be good for gut health. I'd been told Ex B kefir, a fermented milk drink, is a good way to kick things off. It looked like milk, but it smelled interesting – slightly **cheesy** but also vinegary. Tentatively, I poured some into a glass. It had a **creamy** texture, but it was also a little **gritty**. And it tasted like a slightly **acidic**, **fizzy** glass of milk. I'd found something else I could have for breakfast!

Ex B **DAY 6** A Japanese friend had warned me that natto – another probiotic food made from fermented soy beans – is somewhat of an acquired taste. I could see what she meant right away. It looked **slimy** and had a very **pungent** aroma – almost like burned tires. I think the beans actually had a pretty **mild** taste, but the smell Ex C Q2 was so strong that it was hard to tell. [3]I couldn't eat much, so I reached for some gluten-free cakes instead, Ex B which I ate with some kombucha, a sweetened tea that looked a little **murky**. Despite the **cloudy** appearance it was nice, although it didn't exactly taste like tea.

DAY 7 I met some friends for a game of soccer. The jury was still out as to whether the diet had had any effect. Unfortunately, there wasn't much to see. I hadn't morphed into an overnight soccer sensation. So, Ex C Q3 is going gluten-free better for sports performance? It seems highly unlikely. And if you do need to go gluten-free, you should work with a sports nutritionist to create a diet to suit your training needs.

Glossary

appetizing (adj) appetizing food smells or looks very good
morph (v) to change from one thing into another by small and interconnected steps
overjoyed (adj) extremely happy
the jury is still out (phr) used for saying that people have not yet decided what they think about someone or something

8.2 Sports and wellness

READING

A Elicit an example, then put students into pairs to discuss the question. In feedback, ask students to explain their answers. Write on the board any useful language that comes up.

B Set a time limit and tell students to read quickly to answer the question. Let them compare in pairs before feedback.

He ate: grapefruit, lettuce, carrots, gluten-free bread, melon, gluten-free cupcakes, honey, kefir, natto, kombucha tea.
He had to avoid: anything containing gluten, e.g. bread, cereal, pasta, cakes, cookies.

C Tell students to read the article again, more closely this time, and to answer the questions. Again, let them compare with a partner before feedback. In feedback, ask students to refer to the text when giving their answers.

1 *He wanted to test if it had an impact on his ability at sports, because other athletes have found that it has.*
2 *He was frequently hungry, he got bored with the foods he was eating and he didn't like some of the gluten-free products or some of the probiotic food he tried.*
3 *It didn't seem to have any effect on his performance. He recommended that athletes who need to go gluten-free should work with a sports nutritionist.*

D Put students into pairs to discuss the questions. In feedback, ask students who have tried a gluten-free diet to share their experiences with the class. For question 3, elicit as many advantages and disadvantages as you can, and encourage students to agree or disagree with each other.

GRAMMAR

A Focus students on the sentence from the article, and put them into pairs to discuss the questions. In feedback, make sure all students understand how the second *some* refers back to *athletes*. A good way to do this would be to write the sentence on the board and draw an arrow from the second *some* going back to *athletes*.

B Tell students to look at the sentence from Exercise A to help them complete the rules.

C Go through the first underlined sentence with the class as an example, then put students into pairs to work on the rest. In feedback, use the boarding technique again to further clarify if necessary.

1 *more is a determiner; several is a pronoun and = several packages*
2 *some, some are determiners; both is a pronoun and = both grapefruit and melon*
3 *some is a determiner; much is a pronoun and = much natto*

D Direct students to the **Grammar Hub** (see TB93). Use the **Grammar Worksheet** on page W37 for extra practice.

VOCABULARY

A Point out the words in bold in the article, and tell students to put them in the correct place in the table. Explain that some could go into more than one column. Elicit the first one as an example, and tell students to try to use the context to help them work out the meaning of any words they don't know. In feedback, use examples to check students fully understand the meaning of all the adjectives, and check pronunciation where necessary.

B Direct students to the **Vocabulary Hub** (see TB121). Use the **Vocabulary Worksheet** on page W38 for extra practice.

C Put students into pairs to discuss the questions. In feedback, encourage students to expand on their answers and react to each other's anecdotes.

SPEAKING HUB

A Put students into groups and explain the task. Tell them to decide together what type of athlete (e.g. *a sprinter, a marathon runner, a high jumper*) they want to pitch to.

B Tell students to create their plan, using the questions to guide them. Monitor to help or prompt where needed.

C Tell each group to present their plan to the class. Tell the other students to listen carefully and to ask questions at the end of each presentation.

D Put students back into their groups to discuss what they thought of the other groups' plans. Then open this up into a whole-class discussion. Ask students if they think a top athlete would really follow any of these plans and why or why not. Finish with feedback on students' use of language during the activity.

Extra activity
Elicit other examples of diets or eating habits (e.g. *carb-free, vegan*). Put students into groups to discuss which, if any, they have tried and why or why not.

TEACHING IDEA by David Seymour and Maria Popova

Healthy or unhealthy

Use this activity to introduce or extend the theme of nutrition and diet.

Add expressions to this table to show the things you eat and the lifestyle you have.

Things that are good for you		Things that are bad for you	
Food	**Activities**	**Food**	**Activities**
apples	jogging	too much sugar	overworking

In pairs, show each other your tables and discuss what changes you would like to make to your lifestyles.

In groups, throw a ball (or a piece of paper) to another student while saying a kind of food or activity. As you catch it, say if the food or activity is healthy or unhealthy, e.g.

A (throwing) – *Chips.*
B (catching) – *Unhealthy.* (throwing) *Swimming.*
C (catching) – *Healthy*. (throwing) *Playing tennis …*

8.2 Sports and wellness

GRAMMAR HUB

8.2 Pronouns and determiners

- We use determiners before nouns to identify a number, an amount or a group.

  *We have **a few** tomatoes.*

  *I had **a couple of** cups of coffee while I was waiting.*

  *You need to get **some** fresh air.*

- Some common determiners include: *a/an, the, this/that/these/those, all, some (of), none, (a) little, (a) few (of), my/your/their/its/*etc, *any, much, more, both (of), enough, a lot of, other, each/every, one/two/three/*etc, *either (of).*

- We can use some common determiners like *millions of, loads of, tons of* when we want to exaggerate a point, especially in informal English.

  I feel so guilty because I ate a lot of chocolate last night.

- Pronouns can be the same words as determiners but they are not followed by a noun. They replace the noun, often to avoid repeating it.

  You look like you need water – I'll get you some.

  NOT ~~You look like you need water – I'll get you some water.~~

- Some common pronouns include: *I/he/they/*etc, *me/you/him/her/*etc, *this/that/these/those, there, some, mine/yours/his/*etc, *both, several, anyone/something/*etc, *others, none, either.*

- We can also use *one* or *one's* as pronouns to refer to people in general. These are especially used to make generalizations in formal English. *One's* indicates possession.

  *Diets make **one** realize how much food can impact **one's** life.*

Be careful!

- Some pronouns cannot be used as determiners.

  That glass is mine. NOT ~~That is mine glass.~~

- Some determiners cannot be used as pronouns.

  That is my glass. NOT ~~That glass is my.~~

8.2 Pronouns and determiners

A Underline the determiners in each sentence. Some sentences have more than one determiner.

1 I could do with a little help starting this fitness program.

2 The doctor said I should leave the car at home and do more walking.

3 Both of the recreational centers in my area are too far to walk to.

4 There was little point in talking to him since he wouldn't listen.

5 One of the techniques is bound to suit you.

6 The cafeteria had two healthier options but I didn't want either of them.

B Change one determiner into a pronoun in each sentence by crossing out some words.

1 Some people have a gluten-free diet because they genuinely can't eat it without getting sick, but many ~~people~~ believe that avoiding gluten is just healthier.

2 I try to drink a couple of liters of water every day, but I'm pretty sure that I don't drink enough ~~water~~.

3 A lot of people I know are cutting back on sugar and caffeine, but I don't want to cut back on either ~~sugar or caffeine~~.

4 I've started following a vegan diet so I like to try vegan restaurants, but there are only a few ~~vegan restaurants~~ in my area.

5 I prefer fruits and vegetables that have been grown organically to those ~~fruits and vegetables~~ that haven't.

6 The government should make companies that produce food with a lot of sugar use less ~~sugar~~ to help people have better diets.

C Complete each sentence with the correct pronoun. More than one answer is sometimes possible.

1 Jack couldn't decide which of the two sandwiches to get so he just bought ___both___.

2 Some people enjoy running, while ___others/some___ find it really boring.

3 Now I can't tell which shoes are ___mine___ – they look the same as yours.

4 'Which of the two games do you want to watch on TV?' '___Either___ – I really don't mind.'

5 I know we said we'd buy oranges but ___these/they___ don't look very nice.

6 We don't have any soccer shoes in stock but we'll be getting some new ___ones___ in next week.

➤ Go back to page 93.

GRAMMAR
Pronouns and determiners

A Look at the sentence from the article *Should athletes go gluten-free?* Which of the underlined words in the sentence is followed by a noun? What does the word not followed by a noun refer to?

Some athletes have followed suit and switched to a gluten-free diet and some are already swearing by its effects. the first *some*, the second *some* refers to *some* athletes

B Choose the best words to complete the rules.

Pronouns and determiners

Words such as *this, these, many, several* and *some* can be used as both pronouns and determiners. To understand whether the word is being used as a pronoun or determiner, we need to look at the context.

1 Pronouns *are* / *are not* followed by a noun. They are used in place of a noun. We need to use the context to understand what the pronoun refers to.

2 Determiners *are* / *are not* followed by a noun. They are used to say which thing or how many things are being talked about.

C Look at the underlined sentences (1–3) in the article in *Should athletes go gluten-free?* For each sentence, decide which words are pronouns and which are determiners. Then decide which nouns the pronouns refer to.

D Go to the Grammar Hub on page 136.

VOCABULARY
Describing taste

A Complete the table with the words in bold from *Should athletes go gluten-free?* Some words can go into more than one category.

Look	Smell	Taste	Texture
appetizing	cheesy	tangy	crisp
fizzy	pungent	bland	crunchy
slimy		sour	moist
murky		cheesy	sticky
cloudy		acidic	soggy
		mild	creamy
			gritty
			slimy
			fizzy

B Go to the Vocabulary Hub on page 147.

C SPEAK Work in pairs. Discuss the questions.

1 Describe a food you have eaten because you wanted to be healthy. Did it have any effect?

2 Describe a food you have eaten from another country. Did you like it?

3 Describe the most unusual thing you have ever eaten. Would you recommend it to other people?

SPEAKING HUB

A PREPARE Work in small groups. Imagine you are a fitness instructor or personal trainer. You are pitching your services to a famous athlete. To win the pitch, you need to create the best plan to help him or her prepare for an important competition. First decide what kind of athlete you are pitching to.

B PLAN Create a plan to help the athlete. Use the questions to help you.

- What are the best mental techniques to help him or her prepare for the competition?
- What should he or she do to prepare physically?
- What is the best diet for him or her to follow?

C PRESENT Present your plan to the class.

D DISCUSS Discuss the plans with the class. Which plan was the best?

- Talk about sports psychology
- Discuss nutrition and fitness

Café Hub

8.3 Health hacks

Ⓐ– reformulating Ⓢ– repairing misunderstandings

Is it good for you?

A Work in pairs. Look at the picture and discuss the questions.

1 Are these foods healthy? Why?

2 Would you eat the food shown in the picture? Why/Why not?

B Read the terms below. Now watch a video about food packaging. Check (✓) the terms you see or hear.

☑ source of fiber	☐ high in iron
☐ high in vitamins	☑ low in salt
☑ high in vitamin D	☑ source of calcium
☑ gluten free	☑ good
☐ low in calories	☑ 100% natural
☑ OK for veggies	☑ high fiber
☑ nature is power	☐ high in Omega 3
☐ organic	☑ no refined sugars
☑ no added nonsense	☐ veggie-friendly
☑ low sugar	☑ no added salt

Glossary

back up (phrasal verb) to show that an explanation or belief is probably true

bend the rules (phrase) to allow something that is not normally allowed

dupe (v) to trick someone into believing something that is not true or something that is stupid or illegal

manipulate (v) to influence someone or to control something in a smart or dishonest way

tricks of the trade (phrase) quick and effective methods used by experienced people in a particular profession

C Watch the video again. Complete the summary.

A normal grocery store has thousands of products with [1] nutritional information. Food producers cannot make health [2] claims about products unless they can support them with [3] evidence.

However, they often manipulate the [4] consumers/buyers to make their foods appear healthier. People generally only notice certain [5] words when food shopping.

Some terms such as 'good' and 'natural' are [6] unregulated and can be used without any evidence of health [7] benefits.

Glossary

veggie(s) (n, slang) (British) = **vegetarian(s)** (n) (American)

AUTHENTIC ENGLISH

A Work in pairs. Read the sentences from the video and the information in the box. Which of Babita's words has Richard reformulated? duped, fooled

Babita: *So, we're being duped, we're being fooled, are we?*

Richard: *Well, we're being manipulated.*

Reformulating

We reformulate when we want to express that we don't necessarily agree with what another person has said or with their point of view. We frequently reformulate by using *well* and then the same structure the other person has used.

B Match the sentences (1–6) with the replies (a–f).

1 New York's the greatest city in the world. d

2 They're definitely lying to us, aren't they? a

3 What they're doing is illegal. b

4 All health claims on food have to be backed up with scientific evidence. c

5 You hated the movie then? f

6 So, Maria doesn't want to come to the party then? e

a Well, they're not being completely honest.

b Well, they're definitely bending the rules.

c Well, some have to be backed up with evidence.

d Well, it's certainly the most exciting.

e Well, she wants to come but she's working really late.

f Well, I didn't like it very much.

C Work in pairs. Write responses to the sentences. Suggested answers:

1 I bet the movie was amazing, wasn't it? Well, it was interesting.

2 What they're doing is immoral. Well, they're not being very honest.

3 The apartment's filthy. Well, it isn't very clean.

D Work in pairs. Practice the exchanges you wrote in Exercise C.

SAM MALCOLM AMANDA HARRY EMILY

Healthy display

A Work in pairs. Discuss the questions.

1 Where do you get recipes from?

2 Are you good at following recipes or do you prefer to improvise?

B Watch the video. Complete the recipe.

Amanda's

HEALTHY BROWNIE RECIPE

INGREDIENTS

One [1] tablespoon of coconut oil
Two egg whites
[2] Greek yogurt
small amount of sugar
[3] unsweetened cocoa powder
[4] wholemeal flour
[5] chips of dark chocolate chips

METHOD

Step one: [6] pre-heat the oven.
Step two: [7] separate egg whites from yolks.
Step three: [8] mix egg whites, coconut oil, yogurt and sugar.
Step four: Add cocoa powder and wholemeal flour to wet [9] mixture.
Step five: [10] whisk mixture until incorporated.
Step six: Add chocolate chips.
Step seven: Spread the [11] batter in a pan.
Step eight: Put the pan in the oven for [12] twenty/20 minutes at 260 degrees Fahrenheit.

C Where does Harry think he went wrong with the recipe?
He thought the temperature was in Celsius not Fahrenheit.

SPEAKING SKILL

A Work in pairs. Complete the example in the video. Why does Sam use a question tag here?

Sam: Now you did separate the egg whites from the yolks, didn't you?

to make sure Harry has understood the recipe

B Read the information in the box. Which strategy (a–c) has been used in the sentences from the video (1–5)?

Repairing misunderstandings

When we don't understand another person or another person doesn't understand us there are a number of things we can do to repair the misunderstanding.

a Tag questions to check that we have understood correctly or that the other person has understood correctly.

b Clarifying instructions to signal that we are going to go over instructions again.

c Restating to clarify what we mean. We can also say what we don't mean.

1 OK … maybe let's go over them again. b
2 Not whisk … mix. c
3 Remember to add chips … not chunks … chips of dark chocolate. c
4 Hold on, Fahrenheit? You mean Celsius, don't you? a
5 OK, let's go through it one more time. b

C Work in pairs. Take turns reading aloud the sentences (1–5) in Exercise B. Try to copy the intonation of Sam and Harry in the video.

SPEAKING HUB

A PLAN You are going to give instructions on a process you know well. Choose one of the ideas below or use your own idea.

- recipe
- how to repair something
- sport or exercise tips
- professional or academic process

B PREPARE Write notes on how you are going to explain the process to your partner.

C PRESENT Work in pairs. Explain your process to your partner. Ask your partner to retell you the process. Clarify any misunderstandings. Change roles.

Well, no … that's not exactly right. You should make sure you stretch first.

Explain and give instructions about a process

➤ Turn to page 163 to learn how to write a summary of a text about stress.

8.3 Health hacks

Is it good for you?

A Focus students on the pictures, then put them into pairs to discuss the questions.

B ▶ Give students time to read the terms, and make sure they understand them all. Point out the glossary, then tell students to Check (✓) the terms they see or hear on the video.

C ▶ Put students into pairs to try to fill in the blanks in the summary from memory. Then play the video once again for them to watch and check.

AUTHENTIC ENGLISH

A Go through the information in the box about *Reformulating*, then put students into pairs to read and answer the question.

B Elicit the first one as an example, then put students into pairs to do the rest. In feedback, remind students that reformulating is a polite way of disagreeing, and focus on the polite intonation which is used. Model and practice pronunciation of the responses.

C Give one example of your own, then tell students to write their own responses starting with *Well …*

D Put students into pairs. Tell one student to read a sentence from Exercise C and their partner to respond. Students can then swap roles and find out how similar their responses are. In feedback, ask students if their responses were similar, and if not, whose were better and why.

Healthy display

A Give your own example, then put students into pairs to discuss the questions. In feedback, ask students to expand on their answers.

B ▶ Tell students to watch the video and to complete the recipe. Let them compare in pairs before feedback.

C Put students into pairs to discuss the question. You can find the **video script** for *Healthy display* on the Teacher's Resource Center.

SPEAKING SKILL

A Put students into pairs to complete the sentence and to discuss the question.

B Go through the information in the box about *Repairing misunderstandings*, and tell students that there were several examples of this in the video. Put them into pairs to match the five examples to one of the three strategies in the box.

C Model the first one yourself as an example, and make sure students notice your intonation.

SPEAKING HUB

A–C Monitor and help as students work through the exercises individually and then in pairs.

▶ VIDEO SCRIPT

Is it good for you?

B = Babita Sharma R = Richard Hyde F1 = Female 1 F2 = Female 2 M = Male

B: It's all very well having healthier foods, but how do you know what's good and what's bad? Ex C Q1 The average supermarket stocks over 30,000 products, all bombarding us with nutritional information. So does the packaging help us make healthy choices or is it just trying to get into our wallets? Ex C Q2 Food producers are not allowed to make specific Ex C Q3 health claims about products without evidence to back it up. To find out the tricks of the trade, I've come to Stratford-Upon-Avon to meet Richard Hyde, an expert in packaging law from the University of Nottingham. So, we're being duped, we're being fooled, are we?

Ex C Q4 **R:** Well, we're being manipulated. They're using the fact that we only spend a small amount of time thinking about what products we're going to buy in the Ex C Q5 supermarkets. We pick up on those words and we decide to buy it because we think that it's going to be healthy. So this product here says, 'good and counted'. 'Good' isn't particularly a regulated term but it makes you think it's going to be really, really good for you, doesn't it? This one as well, this one says it's 'nature', it brings in the idea of naturalness.

B: And the packaging as well, because all the images that they're using …

R: Oh, look at it! Look at it! The …

B: It shows that you are in the wilderness.

R: Oh, absolutely. There's mountains, there's verdant meadows. It makes you think – well, this is going to be great for me, isn't it? 'No added nonsense' on this one here. Now, of course, that's absolutely not a regulated term.

Ex C Q6 **B:** Terms like 'natural' and 'good' are unregulated and Ex C Q7 don't have to be based on any evidence of health benefits. But there are other terms that are regulated by the government and have to be scientifically backed up. So, do any of us know what those regulated terms mean, or can we still be fooled? We're putting it to the test with some fish.

R: We've got two types of salmon here. Some say they're 'high in' omega 3. And some say they're 'source of' omega 3.

B: 'High in' and 'source of' are both regulated terms that sound similar but mean very different things. The 'source of' omega 3 or 'high in' omega 3?

F1: They're all the same.

F2: Er … I hadn't really thought about it to be honest.

M: It's all the same.

B: All the same.

M: Yeah. Salmon's salmon.

B: Clearly lots of us just don't know the difference. But actually one of these choices is far healthier.

R: 'High in' omega 3 has at least twice as much omega 3 as a 'source of' omega 3 salmon. So if you're really interested in buying things with omega 3 in it, you go for the 'high in' omega 3.

B: So the 'high in' is the winner not the 'source of', did you know that?

M: No.

R: Have you ever thought about it before?

F1: No.

B: Would it make a difference to you?

M: No 'cause I don't like salmon!

B: If you want to be sure of what you're getting, here's some other regulated terms that you can trust. Low-fat foods must have less than three percent fat. Low sugar must be less than five percent sugar. And anything that says it's high in fiber has to have at least six grams of fiber per hundred grams.

8 Writing

Write a summary

W paraphrasing

A SPEAK Work in pairs. How does stress affect the body?

B Read *The effects of stress on the body* and circle the specific health problems the article mentions.

The effects of stress on the body

Chronic stress can affect several different parts of the body, including the musculoskeletal system, the cardiovascular system and the gastrointestinal system.

Stress causes muscles to tense and when this happens for
Ex B an extended period of time, it can cause tension and pain in the back, shoulders and head. For many people, this results in tension headaches and migraines.

It is well known that acute stress causes a temporary
Ex B increase in heart rate and blood pressure. However, long-term stress means that heart rate and blood pressure
Ex B remain high, potentially leading to inflammation of the arteries and an increased chance of hypertension, heart attack or stroke.

Stress can have a direct or indirect effect on the gastrointestinal system. Stress often causes people to eat more unhealthy food than they usually would. This
Ex B can lead to heartburn and acid reflux, which can affect the throat. Stress can upset the stomach too, leading to
Ex B digestive problems, nausea and even stomach ulcers.

In summary, long-term stress puts extra pressure on the body that can lead to health problems for various parts of the body, such as the muscles, the heart and stomach.

C Look at three draft summaries of the article. What are the problems with each of these summaries?

1 Long-term stress can lead to heart attacks and strokes because of the extra pressure it puts on the cardiovascular system. During periods of stress, our heart rate and blood pressure are raised. This is a natural response to stress, but it becomes harmful if it continues for an extended period of time.

2 It is important to use strategies to help you relax, so that stress does not lead to health problems with your muscles, heart and digestive system. For example, having an increased heart rate and increased blood pressure for an extended period of time can result in heart disease or stroke. Stress can also cause headaches, digestive problems and even panic attacks.

3 Chronic stress can affect different parts of the body, including the musculoskeletal system, the cardiovascular system and the gastrointestinal system. Stress causes muscles to tense, and people to eat more unhealthy food, which can upset the stomach.

D Read the information in the box about writing a summary. Then identify the main points in *The effects of stress on the body*.

Paraphrasing

It's important to focus on the main points of the source text, but not just to copy the text. You need to explain the information in your own words.

1 Identify the main points in the piece of text that you want to summarize. In an academic paper, look at the introduction, the topic sentences at the beginning of each paragraph and at the conclusion. In a newspaper article, look at the opening paragraph and the conclusion.

2 Note down any words you need to re-use from the text (i.e. proper nouns, technical words).

3 Explain the information in your own words. Use different structures and different words to make sure you aren't copying from the text. You can also put the information in a different order.

4 Check your summary. Make sure you have not copied parts of the original, introduced new information or changed the meaning.

WRITING

A WRITE Write a short summary of *The effects of stress on the body*. Do not write more than 60 words.

B REVIEW Exchange your summaries. Give your partner any suggestions for improvements.

C EDIT Use your partner's feedback to improve your summaries.

WRITING 163

Answers

Summary 1 does not summarize all the points from the article – it only focuses on heart problems.

Summary 2 does not summarize all the points from the article and it introduces new information (about relaxing) that was not in the original article.

Summary 3 does not summarize all the points from the article and does not paraphrase enough – the first sentence of the text is repeated word for word.

Sample answer

Long-term stress causes health problems all over the body. It can cause pain in our muscles, especially the shoulders, neck and head. Having a raised heart rate and raised blood pressure for a long time can also be a factor in heart attacks and strokes. In addition, stress can cause problems with digestion and make people feel sick.

WRITING

A Elicit one example, then put students into pairs to discuss the question. In feedback, write on the board any useful language that comes up.

B Tell students to read the text and to circle the health problems mentioned.

C Explain that the three summaries are not very good for different reasons. Put students into pairs to decide what the problems are with each one.

D Go through the information in the box about *Paraphrasing*, then put students into pairs to identify the main points in *The effects of stress on the body*.

WRITING TASK

A Instruct students to use the main points of the text that they identified, and the other information in the box, to help them write their summary. Tell them not to use more than 60 words. This could be done as homework if there isn't time to do it in class.

B Students swap summaries with a partner and read each other's. Tell them to make suggestions for improvements, referring again to the tips in the box.

C Students make changes to their summaries, taking their partner's feedback into consideration. Get some feedback, asking students what improvements they made.

Unit 8 Review

VOCABULARY

A Choose the correct word to complete the sentences.

1. I went to see the doctor when I had a ***<u>rash</u>*** / ***sprain*** on my chest.
2. I'm really stressed right now, so my blood ***<u>pressure</u>*** / ***rate*** is a little high.
3. I'm on crutches because I've ***<u>fractured</u>*** / ***pulled*** a bone in my foot.
4. Do you have any eye drops? I've been looking at a screen all day and my eyes are really ***inflamed*** / ***<u>sore</u>***.
5. I ***pulled*** / ***<u>sprained</u>*** my wrist when the ball hit my hand.
6. I think I ***fractured*** / ***<u>pulled</u>*** a muscle at the gym, so I'd better put some ice on it.
7. Do you ever track your heart ***<u>rate</u>*** / ***pressure*** while you're exercising?

B Match the questions (1–12) with the answers (a–l).

1. Do you ever get cold feet before speaking in public? d
2. Do you always give it your best shot when you play sports? a
3. Do you always keep an eye out for good places to eat? j
4. Which sports are not your cup of tea? f
5. Have you heard something that you've had to take with a pinch of salt? h
6. Did you feel like throwing in the towel when it got tough? c
7. When was the last time you felt out of your league? k
8. Who is a sports player who is head and shoulders above his peers? b
9. Do you offer to help out when you see someone making a meal of something? i
10. What was the last thing you read that gave you food for thought? g
11. Are your gut feelings usually right? l
12. Has anyone ever moved the goal posts while you were working on something? e

a Yes, because I'm incredibly competitive.
b Messi is clearly one the best players in history.
c At times in the race I wanted to give up, but you have to keep going.
d No, I don't usually get nervous.
e A teacher once changed the title of an essay.
f I'm not a big fan of football or baseball.
g There was a great article in the paper about innovation the other day.
h Yes, a friend told me a story. But he always exaggerates.
i Not usually, I find it a little embarrassing.
j Not really. I search for things online.
k I once took an exam that was much too difficult for me.
l Rarely. I'm not good at predicting things.

C Choose the correct word to complete the sentences.

1. I don't like soft cookies. They need to be ***<u>crunchy</u>*** / ***tangy*** / ***soggy***.
2. I don't often eat seaweed. It's a little too ***crisp*** / ***murky*** / ***<u>slimy</u>*** for me.
3. Pasta can often be too ***<u>bland</u>*** / ***pungent*** / ***sour***, so I always add a lot of parmesan cheese.
4. I tend to order a ***<u>mild</u>*** / ***gritty*** / ***sticky*** curry when I have Indian food.
5. I like lemon dressing on my salad to give it a ***creamy*** / ***soggy*** / ***<u>tangy</u>*** flavor.
6. I never buy ***mild*** / ***pungent*** / ***<u>fizzy</u>*** drinks in case they've been shaken up.
7. I love eating ***cheesy*** / ***gritty*** / ***<u>sticky</u>*** things like toffee apples and cotton candy.

GRAMMAR

A Correct the mistakes in the sentences.

1. My smartwatch has a feature ~~that~~ whereby you can share your exercise data with friends.
2. There's an app ~~which in~~ in which / with which you can record your fitness data.
3. This is the device that is being used to monitor people's blood sugar levels.
4. The inventor is someone ~~which~~ who / whom people like to read about.
5. I don't know ~~who's~~ whose smartwatch this is.
6. This is the diet tracking service which I subscribe to.
OR This is the diet tracking service to which I subscribe.

B Complete the text with the words or phrases in the box.

a large number of	both	either
most people	one	others	some people

The raw food diet

These days, there are [1] a large number of diets that claim to be the best way to stay healthy. [2] One is the raw food diet. According to this diet, [3] both cooked and processed foods are unhealthy, so people should not eat [4] either. [5] Some people follow a raw vegan diet, whereas [6] others eat animal products, too. The diet includes fruits, vegetables, nuts, seeds and, for the non-vegans, meat. [7] Most people who follow the diet, whether vegan or not, also eat fermented foods, such as sauerkraut and kimchi.

Caught red ... and blue ... and green handed.

Behavior (n) the way that someone behaves.
Synonyms: conduct (n), ways (n)

Goethe means that it is the way we act that shows the kind of person we truly are.

Johann Wolfgang von Goethe (1749–1832) was a German writer of novels, poetry, drama and scientific works.

OBJECTIVES

- talk about group behavior
- discuss factors that affect behavior
- discuss animal behavior
- talk about behavioral experiments
- give and justify your opinion on social engagement
- write a conclusion to an academic report

Work with a partner. Discuss the questions.

1 Look at the picture. How do children learn to behave? What influences our behavior as we grow?

2 Read the quote. What aspects of our image/character might we deliberately try to show through our behavior? What might we reveal accidentally?

3 What would a stranger guess about your character from your behavior? What might they assume incorrectly?

BEHAVIOR 97

OBJECTIVES

Read the unit objectives to the class.

UNIT OPENER QUESTIONS

1 Focus students on the picture and elicit their immediate reaction to it (e.g. are they shocked, amused, annoyed, etc). Then put them into pairs to discuss the questions. In feedback, encourage a variety of different opinions.

2 Go through the quote with the class. Give or elicit an example, then put students back into pairs to discuss the questions. In feedback, encourage students to support their opinions with examples from their own experience.

3 Give your own example and allow students to give their impressions of your character, then put students into pairs to discuss the questions. In feedback, find out if the image they have of themselves matches the image others have of them, and why or why not.

WORKSHEETS

Lesson 9.1 Language and behavior

Vocabulary: Slang (W39)

Grammar: Noun phrases (W40)

Lesson 9.2 Animal behavior

Vocabulary: Verb + object + base form (W41)

Grammar: Participle clauses and verbless clauses (W42)

Vocabulary: Gestures and body language (W43)

9.1 Language and behavior

- Talk about group behavior
- Discuss factors that affect behavior

G noun phrases V slang P pronouncing vague expressions S understanding rapid colloquial speech

VOCABULARY
Slang

A SPEAK Read the dictionary definition. Work in groups and discuss the questions.

1 Can you think of any examples of slang (in English or your language)?
2 What problems can slang cause for language learners?

> **slang** – definition and synonyms
> NOUN Pronunciation /slæŋ/
> Words or expressions that are very informal and are not considered suitable for more formal situations. Some slang is used only by a particular group of people.

9.1 **B** Read and listen to some examples of informal English. In pairs, try to work out the meaning of the underlined slang expressions.

1 I could do with some new wheels but they'd set me back at least ten grand … and I'm completely broke.
I would like/need, a car, cost, thousand, have no money

2 Hey, can you lend me ten bucks? Ah, sweet. That's awesome, dude.
dollars, great, fantastic, a man (informal)

3 I don't mean to gripe, but the office bash last night was a hot mess. I was so bummed!
complain, party, badly organized/not good, extremely disappointed

4 This guy offered me a brand new TV for fifty bucks, so I'm like 'Sounds shady to me – it's probably hot or something.'
man, dollars, I said/thought, suspicious, stolen

5 I wanted to hang out with my buddies tonight but I'm totally beat, so I guess I'll just chill out and crash instead.
socialize/spend time with, friends, exhausted, relax, go to sleep

6 I'm so stoked cuz I got myself a new crib. It's so cool.
glad/happy, because, home, good

9.2 **C** Now listen to a more neutral version of the same sentences to check your ideas.

D DISCUSS Work in small groups. Discuss the questions. Use words in Exercise B.

1 When was the last time you griped about something?
3 What events have you been to that were a hot mess? What happened?
4 When was the last time you felt stoked or bummed? Why?

9.1 Language and behavior

LEAD-IN

Books closed. Put students into pairs to discuss the biggest difficulties they face when trying to understand real English, either written or spoken. Get feedback on their ideas and write on the board any useful language that comes up.

VOCABULARY

A Focus students on the definition of *slang* and put them into groups to discuss the questions. In feedback, ask students to explain the slang they use in their language, by translating it if possible and saying in which situations they use it. If the students are from different countries, find out how similar slang is in their languages. If they are from the same country, find out if they use the same slang in the same situations.

9.1 **B** Tell students to read and listen to the sentences. Do the first one as an example, demonstrating how students can use the context to help work out the meaning, then put students into pairs to try to work out the meaning of the other underlined expressions. Get some feedback on students' ideas, but don't give the correct answers yet.

9.2 **C** Play the recording for students to check their answers. Let students compare in pairs after listening, then get feedback to check they all heard all the answers. Ask students which sentences, the informal ones from Exercise B or the neutral ones from Exercise C, sounded more real, and which they would be more likely to use themselves.

1 *I need a new car but it would cost at least ten thousand dollars and I have no money at all.*
2 *Excuse me, can you lend me ten dollars? Oh great, that's very kind of you my friend.*
3 *I don't mean to complain but the office party last night was badly organized. I was so disappointed.*
4 *A man offered me a brand new television for fifty dollars, so I said that sounds worrying and maybe illegal to me – it's probably stolen.*
5 *I wanted to spend some time with my friends tonight but I'm really tired so I think I'll just relax and go to bed early instead.*
6 *I'm really excited because I have a new apartment. It's so great!*

D Put students into small groups to discuss the questions. In feedback, ask students to expand on their answers and try to prompt them to use more of the expressions from Exercise B. Use the **Vocabulary Worksheet** on page W39 for extra practice.

METHODOLOGY HUB by Jim Scrivener

Dictionary work with all kinds of dictionary

There are many other dictionary-using skills that apply no matter what kind of dictionary – printed or digital – you are using:

- Checking whether your spelling of a word is correct.
- Finding how many syllables a word has.
- Learning where a word is stressed.
- Interpreting definitions.
- Selecting the word that best expresses the meaning you want.
- Selecting between different meanings of the same word.
- Selecting the correct grammatical form of a word.
- Finding the plural of a word.
- Extrapolating from example sentences.
- Making use of collocations.
- Finding idiomatic expressions.

These activities work on different skills. Many of them follow the pattern of students using their knowledge to predict an answer, then using the dictionary to confirm/correct this:

- Guessing spelling: Write out some words with missing letters. Ask students to recall or guess the missing letters …
- Which word?: Give fill-in-the-blank sentences and a choice of two or more possible words (probably unknown to the learners) for each space. Students first guess the answers, then use their dictionaries to decide the best choices.
- Anagrams: Give a list of anagrammed words that have come up in class. Students work out the probable answers …
- Where's the stress?: Write up words. Students predict which syllable has the main stress …
- Dictionary race: Set a number of different challenges (such as the ideas above), perhaps on a worksheet. Students need to work through them quickly within a relatively tight time limit. They try to work accurately and quickly. At the end, students compare with each other to see how they did.

METHODOLOGY HUB by Jim Scrivener

Voice settings

One interesting approach to pronunciation may sound a little odd at first. It's based on the idea that, rather than work on all the small details of pronunciation (such as phonemes, stress patterns, etc), it might be better to start with the larger holistic picture – the general 'settings' of the voice. If you think about a foreign language you have heard a number of times, you are probably able to quickly recall some distinctive impressions about how the language is spoken – the sorts of things that a comedian would pick on if they wanted to mimic a speaker of that language; for example, a distinctive mouth position with the lips pushed forward, a flat intonation with machine-gun delivery, a typical hunching of shoulders, frequently heard sounds, a generally high pitch, etc.

Do your students have such an image about British or American speakers of English? Or Australians? Or Canadians? One useful activity would be to:

(a) watch one or more native speakers on video
(b) discuss any noticeable speech features
(c) try speaking nonsense words using this 'voice setting' ('comedian' style)
(d) practice reading a simple short dialogue in as 'native' a way as they can. (This will probably seem very funny to your students, who will initially tend to do fairly bland copies, never fully believing that a voice setting may be so different or exaggerated compared with their own language; encourage them to risk looking and sounding really like a native speaker.)

There is one important starting question a teacher needs to consider, namely, which pronunciation variety are you going to teach?

9.1 Language and behavior

LISTENING

A Give an example from your own experience. In feedback, encourage students to give examples to support their answers.

B Allow students to compare answers in pairs before feedback.

9.3 C In feedback, ask students to explain why the sentences are true or false by referring to what exactly the speakers said. (See Audio script below.)

D Go through the example sentences 1 and 2.

9.4 E In feedback, ask students to expand on their answers, especially if they come from personal experience

PRONUNCIATION

A Elicit the vague expression in sentence 1 as an example.

9.5 B Give feedback on how well they did this, and if necessary model and practice again, exaggerating slightly at first to make sure students really notice how you're pronouncing the vague expressions.

SPEAKING

In feedback, ask students to share their ideas and try to get the class to agree on the five best overall.

AUDIO SCRIPT

9.3

Listening, Exercise B

L = Lisa G = Greg J = Jake H = Helen

L: Uh, hello.
H: Hey. Come on in. I'm Helen.
J: What's up? I'm Jake.
G: Good morning. How are you doing? I'm Greg.
L: Good, thanks. I'm Lisa. Are you all here for the psychology experiment, too?
Ex C Q1 **G:** Yeah. The organizers offered us 10 bucks, so we signed up.
L: Yeah, same here.
J: I don't know what they're testing, though. Do you?
L: Something about perception skills and stuff like that. Are we supposed to wait for the experimenters?
H: Nah, there were two guys here earlier, psychology professors or whatever, and they were like 'sorry but we have to go and teach.' They left some questions in an envelope.
G: What a hot mess! Should we get going?
J: OK. Task 1: Which line is the same length as the one on the left? Easy. It's line B, isn't it?
H: Yeah, definitely B. It's obvious.
G: Yeah, it's line B. Lisa?
L: Uh, yeah. Line B.
H: Hey, those doughnuts look kind of yummy. Do you think they're for us?
L: I suppose so. Look, there's a note. It says this plate's for
Ex C Q2 the 12 o'clock group and this is for the 11:30 group – that's us.
G: Cool! Mmm, yummy!
H: What's the next task? Let's see: AFC or PTU?
G: PTU, no question. What about you, Jake?
J: Definitely PTU.
H: Yeah, me too. Lisa?
L: Uh, yeah, PTU, I suppose.
J: Great. Those doughnuts were crazy yummy. Can we have some more?
L: Well, the others are supposed to be for the next group.
H: Yeah, but we could just eat them and hide the note!
J: Yeah, whatever.
Ex C Q3 **G:** Fine with me. Lisa?
L: Oh, go ahead then. I mean, they are yummy!
G: Cool! Well done Lisa! You passed the test!
L: What are you on about?
Ex B Q3 **H:** Sorry, Lisa, but it wasn't about perception at all. It was about social pressure and conformity: how groups influence our behavior, and so on.
Ex B Q1 **L:** How do you know? Aren't you participants like me?
Ex B Q2 **J:** Nah, we're the experimenters. We were only pretending. Sorry.
L: So what do you mean, I passed the test?
Ex B Q4 **G:** OK, so the first part was the lines. Did you really think it was line B?
L: Not really. It seemed obvious it was line A, but then you
Ex C Q4 all seemed sort of convinced it was line B. I thought my eyes were playing tricks on me in some way!
H: Yeah, that happens to more or less everyone. Sometimes it's easier to follow the crowd, in a sense, than to trust your own eyes!
L: So it was line A after all?
Ex B Q4 **H:** Yeah, of course it was! OK, so the second test was AFC versus PTU. Why did you go for PTU, Lisa?
L: Cuz you all chose it! I don't even know what PTU stands for. What is it?
J: PTU? Pretending to understand! Most people hate admitting they don't understand something, especially when everyone else is nodding their heads,
Ex C Q5 or something like that, so you pretend. But maybe everyone else is pretending, too! They're all kind of too embarrassed to admit they don't know what's going on!
L: So what's AFC?
J: Ask for clarification! Always ask, even if it makes you feel stupid!
G: Did you enjoy the doughnuts, Lisa?
L: Yeah, they were yummy.
G: Yummy? That's a strange word! Why do you say that?
L: Oh, you got me again! You all called them yummy, didn't you? I never say 'yummy'! Bummer!
Ex B Q4 **G:** Yeah, sorry. We wanted to influence your choice of words. We used loads of slang, too, and stuff like that, to get you to conform to our style of speaking.

LISTENING

A SPEAK **Work in pairs. Do you speak or behave differently depending on who you are with?**

9.3 **B LISTEN FOR GIST** **Listen to a group of people taking part in a psychology experiment. Then answer the questions.**

1 How many participants are in the group?
only one: Lisa

2 Where are the experimenters?
in the room with Lisa

3 What's the purpose of the experiment?
to study social pressure and conformity

4 What five tasks does the experiment include?
length of line; PTU vs AFC; 'yummy' and other slang; the doughnuts; humming

9.3 **C LISTEN FOR DETAIL** **Listen again. Are the statements true (T) or false (F)? Correct the false sentences.**

1 Lisa volunteered to take part for ~~free~~. $10 T / (F)
2 Lisa's group was due to start at 11:30. (T) / F
3 All four members of the group agree to eat the doughnuts. (T) / F
4 Lisa knew for certain that her answer about the lines was wrong. She doubted what she saw. T / (F)
5 Sometimes PTU affects everyone in a group. (T) / F
6 The participants think 'yummy' is a cool word. Nobody suggests it's cool. T / (F)
7 Groupthink is mainly associated with teenagers. also business teams T / (F)
8 The experimenters were surprised by Lisa's behavior. They say most people behave in a similar way. T / (F)

9.4 **D LISTEN TO RAPID SPEECH** **Listen to some extracts from the conversation. Cross out the words and sounds that the speakers leave out. Put brackets [ ] around the phrases they link together. The first two have been done for you. Use the information in the box to help you.**

Understanding rapid colloquial speech

Rapid colloquial English is especially difficult to understand because:

- speakers use a lot of slang and idioms.
- sounds, syllables or even whole words are often left out.
- common phrases like *what do you* and *going to* are linked together.

1 ~~Good~~ morning. How ~~are~~ [you doing?]
2 [~~Don't~~ know] what they're testing.
3 ~~Are~~ we [supposed to] wait?
4 We [~~h~~ave to go] ~~an~~d teach.
5 [Sh~~ould~~ we] get going?
6 [~~It~~'s obvious.]
7 [D~~o~~ you] think they're for us?
8 [What ~~about~~ you,] Jake?
9 [~~Can~~ we ~~h~~ave s~~ome~~ more?]
10 [What ~~are you~~] [going on about?]

E SPEAK **Work in groups and discuss the questions.**

1 Do you think you would respond to the tasks in the same way as Lisa?
2 Have you ever experienced PTU? Think about your experiences as a language learner.
3 Have you ever encountered groupthink or something similar? What happened?

PRONUNCIATION

Pronouncing vague expressions

A **Underline the vague expressions in the extracts from the conversation. Use the information in the box to help you.**

Pronouncing vague expressions

Vague expressions are a way of showing that we're not being too precise. They are especially common in informal English.

Vague expressions are usually pronounced very quickly, with no stressed syllables. The word *of* is often reduced to *a* (e.g. *kinda*, *sorta*). The word *and* becomes *n*.

1 Something about perception skills and stuff like that.
2 There were two guys here earlier, psychology professors or whatever.
3 How groups influence our behavior, and so on.
4 I thought my eyes were playing tricks on me in some way!
5 Sometimes it's easier to follow the crowd, in a sense, than to trust your own eyes!
6 Everyone else is nodding their heads, or something like that.
7 I felt kind of stupid.
8 You must think I'm some kind of sheep!

9.5 **B** **Listen to check your answers. Then practice saying the sentences.**

SPEAKING

DISCUSS **Work in small groups and discuss the question. Use the vague expressions in the list and slang from this lesson in your discussions.**

How can we avoid the problems of group behavior? Think of at least five practical steps.

- and so on
- and stuff like that
- in a/some sense/way
- kind/sort of (+ adjective/verb)
- more or less
- or something (like that)
- or whatever
- some kind/sort of (+ noun)

READING

A SPEAK Work in pairs. Do you think the language you speak could affect any of the areas below? Why/Why not?

- how rich you are
- how you play
- your health

B SKIM Read *Does your language affect your behavior?* Were any of your ideas from Exercise A mentioned?

C READ FOR MAIN IDEA Read the article again. Answer the questions.

1. How did Chen try to show that language (not other factors) affects our behavior?
2. Why does our language affect our behavior, according to Chen?
3. How could Chen's ideas make the world a better place?
4. What other behaviors are connected with our language, according to Chen?
5. What other factor (apart from grammatical structures) might affect how speakers of certain languages behave?
6. What claim is the main focus of the article?
7. What's the problem with the classification of English?
8. Which language feature did Chen use to categorize languages?

D SPEAK Work in groups and discuss the questions.

1. Do you agree with Chen's claims?
2. How else could we explain his correlations?
3. Do you often make long-term plans for the future (e.g. saving for retirement)?
4. Do you consider yourself an impulsive person or someone who likes to plan?

DOES YOUR LANGUAGE AFFECT YOUR BEHAVIOR?

In 2013, Keith Chen, a behavioral economist at Yale University, made headlines around the world with the extraordinary claim Ex C Q6 that the language we speak can have a significant impact on [1]our propensity to save, plan and prepare for the future.

Ex C Q8 Chen divided the languages of the world into two categories: strong FTR (future tense reference) languages, which need markers like 'will' to signal the future, and weak FTR languages, which don't. In English (a strong FTR language), you can't say 'it snows tomorrow'; you usually have to add 'will' or 'going to'. In weak FTR languages like Mandarin, it's normal to say, 'it snows now' and 'it snows tomorrow', using the same verb form in [2]both these cases.

Chen's remarkable finding was that speakers of weak FTR languages save 25% more money for the future than speakers of Ex C Q2 strong FTR languages. Chen's interpretation of this correlation is that for speakers of weak FTR languages, the future feels like part of the present, while speakers of strong FTR languages save much less because the future feels more remote to them.

Ex C Q4 Remarkably, Chen's correlations held not only for savings rates, but also for overeating, smoking, drinking, debt and lack of physical exercise. In each case, speakers of weak FTR languages were significantly healthier and took fewer risks, presumably because they felt [3]a strong connection with their future selves.

While Chen's study provoked considerable interest and enthusiasm from the general public, the backlash from linguists and other academics has been just as striking. One criticism involves the possible confusion of correlation with causation. Ex C Q1 The link between languages and behavior may in fact be due to other factors, such as age, education or income levels. Chen took great care to control for all these factors, by comparing families where the only difference was [4]the language spoken at home. However, many academics still feel deeply uncomfortable with the idea of a causal relationship behind the apparent correlation.

9.1 Language and behavior

READING

A Give your own example, then put students into pairs to discuss the questions. In feedback, encourage students to further question and to agree or disagree with each other.

B Students read the article quickly. Point out that they don't need to understand everything at this stage, but just need to understand enough to check their ideas in Exercise A.

C Put students into pairs to compare answers. In feedback to the questions, ask them to justify their answers with reference to where in the text they found the answers.

D In feedback, encourage students to give examples to support their opinions. If the students speak different languages, find out if their language is a strong or weak FTR language, and if they recognize the typical characteristics of speakers of those language as described in the text. If they speak the same language, find out if they share the same opinion about it.

Extra activity
Ask students to research a talk or video online on the subject of language and behavior. Tell them to write notes and be prepared to discuss what they discovered. At the next class, ask them again if they agree with Chen's claims and encourage them to give evidence to support their opinions.

9.3 (continued)

Ex C Q6 **L:** Ah, yeah. I always thought 'yummy' was uncool, but when you all started using it, I thought maybe it was cool again!

Ex C Q6 **H:** Nah, yummy is always a lame thing to say!

J: How did you feel about eating the other group's doughnuts, Lisa?

L: Not good. But you all convinced me it was fine. It was some kind of trick again, was it?

Ex B Q4 **J:** Yeah, sorry. That was an example of 'groupthink', where people make bad decisions as a group that they wouldn't make as individuals. That's why we agree to things we don't want to do.

Ex C Q7 And it's why many business teams make such terrible decisions.

Ex B Q4 **L:** OK. And what was with that humming at the end?

H: Hah! That was the last task. We wanted to make you copy us. And it worked!

L: Yeah, I know. I felt kind of stupid cuz I didn't know what was going on, so I just joined in. You must think I'm some sort of sheep, copying everything you did!

Ex C Q8 **G:** Chill out, Lisa. Most people are just as bad as you! Anyway, a big pat on the back to you for taking part. You were the bomb! Do you want another doughnut?

GRAMMAR HUB

9.1 Noun phrases

- We can use possessive adjectives, quantifiers, numbers and modified quantifiers before nouns to make noun phrases.

Article/determiner	**Those** researchers are highly qualified.
Possessive adjective	**Their** study is well funded.
Quantifier	**Many** eager participants started immediately
Number	**Two of the five** speakers disagreed.
Modified quantifier	**Almost every single** student showed up early.

- We can use adjective clauses, prepositional phrases, *that* clauses and an infinitive after nouns to make noun phrases.

Adjective clause	**The clinic where she works** just closed.
Reduced adjective clause	**The woman sitting down** is my colleague.
Prepositional phrase	They shared **a wealth of knowledge**.
that clause	I question **the idea that humans are still evolving**.
infinitive	They looked for **a cheap place to eat and sleep**.

- We can use phrases such as *the fact that*, *the idea that* and *the belief that* to turn a sentence into a noun phrase.

A language dies every two weeks. That is regrettable. (= The fact that a language dies every two weeks is regrettable.)

People believe language strengthens social ties. This is supported by research. (= The belief that language strengthens social ties is supported by research.)

9.1 Language and behavior

GRAMMAR

A Put students into pairs to match the examples to the rules. In feedback, elicit that using long noun phrases gives a text a more formal style.

B Direct students to the **Grammar Hub** (see TB100 and below).

C Go through the example step by step to demonstrate how a noun phrase can be built upon. Then put students into small groups to try to make as long a noun phrase as they can for the words in the box. In feedback, write the longest one created for each noun on the board. Use the **Grammar Worksheet** on page W40 for extra practice.

SPEAKING HUB

A Direct students to the **Communication Hub** (see TB121). Put them into groups to discuss the questions.

B Tell students to work individually and choose one of the ideas from Exercise A. Ask them to write down five pieces of evidence to either support or challenge the idea.

C Put students into pairs to tell each other about what they have written. Encourage students to listen to their partner carefully, to ask further questions and to give feedback on what they said.

D Students use their partner's feedback to help make any changes to their presentation before they share it with the class.

E Students present their ideas to the class, while the others listen carefully and ask questions at the end.

F Put students into pairs to discuss which evidence they found most convincing and why. In feedback, ask a few students to explain their opinions.

GRAMMAR HUB

9.1 Noun phrases

A Choose the option which is closest in meaning to the sentence.

1 Lisa questioned many of her professors, and only one gave a clear answer.
   a Many of the professors Lisa questioned only gave one clear answer.
   (b) Only one of the many professors Lisa questioned gave a clear answer.

2 I have two younger brothers, and they are language experts.
   (a) Both of my younger brothers are language experts.
   b Two of my younger brothers are language experts.

3 Very few of the participants enjoyed the study.
   (a) Almost all of the participants disliked the study.
   b Quite a few of the participants enjoyed the study.

4 Jake is standing at the workstation, and he's running reports.
   a The man standing at the workstation is running reports.
   (b) The man standing at the workstation and running reports is Jake.

5 They're looking for a safe location so they can try out their experiment.
   (a) They're searching for a safe location to try out their experiment.
   b They're looking to try out their experiment at a safe location.

6 Many people applied for the trial, but few were qualified to join.
   a Many of the few people applying for the trial were qualified to join.
   (b) Few of the many people applying for the trial were qualified to join.

B Rewrite these sentences using noun phrases. Use the words in bold to help you.

1 I speak **three** languages and **two** of **them** are Latin-based.
   Two of the three languages I speak are Latin-based.

2 I have **little** money, but I save **it all** … well, **almost**.
   I save almost all (of) the little money I have.

3 I've read **very few** pieces of research, but this is **one of them**.
   This is one of the very few pieces of research I've read.

4 **The writer** draws **two** conclusions and they **both** seem dubious to me.
   Both the writer's conclusions seem dubious to me.

5 **The researchers** interviewed **many** people. **Quite a few** had no savings at all.
   Quite a few of the researchers' many interviewees had no savings at all.

6 They **can't conduct the experiment** in peace. That is annoying.
   That they can't conduct their experiment in peace is annoying.

7 That **man** is in charge of the experiment. He's wearing a **white lab coat**.
   The man in the white lab coat is in charge of the experiment.

8 Many linguists **believe language is alive**, and this is factored into their theories.
   The belief that language is alive is factored into linguists' theories.

➤ Go back to page 101.

One alternative possibility is that it's the connotations of a language that affect our behavior, rather than any grammatical properties of the language itself. For example, languages such as English might encourage a live-for-today attitude as a result of people's associations of that attitude with English-speaking countries. Ex C Q5

In a 2010 study, Dirk Akkermans and colleagues set out to find out more by asking bilingual speakers of English and Dutch to play a game. [5]Those who had lived in English-speaking countries were found to be considerably more competitive when playing in English rather than Dutch. However, those who had experienced only limited exposure to the culture of English-speaking countries were found to be no more competitive when playing in English or Dutch, strongly suggesting that it's the culture of English-speaking countries, not the language itself, that is making the difference. Ex C Q5

A second major concern with Chen's study is that his division of the world's languages into two categories, strong and weak FTR, seems overly simplistic. For example, while English does require a future tense marker in predictions like 'it'll rain tomorrow', future markers are optional in other future constructions (e.g. 'I'm leaving tomorrow') and virtually outlawed in conditional clauses (e.g. 'If it rains …'). The future in English is complex, as [6]pretty much every learner can attest, so its classification as strong FTR feels debatable at best. Similar objections could be raised for many other languages. Ex C Q7

Overall, despite [7]the many legitimate concerns, Chen's analysis of the correlation can't be dismissed out of hand. Further research is needed, ideally with a more sophisticated classification of languages. However, if [8]Chen's conclusions that grammar influences behavior prove correct, the implications will be profound. Wouldn't it be great if we could solve [9]all our financial and health problems simply by outlawing words like 'will'! Ex C Q3

"Chen, M Keith. 2013. "*The Effect of Language on Economic Behavior: Evidence from Savings Rates, Health Behaviors, and Retirement Assets.*" American Economic Review, 103 (2): 690-731."

Glossary

backlash (n) a strong, negative and often angry reaction to something that has happened, especially a political or social change
legitimate (adj) fair and reasonable
outlaw (v) to make something illegal
propensity (n) a natural tendency to behave in a particular way
provoke (v) to cause a reaction, especially an angry one
simplistic (adj) treating something in a way that makes it seem much simpler than it really is

GRAMMAR
Noun phrases

A Complete the rules with the examples (1–9) from the text.

Noun phrases

Long noun phrases (NPs) are especially useful in formal and academic writing because they can contain as much information as a full sentence.

Most NPs start with a number, a quantifier (e.g. *some, all*) and/or another determiner (e.g. *the, my, these*).

a *all* and *both* can be used before a determiner without *of*: 2 / 9

b *many, few, little* and numbers can be used after a determiner: 7

c Some quantifiers can be modified with phrases like *almost* or *not exactly*: 6

Common structures at the end of an NP include:

d adjective clauses: 5

e reduced adjective clauses: 4

f preposition phrases: 3

g *that*-clauses: 8

h infinitive: 1

B Go to the **Grammar Hub** on **page 138**.

C **SPEAK** Work in small groups. Build 'monster noun phrases' around the nouns in the box, as in the example.

behavior experiments language

A: My friends' behavior is strange.
B: A lot of my best friends' behavior is strange.
C: A lot of my best friends' behavior when they're tired is strange.

SPEAKING HUB

A **DISCUSS** Work in small groups. Go to the **Communication Hub** on **page 152**.

B **PLAN** Choose one of the ideas in Exercise A. Create a list of at least five pieces of evidence to support or challenge the idea.

C **PREPARE** Work in pairs. Explain your pieces of evidence to your partner. Listen to your partner's evidence. Give feedback and ask questions.

D **PRACTICE** Practice presenting your evidence. Use your partner's feedback to improve your presentation.

E **PRESENT** Report your evidence to the class. Be prepared to answer questions.

F **REFLECT** Decide which evidence you found most convincing and why.

Talk about group behavior
Discuss factors that affect behavior

9.2 Animal behavior

- Discuss animal behavior
- Talk about behavioral experiments

G – participile clauses and verbless clauses
P – intrusive stops
V – verb + object + base form; gestures and body language
S – identifying outcomes of scientific research

READING

A SPEAK Work in pairs and discuss the questions.

chimpanzees | dolphins | crows and jays | dogs

1 Which of the animals listed in the box are intelligent?
2 How do we know?
3 How could we find out?

B SKIM Read *Understanding animal behavior* quickly. What does the writer say about the questions in Exercise A?

Understanding animal behavior

By Peter Aldhous

We gaze into the eyes of a chimp and see a reflection of ourselves. We glance at a crow and see an alien being. Such biases skew our understanding of what non-human intelligence looks like.

The best known experiment designed to probe animal minds is the 'mirror test'. Having been given time to interact with a mirror, chimps Ex C Q1 are marked with a dye and anesthetized. After coming around, they Ex B Q1 & Q2 look into the mirror while touching the marked area. From this behavior, researchers have concluded that the chimps know they are looking at themselves – one of the hallmarks of an advanced mind. Other animals Ex C Q2 that have passed the test include manta rays and dolphins.

My issue with the mirror test isn't the meaning of success, but rather how to interpret failure. Do most animals fail because they lack a concept of self, or is the test irrelevant to species that don't use vision Ex B Q3 for social communication? How would you design a similar test using smells for a dog or ultrasound for a dolphin? When a dolphin **hears its own echoes coming** back in altered form, it might well be thinking: 'Yes, that's me' – but how would we know?

In New Caledonian forests, Gavin Hunt of Massey University **watched** Ex B Q1 & Q2 **crows fashion** twigs into hooks to capture insects from holes. Seeming to understand cause and effect, crows are capable of astounding feats of meta-tool use: using one tool to manipulate another in order to achieve an ultimate goal.

Ex C Q4 In fact, they seem better than chimps at translating their skill in solving one problem to another conceptually similar one. In the trap-tube test, an animal must use a stick to obtain food from a tube. Pushing it in one direction **helps them get** the reward; pushing it in the other **makes the** Ex C Q3 **food fall** into a trap. Crows that have already solved this problem can apply their skills when presented with the trap-table test, which looks different but has the same rule: Don't **let the food drop** down the hole. For chimps, prior experience with the trap tube gives no advantage on the trap table.

Ex B Q3 Understanding the wider scope of corvid cognition meant entering the birds' world to devise experiments to probe their mental processes. Nicky Clayton did this while at the University of California in the late 1990s. After being told confidently by a psychologist colleague that animals lack 'episodic' memory – an ability to remember the 'what, where and when' of past events – Clayton decided to check for herself. While studying western scrub jays, she realized that the birds' habit of burying food provided a prime opportunity to test their memories.

Clayton first **had the jays bury** insect larvae and peanuts in sand-Ex C Q5 filled trays. Having learned that the larvae tasted bad after a few days, if just four hours had elapsed, the jays sought out the places where they had hidden them. But if several days had passed, they Ex B Q1 & Q2 went for the hidden peanuts. This was an impressive demonstration Ex C Q6 of 'episodic-like' memory. Clayton has also found that jays will selectively bury certain types of food when aware that it is likely to be scarce in future. So now we apparently have jays planning ahead, in addition to acting on specific memories of the past.

When I visited Clayton and her scrub jays, it was a while before I **saw one of the birds bury** an item of food – apparently my presence had interrupted them. 'They're checking you out,' Clayton told me. I stared back, struck by the gulf between us. Despite having read the scientific papers and knowing how cognitively sophisticated scrub jays are, I experienced no emotional connection.

Glossary

elapse (v) if time elapses, it passes
feat (n) something impressive and often dangerous that someone does
gulf (n) a large and important difference between people or groups
hallmark (n) typical feature

LEAD-IN

Tell students to imagine they could be any animal. Put them into pairs to tell each other which animal they would choose to be and why. In feedback, encourage students to explain their choices.

READING

A In feedback, encourage students to explain their opinions and to agree and disagree with each other, but don't confirm or reject any answers yet.

B Set a time limit and tell students to read the article to find the answers to the questions in Exercise A. Stress that they only need to read through quickly to do this, and reassure them that they will be able to read the article again more closely later. Let students compare answers in pairs before feedback.

1 & 2

- *Chimpanzees have passed the mirror test but can't apply a rule from one game to another.*
- *New Caledonian crows seem to understand cause and effect and are capable of meta-tool use, etc; western scrub jays seem to have episodic memory and can plan ahead.*

3

- *Dogs: design an equivalent of the mirror test using smells.*
- *Dolphins: design an equivalent of the mirror test using ultrasound.*
- *Corvids: enter the birds' world to devise experiments to probe the mental processes behind their everyday behavior.*

C Go through the information in the box about *Identifying outcomes of scientific research*, then tell students to read the text again and to complete the notes. Again, let students compare answers with a partner before feedback.

D Put students into pairs to discuss the question. In feedback, encourage students to expand on their answers and to agree or disagree with each other.

Extra activity

Ask students to further research the question outside class: *How might research change the way we treat animals?* Ask them to look for two or three examples, like abstracts from academic articles related to animal behavior.

Students can bring these to the next class. Put them into small groups and ask them to summarize any evidence they have found to support their opinions. In whole-class feedback, ask each group to report back on the research discussed and how it may help answer the question.

Extra activity

Give students some well-known idioms involving animals (e.g. *to eat like a horse, as quiet as a mouse, a wolf in sheep's clothing*). Ask them if the same idioms exist in their language or if they have a different one to express the same idea. Put them into pairs to discuss other animal idioms they have in their language. In feedback, ask students to share these, and tell them if the same idioms exist on English. Students could research more for homework and share them in the next lesson.

TEACHING IDEA by David Seymour and Maria Popova

Animal characteristics

Use this activity to introduce or extend the theme of animal behavior.

In pairs, match each animal with the adjective which is traditionally used to describe them.

owl, fox, mouse, monkey, lion, wise, clever, small, bold, proud, dog, bat, ox, donkey, dinosaur, loyal, blind, strong, stubborn, pig, cat, fish extinct, greedy, independent, slippery

How do they compare with popular ideas about animals in your country, e.g. Is an owl considered wise?

Think of animals that these adjectives could describe.

lazy, thoughtful, selfish, kind, sensible, sensitive, fancy, cold, cheerful, impatient, hard-working, easy-going, stylish, reserved, antisocial, moody

Think of another adjective to describe each animal and explain why you chose it.

METHODOLOGY HUB by Scott Thornbury

Clauses

Clauses are to sentences what branches are to trees. That is, they are the largest grammatical unit smaller than the whole sentence. Looked at another way, words are grouped into phrases, the phrases form the components of clauses and one or more clauses comprise a sentence. A simple definition of a clause is any group of words that includes a verb (V). (For exceptions, see below.) Most clauses also contain a subject (S). Other clause elements, identified by their function, are objects (O), complements (C) (also called predicatives) and adverbials (A). Depending on the verb, a clause can be finite or non-finite. A finite clause contains a finite verb, i.e. one that is marked for tense and agrees with its subject: *When the door opens*, you can go in. A non-finite clause is one that has a participle or an infinitive as its verb:

Having opened the door, we went in.

The door being open, we went in.

To open the door, use the key.

Occasionally, the verb can be left out, to form a verbless clause: *Once inside*, we took a look around. = *Once we were inside* …

9.2 Animal behavior

VOCABULARY

A In feedback, use these example sentences from the text to make sure students understand the difference in the use of sense verbs and causative verbs, i.e. the causative verbs are used to show that someone or something is causing something to happen.

B Direct students to the **Vocabulary Hub** (see TB121). Use the **Vocabulary Worksheet** on page W41 for extra practice.

GRAMMAR

A Tell students to cover the article, then put them into pairs to try to complete the sentences from memory.

B Tell students to match the seven sentences from the article to the rules. In feedback, make sure students appreciate that the sentences containing participle clauses give a more formal academic or literary style than the rewritten ones in Exercise A.

C Direct students to the **Grammar Hub**. Use the **Grammar Worksheet** on page W42 for extra practice.

SPEAKING

Give an example of your own, then put students into groups to discuss their experiences and opinions. Once these discussions have generated some ideas, tell them to prepare to report these to the class using participle clauses. Monitor to help if needed as they do this. Then tell each group to report to the class, and encourage other students to listen carefully and to ask questions at the end. Finish with feedback on students' use of language during the activity.

GRAMMAR HUB

9.2 Participle clauses and verbless clauses

- We use present and past participles as well as combinations of both to form participle clauses.

  Feeling unsure of the results, Mary tested the configuration once more.

  Left to their own devices, children can solve complex problems.

  Having just finished his research, Travis went for a walk to relax.

- We can use prepositions such as *before*, *after* and *despite* before participle clauses with present participles (but not past participles).

  Before arriving at the office, Susan texted her boss.
  NOT ~~Before arrived at the office, Susan texted her boss.~~

- We can use conjunctions such as *if*, *when* and *while* before participle clauses with both present and past participles.

  While waiting for the bus, Paula had a marvelous idea.

  When pressed to answer questions, Jonathan became very nervous.

Be careful!

- Participle clauses appear near the nouns they refer to. When that noun is missing, or the clause appears closer to another noun which it doesn't refer to, it becomes a 'dangling participle' and is grammatically incorrect.

  While doing research, Frank noticed the room getting cold. NOT ~~While doing research, the room got cold.~~ (Incorrect: the room wasn't doing research)

- When the participle clause involves using the verb *be*, we can omit the verb altogether and the clause becomes 'verbless'.

  Too impatient to wait, Paul barged in and demanded the results. (= Being too impatient to wait, ...)

- We can start a clause with just a participle, with words such as *when*, *after* or *because* being implied.

  Hearing the news, Alex leaped for joy! (= After hearing the news, Alex leaped for joy!)

9.2 Participle clauses and verbless clauses

A Choose the correct options to complete the sentences.

1. *Sensing* / *Sensed* danger, Henry shut down the machine immediately.
2. *Having already left* / *Leaving the building*, Danielle didn't feel like returning to get her phone.
3. Before *notifying* / *notified* her supervisor, Anna wanted to make sure the experiment was a success.
4. When *asking* / *asked* about the research, Kyle refused to reply.
5. *Too* / *Too being* cautious to take risks, Martin decided to stay on at his job.
6. Despite *handed* / *handing* in her notice, Sarah put in great effort during her last days at work.
7. *Having been told* / *Being told* to speed up the study, David cut corners to make his deadlines.
8. If *successful* / *being successful*, we can publish the results in a science journal.

B Rewrite these sentences using participle clauses or verbless clauses and the word in bold.

1. I understand animal behavior better now that I've read the article. **having**
   Having read the article, I understand animal behavior better.
2. The octopus hid in the coconut shell because it felt threatened. **feeling**
   Feeling threatened, the octopus hid in the coconut shell.
3. These experiments can teach us a lot if you do them properly. **done**
   Done properly, these experiments can teach us a lot.
4. I guessed the answer because I didn't know. **knowing**
   Not knowing the answer, I guessed.
5. The crow had never seen the tool before but used it perfectly. **despite**
   Despite never having seen the tool before, the crow used it perfectly.
6. She wasn't fast enough to win the race, but she came in a close second. **too**
   Too slow to win the race, she came in a close second.

➤ Go back to page 103.

C READ FOR OUTCOMES Complete the notes about the research. Use the information in the box to help you.

Identifying outcomes of scientific research

When you read about scientific research, it's important to distinguish between:

- results (what happened?)
- conclusions (what did we learn?).

You can then decide if you agree with the conclusions.

Mirror test

1 Results: Chimps look in mirror and touch (the) marked area.

2 Conclusions: Chimps know they are looking at themselves.

Trap-tube/-table test

3 Results: Crows can apply their skills from one test to another; for chimps prior experience gives no advantage.

4 Conclusions: Crows are better than chimps at translating skills to conceptually similar problems

Insect larvae vs peanuts

5 Results: Jays went to larvae locations after four hours, but to peanut locations after several days.

6 Conclusions: Jays possess 'episodic-like' memory.

D SPEAK Work in pairs and discuss the question. How might research like this change the way we treat animals?

VOCABULARY

Verb + object + base form

A Look again at the examples in bold in *Understanding animal behavior*. Then complete the rules with verbs from the text.

Verb + object + base form

A very small number of verbs are followed by an object or a base form.

1 Sense verbs: *hear*, *watch*, *see* and *feel* are followed by a base form to describe a complete event, or an *-ing* form to describe a process or series of events.

2 Causative verbs: *have*, *let* and *make*. After *help*, both a base form or an infinitive are possible.

B Go to the Vocabulary Hub on page 147.

GRAMMAR

Participle clauses and verbless clauses

A Complete the sentences from the article with one word.

1 Having been given time to interact with a mirror, chimps are marked with a dye.

2 After coming around, they look into the mirror while touching the marked area.

3 Nicky Clayton did this while at the University of California in the late 1990s.

4 After being told confidently by a psychologist colleague that animals lack 'episodic' memory … Clayton decided to check for herself.

5 Having learned that the larvae tasted bad after a few days … the jays sought out the places where they had hidden them.

6 Clayton has also found that jays will selectively bury certain types of food when aware that it is likely to be scarce in the future.

7 I stared back, struck by the gulf between us.

B Match the sentences (1–7) in Exercise A with the rules (a–c).

Participle clauses and verbless clauses

Participle clauses use participles (e.g. *doing, done, being done, having done, having been done*) instead of a subject + verb.

a When a clause starts with a participle, the meaning is often *when/after* 1, 5 or *because* 7.

b Many participle clauses start with prepositions (e.g. *before, after, despite*) 4.

c After some conjunctions (*if, when, while, although*), we can leave out the subject and *be*. Usually this leaves a participle 2.

When *be* was the only verb, we are left with a 'verbless clause' 3, 6.

C Go to the Grammar Hub on page 138.

SPEAKING

SPEAK Work in groups. Discuss your experiences and opinions of animal intelligence. Then use participle clauses to report back to the class.

LISTENING

A SPEAK Work in groups. Discuss the questions.

1 Do you have any lucky charms that you use before exams or other stressful situations? Do you know anybody who uses these lucky charms?

2 Do you have any lucky rituals or routines that you follow, e.g. before watching your favorite sports team? Do you know anybody who follows these lucky rituals?

9.6 **B LISTEN FOR MAIN IDEA Listen to a radio show about behavioral psychology and answer the questions.**

1 How did the pigeons get food?

____

2 What's the connection between the experiment with pigeons and the one with people?

____

3 How do the three people at the end try to influence events?

____

9.6 **C LISTEN FOR DETAIL Listen again. Choose the correct endings.**

1 In the famous pigeon experiment, the mechanism always delivered food …

a after the same amount of time had passed.

b at random times.

c when the pigeons performed a particular action.

2 As the food continued to be delivered, the pigeons …

a changed their actions.

b became more sure they could affect the delivery.

c became more desperate.

3 The experiment with people …

a showed humans weren't so easily convinced.

b showed very similar results.

c used food as well to trick the participants.

4 The person who seems most convinced of their power to control events is …

a the soccer fan.

b the exam-taker.

c the lottery player.

D SPEAK Work in groups and discuss the questions.

1 Do the behaviors and rituals described in the radio show prove that pigeons and people are stupid/irrational? Or is there a benefit in believing we can influence things beyond our control?

2 What other examples can you think of, where people (or animals) try to control things that are beyond their control?

3 What are some dangers of this type of behavior?

PRONUNCIATION

Intrusive stops

9.7 **A Listen carefully to some extracts from the radio show. Which sound (/p/, /t/ or /k/) can you hear in each of the underlined words?**

1 A kind of bizarre pigeon dance. /p/ /t/ /k/

2 Such actions can influence something beyond our control. /p/ /t/ /k/

3 After completely random lengths of time. /p/ /t/ /k/

4 I was young, and my aunt gave me a lucky hamster toy. /p/ /t/ /k/

B Work in pairs. Practice saying the sentences in Exercise A.

9.8 **C Which six words in the box can have intrusive stops? Listen to check. What's different about the other three words?**

becomes	influence	intense	once
prince	strength	things	warmth	wins

D Work in pairs. Write a sentence using at least three of the words in Exercise C. Then give it to another pair for them to attempt to say correctly.

The more influence the prince has, the more intense he becomes.

9.2 Animal behavior

LISTENING

A Give your own example, then put students into groups to discuss the questions. In feedback, encourage students to expand on their answers and to ask each other further questions.

9.6 **B** Explain that students are going to listen to a radio show about behavioral psychology. Tell them to answer the questions as they listen. Let students compare in pairs before feedback.

1 *They thought they could cause the food to appear, but in fact they could just wait and do nothing.*
2 *They both show how strange behavior can be created from a misplaced belief that we can affect things that are beyond our control.*
3 *By watching soccer games and wearing a soccer jersey and scarf; by placing lucky toys on the desk during exams; by buying lottery tickets at exactly the same time each week*

9.6 **C** Put students into pairs to try to choose the correct answers from memory. Then play the recording again for them to listen and check. In feedback, ask students to justify their answers with reference to what exactly the speakers said in the radio show.

D Put students into small groups to discuss the questions. In feedback, encourage students to give examples to support their opinions and to agree and disagree with each other.

PRONUNCIATION

9.7 **A** Students may find this difficult, so do the first one as an example. Stop the recording after the first sentence and elicit the answer. If students are unsure, play the sentence again and again as many times as necessary. Alternatively, model the sentence yourself, slowing down and exaggerating slightly on the underlined word. When students have it, play the rest of the recording. In feedback, model pronunciation of the underlined words again to make sure students notice the intrusive stops.

B Model one yourself, exaggerating slightly on the intrusive stop to make sure students notice, then put students into pairs to practice saying the sentences. In feedback, ask a different student to read each sentence before the rest of the class repeat. Praise good pronunciation, and correct where necessary.

9.8 **C** Model pronunciation of the first two words as an example, then put students into pairs to do the rest. Encourage them to read the words aloud to help them. Then play the recording for students to listen and check.

D Go through the example with the class, then divide students into pairs to generate their sentences. You could collect all the sentences and hand them out to different pairs for them to read aloud.

Intrusive stops: influence (/nts/), intense (/nts/), once (/nts/), prince (/nts/), strength (/ŋkθ/), warmth (/mpθ/).

The other words (becomes, things, wins) all end in a voiced fricative sound (/z/), so we don't add intrusive stops.

AUDIO SCRIPT

9.6

Listening, Exercise B
P = Presenter M1 = Man 1 M2 = Man 2 W = Woman

P: Hello and welcome to *Human Behavior*. Today, we're looking at one of the most famous experiments of all time. In the 1940s, the leading behavioral psychologist, B. F. Skinner, conducted a remarkable experiment. Some hungry pigeons were placed in a cage with a mechanism that delivered food.
The twist in this particular experiment was that the pigeons' actions had no effect whatsoever on
Ex B Q1 the mechanism, which simply delivered food at
Ex C Q1 regular intervals, regardless of what the pigeons did. The pigeons, of course, didn't know this, so they kept pecking and pushing and so on in a desperate attempt to make the mechanism deliver food. Inevitably, there were occasions when food appeared immediately after the pigeon had performed a particular action. That was enough to convince the pigeon that it was that action that had caused the food to be delivered, so the pigeon kept repeating it again
Ex C Q2 and again. And of course, every time the mechanism delivered another serving of food, the pigeon became more and more convinced that it could influence the mechanism with its actions.
According to Skinner's report, the pigeons swung and moved around a lot, making it look like a kind of bizarre pigeon dance. Surely humans wouldn't believe such actions could influence something beyond our control … or would we?
Ex B Q2 In fact, when the experiment was repeated on
Ex C Q3 humans, who received points instead of food, the results were almost identical. By the end of one experiment, the participants were convinced that they'd gotten a point for a particular combination of shrugging, fidgeting and rocking back and forth. What never seemed to occur to them was that the points were simply awarded after completely random lengths of time. If they'd just sat there and waited, they'd still have won the points just the same, without making themselves look ridiculous in the process. But of course, it wouldn't have been so entertaining to watch.
Does anything like this happen in real life? Let's hear from a few people we interviewed on the street this morning to find out.

Ex B Q3 **M1:** I'm a big soccer fan. I try to watch all my team's games on TV. In fact, pretty much whenever I miss a game, my team loses! So I make sure I'm sitting by the TV in good time for each game, wearing my lucky soccer jersey and scarf, to bring my team luck! And it definitely works – well, most of the time, at least.

W: It started when I was young, and my aunt gave me a lucky hamster toy before a big test. I forgot to take
Ex B Q3 it with me for my next test, which was a disaster! So ever
Ex C Q4 since then, I've always used lucky toys in exams.

Ex B Q3 **M2:** I always buy my lottery tickets at exactly 11:41 on a Thursday morning. I know it sounds crazy, but every time I've won any money on the lottery, it's after buying my ticket at that time. Unfortunately, it doesn't always work, for some reason, but it certainly seems to improve my chances of winning.

P: I'm sure it does. Anyway, join us again next week on *Human Behavior* …

9.2 Animal behavior

VOCABULARY

A Elicit the first one as an example, then put students into pairs to do the rest. In feedback, ask students to mime the gestures to make sure everyone understands.

B Do the first one as an example for the class before putting students into pairs to work on the rest.

C Direct students to the **Vocabulary Hub** (see TB121).

D Put students into small groups to discuss the questions. In feedback, encourage students to explain their answers.

Suggested answers

1 *Happy: You can gaze at something/someone and grin (or smirk).*

Interested: You can raise your eyebrows and nod your head. You might also lean forward toward the speaker.

Bored: You can fidget with something or stare/gaze at something else (e.g. out of the window). You might also fold your arms.

2 *You can fold your arms, cross your legs and lean backwards, away from the speaker.*

3 *You can point to show what you want and beckon to ask the person to come to you. You can nod your head to say 'yes', shake it to say 'no' and shrug your shoulders to say 'I don't know'.*

E Put students into groups. Appoint one *facilitator* in each group, and direct students to the **Communication Hub** (see TB121). When students have read their instructions, instruct them to play the game. Use the **Vocabulary Worksheet** on page W43 for extra practice.

SPEAKING HUB

A Explain that students are going to design and conduct a behavioral experiment. Put them into groups and tell them to choose an assumption to test: either an idea of their own or one of the suggestions given.

B Tell the groups to work out exactly how their experiment will work, using the question as guidance. Monitor to help and prompt if needed.

C Students move around the room, conducting or participating in experiments with students from other groups.

D Tell students to get back into their groups and to compare their findings and evaluate the success of their experiment. In feedback, ask each group to explain to the class what assumption their experiment was testing, what their findings show and how effective their experiment was. Encourage the other students to listen carefully and to comment or ask questions after each presentation. Finish with feedback on students' use of language during the activity.

Extra activity

Put students into pairs to play a simple game. One student asks their partner yes/no questions, and the partner answers. However, in this game *yes* means *no* and *no* means *yes*. How easy do students find this? Tell students to observe their partner's body language as well. Do they still instinctively nod or shake their head?

METHODOLOGY HUB by Scott Thornbury

Lexis

Lexis is a technical term for the vocabulary of a language, as opposed to its grammar. A number of other words relating to vocabulary are derived from the word *lexis*, including the adjective *lexical*, as in the lexical approach. A *lexicon* is a collection of words and is often used to talk about the way vocabulary is stored in the mind, as in *the mental lexicon*. *Lexicography* is the study of words for the purpose of compiling dictionaries.

METHODOLOGY HUB by Scott Thornbury

Lexical item

The term *lexical item* (or, more technically, lexeme) is used in order to get around the fuzziness of the word *word*. For instance, are *go*, *going*, *goes* and *went* all different words, or simply different forms of the same word? Likewise, is *get up* one word or two? And of course, *in case* and *for example* – are these single words or pairs of words?

A lexical item is any item that functions as a single-meaning unit, regardless of its different derived forms, or of the number of words that make it up. So, *go*, *get up* and *for example* are all lexical items. So, too, are idioms like *spill the beans* and *hell for leather*. And *go*, *went*, *been* and *gone* are all forms of the same lexeme (*go*). As a rule of thumb, dictionary entries are organized into lexemes (called headwords or lemmas by dictionary writers), rather than individual words.

METHODOLOGY HUB by Scott Thornbury

Lexical set

Lexical sets are sets of words that share a meaning relationship, e.g. because they relate to a particular topic or situation. Thus, the words *drive*, *steering wheel*, *starter*, *windscreen*, *change gear*, *hand-brake* and *reverse* all belong to the lexical set *car*. Likewise, *menu*, *starter*, *napkin*, *wine glass*, *tip* and *bill* are associated with a restaurant situation. (Note that many words – like *starter* – can belong to more than one lexical set.) Lexical sets can be assembled using a corpus. By looking at the words that co-occur with a key word (such as *car*), and then by looking at the words that co-occur with those words, a network of commonly associated words can be constructed. Most vocabulary teaching is organized around lexical sets (*furniture*, *jobs*, *sports*, etc), on the principle that it is easier both to teach and to learn words that are closely associated. Such a view fits in with what we know about the way words are stored in memory. That is, they are stored in interconnecting networks according to their meaning associations. Sometimes, however, a close association can cause 'interference', so that a learner might say *Bring me the tip* instead of *Bring me the bill*. This has led some researchers to suggest that it might in fact be better to learn vocabulary items which have not been grouped into lexical sets, but which instead have been selected more randomly. Such a view, however, seems to run counter to common sense.

VOCABULARY

Gestures and body language

A **Match the gestures (1–7) with the body parts (a–g). Choose each body part once. When would you use each gesture?**

1 blink / wink e
2 shrug f
3 point / bend / wiggle a
4 nod / shake c
5 fold / cross g
6 cross / bend d
7 raise b

a your finger(s)
b your eyebrows
c your head
d your legs
e your eyes
f your shoulders
g your arm(s)

B **Complete the sentences with the correct form of a verb in the box. Which body part does each verb involve?**

beckon fidget gaze glare grin lean smirk stare

1 Stop staring at those people's clothes! It's really rude! They're looking back now! eyes
2 You look so happy in that photo! You're grinning from ear to ear! mouth (and eyes)
3 I love gazing out to sea and dreaming of what's on the other side. eyes
4 Stop fidgeting with your keys and pay attention! hands
5 During the test, the teacher beckoned for me to come to the front of the class. finger / hand
6 Don't lean against that cupboard! It's not very stable. back
7 When he beat me at tennis, Harry just smirked and said, 'I guess I'm better than you.' mouth / eyes / face
8 I could tell you were angry by the way you glared at me. eyes

C **Go to the Vocabulary Hub on page 147.**

D **SPEAK** **Work in groups and discuss the questions.**

1 Which gestures can you use to show that you're happy/interested/bored?
2 How might you show that you don't like someone?
3 How could you communicate with a stranger who doesn't speak your language?

E **Work in groups to play a game. One of you is the facilitator; the others are players. Facilitator – go to the Communication Hub on page 153. Players – go to the Communication Hub on page 150.**

SPEAKING HUB

A **PREPARE** **Work in groups. You are going to design and conduct a behavioral experiment to test an assumption. You can use one of the ideas below or your own ideas.**

Assumption 1: Our body language communicates more information than the words we use.

Assumption 2: We can't help nodding or shaking our heads when we say *yes* or *no*, or shrugging our shoulders when we say *I don't know*, even if the movements are extremely tiny.

Assumption 3: We can't help mirroring other people's gestures and body language. We copy them subconsciously.

B **PLAN** **Work out how you could test the assumption on other members of the class.**

- How will you set up the experiment?
- What will you tell the participant(s)?
- What will you be looking out for?
- How might your observations confirm or undermine the initial assumption?

C **CONDUCT** **Take turns to conduct your experiments with other members of the class.**

If you're participating in another group's experiment, try to act naturally. Don't try to guess what the experimenters are testing – and don't try to influence their results.

If you're an observer, watch both the experimenters and the participants carefully. Try to work out what the experiment is testing.

D **DISCUSS** **Report back to the class on what you learned from your experiment. Ask other observers for their conclusions. How could you refine your experiment to learn more?**

– Discuss animal behavior
– Talk about behavioral experiments

Café Hub

9.3 Model behavior

A– *end up* S– backtracking and reformulating

All together now

A Work in pairs. Look at the picture and discuss the questions.

1 What is happening in the picture? a shoal of fish swarming

2 Which other animals behave in this way? Why?
Across nature, animals follow the quickest animal to react.

B 00.00–01.51 Work in pairs. Watch the first part of a video. Check your answers to Exercise A.

Glossary

evacuation (n) the process of removing people from a building or an area that is not safe

scenario (n) a situation that could possibly happen

simulate (v) to produce the features of something in a way that seems real but is not

swarm (v) to go somewhere as part of a large crowd

C 00.00–01.51 Watch the first part of the video again. Complete the sentences with the best option (a, b or c).

1 Doctor Ed Codling is a …
  a mathematician.
  b biologist.
  c mathematical biologist.

2 The experiment replicates how people on their own react in …
  a a fire.
  b an earthquake.
  c a plane accident.

3 Doctor Codling wants to observe participants that …
  a look confident and assume they can find the exit.
  b remain calm and find the exit.
  c panic and follow another person.

4 When Doctor Codling blows his whistle he wants them to leave out of …
  a the north exit.
  b the south exit.
  c either the north or south exit.

D Work in pairs. Discuss the questions.

1 What do you think the result of the experiment will be?
A large number of the students went to the wrong exit.

2 How many people do you think will go the right or the wrong way? 12 people

3 Why did people behave in the way they did?
Some of the group influenced the rest of the crowd.

E 01.51–02.35 Watch the second part of the video. Check your answers to Exercise D.

AUTHENTIC ENGLISH

A Work in pairs. Read the sentence from the video. Choose the correct options in the box.

I mean, I've done it before, you just ***end up*** *following someone who looks the most confident in the room.*

end up

We use *end up* to describe being in a particular place or state after doing something or because of doing it. It is used when the subject ***did / didn't*** intend or expect this.

B Work in pairs. Respond to the sentences using *ended up*.

1 You missed your plane. Suggested answers:
I ended up sleeping at the airport.

2 The movie you wanted to see was sold out.
We ended up seeing another one.

3 After traveling around the world for years, Marta unexpectedly settled down in Ireland.
She ended up settling down in Ireland.

4 I thought I'd passed the exam but I failed.
I ended up having to retake the exam.

5 Alan kept on arriving late for work.
He ended up losing his job/being fired.

6 We had booked a vacation but had to cancel it because my boyfriend was sick.
We ended up canceling the vacation.

C Compare your answers with another pair.

Follow the herd

A Work in pairs. What do you think the phrase *follow the herd* means? to do what most other people do

B Watch the video. Answer the following questions.

1. What is Amanda writing an article about? herd mentality
2. What motivated people to use the Social Stairs? social engagement /hanging out with other people
3. What doesn't Harry understand? why we're so impressed by people choosinwg a more fun option
4. Why does Sam want Amanda to tell him what she finds out? to attract more customers to the café

SPEAKING SKILL

A Work in pairs. Complete the examples from the video.

1. Oh, ___you mean___ like that piano staircase in Stockholm?
2. ___Actually___, the piano staircase had an escalator next to it.
3. You ___might be thinking___ about that other example – the Social Stairs or something like that?
4. Oh, yeah. The Social Stairs. ___That was it___.
5. Or ___to put it another way___, they liked hanging out together.

B Watch the video again to check your answers to Exercise A.

C Choose the correct options to complete the information.

Backtracking and reformulating

When we correct something that has been previously said we [1]*backtrack* / *reformulate*. When we say something previously said in a different way we [2]*backtrack* / *reformulate*.

D Work in pairs. Decide which of the examples in Exercise A are backtracking (b) and which are reformulating (r).

1 r   2 b   3 b   4 r   5 r

SPEAKING HUB

A PREPARE You are going to discuss the following question.

Do you think a sense of community is declining in modern society? Why/Why not?

Write notes on what you are going to say and how to justify your opinion. Be prepared to reformulate your arguments.

B DISCUSS Work in small groups. Present your opinion to the rest of the group. Respond to what the other members in your group say.

We've ended up being very isolated ... or to put it another way ... lonely.

C REFLECT Give feedback to the other members of your group. Consider the following points.

- reformulation
- fluency
- pronunciation
- interaction

Give and justify your opinion on social engagement

➤ Turn to page 164 to learn how to write a conclusion to an academic report.

9.3 Model behavior

All together now

A Focus students on the picture, then put them into pairs to discuss the questions. In feedback, encourage students to explain their answers but don't confirm or reject any ideas yet.

B ▶ 00:00–01:51 Point out the glossary, then tell students to watch the first part of the video and check their answers.

C ▶ 00:00–01:51 Put students into pairs to try to answer the questions from memory. Then play the first part of the video again for them to watch and check.

D Students work in pairs to discuss the questions. Get some feedback on their predictions, but again, don't give the correct answers yet.

E ▶ 01:51–02:35 Tell students to watch the second part of the video and check their answers.

AUTHENTIC ENGLISH

A Put students into pairs. Focus students on the sentence from the video, and tell them to use it to help them choose the correct option in the box. In feedback, give more examples of the use of *end up* to help clarify its use.

B Go through the example, then put students into pairs to think of responses to the other sentences. Tell students that there are lots of possible answers, and encourage them to be imaginative.

C Combine pairs to compare their answers. Get feedback on the most interesting responses.

Follow the herd

A Put students into pairs to discuss the question. In feedback, ask students if they have a similar expression in their language.

B ▶ Tell students to watch the video and answer the questions. Let them compare in pairs before feedback. You can find the **video script** for *Follow the herd* on the Teacher's Resource Center.

SPEAKING SKILL

A Put students into pairs to try to complete the sentences from memory.

B ▶ Play the video for students to watch and check their answers.

C Focus students on the information in the box about *Backtracking and reformulating* and tell them to choose the correct options.

D Put students into pairs to look back at the sentences in Exercise A, and decide if they are examples of backtracking or reformulating.

SPEAKING HUB

A Focus students on the question and tell them to work alone to write notes about what they are going to say. Tell them to think about more than one way they can make each point, so that they are able to reformulate if necessary.

B Put students into small groups, and tell each student to present their opinion. Tell the other students to listen carefully and to respond with comments or questions, showing whether they agree with, disagree with or don't understand the points that are made.

C Tell students to give each other feedback in their groups, focusing on the points listed. Finish with whole-class feedback, and ask students who they think made their points most successfully in each group, and why.

Extra activity
Remind students about the expression *follow the herd*, and ask them to think of any times when they have done this and times when they have not. Put them into pairs to discuss this, and ask whether they think following the herd is always a bad thing.

▶ VIDEO SCRIPT

All together now
A = Alok Jha D = Doctor Ed Codlings F = Female M = Male

A: How do birds dance across the sky, changing direction all at the same time? And shoals of fish, a blur of apparently intelligent movement – how do they do it? It turns out this urge to swarm is a fundamental behavior right across nature – even we have it.
So, do we just follow the quickest person to react? Do we swarm like fish? Only one way to find out – join some students for some real science with properly dressed scientists.

D: Hi guys! Thanks for coming along. In a moment, we're going to do an experiment within this blue circle that we've got marked out on the floor.

Ex C Q1 **A:** Doctor Ed Codling is from the University of Essex. He's a mathematical biologist who studies human behavior. To discover how we react as part of a crowd, Ed's experiment will simulate a dangerous
Ex C Q2 situation – a fire alarm. He's watching for people who might not make their own decision but panic
Ex C Q3 and follow someone else, assuming they know the way to the right exit. What if the person you're following doesn't know the way either? I mean, I've done it before, you just end up following someone who looks most confident in the room. Let's try and watch that in action.

D: OK, so, we have the north exit over here, the south
Ex C Q4 exit over there. When I blow the whistle, I want you to leave through the south exit. OK? Off we go!

A: The experiment worked.

D: We had only four people who were told to go in the wrong exit and yet they took twelve with them, I think.

F: I just ran.

M: I just sort of went with everyone else, to be honest. Everyone was sort of heading that way, so …

A: This guy is about to deliberately go the wrong way. The guy next to him reacts instantly and follows.

D: Two-thirds of the group went the wrong way. If this was a real evacuation scenario, they'd have obviously got in trouble there.

A: Does it always happen like this?

D: Er, not always. Obviously, it's a real experiment so sometimes it doesn't quite work out. What we're interested in is, you know, how many people making the wrong decision would then influence quite a large crowd.

9 Writing

Write a conclusion to an academic report

W – linking in academic writing

A SPEAK Work in pairs. Say the following sentences aloud five times. Do they make you feel happier/sadder? Why?

1 Two new blue shoes flew to the moon.
2 These green leaves seem free and easy.
3 Our alarm can't harm the calm farmer.

B Read the conclusion to an academic report. Does it agree with your responses to Exercise A?

CONCLUSION

1 Our research set out to test the facial feedback hypothesis that our facial expressions can affect our moods. Strack *et al* (1988) famously asked respondents to evaluate cartoons while holding a pen in their mouths. Some held it between their teeth, forcing them to smile; others held it between their lips, forcing a frown. The 'smilers' found the cartoons significantly funnier than the 'frowners'. Similarly, Zajonc *et al* (1989), demonstrated a causal relationship between vowel sounds and mood: the repetition of 'smile vowels' (/e/, /iː/) and the 'aha vowel' (/ɑː/) put the respondents in a significantly better mood than 'frown vowels' (e.g. /uː/). However, recent research by Wagenmakers *et al* (2016) has cast serious doubt on this hypothesis.

2 Our own research provides limited support for the hypothesis. We found that repeating sentences with 'smile vowels' did indeed provoke a mood improvement compared to 'frown' vowels. However, in neither case were the results conclusive: the majority of respondents reported no change in mood. The one exception was that the 'aha vowel' had a significant positive effect on almost every respondent's mood.

3 Our evidence suggests that facial expressions do indeed affect mood, but it is principally the open-mouthed 'aha smile' rather than the wide-mouthed grin that has the greatest impact. This may explain the failure of Wagenmakers *et al* to repeat the effects of the pen experiment: they were focusing on the wrong type of smile.

4 If refined and confirmed by further research, the facial feedback hypothesis could be used by psychotherapists and carers to improve patients' moods. Additionally, marketers may use vowel sounds in product names to influence customers' connotations. If products such as 'New You' are renamed as 'Calming Spa', it may well be because of the effect of vowel sounds on our mood.

C Match the topics (a–d) with the paragraphs (1–4).

a Analysis: What did you learn? 3
b Implications: What do your findings mean? 4
c Background: What question were you trying to answer? 1
d Key findings: What information did you collect? 2

D Answer the questions. Use the information in the box to help you.

Linking in academic writing

Use linking words (e.g. *however*) to show the relationships between ideas.

Use colons (:) to show that one idea 'explains' another.

Use semi-colons (;) to show that two related ideas are 'equal' in importance.

1 Find a semi-colon in paragraph 1. In what way are the two ideas equal?
2 Which two linking words in paragraph 1 link all the research together?
3 Find three colons in paragraphs 1–3. How does the second idea explain the first in each case?
4 What linking word in paragraphs 2 and 3 relates expectations to reality? What grammar structure is often used with this word?
5 How does the writer link the main ideas in paragraph 4?

WRITING

A PREPARE Choose one of your own ideas or a piece of academic research from this unit.

B PLAN Write notes about the points you will cover in your conclusion.

C WRITE Write a four-paragraph conclusion. Use linking words, colons and semi-colons in your writing.

D REVIEW Exchange your conclusion with a partner. Do you agree with their analysis? Comment on how they use linking words.

E EDIT Read your partner's comments. Rewrite any parts of your conclusion that you think could be improved.

164 | WRITING

Suggested answers:

1 They both describe the experience of one of the two groups, using very similar words.
2 Similarly and However
3 Paragraph 1 (… a clear causal relationship between vowel sounds and mood: the repetition of 'smile vowels' …): The second part explains what the causal relationship was. Paragraph 2 (… in neither case were the results conclusive: the majority of respondents reported no change in mood.): The second part explains why the results weren't conclusive. Paragraph 3 (This may explain the failure of Wagenmakers et al. to repeat the effects of the pen experiment: they were focusing on the wrong type of smile.): The second part explains why Wagenmakers et al. failed.
4 Indeed; emphatic do
5 Additionally

Refer students to this conclusion as a model for the writing task.

Remind students to refer back to the linking devices in the box when they evaluate their partner's work.

WRITING

A Put students into pairs to follow the instructions and discuss the question. In feedback, ask students to explain their feelings and find out how similar the group's responses were.

B Tell students to read the conclusion to the report to find out if it agrees with their responses. In feedback, elicit students' reaction to the research.

C Students read the conclusion again and match the four paragraphs to the topics.

D Go through the information in the box about *Linking in academic writing*, then put students into pairs to answer the questions.

WRITING TASK

A Tell students that they are going to write their own conclusion to an academic report. Tell them to choose a piece of academic research to write about, either from something previously mentioned in this unit or an idea of their own.

B Students make notes about the points they will include. Remind them of the topics that were covered in the different paragraphs of the model text.

C Remind students about the organization of the model text and the linking devices used. Tell students to write their conclusion in four paragraphs. This can be done for homework if there isn't time in class.

D Students swap their conclusions with a partner and read each other's. Ask them to write comments, both about how far they agree with the content and how well linking words have been used.

E Students read their partner's comments and make any changes they would like to make. In feedback, ask students what changes they made and why.

Unit 9 Review

VOCABULARY

A Complete the conversation with the words in the box.

awesome	bucks	bummed	chill out	
dude	guy	mess	shady	stoked	was like

A: Hey, [1] ___dude___. You look happy. What's up?

B: I'm so [2] ___stoked___! I just got ten [3] ___bucks___ for taking part in an experiment.

A: [4] ___Awesome___! What did you do?

B: I had to use sticks to push food out of a tube, but it kept dropping into a hole. It was a hot [5] ___mess___! I was so [6] ___bummed___, but the [7] ___guy___ who was in charge [8] ___was like___, [9] '___chill out___, man! Don't worry!'

A: Sounds a little [10] ___shady___ to me. What were they testing?

B: Whether people are smarter than crows! Crazy, huh!

B Find and correct the mistake in three of the sentences.

1. The researchers watched one chimp hide the food.
   correct
2. We weren't let to watch the experiment.
   We weren't allowed to . . .
3. I'll have my assistant to contact you next week.
   I'll have my assistant contact . . .
4. I felt a mosquito bite me last night.
   correct
5. I can't help you pass the exam, but I can help you avoid mistakes.
   correct
6. A crow was seen use one tool to make another.
   A crow was seen using . . . / was seen to use . . .

C Choose the correct words to complete the blog post.

How to listen – and show you care

- [1] ***Lean*** / ***Glare*** / ***Raise*** toward the other person slightly.
- Don't [2] ***fold*** / ***gaze*** / ***wink*** your arms or [3] ***fidget*** / ***shake*** / ***wiggle*** with pens, keys, etc.
- Keep neutral facial expressions – a smile might look like a [4] ***gaze*** / ***raise*** / ***smirk***.
- Don't speak. Instead, [5] ***bend*** / ***nod*** / ***wink*** your head slowly to show understanding, [6] ***cross*** / ***point*** / ***raise*** your eyebrows to show interest, or [7] ***bend*** / ***shrug*** / ***wiggle*** your shoulders to show you don't know.
- Keep eye contact but don't [8] ***cross*** / ***grin*** / ***stare***. You're allowed to [9] ***beckon*** / ***blink*** / ***glare***!

GRAMMAR

A Reorder the sentences to make noun phrases.

1. You usually have to use / forms / available / future / the / two / that / of / one / are /
   You usually have to use one of the two future forms that are available.
2. The research focused on / for / are making / the / that / worrying / of / preparation / the future / lack / extremely / most people / The research focused on the extremely worrying lack of preparation that most people are making for the future.
3. all / behavior / Practically / into / research / my / animal / shows they're smarter than we think
   Practically all my research into animal behavior shows they are smarter than we think.
4. The accident occurred because of / the event / for / failure by / such / the organizers / almost / to plan / the / large crowds / complete / to attend / The accident occurred because of the almost complete failure by the organizers to plan for such large crowds to attend the event.
5. problem / the / ways / these / approaching / Both / of / are flawed
   Both these ways of approaching the problem are flawed.
6. We are aware of / that / be expressed / the / only / animal intelligence / of / many / a / can / few / ways /
   We are aware of only a few of the many ways that animal intelligence can be expressed.

B Complete the sentences with participle clauses. Use the verbs in parentheses.

1. ___Having eaten___ a big breakfast earlier, I skipped lunch. (*eat*)
2. The octopus uses a coconut shell as a shelter if ___attacked___. (*attack*)
3. ___Seeming___ to understand the rules, the pigeon solved the puzzle quickly. (*seem*)
4. ___Having been told___ to be at the airport at 4 am, we weren't happy about the 10-hour delay. (*tell*)
5. When ___packing___ your bags, remember to leave space for souvenirs. (*pack*)
6. Despite not ___having studied / studying___ at college, she has produced some excellent research. (*study*)

10 SOCIETY

Society exists only as a mental concept; in the real world there are only individuals.
Oscar Wilde

A castle village in Burj Al Babas, Bolu, Turkey

Society (n) people in general living together in organized communities, with laws and traditions controlling the way they behave toward one another. Synonyms: community (n), humankind (n)

Oscar Wilde means that society is a human creation, but that it in turn influences the behavior of individuals.

Oscar Wilde (1854–1900) was an Irish poet, playwright and novelist.

OBJECTIVES

- discuss issues related to tourism
- present solutions to urban problems
- talk about political activism
- discuss how to make a difference
- debate for and against a motion
- write a persuasive essay

Work with a partner. Discuss the questions.

1 Look at the picture. What type of person might live in a place like this?
2 Read the quote. What do you think Wilde means? Do you agree?
3 What would be the advantages and disadvantages of living in an unusual place like the one in the picture?

SOCIETY 109

OBJECTIVES

Read the unit objectives to the class.

UNIT OPENER QUESTIONS

1 Focus students on the picture and elicit what it shows. Put them into pairs to discuss the question. In feedback, elicit as many different opinions as you can.

2 Focus students on the quote and put them into pairs to discuss the question. There are several different interpretations of its meaning, so point this out and encourage students to express different views and to agree and disagree with each other.

3 Elicit one example, then put students back into pairs to discuss the question. In feedback, write on the board any useful language that comes up.

WORKSHEETS

Lesson 10.1 Urban problems

Vocabulary: Culture and heritage (W44)

Grammar: Discourse markers (W45)

Vocabulary: Nouns with *to* (W46)

Lesson 10.2 How to change the world

Vocabulary: Word building (W47)

Grammar: Ellipsis and substitution (W48)

10.1 Urban problems

- Discuss issues related to tourism
- Present solutions to urban problems

G – discourse markers
P – introducing new information
V – culture and heritage; nouns with *to*
S – integrating information from different texts

READING

A SPEAK Work in pairs. What are some advantages and disadvantages of increased tourism for a city?

B SCAN Read the three newspaper articles. What problem of tourism are they discussing?
overtourism – crowding at tourist sites

Has tourism reached its limit?

Being **designated** as a UNESCO World **Heritage** site helps **preserve** a site and **refurbish** its facilities – as well as boosting tourism. Yet, it can end up **endangering** the site. A famous example is Machu Picchu, the **ruins** of an Inca **settlement** in Peru, which is being destabilized owing to tourists littering, climbing on the ruins or even taking pieces of it home. Ex B

In response to similar problems, Venice has capped the number of tourists allowed to enter its most famous areas. Niagara Falls requires visitors to buy tickets which say when they can enter the site, whereas the Taj Mahal has increased entrance fees for tourists to actually try to put people off visiting.

Glossary

booming (adj) if an activity is booming, it is becoming very popular

destabilize (v) to cause problems for a country, government, or person in authority so that they become less effective

elitist (adj) supporting or based on a system in which a small group of people have a lot of advantages and keep the most power and influence

C SYNTHESIZE INFORMATION Imagine that you are writing an essay about tackling the problem you identified in Exercise B. Complete the notes using information from all three articles. Use the information in the box to help you.

Integrating information from different texts

Sometimes you need to get information from multiple sources to understand a topic.

- Be clear about your purpose for reading. What questions are you trying to answer?
- Underline the main ideas in the texts and look for arguments connected to your topic.
- Use headings to organize the information you are looking for. Write notes under these headings as you read more texts.

Notes

Issues caused by the problem Suggested answers: damage to sites, strain on the infrastructure, overcrowding

Ideas for dealing with the problem limiting visitor numbers, charging a tourism tax, using apps

Criticism of these ideas increased prices are elitist, the tourism tax is unfair, limiting the number of visitors is too extreme

D DISCUSS Work in pairs. Look at your notes in Exercise C and discuss the best methods for solving the problem.

Is tourism tax fair?

The New Zealand government recently announced that it will start charging tourists a tax of approximately NZ$35 (£18). The government claims this **fund** will be spent on infrastructure and the natural **habitat** of New Zealand's wildlife. Ex B

Is this reasonable? Tourists already contribute to the economy by paying for hotels, food and souvenirs. It's not as elitist as charging higher entrance fees to attractions, but it is still enough to put some tourists off.

Some might question if the fee is masking a failure to manage tourism properly. Should governments be responsible for not only attracting tourists, but better ensuring they are able to handle the influx of visitors?

10.1 Urban problems

LEAD-IN

Books closed. Put students into pairs to discuss what they think the five most visited cities in the world are. Get feedback, and then tell them that in 2018 they were Bangkok, London, Paris, Dubai and Singapore. Put students back into pairs to discuss which of those cities they have been to or would like to go to. In feedback, ask students to share their experiences or opinions.

READING

A Elicit one example of an advantage and a disadvantage of tourism for a city, then put students into pairs to think of more. In feedback, ask students to explain their answers and to give examples where necessary. Write on the board any useful language that comes up.

B Set a time limit and tell students to read the three articles quickly to find out what problem they are discussing. Remind students that they don't need to read and understand every word in order to do this, and reassure them that they will have an opportunity to read the articles more closely later.

C Go through the information in the box about *Integrating information from different texts*, and tell students to complete the notes using information from all three articles. Put students into pairs to compare notes before feedback. In feedback, write on the board the key points to make sure all students have them for easy reference.

D Put students into pairs to look at their notes again and to discuss which method for solving the problem they think is best. In feedback, encourage students to expand on their answers and to agree and disagree with each other.

TEACHING IDEA by David Seymour and Maria Popova

Tourist trail

Use this activity to introduce or extend the theme of tourism.

I'm going to name a country. Take turns around the class naming a tourist attraction there, and then a new country for the next student, e.g.

T – *France.* A – *The Eiffel tower. India.* B – *The Taj Mahal. America.* C – *The Grand Canyon. Brazil …*

In small groups, discuss which of them you have seen or would like to see. Add some more things you like to look at when you travel, e.g. *paintings, street performers.*

On your own, write 100–250 words (choose according to the level of the class) about a time you visited a tourist attraction.

GRAMMAR HUB

10.1 Discourse markers

- We use discourse markers to connect ideas, or to give further information regarding our attitude to what we're saying or writing.
- We use some discourse markers to join two clauses within a sentence. They can be positioned either at the beginning of a sentence (followed by a comma) or in between the two clauses. They may be used to express cause and consequence, or to describe a contrast.

despite	**Despite** having a degree in Business Studies, Karla didn't get the job. Karla didn't get the job **despite** having a degree in Business Studies.
owing to	**Owing to** his lack of certifications, Omar was unable to find a job in the field. Omar was unable to find a job in the field **owing to** his lack of certifications.
whereas	**Whereas** Kim is determined to succeed, her sister lacks ambition. Her sister lacks ambition, **whereas** Kim is determined to succeed.

- We use some discourse markers to connect ideas in two separate sentences. These discourse markers can be positioned at the beginning of the second sentence, in which case they should be followed by a comma. Some can also be placed after the subject of the second sentence, and should in this case be followed by a comma, or at the end of the second sentence.

as a matter of fact	He's doing research into Arctic animals. **As a matter of fact**, he's leaving for Greenland next week. / He's leaving for Greenland next week, **as a matter of fact**.
conversely	The novel was a huge bestseller. **Conversely**, the movie version was never as successful. / The movie version, **conversely**, was never as successful.
for instance	Mediterranean resorts are making a comeback. **For instance**, Mykonos is now seen as a vacation hotspot for Europe's young celebrities. / Mykonos, **for instance**, is now seen as a vacation hotspot for Europe's young celebrities. / Mykonos is now seen as a vacation hotspot for Europe's young celebrities, **for instance**.
in any case	It seems that no crime had taken place. **In any case**, it wasn't a matter for the police. / It wasn't a matter for the police, **in any case**.
moreover	Tax income increased because of tourism. **Moreover**, it has created hundreds of new jobs. / It has, **moreover**, created hundreds of new jobs.

10.1 Urban problems

VOCABULARY

A Ask students to match the words in bold to the definitions. Elicit the first one as an example, demonstrating how to use the context provided by the articles to work out the best meaning and to check whether it makes sense. Then put students into pairs to work on the rest. In feedback, give more examples to fully clarify or check understanding.

B Direct students to the **Vocabulary Hub** (see TB121).

C Students work in pairs to discuss the questions. In feedback, encourage them to give reasons and examples to support their opinions. Use the **Vocabulary Worksheet** on page W44 for extra practice.

GRAMMAR

A Elicit that the bold words are all discourse markers. Do the first one as an example, and show students how to use the examples provided in the articles to work out the meaning / use of the discourse markers.

B Tell students to use the examples in Exercise A to help them complete the rules. In feedback, refer back to these sentences, as well as the examples from the articles, to make sure students understand how to use the discourse markers.

C Direct students to the **Grammar Hub** (see TB110 and below).

D Elicit the first one as an example, then tell students to complete the other sentences with their own ideas. Put students into pairs to compare sentences. Use the **Grammar Worksheet** on page W45 for extra practice.

SPEAKING

A Put students into pairs to discuss the questions. Get feedback only on question 1 at this stage, and ask students to give examples in their answers.

B Put students into larger groups and go through the steps to reaching a consensus. You could appoint a stronger student in each group as chairperson to ensure the steps are followed. When time is almost up, prompt the chairperson to establish agreement within each group.

C Ask each group to present and justify their position to the class. Tell the other students to listen carefully and to ask questions at the end of each presentation. When each group has presented, find out if the whole class is able to reach a consensus. Finish with feedback on students' use of language during the activity.

Extra activity

Put students into small groups to design the perfect tourist city. Elicit and write on the board a few ideas of the kind of attractions and facilities that make a city attractive to tourists.
Tell them to think not only about the tourists' experience but also how to keep the city a good place for local people to live in. Allow students time to prepare and if appropriate to do research on their phones or online. In feedback, ask students to present their ideas. As a class, vote on the best city to:

- visit as a tourist
- live in as a resident.

GRAMMAR HUB

10.1 Discourse markers

A What is the function of the discourse markers in bold? Read the sentences and choose the correct options.

1 Large hotel complexes consume huge amounts of water, **whereas** smaller family-run hotels tend to use less.
  (a) contrasting two different ideas
  b comparing two related ideas

2 Walking vacations, **for instance**, are an environmentally-friendly choice.
  a suggesting a possibility
  (b) giving an example

3 Huge building projects tend to attract investors. **Conversely**, small businesses sometimes struggle to raise money.
  a repeating and reinforcing an idea
  (b) contrasting two different ideas

4 The room wasn't expensive at all. **As a matter of fact**, it was one of the cheapest places we stayed.
  (a) adding more information
  b giving an example

5 Farmers are warning that crops may fail **owing to** the lack of rain.
  (a) offering an explanation
  b trying to persuade someone

6 **Despite** placing advertisements on various websites, Aisha didn't manage to sell her products.
  a describing a situation
  (b) contrasting two different ideas

B Choose the correct options to complete the sentences.

1 We haven't visited all the monuments yet. *Owing to* / *In any case*, Farid isn't that interested in sightseeing.

2 We managed to visit all the most important museums in the city *whereas* / *despite* our limited budget.

3 Because the cost of living in Venice is so high, many people are leaving. *Moreover* / *For instance*, many inhabitants are worried about the danger of flooding.

4 Many of the streets in Venice are very narrow. The 'Calleta Varisco', *conversely* / *for instance*, is just 53 centimeters wide!

5 *Owing to* / *Despite* rising water levels, Venice city authorities are building flood barriers to protect the city.

6 Riding on a gondola is a bucket list experience for many visiting Venice. Some say it is one of the most iconic tourist experiences, *as a matter of fact* / *moreover*!

➤ Go back to page 111.

VOCABULARY

Culture and heritage

A **Match the words in bold in the articles with the meanings (1–10).**

1. habitat = the type of place where an animal lives or a plant grows
2. ruins = the parts of a building that remain after it has been damaged
3. fund = a large amount of money
4. preserve = to take care of something and prevent it being damaged
5. settlement = a place where people live
6. architectural = relating to the style or design of a building
7. designate = to formally choose someone or something for a role or special status
8. heritage = objects, traditions and beliefs important to a society's history or culture
9. endanger = to put something at risk of being destroyed or becoming extinct
10. refurbish = to repair or improve a building

B **Go to the Vocabulary Hub on page 148.**

C **SPEAK Work in pairs and discuss the questions.**

1. Are there any habitats where endangered species live in your country?
2. Should your country's government provide a larger fund to preserve cultural sites?
3. How important is architectural style to your country's heritage?

Tackling tourism with tech

Tourism in Amsterdam is booming, with over 14 million visitors a year to enjoy the canals and the mix of **architectural** styles. The Amsterdam tourism board felt limiting tourist numbers was too extreme, so they turned to technology to deal with potential overcrowding. Ex B

Many tourists visit the Van Gogh Museum in the morning and take a cruise on the canal in the afternoon. So the tourism board has launched an app providing information on how busy the attractions are and suggesting alternative destinations.

GRAMMAR

Discourse markers

A **Choose the correct discourse markers to complete the sentences.**

1. A top tourist attraction is the Grand Bazaar in Istanbul *owing to* / *despite* its spectacular architecture and wide range of stores.
2. The Zócalo in Mexico, another very popular attraction, hosts a large number of events throughout the year. *Yet* / *Moreover*, it is home to the Metropolitan Cathedral and the National Palace.
3. Some of the most popular tourist attractions are in the US – *as a matter of fact* / *namely* Times Square, Central Park and Union Station.
4. Theme parks are also among the most popular tourist destinations. Walt Disney World in Florida, *in any case* / *for instance*, is a very popular destination.
5. *Conversely* / *Whereas* several of the world's most popular tourist attractions are in the US, one of the most popular destinations in Europe is Paris.

B **Complete the rules with words and phrases in Exercise A.**

Discourse markers

1. Use *despite*, owing to and whereas to join two clauses. They can come at the beginning of the sentence (followed by a comma) or in between the two clauses.
2. Use *as a matter of fact*, *conversely*, *in any case*, for instance and moreover to connect ideas in two sentences.

C **Go to the Grammar Hub on page 140.**

D **Work in pairs. Make sentences using the prompts below plus a discourse marker.**

1. there are some great tourist sites in my city
2. people who live near tourist sites often get angry with tourists
3. tourists have a reputation for bad behavior
4. many cities around the world are eager to attract tourists

SPEAKING

A **SPEAK Work in pairs and discuss the questions.**

1. How important is tourism to your country?
2. Do you believe tourism is mainly good or bad for a city? Why?

B **DISCUSS Work in groups. Try to gain a consensus on question 2 in Exercise A. Use the steps below to help you.**

- Get everyone's view.
- Allow speakers time to justify their views.
- Establish agreement: think about ways of doing this fairly.

C **PRESENT Present and justify your position to the class.**

LISTENING

A SPEAK **Work in pairs and discuss the questions.**

1 What kind of place do you like to work or study in? Why do you like this place?

2 What are your favorite buildings in your city? Why do you like them?

10.1 **B LISTEN FOR GIST** **Listen to the first part of a radio report about building design. Generally speaking, how can the design of a building affect people?**

10.2 **C LISTEN FOR DETAIL** **Listen to the next part of the radio report and note down how these specific features can affect people.**

1 Light: People prefer daylight/windows when working.

2 Shapes and lines: People are more comfortable with curved lines/shapes. Straight lines cause feelings of fear.

3 Colors: Red walls are better for tasks that require attention to detail. Blue walls are better for creative tasks.

4 Store facades: Lively and interesting facades relax people, but monotonous ones make them anxious.

5 Spaces between buildings: Wide spaces can prevent people from interacting and prevent a sense of community.

D SPEAK **Work in pairs and discuss the questions.**

1 What do you think of the different ideas? Do you think they make a difference?

2 Why do you think many buildings don't follow the recommendations discussed in the program?

VOCABULARY

Nouns with *to*

A Circle the nouns followed by *to* in the extracts from the radio program. Use the information in the box to help you.

Nouns with *to*

Several nouns are often followed by an infinitive. You can remember which ones they are by thinking about the adjective or verb forms of these words – because they are also normally followed by an infinitive, e.g. *Architects normally start with the wish to design innovative buildings.*

1 And if people feel better about their environment, they have a higher (inclination) to interact positively with the people around them.

2 People have a (tendency) to be less productive if their desk is more than 7.5 meters away from a window.

3 … whereas plain, monotonous facades make people anxious and give them the (urge) to hurry past.

4 The project's failings were a (reminder) for architects to think not just about the look of buildings, but also about how people would interact within the spaces they create.

B Match the underlined nouns (1–10) with their meanings (a–j).

1 Most architects have a desire to create beautiful rather than functional buildings. e

2 Most people in big cities show a reluctance to talk to strangers. b

3 Governments have an obligation to limit the population of their cities. h

4 Cities need to be doing a lot more in readiness to deal with swelling populations. c

5 The refusal of many cities to provide seating in public places is a mistake. f

6 A failure to learn from environmental psychology will lead to higher crime rates. d

7 People need frequent reminders to behave considerately in cities. a

8 Companies have a responsibility to make sure building design has a positive effect on their staff. j

9 People in cities have a tendency to feel isolated because they are too busy to socialize. i

10 There should be a greater urge to limit noise and sound pollution in cities. g

a something that helps you remember something

b an unwillingness

c preparation

d not doing something that you were expected to do

e a wish

f saying that you will not do something

g a strong feeling of wanting or needing to do something

h responsibility

i a habit of behaving in a particular way

j a duty

C Work in pairs. Do you agree with the sentences in Exercise B?

D Work in pairs. Complete the sentences with your own ideas.

1 Architects have a tendency to …

2 In my city, most people show a reluctance to …

3 Most people have no desire to …

4 Local planners have a responsibility to …

10.1 Urban problems

LISTENING

A–B 10.1 *It can affect how people feel and act, and make them healthier, happier and more productive. It can make them less stressed. If people feel better, they are more likely to interact positively.*

C–D 10.2 Students check in pairs before whole-class feedback.

VOCABULARY

A Elicit the first one, then tell students to circle the other examples.

B In feedback, give further examples to clarify the phrases.

C Put students into pairs to discuss the sentences.

D Use the **Vocabulary Worksheet** on page W46 for extra practice.

AUDIO SCRIPT

10.1

Listening, Exercise B
D = Denise

D: Walking along the streets of Beijing, you really get the sense of a city going through a rapid period of change. Huge skyscrapers dominate the skyline, while construction work continues all around. As the city evolves, its population has swelled to over 21 million, making Beijing one of the most populated cities in the world. And the more people there are, the more challenging it becomes to provide comfortable environments for people to live and work in. Fortunately, researchers at the Well Living Lab on the northern outskirts of Beijing are conducting an extensive research project to identify ways

Ex B that building design can make people healthier, happier and more productive. And if people feel better about their environment, they have a higher inclination to interact positively with the people around them. Inside an unassuming office building, human guinea pigs are being carefully monitored inside a simulation of a typical office environment. I talked to environmental psychologist Wang Wei about how this kind of research can help with building design.

10.2

Listening, Exercise C
W = Wang D = Denise

D: So, Wang Wei, what research is being done at the Well Living Lab here in Beijing?

W: They're looking at how small changes to the environment, such as changes to the lighting, air quality or noise levels, affect people. They're observing people's emotional responses and using wearable technology to monitor people's physical reactions.
For example, recently, they've been looking at what kind of light makes workers most productive. They experimented by using different kinds of light.

Ex C Q1 They found that people strongly preferred daylight to electric light – and, as a matter of fact, other research has shown that people have a tendency to be less productive if their desk is more than 7.5 meters away from a window. They also found that certain kinds of blue lighting can have a positive effect on workers' moods.

D: What other things have psychologists learned about office environments?

W: Some fascinating research has focused on shapes and lines.

Ex C Q2 Apparently, people feel more comfortable in places with round shapes and curved lines. On the other hand, straight lines and sharp edges have been shown to create feelings of fear. Other

Ex C Q3 research has looked at colors. Red walls have been shown to be better suited for tasks that require accuracy and attention to detail – perhaps because people associate the color red with danger, so they're more alert. Conversely, blue walls suit creative tasks – in fact, people trying to be creative in rooms with blue walls had twice as many ideas as those working in rooms with red walls.

D: And what have we learned about the design of the city?

W: People living in cities tend to have higher levels of stress, so unsurprisingly a lot of the research has looked at what can be done about this. One

Ex C Q4 interesting study showed that people are more relaxed when they see lively and interesting store facades, whereas plain, monotonous facades make people anxious and give them the urge to hurry past. Other studies have looked at how spaces can facilitate more communication – because cities

Ex C Q5 can be very isolating places. Some ideas include arranging spaces that encourage interaction between strangers, such as providing more seating in communal spaces. It sounds simple, but many places have had this kind of seating removed in recent years and people didn't realize the impact this would have.

D: If you don't believe the importance of thinking about these details, you only need to look back at the story of the Pruitt-Igoe housing complex that was built in Missouri in the US in the 1950s. When it opened, the complex was lauded as magnificent architectural design. Yet, when people actually began to live there, several problems with how people interacted in the space became evident – for example, the wide spaces between the different apartment blocks in the complex meant people in different blocks had little chance to interact. This meant there was no sense of shared community between residents of different blocks, and as a result, the complex quickly became a hostile and unpleasant place to live in. The project's failings were a reminder for architects to think not just about the look of buildings, but also about how people would interact within the spaces they create. Today, architects and designers are much more aware of the importance of psychology when designing buildings. Various studies, like the ones being carried out in Beijing, are looking at how places make people feel and act. This research is vital for creating the buildings of the future. With so many people living close together, the environment should encourage positive feelings.

10.1 Urban problems

PRONUNCIATION

10.3 **A** Students listen carefully to the four extracts, and decide if the pitch of the speaker's voice goes up or down on the underlined words. In feedback, model the pronunciation yourself, exaggerating slightly, to make sure all students have noticed what happened.

B Put students into pairs to practice saying the sentences. Tell them to listen carefully to their partner and to give feedback on whether they changed pitch appropriately.

SPEAKING HUB

A Put students into small groups and explain the situation. Tell them to work together to imagine what problems their city is facing and to brainstorm solutions for each one. Monitor to help or prompt if needed.

B Students work in their groups to prepare a speech about their candidate. Go through the points they need to consider as they do this. Again, monitor to help or prompt if needed.

C Tell each group to make their speech. Encourage the other students to listen carefully and to ask questions at the end of each one.

D Put students back into their groups to discuss which of the other speeches they thought was the best and why. Get some whole-class feedback, and encourage students to explain what they liked or didn't like about the other speeches. Finally, hold a vote to decide which candidate the class would elect. Finish with feedback on students' use of language during the activity.

Extra activity

Elicit an example of good design and of bad design, then put students into pairs to think of more. Ask them to come up with at least two examples of each. These examples could be buildings or features of cities, but they could also be examples of everyday objects. Monitor to help and prompt if needed. In feedback, ask students to explain their choices and to agree or disagree with each other. As a class, you can vote on the best and worst examples of design.

METHODOLOGY HUB by Adrian Underhill

Key

Every speaker has a characteristic pitch range within which most of their pitch variations take place. Some speakers have a narrow range, others have a wide range. According to the discourse approach to intonation, speakers distinguish three significant pitch levels within their individual and characteristic pitch range. And every tone unit that is uttered is assigned to one of these three levels, or keys.

Key is determined by the first (or only) prominence in the tone unit, compared with the first (or only) prominence in the preceding tone unit. A tone unit is in high key if its first prominence is at a higher pitch than the first prominence in the preceding tone unit. It is in mid key if it is the same pitch, and it is in low key if lower. Thus all key choices are high, mid or low relative to the pitch choice of the previous tone unit.

The meaning of key

Each tone unit selects a new key choice and this adds a meaning independent of the rest of the pitch movement.

- High is contrastive. The tone group contains information that contrasts with what speaker or hearer might expect.
- Mid is additive. The matter is additional to what has gone before.
- Low is equative. The content follows naturally from the content of the previous tone unit. It has no new impact.

Mid key does not mean normal or average; it is the neutral or unmarked key against which the choice of high and low is significant.

The use of key

Make the following statement with two tone units, each with only one prominence (i.e. on the tonic syllable). The first unit is referring, and the second one is proclaiming.

↘↗ On SUNday ↘ it SNOWED

1 Try it like that.

2 Now try it first with high key.

↘ it SNOWED

↘↗ On SUNday

This means that regardless of the pitch movement on each tonic unit, the starting pitch of the second is higher than the starting pitch of the first. When you get this it can give the impression of *What a surprise! Who would have expected it to snow?*

3 Now try with mid key.

↘↗ On SUNday ↘ it SNOWED

The starting pitch of the second tonic is the same as that of the first. This gives the impression of additional information, but no great surprise. Oh, by the way, another thing about Sunday is that it snowed.

4 Now try with low key.

↘↗ On SUNday

↘ it SNOWED

The starting pitch of the second tonic is lower than that of the first. This can give the impression: *It practically goes without saying that it should have snowed – what else would you expect?*

Google Global HQ

PRONUNCIATION

Introducing new information

10.3 **A Listen to the extracts from the radio program. Does the pitch of the speaker's voice go up or down on the underlined words?**

1 As the city evolves, its population has swelled to over 21 million, making Beijing one of the most populated cities in the world. <u>And</u> the more people there are, the more challenging it becomes to provide comfortable environments for people to live and work in. up

2 They found that people strongly preferred daylight to electric light – and, <u>as a matter of fact</u>, other research has shown that people have a tendency to be less productive if their desk is more than 7.5 meters away from a window. up

3 Apparently, people feel more comfortable in places with round shapes and curved lines. <u>On the other hand,</u> straight lines and sharp edges have been shown to create feelings of fear. down

4 One interesting study showed that people are more relaxed when they see lively and interesting store facades, <u>whereas</u> plain, monotonous facades make people anxious and give them the urge to hurry past. down

B Work in pairs. Practice saying the sentences. Listen carefully. Did your partner use a higher pitch on the correct word?

1 Although most people think that living in a city is exciting, it's actually fairly boring for many people.

2 Rather than developing urban areas, we should be developing rural areas.

3 Companies are now embracing ideas from environmental psychology rather than ignoring them.

4 The offices of large companies are being designed to encourage positive feelings in staff. People's homes, however, are much less likely to receive the same attention.

SPEAKING HUB

A PLAN Work in small groups. Imagine that your city is holding an election for a new mayor. Make a list of some of the biggest problems about living in your city and brainstorm some solutions to these problems.

B PREPARE You support a candidate in the election. Prepare a short speech to try to persuade people to vote for your candidate. You should:

- decide which three problems your candidate will solve
- be ready to explain the problems
- be ready to explain how your candidate will fix them
- make sure that each member of your group has something to say.

C PRESENT Give your speeches and listen to the other groups' speeches.

D DISCUSS As a class, decide which candidate you want to be mayor.

For me, the best speaker by far was ...
While I liked all the candidates, the one that really stood out was ...

Discuss issues related to tourism
Present solutions to urban problems

10.2 How to change the world

- Talk about political activism
- Discuss how to make a difference

G ellipsis and substitution **V** word building **P** managing conversations **S** recognizing shifts in register

READING

A SPEAK Work in pairs and discuss the questions.

1 If you were concerned about a local issue, would you contact your local politician about it?

2 Do you think that political activism (e.g. demonstrations or petitions) can make a difference?

B READ FOR MAIN IDEA Read the article *Political activism* and choose the best summary.

1 The younger generation is becoming very active in politics and many are choosing to become politicians so they can make the world a better place.

2 The younger generation is more interested in campaigning for specific causes than getting behind a particular political party.

3 The younger generation is completely uninterested in politics and prefer to focus on their friendships, hobbies and interests.

C READ FOR DETAIL Read the article again and answer the questions.

1 Is the writer part of the younger or older generation?

2 Why is the younger generation disillusioned with the political system?

3 What three issues has the Harry Potter Alliance taken an interest in?

4 What does the writer mean when he says that 'we're moving from a vision of civics that is party-based and partisan to one that's personal and pointillist'?

D SPEAK Work in pairs. Discuss the question. Some people label the kind of political activism described in the article as 'slacktivism'. Do you think this is a fair criticism?

Political activism is as strong as ever, but now it's digital – and passionate

The new generation of digital natives are not apathetic about politics, but they see online campaigns as more effective than lobbying a politician or joining a party.

Ex C Q1 Like most Americans of my generation – born in 1973 – I learned about civics from television. On Saturday mornings, our childhood diet of cartoons was regularly interrupted for *Schoolhouse Rock*, three-minute animated musical lessons on science, grammar and the workings of government. Today, it's hard to teach civics in three-minute snippets because the way we participate in civic life is changing shape – and changing very Ex C Q1 quickly. The vision of participatory citizenship that I grew up with – read a newspaper, vote in elections and if you're really incensed, write to your congressional representative – is utterly unpersuasive and unappealing to the students Ex C Q2 I teach. Digital natives, born and raised in an atmosphere of interactivity, are acutely aware of how insensitive most governments are to participation and how little meaningful interaction they can expect from their elected representatives and other government officials.

This distaste for participation in dysfunctional political systems is easily misread as apathy, leading legislators and educators to declare 'a crisis in civics' as young people participate in elections at a much lower rate than their parents. But that misses a key shift: Digital natives are participating in civic life in ways where they feel they can have an impact and these points of impact are often outside government.

Take the Harry Potter Alliance, a group of teen and twenty-something fans of J.K. Rowling's books and movies, who are organizing online and searching for ways to live out the values of Harry Potter and Dumbledore's Army here in the Muggle world. Their Ex C Q3 past campaigns have purchased thousands of books for underfunded public libraries and sent planeloads of health supplies for Haitian crisis response. Now they're working to persuade Warner Bros. to buy fair-trade chocolate for the candies sold as tie-ins to the movies, bombarding the company with 'howlers', open, digital letters that demand it consider the ethical concerns of Harry Potter's fans.

10.2 How to change the world

LEAD-IN

Books closed. Ask students to think of one thing they would like to change about where they live and what they could do to try to make this happen. Put them into pairs to tell each other their ideas.

READING

A Put students into pairs to discuss the questions.

B Set a time limit and tell students to read the article. When the time is up, let students compare answers in pairs.

C Tell students to read the article again and to answer the questions. Let them compare answers in pairs before feedback.

1 *He says he was born in 1973 and that he teaches students – so he is likely to be a university professor.*
2 *Because politicians and governments don't interact enough with voters.*
3 *Purchasing books for public libraries, sending supplies to victims of the disaster in Haiti and supporting fair trade.*
4 *He means people choose to support the issues they believe in rather than the issues their party believes in.*

D Check students understand what is meant by *slacktivism*, then put them into pairs to discuss the question. In feedback, encourage students to expand on their answers and to agree or disagree with each other.

Extra activity

Following on from the discussion on political activism, there is a good opportunity for a class debate. Write *Today, younger people are too apathetic about politics* on the board. Decide who in the class will be for and against the motion.

Put students into groups to write notes for their side of the argument. Allow students time to prepare their arguments and decide who will speak and in what order. Monitor during this stage and provide help if needed.

Ask the groups to join together to debate the motion. During the debate, encourage students to listen and respond to the arguments of the other side. Include a brief feedback stage when each group has finished to highlight examples of good language use. At the end, encourage students to hold a vote to determine whether they are still for or against the motion.

TEACHING IDEA by David Seymour and Maria Popova

A perfect world

Use this activity to introduce or extend the themes of global problems and political activism.

In small groups, make a list of ten problems in the world and briefly explain them, e.g. 1) War – *There isn't enough cooperation between governments.* 2) Pollution – *People drive their cars too much.* Do this on the left-hand side of a piece of paper.

Swap lists with another group. Discuss solutions and write them on the right-hand side, e.g. 1) *We need to give more power to the UN.* 2) *More people should ride bicycles.*

Swap lists again to see if you agree with the other group's solutions.

TEACHING IDEA by David Seymour and Maria Popova

Projects

Use this activity to introduce or extend the themes of the media and political activism.

Write notes about a major political story happening at the moment. Sources can include TV/radio news, newspapers, the internet or conversations with other people who are interested in the same story. Compose a news report to read out to the class. If there are two of you interested in the same story, do it as newsreader and an on-the-spot reporter.

METHODOLOGY HUB

Extensive reading

There is a great deal of evidence that extensive reading (i.e. reading longer texts, such as a novel, over time) has a powerful impact on language learning. The more someone reads, the more they pick up items of vocabulary and grammar from the texts, typically without realizing it, and this widening language knowledge seems to increase their overall linguistic confidence, which then influences and improves their skills in other language areas, too (though this is probably only true in cases where the material they read is self-chosen and is genuinely relevant and interesting to them).

So, there are strong arguments for actively encouraging students to read a lot in the target language, both in and outside the classroom. We can help by:

- providing a library of readers (see below), magazines, newspapers, flyers, etc
- training learners how to select suitable reading material and in ways to read it
- creating a 'book club' environment that encourages learners to choose what books to purchase, talk about favorite books, share them with each other, write brief recommendations, etc
- allowing sections of classroom time purely for students to read; some teachers who have five or six lessons a week set aside one of these lessons as quiet reading time.

A library doesn't need to be large. It can be something as simple as a small box of books and magazines. However, it's important to include items that are relevant and suitable for your class. Unabridged old copies of worthy classics are probably not a good choice. Better to have a few recent magazines on themes that students like (e.g. movies, pop stars, computer games, etc for a teen class) and a small set of graded readers.

VOCABULARY

A Go through the information in the box about *Word building*, and elicit the first one as an example. In feedback, draw attention to word stress, especially where it changes from one word class to another (e.g. *politics/political*), and practice pronunciation.

B Direct students to the **Vocabulary Hub** (see TB121). Use the **Vocabulary Worksheet** on page W47 for extra practice.

SPEAKING

Put students into small groups to discuss the questions. Before feedback, you could regroup students and tell them to compare ideas to see if they chose the same problems and solutions.

Extra activity

Put students into pairs to think of more ways that the lifestyles and attitudes of the younger generation are different from those of the older generation. Monitor to help with language as needed.

Get some feedback, then put students back into pairs to predict how the lifestyles and attitudes of the next generation will be different from those of today. Again, get some feedback, and write on the board any interesting language that comes up.

METHODOLOGY HUB by Christine Nuttall

Morphology

The morphology or internal structure of a word may offer valuable clues to its meaning, so it is well worth learning something about it. In English, this involves the study of affixation and of the ways in which compound words are built, maybe also of the way phrasal verbs are put together. You can start making students aware of affixes as soon as they meet the simple ones such as UNhappy, teachER, DISagree, examinATION. However, unless you approve of learning uncontextualized lists, organized study must be postponed until they have a reasonable vocabulary. Serious work can begin when students have a big enough vocabulary to provide other examples of the same affix (UNwilling, UNkind, UNwrap, etc) and of bases (i.e. the words or parts of words to which affixes are attached: *willing*, *kind*, *wrap*, etc). Students need to know which affixes can combine with what bases, which affixes can co-occur (UNwillingNESS, DISagreeMENT, etc), what changes in spelling or pronunciation occur when affixes are added and so on. An analytical approach to morphology pays big dividends in enabling students to work out the meaning of new words. Some recipes for exercises follow.

1 Supply an affix (e.g. UN-) and a number of bases (e.g. *happy*, *slow*, *neat*).

   Task: Indicate or find out from a dictionary which of the bases can take the affix.

2 Supply a base (e.g. *sharp*) and several affixes (e.g. UN-, -LY, -EN, -MENT, -NESS).

   Task: Indicate/find out which of the affixes the base can take.

3 Supply a list of affixes of similar function (e.g. the adjective-forming suffixes -FUL, -OUS,-Y, -ISH) and a list of bases.

   Task: Indicate/find out which basewords take which affixes, and if more than one is possible, what variations in meaning are involved (e.g. *manful*, *mannish*, *manly*).

4 Supply an incomplete table of forms consisting of basewords with various affixes.

   Task: Complete the table by filling in the blanks.

5 Supply sentences containing words of a particular form, e.g. verbs.

   Task: Rewrite the sentences in a specified way entailing the use of a different form of the given word (e.g. nouns instead of verbs).

There is a finite set of affixes and many of them are highly productive (i.e. a great many words can be produced by means of them). Hence they repay study. Studying affixes also requires the study of bases; but roots are a different matter. In English, many words (especially in academic terminology) contain roots which cannot stand alone, for example, *educ-* (or *-due-*) in the words *education*, *educator*, etc.

How far students need to know such roots depends on their field of study. For instance, a biology student might find it useful to understand the meaning of *cyt*, as in *cytoplasm*, *cytology*, *leucocyte*. But students who rarely encounter these words would do better to treat each as a whole.

Nevertheless, the relationship between words like *edible*, *edibility* and *inedible* can still be recognized, without troubling to identify the root: as long as *edible* is understood, the others can also be interpreted. Students can practice deducing the meaning of an affix (or a root, if worthwhile) by studying well-known words in which it occurs; what they find out for themselves will be better remembered.

As well as investigating the structure of complex words (i.e. those produced by affixation), students need to understand the patterns of compound words, those formed by combining two normally independent words, such as *software*, *gunsmith*, *painstaking*, *second-hand*, *spoon-feed* and *dry-clean*. It is worth drawing attention to compounds encountered in texts, because the meaning can often be worked out from the meanings of the component parts. It is also worth studying the ways they are formed, as patterns that are permissible in one language may be impossible in another: it is important to distinguish a *houseplant* from a *planthouse*, for instance.

VOCABULARY
Word building

A Complete the Example column with words from the article. Use the information in the box to help you.

Word building

We use suffixes to change the form of words. For example, we can add *-ness* to the end of an adjective to turn it into a noun (*ready* becomes *readiness*). Being aware of different suffixes can help you to understand what kind of word is being used.

Suffix	Add to ...	to make...	Example
-al	a noun	an adjective	dysfunctional, formal, personal, ethical, political, congressional
-ate	a noun	an adjective	passionate
-ic	a noun	an adjective	apathetic, civic, public
-ical	a noun	an adjective	musical, ethical
-ive	a verb	an adjective	effective, insensitive, active, unpersuasive
-hood	a noun	a noun	childhood, neighborhood
-ity	an adjective	a noun	interactivity, security, community, identity
-ship	a noun	a noun	citizenship, entrepreneurship

B Go to the **Vocabulary Hub** on **page 148**.

SPEAKING

DISCUSS Work in small groups. Discuss the questions.

1 What do you think are some of the biggest problems in the world today? Make a list and rank the problems.

2 What could people do to raise awareness of the top three issues on your list? How could people try to get companies, individuals or governments to change their behavior?

3 If a friend of yours wanted to become involved in political activism, would you encourage him or her or dissuade him or her from doing so? Why?

Not every digital native is an engaged, active citizen (and not every young person is a digital native) and not every online campaign has an impact. But it's too easy to dismiss digitally-rooted activism as naive 'slacktivism'. Online activism is having an impact, but it frequently focuses on areas outside formal political participation. Civic participation of the young uses a broad suite of tools to affect a wide range of targets.

Coders write open-source security software in the hope of frustrating NSA surveillance, while community organizers fund neighborhood gardens through Kickstarter. This emergent civics targets governments, corporations, communities and the media. It harnesses social media, crowdfunding, social entrepreneurship and open-source software as well as law and politics, to bring about change.

No wonder it's hard to get our heads around it. Ex C Q4 We're moving from a vision of civics that's party-based and partisan to one that's personal and pointillist. Parties offer a way to have an opinion (often an ill-informed one) on every issue, while participatory civics centers on issues that people are passionate about. While my generation tends to see the world in terms of issues important to Republicans or Democrats, my students often see the world in terms of the issues their friends care about, a political identity built on the passions of people important to them. This isn't civics in crisis – it's civics in flux, civics that's changing with the people who practice it.

Glossary

dysfunctional (adj) not working normally
howler (n) a silly and embarrassing mistake
incensed (adj) extremely angry
lobby (v) try to influence politicians or people in authority on a particular subject
snippet (n) a small piece of something, especially information or news

LISTENING

A SPEAK Work in pairs. Discuss the questions.

1 What job did you want to do when you were younger?

2 Do you still want to do that job? Why/Why not?

10.4 **B LISTEN FOR MAIN IDEA** Listen to a conversation about finding a job after college. Answer the questions below.

1 What kind of job was Robin interested in before?

something in business, possibly a management trainee program

2 What kinds of jobs is Robin thinking about doing now?

working for a charity, working in politics, doing social work

10.4 **C LISTEN FOR DETAIL** Listen again and answer the questions.

1 What made Robin think about pursuing a different career?

talking to his cousin, who does charity work

2 What does Joanna think about the jobs Robin is thinking of applying for?

They would be poorly paid, boring or very difficult.

3 What advice does Mr. Evans give Robin about finding the job he wants to do?

He should start doing some volunteer work now.

4 How did the philosophy graduate decide to help people?

He decided to get a high-paying job and donate.

5 Does Joanna agree with Mr. Evans' advice?

Joanna thinks it's good advice but they are both uncertain about giving money away.

10.5 **D LISTEN TO REGISTER** Listen to extracts from the conversation. For each, decide if Robin is using formal or informal register. Use the information in the box to help you.

Recognizing shifts in register

People speak differently in formal and informal/casual situations.

In formal situations, speakers:

- use longer, more complete sentences
- use careful pronunciation
- are less direct
- use formal words and phrases.

In informal/casual situations, speakers use:

- short sentences, contracted forms and often omit words
- less careful pronunciation
- more informal words and phrases (phrasal verbs, vague language and slang).

1 *informal* / *formal*

2 *informal* / *formal*

3 *informal* / *formal*

4 *informal* / *formal*

5 *informal* / *formal*

6 *informal* / *formal*

E SPEAK Work in pairs and discuss the questions.

1 What kind of job do you think Robin should pursue? Why?

2 What do you think about the idea of working in finance to help charities?

3 If you want to donate to charity, what's the best way to choose the charity?

10.2 How to change the world

LISTENING

10.4; 10.5 **A–D** Put students into pairs to discuss the questions and check their answers before whole-class feedback.

E Put students into pairs to discuss the questions. Monitor to help if necessary. Then try to encourage a range of ideas and opinions during feedback.

AUDIO SCRIPT

10.4

Listening, Exercise B

R = Robin J = Joanna Mr. E = Mr. Evans

J: A few weeks to go and then we're done with college for good. Can't believe it.

R: Me neither. The end of an era. So … you going to work at your dad's company then?

J: Hmm … hope not. Not if I can help it, anyway. But yeah … may need to. Any idea what you're going to do?

R: Well, funny you should ask that. I've just been trying to look over my résumé and looking for some interesting stuff to apply to. The thing is I really want to do something to help people. But I haven't seen too much of that sort of thing.

Ex B Q1 **J:** Really? Oh OK, thought you were going to apply for something in business though, like one of those management trainee programs.

Ex C Q1 **R:** I don't know. I don't think all that is really for me. I'd like to make some kind of a difference to the world.

Ex B Q2 You know my cousin works for a charity, right?

J: Oh yeah?

Ex B Q2 **R:** Yeah, a clean water organization. Anyway, we've been talking a lot recently about all the stuff she's doing and it kind of made me want to do something similar, too.

Ex C Q2 **J:** Oh, OK got you. But you wouldn't earn that much working for a charity. At least not at first. Any other ideas?

Ex B Q2 **R:** Well, yeah I thought about politics, too.

Ex C Q2 **J:** Hmm. Don't know. I mean all they seem to do is argue with each other. Just don't know how much of a change you'll be making.

Ex B Q2 **R:** OK … and there's also social work. You know, looking out for children, vulnerable people …

J: Hmm OK …

R: I take it you're not convinced then?

Ex C Q2 **J:** I just think that looks like a tough job, coping with a lot of difficult situations. I couldn't do it myself personally. I was thinking … what about teaching? You'd be a great teacher. You could train to be a teacher or just volunteer in your spare time.

R: Yeah … I guess.

J: Hey, there's Dr. Evans. Isn't he the new career's advisor? Why don't you talk to him?

R: Good idea. Hang on sec … Excuse me, Dr. Evans. Would you have a minute to talk?

Mr. E: Oh hello Robin. Sure. How can I help?

R: I was wondering if you could offer me some advice. I've just been considering what to do after graduation.

Mr. E: OK. So what are you interested in doing?

R: Well I think … first and foremost I want to do a job which involves helping people, you know, that are less fortunate than myself. So I was really interested in applying for a position with a charity.

Mr. E: Ah. OK. So my first question then would be: what kind of charity do you have in mind?

R: So, ideally one that campaigns for clean water … or maybe disease prevention.

Mr. E: So second question: what do you see yourself doing for them?

R: Well … I'd like to be assisting with policy making, I guess.

Mr. E: OK let me just stop you there. Of course that is one area of charity work. But it's highly competitive. And you don't have experience or a specialist certification. You're more likely to be involved in fundraising, persuading people to donate money,

Ex C Q3 at least initially. And even then, it would definitely strengthen your application if you can show some commitment to their particular work.

R: Like volunteering maybe. I was thinking about some kind of voluntary work.

Mr. E: You should definitely do it.

R: Great, thanks Mr. Evans. I can look into it.

Mr. E: But let me get to my final point. You should bear in mind that working for a charity isn't the only way you can help people. If you're likely to be

Ex C Q3 helping the organization get money, you may actually be able to make more of a difference pursuing a career in business. Especially with your background. Then you can commit to donating a portion of your salary to your chosen charity.

R: Right … I hadn't thought of that before.

Mr. E: Yes, there's a very, very interesting book about a Wall Street trader, called *The Most Good You Can Do*. If you haven't read it, you should do. The guy was a philosophy student, really smart in fact. Just like you he was thinking how to make a difference. He decided that the way he could make the biggest

Ex C Q4 impact was by working hard in finance and donating money to charity. He's been able to donate over $100,000 a year to his chosen charities – and as a result touched many people's lives.

R: Thank you, I'll look it up. And thanks for the advice Mr. Evans, it's much appreciated. I definitely have a lot to think about.

Mr. E: You're welcome.

J: So, come on then. What did he say?

R: Not what I expected. At all. He said it might be better to get a normal job, you know, an office job or something like that.

J: Told you so.

R: No, but then give the money to charity.

J: Oh. Great.

R: Yep, that's what he said. Apparently, there's a guy who does that and has given over a hundred grand a year away.

J: No way!

R: Yeah I know. Crazy, right?

Ex C Q5 **J:** Well, it's kind of good advice. The part about an office job. I'd do that. I'm just not sure about the giving away part.

10.2 How to change the world

GRAMMAR

A–F Where appropriate, elicit the first question of the exercise as an example, before putting students into pairs to complete the rest of the questions. Direct students to the **Grammar Hub** (see below). Use the **Grammar Worksheet** on page W48 for extra practice.

PRONUNCIATION

10.6 **A–B** During the speaking stage, model and practice pronunciation, exaggerating slightly if necessary, to make sure students really get into the spirit of it. Give students time to think of their own anecdote, then put them into pairs to tell them to each other and to respond appropriately.

SPEAKING HUB

A–D Monitor to help at each stage and to make sure students change partners regularly during Exercise B.

Extra activity

Ask students if there are street fundraisers in their country, and if they have a good or bad reputation. Then put students into groups to think of ways of improving the image of street fundraisers or of alternative methods of raising money.

GRAMMAR HUB

10.2 Ellipsis and substitution

- Ellipsis involves leaving out words and phrases to avoid repeating them.
- In written English, there are a number of grammatical items that are often left out.

repeated subject	**He**'s into politics and (**he**) is passionate about activism.
repeated subject + modal	**They should** organize a campaign and (**they should**) create some positive publicity.
repeated subject + auxiliary verb	**We're going to** start a petition and (**we're going to**) organize a protest meeting.
repeated verb phrase	'I thought you were **going on the march**.' 'Yes, I am (**going on the march**).'
repeated adjective	So many students are **apathetic**, but Kiera isn't (**apathetic**).

- In spoken English, we can also leave out some grammatical items for the sake of brevity, when it's clear who/what we're talking about.

  subject: *Can't believe we managed to save the forest from developers! (= I can't believe …)*

  auxiliary verb: *You planning to join the group? (= Are you planning …)*

  auxiliary verb + subject + verb: *Any preference as to which route we take? (= Do you have any preference …)*

- We often substitute the following words and phrases to avoid repeating words.

  do: *Are you going into town? Will you post my letter if you **do**?*
  (to avoid repeating 'go into town')

  not: *I may have to organize the campaign, but I hope **not**.*
  (to avoid repeating 'that I don't have to organize the campaign')

  do so: *Deactivate the security alarm. In order to **do so**, you'll need to key in this code number.*
  (to avoid repeating 'deactivate the security alarm')

  do it: *I often read English-language newspapers. I **do it** to improve my vocabulary.*
  (to avoid repeating 'read English-language newspapers')

  do that: *I specifically asked you not to read my emails. Why did you **do that**?*
  (to avoid repeating 'read my emails')

10.2 Ellipsis and substitution

A Cross out the words that can be omitted in the conversation.

Dom: ~~Do you know~~ who I saw the other day? Know

Ali: No, who ~~did you see~~?

Dom: Klaus.

Ali: ~~Do you mean your~~ old roommate from college? Your

Dom: Yeah! I can't believe it – ~~I saw him again~~ after all these years.

Ali: What happened ~~when you saw him~~?

Dom: He gave me his phone number and ~~he gave me his~~ email address.

Ali: ~~Are you planning~~ to meet up soon? Planning

Dom: He's going to be visiting the area again next month, so he'll give me a ring when he does ~~visit the area again~~.

B Replace the phrases in bold with the words and phrases in the box.

do | do it | do so | doing that | don't

1 'Do you have time to help out at the animal shelter?'
'No, I'm afraid I **don't have time to help out at the animal shelter**.' don't

2 'I'd like to volunteer with you on the weekend.'
'That's great. You'll have to fill out this form in order to **volunteer with us on the weekend**.' do so

3 'I volunteer at an animal shelter every weekend.'
'I really admire you for **volunteering at the animal shelter**.' doing that

4 'Are you enjoying your volunteer work?'
'Yes. I didn't know how fulfilling it would be, but now I **know how fulfilling it is**.' do

5 'I've always wanted to volunteer at the Cats' Home.'
'So why don't you **volunteer at the Cats' Home**?' do it

➤ Go back to page 117.

GRAMMAR
Ellipsis and substitution

A **Look at the extracts from the conversation. The speakers omitted some words. Complete the sentences with the omitted words.**

1 I've just been trying to look over my résumé and ___I've been___ looking for some interesting stuff to apply to.

2 ___Do you have___ any idea what you're going to do?

3 You could train to be a teacher or ___you could___ just volunteer in your spare time.

B **Look at the underlined words in the sentences. What words do they replace?**

1 **A:** So … you going to work at your dad's company then?
B: Hmm … hope not. I'm not going to work at my dad's company

2 If you haven't read it, you should do. read it

3 **A:** I was thinking about some kind of volunteer work.
B: You should definitely do it. do some volunteer work

C **Complete the rules using examples in Exercises A and B.**

Ellipsis and substitution

Ellipsis means omitting unnecessary words. We can omit:

1 the subject + modal: ___you could___
2 the subject + auxiliary verb: ___I've been / Do you have___
3 a verb phrase
4 an adjective: ___really (rich)___.

In spoken English, it's also common to leave out words if our meaning is obvious from the context. We can omit:

5 the subject
6 the subject + auxiliary verb.

Substitution means avoiding repeating something by using words like:

7 *do:* ___read it___
8 *not:* ___I'm not going to work at my dad's company___
9 *do so / do it / do that:* ___do some kind of volunteer work___.

D Go to the **Grammar Hub** on **page 140**.

E **SPEAK** **Work in pairs. Cross out the words that can be omitted in these sentences. Then discuss whether you agree or disagree with them.**

1 Charity workers should not receive high salaries and ~~they should~~ not get bonuses.
2 Some charity workers are very persistent and I wish they weren't ~~so persistent~~.
3 Animal charities often receive the most money, but they shouldn't ~~receive the most money~~.

F **Work in pairs. Replace parts of the questions with *do so*, *not* or *so*. Then ask your partner the questions.**

1 Would you ever go overseas to do volunteer work? If ~~you went overseas to do volunteer work~~ so, where would you go?
2 Do you think having volunteer work on your résumé makes a big difference to recruiters or ~~does it not make a big difference to recruiters~~ not?
3 If your company or college allowed you to take a week off to do volunteer work, would you ~~take a week off to do volunteer work~~ do so?

PRONUNCIATION
Managing conversations

10.6 **A** **Listen to extracts from the conversation. For each extract, decide if the intonation on the second speaker's words rises (↗) falls (↘) or rises then falls (↗↘).**

1 ↗↘ 2 ↘ 3 ↗ 4 ↗ 5 ↘

B **SPEAK** **Work in pairs. Think of an anecdote for one of these topics. Listen to your partner and use appropriate reactions to keep the conversation going.**

- some good advice a teacher gave me
- a time I made a difference

SPEAKING HUB

A **PREPARE** Work in two groups. You are going to role-play an event where charities look for funding. Group A – you are fundraisers for a charity. Decide what type of charity you work for. Group B – you are funding organizations. Decide what types of charities you want to give money to and why.

B **PLAN** Group A – plan how you will persuade people to support your charity. Group B – think of questions you will ask charities that want your funding.

C **PRESENT** Talk to students from the other group. Try to persuade them to support your charity or ask them questions about their work.

D **REFLECT** Who was able to convince the most people to support their charity? Why were they successful?

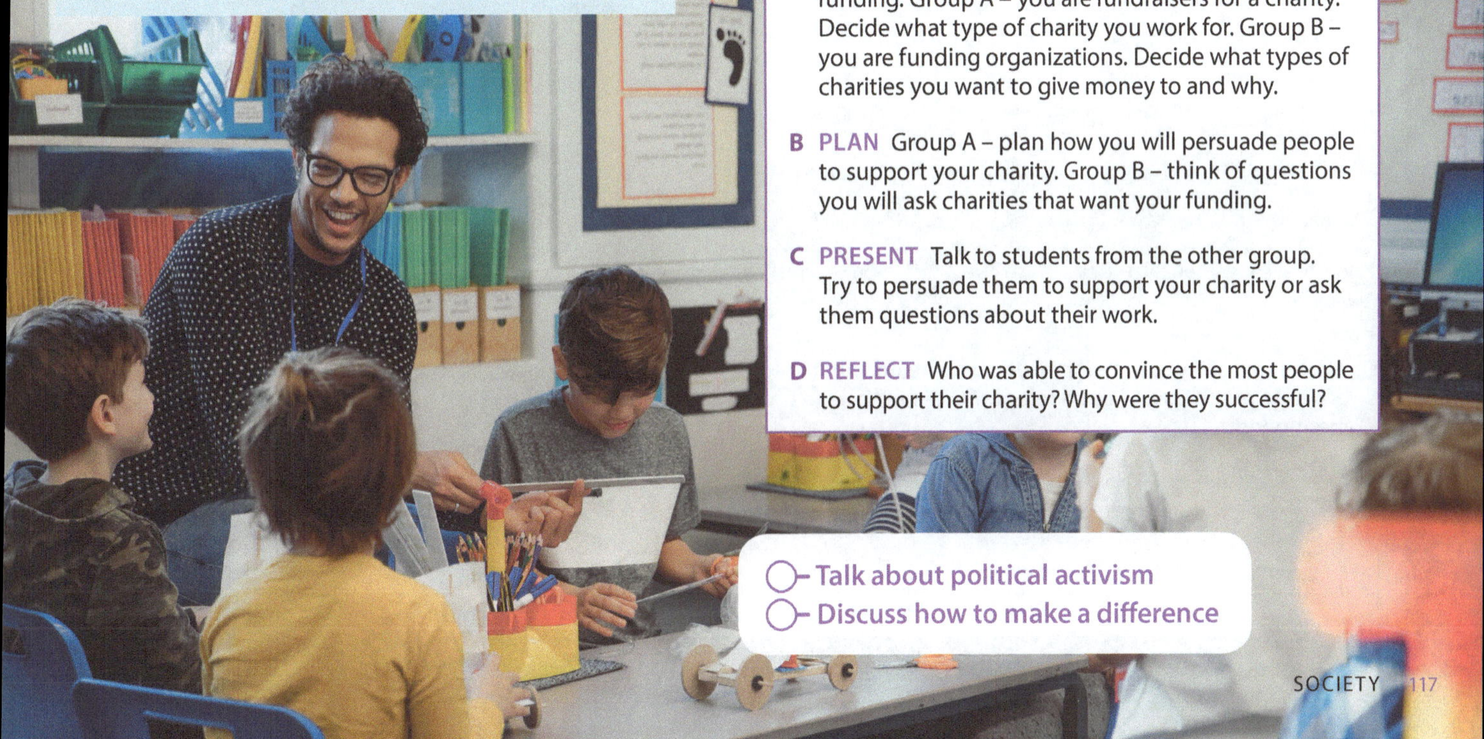

- Talk about political activism
- Discuss how to make a difference

10.3 Changing cities

Ⓐ– describing a scene in real-time Ⓢ– using vague language

Mexicable

A Work in pairs. Look at the pictures and discuss the questions.

1 What are some of the different uses of cable cars?

2 Are there cable cars in your city or country? How are they used?

B Watch the video. Check (✓) which of the following you see.

1 A man admiring spectacular views from a cable car. ✓
2 A man in a wheelchair going up a ramp. ☐
3 A man in a wheelchair entering a cable car. ✓
4 Tourists taking photos from a cable car. ☐
5 Mechanics repairing an engine. ☐
6 A man wheeling himself along a sidewalk. ✓

C Watch the video again. Complete the sentences with between one and three words.

1 Ade likes the cable car station because there's a wheelchair entrance and ___a ramp___.

2 From the cable car, Ade points out a mural of ___an elephant___.

3 The cable cars from Stations 1 to 4 are moved by ___one engine___.

4 *Mexicable* connects some of the poorest and ___most isolated___ areas of the city.

Glossary

feat (n) something difficult needing a lot of skill, strength, bravery, etc to achieve it
haphazard (adj) done in a way that does not seem to be carefully planned or organized
loop (n) a round shape or curve made by a line curling back toward itself
mural (n) a large painting on the wall of a room or building

D Work in pairs. Try to remember what you heard. What do these numbers and dates refer to? One number isn't mentioned.

1 22 million ___people___
2 2016 ___system completed___
3 6 ___pesos___
4 26 ___not mentioned in the video___
5 30,000 ___passengers a day___
6 4 ___stations (moved by one engine)___
7 7 ___stations in total___
8 3 ___miles (the cars run for)___

AUTHENTIC ENGLISH

A Work in pairs. Read the sentence from the video and the information in the box. Underline the descriptive words. What do they mean?

The views from the Mexicable – you've got this <u>sprawling</u> city and these murals and <u>the amazing</u> colors on the houses, it's just <u>breathtaking</u>!

sprawling: covering a wide area; amazing: very good or pleasant; breathtaking: extremely impressive or beautiful

Describing a scene in real-time

When we describe a scene in real-time we often use visually descriptive language to bring the scene to life and paint a mental picture in the listener's mind.

B Read the sentences. What is being described in each sentence?

1 There's this sea of golden shifting sand, spectacular dunes and a fierce, burning sun. a desert

2 Just look at the gorgeous lush green meadows and peaceful grazing sheep. the countryside

3 I've never seen such deep valleys and magnificent snow-capped peaks. a mountain/mountain range

4 Everywhere you look there are towering skyscrapers, bustling streets and stunning street art. a city

5 You have these picturesque narrow streets, an enchanting medieval square and beautiful, cozy cottages. a village

C Work in pairs. Describe a scene to each other using descriptive language. Student A – go to the Communication Hub on page 152. Student B – go to the Communication Hub on page 155.

Everything's changing

SAM MALCOLM AMANDA HARRY EMILY

A Work in pairs. Discuss the questions.

1. What developments are happening where you live?
2. Are the developments positive or negative? Why?

B Watch the video. Does everybody have a similar opinion about the new cable car? No, Harry likes the idea.

C Watch the video again. Answer the following questions.

1. Why is parking and traffic worse according to Emily? Because they pedestrianized a couple of the roads.
2. What is being built over the river? a cable car
3. What does Malcolm say will happen to the area soon? It will be gentrified.
4. How much would it cost Emily to rent a bigger office? £2,000 a month
5. Why is Harry looking forward to the cable car? fun, reduce traffic, encourage tourism
6. What improvements have there been to the area according to Amanda? Crime/unemployment has been reduced.
7. How was Sam able to set up his café according to Harry? He was able to set up the café on a government scheme/ program to encourage small businesses in the area.

SPEAKING SKILL

A Work in pairs. Look at the extracts from the video. Why have the speakers used the underlined phrases?

Amanda: Also, the area was quite run down with high unemployment and all the rest of it.

Malcolm: I had to park all the way over on whatsitsname and walk here.

Amanda can't think of other exact examples of how the area has declined, so she uses *all the rest of it* to mean other similar things.

B Read the information in the box. Underline the vague language in the sentences from the video.

Using vague language

We often use vague words when we can't find the exact expression we need.

- **a** List completers – when someone is unable to complete everything on a list.
- **b** Placeholders – a speaker cannot remember something.
- **c** Evasion – not wanting to say something exactly.
- **d** Quantities – when we're not sure of the exact figure.

1. It doesn't help either that they're building that thingy over the river. b
2. I hardly recognize the neighborhood any more with all the new shops, the road system and stuff like that. a
3. It was two thousand odd pounds for the month. d
4. Well, yeah, sort of … it is convenient … but if I can't afford to stay in the area they won't be much good to me. c
5. It will also encourage tourism and who knows what else. a
6. Crime in the area is down about 20% in the past four years. d

C Work in pairs. Match the examples (1–6) from the video with the functions (a–d) in the box.

SPEAKING HUB

A **PREPARE** You are going to debate the following motion. Decide who in the class will be *for* and *against* the motion.

All vehicles should be banned from city centers.

B **PLAN** In your groups, write notes for your side of the argument. Think about:

- environment
- public transportation
- convenience
- cost

C **PRESENT** Join together with the other group and hold a debate.

Without cars you could have more public spaces, street cafés and all the rest of it.

D **REFLECT** Hold a vote on whether you agree or disagree with the motion.

Debate for and against a motion

➤ Turn to page 165 to learn how to write a persuasive essay about living in the city or country.

10.3 Changing cities

Mexicable

A Focus students on the pictures, then put them into pairs to discuss the questions. In feedback, find out how much personal experience students have of cable cars, if any, and how they feel about them.

B ▶ Point out the glossary, then instruct students to watch the video and to check what they see.

C ▶ Put students into pairs to try to complete the sentences from memory. Then play the video again for them to watch and check.

D Put students into pairs to try to remember what the numbers and dates refer to. Play the video once again if necessary before feedback.

AUTHENTIC ENGLISH

A Go through the information in the box about *Describing a scene in real-time*, then tell students to underline the descriptive words in the sentence from the video and to decide what they think they mean.

B Elicit the first one as an example, then put students into pairs to do the rest.

C Put students into pairs. Direct students to the **Communication Hub** (see TB121). Make sure they can't see each other's page, and tell them to describe their pictures to each other in as much detail as possible. You could tell students to try to draw the scene as their partner describes it, and then compare their drawing with the picture afterwards. In feedback, find out whose descriptions were the most vivid or whose drawings were the most similar to the photos.

Everything's changing

A Put students into pairs to discuss the questions. In feedback, encourage students to expand on their answers and to give examples.

B ▶ Students answer the questions as they watch the video. Let them compare answers in pairs before feedback.

C ▶ Allow students to compare their answers again before whole-class feedback. You can find the **video script** for *Everything's changing* on the Teacher's Resource Center.

SPEAKING SKILL

A Put students into pairs to look at the example from the video and to answer the question.

B Go through the information in the box about *Using vague language*, then tell students to underline the examples in the sentences from the video.

C Put students into pairs to match the eight sentences with one of the four functions of vague language in the box.

SPEAKING HUB

A Explain that the students are going to have a debate and divide the class into two equal groups. Tell one group that they're going to argue in favor of the motion, and the other group that they're going to argue against.

B Students work in their groups (for a large class, divide them into smaller groups) to prepare ideas for the debate. Tell them to think about the points listed, as well as any more of their own ideas. Monitor to help or prompt if needed.

C Put each group arguing for the motion together with one arguing against to have the debate. Monitor to ensure everyone gets a chance to express their opinion but also encourage students to react to what the other group says.

D As a whole class, ask students what the best arguments for or against they heard were. Take a vote to find out the students' real opinion. Finish with feedback on students' use of language during the activity.

Extra activity

Put students into pairs to discuss what others they think should or will be banned in cities in the future. In feedback, encourage students to explain their answers and to agree or disagree with each other. If students are engaged by one particular theme during the discussion, this activity could easily be expanded into a debate. Write the motion on the board in the form: *. . . should be banned from cities in the future.* Put students into groups to prepare their arguments before allowing the class to debate the motion.

▶ VIDEO SCRIPT

Mexicable

A = Ade Adepitan V = Victor Jasso

A: Getting 22 million people in and out of the crowded city every day is a challenge, especially with its haphazard bus service. But I've come to the suburb of Ecatepec to discover that almost anything can be built in this spirited city.
Well, wow! Look at this, it's just like everything else here in Mexico City – a big surprise! The last thing
Ex C Q1 I was expecting to find here is a cable car. It's accessible as well, there's a wheelchair entrance, there's a ramp – I'm loving it already.
The views from the Mexicable – you've got this sprawling city and these murals and the amazing colors on the houses, it's just breathtaking!
This cable car system was only completed in 2016. It costs just six pesos to ride and already nearly 33,000 people are using it every day.
Ex C Q2 Victor Jasso is the engineer who keeps the system running smoothly.
Can you tell me about the mechanics?

V: Yeah.

A: What goes into this? 'Cause it looks like an enormous engineering feat.

Ex C Q3 **V:** This cable car is moved by an engine. The engine is the big red one thing, over there, the station, and with that engine we move the whole loop between Station 4 and Station 1.

A: So, that one engine moves all of these cars across four stations?

V: Yes.

A: Wow! There are seven cable car stations in total
Ex C Q4 running just over three miles connecting some of the city's poorest and most isolated hillside neighborhoods.

10 Writing

Write a persuasive essay

W using counter-arguments and rebuttals

A SPEAK Work in pairs. Look at the essay title and discuss the questions.

1 What is gentrification?
2 What do you think of gentrification? Is it a good or bad thing?

B Read the example essay and answer the questions.

1 What is the writer's opinion of gentrification?
2 What reasons does the writer give for her opinion?
3 What reason to support the opposite opinion on gentrification does the writer mention?

DOES GENTRIFICATION HAVE A POSITIVE OR NEGATIVE IMPACT ON CITIES?

In cities all over the world, 'gentrification' is changing entire neighborhoods. Some people argue that this improves the areas by making them cleaner and safer. However, on the whole, gentrification actually has a negative impact. It prices people out of the areas where they have lived for years, destroys the unique character of neighborhoods, and it only benefits the rich.

The most obvious negative impact of gentrification is that it forces long-term residents to move away from their homes. As an area becomes trendy, landlords are able to increase the rent and attract wealthier tenants to the area. Meanwhile, lower income families are forced to move away from their friends, schools and jobs to find cheaper places to live.

Gentrification also results in the area losing its individual character. People may have first been attracted to an area by its unique stores and restaurants. However, as this area becomes gentrified, these establishments are unlikely to be able to pay increased rent. Gradually, these stores and restaurants are replaced by clothing chains so the area becomes just like many other neighborhoods in the city.

Some people argue that gentrification has a positive impact because the area becomes cleaner and safer. While it is true that gentrification leads to less crime and better facilities, the local people who deserve to benefit from these changes are unable to stay in the area. Rather than improving the city for all, gentrification only benefits the wealthiest.

In conclusion, gentrification predominantly has a negative impact on cities. It forces long-term residents from their homes, results in areas losing their individual character, and only provides real benefits for those with the most money. The government needs to find a way to ensure that redevelopment of the city can have a positive effect for everyone.

C Find the phrases the writer used to introduce the counter argument and rebuttal in the example essay. Use the information in the box to help you.

Using counter-arguments and rebuttals

In order to strengthen your argument in a persuasive essay, you can anticipate the points that could be used to support the opposite side of the argument (the counter-arguments) and respond with your answer to those arguments (a rebuttal). The rebuttal must respond directly to the counter argument.

Introduce a counter argument with phrases like:

- *Opponents/Supporters of .... claim/argue/believe that ...*
- *Some studies have shown that ...*
- *There is an argument that ...*

Introduce a rebuttal with phrases like:

- *However, this is only partially true.*
- *Studies have shown this is not true.*
- *Nevertheless, ...*

WRITING

A PREPARE Work in pairs. Look at the essay prompt and brainstorm reasons to support each side.

Which is better: living in the city or living in the country?

Reasons why living in the city is better	Reasons why living in the country is better
more jobs, better facilities, better entertainment, easier travel	cleaner air, nicer scenery, more outdoor activities, cheaper property

B PLAN Decide on your best points from Exercise A and make a plan of your essay.

C WRITE Write a persuasive essay to answer the essay prompt. Use a counter-argument and rebuttal in the third body paragraph. Use the example essay to help you.

D REVIEW Exchange your essay with a partner. How could your partner's essay be improved? How effective are their counter-arguments and rebuttals?

E EDIT Read your partner's comments. Rewrite any parts of your essay you think can be improved.

WRITING 165

Answers

1 They think it has a negative impact on cities.
2 It prices people out of the areas where they have lived for years, destroys the unique character of different areas, and it only benefits the rich.
3 That gentrification makes cities cleaner and safer.

Answers

The counter-argument was introduced with 'Some people argue that ...', whereas the rebuttal was introduced with 'While it is true that ...'

Refer students to this essay as a model for the writing task.

WRITING

A Put students into pairs to discuss the questions. In feedback, encourage students to expand on their answers and to agree or disagree with each other.

B Tell students to answer the questions as they read the essay. Let them compare answers in pairs before feedback.

C Go through the information in the box about *Using counter-arguments and rebuttals*, then ask students to find phrases used to introduce these in the essay.

WRITING TASK

A Put students into pairs to brainstorm ideas for both sides of the argument. In feedback, write on the board as many ideas as students can give. Ask students to explain their answers where necessary.

B Students choose the points they want to include in their essay and make a plan.

C Tell students to write their essay. This can be done as homework if there isn't time to do it in class. Remind students to use their plan to help them, and to use the same structure as the example essay, especially by putting a counter-argument and rebuttal in the third paragraph.

D Ask students to exchange their essays with a partner. Tell them to read the essay and to make comments on possible improvements to the content, language or organization.

E Encourage students to read their partner's comments and to make any changes they feel are necessary. In feedback, ask students what changes they made and why, and what they liked about their partner's essay.

Unit 10 Review

VOCABULARY

A Complete the article with the words in the box.

architectural designated endangered fund habitat heritage preserve refurbish ruins settlement

UNESCO

World Heritage Sites

The goal of the World [1] Heritage list is to help countries [2] preserve sites of 'outstanding universal value'. To be [3] designated as a World Heritage site, a place must meet one of ten criteria, such as being an [4] architectural masterpiece, a human [5] settlement or the [6] ruins of one representative of a particular culture, a place of exceptional natural beauty, or a place that is the natural [7] habitat of an [8] endangered species.

Once a site is selected for the list, the World Heritage [9] Fund can provide money to protect or [10] refurbish the site – and being on the list usually provides a significant boost to the number of tourists visiting the site.

B Choose the correct words to complete the sentences.

1 Architects have *an urge* / *a responsibility* to provide people with enough daylight.

2 People have a *reluctance* / *tendency* to be less productive if there is background noise.

3 The government needs frequent *desires* / *reminders* to tackle the problem of air pollution.

4 The government's *readiness* / *refusal* to invest in rural areas has led to overcrowding in cities.

5 Architects have *a failure* / *an obligation* to talk to the people who will use a building before they design it.

C Choose the correct words to complete the sentences.

1 Young people don't like politics because it is too *formal* / *formality*.

2 People often vote for the person with the strongest *personal* / *personality* rather than the best plans.

3 The *public* / *publicity* should have a vote on major political decisions.

4 Social media enables much easier *interactive* / *interactivity* with politicians.

5 Politicians' *personal* / *personality* lives should remain private.

6 People who don't vote have let down their *communal* / *community*.

GRAMMAR

A Complete the article with the words or phrases in the box. There are five you do not need to use.

as a matter of fact conversely despite for instance in any case moreover namely owing to whereas yet

Tourist sites go through similar stages as they grow. First of all, adventurous tourists start coming to a place. [1] Owing to this interest, local people set up businesses to cater for tourists. They open hotels and restaurants, [2] for instance. After that, larger companies start to invest in the area – [3] namely, by building large hotels and catering to large groups. The tourism industry begins to dominate the area, while, [4] conversely, other industries begin to shrink. As the number of visitors increases, the area becomes less attractive and visitors begin to go elsewhere. [5] Moreover, the facilities begin to become dated and damaged. If there is no further investment, the area will go into decline.

B Match numbers (1–6) to letters (a–f) to form full sentences.

1 It's better to give money to a charity than d

2 You should donate clothes or a

3 Some charities are really wasteful with their donations e

4 If a friend asks you to donate to a charity, c

5 Some people are really good at volunteer work, f

6 It's a good idea to choose one or two charities to support b

a volunteer your time rather than give money.

b and when you do, you can give bigger donations.

c you should do so.

d to an individual.

e and I wish they weren't.

f but I'm not.

Vocabulary and Communication Hub

Contents

Vocabulary Hub

1.1 Clothes and fashion

A Choose the correct word to complete the sentences.

1 There is a *dress code* / *uniform* at my work – for example, we aren't allowed to wear torn jeans or shorts. A uniform requires everyone to wear exactly the same clothes.
2 Many people try to copy Audrey Hepburn's style – she was a real trend *setter* / *follower*. After a trend has been set/started, people follow it.
3 The theme of the party is *Superheroes* – everybody has to wear a(n) *outfit* / *costume*. A costume is for somebody pretending to be someone else.
4 You need a new pair of pants – those are so old and *scruffy* / *casual*. Scruffy clothes may be dirty/damaged; casual clothes are comfortable.
5 People who work in fashion usually dress boldly to *fit in with* / *stand out from* the crowd. fit in = look the same/similar; stand out = look different
6 I like *baggy* / *oversized* clothes in the summer because they keep you cool. baggy = deliberately loose-fitting; oversized = too big

B Work in pairs. Look again at both options in Exercise A. What is the difference between each option? What do they have common? See Ex A for answers.

➤ Go back to page 2.

1.2 Experimenting with prefixes and suffixes

Add the correct prefix or suffix from the box to the words in bold to complete the sentences.

friendly ish prone proof re resistant savvy super

1 It doesn't matter if he dropped the camera in the pool – it's **water**__proof__ and **shock**__resistant__.
2 She's really up-to-date with new recording and video equipment. She's very **tech**__savvy__.
3 The sound quality is awful and it looks like it was made at home. It's just too **amateur**__ish__ to be taken seriously.
4 She has a lot of experience making vlogs. She has every reason to feel __super__**confident** about her abilities.
5 He's always breaking the stuff on the set. I guess he's just **accident**__prone__.
6 The themes on the show are too adult. I couldn't show my children that – it's not **family**__friendly__.
7 You've made a mess of that video. You'll have to __re__**start** it.

➤ Go back to page 8.

2.1 Describing art

Choose the correct words to complete the sentences. Then discuss the sentences with your partner. Do you agree?

1 Some people enjoy looking around galleries, but I find it very *tedious* / *unconventional*.
2 Some modern theater is incredibly *pretentious* / *groundbreaking* – it's more about making the writer feel smart than actually saying anything important.
3 Art needs to be *hilarious* / *thought-provoking*. Without a deeper meaning, it's just a pretty picture.
4 Some of the most *iconic* / *sensational* photographs can be disappointing when you see them up close.
5 When a writer uses the same idea in his or her work too many times, it feels really *repetitive* / *overrated*.

➤ Go back to page 14.

2.2 Compound adjectives

Make compound adjectives with the words in the box to complete the sentences. Use each word only once.

highly late open part self thick well world

1 I work for a company now, but, in the future, I'd like to be __self__**-employed**.
2 Traveling can introduce you to new ways of seeing the world and make you more __open__**-minded**.
3 Sandra's looking for a __part__**-time** job so she can study and work at the same time.
4 Sometimes as a writer you need to be __thick__**-skinned** – you can't take criticism personally.
5 Rob is a __highly__**-motivated** person who loves his job and wants to excel at it.
6 It's important that my job is __well__**-paid**, so I have some disposable income after I pay all my bills.
7 He is definitely a celebrity in his own country, but he isn't __world__**-famous** yet.
8 There is a __late__**-night** convenience store below our apartment that will be open.

➤ Go back to page 20.

3.1 Sustainability

Complete the text with the words in the box.

biodegradable consume emission exploitation neutral offsetting renewable

Home Articles About Contact

How to be green

[1] Renewable energy from sun, wind, rain and waves is one possible solution to the environmental problems we face today. It helps us to address the over-[2] exploitation of natural resources that are finite like minerals, oil, natural gas and coal. Some businesses and organizations aim to be carbon-[3] neutral by [4] offsetting the amount of carbon they release. There are even some zero-[5] emission buildings which actually create as much energy as they [6] consume. Also using [7] biodegradable materials, for example, in food packaging, is another important step because these materials break down naturally and cause less waste.

➤ Go back to page 26.

3.2 Verb–noun collocations

Cross out the incorrect word or phrase in each group.

1 We managed to *achieve* / *attain* / *deliver* / ~~*perform*~~ / *meet* our goals.
2 We have made *a concerted effort* / *limited progress* / *reasonable headway* / *advances in the right direction* / ~~*room for improvement*~~.
3 They performed ~~*impressively*~~ / *particularly* / *reasonably* / *relatively* / *surprisingly* poorly.
4 The statistics *demonstrated* / ~~*hindered*~~ / *displayed* / *showed* a marked imbalance.
5 We should set ~~*significant progress*~~ / *realistic goals* / *clear objectives* / *measurable targets*.
6 We have seen *little movement* / ~~*a deadline*~~ / *a new record* / *regression* / *incremental progress*.

➤ Go back to page 33.

4.2 Science and research

Choose the correct word to complete the sentences.

1 What are some examples of social *findings* / *norms* in your social group?
2 Can you *conduct* / *speculate* how most people would react if they were publicly told they had a low score on a test?
3 Do you think the study above proved the theory that the researchers *demonstrated* / *hypothesized*?
4 What did this study *conduct* / *demonstrate*?
5 Can you think of another idea for *an experiment* / *some findings* to prove the hypothesis?
6 Is it important to read the *findings* / *participants* of a study to understand the conclusions?
7 Have you ever *conducted* /*speculated* an experiment at school or college?
8 What have you *concluded* / *conducted* about embarrassment by reading the texts?

➤ Go back to page 43.

4.2 Thinking

Choose the correct options to complete the sentences.

1 While she is very smart, she just isn't very practical. She doesn't have much ***common sense*** / ***wishful thinking***.

2 I was lying on the beach when I had an amazing idea for my business – it was a ***eccentric*** / ***eureka*** moment.

3 He is very ***eccentric*** / ***absent-minded*** – he really stands out from the crowd and doesn't mind doing things in his own unique way.

4 I'd say I'm a little ***curious*** / ***absent-minded*** – for example, I left my key card at home this morning and couldn't get into my office.

5 If you make a resolution but put no effort into planning how to achieve it, then your idea is just ***wishful thinking*** / ***common sense***.

6 We need someone who can analyze and solve serious problems – in other words, ***troubleshooting*** / ***overthinking*** skills are essential for this job.

7 Lara always ***troubleshoots*** /***overthinks*** things; sometimes she should just follow her instincts.

8 Tim describes himself as ***curious*** / ***eccentric***, but I would describe him as nosy.

➤ Go back to page 44.

5.1 Competition and cooperation

A **Read the definition of *outmaneuver*. What does the prefix *out-* mean?** The prefix means 'more than' or 'better than'.

> **outmaneuver** – definition and synonyms
> VERB Pronunciation /ˌaʊtməˈnuːvə(r)/
> to defeat or gain an advantage over someone by being more smart or skillful than they are

B **Complete the sentences with the correct form of the verbs in the box.**

outdo outnumber outplay outrun outsmart outweigh

1 You'll need to be fast to outrun your rivals and win the race.

2 When we played tennis, she completely outplayed me, and I lost every game.

3 It's not perfect, but on balance, the advantages outweigh the disadvantages.

4 When I bought a new car, my neighbor didn't want to be outdone, so he bought one too!

5 I managed to outsmart my opponent by solving the clues faster.

6 In my class, women outnumber men by three to one.

➤ Go back to page 53.

5.2 Reporting verbs

Complete the second sentences with a reporting verb from the box and reported speech.

alleged boasted clarified doubted speculated

1 'The new bridge is supposed to reduce traffic congestion, but I don't think it will.'
Daniel doubted whether the new bridge would reduce traffic congestion.

2 'Sorry – I think you misunderstood me. I didn't offer to do all the work for you.'
Tania clarified that she hadn't offered to do all the work for me.

3 'Who knows? If you'd studied harder, you might have gotten a better grade.'
Max speculated that I might have gotten a better grade if I'd studied harder.

4 'I was awesome at the Take or Share game! I made over $200!'
Victoria boasted that she'd been fantastic at the Take or Share game.

5 'I can't prove it, but I know that Andy lied on his résumé to get the job.'
Michael alleged that Andy had lied on his résumé to get the job.

➤ Go back to page 55.

5.2 Motivation and manipulation

Complete the text with the correct form of the phrases in the box.

act coax go nuts inclined spur steer tap into

A day in the life of... a salesman

I wouldn't say my job involved [1] __coaxing__ people into buying things that they don't actually want. I would never convince someone to buy a faulty product or [2] __act__ against their best interests. But I totally believe in the quality of our products – they have been well-designed and [3] __tap into__ what the market really wants. My job is just to [4] __steer__ people toward the most appropriate products in our range to meet their needs. To be honest it's not difficult. The products sell themselves. Customers are [5] __going nuts__ for them. It is the quality of the product that [6] __spurs__ me on to do my job as well as I can. If the product is no good, you're not [7] __inclined__ to make the same effort to sell it.

➤ Go back to page 56.

6.1 Journeys and adventures

A Complete the sentences with a word or phrase. Use the definitions in parentheses to help you.

1 Can you think of a time that you went __off the beaten path__ (*away from frequently visited places*)?
2 How do/would you pass the time on a __long-haul__ (*long distance*) flight?
3 Do you prepare in advance before you __embark__ (*leave*) on a trip? What do you do?
4 Is there any __uncharted territory__ (*places not covered by maps*) left in the world? Where?
5 Imagine you had to camp in the __heart__ (*middle*) of a rainforest. What __provisions__ (*supplies of food, drink, equipment*) would you take with you?
6 Would you like a job that required you to be a __globetrotter__ (*frequent traveler*)? Why/Why not?

B Work in pairs. Discuss the questions in Exercise A.

➤ Go back to page 63.

6.2 Binomial expressions

Work in pairs. Complete the sentences with a binomial expression from the box.

by and large far and wide heart and soul life or death safe and sound side by side slowly but surely time after time

1 Marco Polo traveled __far and wide__ in Asia.
2 Brothers Louis and Auguste Lumière worked __side by side__ to create motion pictures.
3 Edmund Hillary and Tenzing Norgay were the first to climb Mount Everest and return __safe and sound__.
4 The American conservationist Dian Fossey won the trust of the gorillas __slowly but surely__.
5 The German physicist Albert Einstein is, __by and large__, thought to be the smartest person that ever lived.
6 Passengers on the sinking *Titanic* faced a __life or death__ situation.
7 __Time after time__, numerous climbers have tried to reach the summit of the mountain. But all have failed.
8 Van Gogh put his __heart and soul__ into his art and inventions, working tirelessly on both.

➤ Go back to page 69.

Vocabulary Hub

7.1 Feelings

Choose the correct options to complete the text.

Home Articles About Contact

The psychology of everyday life

Extreme and stressful situations can always be difficult to cope with. But it's actually how we deal with mundane, everyday tasks, that has the biggest impact on our well-being. Here are some tips on how to cope.

- Learn to control your emotions – be the calm and collected person rather than the [1]***hysterical*** / ***courageous*** / ***devastated*** one when the pressure is on.
- Try not to fire back emails when you're [2]***humble*** / ***grumpy*** / ***resilient*** – an angry message may make you feel better immediately. But, you'll be [3]***indifferent*** / ***disgusted*** / ***devastated*** when your boss fires you and you're suddenly jobless.
- If you just aren't getting anywhere with something and are [4]***frustrated*** / ***devastated*** / ***disgusted***, recognize that you may need a break or even to ask for help.
- Sometimes it's important to be [5]***courageous*** / ***humble*** / ***superior*** and take risks rather than play it safe. Bravery is something you can practice and get better at.
- Just because you are busy, don't be [6]***indifferent*** / ***hysterical*** / ***resilient*** to other people's problems – it's important to help out the people around you.
- No matter how well you think you're doing right now, try to stay [7]***humble*** / ***courageous*** / ***resilient*** about your achievements. Nothing annoys people more than a [8]***superior*** / ***disgusted*** / ***hysterical*** attitude.

➤ Go back to page 76.

7.2 Polysemy

Complete the sentences with the correct form of one of the words from page 79. You can use some words more than once.

1 It can be difficult to ___land___ a job with the right balance between intellectual challenge and not too much ___pressure___ to succeed.

2 One of the most important ___applications___ of barometers (which measure atmospheric ___pressure___) is to calculate the height at which a plane is flying.

3 There's too much ___competition___ between hundreds of people who have sent in their ___application(s)___ for the job; there should be a ___competition___ to find the successful candidate instead!

4 The pilot says he will ___land___ the plane shortly as ___conditions___ have improved.

➤ Go back to page 79.

7.2 Intensifiers

Choose the correct intensifiers to complete the advice about job interviews. What other intensifiers are used?

1 It's perfectly normal to exaggerate your achievements *remarkably* / *somewhat*, but you should never tell *noticeably* / *outright* lies.

2 If you're not *altogether* / *immensely* sure what the interviewer is asking, it's completely fine to ask for clarification.

3 *Practically* / *Radically* all interviews are highly stressful, but as long as you're extremely well-prepared, it should be *relatively* / *utterly* painless.

4 Remember that for the interviewers, it's *practically* / *exceptionally* boring to hear the same answers from every single interviewee. If you give *immensely* / *radically* different answers, you'll stand out from the crowd.

➤ Go back to page 81. Other intensifiers: perfectly, completely, highly, extremely, single

8.1 Health problems

Cross out one word in each sentence which does not make a collocation.

1 Tony fractured a(n) ~~*muscle*~~ / *arm* / *bone* when he went skiing last year.
2 Do you sell anything for a ~~*twisted*~~ / *sore* throat?
3 Some studies have claimed that *low* / ~~*slow*~~ blood pressure may be more common among athletes.
4 When I was running I may have *pulled* / ~~*dislocated*~~ / *sprained* a muscle.
5 After intense exercise your ~~*skin rash*~~ / *blood pressure* / *heart rate* is usually higher.
6 You can buy a number of products over the counter to help relieve skin ~~*fractures*~~ / *inflammation* / *rashes*.

➤ Go back to page 86.

8.2 Describing taste

Complete the sentences with words from Exercise A. More than one answer is possible for some sentences.

1 I love ___fizzy___ drinks, but I'm trying to be healthy so I usually order sparkling water at restaurants.
2 I know I should eat more citrus fruits to get my daily dose of Vitamin C, but they are just too ___acidic___ for me.
3 Presentation is so important for me – if food doesn't look ___appetizing___, I can't eat it.
4 I ate a delicious curry on the weekend, which wasn't too spicy at all – in fact, it was fairly ___mild___.
5 My dad loves blue cheese, so I get some really ___pungent___ aromas when I open the fridge sometimes.
6 I try to eat salad for lunch occasionally, but it doesn't taste like much. It's really ___bland___ unless I put some unhealthy dressing on the top.
7 I'm trying to eat healthy snacks, like carrot sticks – they're nice and ___crunchy___.

➤ Go back to page 93.

9.2 Verb + object + base form

Complete the sentences with the correct form of the verbs in parentheses.

1 The scientists observed the dolphin ___admiring___ itself in the mirror for hours. (admire)
2 Snakes' heat sensors help them ___to detect___ prey ___approaching___. (detect, approach)
3 Scientists must be seen ___to follow___ procedures very carefully. (follow)
4 Oh! You're here! I didn't notice you ___arriving___! (arrive)
5 I woke up because I could feel a spider ___crawling___ on my arm. (crawl)
6 I was made ___to wait___ for over an hour before they let me ___come___ in. (wait, come)
7 The experimenters had the participants ___sign___ a form before they could start. (sign)

➤ Go back to page 103.

9.2 Gestures and body language

Complete the sentences with the correct form of the words in the box.

beckon	fidget	glare	grin	lean	wink	nod	gaze

1 Sally was ___gazing___ across the bay, looking at nothing in particular, when the ship suddenly came into view.
2 Phillip just can't sit still in meetings – he's always ___fidgeting___.
3 James ___winked___ at Emma, so she knew he was joking.
4 'Shhh … we have to be quiet … just ___nod___ if you agree with me.'
5 The bookshelf fell over when I ___leaned___ against it.
6 Steven was so happy when he got the job that he couldn't stop ___grinning___.
7 The teacher ___beckoned___ his student over to the board.
8 Elizabeth was so angry that she just ___glared___ at them without saying a word.

➤ Go back to page 105.

10.1 Culture and heritage

Complete the text with the words in the box.

architectural endangered funding habitat heritage preserve refurbishment settlement

HOMETOWN GLORY

My hometown has a very rich history – it is where a famous treaty was signed and is close to the site of an ancient [1] ___settlement___. In fact some of ruins of the site are still standing today and are of special [2] ___architectural___ interest as they show the precise engineering methods of the Romans.

For these reasons alone, the town is a very important part of my country's national [3] ___heritage___. The nearby forests are the [4] ___habitat___ of a lot of different wildlife, including some rare species which are unfortunately now [5] ___endangered___. As such they have been designated as an area of outstanding natural beauty and are protected.

Unfortunately we don't receive a lot of [6] ___funding___ from the government to [7] ___preserve___ areas of the old town. Some of the unlisted buildings are in real need of [8] ___refurbishment___ – so please come and visit us. Tourism is a valuable source of income and helps us to keep our heritage and culture alive!

➤ Go back to page 111.

10.2 Word building

A Write the correct form of the word in parentheses to complete the sentences.

1 A good politician is someone who grew up in the ___community___ (commune) that they represent.
2 Most politicians are more interested in ___personal___ (person) success than helping the public.
3 Becoming ___active___ (act) in politics is the best way to make a difference in the world.
4 I feel ___passionately___ (passion) about politics and follow the news closely.
5 Most people's political beliefs are formed during their ___childhood___ (child) by listening to their parents.
6 Many people are ___apathetic___ (apathy) about politics, because they don't trust politicians.
7 The best politicians are those who had other careers before entering ___political___ (politics) life.
8 Local politics is often more ___effective___ (effect) at improving people's lives than national politics.

B Work in pairs. Do you agree with the sentences in Exercise A? Why/Why not?

➤ Go back to page 115.

2.2 Students A and B

Read what your answers to the quiz say about you.

ARE YOU CUT OUT FOR FAME?

MOSTLY 1S
You have a very clear vision for your future and nothing will stop you from achieving it. You welcome negative feedback as a way to improve and grow as a person. You want to be well-known, even if this won't necessarily make you rich.

MOSTLY 3S
You feel comfortable among large groups of people and don't need a lot of alone time. That being said, you would not particularly enjoy your private life being discussed online. You are fairly ambitious and would like to be respected in your field. But you also have other interests in your life which are important to you. Fame might not be for you.

MOSTLY 5S
You don't enjoy being the center of attention and value privacy. For you, work is a small part of your life, secondary to spending time with friends and family. The purpose of working is to earn money to do the things you enjoy. Fame isn't for you.

➤ Go back to page 20.

4.1 Students A and B

BRAIN TEASERS

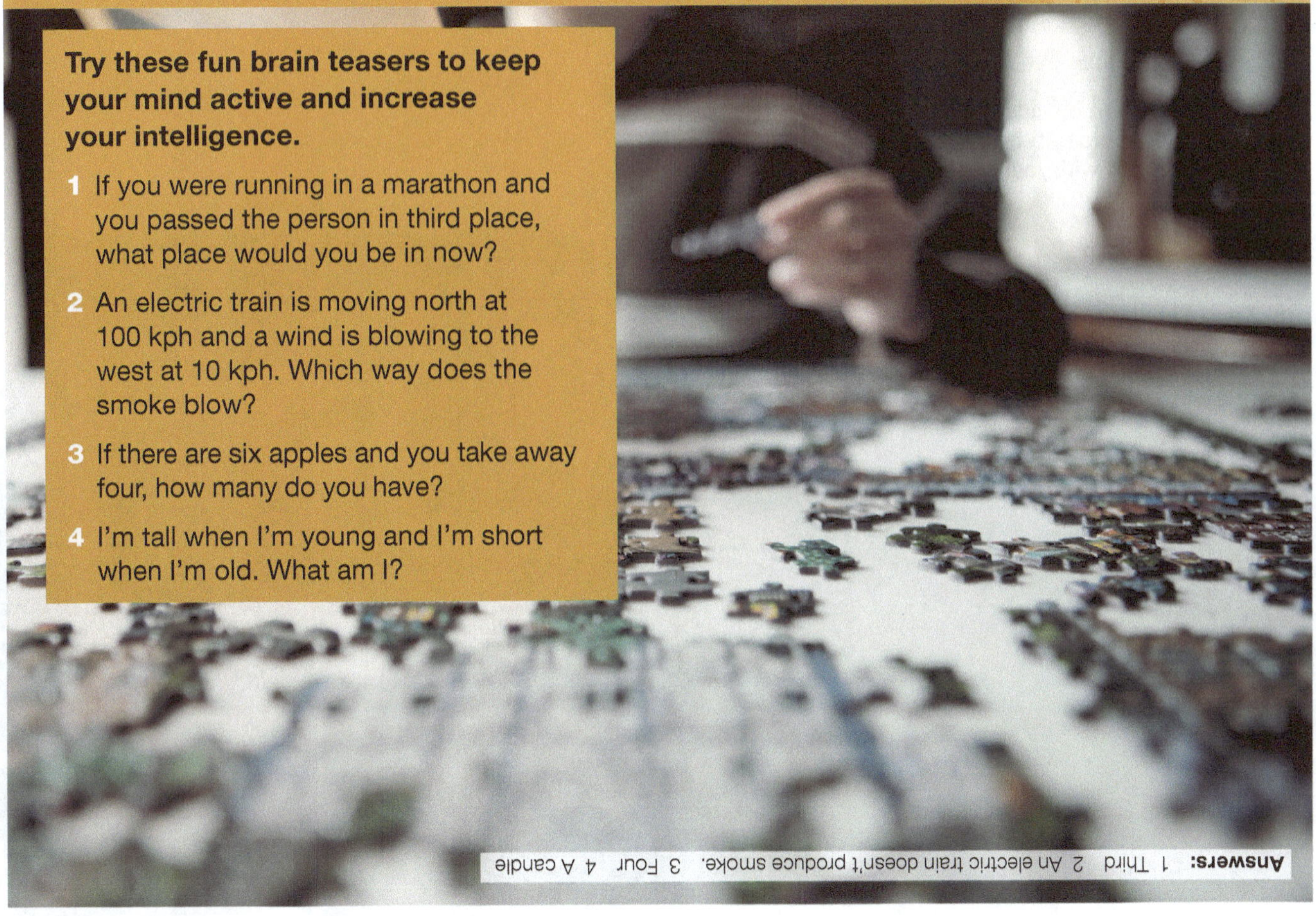

Try these fun brain teasers to keep your mind active and increase your intelligence.

1 If you were running in a marathon and you passed the person in third place, what place would you be in now?

2 An electric train is moving north at 100 kph and a wind is blowing to the west at 10 kph. Which way does the smoke blow?

3 If there are six apples and you take away four, how many do you have?

4 I'm tall when I'm young and I'm short when I'm old. What am I?

Answers: 1 Third 2 An electric train doesn't produce smoke. 3 Four 4 A candle

➤ Go back to page 38.

Communication Hub

9.2 Players

You have three minutes to get ten points, but you have to work out the rules to the game by yourselves. For example, maybe you get a point for nodding your head, for blinking your eyes or for saying a particular word (or possibly all three at the same time). Work as a team to see if you can win ten points in three minutes. Good luck!

➤ Go back to page 105.

4.1 Student A

Using your own words, explain each situation to your partner. Then decide what you would do in pairs.

Situation 1

Imagine that a company begins selling brain implants. They allow you to learn and remember information quickly. For example, some people use them to learn languages or other skills instantly. However, the implants have also caused people to lose some of their memories. Would you buy one?

Situation 2

Imagine that a company begins selling highly advanced robots. These robots will take on any tasks that you need them to do, provide companionship for people who live alone, and protect you and your house. They are also smart enough to learn and use their initiative. Would you get one of these robots?

Situation 3

Imagine that artificial intelligence is used for both medical check-ups and treatment in the future. The AI has a higher rate of accurate diagnoses than human doctors. You have the choice between a human doctor or an artificial intelligence system. Which would you pick?

➤ Go back to page 41.

4.2 Students A and B

Think of a time when you did something you regret. Use the prompts below or your own ideas. Discuss it with your partner.

- You failed a test.
- You forgot something.
- You lost something.
- You missed an appointment.
- You sent an email or message to the wrong person.
- You wore the wrong type of clothes.

➤ Go back to page 43.

5.2 Students

Work in small groups to solve the puzzles.

PUZZLE A: THE TAKE OR SHARE IT GAME

You and a stranger are both offered a choice: **TAKE or SHARE.**

If only one player chooses **TAKE**, they keep $1000.

If both players choose **SHARE**, they get $500 each.

But if both players choose **TAKE**, they get nothing.

You can't communicate with each other.

What's the best strategy if you play once?

What if you play multiple times?

PUZZLE B: THE TALENT SHOW DILEMMA

You're watching a TV talent show. The two candidates with the most votes will go through to the final. Your favorite contestant is so popular she's almost certain to win. Your second favorite contestant also deserves to be in the final. You have only one vote. Who should you vote for?

PUZZLE D: THE ROAD NETWORK

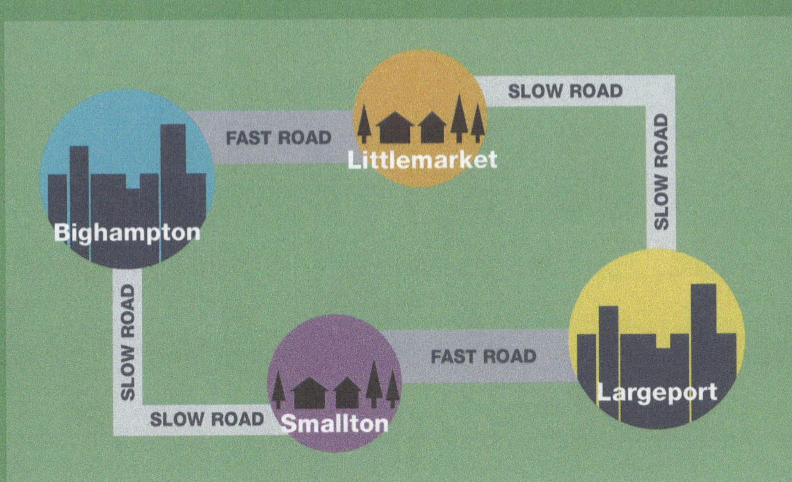

The map shows the road network between four towns. Where (if anywhere) should you build a new road to solve the towns' traffic problems?

➤ Go back to page 54.

9.1 Students

In your groups, discuss the questions.

- Experiments have shown that speaking English encourages people to be more competitive, thanks to the connotations of English-speaking countries. What effect might your own language have on its speakers?
- Unlike English, many languages have formal and informal words for *you*, so you always have to think about your relationship with the other person before speaking to them. How might that affect your behavior?
- The present perfect in English treats past events as part of the present. How might that affect English speakers' view of the past … and their behavior?

➤ Go back to page 101.

4.1 Student B

Using your own words, explain each situation to your partner. Then decide what you would do in pairs.

Situation 1

Imagine that a company begins selling body upgrades. You can use its technology to make you stronger, faster and more skillful. People can use the upgrades to fix their sight and hearing, or repair injuries. However, the new parts don't look natural, so it will be clear you have had upgrades. Would you use this service?

Situation 2

Imagine that a company begins offering a memory back-up service. You can download the memories from your brain onto its servers and then view the memories whenever you want. You can also share selected memories with others. However, you don't get to choose which memories are downloaded. Everything has to be downloaded together. Would you use this service?

Situation 3

Imagine that a highly advanced robot in the future demanded the same rights as a human. The robot argues that it is as conscious as a human being. Would you support the demands of the robot?

➤ Go back to page 41.

10.3 Student A

SPEAK Describe the following scene to your partner.

➤ Go back to page 118.

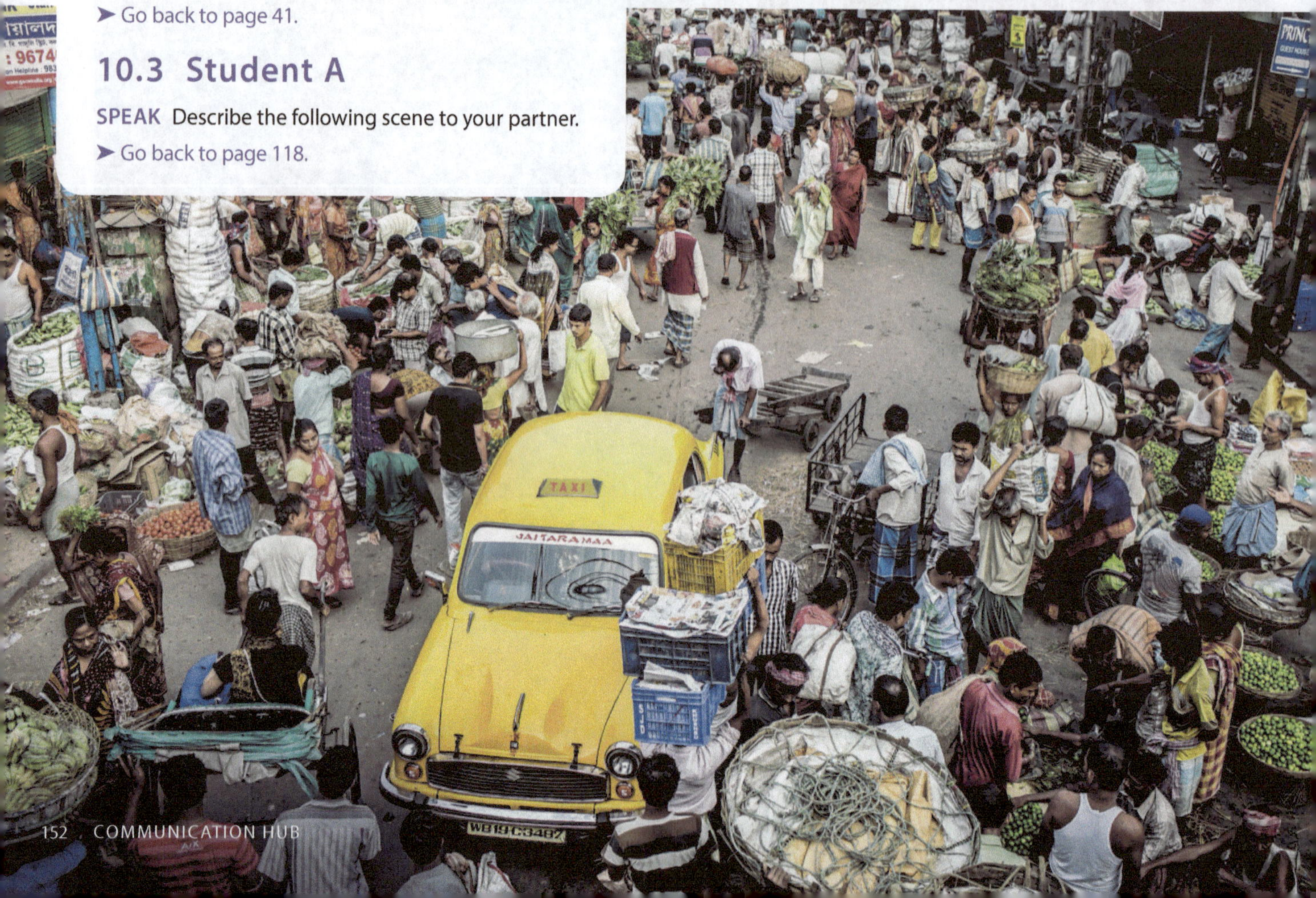

4.3 Students

Low frequency sounds, like number 1, are connected to earthy tones like browns and reds. High frequency sounds like, number 2, are connected to violet tones like blue and purple.

➤ Go back to page 46.

9.2 Facilitator

The 'game' is in fact an experiment to see if you can trick the players into behaving strangely. They think they have to 'win' points, but in fact they simply get a point at regular intervals. When the game starts, count to ten slowly and silently in your head, again and again, saying 'one point' aloud every time you reach ten. Don't let the players work out the real rules – but you can share the secret with them at the end!

➤ Go back to page 105.

6.1 Group A

Work in small groups. Read about a historical mystery. Speculate about what happened.

THE LOST COLONY OF ROANOKE

In 1585, an English settlement was established on a small island off the Eastern coast of the US. In the first year there, they began to run out of food, so the Mayor returned to England to get supplies – but it was three years before he could come back. He left behind his daughter, son-in-law and grandchild among the colonists.

When he returned, the colony and all 117 members of the colony were gone. The only thing left was a fence around the area and a newly built fort on the other side of the island. He never saw or heard from the colonists again.

The Mayor had told the settlers to carve a symbol into a tree if they had been forced to leave the area, but he only found the word CROATOAN. Croatoan was the name of a nearby island, inhabited by a tribe of indigenous people with the same name.

In recent years, some objects of European origin from that period were found at two different locations. Part of a sword was found on Croatoan Island and some pottery was found about 50 miles inland.

Despite modern efforts to solve the mystery, nothing of the actual colonists is known for sure. Several theories exist, but the quest to find out what happened continues.

➤ Go back to page 63.

4.3 Students

Both pictures are brightness illusions known as Munker's illusion. Although the shapes appear to vary in brightness, they are actually the same. It is the colors next to them that make them appear different.

➤ Go back to page 46.

3.2 Student B

Read the situation and prepare what you will say.

You're being interviewed for a radio program about progress. You feel that while there have been a lot of advances, overall life in the modern world is getting worse. You can think about the following points or use your own ideas to prepare:

- the impact of technology
- community
- quality of life
- cost of living
- employment
- the environment

Complain to the interviewer about how life is getting worse in the modern world.

➤ Go back to page 31.

6.3 Students

Underline examples of summarizing, repetition and dynamic words in the transcript.

Hydrogen atoms, carbon atoms, oxygen and sulphur atoms – these basic building blocks react and combine to make everything.

A forest is a complex place – there are oak trees and grass and mosses and ferns, and countless animals and plants all living together in a tangled ecosystem. But there's a simpler level of description – everything is made of atoms. So an oak tree is really just carbon, nitrogen, oxygen and hydrogen and a few other things mixed together. So, when you look at it like that, it's really not that complicated at all. *(Repetition; Summarizing)*

The atoms that make up this forest have been on an extraordinary journey to get here. Think of a carbon atom in this acorn. It was assembled in the heart of a star billions of years ago out of protons that were built just after the Big Bang. It got thrown out into the universe in a supernova explosion, collapsed as part of a dust cloud to form the sun and then the earth four and a half billion years ago. *(Dynamic words)*

It will have spent a lot of time in rocks. It was probably part of some of the first living things on Earth. It would have been breathed out as carbon dioxide by someone that walked through this forest 400 years ago. It will have entered into some ancient oak tree through the action of photosynthesis constructed into this acorn and fallen down to the ground. And there it is. It's got a history that goes back billions of years. In fact, a history in terms of the building blocks of carbon, the protons, that goes back right to the origin of the universe. And in billions of years time when the sun dies and the Earth is vaporized they'll be thrown back out into space and probably condensed into a new world billions of years in the future. *(Repetition; Repetition; Dynamic words)*

So life is just a temporary home for the immortal elements that build up the universe. *(Summarizing)*

➤ Go back to page 70.

10.3 Student B

SPEAK Describe the following scene to your partner.

➤ Go back to page 118.

6.1 Group B

Work in small groups. Read about a historical mystery. Speculate about what happened.

THE NAZCA LINES

Approximately 2,000 years ago, people living in southern Peru drew pictures of shapes and animals into the dry desert landscape by removing red rocks to reveal the white sand below.

Some of the pictures are as large as the Empire State Building, but when seen from above are very accurate. How did the people draw the pictures without being able to see them from above? And since the pictures are not visible from the ground, who was supposed to see them?

One scientist found that one of the lines pointed directly to the sun during the winter solstice.

Another scientist believes the drawings were used to mark the location of underground rivers and wells.

One image is of a spider, but this species of spider is not found in this area. It comes from the Amazon, over 900 miles away.

➤ Go back to page 63.

1.1 Vocabulary

Clothes and fashion

Student A

A Write your ideas about the following topics.

1 The uniform you most like the look of. ______________

2 A trend you regret following when you were younger. ______________

3 A situation where it is OK to wear scruffy clothes. ______________

4 An outfit you wore for a special occasion. ______________

5 A time you really wanted to fit in. ______________

6 How you feel about wearing oversized clothes. ______________

B Swap your responses with Student B. Ask each other questions to find out more information.

C Share the most interesting piece of information you found out about your partner with the class.

Student B

A Write your ideas about the following topics.

1 A costume you have worn, or would wear, to a party. ______________

2 A time when it's good to stand out from the crowd. ______________

3 A trendsetter whose style you admire. ______________

4 Somewhere where there is a dress code. ______________

5 What you associate baggy clothes with. ______________

6 A situation where casual clothes aren't appropriate. ______________

B Swap your responses with Student A. Ask each other questions to find out more information.

C Share the most interesting piece of information you found out about your partner with the class.

American Language Hub Level 5 Teacher's Book.
Published by Macmillan Education Limited. © Macmillan Education Limited, 2020. This page may be photocopied and used within the class.

Nominal clauses

A Put the words in the correct order to make sentences.

1 they are / a lot / someone / the kind of person / about / how / tells you / dresses / .

____

____

2 available / of / the experience / should be / to everyone / looking good / .

____

____

3 that / you look / the idea / isn't important / how / is ridiculous / .

____

____

4 weak person / and trends / following / is a sign / fashion / of a / .

____

5 in developing / bad for / cheap clothes / making / countries is / the environment / immoral and / .

____

6 people buy / that / extremely worrying / the fact / cheaply produced / clothes is / so many / .

____

B Get into groups of four and divide into pairs. Decide who will be pair A or B and then follow the instructions below.

Pair A: Think of reasons to agree with sentences 1–3 and to disagree with sentences 4–6 in Exercise A.

Pair B: Think of reasons to disagree with sentences 1–3 and to agree with sentences 4–6 in Exercise A.

C Work with someone from the other pair and try to persuade them to agree with you.

D Complete the sentences below with your own ideas.

1 How someone ____________ tells you a lot about the kind of person they are.

2 The experience of ____________ should be available to everyone.

3 The idea that ____________ is ridiculous.

4 ____________ is a sign of a weak person.

5 ____________ is bad for the environment.

6 The fact that ____________ is extremely worrying.

E Compare your sentences in Exercise D with a partner. Do you agree with each other?

Published by Macmillan Education Limited. © Macmillan Education Limited, 2020. This page may be photocopied and used within the class.

Metaphors

a

b

c

d

e

f

g

h

A Match the following metaphors (1–8) to the literal meaning pictures (a–h).

1 a breeze ___

2 buy something for peanuts ___

3 catch someone's eye ___

4 get wound up ___

5 off-the-shelf ___

6 a tight budget ___

7 tailor-made ___

8 throw money down the drain ___

B Work in pairs. Discuss the meaning of the metaphors in Exercise A. Which of the metaphors would be appropriate in the following situations? How exactly could you use them?

1 You want to renovate your house, but you don't have much money to spend.

2 Your friend has bought something you know they could have gotten cheaper elsewhere.

3 You were worried about an exam, but it turned out to be really easy.

4 You went on a tour with a guide who planned the tour especially for you.

5 You weren't planning to buy something, but you noticed it as you went past a store.

6 You bought something for a price you think is incredibly low.

7 You see a box of sneakers that looks exactly the same as others you have seen before.

8 You're really annoyed about the behavior of someone you live with.

C Work with a different partner. Discuss whether you have experienced any of the situations in Exercise B. If so, give details.

Published by Macmillan Education Limited. © Macmillan Education Limited, 2020. This page may be photocopied and used within the class.

1.2 Grammar

Comparatives and superlatives

A GROUP A Think of ideas to support the following opinions.

- The 80s was the best decade for fashion.
- Cassettes are the best way to listen to music.
- The most important app to have is (*your idea*).

Use the phrases below to explain and justify your statements.

twice as … as … by far the best … a great deal more than …

B Get into a new group, with someone from Groups B and C.

A GROUP B Think of ideas to support the following opinions.

- The 90s was the best decade for fashion.
- CDs are the best way to listen to music.
- The most important app to have is (*your idea*).

Use the phrases below to explain and justify your statements.

every bit as … as … our very best … considerably more than …

B Get into a new group, with someone from Groups A and C. Discuss the opinions and try to persuade the other members of your group to agree with you.

A GROUP C Think of ideas to support the following opinions.

- The 2000s was the best decade for fashion.
- Vinyl is the best way to listen to music.
- The most important app to have is (*your idea*).

Use the phrases below to explain and justify your statements.

easily as … as … far and away the best … the more you …, the more you …

B Get into a new group, with someone from Groups A and B. Discuss the opinions and try to persuade the other members of your group to agree with you.

Published by Macmillan Education Limited. © Macmillan Education Limited, 2020. This page may be photocopied and used within the class.

Experimenting with prefixes and suffixes

1

re
super
ish
prone
savvy
proof
friendly
y

2

amateur
lucky
trash
tech
think
disaster
water
user
media
child
idiot
start
cheese
confident
accident
environmentally

A Match each prefix or suffix in circle 1 to two words in circle 2 to make 16 words or phrases.

B Use one of the words or phrases from Exercise A to complete questions 1–8.

1 Are there any ________________ habits you've grown out of? If so, what?

2 Who's the most ________________ person you know? What has happened to them?

3 Have you ever felt ________________ before an exam, an interview, a game or a competition? Was it justified?

4 Is there an area of your life that needs a________________? Why isn't it working right now?

5 How important is it for young people to be ________________ these days? Does it damage their life chances if they aren't?

6 How ________________ is your country? Is there anything more that can be done to make it more so?

7 Are you a fan of ________________ music or do you prefer something more serious?

8 What's the most ________________ gadget you own? Is it simple enough for anyone to use it?

C Ask three different classmates each question in Exercise B. Write a note about their answers in the grid below each question.

D Compare your results with a partner and discuss who in the class you have most in common with.

Published by Macmillan Education Limited. © Macmillan Education Limited, 2020. This page may be photocopied and used within the class.

Describing art

A Complete the table with adjectives from the box which you would most associate with that art form.

acclaimed appalling awesome groundbreaking hilarious iconic overrated pretentious repetitive sensational tedious thought-provoking unconventional underrated

Painting/Sculpture	Movie	Book	Song

B Work in pairs. Compare your answers to Exercise A. Give reasons for your answers.

C Complete the sentences with one of the adjectives from Exercise A. Use the definitions in parentheses to help you.

1 It's really ______________ (*makes you think*). It changed the way I see things.

2 I left half way through because it was so ______________ (*not interesting at all*).

3 The critics liked it but I just thought it was ______________ (*trying to be more clever than it really is*).

4 Hardly anyone I know has heard of it, and those that have don't like it. I think it's great and totally ______________ (*not valued as highly as it should be*).

5 It's not for everyone. It's fairly ______________ (*not typical*).

6 It's really ______________ (*famous and popular*). It's one of the first things people mention when I tell them where I'm from.

7 Some people complain that it's ______________ (*the same thing again and again*). But that's why I like it.

8 It was really ______________ (*original and influential*). So much that came after was inspired by it.

D Think of an example which is true for you for each sentence in Exercise C.

E Work in groups and discuss your choices from Exercise D.

Published by Macmillan Education Limited. © Macmillan Education Limited, 2020. This page may be photocopied and used within the class.

2.1 Grammar

Narrative tenses

A Complete the sentences with the correct form of the verbs in parentheses.

1 They ______________ (*planning*) the project for years before they finally got started.

2 Luca was devastated when his computer broke and he realized all his work ______________ (*lose*).

3 She came up with the idea while she ______________ (*try*) to solve a completely different problem.

4 I ______________ (*never consider*) myself a creative person until I started painting.

5 Sam ______________ (*never teach*) how to play the piano. He just picked it up.

6 Beth ______________ (*always want*) to have a creative job, so it was a dream come true when she got one.

7 I ______________ (*only work*) for the company for a few weeks when I had my biggest success.

8 So much progress ______________ (*make*) in art and design during the 20th century.

B Work in pairs. Complete the following sentences with guesses about your partner.

- You were really embarrassed once because …
- You were really annoyed once because …
- You couldn't sleep once because …
- You had a falling out with someone once because …
- You were very lucky once because …

C Read your sentences to your partner and find out how many are true. If the sentence is true, ask for more information. If it is not true, ask if your partner has had the experience for a different reason.

American Language Hub Level 5 Teacher's Book.
Published by Macmillan Education Limited. © Macmillan Education Limited, 2020. This page may be photocopied and used within the class.

2.2 Vocabulary

Ideas and inspiration

A Match the halves to complete the phrases.

1	get into	**a**	a wall
2	run	**b**	ideas off someone
3	work	**c**	the right state of mind
4	bounce	**d**	yourself in something
5	draw	**e**	your instincts
6	jump	**f**	with an idea
7	immerse	**g**	a fresh perspective on something
8	get	**h**	start your creativity
9	hit	**i**	inspiration from something or someone
10	trust	**j**	from a blank canvas

B Complete the text below with the correct form of phrases from Exercise A.

Miguel had been trying to get started on a new project, but he just couldn't [1] ____________ and he'd [2] ____________. Since he frequently [3] ____________ his friends, he decided to talk to someone else to [4] ____________, and it's always good to have someone to [5] ____________. Since he'd started with nothing, he was [6] ____________, but he [7] ____________ and [8] ____________ whatever ideas came to him.

C Work in groups and tell each other about:

- someone you bounce ideas off
- something that helps you get a fresh perspective on things
- someone or something you draw inspiration from
- a time when you trusted your instincts
- something you enjoy immersing yourself in

Published by Macmillan Education Limited. © Macmillan Education Limited, 2020. This page may be photocopied and used within the class.

Compound adjectives

A Form compound adjectives from boxes a and b to complete the definitions 1–8.

a highly late open part self thick well world

b employed famous minded motivated night paid skinned time

1 A ________________ store doesn't close early.

2 Someone who really wants to succeed is ________________.

3 Someone or something that is known everywhere is ________________.

4 Someone who works for themselves is ________________.

5 Someone with a very high salary is ________________.

6 Someone who doesn't get offended or upset easily is ________________.

7 Someone who only works a few hours a day or a few days a week is ________________.

8 Someone who welcomes new ideas is ________________.

B Rank the following statements from 1 to 5 according to how much you agree with them (1 = strongly disagree, 5 = strongly agree).

- I'd love to be self-employed.
- I'd work part time if I could.
- It's very important for me to have a well-paid job.
- I'm highly motivated in everything I do.
- Most people in my country are fairly open-minded.
- There are plenty of late-night facilities where I live.
- You need to be thick-skinned to be successful in life.
- World-famous brands aren't necessarily the best.

C Work in pairs. Compare and give reasons for your answers in Exercise B. How similar are you?

American Language Hub Level 5 Teacher's Book.
Published by Macmillan Education Limited. © Macmillan Education Limited, 2020. This page may be photocopied and used within the class.

Future in the past

Student A

A Write an explanation for each of the situations below in three sentences. Do not use any of the words given in the bullet points. Use the sentence prompts in the *Useful phrases* box to help you.

- You lost your job.
- You had a lucky escape.
- You spent all your money.
- You took up a new hobby.

Useful phrases

I was about to …
I was going to …
I didn't think I'd have time to …
I was supposed to …
I knew I wouldn't be able to …
I decided I would … instead

B Work in pairs. Read your sentences to your partner. Can they guess the situation?

Student B

A Write an explanation for each of the situations below in three sentences. Do not use any of the words given in the bullet points. Use the sentence prompts in the *Useful phrases* box to help you.

- Your car broke down.
- You changed careers.
- You had an argument with a friend.
- You won a prize.

Useful phrases

I was about to …
I was going to …
I didn't think I'd have time to …
I was supposed to …
I knew I wouldn't be able to …
I decided I would … instead

B Work in pairs. Read your sentences to your partner. Can they guess the situation?

Published by Macmillan Education Limited. © Macmillan Education Limited, 2020. This page may be photocopied and used within the class.

Sustainability

A Reorder the letters in bold to make words.

Can you think of:

1 a **roze-monisesi** method of transportation?

2 a **gloabeadierdb** material?

3 a natural resource which is **rove-opetildex**?

4 a **webarelen** source of energy?

5 a **nisulabaste** method of food production?

6 a consequence of the **potinedel** of the ozone layer?

7 an everyday activity that is **flurham** to the environment?

8 something you can do to attempt to be **bronac-turnale**?

9 something you can do to **festof** the pollution caused by tourism?

10 a way to prevent plastic from **migucalanuct** in the environment?

B Work in pairs. Discuss the questions in Exercise A.

C Work in groups and choose the three best ideas on how to make where you live more environmentally friendly. Prepare to present these ideas to the class.

D Present your ideas and listen to the other group's presentations. Whose presentation was the best? Why?

American Language Hub Level 5 Teacher's Book.
Published by Macmillan Education Limited. © Macmillan Education Limited, 2020. This page may be photocopied and used within the class.

3.1 Grammar

Future structures

A Decide if the sentences are grammatically correct or incorrect. Rewrite the incorrect ones.

1 I hope I'll have been retiring by the time I'm 60.

2 I expect I'll be living in the same place ten years from now.

3 By the end of this year, I'll be studying English for ten years.

4 We can't save the planet unless we dramatically change our lifestyles.

5 We could have discovered life on other planets by the end of this century.

6 People might only have driven electric cars by 2030.

7 We are on the verge of become a cashless society.

8 Before long, it will be impossible to get on in life if you couldn't speak English.

B Work in pairs. Compare your answers to Exercise A.

C Discuss with your partner whether you agree or disagree with the sentences in Exercise A.

Published by Macmillan Education Limited. © Macmillan Education Limited, 2020. This page may be photocopied and used within the class.

Forming verbs from adjectives

A Work in pairs. Explain one of the verbs below to your partner. Do not use the verb or the adjective it comes from in your explanation.

broaden ensure strengthen SOLIDIFY equalize visualize purify enlarge tighten enable deepen formalize shorten simplify

B Complete the sentences with the correct form of a verb from Exercise A.

1 Do you agree that travel ____________ the mind? How?

2 Have you ever had to ____________ your budget? Why?

3 Do you find it easy to ____________ your future self?

4 What can you do to ____________ your understanding of a country or culture?

5 What's the best way to ____________ a business is successful?

6 What does technology ____________ you to do that you couldn't do five years ago?

7 What's the best way to ____________ your everyday life so that it is less complicated?

8 Is there an event that you think should be ____________ by a few hours or days?

C Discuss the questions with your partner.

American Language Hub Level 5 Teacher's Book.
Published by Macmillan Education Limited. © Macmillan Education Limited, 2020. This page may be photocopied and used within the class.

3.2 Grammar

Negative inversion

A **Rewrite the sentences so that they have the same meaning to the first.**

1 She'd never kill a wild animal.

Never in a million years ______________________________.

2 I've never been in a helicopter, and I don't know anyone who has.

No one I know ______________________________,

and neither ______________________________.

3 Sam plays the piano and speaks fluent Italian.

Not only ______________________________.

4 I don't think I'd ever be able to do a skydive.

No way ______________________________.

5 Blanca really doesn't think hitchhiking is a good idea.

By no means ______________________________.

B **Complete the following sentences so that three are true and two are false.**

- Never in a million years would I ______________.
- No one I know has ever ______________, and neither have I.
- Not only do I ______________, but I also ______________.
- No way could I ever ______________.
- By no means do I think ______________.

C **Work in pairs. Read your sentences in Exercise B to your partner and listen to theirs. Ask questions to find out more information, then guess which sentences are true and which are false.**

Published by Macmillan Education Limited. © Macmillan Education Limited, 2020. This page may be photocopied and used within the class.

Verb–noun collocations

A Match the nouns/noun phrases with the verbs in the table to form collocations.

a concerted effort advances in the right direction benefits home measurable targets more harm than good realistic goals shape the initiative the myth the opportunity the stereotype the time your best

Bring	Do	Make	Take

Seize	Set	Perpetuate

B Complete the text with collocations from Exercise A, using the verb in the correct form.

I've spent a long time thinking about my future, and my plans are finally starting to 1________________. I graduated last year, and I don't want to 2________________ that young people are lazy, so I've been 3________________ to find the right next step for me. I'm still living at home, and I think it's important to be able to 4________________ a salary to help contribute.

I also want to be ready to 5________________ when the right job comes up.

I want a job that will 6________________ not only to me but also to the whole community, and it's important to have some training, as without it I could end up 7________________. It might 8________________, but that's OK as I'm not in a hurry.

C Work in pairs. What job do you think the person in Exercise B should do?

D Work in groups. Roll two dice. Talk about the topic (1–12) that matches the number you roll for one minute. Use as many of the collocations from Exercise A as you can.

Topics

1 sports
2 crime
3 the economy
4 the weather
5 clothes and fashion
6 public transportation
7 health
8 food
9 art and literature
10 science and technology
11 music
12 movies

American Language Hub Level 5 Teacher's Book.
Published by Macmillan Education Limited. © Macmillan Education Limited, 2020. This page may be photocopied and used within the class.

4.1 Vocabulary

Conceptual metaphors

A Choose a shape at random and write the following in each one.

- something in the future you would like to invest time in
- a time you had to defend your position
- someone you know who has a fiery temper
- an issue you think a lot of people are in the dark about
- something you think is a waste of time
- a good strategy for expanding your vocabulary
- what you do when you need to cool down
- a person you used to know who was hot-tempered
- someone you know who is very bright
- what you spend most of your free time doing
- something you would like an expert to shed some light on
- someone whose arguments you'd like to shoot down

FOLD

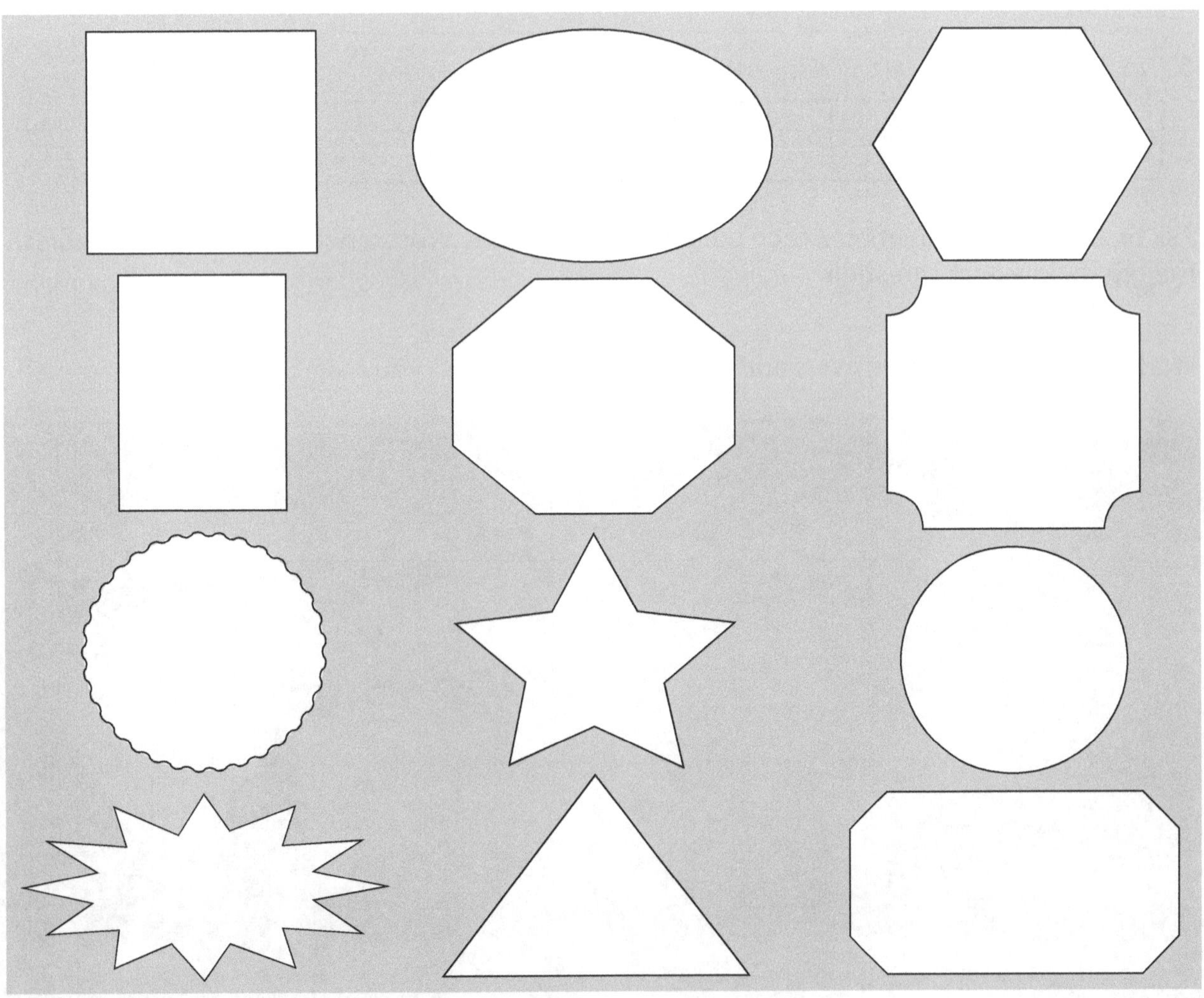

B Fold your page and swap sheets with your partner. Ask them the reason(s) why they wrote what they did in each shape. Ask further questions to find out more information.

American Language Hub Level 5 Teacher's Book.
Published by Macmillan Education Limited. © Macmillan Education Limited, 2020. This page may be photocopied and used within the class.

Conditionals without *if*

A Find and correct the mistake in each question (1–6) by deleting or changing one word.

1 Supposed money was no object, where would you go on your next vacation?

2 Should there to be an election tomorrow, do you know how you would vote?

3 Were you been born in a different country, how would your life be different?

4 Were you an animal, what animal would you like to be?

5 Imagining time travel became possible, what era would you like to visit?

6 Would your safety guaranteed, what dangerous activity would you most like to try?

B Ask three different classmates each question in Exercise A. Write a note about their answers in the grid below each question.

C Work in pairs. Compare answers and discuss who in the class you have most in common with.

Published by Macmillan Education Limited. © Macmillan Education Limited, 2020. This page may be photocopied and used within the class.

Science and research

A Reorder the letters in bold to make words that complete the sentences.

1 We decided to **nudtocc** an **retemexinp**.

2 Mark found a group of **tinpascripat**.

3 They wanted to test a social **ormn**.

4 She **hostezdhipye** and **dlutacesep** beforehand.

5 Unfortunately, the **gisnindf** didn't **totemedsran** what I had hoped.

6 Julia didn't manage to **lecnudco** anything.

B Complete the text with the correct form of words from Exercise A.

Maria has always loved science, probably because she's a very curious person and she's always [1]__________ and [2]__________ about the world around her. Whenever she reads about a new [3]__________ being [4]__________ that they need [5]__________ for, she always volunteers as she'd love to be able to help in a new discovery. In the last one she was involved in, the [6]__________ seemed to [7]__________ something amazing, although more research is needed before they're able to [8]__________ anything definitively.

C Work in groups. Discuss the hypotheses below about social norms. Do you agree or disagree with them? How might you test them?

- People feel uncomfortable if you shake hands and maintain eye contact for more than three seconds.
- People hate it when someone cuts in line, but when they do it themselves, they always think there's a good reason.
- People don't like it if you sit next to them on public transportation or in a movie theater when there are other seats free farther away.
- If you're next to the doors in an elevator, it's weird to stand facing inward toward the other people.
- Everybody loves talking about how much they're afraid of clowns.

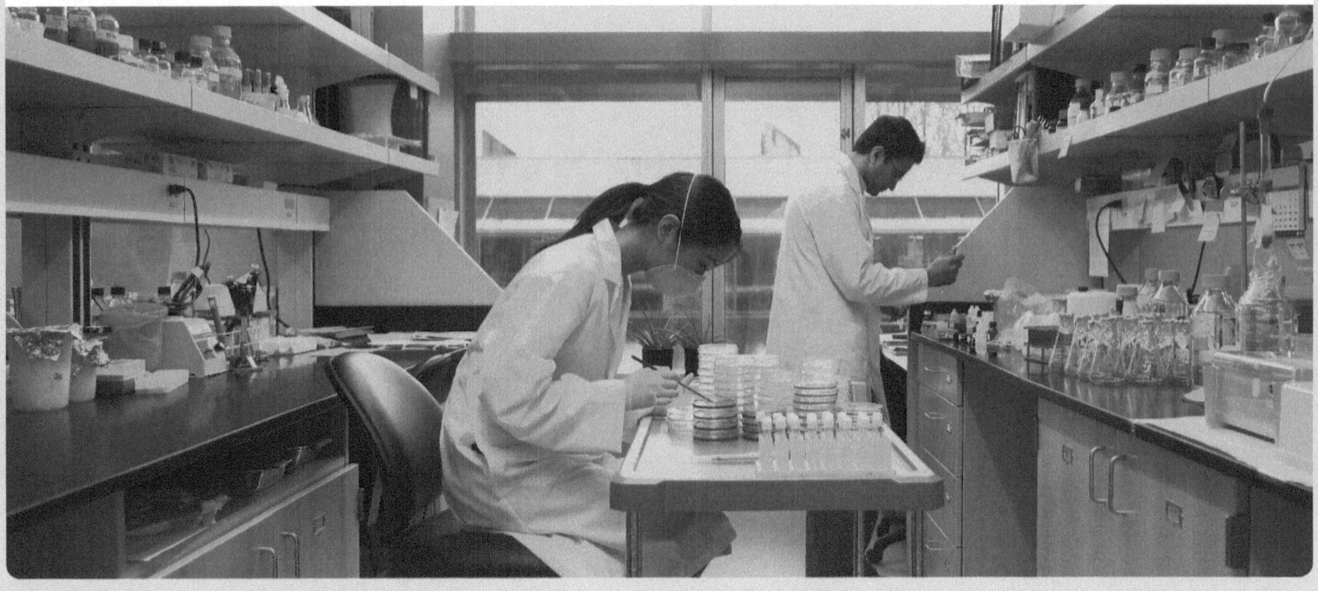

Published by Macmillan Education Limited. © Macmillan Education Limited, 2020. This page may be photocopied and used within the class.

4.2 Grammar

Wishes and regrets

A Rewrite the sentences so that they have the same meaning to the first.

1 I'm not as tall as I'd like to be.

I wish ______________________________.

2 It was a big mistake to ignore that message.

If only ______________________________.

3 The problem was that I wasn't paying attention when she was explaining how to do it.

I should ______________________________.

4 I think my life would be better if I'd studied something different.

I'd prefer ______________________________.

5 I regret not doing more research before agreeing to do this.

I wish ______________________________.

6 It's a real shame I can't swim.

If only ______________________________.

7 It was my fault that I didn't get the job. I wasn't well enough prepared for the interview.

I should ______________________________.

8 It's a pity I didn't start learning English when I was much younger.

I'd love ______________________________.

B Work in small groups. Discuss whether you have any of the same wishes and regrets mentioned in Exercise A.

C Work in pairs. Imagine the things below have happened to you. Write sentences about what you wish or regret. Read your sentences to your partner. Can they guess what has happened?

- You've lost your job.

  If only I hadn't been rude to my boss.
- You've fallen out with a good friend.
- You've broken something expensive.
- You've burned your dinner.
- You've spent a lot of money on an outfit you don't like.
- You've missed your flight.
- You've lost a book you borrowed from a friend.
- You've had a terrible haircut.
- You're lost.
- You have food poisoning.

American Language Hub Level 5 Teacher's Book.
Published by Macmillan Education Limited. © Macmillan Education Limited, 2020. This page may be photocopied and used within the class.

4.2 Vocabulary

Thinking

A Complete the sentences with one of the words or phrases in the box.

absent-minded	common sense	curious	overthink

1 Are you ________________ about other countries or cultures? If so, which ones?

2 Do you consider yourself to be ________________? If so, what kinds of things do you forget? If not, do you know someone who is?

3 Do you tend to ________________ things? If so, what things? If not, how do you manage not to?

4 Do you rely on your ________________ when making important decisions?

eccentric	eureka moment	troubleshoot	wishful thinking

5 Who is your most ________________ relative? Why?

6 When did you last have a ________________? What about?

7 Do you think the idea that the world will be a better place in ten years is just ________________? Why/Why not?

8 Are you able to ________________ technical problems easily? If so, how did you learn to do this? If not, who do you ask for help?

B Work in groups. Discuss the questions in Exercise A. Who do you have most in common with?

Published by Macmillan Education Limited. © Macmillan Education Limited, 2020. This page may be photocopied and used within the class.

5.1 Grammar

The passive voice

A Complete the sentences with the correct passive voice form of the verb in parentheses.

Find someone who:

1 hates ______________ ______________ (*correct*).

2 is expecting ______________ ______________ ______________ (*give*) a prize or an award soon.

3 has ______________ a professional photo ______________ (*take*) or portrait ______________ (*paint*).

4 has ______________ their bag ______________ (*steal*).

5 has ______________ ______________ (*ban*) or ______________ (*block*) on social media.

6 has been ______________ (*make*) ______________ ______________ (*eat*) something horrible.

7 thinks they should have ______________ ______________ (*teach*) something better.

8 thinks they ______________ ______________ ______________ (*underpaid*).

B Find someone who matches with each sentence in Exercise A.

C Share the most interesting thing you found out with the class.

5.1 Vocabulary

Competition and cooperation

Work in groups of three. Choose one of the words in your list below, but do not say what it is. Explain the word to the others in your group.

If their first guess is correct, they get five points. If their second guess is correct, they get four points and so on.

For the second word, the first guess is worth four points. For the third word, the first guess is worth three points, etc.

Student A	Student B	Student C
opponents	rivals	allies
collaborate	cooperate	coordinate
outplay	outsmart	outdo
outmaneuver	outnumber	outweigh
overcome	prevail	outrun

American Language Hub Level 5 Teacher's Book.
Published by Macmillan Education Limited. © Macmillan Education Limited, 2020. This page may be photocopied and used within the class.

Reporting verbs

A **Choose the correct alternative to complete each question.**

1 Is there anything you would ***urge / assert*** visitors to your country to do or not to do?

2 Are you the kind of person who ***instructs / boasts*** about your achievements? Why/Why not?

3 Do you ***allege / acknowledge*** any flaws in your character? If so, what are they?

4 Do you find it easy to ***imply / clarify*** complicated ideas? If so, how?

5 Is there anything you ***speculate / doubt*** will happen, even though it should?

6 Do you think it's more effective to be direct, or to ***instruct / imply*** something, when you want to persuade or convince someone to do something?

7 Do you know any politicians or celebrities who are ***alleged / speculated*** to have done something wrong? Who? What?

8 From your experience, what do you ***conclude / clarify*** is the best way to support or motivate classmates or team members?

B **Discuss the questions with a partner.**

C **Change partners and tell them what your previous partner said.**

Published by Macmillan Education Limited. © Macmillan Education Limited, 2020. This page may be photocopied and used within the class.

5.2 Grammar

Passive voice reporting structures

A **Complete the sentences below about your classmates, without asking anyone to check if they are true.**

- ______________ is rumored to have ______________.
- ______________ is expected to ______________.
- ______________ is assumed to be ______________.
- ______________ is known to like ______________.
- ______________ is understood to be ______________.
- ______________ is considered to be ______________.
- ______________ is thought to have ______________.
- ______________ can be assumed to have been ______________.

B **Speak to the people you have written about and check if your sentences are true.**

5.2 Vocabulary

Motivation and manipulation

a act   be inclined   coax   go nuts   spur   steer   tap

b against   for   into   into   on   to   toward

A **Complete the questions with a verb/verb phrase from box a and a preposition from box b. Use the correct form of the verb.**

1 What are young people ______________ these days?

2 What can cause someone to ______________ their own best interests, even when they know it's a bad idea?

3 What popular movements have advertisers or politicians tried to ______________ in order to influence people?

4 What ______________ you ______________ when you are lacking motivation?

5 What characteristics or behavior can someone adapt to make people ______________ believe or agree with them?

6 What tactics do stores employ to ______________ people ______________ buying certain products?

7 Would it be difficult to ______________ you ______________ doing karaoke?

B **Work in pairs. Discuss the questions in Exercise A.**

Published by Macmillan Education Limited. © Macmillan Education Limited, 2020. This page may be photocopied and used within the class.

6.1 Vocabulary

Journeys and adventures

offthebeatenpathlong-haulembarkonintheheartofglobetrottersprovisionsimpenetrableunchartedterritory

A Complete the questions below using the words in the word snake above.

1 Do you admire ________________ or do you think they're irresponsible? Would you like to be one, or are you happier at home?

2 Are there any more environmentally friendly ways to travel the world than ________________ flights? Have you tried any of them? If not, would you?

3 Are any parts of your country ________________? Why is it so difficult to go there?

4 What ________________ would you always take with you on a long journey?

5 What little known place in your country would you recommend for someone who likes to go ________________?

6 Do you like to stay ________________ of a city, or do you prefer somewhere quieter?

7 Are you comfortable going into ________________ or do you prefer more familiar places or activities?

8 Do you think you will ________________ a new project or career in the near future?

B Ask three different classmates each question in Exercise A. Write a note of their answers in the grid below each question.

C Compare your findings from Exercise B with a partner and discuss who in the class you have most in common with.

Published by Macmillan Education Limited. © Macmillan Education Limited, 2020. This page may be photocopied and used within the class.

Past modals for speculation and deduction

A Work in pairs. Complete the sentences to explain each situation in bold.

1 **Your friends are coming to visit you at your new house, but they're half an hour late. They've never been to the area before.**

They may well ______________________________.

2 **You can't find your phone. You've looked everywhere for it. The last time you had it, you were in a taxi.**

______________________________ in the taxi.

3 **You saw your friend on the street and yelled to him, but he ignored you.**

He couldn't ______________________________.

4 **You sent a message to your friend last night suggesting you go out. She didn't reply and when you tried to call her, she didn't answer.**

She can't ______________________________.

5 **A colleague hasn't come to work today. It was his birthday yesterday.**

He ______________________________.

B Write a situation that could be explained by the sentences.

1 ______________________________

She can't have been paying attention.

2 ______________________________

There's a distinct possibility that he cheated.

3 ______________________________

It could have been a genuine mistake.

C Read your situations to your partner. Can they explain them? Give further information to help if necessary.

American Language Hub Level 5 Teacher's Book.
Published by Macmillan Education Limited. © Macmillan Education Limited, 2020. This page may be photocopied and used within the class.

Three-part phrasal verbs

A Match a word from each column (a, b and c) to make three-part phrasal verbs.

a	b	c
be	up	from
get	up	from
get	up	on
come	out	on
look	off	for
find	away	to
switch	back	about
brush	around	against

B Complete the sentences with the correct form of a phrasal verb from Exercise A.

1 Lara was feeling stressed at work and decided she needed to ______________ it all for a while.

2 I never get around to traveling, and I don't want to ______________ my life when I'm older and regret anything.

3 We've decided to plan a big trip. We asked a couple of friends to come with us, but they ______________ it so we're going by ourselves.

4 Tom's done some research to ______________ everything he needs to know before his ski trip.

5 This week, I feel prepared for any problems I may ______________ with work.

6 They just need to ______________ their Spanish before they move to Madrid.

C Fill in the blanks with one of the three-part phrasal verbs from Exercise A.

Tell your partner about:

1 a trip you ______________ fondly.

2 a country you'd like to ______________.

3 a language you'd like to ______________.

4 a good place to ______________ crowds.

5 something new you ______________ trying.

6 what helps you ______________ bad choices.

7 a difficulty you've ______________.

8 something you never ______________ doing.

D Discuss the topics in Exercise C with your partner.

Published by Macmillan Education Limited. © Macmillan Education Limited, 2020. This page may be photocopied and used within the class.

-ing and infinitive forms

A **Complete the sentences with the correct form of verbs in the box.**

book	do	find	make	put	start	sunbathe	worry

1 It's really worth ____________ in advance, as it gets really busy.

2 It's very difficult ____________ somewhere to stay at this time of year.

3 If you don't have anything ____________, can you give me a hand with this?

4 I spend most of my time ____________ when I'm on vacation.

5 This book tells you everything you need to know about ____________ your own business.

6 I didn't have much fun ____________ it together, but I'm happy with my wardrobe now.

7 I don't think I have enough information ____________ a final decision.

8 There's no point ____________ about something you can't do anything about.

B **Complete the sentences so that they are true for you.**

- I usually have fun ________________.
- I spend a lot of time ________________.
- But I don't have time ________________.
- I find it very motivating ________________.
- I'm not remotely interested in ________________.
- I have far too many/much ________________.
- If you ask me, it's not worth ________________.
- And there's definitely no point ________________.

C **Work in groups and read each other's sentences. How similar are you? Ask others about the reasons for their answers.**

Published by Macmillan Education Limited. © Macmillan Education Limited, 2020. This page may be photocopied and used within the class.

6.2 Vocabulary

Binomial expressions

A Work in pairs. Find the mistakes in the questions below. Re-write the questions correctly.

1 Are there any mistakes you make time after wide?

____

2 By and away, are you optimistic about the future?

____

3 Did your English improve suddenly or slowly but sound?

____

4 Can you think of an example of a rags-to-time story?

____

5 Have you ever been in a life-or-soul situation where you've been relieved to emerge safe and time?

____

6 Who or what from your country is well known far and large?

____

7 What would you say is far and surely the most beautiful place you've ever been?

____

8 Can you think of a job that you'd really have to put your heart and death into?

____

B Predict the answer that you think your partner would give to each question.

C Discuss your predictions from Exercise B with your partner. Ask further questions to find out more information.

D Compare answers as a whole class. Whose predictions were the most accurate? What was the most common answer for each question?

Published by Macmillan Education Limited. © Macmillan Education Limited, 2020. This page may be photocopied and used within the class.

it clefting

A Put the words in the correct order to make sentences.

1 most of it's afraid spiders I'm that

____

2 quality free it's that's important the of factor life time most in

____

3 going time was way for changed it the abroad I the that first think really

____

4 parents most I who it's owe to my

____

5 effect confidence that it's has English biggest on the your

____

6 weather down me that it's gets bad most

____

B Are the sentences in Exercise A true for you? Work with a partner and explain why or why not.

C Ask and answer the questions with a partner, correcting the information where appropriate.

1 Do you get along best with your brother?
2 Is your favorite sport baseball?
3 Was your best ever vacation to Australia?
4 Are you really good at dancing?
5 Did you use to play the drums?
6 Would you like to learn to fly a helicopter?

American Language Hub Level 5 Teacher's Book.
Published by Macmillan Education Limited. © Macmillan Education Limited, 2020. This page may be photocopied and used within the class.

7.1 Vocabulary

Feelings

Student A

A Take turns explaining the words in the table below. Explain your words to your partner. Listen to your partner's explanations and write their words on the other side of the table.

Your words	Your partner's words
courageous	
disgusted	
grumpy	
superior	
humble	

B Work in groups. In turns, choose one of the topics below to talk about for 30 seconds. How many of the adjectives from Exercise A can you use?

art birthdays childhood family Monday mornings nature shopping space the economy traffic

Student B

A Take turns explaining the words in the table below. Explain your words to your partner. Listen to your partner's explanations and write their words on the other side of the table.

Your partner's words	Your words
	frustrated
	devastated
	indifferent
	resilient
	hysterical

B Work in groups. In turns, choose one of the topics below to talk about for 30 seconds. How many of the adjectives from Exercise A can you use?

art birthdays childhood family Monday mornings nature shopping space the economy traffic

Published by Macmillan Education Limited. © Macmillan Education Limited, 2020. This page may be photocopied and used within the class.

7.2 Vocabulary

Polysemy

A Complete the pairs of sentences with the correct form of the same word.

1 a I need to sit down. I feel ____________.

b He thinks he's ____________ but I find him offensive.

2 a I'm going to ____________ myself to an ice cream.

b My boss ____________ me really badly.

3 a You need to make a big ____________ to your lifestyle.

b I need some ____________ for the machine.

4 a He has nothing interesting to say. He's really ____________.

b It doesn't hurt a lot. It's more of a ____________ ache.

5 a I need someone to ____________ my car.

b Can you ____________ this mirror in place?

6 a Is this made of ____________?

b Let's go for a walk in the ____________.

B Try to make some similar pairs of sentences with the words below. Give them to your partner to try to fill in the blanks.

bright	flight
dim	man
force	book
drive	bank

C Can you think of any examples of polysemes in your language? Tell your partner.

American Language Hub Level 5 Teacher's Book.
Published by Macmillan Education Limited. © Macmillan Education Limited, 2020. This page may be photocopied and used within the class.

what clefting and *all* clefting

A Match the sentence halves to make complete sentences.

1 What I love about the weekend is
2 What I always do before going to bed is
3 All you need to bring to my party is
4 All I want for my birthday is
5 What I'd really like to know is
6 All I know is
7 What you should know before you come to my town is
8 All I need is

a what I learned from my parents.
b not having to get up early.
c whatever you want to eat and drink.
d read for half an hour.
e where you were last night.
f a little more time to finish.
g that it's very dangerous at night.
h world peace.

B Rewrite the sentences in Exercise A so that they are true for you.

C Ask the following questions to three other students and write down their answers in the table.

	Student 1	Student 2	Student 3
What do you love about weekends?			
What do you always do before going to bed?			
What do I need to bring to your party?			
What do you want for your birthday?			
What would you really like to know?			
What do you know?			
What should I know before coming to your town?			
What do you need?			

D Share the most interesting piece of information you found out in Exercise C with the class.

Published by Macmillan Education Limited. © Macmillan Education Limited, 2020. This page may be photocopied and used within the class.

7.2 Vocabulary

Intensifiers

A Fill in the blanks in the sentences with an appropriate intensifier.

altogether outright somewhat

1 Have you had a meal that was ____________ disappointing recently? Why?

2 Have you ever had to abandon a vacation or trip ____________? Why?

3 Is there anything you would like to see a(n) ____________ ban imposed on? Why?

immensely radically remarkably utterly

4 Is there anything that would ____________ transform your life? What? How?

5 Has anything you weren't looking forward to ever ended up going ____________ well?

6 Have you heard any ____________ absurd ideas or suggestions recently? What were they?

7 Have you ever felt ____________ proud of yourself? Why?

noticeably practically relatively

8 Has your English ____________ improved over the last month?

9 Is there anything you would like to do but feel it would be ____________ impossible?

10 Compared to English, would it be ____________ easy for a foreigner to learn your language?

B Work in groups. Discuss the questions in Exercise A.

American Language Hub Level 5 Teacher's Book.
Published by Macmillan Education Limited. © Macmillan Education Limited, 2020. This page may be photocopied and used within the class.

8.1 Vocabulary

Health problems

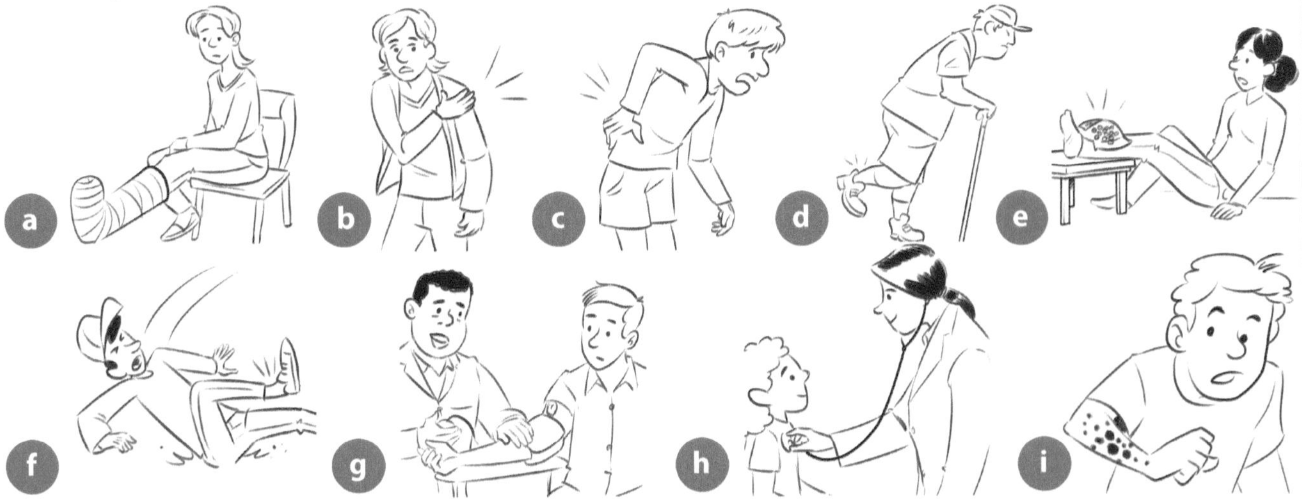

A Match the halves to form phrases, then match each phrase to one of the pictures.

1 pull	**a** rash
2 have a skin	**b** blood pressure
3 sprain	**c** throat / back
4 have a fast / slow	**d** joint / skin
5 have high / low	**e** a rib / your leg
6 dislocate	**f** heart rate
7 have an inflamed	**g** your ankle / your wrist
8 fracture	**h** your shoulder / thumb
9 have a sore	**i** a muscle

B Choose one of the complaints from Exercise A. Describe the symptoms and what you are doing now. Can your partner guess what the complaint is?

It's swollen. I can't walk on it. I have a bandage on it.

Have you sprained your ankle?

C Complete the text with the correct form of phrases from Exercise A.

Some people might say we're a clumsy family, or a bunch of hypochondriacs, but I just think we're very unlucky. We all play sports, so it's fairly common for one of us to be limping because we've [1] ______________, or not able to walk at all for a few days because we've [2] ______________. Last year, I [3] ______________ and it was in a cast for six weeks! I also ride a motorcycle, and I fell off and [4] ______________, which was incredibly painful although the doctor managed to put it back into place pretty easily. We have a lot of allergies, so someone usually comes out in a [5] ______________ or has [6] ______________ from something we've eaten. We don't go to the doctor for everything, as I usually have a [7] ______________ which I can treat myself with a lozenge or a hot drink, but we do have some more serious problems. I have [8] ______________, so I have that taken regularly, and I also take medication for a [9] ______________, which is probably my biggest worry.

Published by Macmillan Education Limited. © Macmillan Education Limited, 2020. This page may be photocopied and used within the class.

Adjective clauses with complex relative pronouns

A Complete each sentence (1–10) with a relative pronoun.

	My answer	Student 1	Student 2
1 Someone ____________ lifestyle you envy			
2 Someone with ____________ you spent an unenjoyable evening			
3 A method ____________ you can make a lot of money			
4 Someone ____________ you've learned a lot from			
5 Someone ____________ job you would hate to have			
6 An activity ____________ you can grow as a person			
7 Someone with ____________ you'd hate to be stuck in an elevator			
8 Someone ____________ habits annoy you			
9 Someone from ____________ you'd never borrow money			
10 A fictional character to ____________ you relate strongly			

B Write your answers in the table in Exercise A.

C Ask questions to two different people to find out what they wrote. Write a note about their answers in the table in Exercise A.

Whose lifestyle do you envy?

D Compare your findings with a partner and discuss who in the class you have most in common with.

American Language Hub Level 5 Teacher's Book.
Published by Macmillan Education Limited. © Macmillan Education Limited, 2020. This page may be photocopied and used within the class.

8.2 Vocabulary

Idioms

A Complete the sentences with the words in the box.

depth	eye	feet	food	goalposts	gut	head and shoulders	meal	salt	shot	tea	towel

1 When I'm shopping, I always keep an ____________ out for …

2 I once felt out of my ____________ when …

3 You have to take what … says with a pinch of ____________.

4 … really gave me ____________ for thought.

5 I once felt like throwing in the ____________ when …

6 I have a ____________ feeling that …

7 Someone close to me once moved the ____________ by …

8 I once got cold ____________ when …

9 I always give my best ____________.

10 … isn't really my cup of ____________.

11 It really annoys me when people make a ____________ of …

12 In school, I was ____________ above everyone else at …

B Complete the sentences in Exercise A with your own ideas.

C Work in pairs. Discuss your answers from Exercise B. Ask questions to find out more information.

Published by Macmillan Education Limited. © Macmillan Education Limited, 2020. This page may be photocopied and used within the class.

Pronouns and determiners

A Match the first half of the conversations with the replies.

1 How many people are coming?
2 Do you want this one or that one?
3 How much do you have?
4 How many times have you been here?
5 What did everyone think of the movie?
6 Whose is that?
7 I need a drink.
8 Why don't you apply for those jobs?

a Some liked it, some didn't.
b Not as many as I hoped. Several people have dropped out.
c Not mine.
d I can't decide. Can I have both?
e I'll get you one.
f Neither one particularly appeals to me.
g Several. I've lost count.
h Just a little. But enough.

B Tell your partner about:

- a choice you had to make where both alternatives were tempting.
- a choice you had to make where neither alternative was tempting.
- something you're definitely going to do one of these days.
- something several people have tried to do, but none have managed.
- something that not many people like, but you do.
- something that not many people can do, but you can.
- something that some people do one way and some do another.
- something that a little is enough of.

American Language Hub Level 5 Teacher's Book.
Published by Macmillan Education Limited. © Macmillan Education Limited, 2020. This page may be photocopied and used within the class.

8.2 Vocabulary

Describing taste

A Choose the correct alternative to complete the sentences.

1. This needs more salt. It's a bit ***bland*** / ***sour***.
2. It may not look very ***gritty*** / ***appetizing***, but it tastes delicious.
3. That doesn't look right. Surely, it shouldn't be so ***tangy*** / ***cloudy***.
4. These must be stale. They're supposed to be ***sticky*** / ***crunchy***.
5. I don't care how good it tastes. I can't eat anything that smells so ***pungent*** / ***cloudy***.
6. This might be bad. Is it supposed to be ***sour*** / ***spicy***?
7. This is perfect, and nice and ***slimy*** / ***moist*** in the middle.
8. I'm not very adventurous with flavors, so I usually choose something ***mild*** / ***soggy***.

B Work in pairs. What do you think is being described in each sentence in Exercise A?

C Work in groups. Decide what food you would associate with each of the adjectives in the box.

acidic appetizing bland cloudy crisp crunchy gritty mild moist
murky pungent slimy soggy sour sticky tangy

D Work in pairs. Discuss the following ideas in relation to food and drink you have tried. Give details about the experience.

Where did you eat/drink it? Would you order it again?

- blandest
- tangiest
- slimiest
- crunchiest
- stickiest
- moistest
- most pungent
- most appetizing
- most acidic
- sourest

Published by Macmillan Education Limited. © Macmillan Education Limited, 2020. This page may be photocopied and used within the class.

Slang

A Work in pairs. Rewrite the conversation below to make it more informal.

A: ~~What are your plans for tonight?~~

What are you up to tonight?

B: I'm going to a friend's birthday event. How about you?

A: I'm very tired so I'm just going to relax at home and watch television. I'll probably go to bed very early.

B: I require something to wear. There's a nice dress I want, but it would cost a hundred dollars and I'm a little short of money right now.

A: Don't complain. You have a lot of wonderful clothes. I'd be delighted if I had so many.

B: OK. I've chosen what I'm going to wear anyway, so that problem is solved.

A: Is that suspicious man going to be there?

B: I hope not. I'll be disappointed if he is.

A: Let's spend some time together on the weekend.

B: Yes, let's.

B Discuss the following questions with your partner.

- Do you use a lot of slang when speaking in your language?
- In what situations do you or would you use slang? And when don't you or wouldn't you?
- Does slang date well? Do you still use the same slang expressions you were using ten years ago?
- What impression does it give when someone uses a lot of slang?

Published by Macmillan Education Limited. © Macmillan Education Limited, 2020. This page may be photocopied and used within the class.

Noun phrases

Student A

A On a separate piece of paper, add as much information as you can to the nouns in the sentences below. Use the example to help you.

- The scientist carried out some research.

The *highly acclaimed 70-year-old Nobel prize-winning Romanian* scientist*, who has recently retired,* carried out some research *at the University of Liverpool, where many other great people have studied, into our ability to learn languages that changed how we understand the subject*.

- The doctor treated the patient.
- The monkey climbed the tree.
- The team won the cup.

B Swap your rewritten sentences with Student B. Read each other's sentences and try to shorten them back down to the original that they started with.

Student B

A On a separate piece of paper, add as much information as you can to the nouns in the sentences below. Use the example to help you.

- The scientist carried out some research.

The *highly acclaimed 70-year-old Nobel prize-winning Romanian* scientist*, who has recently retired,* carried out some research *at the University of Liverpool, where many other great people have studied, into our ability to learn languages that changed how we understand the subject*.

- The mechanic fixed the car.
- The dog chased the cat.
- The player won the tournament.

B Swap your rewritten sentences with Student A. Read each other's sentences and try to shorten them back down to the original that you started with.

American Language Hub Level 5 Teacher's Book.
Published by Macmillan Education Limited. © Macmillan Education Limited, 2020. This page may be photocopied and used within the class.

Verb + object + base form

A Put the words into the correct order to make questions.

Have you ever:

1 committing / seen / crime / someone / a / ?

2 on / an / crawling / you / felt / insect / ?

3 cheat / exam / someone / in / helped / an / ?

4 do / you / someone / made / homework / your / for / ?

5 who / someone / you / them / didn't / watching / were / watched / know / ?

When did you last:

6 by / watch / world / sit / go / and / the / ?

7 you / someone / a / have / favor / do / ?

8 for / make / wait / long / a / someone / time / you / ?

9 lie / someone / a / hear / telling / ?

10 something / street / see / strange / the / happening / on / ?

B Ask and answer the questions in Exercise A with your partner.

Published by Macmillan Education Limited. © Macmillan Education Limited, 2020. This page may be photocopied and used within the class.

9.2 Grammar

Participle clauses and verbless clauses

A Match the sentence halves to make complete sentences.

1 While in college,
2 Having grown up in a big city,
3 When on vacation,
4 When studying,
5 Only after having done all my housework
6 Not having read the book,
7 After being shown how to do something once,
8 Getting home after a busy day at work,

a I don't want to see the movie until I have.
b I like to relax and not do much.
c I didn't work as hard as I could have.
d I frequently take a long bath.
e I don't find it difficult to use public transportation.
f I can remember it pretty well.
g I can't concentrate unless there's complete silence.
h can I really relax.

B How many of the sentences in Exercise A are true for you?

C Complete the sentences below with your own ideas.

- Being a …
- Having been …
- While on vacation …
- While at work / at school …
- Not having …
- When …, I usually …
- Not being …
- Not wanting to …

D Work in pairs. Compare your answers to Exercise C.

Published by Macmillan Education Limited. © Macmillan Education Limited, 2020. This page may be photocopied and used within the class.

Gestures and body language

A Match the verbs in the box to the body parts (1–8) they involve. Some verbs can go with more than one body part.

beckon bend blink cross fold gaze glare grin nod
point raise shake shrug smirk stare wiggle wink

1 **fingers:** ______, ______, ______, ______

2 **arms:** ______, ______

3 **shoulders:** ______

4 **legs:** ______, ______

5 **head:** ______, ______

6 **eyes:** ______, ______, ______, ______, ______

7 **eyebrows:** ______

8 **mouth:** ______, ______

B Work in pairs. What would you do in the following situations?

1 You're in a long, boring lecture.

2 You're trying to get the attention of a group of children.

3 You're listening to a speech you disagree with.

4 You've just stepped outside into the sunshine after two hours in the movie theater.

5 Your friend is about to put their foot in their mouth and say something awkward.

6 The zipper on someone's pants is undone and they haven't noticed.

7 You've been sitting in the same position for a long time.

8 You see someone you find very attractive.

C Work in groups. How international are the gestures in Exercises A and B? If you are from different countries, discuss what different gestures you use. If you are from the same country, what do you know about different gestures in different countries?

American Language Hub Level 5 Teacher's Book.
Published by Macmillan Education Limited. © Macmillan Education Limited, 2020. This page may be photocopied and used within the class.

10.1 Vocabulary

Culture and heritage

A Complete the sentences with the correct form of the words in the box.

architectural	designate	endanger	fund	habitat	heritage	preserve	refurbish	ruins	settlement

1. A building you think should be ____________.
2. An important part of your country's cultural ____________.
3. A place famous for its ancient ____________.
4. Somewhere you would ____________ as a World Heritage site.
5. An ____________ style you like.
6. The oldest ____________ you have visited.
7. Something everyone can do to help ____________ the natural world.
8. Something that ____________ the planet.
9. An animal whose natural ____________ is in your country.
10. A charity ____________ you have donated to.

B Write an example for each sentence in Exercise A.

C Work in pairs. Take turns telling your partner your examples from Exercise B in a random order. Try to guess which sentence each of your partner's examples goes with. Ask more questions to find out reasons for each others' choices.

Published by Macmillan Education Limited. © Macmillan Education Limited, 2020. This page may be photocopied and used within the class.

Discourse markers

A Complete the texts with one of the discourse markers in the box.

as a matter of fact	conversely	despite	for instance	in any case	moreover	owing to	whereas	yet

Kim

My favorite place for a vacation would be somewhere wild and unspoiled. 1 ______________, I'm going to New Zealand next month, where I can do some extreme sports like bungee jumping, 2 ______________. 3 ______________, I love walking in the wilderness and breathing in fresh air.

David

My wife and I are very different in our vacation tastes. I love big all-inclusive hotels, 4 ______________ she likes self-service apartments. We very rarely argue, 5 ______________ our differences. 6 ______________, we're lucky enough to be able to afford two vacations a year so we can choose one each!

Jessica

There are two sides to me. I love clubbing and staying out all night, and 7 ______________ I love peace and quiet. Ibiza is the perfect place for me, 8 ______________ the fact that it has an amazing nightlife 9 ______________ you can also find plenty of deserted places to relax.

B Work in pairs. Discuss which person in Exercise A you are most similar and dissimilar to.

C Write a paragraph about what you like to do on vacation.

D Work in groups and read each other's paragraphs. How similar are you?

American Language Hub Level 5 Teacher's Book.
Published by Macmillan Education Limited. © Macmillan Education Limited, 2020. This page may be photocopied and used within the class.

Nouns with *to*

A Choose the correct alternative to complete the sentences.

1. When visiting a new city, I often have a strong ***urge*** / ***obligation*** to climb a high tower to get a great view.
2. A lot of people show a ***reluctance*** / ***reminder*** to learn the local language when they travel.
3. Tourists have a ***tendency*** / ***readiness*** to ignore local people and local issues when they travel.
4. I get frustrated by people's ***desire*** / ***failure*** to plan appropriately for the future.
5. People living in cities have a ***responsibility*** / ***refusal*** to reduce their carbon footprint.

B Complete the sentences with your own ideas.

- I've always had a tendency to ____________________.
- I have no desire to ____________________.
- I sometimes have a strong urge to ____________________.
- I feel a responsibility to ____________________.
- I need frequent reminders to ____________________.
- I wouldn't like to have an obligation to ____________________.
- I get annoyed by some people's refusal to ____________________.
- I'm surprised by some people's reluctance to ____________________.
- I'm studying in readiness to ____________________.
- I'm disappointed by my failure to ____________________.

C Work in pairs. Read the endings of your sentences in Exercise B to your partner. Can they guess which sentence opening they match with?

A: Go skydiving

B: You have no desire to go skydiving?

A: That's right.

B: Why not?

Published by Macmillan Education Limited. © Macmillan Education Limited, 2020. This page may be photocopied and used within the class.

10.2 Vocabulary

Word building

A Use the same suffix for each pair of words (1–7) to make new nouns or adjectives. Make any other spelling changes necessary.

-al -ate -hood -ic -ity -ive -ship

1 music ____________
person ____________

2 passion ____________
consider ____________

3 sympathy ____________
apathy ____________

4 effect ____________
act ____________

5 flexible ____________
responsible ____________

6 child ____________
neighbor ____________

7 citizen ____________
entrepreneur ____________

B Complete the sentences with one of the words from Exercise A.

1 I love where I live. It's such a friendly ____________.

2 We need to encourage more ____________ to improve the economic situation of the country.

3 I think it's extremely bad manners to ask ____________ questions to someone you hardly know.

4 Most people I know are ____________ about politics. They're just not interested in it at all.

5 I wish people would be more ____________ on public transportation and not listen to loud music, talk loudly on their phones or eat smelly food.

6 The most ____________ way to learn a language is to go to a country where it's spoken and try to immerse yourself.

7 The most important quality to have if you want to be successful is ____________. You have to be able to adapt to new situations and take on new challenges.

8 ____________ is the best time of your life. When you get older, there's just too much ____________.

C Work in pairs. Are the sentences in Exercise B true for you?

American Language Hub Level 5 Teacher's Book.
Published by Macmillan Education Limited. © Macmillan Education Limited, 2020. This page may be photocopied and used within the class.

10.2 Grammar

Ellipsis and substitution

A Make these sentences sound more natural by deleting any unnecessary words.

1 I've always wanted to go traveling and next year, I'm going to go traveling.

____

2 I've never watched a baseball game and I never want to watch a baseball game.

____

3 It might rain tomorrow but I hope it doesn't rain tomorrow.

____

4 By the end of this year, I will have gotten a new job, I will have moved to a new house and I will have gotten married.

____

B Make these sentences sound more natural by deleting or using substitution.

1 I don't like spicy food and my partner doesn't like spicy food.

____

2 I don't buy a lot of organic products but I should buy a lot of organic products.

____

3 Will my country win the next World Cup? I hope my country will win the next World Cup.

____

4 I don't know if the economy is improving but I hope the economy is improving.

____

C Work in groups. How many of the sentences in Exercises A and B are true for you?

Published by Macmillan Education Limited. © Macmillan Education Limited, 2020. This page may be photocopied and used within the class.

Answer key

1.1 Grammar

A

1 How someone dresses tells you a lot about the kind of person they are.
2 The experience of looking good should be available to everyone.
3 The idea that how you look isn't important is ridiculous.
4 Following fashion and trends is a sign of a weak person.
5 Making cheap clothes in developing countries is immoral and bad for the environment.
6 The fact that so many people buy cheaply produced clothes is extremely worrying.

1.1 Vocabulary

Metaphors

A

1 g 2 d 3 c 4 b
5 h 6 e 7 f 8 a

B

1 I'm on a tight budget.
2 You're throwing money down the drain.
3 It was a breeze.
4 It was tailor-made.
5 It caught my eye.
6 I bought it for peanuts.
7 It's an off-the-shelf design.
8 They really wind me up.

1.2 Vocabulary

A

amateurish; childish; disaster-prone; accident-prone; idiot-proof; waterproof; re-start; re-think; super-lucky; super confident; tech-savvy; media-savvy; user-friendly; environmentally friendly; cheesy; trashy

B

Suggested answers

1 childish
2 accident-prone
3 super confident
4 re-think
5 tech-savvy
6 environmentally friendly
7 cheesy
8 idiot-proof

2.1 Vocabulary

C

1 thought-provoking
2 tedious
3 pretentious
4 underrated
5 unconventional
6 iconic
7 repetitive
8 groundbreaking

2.1 Grammar

A

1 'd/had been planning
2 had been lost / was lost
3 was trying
4 'd/had never considered
5 was never taught
6 'd/had always wanted
7 'd/had only been working
8 was made

2.2 Vocabulary

Ideas and inspiration

A

1 c 2 f 3 j 4 b 5 i
6 h 7 d 8 g 9 a 10 e

B

1 get into the right state of mind
2 hit a wall
3 draws inspiration from
4 get a fresh perspective / bounce ideas off
5 bounce ideas off
6 working from a blank canvas
7 trusted his instincts
8 ran with

2.2 Vocabulary

Compound adjectives

A

1 late-night
2 highly motivated
3 world-famous
4 self-employed
5 well paid
6 thick-skinned
7 part-time
8 open-minded

3.1 Vocabulary

Sustainability

A

1 zero-emission
2 biodegradable
3 over-exploited
4 renewable
5 sustainable
6 depletion
7 harmful
8 carbon-neutral
9 offset
10 accumulating

3.1 Grammar

A

Suggested answers

1 ~~have been~~ be 2 correct
3 ~~be~~ have been 4 correct 5 correct
6 ~~might only have driven~~ will be driving
7 ~~become~~ becoming 8 ~~couldn't~~ can't

3.1 Vocabulary

Forming verbs from adjectives

B

1 broadens 2 tighten 3 visualize
4 deepen 5 ensure 6 enable
7 simplify 8 shortened

3.2 Grammar

A

1 would she kill a wild animal
2 has ever been in a helicopter; have I
3 does Sam play the piano, but he also speaks fluent Italian
4 could I ever do a skydive
5 does Blanca think hitchhiking is a good idea

3.2 Vocabulary

A

Bring: benefits; home
Do: more harm than good; your best
Make: a concerted effort; advances in the right direction
Seize: the initiative; the opportunity
Set: measurable targets; realistic goals
Perpetuate: the myth; the stereotype
Take: shape; the time

B

1 take shape
2 perpetuate the myth / stereotype
3 doing my best
4 bring home
5 seize the opportunity
6 bring benefits
7 doing more harm than good
8 take time

4.1 Grammar

A

1 ~~Supposed~~ Supposing
2 ~~to~~
3 ~~Were~~ Had
4 ~~Were you an animal~~ Were you to be reincarnated
5 ~~Imagining~~ Imagine / Supposing
6 ~~Would~~ Were

4.2 Vocabulary

Science and research

A

1 conduct; experiment
2 participants
3 norm
4 hypothesized; speculated
5 findings; demonstrate
6 conclude

B

1 speculating/hypothesizing
2 hypothesizing/speculating
3 experiment
4 conducted
5 participants
6 findings
7 demonstrate
8 conclude

Published by Macmillan Education Limited. © Macmillan Education Limited, 2020. This page may be photocopied and used within the class.

4.2 Grammar

A

Suggested answers

1 I was a little taller
2 I hadn't ignored that message
3 've been paying more attention
4 to have studied something different
5 I'd done more research
6 I could swim
7 've been better prepared
8 to have started studying English when I was younger

4.2 Vocabulary

Thinking

A

1 curious
2 absent-minded
3 overthink
4 common sense
5 eccentric
6 eureka moment
7 wishful thinking
8 troubleshoot

5.1 Grammar

A

1 being corrected
2 to be given
3 had; taken; painted
4 had; stolen
5 gotten/been banned; blocked
6 made to eat
7 been taught
8 're/are being underpaid

5.2 Vocabulary

Reporting verbs

A

1 urge 2 boasts 3 acknowledge
4 clarify 5 doubt 6 imply
7 alleged 8 conclude

5.2 Vocabulary

Motivation and manipulation

A

1 going nuts for
2 act against
3 tap into
4 spurs; on
5 be inclined to
6 steer; toward
7 coax; into

6.1 Vocabulary

Journeys and adventures

A

1 globetrotters
2 long-haul
3 impenetrable
4 provisions
5 off the beaten path
6 in the heart
7 uncharted territory
8 embark on

6.1 Vocabulary

Three-part phrasal verbs

A

be up for; get away from; get around to; come up against; look back on; find out about; switch off from; brush up on

B

1 get away from / switch off from
2 look back on
3 weren't up for
4 find out about
5 come up against
6 brush up on

C

1 look back on
2 find out about
3 brush up on
4 get away from
5 're/are up for
6 switch off from
7 come up against
8 get around to

6.2 Grammar

A

1 booking 2 to find 3 to do
4 sunbathing 5 starting 6 putting
7 to make 8 worrying

6.2 Vocabulary

A

1 ~~wide~~ time
2 ~~away~~ large
3 ~~sound~~ surely
4 ~~time~~ riches
5 ~~soul~~ death; ~~time~~ sound
6 ~~large~~ wide
7 ~~surely~~ away
8 ~~death~~ soul

7.1 Grammar

A

1 It's spiders that I'm most afraid of.
2 It's free time that's the most important factor in quality of life.
3 It was going abroad for the first time that really changed the way I think.
4 It's my parents who I owe most to.
5 It's confidence that has the biggest effect on your English.
6 It's bad weather that most gets me down.

7.2 Vocabulary

Polysemy

A

1 funny; funny
2 treat; treats
3 change; change
4 dull; dull
5 fix; fix
6 wood; woods

7.2 Grammar

A

1 b 2 d 3 c 4 h
5 e 6 a 7 g 8 f

7.2 Vocabulary

Intensifiers

A

1 somewhat 2 altogether 3 outright
4 radically 5 remarkably 6 utterly
7 immensely 8 noticeably 9 practically
10 relatively

8.1 Vocabulary

A

1 i; Picture d
2 a; Picture i
3 g; Picture f
4 f; Picture h
5 b; Picture g
6 h; Picture b
7 d; Picture e
8 e; Picture a
9 c; Picture c

C

1 pulled a muscle / sprained an ankle
2 sprained an ankle / pulled a muscle
3 fractured my leg
4 dislocated my shoulder
5 skin rash
6 inflamed skin
7 sore throat
8 high blood pressure
9 fast heart rate

8.1 Grammar

A

1 whose 2 whom 3 whereby
4 who 5 whose 6 whereby
7 whom 8 whose 9 whom
10 whom

8.2 Vocabulary

Idioms

A

1 eye
2 depth
3 salt
4 food
5 towel
6 gut
7 goalposts
8 feet
9 shot
10 tea
11 meal
12 head and shoulders

8.2 Grammar

A

1 b 2 d 3 h 4 g
5 a 6 c 7 e 8 f

8.2 Vocabulary

Describing taste

A

1 bland 2 appetizing 3 cloudy
4 crunchy 5 pungent 6 sour
7 moist 8 mild

Published by Macmillan Education Limited. © Macmillan Education Limited, 2020. This page may be photocopied and used within the class.

9.1 Vocabulary

Slang

A

A: What are you up to tonight?
B: I'm going to a friend's birthday party. How about you?
A: I'm beat so I'm just going to chill at home and watch TV. I'll probably crash early.
B: I could do with something to wear. There's a nice dress I want, but it would set me back a hundred bucks and I'm broke.
A: Don't gripe. You have a ton of awesome clothes. I'd be jazzed if I had so many.
B: OK. I've chosen what I'm going to wear anyway, so that's sorted.
A: Is that sketchy guy going to be there?
B: I hope not. I'll be bummed if he is.
A: Let's hang out on the weekend.
B: Yes, let's.

9.2 Vocabulary

Verb + object + base form

A

1 seen someone committing a crime?
2 felt an insect crawling on you?
3 helped someone cheat in an exam?
4 made someone do your homework for you?
5 watched someone who didn't know you were watching them?
6 sit and watch the world go by?
7 have someone do you a favor?
8 make someone wait a long time for you?
9 hear someone telling a lie?
10 see something strange happening on the street?

9.2 Grammar

A

1 c 2 e 3 b 4 g
5 h 6 a 7 f 8 d

9.2 Vocabulary

Gestures and body language

A

1 **fingers:** point; bend; wiggle; beckon
2 **arms:** fold; cross
3 **shoulders:** shrug
4 **legs:** cross; bend
5 **head:** nod; shake
6 **eyes:** blink; wink; gaze; glare; stare
7 **eyebrows:** raise
8 **mouth:** grin; smirk

10.1 Vocabulary

Culture and heritage

A

1 refurbished
2 heritage
3 ruins
4 designate
5 architectural
6 settlement
7 preserve
8 endangers
9 habitat
10 fund

10.1 Grammar

A

1 As a matter of fact
2 for instance
3 Moreover
4 whereas
5 despite
6 In any case
7 conversely
8 owing to
9 yet

10.1 Vocabulary

Nouns with *to*

A

1 urge 2 reluctance 3 tendency
4 failure 5 responsibility

10.2 Vocabulary

Word building

A

1 musical; personal
2 passionate; considerate
3 sympathetic; apathetic
4 effective; active
5 flexibility; responsibility
6 childhood; neighborhood
7 citizenship; entrepreneurship

B

1 neighborhood
2 entrepreneurship
3 personal
4 apathetic
5 considerate
6 effective
7 flexibility
8 Childhood; responsibility

10.2 Grammar

A

1 I've always wanted to go traveling and next year, I'm going.
2 I've never watched a baseball game and I never want to.
3 It might rain tomorrow but I hope it doesn't.
4 By the end of this year, I will have gotten a new job, moved to a new house and gotten married.

B

1 I don't like spicy food and neither does my partner.
2 I don't buy a lot of organic products but I should do.
3 Will my country win the next World Cup? I hope so.
4 I don't know if the economy is improving but I hope it is.

American Language Hub Level 5 Teacher's Book.
Published by Macmillan Education Limited. © Macmillan Education Limited, 2020. This page may be photocopied and used within the class.